Continuing Issues in Early Childhood Education

Third Edition

Stephanie Feeney
Professor Emerita, University of Hawaii

Alice Galper
Educational Consultant

Carol Seefeldt
Professor Emerita, Late of the Institute for Child Study
University of Maryland, College Park

Merrill
is an imprint of

Upper Saddle River, New Jersey
Columbus, Ohio

Library of Congress Cataloging in Publication Data

Continuing issues in early childhood education / [edited by]
Stephanie Feeney, Alice Galper, Carol Seefeldt.—3rd ed.
p.   cm.
Includes bibliographical references and index.
ISBN-13: 978-0-13-234098-4
ISBN-10:   0-13-234098-4
1. Early childhood education—United States.   2. Early childhood education—United States—Finance.
3. Teachers—Training of—United States.   4. Early childhood education—Curricula—United States.   5. Early childhood education—United States—Evaluation.   I. Feeney, Stephanie.   II. Galper, Alice.   III. Seefeldt, Carol.
LB1139.25.C66 2009
372.21—dc22   2008011441

Vice President and Executive Publisher: Jeffery W. Johnston
Acquisitions Editor: Julie Peters
Editorial Assistant: Tiffany Bitzel
Senior Project Manager: Linda Hillis Bayma
Production Coordination: TexTech International
Design Coordinator: Diane C. Lorenzo
Cover Designer: Candace Rowley
Cover Image: Jeff Reese
Operations Specialist: Laura Messerly
Director of Marketing: Quinn Perkson
Marketing Manager: Darcy Betts Prybella
Marketing Coordinator: Brian Mounts

This book was set in Zapf Calligraphic by TexTech International. It was printed and bound by
R. R. Donnelley & Sons Company.

Photo Credits: Page 7, Jeff Reese; all other interior photos courtesy of Leeward Community College Children's Center, photographers Eva Moravcik, Steve Bobilin, and Jackie Rabang.

Pearson® is a registered trademark of Pearson plc
Merrill® is a registered trademark of Pearson Education, Inc.

Pearson Education Ltd., London
Pearson Education Singapore, Pte. Ltd.
Pearson Education Canada, Inc.
Pearson Education–Japan
Pearson Education Australia PTY, Limited

Pearson Education North Asia, Ltd. Hong Kong
Pearson Educación de Mexico, S.A. de C.V.
Pearson Education Malaysia, Pte. Ltd..
Pearson Education Upper Saddle River, New Jersey

Merrill
is an imprint of

10 9 8 7 6 5 4 3 2 1
ISBN-13: 978-0-13-234098-4
ISBN-10:   0-13-234098-4

This book is dedicated to Carol Seefeldt, who was lead editor for the first and second editions of *Continuing Issues in Early Childhood Education*. A consummate professional, Carol understood, more than most, that early childhood education is a serious endeavor. She strongly believed that only through discussion of numerous issues could we develop the expertise necessary to do the very best for the young children that we serve. She is missed by the profession, but her legacy continues with the publication of this third edition.

About the Authors

Nancy Barbour is a professor and associate dean in the College of Education, Health, and Human Services at Kent State University. She teaches early childhood courses in the Department of Teaching, Leadership, and Curriculum Studies. Her focus is on preparing teachers to work with young children and families in preschool settings.

Margaret Beneke is an early childhood educator who has taught preschool, kindergarten, first, and second grade in both public and private settings. She received her M.A.T. in child development from Tufts University, where she co-developed and co-taught a community arts program and researched children's ethnic identity. Her current interests are documentation and making learning visible in public education.

Sue Bredekamp is the director of research at the Council for Professional Recognition in Washington, DC. She is the former director of professional development and accreditation for the National Association for the Education of Young Children (NAEYC).

Linda Buck is professor and coordinator of early childhood programs at Honolulu Community College. She has been involved in advocacy and policy work in Hawaii for 20 years, including serving as the state's first early childhood education and childcare coordinator in the Governor's Office of Children and Youth.

Stephanie Feeney is professor emerita of education at the University of Hawaii at Manoa. Her publications include the textbook *Who Am I in the Lives of Children?* (going into its 8th edition), a curriculum for young children, the NAEYC Code of Ethical Conduct, and two books about professional ethics published by NAEYC. She does research and writes in the areas of curriculum, children's literature and professional ethics.

Gale Flynn is a long-time child and family advocate whose career spans across the fields of child welfare, mental health, family support and early childhood education. Gale is currently an educational consultant working toward integrating health, education, and family support systems for young children and families at both the policy and program development levels.

Nancy K. Freeman is associate professor of early childhood education and director of the University of South Carolina Child Development Research Center. She coauthored two books on professional ethics and has published and presented widely on this topic. She has served on the executive committee of the National Association of Early Childhood Teacher Educators.

Alice Galper was a professor of human development, teaching graduate and undergraduate courses in early childhood and human development at Mt. Vernon College, Washinton, DC, for nearly 20 years, and at the University of Maryland. Her research revolved around intergenerational attitudes and program evaluation. She has written many articles with Carol Seefeldt for such journals as *Child Development,* and the *Early Childhood Research Quarterly,* and collaborated with her on several teacher education books.

Janet Gonzalez-Mena was a full-time faculty member at Napa Valley College in the Child and Families Studies Program until she retired. She has been a preschool teacher and a child care director and is author of college textbooks about early childhood education and a parenting book called *Dragon Mom.*

Erica Greenberg is research assistant to Sharon Lynn Kagan at the National Center for Children and Families at Teachers College, Columbia University. Her research interests include early childhood accountability and improvement strategies and the impact of preschool expansion on K-12 education.

Sharon Lynn Kagan is the Virginia and Leonard Marx Professor of Early Childhood and Family Policy, codirector of the National Center for Children and Families, and associate dean for policy at Teachers College, Columbia University, and professor adjunct at Yale University's Child Study Center. A scholar advocate, she has used research to help influence practice in early care and education in the United States and in countries throughout the world.

Kristie Kauerz is the early childhood/P-3 policy director for the Office of the Lieutenant Governor in Colorado. She is also pursuing her doctorate in early childhood education policy at Teachers College, Columbia University. She has extensive experience working with state-level policy makers on early childhood issues and was program director of early learning at the Education Commission of the States.

Martha Lash is an assistant professor in the College of Education, Health, and Human Services at Kent State University, where she has taught since 2003. She teaches early childhood and curriculum courses in the Department of Teaching, Leadership, and Curriculum Studies. Her areas of study are children's social development, preschool teachers' beliefs and practices, and professional development of early childhood educators.

Bruce L. Mallory is provost and executive vice president at the University of New Hampshire, where he has been a professor of early childhood and special education since 1979. His scholarly work focuses on social policies affecting young children with disabilities and their families, rural early intervention program design, reconceptualizing theory and practice in early childhood education, and cross-cultural studies of early education.

Eva Moravcik is professor of early childhood education at Honolulu Community College. She teaches courses in early childhood foundations and curriculum and directs the Children's Center at Leeward Community College. She is coauthor of *Who Am I in the Lives of Children?*, a social studies–based curriculum for young children, and an NAEYC book on teaching professional ethics.

Rebecca S. New, previously at Tufts University, has assumed a joint appointment at the Frank Porter Graham Child Development Research Institute and the School of Education at the University of North Carolina, Chapel Hill. She has worked in the field of early childhood education for over three decades as a classroom teacher, teacher educator, and researcher. Currently she is drawing on her knowledge of Italian early childhood education to expand interpretations of quality childcare and developmentally appropriate educational practices.

Cynthia Paris is assistant professor of early childhood education in the Department of Human Development and Family Studies at the University of Delaware. Her research and advocacy focuses on the ways in which teachers grow toward and sustain child- and family-focused teaching across the professional life span.

Sandra Petersen is a writer and program analyst for the Early Head Start National Resource Center at Zero to Three. She created and teaches the special needs workshop for the Program for Infant Toddler Care. Her career in early childhood includes work in child care, early intervention, infant-parent psychotherapy, and policy.

Stuart Reifel is professor of curriculum and instruction and educational administration at The University of Texas at Austin, where he holds the W.K. Kellogg Endowed Fellowship. He studies and teaches about children's play, early childhood curriculum, and early childhood research. His interests in play stem from his years teaching nursery school and kindergarten.

Beth Rous is associate professor in educational leadership studies in the College of Education and director of early childhood at the Human Development Institute at the University of Kentucky. She has been in the field of early childhood and early childhood special education for more than 25 years as a teacher, trainer and researcher. She is the former president of the National Division for Early Childhood of the Council for Exceptional Children.

Frances O'Connell Rust is senior vice president for academic affairs and dean of faculty at the Erikson Institute. Her research and teaching focus on teacher education and teacher research. Much of her work has been done in New York City, where for 17 years she was professor of education at New York University.

Diana Schaack is the director of research for a Colorado-based child care quality improvement initiative. She is also a doctoral student in child development at Erikson Institute/Loyola University Chicago. Her primary areas of work focus on measuring quality in early childhood settings and ways in which to improve child care quality.

Catherine Scott-Little is an assistant professor in the Department of Human Development and Family Studies at the University of North Carolina at Greensboro, where she teaches in the birth through kindergarten teacher education program. Her most recent research focuses on early learning standards for infants, toddlers, and preschoolers.

Annette Sibley is president of Quality Assist, Inc., an Atlanta-based consulting firm. She specializes in research, program evaluation, training, and technical assistance relating to quality improvement in early care and education programs. She was instrumental in the development of the accreditation system for the National Association for Family Child Care and is coauthor of the *Assessment Profile for Early Childhood Programs,* an evaluation tool for early childhood programs, and the *Assessment Profile for Family Child Care Homes.*

John A. Sutterby is an associate professor in curriculum and instruction at the University of Texas at Brownsville/Texas Southmost College. His research interests include bilingual programs, child care, children's play, and family involvement.

Kate Tarrant is a graduate research fellow at the National Center for Children and Families at Teachers College, Columbia University, and a third-year doctoral student in the Department of Curriculum and Teaching. Her research focuses on the intersection of early childhood policy and practice.

Gerrit Westervelt is executive director of the Build Initiative, a foundation-driven project to help states create comprehensive early learning systems. He has been involved in K–12 and early childhood policy for 20 years as a policy analyst, lobbyist, and nonprofit leader.

Barbara A. Willer is a deputy executive director for the National Association for the Education of Young Children (NAEYC). She has held a number of leadership positions during her 20-year tenure with NAEYC. Dr. Willer is the author of numerous publications regarding early childhood program quality and public policy issues affecting young children and their families.

Donna S. Wittmer has been a professor of Early Childhood Education at the University of Colorado Denver for 17 years. She and Sandra Petersen are the authors of the textbook, *Infant and Toddler Development and Responsive Program Planning: A Relationship-Based Approach.*

PREFACE

Welcome to the third edition of *Continuing Issues in Early Childhood Education*. Stephanie Feeney has joined Alice Galper as coeditor of this book due to the loss of our friend and colleague Carol Seefeldt. In this edition we honor Carol's commitment to young children and her vision for this book. We also incorporate her contributions to the previous edition whenever possible. We have added some new authors and have updated several chapters from the previous edition so that this revision will provide a current perspective on some of the many continuing issues encountered in the field of early childhood education.

Issues remain the focus of this book. *Issues* can be defined as matters for discussion or concern, and/or the central or most important topics in a discussion or debate. The third edition, intended to provide a broad overview of critical issues facing the early childhood field today, is designed for graduate students or advanced undergraduates in early childhood education programs as well as for practicing early childhood professionals. We hope that it will foster lively discussions, give readers new insights into what is happening in the field, and enhance their ability to articulate their understandings of the needs of young children and the nature of early childhood education today. This may in turn lead to expanding and refining current understandings, generating new questions, and identifying new issues. This process will lead to an ever-clearer understanding of how to best care for and educate young children.

Today's early childhood educators exercise a great deal of responsibility and are called on to make numerous decisions every day. They interact with children, families, colleagues, administrators, and policy makers. To be effective, they cannot base decisions on their own personal inclinations and biases, nor on uninformed opinions. Rather, action should be informed by understanding of the complexities related to each new, potentially controversial issue and by evidence from current research about child development and best practices in early childhood programs.

This third edition of *Continuing Issues in Early Childhood Education* consists of 18 chapters organized into eight parts. Each part addresses a significant question in the early care and education field. The chapters in each section provide background, impart current knowledge about the subject including relevant research, examine current issues, and explore prospects for the future. The book is designed to assist advanced students to become knowledgeable practitioners and reflective decision makers. We hope that it will provide veteran early childhood educators with a context for understanding some of the challenges they encounter in their work, and newcomers with insights into some of the issues they may encounter as they begin to work with young children and families.

THE AUTHORS

Authors of the contributed chapters include scholars, teacher educators, researchers, policy specialists, and practitioners who work with children and families. They agreed to share their expertise because they thought that providing information about their topics would help advanced students gain a greater understanding of the complexities of the early childhood field and offer a basis for constructive action. Having multiple authors adds richness to the book by offering a variety of perspectives. You will find that the writing styles range from formal and scholarly to personal and anecdotal. Although the authors' approaches and styles are different, all of them are known and respected for their expertise in early care and education and in the areas they write about. We are very grateful to all of them for taking time from their other commitments to contribute to this book.

USING THIS BOOK

This book is designed for use in advanced courses in early care and education, though it might be helpful to any early childhood educator seeking better understanding of current issues in the field. These issues include the use of child development research, recruitment and retention of staff, professional development, the importance of program quality and how to evaluate it, reconciling child-friendly pedagogy and assessment techniques with current demands for accountability and the use of standards-based curricula. Other urgent issues are the role of families in early care and education, meeting the needs of all young children, and how best to advocate for comprehensive quality programs.

TO THE INSTRUCTOR

The questions that introduce each section of the book can be used as the organizing structure for a course and as a springboard for in-depth engagement with the topics. In class sessions students can discuss their reactions to chapter content, hear from guest speakers addressing local policy initiatives, and relate to what they have read to their own communities. Students can discuss and write reflections based on the list of questions in the introduction to each section, explore a topic further by writing a report on a book listed in the chapter references, write a research paper on a topic of interest, or gain first-hand experience with a topic by doing a community exploration (for example, visiting a program or interviewing a professional).

ACKNOWLEDGMENTS

We wish to give a special thank you to Julie Peters, Acquisitions Editor at Pearson / Merrill, who believed in the book and the importance of the issues it raises.

Brief Contents

CONTENTS

Chapter 7
The Professional Development of Teachers of Young Children   158

Nancy Barbour and Martha Lash

Chapter 8
What Do Early Childhood Educators Need to Know and Do to Work in Urban Settings?   184
Frances O'Connell Rust

Chapter 9
Professionalism and Ethics in Early Care and Education   196
Nancy Freeman and Stephanie Feeney

Part 6: How Will Early Childhood Education Be Evaluated?   325

Part 7: What Is the Role of Families in Early Care and Education?   365

Chapter 17
Family-Centered Early Care and Education   369

Janet Gonzalez-Mena

Note: Every effort has been made to provide accurate and current Internet information in this book. However, the Internet and information posted on it are constantly changing, and it is inevitable that some of the Internet addresses listed in this textbook will change.

INTRODUCTION

The chapters in *Continuing Issues in Early Childhood Education* address vital issues that confront early childhood educators in our nation today. Some of these issues have been ongoing since the early days of the field; others emerged from current events. The topics were chosen because they are significant, frequently encountered, and have an impact on the lives of children and those who care for and educate them. Taken together, they provide a big picture of where we are as a field and point to some of the challenges we may face in the future. When the same issue or topic comes up in several chapters it indicates that this is currently a "hot" topic.

The reader may notice some lack of consistency in the terms used in this book. This is because there is, at this time, no agreed-on terminology regarding who we are and what we do in early care and education. We, the editors, have attempted to follow some conventions that are widely used (but not completely accepted). We use the term *early care and education* to refer to all programs that support the development and learning of children between birth and age 8. This term was introduced in the 1990s to try to bring together the two primary purposes for early childhood programs—caring for children while family members were at work or at school, and providing learning experiences. The *field of early care and education* is a broadly inclusive term used to refer to those who provide programs and services for young children. When we talk about members of the early childhood workforce, we generally use the term *early childhood educator*, and attempt to limit use of the term *professional* to those who have completed a formal training program. The term *caregiver* or *provider* is often used to describe those who work with infants and toddlers, and *teacher* for those who work with preschool, kindergarten, and primary-grade children, though the setting also influences this terminology.

We believe that if early childhood educators are ever to speak with a persuasive voice and be clearly understood, the issue of terminology needs to receive serious attention in the future.

In this edition, we have expanded the number of sections in the book from five to eight in order to give the topics of families, diversity, and advocacy more significance by placing each of them in a separate section. The eight questions listed below provide the organizing framework for the book.

Part 1: Who Is Responsible for the Care and Education of Young Children?

Who in our society is responsible for funding, operating, and monitoring care and education programs for young children? Who is responsible for providing positive learning experiences and assisting families in learning about child development and effective parenting? The issue of responsibility for children is as old as our nation.

Years ago the issue of responsibility for young children prior to entrance into elementary school came to a head when President Nixon vetoed the child care bill of 1971. In so doing, Nixon carefully selected his words, saying that, as a nation, we are not ready to "communize" our children through group care and education. For a number of years federal, as well as local and state, governments were cautious about assuming responsibility for children prior to their entry into elementary school.

Today, there is more widespread recognition than ever before of the importance of early experiences and the value of high-quality programs and services for young children and their families. More and more local and state agencies are supporting early childhood programs. At the time of this writing, a fundamental change is taking place, as many states are beginning to assume responsibility for programs for 4-year-olds. Some are even including 3-year-olds in state-funded programs. There is also more support from the federal government and from the private sector. Religious institutions, private associations, local and state governments, and the federal government are all involved in promoting the well-being of children. Much of the discussion about early care and education today focuses on the proper role of each of these entities in funding, implementing, and monitoring programs that effectively serve children and provide their families access to the services they need.

In this first section of the book we explore the issue of the responsibility for early care and education from two vantage points. Two chapters explore what programs and services are needed to support positive development in young children, and the role of different groups in society for providing for their needs. Chapter 1 focuses on the issues of governance and coordination and Chapter 2 offers an international perspective on this topic.

Part 2: What Kinds of Programs Do Children Need to Support Their Development?

The importance of the early years in later development is supported by findings about the physiology of the infant brain and growing evidence that cognitive and emotional development are powerfully impacted in the first years of life. While there is general agreement today that many benefits result from nurturing and stimulating early learning environments for young children (especially those at risk of school failure), there is still a great deal of discussion regarding the kinds of programs and practices that produce long-lasting developmental benefits for young children. In Part 2 of this book we explore the kinds of experiences children need to support their development at different stages in the early years, with a special focus on current research.

Chapter 3 focuses on the challenges involved in providing optimal care for our youngest and most vulnerable children and emphasizes the important role of positive relationships and responsive caregiving in infant/toddler development.

Chapter 4 looks at the issue of quality as it applies to all programs for children under the age of 5. The authors conclude that many children are being cared for in poor or mediocre child care environments that might be harmful to their development, and provide information about some initiatives that are currently under way to increase program quality.

Chapter 5 discusses how parties define the term *readiness* and explores the impact of educational accountability on ideas and practices relating to school readiness. The chapter concludes with a call for a multifaceted definition of readiness that expands it from a focus on the characteristics of the child to a broader view that includes family, school, and community supports available to children as they enter and attend kindergarten.

Part 3: Who Will Teach Young Children?

What knowledge, personal qualities, experiences, skills, and training are necessary to work effectively with young childen? How can teachers acquire these things? The kinds of teachers that young children need and the best ways to prepare them are long-standing issues in the field of early care and education. Some believe that anyone can teach young children, though it helps if the person is warm and nurturing. Others demand that only the most highly trained, skilled, and knowledgeable people be considered qualified to teach our youngest children.

Today this discussion has expanded to address not only the personal qualities and qualifications of individual teachers but also the issue of developing an early childhood workforce to meet the growing need for trained program personnel. Some recurring questions include: How can we recruit people into the field who will provide the kind of positive experiences we want for our children? How can we provide them with ongoing professional development? And, the greatest challenge of all, how can we retain early educators in the workforce of a field that does not provide adequate compensation for many of its workers?

Chapter 6 explores the current status of the early childhood workforce and discusses some critical issues related to recruiting and retaining well-trained educators.

Chapter 7 discusses the definition of the term *professional development*, examines characteristics of adult learners and theories regarding how they learn, and reviews the history of professional development in the field. The authors also describe some views about appropriate content for training teachers of young children and review research on the impact of professional development on programs and children.

Chapter 8 offers guidance to teachers about how to work effectively with low-income and inner-city children. Though the focus is on acquiring dispositions and skills that will be helpful to teachers who work in urban settings, sage advice is provided that could be helpful to all teachers of young children.

Chapter 9 looks at the nature of professions, explores whether early care and education is a profession, and discusses some of the costs and benefits of professional status. The chapter goes on to discuss the role of codes of ethics in professions and provide an overview of the NAEYC Code of Ethical Conduct. The authors conclude the chapter with a call for all early childhood educators to learn to behave ethically in their dealings with children and families.

Part 4: What Is the Early Childhood Curriculum?

The fourth part of the book addresses three interconnected topics relating to the content and process of teaching in early childhood programs. The chapters address the planned curriculum, the role of play in early childhood programs, and the role of early learning standards in shaping the curriculum in early childhood programs.

Chapter 10 offers a broad overview of the early childhood curriculum including its history, an examination of implications of constructivist and behaviorist theories, and an overview of some influential ideas about the purpose of early childhood curriculum. Some widely used curricular approaches are examined, and ways in which early childhood educators can provide a rich and meaningful program for children, while at the same time addressing early learning standards, are presented.

Chapter 11 explores a long-standing commitment to play as an essential component of early childhood education. It recounts the history of play, examines a large body of research on the impact of play on children's development, discusses the educational purposes of play materials, presents a number of issues relating to play, and reflects on contemporary directions for play.

Chapter 12 looks at potential negative consequences and positive benefits of early learning standards, examines the relationship between standards and accountability, and explores the relationship of developmentally appropriate practice to these standards. The author calls for the integration of curriculum in the interests of more meaningful, connected learning, and highlights the need for robust content in curricula for young children.

Part 5: How Can We Meet the Needs of All Young Children?

Chapter 13 argues that full inclusion for young children with "developmental disabilities" is the only right, democratic, and ethical thing for our schools and society, though it remains a difficult reality to achieve for financial, attitudinal, and method-ological reasons.

Chapter 14 presents a broad view of diversity as both a challenge and a resource for early childhood education. Traditional challenges associated with race and class haven't gone away, and new patterns of immigration and acculturation have a powerful influence on children's school achievement. Inclusive educational policies and practices will require that we embrace a new theory of human devel-opment that highlights the dynamic relationship between sociocultural contexts and children's learning and growth.

Part 6: How Will Early Childhood Education Be Evaluated?

Chapter 15 outlines the continuing debate between those who favor formal assess-ment using only intelligence or achievement tests and those who argue for authentic or performance-based assessments that employ investigation, anecdotal records, and portfolios. The chapter highlights the importance of clarifying what child out-comes should be measured, by whom, and for what purpose.

Chapter 16 discusses the need for well-enacted evaluations as a tool for build-ing high-quality programs for all children birth through age 8. The author discusses issues involved in program evaluation, and cautions that whereas evaluation tools have improved, there is an imbalance between high-stakes decisions and the limited but improving tools and processes available at this time.

Part 7: What Is the Role of Families in Early Care and Education?

In adding this new section of the book, the editors acknowledge the great impor-tance accorded by professionals today to the role of families in early care and educa-tion. Chapter 17 paints a complex picture of families and early care and education professionals, including the benefits of bringing the two groups together and some of the issues that get in the way. The author asks teachers to step out of their com-fort zone to work on relationships with diverse family groups.

Part 8: How Can We Advocate for Young Children?

We have moved advocacy from the first to the last section of the book. We did this because when we taught using this book, students were interested in knowing what they could do to support the agenda for children and their families after learning about all of the issues. The motivation to learn about advocacy is stronger when readers know about the issues. Chapter 18 emphasizes the ethical impera-tive for all early childhood professionals to advocate for the well-being of children. The authors discuss the three spheres of influence—personal, private, and public policy—and provide three overarching advocacy strategies that can be utilized by early childhood professionals.

PART 1

WHO IS RESPONSIBLE FOR THE CARE AND EDUCATION OF YOUNG CHILDREN?

*P*art I of *Continuing Issues in Early Childhood Education* addresses the question, Who Is Responsible for the Care and Education of Young Children? This question about responsibility for the very young is an issue almost as old as our nation. Although a free public education financed by the states and supported by the federal government was far from the Puritans' minds, their concern with religion and the ability to read the Bible led to the passage of the Old Deluder Satan Act of 1647 (Cohen, 1974), which mandated that every town of 50 households appoint and pay a teacher of reading and writing, and that every town of 100 households provide a grammar school to prepare youths for the university. Education until then had taken a variety of forms, from the dame school to apprenticeships. Before the creation of the public elementary school, most young children continued to learn by modeling the skills used by their mothers in the home and their fathers on the farm or in a business. Minorities, the poor, and girls fared poorly in the educational system of Colonial America.

Times have changed. In our society, we have made a commitment over the years to government's responsibility for the education of children once they reach elementary school. A well-defined legal structure, within a framework of constitutional provisions and laws, outlines the authority and responsibility of the federal, state, and local governments for the education of children 5 years of age and older. Given this framework, public education for children older than 5 is generally agreed to be the responsibility of the states. The responsibility for children under the age of 5 was traditionally agreed to reside with their families.

The role of government in the care and education of the very young has vacillated throughout our history. Generally, before the 1960s, government assumed a small role in programs for children under kindergarten age. In response to specific problems, the federal government formulated public policies and created and funded initiatives designed to address the welfare of children at risk for school failure and those with disabilities. For example, the federally funded Head Start program for low-income children was created in 1965. This exemplary program for poor children was never funded to serve the entire eligible population, however, and limited financial assistance was afforded to most low- and middle-income families during the 1970s and 1980s. Beginning in the 1990s, we have seen an increasing partnership between families, the public sector (including federal, state, and local governments), and the private sector in funding early care and education.

Since the 1990s a number of states and cities have initiated early care and education initiatives targeting children prior to their entrance into kindergarten. In spite of these efforts, the number of early childhood programs in most communities did not meet existing needs. Some kinds of care were (and continue to be) in extremely short supply—care for children of parents who work nonstandard hours, infants, children who are ill, and before and after school care. A recurring issue that is highlighted in several places in this book is that the supply of good quality early care and education programs still does not meet the demand for them. Another persistent issue is that most families cannot pay the full cost of care without some additional support from the public and private sectors. This situation was exacerbated by the 1996 Personal Responsibility and Work Opportunity Act, which restricted welfare and required that women who had previously received public assistance return to the workforce. Though all levels of government have consistently acknowledged the need for and importance of programs that address the educational needs of young children and their families, investments and supporting policies have never come close to meeting the increasing demand for such programs.

Recognition of the importance of early education is fairly widespread and new public and private funding sources have emerged in the last few years. Nevertheless, some children in our country still do not have access to adequate early care and education programs.

The first of the two chapters in Part I, "Governing American Early Care and Education: Shifting from Government to Governance and from Form to Function," written by policy experts Sharon Lynn Kagan and Kristie Kauerz, reviews the role of government in early care and education in the United States and historical attitudes toward it, and then examines some of the changes that began in the 1990s. The authors argue that the critical queston today is not *if* government should be involved in early care and education. They say that government *is* involved and the question now is what needs to be done to make it work.

The authors discuss the current proliferation of state and federally funded programs and the large of number of public and private agencies involved in providing programs and services for young children, each of which has its own mandates and guidelines. In summing up the issue they write, "The multiplicity of programs—each linked to different standards, rules, and regulations—has led to a hodgepodge of efforts that are confusing to parents and policy makers, troublesome to providers, and patently inefficient" (p. 14). What we find today is a "convoluted nonsystem of ECE services . . . those of sound mind would never have deliberately chosen to create" (p. 14).

Kagan and Kauerz discuss the serious lack of leadership and coordination for creating a workable delivery system for early care and education programs. The question that we should be asking today, they say, is how to coordinate all the players to maximize outcomes for children. The question of responsibility focuses on the importance of *governance*, which is described as "How programs and entities are managed to promote efficiency, excellence, and equity. It comprises the traditions, institutions, and processes that determine how power is exercised, how constituents are given voice, and how decisions are made on issues of mutual concern" (p. 15). The authors believe that the critical issue at this time is the creation of viable new governance forms that will meet the demands of a rapidly changing field and alignment of these forms with functions that states hope to create or strengthen.

The chapter concludes with issues to consider, including the importance of balancing authority and accountability, the importance of durability in governance structures, adequate funding, building public support, and finally, and perhaps most important, the need for our society to examine its values and make a commitment to the welfare of young children—a theme that will resonate through the chapters that follow.

This chapter will be of interest not only to advanced students in early childhood courses but also to those involved in formulating policies relating to the provision of early care and education programs. We urge you to share it with anyone in your community addressing the issue of governance.

Chapter 2, "The Role of Government in Early Childhood Education and Care: An International Perspective," written by Gale Flynn, looks at government's role from a broader vantage point. Flynn discusses the powerful influence on government support for early care and education exerted by the UN Convention on the Rights of the Child (a document that has been ratified by every country except the United States and Somalia). She then highlights findings from some of the cross-national studies conducted by the Organization of Economic Co-operation and Development (OECD), an international think tank that has investigated policy related to early care and education in 24 industrialized countries.

Some of the compelling reasons that countries provide support for early care and education are described as the kinds of programs and services that are supported. These can be put into two categories: programs in which funding goes directly to families to aid them in child rearing, and programs in which someone outside the home is paid to care for and educate young children, including family child care, center-based care, and preprimary education.

Flynn goes on to elaborate on topics introduced in Chapter 1 with a discussion of governance functions in early care and education including policy development, coordination, and quality assurance. Mechanisms for funding these functions are discussed, along with examples of how these issues are addressed in a number of different countries. Flynn concludes that there has been a steady trend of increasing government involvement in the care and education of young children and that most countries, inspired by the UN Convention on the Rights of the Child, have strengthened their commitment and are moving toward better integration of services.

These first two chapters remind us that early care and education occur in a larger societal context and provide a broad overview of the kinds of organizational structures that are needed if all young children are to have a good foundation for healthy development. They also presage some themes that emerge throughout this book: the need for an adequately trained and compensated workforce, the need for examination of societal values leading to greater awareness of the importance of the early years, and willingness to invest in children at this critical time in their lives.

APPLY WHAT YOU LEARNED

As you read the following chapters, think about, talk about, and do additional reading and research regarding these questions:

❑ What is the role of the local government in the care and education of young children in your community? In your state?

❑ How might the federal government fulfill the constitutional requirements to provide for the general welfare of young children given our current political system?

❑ What structures exist in your community/state for the governance of care and education programs for children under the age of 5? How did they evolve?

❑ What mechanisms exist in your community for coordination between programs and services and transition between different care and education settings?

❑ What are some significant differences between attitudes and practices regarding early care and education in the United States and in other countries discussed in Chapter 2?

❑ Which of the programs and practices described in Chapter 2 do you think could be adopted in the United States?

REFERENCES

Cohen, S. (1974). *A history of colonial education, 1607–1776.* New York: Wiley.

Johnson, J. (1998). "The role of government in early care and education: Who decides?" In C. Seefeldt & A. Galper (Eds.), *Continuing issues in early childhood education* (2nd ed., pp. 7–28). Upper Saddle River, NJ: Merrill/Prentice Hall.

Steiner, G. Y. (1976). *The children's cause.* Washington, DC: Brookings Institution.

CHAPTER 1

GOVERNING AMERICAN EARLY CARE AND EDUCATION: SHIFTING FROM GOVERNMENT TO GOVERNANCE AND FROM FORM TO FUNCTION

Sharon Lynn Kagan
Teachers College, Columbia University

Kristie Kauerz
Office of the Lieutenant Governor in the State of Colorado

In past editions of this book, the role of government in the development and delivery of services to young children and their families has been explored thoroughly. Chapters in previous editions have addressed critically important questions regarding the role that government should play in early care and education (Goffin, 1990; Johnson, 1998).

Our intent in this chapter is quite different. We contend that for decades the debate has focused on the appropriate role of government in early care and education (ECE), with particular emphasis on the degree to which it should provide funding, regulate, and be held accountable for young children's programs and services. Our thesis holds that, while important, these questions are presently moot. The great proliferation of early childhood programs at all levels of government means that, de facto, the issue of government's role is being etched out in different ways, state by state. With the rapid expansion of ECE programs, and with highly idiosyncratic patterns of government engagement, we suggest today's issue is *governance*. We accept that states will have different patterns of who funds what; similarly, we posit that states need to grapple with how multiple funding streams are treated.

We review the history of governance in ECE, examine contemporary governance approaches, delineate essential functions of governance, and make recommendations regarding provisions that must be established if American early care and education is to be governed effectively and equitably.

GOVERNMENT'S ROLE: TAKING STOCK, PAST AND PRESENT

America's founding fathers did not establish the country as a social welfare state, heavily dependent on government involvement in family life. To the contrary, early pioneers came to this land to escape the tyrannies of oppressive governments. It is not strange that the privacy and primacy of the family reigned and, with it, a strong preference for individual initiative and self-sufficiency. Social services, therefore, were established, largely in the private sector, for those who could not fend for themselves. At the same time, the United States was a country that valued a common education as a cornerstone of democracy. Over the years, America manifested this commitment in the development of the world's most comprehensive, compulsory K–12 public school system that serves nearly all children. Somewhat uniquely, early care and education (as the very name implies) has a firm foot in both the social service and education worlds, with this division rendering the question of government responsibility for ECE fuzzy.

Any history of American child care and/or early education reflects this duality. From the earliest times, questions of whether government had a responsibility for children's well-being were front and center. Essentially decided by public inaction, except in times of national crisis, government's role remained marginal to that of the private sector. For all intents and purposes, private programs were funded, managed, and controlled by the settlement houses, churches, and nonprofit agencies that brought them to life. As demand grew, the for-profit sector entered the market, adding to the supply of private services for young children. In the 1960s, when America's social conscience reached its zenith, government—primarily federal, but also some states—stepped in to provide programs for economically disadvantaged children. Serving only a small percentage of the population, these programs evoked questions regarding the extent to which government would assume a fair share of responsibility for helping, in partnership with families, to structure children's child-rearing environments and experiences.

Issues of government's role in early care and education reached another turning point in the 1990s, in part because elementary and secondary education was surging to the forefront of the policy agenda, in part because the federal government was assuming a larger policy role in general, and in part because new data testified to the effects of high-quality early childhood programs. Bringing young children to the fore, the National Education Goals Panel, in its first goal, historically called for the nation to prepare its young children for school. Controversial, this goal was the prelude to much discussion and, along with new research and organized advocacy, to an expanded federal investment in services for young children. In fiscal year 1999, a General Accounting Office (2000) report showed that 69 federal programs provided or supported education and care for children under age 5. Nine different federal agencies and departments administered these programs, though the Departments of Education and Health and Human Services operated most of them.

Since the 1990s, in addition to federal investment and involvement, states have also expanded their policies and programs that serve young children—indeed, at a rate that outpaces the federal government. Many states now have state-funded prekindergarten, home visiting, family support, child nutrition, and other programs. For example, in 2006, 38 states had launched state-funded prekindergarten programs to provide educational services to a portion of their 4- (and, in some cases, 3-) year-olds; a handful of states have made these programs universally available (Barnett, Hustedt, Hawkinson, & Robin, 2006). States are also making considerable investments in the infrastructure to support these efforts, including efforts to improve the quality and retention of the workforce, to improve the quality of programs, to make programs accessible to parents via resource and referral efforts, and to improve accountability. For example, governments have established quality standards (for both programs and teachers), eligibility requirements and, in some cases, expectations for what children will experience and learn as a result of their participation in these initiatives. Finally, at the same time that government involvement has been increasing, there has been a proliferation of private programs and initiatives.

THE CONSEQUENCES OF GOVERNMENT ACTION/ INACTION AND THE NEED FOR GOVERNANCE

The multiplicity of programs—each linked to different standards, rules, and regulations—has led to a hodgepodge of efforts that are confusing to parents and policy makers, troublesome to providers, and patently inefficient. Confusion exists because (1) parents have trouble accessing and understanding differences among program offerings, and (2) policy makers are not sure of the comparative quality and outcomes of the programs and, consequently, of the comparative value of their investments. Inefficiency results from different institutions, authorities, and programs acting independently while providing, and often duplicating, the same tasks and services for young children and families. Alternatively, sometimes programs have contradictory regulatory standards that raise serious issues of equity for providers (e.g., different pay scales for the same work). Complicating matters, these efforts take place within a broader education policy context that emphasizes equity and high-quality experiences for all children. Despite these good intentions, decades of uncoordinated policy making have rendered a convoluted nonsystem of ECE services that does not meet these goals; indeed, this nonsystem is one that those of sound mind would never have deliberately chosen to create.

That this situation has emerged is no one's fault. In part, it resulted from the fundamental American value of parental choice. Multiple programs provide a bevy of options from which parents can choose to enroll their children at different ages and different times of the year (e.g., half- or full-day; year-round or school calendar only; community- or school-based). In part, it resulted from the quintessentially democratic principle of compromise; the field wanted more regularized and organized funding but, due to a lack of resources, it captured the various limited funds that were made available, along with their accompanying, and often discrepant, mandates. In part, the nonsystem flourished because of federalist issues. Finally, we contend, it emerged because there was no centralized locus of governance for early care and education. Stated simply, there was no single agency of government, no single committee of Congress or of state legislatures, and no single state board around which people and policies could coalesce.

Given these realities, the burning question is no longer solely what role government should play, but how the multitude of public and private actors and initiatives can be configured to maximize efficiency, outcomes, equity, excellence, and individuality. Enter governance. The relevant question today is one of governance: *How can the multitude of federal, state, local, and nongovernmental ECE programs be governed together?*

DEFINING AND UNDERSTANDING NEW GOVERNANCE APPROACHES

Defining Governance: What Is It and How Is It Different from Government?

Governance is both a pervasive and slippery term. Most agree that governance is an inherent characteristic of societies, communities, and organizations, and that it exists in both the public and private sectors. Broadly, it has been defined as the means by which actors use purposeful efforts to guide, steer, control, or manage sectors or facets of society (Kooiman, 1993b). It has been defined as the process whereby a collective group makes important decisions (many regarding resources), determines who to involve in decision-making processes, and establishes how it will account for its efforts (Institute on Governance, 2005). In the public sector, it has been defined as the process by which nations allocate responsibility for decision making and delivery within and across administrative departments, levels of government, and public and private actors (Neuman, 2007). Governance is different from government, with "the latter stressing hierarchical decision-making structures and the centrality of public actors, while the former denotes the participation of public and private actors, as well as non-hierarchical forms of decision making" (Kohler-Koch & Rittberger, 2006).

More specific to early care and education, governance works to ensure that *all* programs are expected and supported in their efforts to attain quality standards for themselves and for their teachers, to be affordable and meet the needs and demands of the local community, to be cost-effective, and to provide children with meaningful experiences that prepare them to be successful lifetime learners (Kagan & Cohen, 1997). In sum, as these definitions suggest, governance refers to how (often multiple) programs and entities are managed to promote efficiency, excellence, and equity. It comprises the traditions, institutions, and processes that determine how power is exercised, how constituents are given voice, and how decisions are made on issues of mutual concern.

Understanding New Approaches to Governance

Complex as the ECE field may be, it is not alone in its quest for new approaches to governance. Societal shifts—decentralization and a preoccupation with efficiency as a criterion for public action—coupled with the ever-increasing complexity and costs of public problems have limited government's ability to handle solutions in the public sector alone (Salamon, 2002). Consequently, there is increasing reliance on "indirect government" in which third parties (e.g., nongovernmental organizations, collaborative initiatives, and private industry) help to deliver publicly financed services and pursue publicly authorized purposes. As such, America is witnessing an increasing hybridization of the public and private sectors and an increased sharing—between government and third-party, private-sector actors—of basic government functions, including the exercise of discretion over the use of public authority and the delivery of services using public funds (Salamon, 2002). This interplay of public and private actors can be found around the world and in areas such as social welfare, environmental protection, education, and physical planning (Kohler-Koch & Rittberger, 2006; Kooiman, 1993a; Peters & Pierre, 1998). Because of these dramatic shifts, contemporary public sector governance structures are collaborative in that they often transcend any single agency or program by establishing interdependencies between public agencies and a range of third-party actors. This shift can be characterized as one from "public versus private" to "public plus private." New forms of governance have been termed "on the borderline between government and society" (Kooiman, 1993b). In short, the fundamental developments and structural characteristics of the society in which we live are pushing us toward new forms of governance across the globe, the country, the sectors, and the professions.

Contemporary governance theories stress several fundamental principles:

1. Decision making is more often than not done collaboratively; top-down approaches of the past have given way to shared or even bottom-up policy making (Kohler-Koch & Rittberger, 2006).

2. Legitimacy is derived from the democratic process and the rule of law, not the force of a dominant individual; "there seems to be a shift away from more traditional patterns in which governing was basically seen as 'one-way traffic' from those governing to those governed, toward a 'two-way traffic' model in which aspects, qualities, problems, and opportunities of both the governing system and the system to be governed are taken into consideration" (Kooiman, 1993b, p. 4).

3. The autonomy of individual entities is protected as collaborative policies are developed.

These principles set apart new approaches to governance from those of the past.

GOVERNANCE IN EARLY CARE AND EDUCATION

ECE Governance—Contextual Factors

In early care and education, the framing of and work around governance have been evolutionary enterprises. Initially, the field took a very narrow approach to governance, focusing only on the governance of individual programs (Phase I).

With the proliferation of programs, the field recognized a need for cooperation and collaboration across programs and funding streams, leading to the establishment of loosely configured entities to achieve effective linkages (Phase II). As demands for equity and efficiency have grown, the field has begun to explore broad new governance models and structures (Phase III). Today, all three approaches to governance still exist in the ECE field. With each of the 50 states having its own history, values, and priorities, there is a wide range of approaches from which we can and have learned. To most, however, governance is a knotty concept; it involves tackling tough issues such as power, influence, turf, and money. Despite its importance and the energy invested in it, early childhood governance has received little analytic or evaluative attention. It is similar to the proverbial blind men and the elephant, with researchers, practitioners, and policy makers touching all parts of it and garnering different understandings. With these understandings, the following description of existing approaches to ECE governance is just that—descriptive, not evaluative.

ECE Governance—Phase I: The Programmatic Approach

Prior to the 1960s, governance, to the degree it existed, was limited to program and sometimes fiscal oversight by the boards of private nonprofit programs or the religious or community-based programs that housed or sponsored them. Publicly funded child care had its own regulations handled through state regulators, who were often legally compelled to monitor programs. From the governance perspective, Head Start parachuted onto this scene in a revolutionary way. While continuing the tradition of the past, in that legislation promulgated rules for Head Start only, the rules were startling. Programs were to meet Program Performance Standards and periodic monitoring was required; policy councils were to have the final word on major decisions regarding the program, including hiring and budget decisions; and parents were to comprise over half of the membership of each policy council. These governance provisions pertained just to Head Start and were highly regarded as a key to its distinctiveness and success.

In Phase I, other smaller ECE programs emerged, each with its own approach to governance. Prekindergarten, early intervention/special education, family support, family literacy, health, and mental health programs all had their individual approaches to governance. Boards, committees, and commissions oversaw the performance of single programs or groups of programs targeted at limited populations of children.

The consequence of this programmatic approach to governance—a nonsystem of services for young children—has been discussed and cited often (Bruner, Stover Wright, Gebhard, & Hibbard, 2004; Gallagher, Clifford, & Maxwell, 2004; Kagan & Cohen, 1997). With each program adhering to its own program standards, its own expectations for children, its own criteria for teacher qualifications, and its own system of monitoring and improvement, no early childhood "whole" could emerge. Programs competed with each other for resources, for personnel and, in some communities, even for children. Often, the competition was rancorous, as staff moved en masse from one program to another for pennies-per-hour wage increases.

ECE Governance—Phase II: Coordination and Collaboration

Recognizing the challenges that resulted from a lack of coordination and collaborative planning, a series of efforts that hallmarked the onset of Phase II took hold in the mid-1980s. Labeled "systems efforts," "joint planning," or "partnerships," these efforts aimed to bring sponsors and providers of different programs together to achieve common goals. These coordinating efforts take several different forms: (1) within-government cabinets, (2) within-government management teams, (3) state-level collaboratives, (4) managing partnerships, and (5) state-local partnerships.

Quite popular, within-government cabinets generally are established by governors and composed of the top-ranking executives of state agencies responsible for programs and services related to young children. Often called "children's cabinets," these groups promote coordination across agencies; mobilize resources around the governor's priorities for children and families; facilitate a holistic approach to serving children; and strengthen partnerships with the nonprofit and private sectors (Segal, Grossman, & Lovejoy, 2004). At least 16 states currently have a within-government cabinet focused on early childhood issues. Most include key leaders from state agencies that serve children and families, including child welfare, health and human services, mental retardation, mental health, and education. Some also involve leadership from economic development, administration, labor, and employment departments. Other cabinets include representatives from outside the executive branch, involving leaders from the courts and justice system, the attorney general, and the state treasurer. Children's cabinets can move an agenda swiftly, develop shared visions, and foster public awareness. While many cabinets consider the allocation or reallocation of resources and make funding recommendations to the governor and independent state agencies, most cabinets lack authority and accountability to implement such changes.

Within-government management teams are often established to complement the work of the within-government cabinets, although some states established them independently. Composed of midlevel bureaucrats from state agencies responsible for administering early childhood programs, these management teams provide a forum for administrators with direct management oversight of various programs, initiatives, and funding streams to plan and work together. The Head Start collaboration director generally is included in these efforts. Although these teams provide a collaborative forum for sharing ideas and setting priorities, they often lack authority and accountability to implement and sustain meaningful, system-level policy change. One example of this is Maryland's Subcabinet on Children, Youth, and Families, established in statute in 1993 to improve the structure and organization of state services; the subcabinet was elevated to a children's cabinet in 2005.

Moving beyond the confines of government, a number of states have established initiatives that involve the hybridization of public and private sectors. These efforts are known as collaborations, task forces, or councils and often are established to meet a single need (e.g., to plan a new project, create a strategic plan, or address a legislative issue). Examples include the coordinating councils established by all 50 states to guide the Early Childhood Comprehensive System Grants, funded by the Maternal and Child Health Bureau; the leadership teams established by those states participating in the BUILD Initiative; and the multitude of task forces and study commissions established by executive order or legislation each year. Membership is usually composed of both in- and out-of-government people. Frequently, these groups are part of a special foundation initiative. While effective in meeting short-term needs and/or crafting long-term recommendations, such bodies typically are not durable and often do not have authority to implement meaningful system change.

A fourth approach to governance includes managing partnerships created to oversee new large-scale and long-term programs. Because program oversight is involved in these cases, the efforts typically have staff and considerable resources. The most notable example is North Carolina's Partnership for Children (NCPC), established in 1993 to provide statewide oversight of the Smart Start initiative. The NCPC is a private, nonprofit 501(c)(3) organization with an executive director and board of directors that brings together government, the nonprofit sector, business, civic, and community groups. NCPC receives annual appropriations from the state and significant investments from the private sector. These funds are used to provide technical assistance and training for local Smart Start partnerships in the areas of program development, administration, organizational development, communication, fiscal management, technology, contracts management, and fund-raising. In addition, the NCPC funds local Smart Start partnerships. This kind of managing partnership has significant authority to manage funds, set policies, and oversee service delivery. In some cases, these managing partnerships are imbued with the authority to do comprehensive state planning that impacts all early care and education programs, but lack the authority to implement—and enforce—priorities.

A fifth governance approach that characterized Phase II comprises those efforts that have a state entity, typically a council or apparatus (discussed in the third and fourth approaches above), along with local counterparts. In this approach, local entities have specific responsibilities germane to their geographic area that are coordinated with the state entity. Often these entities are created in legislation and are responsible for planning. Smart Start North Carolina is one example of this, combining the state-level Partnership for Children with 80 local partnerships that serve all 100 of the state's counties. Another example is Iowa's Community Empowerment Initiative that comprises the Iowa Empowerment Board (with members from state agencies and the state legislature, as well as nongovernmental representatives) and 58 local community empowerment boards that serve all 99 counties.

Taken together, these five approaches characterized the bulk of "governance" activity in the 1980s and 1990s. While vibrant and exciting in their time, many of these approaches have serious shortcomings. For the most part, these efforts are not really "governance." That is, they lack the durability, authority, and accountability associated with true governance. With regard to durability, some are not imbued in state legislation and consequently often disappear with the arrival of new political leaders who advance their own agendas and approaches. In addition, Phase II efforts regularly lack real authority. Without a clear directive based in legislation or other durable policy, they lack clout and a clear sense of mission or purpose. Groups flounder, spending hours of time developing mission statements while members with busy schedules lose interest, fueling group inertia. But perhaps most important, many of the Phase II efforts lack authority for systemwide accountability. They have planning and recommending powers but, for the most part, are not fully responsible for systemwide programs, budgets, and outcomes. Lacking such fiscal and performance accountability, the entities cannot make the deep policy changes that are needed to unify early care and education into a structured system.

Having noted their shortcomings, it is important to acknowledge that Phase II approaches are important midstream efforts; they truly catapulted governance from a program approach to one that facilitated holistic planning across the ECE field. In many cases, these "governance" approaches improve the coordination of direct services and foster the development of the early care and education infrastructure. They also improve collaboration across agencies, initiatives, and programs. Finally, immeasurably valuable, they have unified the field at a conceptual level, illuminating the failings of impermanent structures and paving the way for much more sophisticated governance structures that characterize Phase III.

ECE Governance—Phase III: Moving Toward Shared Responsibility and Accountability

During the late 1990s and into the new millennium, discourse around the creation of an early childhood system took hold, as did growing recognition that existing governance approaches, while helpful, were not adequate to meet the growing demands of the field. Some were too informal and lacked fiscal authority; others lacked staying power, deflating when the founding elected official was no longer in office. But perhaps most significant, there was growing recognition that the rapid expansion of early care and education that took place in the early to mid-2000s placed unfair burdens on structures established to coordinate, but not imbued with the authority needed to govern. Goffin and Washington (2007) characterize the era as one during which "almost every facet of the field's work is undergoing change." Like other new realities, they suggest that "early care and education must organize itself as an effective delivery system" and call for the establishment of accountability and governance structures.

Motivated by recognition of the need to increase equity, efficiency, and accountability, states have begun to examine the nature of governance, with many developing new ideas and approaches. Some states have been quite inventive and have implemented structural changes that alter ECE governance. These have taken on different forms and functions, much like their precursors in Phases I and II. In an effort to chronicle the contemporary governance scene in the United States, we turn to a rubric advanced for an analysis of governance abroad.

In reviewing the literature and examining governance approaches used in OECD countries, Neuman (2007) suggests that governance has three dimensions across which countries vary in their efforts. The first, administrative integration, refers to the degree to which a single administrative agency is responsible for early care and education. For example, in several European countries, programs and services associated with child care, which traditionally have been lodged in ministries of social services, are being moved into ministries of education. A second dimension to governance is decentralization, which refers to alterations in the balance of authority and autonomy among different levels of government. For example, responsibility for early education that was highly centralized at the state government level in Sweden has been moved to the local level, thereby significantly altering the governance of early care and education in that country. Finally, a third governance dimension is privatization, referring to the degree to which governing functions are assigned to the public and private sectors. For example, in France, services that had been primarily the responsibility of government are now being incentivized so they are more appealing to the private sector. It is important to note that in both Europe and the United States, these three dimensions of governance do not function in isolation; it is quite common to have governance reforms that simultaneously devolve authority to localities (decentralization) and to the private sector (privatization). These three dimensions provide a useful lens through which to examine governance trends in the United States.

Administrative Integration.   To better describe trends in the United States, we have subdivided the first governance dimension—administrative integration—into three: *stand-alone administrative integration,* wherein one lead agency is given authority for ECE; *blended administrative integration,* wherein a new entity that has authority to link existing agencies oversees ECE; and *subsumed administrative integration,* wherein a subunit (e.g., a division or department) of a single agency is given authority for ECE. Although they each represent a kind of administrative integration, they are quite different and therefore are discussed separately.

Stand-Alone Administrative Integration or the Entirely New State Agency Approach.   One recent approach to governance in early care and education is the unification of complementary programs, services, and initiatives into a new, free-standing executive state agency or department. These newly established executive branch agencies have powers similar to other state departments (e.g., education, human services). The department is represented by a secretary or commissioner on the governor's cabinet, thereby granting departmental status to early care and education equal to that given K–12 and higher education. The agency has its own staff, administers programs, and has monitoring, regulatory, and enforcement duties. This approach to governance accords the state agency substantial degrees of both authority and accountability (fiscal and results) that pertain to a broad array of services and infrastructure that comprise the system. Three states have recently created new state agencies: Massachusetts, Georgia, and Washington. Washington is not discussed here, as it is discussed later to highlight how its efforts reflect the trend toward privatization.

Massachusetts. The state's General Assembly established a new state department and accompanying independent board—the Department and Board of Early Education and Care—in July 2005. The new department consolidates all ECE services into one streamlined agency, combining the authority and functions of the Office of Child Care Services with those of the Early Learning

Services Division at the Department of Education (except for kindergarten, mental health, and autism grant programs that serve school-aged students). The creation of the department is part of an overall plan to develop universal access to voluntary, high-quality early childhood education, delivered through a mix of public and private providers, for all preschool-aged children in Massachusetts. The department holds (a) fiscal accountability through its administration of child care subsidies; (b) program accountability by licensing more than 12,000 child care and early education facilities that serve over 220,000 children statewide; (c) child/student accountability by overseeing the development of a kindergarten readiness assessment system and a comprehensive evaluation of early education and care programs; and (d) teacher accountability through its management of a workforce development system that supports the education, training, and compensation of the ECE workforce, including all center-based, family child care, and infant, toddler, preschool, and school-age providers. In order to ensure continuity of expectations and leadership across the full education continuum, from birth through postsecondary, Massachusetts's Commissioner of Early Education and Care serves on the state's Board of Higher Education and Board of Education.

Georgia. The state's department, Bright from the Start: Georgia Department of Early Care and Learning, assumes the responsibilities of the Office of School Readiness, the Georgia Child Care Council, and the Child Care Licensing Division of the Office of Regulatory Services in the Department of Human Resources. As such, it is the state agency with authority to oversee child care and educational services for Georgia's children ages birth through 4 and their families and to administer nutrition programs for children and adults. The department holds both fiscal and performance accountability: it oversees Georgia's Pre-K Program for 4-year-olds; licenses approximately 3,000 child care centers and group child care homes; registers over 5,000 family child care homes; administers two federal nutrition programs (the Child and Adult Care Food Program and the Summer Food Service Program); houses the Head Start State Collaboration Office; and implements the Standards of Care Program and Homes of Quality Program to enhance the quality of child care provided to infants, toddlers, and 3-year-olds. In addition, the department administers the federal Even Start family literacy program; funds and partners with the child care resource and referral agencies; collaborates with Smart Start Georgia and other entities to enhance early care and education with blended federal, state, and private monies; and distributes federal Child Care Development Funds.

While this model of governance creates clear, visible lines of authority, it also presents challenges. Integration from one perspective is dis-integration from another. By consolidating programs and services from other state agencies into a single new agency, these efforts create the need for all new patterns of cross-agency coordination and collaboration. Departments of human services still provide meaningful and relevant services to families and children, as do departments of education and health. In addition, after creating single agencies, these states must ensure that the ECE agency garners the resources and clout necessary to compete with welfare, transportation, homeland security, and other major state policy priorities.

Blended Administrative Integration.   A second approach to administrative integration is in the establishment of an executive branch office to lead and manage ECE efforts across state departments, blending management functions across multiple agencies. Here, a single office brings together programs and staff from diverse departments while funding from the individual departments remains separate. The governance entity appears on the organizational charts of both departments, and the leader of the office reports jointly to both departments' executive directors. The governance entity performs regulatory and administrative functions, with a heavy emphasis on creating a coherent strategy and ensuring its implementation in the respective agencies. In so doing, it seeks to avoid the duplication of functions across departments. Inventive, blended administrative integration represents an advancement over Phase II governance approaches discussed earlier without realigning existing major funding streams or deconstructing the boards of the individual agencies. This approach is most effective when the governor has appointment authority for the executive directors of all of the affected state agencies.

> **Pennsylvania.** The Office of Child Development and Early Learning was established in December 2006 to coordinate initiatives within the Departments of Education and Public Welfare dedicated to early learning and development for children birth through 5 years old. The office incorporates programs formerly housed in the Department of Education (Head Start, prekindergarten, full-day kindergarten, and preschool intervention programs for children ages 3–5) and in the Department of Public Welfare (child care, early intervention for children from birth to 3, and family support). Four bureaus carry out the work of the office: the Bureaus of Certification Services, Early Learning Services, Subsidy Child Care Services, and Early Intervention Services. There is also a finance, planning, and evaluation unit. More specifically, the Bureau of Certification Services regulates all child care centers, group homes, and family child care homes through regional offices. The Bureau of Early Learning Services connects programs and develops strategies to support public-private sector collaborations; it administers pre-K, Keystone STARS, state-funded Head Start, the Children's Trust Fund, Nurse Family Partnership, Parent Child-Home Program, and T.E.A.C.H. The Bureau of Subsidy Child Care Services organizes the subsidized child care and parent counseling services. The Bureau of Early Intervention Services oversees the early intervention programs for children from birth to age 5.

Subsumed Administrative Integration: The New Unit Approach.   A third contemporary approach to governance in early care and education is the bringing together of complementary programs, services, and initiatives in a new division that is housed within an existing state agency. Here, programs and funding are consolidated within a unit with its own staff that administers programs, and may have monitoring, regulatory, and enforcement duties. Currently, administratively integrated divisions dedicated to early care and education have been created within the

Departments of Education in Tennessee and Maryland, within the Department of Human Services in Arkansas, and within the Governor's Office in North Carolina.

Maryland. In 2005, the state's General Assembly passed a bill establishing a new Division of Early Childhood Development within the Maryland State Department of Education. This required transferring certain programs from the Office for Children, Youth, and Families and from the Department of Human Services to the Department of Education. Specifically, the Division of Early Childhood Development took on authority for licensing, registering, and monitoring family child care homes and child care centers. In addition, the new division now provides oversight to the Child Care Resource Network, the Family Support Centers Network, and the Child Care Credential. The Child Care subsidy program remains in the Department of Human Resources, leaving fiscal accountability for early childhood services divided across state agencies. The rationale for housing the Early Childhood Development Division within the Department of Education was, in part, based on the department's long-held goal that all children arrive at school with the skills and competencies needed to succeed in life. Furthermore, the department has responsibility for ensuring educational achievement for all children under the No Child Left Behind Act, and the legislature believes that early childhood programs can be aligned more efficiently with K–12 education goals if housed under the same state agency ("An Act Concerning Education," 2005). An Early Childhood Development Advisory Council, established in state law to guide the division, does not have direct policy-making authority but suggests priorities to the State Superintendent of Education.

This approach provides administrative integration and facilitates the coordination of efforts within an existing state agency, but it does not provide the same degree of autonomy, authority, and political leverage as does the creation of an entirely new state agency. Inherent in this approach is selection of the agency wherein the new unit will be located. As Rigby, Tarrant, and Neuman (2007) point out, the very choice of which department the division is subsumed under can bias the underlying values and principles of its future work. For example, integration within an education department may help to garner political and financial resources to expand access toward universal education that may be unattainable within a social services department (because K–12 education is widely accepted as being a fundamental right available to every child), yet may also lead to downward pressure of school-like methods and practices (Neuman, 2007). In contrast, while integration within a human services or social welfare department may limit access to children most at risk (because these agencies primarily provide safety-net services and programs to vulnerable populations), it may be better able to maintain a comprehensive focus on meeting the full developmental needs of children and families, not just their "education" needs.

Decentralization.   A second dimension of ECE governance is decentralization, whereby states empower local communities to initiate and implement efforts that integrate care and education. These efforts reflect theories of federalism that argue local governments and communities are best equipped to design and administer programs and policies that must meet the needs of local residents (Peterson, 1995). Similar to the state-local partnerships discussed above in Phase II efforts and exemplified by North Carolina and Iowa, more recent forms of decentralized governance permit local communities not only to implement specific programs but also to be innovative in crafting policy solutions.

Colorado. In response to federal welfare reform and trends to devolve decision making, Colorado initiated an innovative effort to support local communities in their efforts to build high-quality ECE systems. In 1997, the Colorado General Assembly authorized the creation of local early childhood councils in 12 communities. By 2007, additional legislation increased the number of communities to 31, serving 60 of the state's 64 counties. The intention behind the establishment of the local councils was to create laboratories for exploring, defining, and implementing the critical components of an ECE system. By statute, the councils are asked to (a) improve coordination between local, county, state and, where possible, federal resources; (b) ensure collaboration among public and private stakeholders in the delivery of services; (c) partner with K–12 education stakeholders to ensure linkages between early childhood education, kindergarten, and grades 1 to 3; (d) include program components that expand the quality of ECE programs; and (e) be responsive to the needs of working parents. Each council's responsibilities include assessing community needs, focusing planning and activities around those needs, and implementing policies and programs that will not only meet the local needs but also inform the state's overall system-building efforts. In addition to grants and ongoing technical assistance from the state, the authorizing legislation allows councils to request waivers to any state law, rule, or regulation that hinders their efforts to provide comprehensive services for children and their families.

The advantage of decentralized efforts is that local communities' policy innovations can be transferred to policy makers at the state level. Because these ideas have been vetted and implemented at the local level, policy construction at the state level can be less politically controversial. One challenge, however, is that not all localities have the political will, the advocacy leadership, or the resources to form strong councils. Decentralization can also increase inequities. In states with strong traditions of local control, some communities may be more willing than others to exert local taxing authority to increase and improve services; in states without local control, more powerful locales can advocate more effectively for state resources, leading to unevenly distributed services across communities. Further, decentralized efforts often emerge when there are not enough resources at the state level to mandate statewide access or compliance. As such, the efficacy of decentralization is dependent on a system of incentives and guiding policies that support and encourage, but do not require, meaningful statewide policy change.

Privatization. The third dimension of governance is privatization, whereby the state transfers provision, financial, and/or regulatory responsibility to actors outside the public sector, including both nonprofit and for-profit organizations

(Neuman, 2007). For the most part, this occurs in partnership—rather than in competition—with the state.

> **Washington.** In 2005, the Washington state legislature established the Washington Early Learning Council, asking it to create an adequately financed, high-quality, accessible, and comprehensive ECE system. Based on the council's recommendations, two major new entities were created: an entirely new state agency devoted to early care and education, the Department of Early Learning (DEL), and a public-private partnership, Thrive by Five Washington. The department was established in statute and the public-private partnership was established by a memorandum of understanding signed by business, philanthropic, and government leaders. This model recognizes that private organizations can undertake specific activities more efficiently and effectively than can state government. To this end, Thrive by Five encourages increasing both the supply of quality ECE services and parents' understanding of and demand for quality services. Thrive by Five has four priorities: (1) supporting two demonstration communities; (2) identifying other promising models of collaboration across the state that are developing coordinated ECE approaches to inform and shape state-level policy; (3) encouraging statewide system building through public education and advocacy efforts; and (4) providing parents and community members with information about the quality of care they should expect and demand for their children.

In the best of cases, "government organizations remain a part of . . . these emerging models of governance, but they are conceptualized as dependent on the other actors to the same extent that those actors are dependent on government" (Peters & Pierre, 1998, p. 226). These public-private partnerships usually have substantial authority and accountability over the initiatives for which they were created, but their influence does not extend to other programs or initiatives in the system. In the worst of cases, therefore, this approach to governance can exacerbate the splintered nature of the system by providing yet another "silo" with its own mission, funding, and accountability standards.

ECE Governance—Current Issues

New governance forms need to be, and are being, developed to meet the demands of a rapidly changing field. The examples provided here illustrate how significantly the field is advancing, with states and localities etching vibrant new strategies and structures. As we have seen, each approach has clear benefits and, as program implementers know too well, serious challenges. In addition to conducting informal assessments of their efforts, states are monitoring their new governance structures with systematic evaluations—some of which are mandated in legislation.

Fortunately, the field can learn much from these pioneering states. Given that states are so different, it is highly unlikely that one approach will fit all. Indeed, the diversity of approaches already in process clearly signals the diversity that is likely to unfold. Questions persist: How does a state know which, if any, of these governance approaches to use? What issues must states consider as they craft new approaches to governance? What guidance can be rendered to ease the development of new and effective governance structures?

Using the words and constructs of master architect Ludwig Mies van der Rohe, we believe that form should follow function. In other words, the form of the governance structure adopted should be aligned with the functions a state hopes to institute and/or strengthen by creating a new governing entity. However simple this sounds, it is difficult to implement because of the general lack of clarity on the functions of governance in general, and of governance in early care and education in particular. Consequently, we now turn to examining governance functions.

SHIFTING FROM FORM TO FUNCTION

If we have learned anything from the history of ECE governance, it is that the field has been remarkably adaptive and inventive. Even this brief review suggests that the field has created and re-created governance entities, learning from the work of others over time and across states. Changes in governance are becoming increasingly more prevalent and sophisticated. As governance gains currency, however, it also raises concerns. Because governance realigns power and resources and because it evokes significant structural and operational changes, it is often the most controversial component of an early childhood system. Moreover, there is frequently confusion about the precise functions that a governance structure should undertake.

In discussing these functions, it is important to note that they must be present if the entity is to be a successful *governance* vehicle. This is not to say that entities lacking these functions are not important and effective; they well may be strong collaborative entities, but they do not exercise governance. (It should be noted that some entities labeled collaborations or partnerships may indeed execute governance functions.) In discussing governance, then, we care more about the functions being carried out than the name of the entity. Specifically, to distinguish functional governance entities from other collaborative entities, we suggest that two key functions must be present in their entirety: authority and accountability. Both should exist durably, clearly, and visibly; they must not be subject to frequent changes, obfuscated language, or limited exposure. Both authority and accountability have several components, all of which should be present if we expect governance entities to be effective.

Authority: The Power to Act

Webster's defines *authority* as "the power or right to give commands, to enforce obedience, take action, or make final decisions; jurisdiction." Authority legitimately empowers entities to implement policy change; it allows them to make—and enforce—critical decisions on priorities including: (1) regulations, (2) finances, and (3) data.

The Authority to Develop and Enforce Regulations.   Governance entities must possess regulatory authority. That is, they must have the power to establish and enforce regulations that enable people and organizations to operate within the ECE field. Such regulations must be imbued in state law and must pertain to all those individuals, facilities, and programs over which the government exercises authority. Examples of regulatory authority include the power to develop and enforce the regulations that: (1) entitle and govern facilities' operation; (2) enable individuals to practice early care and education, including the establishment of criteria that reflect the necessary competencies and qualifications to teach; (3) influence the distribution of services (e.g., eligibility levels, parental fees); and (4) establish aligned early learning standards (e.g., specifications of what young children should know and be able to do), curriculum guidelines, and assessment efforts.

The Authority to Budget, Allocate, and Manage Fiscal Resources.   Governance entities must possess fiscal authority—the ability to garner fiscal resources and then to administer, allocate, and manage the funds. They must have adequate resources to carry out effectively all the functions presented herein. Moreover, because multiple funding policies and programs currently characterize early care and education, some consolidation of funding will be necessary. Such consolidation should not result in funding reductions but should yield a more efficient and effective use of resources.

The Authority to Collect, Interpret, and Release Data.   Governance entities must possess authority to collect, store, track, and analyze data. Data are the sine qua non of effective administration. Such data need to transcend individual programs and must be collected and analyzed in conjunction with one another. Data should reflect the different kinds of authority just discussed, with accurate, current, and accessible data available on program availability and accessibility, program quality, teachers, fiscal resources, and children. To be maximally effective, individual ECE student, teacher, and program identifiers should be developed irrespective of funding sources. Moreover, the collection of data should be consistent across programs.

Accountability: The Power to Know

Webster's defines *accountability* as "being obliged to account for one's acts: responsible, explainable." Governance includes accountability *to* someone or some entity and accountability *for* something (Posner, 2002). Taking the "to" first, a governance entity has accountability to those who have a stake in the performance of the governed endeavor. For example, governance can involve accountability to elected officials, interested groups, clients of the direct services provided, the media, and others. The range of people to whom accountability is accorded largely determines which interests frame the debate and the ultimate objectives of the effort(s). Governance "for" something typically translates into two kinds of accountability: (1) fiscal accountability, which chronicles whether money is spent efficiently and for those purposes it was intended; and (2) performance accountability, which chronicles the effectiveness or achievement of desired results.

In early care and education, the "to" and the "for" present interesting and changing issues. Typically, early childhood programs are accountable to their funding source(s), and since there are many different funding sources, there are many agents to whom programs must render accountability. Multiple funding streams significantly complicate coherent governance. By contrast, the current need for unified accountability systems that are consistent from institution to institution and program to program is paramount. Turning from the "to" to the "for," early care and education historically has been accountable for program quality, with the empirically driven understanding that programs of higher quality are more likely to achieve better child outcomes. Today, however, the press for results is evident in calls for four different forms of accountability, each of which must be addressed by the governance entity. Moreover, an ideal governance structure would recognize that all four types of accountability are inextricably linked; it would not only establish each of the four types but also ensure that all were aligned with one another.

Fiscal Accountability.   Governance entities must not only possess the authority to budget and allocate resources but also be accountable for ensuring that programs and services remain fiscally responsible. This means that funds must be managed and used according to prescribed goals (e.g., making services affordable and accessible to families). Fiscal accountability is an ongoing effort that must be funded as part of the efforts of the governance entity.

Program Accountability.   Governance entities must either provide oversight to programs directly or provide for the provision of such oversight. Program accountability ensures that the quality of all programs, irrespective of funding stream, is monitored regularly and reliably. The establishment of quality rating systems and accreditation facilitation projects supports measurement and implementation of program improvement. Accountability ensures that such efforts are monitored to discern their impact on program quality. Embedding these efforts in, or linking them to, a governing entity ensures that program quality is equitable.

Workforce Accountability.   Governance entities must monitor the capacity of the workforce to deliver the intended quality of services to children and their families. Such accountability takes the form of assessing the nature and quality of teacher preparation efforts, as well as the degree to which teachers in the state adhere to prescribed standards.

Child/Student Accountability.   Perhaps most controversial of all, governance entities need to be sure that children are making developmental progress toward achieving the state's prescribed early learning standards. Such child accountability takes different forms, as well documented by the National Task Force on Early Childhood Assessment and Accountability (in press). Governance entities have the responsibility to design and implement child accountability systems that will provide data about children's progress to policy makers while honoring the rights of young children. Given the controversy surrounding this issue, the establishment of accountability for children is typically carried out only after thorough deliberation and input.

ISSUES TO CONSIDER

This comprehensive approach to governance is set forth for debate and consideration. Certainly, to date, no single early care and education governing entity has been imbued with all authority and accountability functions suggested herein.

However, this does not mean that such an entity is not possible. K–12 education has an elaborate and, despite criticism, well-honed governance system. Within most state departments of education, the authority and accountability functions described above exist. To build such authority and accountability into governance entities in early care and education, what issues need to be considered? We present five below.

The Issue of Balance

In their efforts to advance early care and education governance, many states have created entities that have mixed governance authorities and accountabilities. For example, governance approaches may be designed to have authority for regulations and accountability for finances. Alternatively, they may have the reverse. In designing a governance entity, it is important to align the authority with the accountability functions, so that, for example, if fiscal authority is granted, it is accompanied by fiscal accountability, enabling a balanced approach to governance. In other words, accountability should be accorded only when commensurate authority exists.

The Issue of Durability

To be effective, governance entities must have durability. Governance entities cannot be regarded as the brainchild of, or be dependent on, a small number of visionary and dedicated individuals. During initial developmental stages of new governance structures, it is important to ensure that both their creation and dissolution require stakeholder input, bipartisan agreement, and official action by a political institution. In addition, new governance structures must be given adequate time to become well-established and to work out the inevitable kinks that change brings. Given America's penchant for quick fixes, one worrisome trend is that if a governance entity does not meet all of its goals immediately, it is deemed a failure. Good governance is not simple, particularly when it demands the realignment of established agencies, departments, and patterns of activity.

We suggest evaluating all governance entities after they have been in existence for at least two years. Modifications can be made based on such evaluations, but once established, a governance entity should be given at least a decade of life. This kind of sustainability will provide governance durability and legitimacy across changes in political leadership; it will temper the ever-changing, often flip-flopping policies and priorities caused by change in political leadership that is only exacerbated as term limits for elected officials become more prevalent across the nation.

The Issue of Funding

Because it is often argued that increased funding for early care and education should improve direct services for children and families, it is easy to forget that governance entities need and deserve funding. Indeed, funding for governance should be regarded as an investment that yields more effective, efficient, and equitable utilization of monies. Routinely, funding is accorded to the governance of other policy priorities (e.g., state departments of education, higher education, human services, health, and transportation). Providing adequate funding for ECE governance entities should be, therefore, self-evident.

The Issue of Public Support for Governance

Governance is not a sexy topic. Nor is there a good way to talk about it without dredging up images of bureaucratic mumbo jumbo that is far removed from what children and families really need. And yet, the public is affected—positively—by good governance on a daily basis. A challenge for the future will be to build public support that accepts and embraces governance entities as necessary and credible components of an ECE system.

The Issue of Values

In making the case for accountability, it has often been said that a society measures what it treasures. By taking serious stock of program efficacy and the impacts of such programs on young children, early care and education has been able to legitimize increased funds. With such accountability, however, must come increased, organized authority. If the country values young children the way it professes, it must ensure—without debate—that the programs that serve them are of high quality, are efficiently managed and monitored, and are readily and easily accessible to all. Unfortunately, and unlike our European counterparts, the United States generally has not seen fit to invest in ECE governance. In so doing, our actions speak louder than our words; we seem to value young children only to the extent that we can most modestly serve them.

CONCLUSIONS

In this chapter, we have attempted to discuss governance from historical, theoretical, and practical perspectives. We note the importance of governance to the effective delivery of services; in fact, we contend that effective governance is the centerboard that keeps the early childhood ship afloat. We would even go so far as to contend that without attention to effective governance, we should not launch new initiatives. Governance is glue; it is the essential ingredient that will enable American early care and education to survive and thrive.

This does not mean that all governance entities will look alike. We hope not. We do hope, however, that our explication of diverse authorities and accountabilities presents the range of what is possible and will serve to guide deliberations as states and localities accord more necessary attention to governance. In so doing, we hope to have shifted the discourse from government to governance and from form to function.

REFERENCES

An act concerning education—Child care administration and Office for Children, Youth, and Families and Maryland Family Support Centers Network—Transfer to State Department of Education, Maryland General Assembly, 419th Sess. (2005).

Barnett, W. S., Hustedt, J. T., Hawkinson, L. E., & Robin, K. B. (2006). *The state of preschool 2006: State preschool yearbook.* New Brunswick, NJ: National Institute for Early Education Research.

Bruner, C., Stover Wright, M., Gebhard, B., & Hibbard, S. (2004). *Building an early learning system: The ABCs of planning and governance structures.* Des Moines, IA: State Early Childhood Policy Technical Assistance Network, Child & Family Policy Center.

Gallagher, J. J., Clifford, R. M., & Maxwell, K. (2004). Getting from here to there: To an ideal preschool system. *Early Childhood Research and Practice, 6*(1).

General Accounting Office (GAO). (2000). *Early education and care: Overlap indicates need to assess crosscutting programs* (No. GAO/HEHS-00-78). Washington, DC: Author.

Goffin, S. G. (1990). Government's responsibility in early childhood care and education: Renewing the debate. In C. Seefeldt (Ed.), *Continuing issues in early childhood education* (pp. 9–26). Upper Saddle River, NJ: Prentice Hall.

Goffin, S. G., & Washington, V. (2007). *Ready or not: Leadership choices in early care and education.* New York: Teachers College Press.

Johnson, J. C. (1998). The role of government in early care and education: Who decides? In C. Seefeldt & A. Galper (Eds.), *Continuing issues in early childhood education* (2nd ed., pp. 7–28). Upper Saddle River, NJ: Merrill/Prentice Hall.

Kagan, S. L., & Cohen, N. E. (1997). *Not by chance: Creating an early care and education system for America's children.* New Haven, CT: Bush Center in Child Development and Social Policy, Yale University.

Kohler-Koch, B., & Rittberger, B. (2006). Review article: The "governance turn" in EU studies. *Journal of Common Market Studies, 44,* 27–49.

Kooiman, J. (1993a). *Modern governance: New government-society interactions.* London: Sage.

Kooiman, J. (1993b). Social-political governance: Introduction. In J. Kooiman (Ed.), *Modern governance: New government-society interactions* (pp. 1–8). London: Sage.

National Task Force on Early Childhood Assessment and Accountability (in press). *Final report.* Washington, DC: Pew Charitable Trusts.

Neuman, M. J. (2007). *Governance of early care and education: Politics and policy in France and Sweden.* Unpublished doctoral dissertation, Columbia University.

Peters, B. G., & Pierre, J. (1998). Governance without government? Rethinking public administration. *Journal of Public Administration Research and Theory, 8*(2), 223–243.

Peterson, P. E. (1995). *The price of federalism.* Washington, DC: Brookings Institution.

Plumptre, T., & Graham, J. (1999). *Governance and good governance: International and aboriginal perspectives.* Retrieved December 9, 2005, from www.iog.ca

Posner, P. L. (2002). Accountability challenges of third-party government. In L. M. Salamon (Ed.), *The tools of government: A guide to the new governance* (pp. 523–551). New York: Oxford University Press.

Rigby, E., Tarrant, K., & Neuman, M. J. (2007). Alternative policy designs and the socio-political construction of childcare. *Contemporary Issues in Early Childhood, 8*(2), 98–108.

Salamon, L. M. (2002). The new governance and the tools of public action: An introduction. In L. M. Salamon (Ed.), *The tools of government: A guide to the new governance* (pp. 1–47). New York: Oxford University Press.

Segal, A., Grossman, L., & Lovejoy, A. (2004). *A governor's guide to children's cabinets.* Washington, DC: National Governors Association.

CHAPTER 2

The Role of Government in Early Childhood Education and Care: An International Perspective

Gale Flynn

Educational Consultant

As societies become more developed, countries have witnessed a slow but steady growth in governmental support for families in the provision of care and education of young children. Generally, the growth has been spurred by increasing female participation in the labor force as well as societies' recognition that proper care and education are a child's basic human right. In 1989, the United Nations adopted the Convention on the Rights of the Child (CRC), which was the most widely ratified human rights document in world history (UNICEF, 1989). Only the United States and Somalia have yet to ratify the CRC. Article 18 of the CRC calls on nations to provide assistance to parents and legal guardians in their child-rearing responsibilities and to make child care services and facilities available, especially to working parents. More recently, in 2005, the Office of the United Nations High Commissioner for Human Rights extended these early childhood recommendations by reminding parties to develop comprehensive policies covering health, care, and education that provide assistance to parents and caregivers, including parenting education, counseling, and quality child care services backed by monitoring systems (Paragraphs 20, 21; OHCHR, 2005).

Across the globe, countries have made steady strides in adopting policies toward fulfilling these obligations to their youngest citizens. Many Western European nations, as well as Canada, provide universal health care, a considerable first step in ensuring children's optimal development. Within the context of adequate health care, public early childhood education and care (ECEC) efforts can be categorized into two somewhat distinct areas of policies and programs:

1. Those that enable parents to directly care for and educate their young children
2. Those that engage others in the provision of ECEC

Examples of government policies that enable parents to directly care for and educate their children include the provision of paid parental leave, family cash allowances, and support for parenting education. Government policies designed to help families engage others in the care and education of young children usually take the shape of programs that offer family day care, center-based care, preprimary education, and out-of-school provision (or before and after school care).

Our understanding of international policies regarding ECEC has been greatly enhanced due to the educational monitoring efforts of the United Nations Educational, Scientific, and Cultural Organization (UNESCO) as well as cross-national studies that have been undertaken by the Education Committee of the Organization of Economic Cooperation and Development (OECD). The OECD is an international think tank consisting of representatives from 30 industrialized countries committed to democratic and market economies. Their work focuses on addressing the challenges of economic, social, and environmental globalization.

In 1998, the OECD launched the "Thematic Review of Early Childhood Education and Care (ECEC) Policy" with 12 countries participating: Australia, Belgium (Flemish and French communities), the Czech Republic, Denmark, Finland, Italy, the Netherlands, Norway, Portugal, Sweden, the United Kingdom, and the United States. The impetus for the review followed recognition that ECEC was necessary not only to ensure the access of women into the marketplace but also to support early human development as a foundation for lifelong learning. The review formed the basis for a comparative report published by the OECD Secretariat, entitled "Starting Strong: Early Childhood Education and Care" (OECD, 2001). A follow-up 2002 review, examining additional topics, included eight more countries: Austria, Canada, France, Germany, Hungary, Ireland, Korea, and Mexico. Therefore, during the period from 1998 through 2004, 24 countries have participated in these reviews, offering significant insights regarding the effectiveness of government policies and ECEC systems in caring for their youngest citizens. This chapter attempts to highlight some of the findings of these and other cross-national studies to add perspective and to enrich ongoing discussions regarding the development of more coherent ECEC systems.

WHY COUNTRIES SUPPORT ECEC

As mentioned earlier, most countries have adopted the UN Convention on the Rights of the Child as a fundamental guide for developing policies and programs that ensure young children receive health services, care, and education. These rights correspond with strong social welfare ideologies that have permeated European countries following their recovery from the devastating effects of World War II. Beyond these philosophical principles, other special circumstances unique to each country have stimulated further investments in ECEC. Many countries recognize that ECEC is a valuable tool for maintaining adequate levels of female participation in the labor force, addressing declining fertility rates, and improving social equity for the disadvantaged.

Issues of Female Workforce Participation and Gender Equity

A major economic concern in more developed countries is the need to sustain and support contemporary levels of women in the workforce. Female participation in the labor market has grown significantly over the past 30 years, and currently ranges from 60 to 70 percent in most industrialized nations.

For example, Ireland's gross domestic product (GDP) surged 7.8 percent annually during the 10-year period between 1993 and 2003, and women contributed significantly to this growth (National Women's Council of Ireland, 2005). Access to quality child care must parallel economic expansion for production levels to be sustainable. Ireland's ECEC package includes 18 weeks of paid maternity leave, and free half-day preprimary classes within primary schools for children aged 4–6. Parents pay approximately 51 percent of the average cost of child care for children in the 0–3 age group. The offering of partial care and education may explain why 35.1 percent of women in Ireland's workforce engage in part-time versus full-time employment (OECD, 2006).

As in Ireland, many women reconcile the tension between work and family by engaging in part-time or casual employment, sometimes paid on a cash basis. Though this strategy may support more immediate family needs to care for young children, in the long run, women's life-course earnings and social pensions are usually sacrificed and they become more dependent on others in their senior years. Their more casual or interrupted participation in the workforce generally contributes to lower professional attainment and decreased earnings than that of men, thereby sustaining the gender divide.

Issues of Demographic Challenges

Demographic challenges of declining fertility are being experienced worldwide but with more dramatic implications in developed countries. On average, women must have two children during their childbearing years in order for a country's population to remain stable. Demographers note that those nations whose total fertility rates (TFR) are less than 2 will likely witness declining populations within a relatively short time frame. Falling populations ultimately lead to declines in economic productivity unless countries act to recruit new sources for their labor force and future tax bases (Wattenberg, 2004). Those with falling fertility rates may be inclined to widen the doors of immigration to offset impending labor shortages. Others may prefer a more long-term solution of enticing natural-born citizens to reproduce by offering them an array of support for child rearing.

In 2005, the TFR for the United States was 2. Coupled with a steady influx of immigrants, the TFR has produced no looming concern over the consequences of population decline. Other industrialized countries, however, are experiencing serious fertility problems as noted in the following TFRs: France, 1.8; Sweden, 1.6; Germany, 1.4; Italy, 1.3; Japan, 1.3; and Russia, 1.3. Several countries have approached the issue by establishing or strengthening their existing pro-family policies.

The French are especially concerned that their falling native population will eventually threaten the very existence of French language and culture. They have established several pro-natal policies including universal health care, paid parental leave, and family cash allowances, together with an ECEC system that deliberately promotes French identity and citizenship. Universal care and education is available as early as age 3 and will over time reach all two-year-old children. The French ECEC system provides a vehicle to promote a heavily centralized standard curriculum and teacher-training program that focuses on critical elements of perpetuating French culture.

In addition to falling birth rates, citizens of more developed countries are experiencing longer life spans, requiring significant health and social supports for an increasingly aging population. Governments with more generous social welfare policies are hard-pressed to reconcile the growing demands of both their younger and older dependent citizens. The impact of the dependent population squeeze is a concern for ECEC advocates as aging citizens have the advantage of political power (the vote) over their younger counterparts.

Issues of Social Equity

In most societies, government is expected to lead efforts to control and effectively diminish the impacts of social ills such as poverty, crime, delinquency, and so on. The costs of remedial social welfare programs can take a considerable chunk out of national budgets and therefore governments tend to pay attention when there is strong evidence of potential cost savings through investments in preventive efforts. Several longitudinal studies, particularly in the United States and the United Kingdom, have demonstrated the long-term educational, social, and economic benefits of quality child care, particularly for disadvantaged children. Nobel Prize–winning economist James Heckman (2000, 2006) successfully translated these benefits into returns on investment, prompting new interests in increasing access to ECEC particularly for children at risk for educational failure.

Though most European countries offer ECEC programs on a universal basis, several enhance these provisions with supplemental resources that target low-income and disadvantaged children as a means of mediating disparities and ensuring a "fair start" in life. France provides more funding (currently 10 percent) to areas that are socially and economically disadvantaged called "priority education zones." Local governments utilize these resources to lower child-staff ratios, hire resource specialists, or develop innovative programs to address identified needs. The French government also provides additional recruitment and retention incentives to staff who work within these zones (Neuman & Peer, 2002).

In the United States, only a few states have enacted laws providing universal access to preprimary programs, although there is steadily growing interest and funding for ECEC programs that target "at-risk" children. The national Head Start program was designed specifically to help compensate for educational disparities found between children of poverty and those of greater means by providing poor children with quality preschool experiences. Though Head Start has proven its success in leveling the playing field upon school entry, after 40 years it remains underfunded with only 50–60 percent of eligible children enrolled (Zigler, Gilliam, &

Jones, 2006). The lack of political will to finance and enroll all eligible children accounts for Head Start's continued restricted availability to children in poverty and those with special education needs, despite the fact that research has demonstrated that low-income preschool children do better in more integrated socioeconomic environments (Schechter, 2002).

England is implementing a "progressive universalism" ECEC policy, which currently entitles all 3- and 4-year-old children to 12.5 hours per week of an educational program in state-maintained nursery schools for a period of 33 weeks (OECD, 2006). In 1998, the government initiated a major strategy to eradicate child poverty by 2020 through an early childhood initiative named Sure Start. The initiative offers an array of health, early care, and education and family support services to disadvantaged families with young children living in the most deprived areas of the country.

WHAT TYPES OF ECEC PROGRAMS DO GOVERNMENTS SUPPORT?

Though there are a variety of government-supported ECEC programs, most fall into one of two broad categories that can be distinguished by simply examining who is providing the care and education of the young child: either the child's parent or someone else. Policies that support paid parental leave, family allowances, parenting education, and parent participation in playgroups fall into the first category of enabling parents to directly care for and educate their young child for a period of time rather than engage in labor market activity. As parents move into the labor force and as nations recognize children's own rights to quality early education experiences, governments establish policies and programs to support other caregivers and educators in offering ECEC.

Supporting Parents to Directly Care for and Educate Their Children

Paid Parental Leave. Government labor policies offering paid parental leave not only support the physical care of young children but also enable families to secure a strong social-emotional foundation for the child during the earliest and most critical period of development. In 1996, the European Council (the highest political body of the European Union) agreed that its member nations would introduce legislation enabling parents to care full-time for their child over a minimum 3-month period. Most OECD countries offer employees who have worked for a specified period of time prior to becoming pregnant, paid maternal and parental leave benefits.

Figure 2–1 provides an overview of the "effectiveness" of parental leave policies in 18 nations by considering how adequately each nation compensates parents during their entitled leave period. The assumption is that parents are more likely to take leave when their benefits are closer to the compensation levels they received during active employment. There are greater parental leave provisions in countries

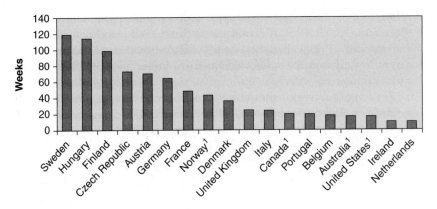

FIGURE 2–1

Effective Parental Leave Provision

Note: The degree of parental leave effectiveness is calculated by weighing the length of parental leave by the level of payment: Effective parental leave = [(maternity leave in weeks – 14 weeks) * % payment benefit) + (total parental leave in weeks * % payment benefit)].

[1]Data taken from Cleveland and Krashinsky (2003).

Source: Deven and Moss (2005); Platenga and Siegel (2004).

such as Sweden and Hungary and therefore more incentive for parents in these countries to take leave and remain at home with their children. France has established the *Allocation parentale d'éducation* for parents with two or more children, in which a flat rate stipend is paid to allow working parents to remain at home. If the parent decides to return to work part-time, the stipend is reduced by one-half, rather than discontinued.

Across the lower end of the economic spectrum, parents residing in countries that allow parental leave, but with lower compensation levels, are less likely to accept the benefit. The United States does not require paid maternity leave, or paid parental leave. What the government does require of employers with 50 or more employees, is a guarantee that after a maximum of 12 weeks of family leave, the employee may return to the same job with the same pay and benefits.

Family Allowances.   Another vehicle that governments utilize to assist parents with their responsibility for child rearing is a family allowance that provides monthly cash assistance or subsidies to families based on the birth of a new child. Sweden provides child allowances to each child born into the family regardless of household income. In France the family allowance begins with the birth of a second child and increases with additional children. The subsidy continues until children reach 20, as long as they are enrolled in school or a work-apprenticeship program.

Parenting Education.   Parenting education aimed at families with children under the age of 3 years, particularly the home visitor model, has proliferated in various regions over the past 10 years. The strategy is designed to enrich the home environment and support parents with information and skills that promote their child's developmental needs. In Dublin, Ireland, Community Mothers visit first- and second-time parents of children from birth to 2 years (Molloy, 2002). They are often experienced mothers who are employed as paraprofessionals and trained and supported by family development nurses while utilizing a curriculum focused on child health, nutrition, and overall development. England established the Sure Start program consisting of outreach and home visits to strengthen young families, along with child care, early education, and after school care, as part of an overall antipoverty strategy. Parenting education is also provided in various group formats. Parenting services have the added benefit of breaking down the isolation many homebound parents may experience in more developed economies while ensuring that additional family needs are addressed through proper linkages with community resources.

Playgroups.   Playgroups, which require a family member to participate with the child, vary in formality, but in general offer toddlers and older children an opportunity to play with each other while being supervised by an educator or parent. Countries vary in their regulation of playgroups, depending on their purposes and pedagogy. More formal playgroups may focus on both parenting education and early childhood education and offer structured learning environments and activities. Playgroups operate in response to the varied needs and interests of families within each community and offer a more socialized experience than home-based early learning models. In England, playgroups are a major type of ECEC service to children under compulsory school age.

Support for Others to Care for and Educate Young Children

Government policies that support entities other than parents to care for and educate young children generally take the form of subsidizing various care arrangements including family child care, center-based care, preprimary education, and out-of-school provision. Though each of these services is regulated by government agencies to ensure the basic health and safety of children, the center-based care and preprimary education programs tend to be more formally organized than family child care and out-of-school provision.

Family Child Care.   Family child care is usually provided to a small group of children in the private home of a regulated and licensed caregiver, on a partial-day or full-day basis. It is a critical component in the early care system for children under the age of 3; however, most OECD countries acknowledge that it is of mixed quality and in short supply. In England approximately 30 percent of children between the ages of 1 and 3 attend child minders or private day nurseries and receive vouchers or subsidies through government or employer sources for the care. In France, families with children younger than 6 who place their children in a family child care provider's home are eligible for an allowance, *Aide a la famille pour l'emploi d'une assistante maternelle* (AFEAMA) of between 203 and 133 EUR (in 2007, approximately $280 to $184 U.S.) depending on income, for children under the age of 3. The allowance is reduced by one-half for children between 3 and 6 (OECD, 2006).

Center-Based Care.   Centers offer group care for children from birth to primary school entry in a licensed institutional setting, as distinguished from a home in a family child care setting. Centers may be public or private and operate on a partial or full-day schedule, and in general are less structured and directed toward prescribed learning activities than are preprimary schools. Traditionally, they have been designed to meet the needs of working parents, while preprimary schools were designed to transition children to the social and academic expectations of primary education.

Denmark has the distinction of enrolling the largest percentage (83 percent) of children between the ages of 1 and 2 in day care facilities (*Vuggestuer-crèche*), which are predominantly funded and operated by public, municipal authorities. The Danes begin utilizing the Vuggestuer-crèche from the time a child is about 6 months old but are also given the option of utilizing age-integrated (0–6 years) centers known as *aldersintegrerede institutioner*. Parental fees are capped at 30–33 percent of the center's costs and are further reduced for low-income families. Access to center-based care for Danish children ages 3–5 was nearly universal, at 94 percent as of 2004 (OECD, 2006).

Preprimary Education.   The International Standard Classification of Education (ISCED) defines preprimary education (ISCED level 0) as all programs that, in addition to providing care, offer a structured and purposeful set of learning activities, either in a formal institution or in a nonformal setting (UNESCO, 1997). Preprimary programs are usually for children age 3 and older and are held for the equivalent of at least 2 hours a day for at least 100 days a year.

According to UNESCO's 2007 *Education for All Global Monitoring Report*, there was a 10.7 percent worldwide increase in children enrolled in preprimary education over the 5-year period from 1999 to 2004. Table 2–1 reflects these increases in various regions of the world and indicates that the most dramatic increase took place in the Caribbean, where gross enrollment ratios (the ratio of children enrolled within the population age cohort) have achieved 100 percent levels and now surpass North American and Western European nations.

Most OECD countries provide their children with 2 years of free preprimary experience before they enter the compulsory primary school system.

Out-of-School Provision (OSP).   Care generally provided to school-aged children, before and after school hours or during intersession periods, is known as out-of-school provision, or OSP. Nearly 33 percent of children ages 6–12 in the Belgium French community have access to OSP services; however, in 2003 the government launched a 10-year plan with significant new funding to improve both access and quality. In addition, a 2004 education statute supports the financing of homework clubs as an additional OSP service. Approximately 40 percent of Hungarian students attend OSP services organized by their elementary schools. They include both before- and after-school programs as well as summer camps where a school may have access to a recreational site in the countryside. Programs can be either leisurely or educational and camps usually include school faculty and parents. Sweden offers leisure-time centers (*fritidshem*) to children ages 6–12 and nearly 50 percent of students enroll in them.

TABLE 2–1

Preprimary gross enrolment changes between 1999 and 2004, by region

| Region | Total Enrollment (000) | | Change between 1999 and 2004 (%) |
| | School Year Ending in | | |
	1999	2004	
World	111,722	123,685	10.7
Sub-Saharan Africa	5,129	7,359	43.5
Arab States	2,356	2,625	11.4
Central Asia	1,450	1,482	2.1
East Asia	36,152	32,836	−9.2
Pacific	416	520	25.0
South and West Asia	22,186	31,166	40.5
Caribbean	673	965	43.4
Latin America	15,720	18,154	15.5
N. America / W. Europe	19,151	19,408	1.3
Central / East Europe	8,538	9,176	7.5

Source: UNESCO, EFA Global Monitoring Report, 2007.

THE ROLES OF GOVERNMENTS IN ECEC

Governance: Policy Development, Coordination, and Quality Assurance

Early childhood care and education programs have evolved across both the public and private sectors and among various layers and ministries of government. As was discussed in Chapter 1, effective early childhood education and care systems require a governance infrastructure that supports good policy development, coordinates programs so that they satisfy families' needs and assures them of quality no matter where or when they may take up the service.

Policy Development

Policy making in democratic societies is a participatory process in which varied interests assemble and contribute to decisions that will affect their well-being. Ideally, ECEC policies should reflect a collective philosophy regarding the nature of childhood and the rearing of children, and offer a guiding framework for the provision of services to young children. Several countries have established national or regional pedagogical frameworks, based on a strong vision and a set of beliefs and principles about the period of early childhood itself. These frameworks serve as the basis for a coherent system of early childhood programs. When established at the national level, philosophical and pedagogical frameworks provide ample justification for public expenditure and help set clear policies for and identify the key goals of early childhood services. As nations develop these principles and frameworks, we can identify some differentiation in curricular emphases, with some countries taking a more holistic, social, and civic focus (Sweden, Denmark) while others stress school readiness and emphasize critical learning areas, particularly in literacy and math (England, United States).

For example, in Sweden, early childhood is considered to be a precious time, during which children should experience the innocence of childhood rather than be rushed into adulthood, where they can understand their right to be cared for and to be responsible for the care of others and where they can expect to share their views and to respect the views of others (Kagan & Hallmark, 2001). Programs therefore emphasize broad developmental goals and assist children to recognize the rights and responsibilities of citizenship. Swedes are careful to guard against the "schoolification," or imposition of primary education goals on young children and have resisted assessments that focus on cognitive development.

Italy has defined a vision of young children who can think and act for themselves and who are connected to their family and community. Within this national vision, the Reggio Emilia community emphasizes a child "rich in potential, strong, powerful, competent, and most of all connected to adults and other children" (Malaguzzi, 1993, p. 10). The Reggio Emilia schools have adopted a "pedagogy of listening" that honors the child's natural learning dispositions and resists predefined outcomes for young children (Rinaldi, 2006).

Research demonstrating the powerful educational and social benefits of quality preschool education on young impoverished children has moved both the United Kingdom and the United States to promote a school readiness model that promises to better prepare young children for the expectations of the primary school setting. Clear national policies also help to promote a more even level of quality across age groups and various program settings. Most governments further devolve the responsibility for developing program standards, including curricula and professional training standards, to local levels of government.

Coordinating Care and Education

Policies for the "care" and "education" of children have historically developed separately under a variety of governmental ministries, resulting in a fragmented service system for children and families. In general, children in the 0–3 age group have been served under the auspices of child care policy agencies while children of preprimary (4–6) ages have been served under educational agencies. ECEC services tend to be even more disjointed under governments that see early care as a private responsibility of parents rather than a shared responsibility between families and the larger society.

In recent years, many governments have recognized the need for a better coordinated system and have assumed a lead role in designing overall ECEC frameworks to ensure that services are coherently delivered. These systems are complex, usually crossing various ministries (health, labor, education, and social welfare) and governance levels (national, regional, and municipal). The process of system coordination and integration is difficult, and there is no one model suitable for all. There are, however, valuable lessons on system integration that can be gleaned from international efforts that are currently taking place.

Several countries, such as Denmark, Finland, Norway, and Sweden have decided to take a single-ministry approach to help build a more cohesive and holistic system. In these countries, coordination takes place under a ministry at the national level focused on both development and education. Those countries that view ECEC as part of the larger education continuum prefer to house the early childhood system within their education ministries where there is infrastructure for ensuring quality, such as a training authority, an evaluation section, pedagogical inspection, and monitoring units. In the late 1990s, England, Scotland, and Sweden transferred national responsibility for ECEC from their welfare to their education ministries. Scotland has undertaken a "New Community School Initiative," which attempts to integrate child care, early education, and school-aged education with health and family support. The country's child welfare services have also been placed under their department of education (Cohen & Wallace, 2003).

Sweden has had a long history of well-funded and integrated care and education services under its Ministry of Education and Science. Its strong holistic pedagogical tradition resulted in distinct preschool curricula emphasizing care, nurturing, and learning. The ministry takes a comprehensive view of learning from the early years through primary and secondary levels, thereby enabling smooth transitions. Sweden has developed "whole-day schools" with distinct national curricula for children in the early years (1–5 years old) and school-aged, and at "leisure time centers" (out-of-school provision). More recently, in 2001 Sweden's centralized teacher-training system established a "new teacher qualification" that unified the training of preschool teachers, school teachers, and leisure time pedagogues into a single scheme that ensures a common and appropriate pedagogy across each of these settings. Concerns regarding the overemphasis of academics or "schoolification" of young children within the education ministry were addressed by specifying policies that clearly identified pedagogy and training teachers to work within these parameters. Single-ministry approaches have resulted in more effective and coherent policy making, greater public investments, and consequently greater consistency in the levels and quality of service provision across sectors, age groups, and settings.

Other than restructuring existing agencies, countries have also created interagency councils, sometimes referred to as coordinating mechanisms (COMs), that maintain individual responsibility for their respective programs but attempt to coordinate their efforts at a national, regional, and even municipal level. In Singapore, where preschool education programs are provided by the Ministry of Education as well as the Ministry of Community Development and Sports, a COM was established to help develop a joint training framework for preschool teachers across both ministries. COMs have been effective in coordinating sectors to handle specific programs and tasks (e.g., gathering information and developing training standards); however, they have not been very successful in promoting a coherent overall policy and administrative framework (Choi, 2003). This is in part due to their temporary status, as well as their lack of authority to make necessary policy, programmatic, or funding changes.

Some governments devolve interagency decisions to a level closest to the family, based on the premise that parents and local communities should be involved in the design of services to meet their particular needs. Though decentralized decision making and design efforts allow for flexible responses to local needs, they also tend to increase variability in services regarding who has access, what standards are required, and how well programs are monitored.

It appears that effective systems require a stable mechanism at a rather high (national) level for conceiving a coherent set of early childhood policies, goals, strategies, and funding requirements to ensure that all children have access to quality care and education services. Then some level of devolution of power and resources can be assumed by local authorities who design the specifics of the system.

Setting and Monitoring Quality

As governments increase their investments in ECEC services, they also take a more proactive role in defining health, environmental, and program standards to ensure that young children receive the desired quality and level of services. In many countries, the responsibility for setting standards and regulations, monitoring to review compliance, and evaluating to understand their impacts rests with regional or local authorities. The exceptions to this practice are France, the United Kingdom, and New Zealand, where ECEC is currently more highly centralized. Nordic countries are beginning to devolve their regulatory functions to local levels, but are doing so after having established a history of high-quality services popular among the people. Definitions of quality are not universal either across or within countries, and are more or less dependent on each local area's unique interests, cultural values, and views of early childhood. In determining these standards, local governments not only examine the relevant research but also seek broad consultation from major stakeholders including parents, experts within the early childhood field, program providers, and professionals who work with young children.

Despite regional variations in the definition of *quality*, several key features are commonly found in government regulations. They include:

❑ Structural quality, such as child-adult ratios, group size, staff qualifications, level of funding, working conditions, and environmental requirements for health and safety

❑ Process quality, which generally focuses on activities offered, schedules, and the relationships and type of social interactions among children, adults, and parents

❑ Outcomes, which may include predefined child learning outcomes, broader developmental outcomes, social cohesion, or measures of parent satisfaction with services (Mooney et al., 2003).

As countries define and monitor their quality standards, they are increasingly improving their provision of technical assistance to providers of ECEC services to help them reach required benchmarks. In the Nordic countries, regulatory inspectors have been replaced by advisors who offer assistance and work alongside program personnel and parents. In the United States, where regulatory staff work-loads are relatively high, the emphasis is on compliance rather than support for the provider (Gormley, 2000). Overall, government through its legislative and regula-tory authority and ability to finance the achievement of standards is in a unique position to ensure quality in the ECEC system.

Funding of ECEC

Effective policies must be backed by adequate resources in order to fulfill their intended purposes. Therefore, one of the primary roles of government is to ensure sufficient and stable funding not only for ECEC programs but also for the gover-nance requirements to properly manage those services.

Sharing the Cost: Public, Private, and Parents.   While many governments pay the majority of the costs for early care and education, most share this cost to varying degrees with parents and private sources such as corporations, foundations, and nongovernmental organizations (NGOs). In general, there is greater government assumption of costs associated with educational, preprimary programs than there is for child care. However, in the Nordic countries, state and local government sub-sidies assume nearly 85 percent of child care costs, with parents paying most of the remaining cost. As children progress toward the educational side of the service spectrum, government assumes nearly 100 percent of the cost.

On average, parents who reside within the European Union pay about 25 percent of the cost of nonkindergarten care and education (Bennett, 2004). In countries with less government support, such as the United States, parents pay the lion's share of ECEC costs (ranging from 60 to 80%), with government targeting its support toward disadvantaged populations (those living in poverty and the dis-abled). This translates into young families having to pay 15–18 percent of their total income for child care as compared to an average of only 5–7 percent of family income spent on college tuition.

In 1996, the European Commission Network on Childcare recommended European countries invest at least 1 percent of their gross domestic product (GDP) in order to ensure a rather minimum provision of care. Table 2–2 illustrates a select group of countries' expenditures on ECEC services for children from birth to age 6, based on their responses to a 2004 OECD survey. Government investment in ECEC as a percentage of GDP is highest in northern European countries, but many coun-tries have not yet reached this benchmark.

When governments do not assume a level of funding that ensures universal access to quality ECEC, and parents are hard-pressed to do so, the private sector, con-sisting of businesses, communities, and social organizations, are asked to fill the void. Private-sector support for ECEC services takes several forms. Corporations may offer "family-friendly" work benefits such as flexible hours, job-sharing, home-based work sites, vouchers to subsidize child care expenses, on-site or contracted child care, matching employee contributions to nongovernmental organizations targeting ECEC benefits (e.g., United Way), and parenting education workshops (Myers, 2002). Governments may entice corporations to adopt family-friendly policies by

TABLE 2–2
2004 Public expenditures
on ECEC services (0–6)

Country	Public Expenditure as a Percent of GDP
Denmark	2.0
Sweden	1.7
Norway	1.7
Finland	1.3
France	1.0
Hungary	0.8
Austria	.55
United Kingdom	0.5
United States	.48
Netherlands	.45
Germany	.45
Italy	.43
Australia	0.4
Canada	.25

Source: OECD, *Starting Strong II*, 2004 survey.

providing them with tax benefits for doing so (e.g., offering tax credits for providing on-site child care facilities).

Some countries establish tax schemes whereby government, private corporations, and employees all contribute toward a social security fund that includes the provision of paid parental leave benefits and other ECEC services. Mexico and Sweden have earmarked taxes in this way and Colombia has established a 3 percent payroll tax designated for a broad array of services to young children, including child care.

Supply-Side versus Demand-Side Funding.   In general, governments have developed two means of funding ECEC services. One means, called *supply side,* directly funds the provision of services that can be operated by public entities (e.g., traditional public schools) or by private entities through a contracting process (e.g., Head Start in the United States). In this approach, governments have greater control over access to and the quality of services as they are more directly involved in supplying, designing, and monitoring programs. They can choose to fund entire operations (operations grants) or target their resources to supplement operations such as through quality-enhancement grants, wage-enhancement grants, capital equipment grants, or overall tax relief. Qualifications of personnel and compensation for staff are more uniform and closer to that of the primary education system when supply-side funding mechanisms are utilized. On the other hand, the costs of directly operating these services are rather high, and bureaucracies can add long delays to the procurement and start-up of new services.

The approach of funding private entities to enter the market under specified program conditions is viewed as a lighter and more responsive method of meeting demand for services. It has the advantage of targeting public resources to populations or areas determined to have greater needs, or where market failure has taken place. In 1990, New Zealand established a new policy intended to increase both overall quality and equity of access to services for rural Maori and Pacific Island children. The Ministry of Education funds larger grants-in-aid to entities that have lower staff-child ratios, have better qualified teachers, serve low-income communities, or operate in a language other than English. Most children with disabilities are enrolled in private programs with the Ministry of Education providing advice and support (Meade & Podmore, 2004).

Another means, called *demand side,* provides funding directly to parents through tax deductions or credits for ECEC expenses, or through government vouchers or subsidies that enable parents to purchase ECEC services that best meet their needs. These subsidies are usually set *below* the actual cost of services. There has been a growing trend in developed countries to move toward the demand-side approach, as it is less expensive, more flexible in allowing for parental choice, and can draw new suppliers into the market if subsidies are priced at a reasonable level relative to costs. This approach is more effective when parents are provided with good information on how to select a high-quality ECEC program. Problems occur when parents choose low-quality care, either because they are unaware of the negative impacts on their children, or simply because quality providers are unavailable within their local market. In this free-market model, private providers may be reluctant to invest in poor neighborhoods where, despite having subsidies, there is an insufficient number of consumers who can afford the true cost of quality care. They may also be reluctant to serve special needs children who generally require higher-intensity services, resulting in greater costs. A serious effect of the demand-side model therefore is a less integrated care and education system.

The OECD review concluded that direct public funding of services offers more effective control, the advantages of scale, better national quality, more effective training for educators, and a higher degree of equity in access and participation than consumer-subsidy models (OECD, 2006). As to whether a government should operate services itself or purchase services from the private sector, some economists suggest that this decision should be based on the existing quality of services provided by the private-sector market, and whether government can effectively monitor and control this quality. If it cannot, then publicly provided services make more sense (Cleveland & Krashinsky, 2003). A more long-term view would be for government to invest in public ECEC services, while simultaneously supporting private-sector integration and quality enhancements.

Most countries have developed a mix of supply-side and demand-side approaches. In the earlier example of New Zealand, the government adopted a mixed funding model with supply-side funding being offered through its Ministry of Education and demand-side child care subsidies being offered through its Ministry of Social Welfare.

Developing the ECEC Workforce

There is no question that the key to a quality ECEC program is a caring and competent teacher, pedagogue, or child minder who can offer nurturing and stimulating experiences to young children. Research has demonstrated that better training and fair compensation for staff members result in positive outcomes for young children (Helburn, 1995).

In countries with more integrated care and education systems, two core lead professionals have emerged across the 1–6 age group. One is an *early childhood teacher* with a minimum 3-year tertiary degree who is often assisted by a trained auxiliary considered an equal member of the team (Martin-Korpi, 2005). The other is the *pedagogue,* a professional working with the theory and practice of pedagogy, addressing the whole child: body, mind, emotions, creativity, history, and social identity (Moss & Petrie, 2002). Denmark's pedagogues have completed a 3.5-year tertiary training and are certified to work in day care, kindergarten, and OSP settings. Early childhood staff profiles and qualifications appear to be weakest in countries that have split systems of care and education and where services exist within a free-market economy (Australia, the Netherlands, the United States).

Where government has assumed a strong role in the provision of ECEC services, there is a consequent high investment in the preparation, continuing education, and compensation of those who make up the workforce. In France's highly centralized system, the Ministry of Education sets educational goals, and additionally defines standards, determines curriculum, and provides systematic teacher training. Local governments are responsible for sponsoring facilities, support staff, and out-of-school provision services. French teachers serving the nation's public preschools, called *école maternelle,* are well trained with bachelor's and master's degrees in education, qualifying them to work with children ages 2 to 11. They are employed by the national government, which compensates them on par with primary education teachers. Those teachers who work in high-risk areas, called Priority Education Zones, receive additional bonuses. French teachers have access to 36 weeks of paid in-service training over their careers (Neuman & Peer, 2002). Teachers also receive 4 half-day, obligatory trainings annually, provided by pedagogical counselors.

Ireland, Jamaica, the United Kingdom, and Sweden each have joint training of ECEC and primary teachers, with graduates qualified to work in preprimary and primary school settings. In contrast, child care providers in many countries are poorly trained, endure inferior working conditions, are modestly compensated, and are less likely to have access to in-service training (Neuman & Bennett, 2001).

Governments are utilizing a variety of approaches to build their child care workforce, but most rely on the leverage of regulations and subsidies to do so. In France, where families may receive an allowance to purchase family day care from a licensed *assistante maternelle,* compensation is far below that of teachers in *l'école maternelle.* In an effort to enhance the quality of *assistante maternelle,* municipal governments are required to provide them with training, as well as a guaranteed living wage and health insurance. Early childhood practitioners who work in center-based *crèche,* serving children from birth to 3 years of age, receive a year of professional training in nursing and are certified by the Ministry of Health. Most are public employees working in community organizations or nonprofit associations and have the right to professional development.

The United Kingdom is working toward greater integration of their care and education systems and has developed national qualifications and training standards for under-8 day care and child-minding providers. The United Kingdom offers both supply-side and demand-side subsidies and has increased subsidy funding and relaxed child-staff ratios if providers meet higher qualifications. Several countries have taken the position that raising the quality of teachers is a more significant program standard than lowering child-adult ratios. The United Kingdom also introduced a national minimum wage for ECEC employment and is in the process of developing a "Common Core" of skills and knowledge necessary for those who work with children, young people, and families, which will cut across the health, education, and social welfare sectors. In 2004, England implemented the National Professional Qualification and Integrated Center Leadership program as part of their overall strategy of system integration. The program pays senior staff of England's expanding network of "Children's Centers" (a multiservice family resource center) to take coursework in leadership and management leading to a new qualification in administration that will be recognized across education, health, and social services.

Other examples of workforce quality initiatives include Austria's requirement that family child care providers complete basic coursework in addition to being licensed. A Korean statute requires that kindergarten teachers take a minimum of 80 hours of staff development over a 3-year period and that child care workers take 40 hours. Belgium decided to eliminate child care subsidies and child care tax breaks to families who elected not to utilize licensed and regulated family day care providers. In Denmark, municipalities offer their family child care providers biweekly training through their local kindergarten programs (OECD, 2006). The New Zealand government provides a subsidy to institutions of higher education for each ECEC student who has completed a full-time course schedule.

Some governments are also taking initiative to diversify the ECEC workforce by implementing strategies to recruit more males, ethnic minorities, and indigenous staff members to better reflect the profiles of their local communities.

CONCLUSIONS

Clearly ideological, social, and economic contexts have set the backdrop for the steady trend of increasing government roles and responsibilities in the care and education of their youngest citizens. Most countries have formally adopted the UN Convention on the Rights of the Child as a foundation for codifying their own policies and establishing goals and strategies for strengthening their ECEC systems.

This chapter has attempted to highlight the comprehensiveness of ECEC policies in industrialized countries and demonstrate their effect in supporting rather than supplanting the child-rearing role of parents. Ideally, early childhood provisions enable parents to comfortably negotiate the tensions between their participation in the labor market and obligations to their family either by supporting them to directly care for their children, or by offering them choices in quality care and education provided by others.

Governments have assumed a primary role in ECEC system development and we are witnessing a gradual evolution toward better integration of early childhood programs. New governance infrastructure models are clarifying pedagogical frameworks, promoting coherent policies, attending to program quality and work-force development, and advocating for necessary funding requirements to ensure system stability.

REFERENCES

Bennett, J. (2004, May). Early education financing: What is useful to know? *UNESCO Policy Brief on Early Childhood*, No. 23.

Choi, S. (2003, January). Cross-sectoral coordination in early childhood: Some lessons to learn. *UNESCO Policy Brief on Early Childhood*, No. 9.

Cleveland, G., & Krashinsky, M. (2003). Financing ECEC services in OECD countries. Paris: OECD.

Cohen, B., & Wallace, J. (2003, April). Reforming education and care in England, Scotland and Sweden. *UNESCO Policy Brief on Early Childhood*, No. 12.

Deven, F., & Moss, P. (Eds.). (2005). *Leave policy and research: Overviews and country notes* (CBGS Work documentary 2005 / 3), available at www.cbgs.be/repository/WD_2005>03.pdf

Gormley, W. T. (2000). Early childhood education and care regulation: A comparative perspective. *International Journal of Educational Research, 33,* 55–74.

Heckman, J. J. (2000). Policies to foster human capital. *Research in Economics, 54*(1), 3–56.

———. (2006, January 10). *Investing in disadvantaged young children is an economically efficient policy.* Paper presented at the Committee for Economic Development/Pew Charitable Trust/PNC Financial Services Group Forum on Building the Economic Case for Investments in Preschool, New York.

Helburn, S. W. (Ed.). (1995). *Cost, quality, and child outcomes in child care centers.* Denver: Department of Economics, University of Colorado.

Kagan, S. L., & Hallmark, L. (2001). Early care and education policies in Sweden: Implications for the United States. *Phi Delta Kappan, 83*(3), 237–246.

Malaguzzi, L. (1993, November) Fundamentals of the Reggio Emilia approach to early childhood education. *Young Children,* 9–12.

Martin-Korpi, B. M. (2005, September). The foundation for lifelong learning. In *Children in Europe, Curriculum and Assessment in the Early Years,* Issue 9, Children in Scotland, Edinburgh.

Meade, A., & Podmore, V. N. (2004, April). Funding strategies for equitable access to early childhood education: The case of New Zealand. *UNESCO Policy Briefs on Early Childhood,* No. 22.

Molloy, B. (2002). *Still going strong: A tracer study of the community mothers program.* Dublin and The Hague: Bernard van Leer Foundation.

Mooney, A., Candappa, M., Cameron, C., McQuail, S., Moss, P., & Petrie, P. (2003). *Early years and childcare international evidence project: A summary.* London: DfES.

Moss, P., & Petrie, P. (2002). *From children's services to children's spaces: Public policy, children and childhood.* London: Routledge Falmer.

National Women's Council of Ireland. (2005). *An accessible childcare model.* Dublin: Author.

Neuman, M., & Bennett, J. (2001). Starting strong: Policy implications for early childhood education and care in the United States. *Phi Delta Kappan, 83*(3), 246–255.

Neuman, M. J., & Peer, S. (2002). *Equal from the start: Promoting educational opportunity for all preschool children—Learning from the French experience.* New York: French-American Foundation.

OECD. (2006). *Starting strong II: Early childhood care and education.* Paris: Author.

Peisner-Feinberg, E. S., Burchinal, M. R., Clifford, R. M., Culkin, M., Howes, C., Kagan, S. L., Yazejian, N., Byler, P., & Rustici, J. (1999). *The children of the cost, quality, and outcomes study go to school: Technical report.* Chapel Hill: Frank Porter Graham Child Development Center, University of North Carolina.

Plantenga, J., & Siegel, M. (2004, October 21–23). Childcare in a changing world. Position paper prepared for the *Child Care in a Changing World* Conference, sponsored by the Dutch Presidency, Gronengen, the Netherlands. Available at www.childcareinachangingworld.nl

Rinaldi, C. (2006). *In dialogue with Reggio Emilia: Listening, researching and learning.* London and New York: Routledge.

Schechter, C. (2002). *Language growth in low-income children in economically integrated versus segregated preschool programs.* West Hartford, CT: St. Joseph's College.

UNESCO. (2006). *Strong foundations: Early childhood care and education, Education for all global monitoring report 2007.* Paris: Author.

UNESCO. (2006). International Standard Classification of Education, 1997. Retrieved from www.uis.unesco.org

UNICEF. (1989). The Convention on the Rights of the Child. Available at www.unicef.org/crc/fulltext.htm

Wattenberg, B. J. (2004). *Fewer: How the new demography of depopulation will shape our future.* Chicago: Ivan R. Dee.

Young, M. E. (Ed.). (2002). From early childhood development to human development. In *Role of the private sector in early child development.* Washington, DC: World Bank.

Zigler, E., Gilliam, W. S., & Jones, S. M. (2006). *A vision for universal preschool education.* New York: Cambridge University Press.

PART 2

WHAT KINDS OF PROGRAMS DO CHILDREN NEED TO SUPPORT THEIR DEVELOPMENT?

*"T*rain up a child in the way he should go; and when he is old, he will not depart from it" (Prov. 11:3). Since the beginning of recorded time, philosophers have extolled the importance of the early years for future growth and development. Whether you start with the Bible, Aristotle, Rousseau, or Locke, the idea that what happens during the early years of life will affect later development has been a prevalent theme. From birth through age 6, the child learns all the rudiments of knowledge, wrote Comenius in *The School of Infancy* in the 1600s. In the early 1900s, McMillan wrote that "at last the world seems to be awakening to the fact that human destiny is largely shaped by the nurture or neglect of early infancy and childhood" (p. v). The kindergarten, as well, was seen as a "child saver." Through the experiences of the kindergarten in the United States, children, especially those of the poor and immigrants, were socialized for citizenship in a democracy.

The authors whose chapters comprise Part 2 examine the nature of care and education programs for children at different stages of early childhood and the impact of these programs on learning and development. These authors agree that all children should have an opportunity to experience optimum environments during their early years and that it is during this period that deprivation can be the most harmful. The chapters in Part 2 underscore the importance of respectful and nurturing relationships between children and their adult caregivers and the importance of stimulating learning environments, experiences, and materials. These authors also agree that high-quality early care and education should be available to all children in our society who need it because mothers continue to enter the workforce in record numbers and more children than ever are at risk for school failure because they live in poverty and/or in families where English is not the primary language.

While out-of-home care for children over the age of 3 whose mothers work has been grudgingly accepted since large numbers of women began entering the labor force in the 1960s, there was a widespread feeling that out-of-home care was not desirable for infants and toddlers. Much of the early research on programs for the very young was intended to demonstrate that out-of-home care could damage the mother-child relationship and result in children failing to become securely attached to their mothers. Over the years, the debate has moved from condemning all infant and toddler care to examining the quality of care and the kinds of experiences that support positive growth as opposed to those that produce detrimental effects. Since the 1990s, research has focused on identifying and measuring the critical features of child care quality. Today, the focus is shifting again, with a growing emphasis on measuring child outcomes and school-readiness.

Chapter 3, "Programs for Infants and Toddlers," coauthored by Donna S. Wittmer and Sandra Petersen, looks at what children need in programs at this early stage in their development and explores some of the resources available for families whose children are at risk for school failure or who have special needs. Wittmer and Peterson believe that new understandings about the nature of development in the early years should inform decisions about infant care and education. For all aspects of development, they stress the powerful role that adult caregivers play in the lives of the very youngest and most vulnerable children—particularly with regard to children's need for emotional support and stimulating materials and experiences.

The authors also focus on the potential dangers of exposing children to situations that cause undue stress.

Wittmer and Petersen examine the quality and availability of programs for infants and toddlers and some of the options that are currently available for families. They discuss characteristics of programs that support children's optimal development and come to the distressing conclusion that the type of early care and education programs available for infants and toddlers is quite far removed from the description of quality supported by research. They also examine some current initiatives for improving the quality of infant and toddler care.

Introducing a recurring issue in this book, the authors discuss the lack of adequately trained and compensated caregivers for young children. They emphasize the need for caregivers to have sound knowledge of infant development, and even more important, to have personal qualities that enable them to be responsive and nurturing in their work with young children. They highlight the need for ongoing professional development (another theme pervading this book) that includes awareness and appreciation of culture and diversity, knowledge of language acquisition, a solid background in infant and toddler development, and strategies for creating responsive programs based on this knowledge. The chapter concludes with a call for more awareness of the importance of quality programs for young children and their families, for well-trained and compensated caregivers, and for adequate funding to ensure that all children receive a good beginning.

Chapter 4, "Quality in Early Childhood Programs," written by Gerrit Westervelt, Annette Sibley, and Diana Schaack, explores the nature of quality care and its impact on the development of young children (with a focus on birth to age 5). These authors discuss the increasing need for out-of-home care for young children and make a strong case that not just any care will do. They report that current research demonstrates that children need quality care because it "affects children's well-being and developmental progress." They state that it is, however, difficult to define what "high quality" means because different groups of people, including family members, program personnel, and policy makers, value different aspects of child care.

The authors describe different components of quality and a new research focus—identifying the critical aspects of care settings that promote positive outcomes for children. A number of significant studies are reviewed. Westervelt and his colleagues go on to examine research on factors in child care that can be used to predict the quality of settings for young children. These include training for early childhood educators, ratios and group sizes, and the nature of the work environment. They also explore the percentage of programs that can be defined as having "high quality" and decry the great number of children cared for in settings that do not meet minimum standards. They conclude the chapter with a discussion of some things that are being done, and what could be done, to improve the quality of care. These include systems for rating quality and providing greater reimbursement to programs that meet standards, more and better professional development for the early childhood workforce, adequate compensation for personnel, and technical assistance to programs. They too reiterate the theme that what is needed most is greater awareness of the needs of young children and commitment to providing them with the best possible programs in the early years.

The third chapter in this section focuses on children who are about to enter kindergarten and examines the complex and politically charged topic of school readiness. In Chapter 5, Catherine Scott-Little discusses the evolution of current interest and concern with school readiness. She explores different lenses for viewing readiness that are used by child development theorists, educators, parents, and policy makers. And she discusses a variety of definitions of *readiness*—a term like *quality,* which is subject to multiple interpretations. Scott-Little goes on to summarize research on children's readiness for school success in the areas of health and physical development; social and emotional development; approaches toward learning, language and literacy; and cognitive development. She examines factors that contribute to the wide variation in skills and abilities that children bring to kindergarten.

Scott-Little looks at the impact of views of readiness on decisions about whether children should enter kindergarten, especially the practice of *red-shirting* (holding children out of kindergarten to give them an extra year) and kindergarten retention. The chapter ends with pleas for more refined views of children's readiness for school, for careful attention to transition practices that smooth children's entrance into school, for more responsive relationships, and for child-friendly learning environments and curricula.

Together these chapters highlight the need for mechanisms to weave all of the various program strands into a coherent system. Each of the chapters reminds us that important policies, practices, and collaborations must be in place before we can say with confidence that early education will benefit every child. Other recurring themes are children's need for high-quality programs and the importance of an adequately trained workforce. The authors in this section also express the hope that more societal awareness of the importance of the early years will lead to greater respect and compensation for those who work in the early care and education field.

Another significant issue that emerges is the need for attention to transitions. Never before in history have young children been exposed to such a multiplicity of settings from infancy onward. This suggests that we must be concerned not only with the quality of each setting but also with support for children in making successful transitions from one setting to another. In order to serve children's best interests there must be coordinated linkages between homes, early childhood programs, elementary schools, and communities.

APPLY WHAT YOU LEARNED

As you read the following chapters, think about, talk about, and do additional reading and research regarding these questions:

❑ How could our society best provide for the early care and education of infants and toddlers?

❑ What kinds of infant and toddler programs are available in your community? Learn what you can about the kinds of programs and the quality of these programs.

❑ How could our society provide for the optimal development of all young children?

❑ What kinds of provisions are there in your community for improving the quality of child care programs?

❑ What kinds of policies could be put into place to ensure that all children have a good chance of being successful when they enter kindergarten?

❑ What is the prevailing view about the nature of school readiness in your community? What provisions are available to help children enter kindergarten ready to be successful?

❑ What is the kindergarten curriculum like in your community? Does it address a wide range of developmental differences?

❑ What provisions are available in your community to help young children make smooth transitions between educational settings?

REFERENCE

McMillan, M. (1919). *The nursery school.* London: L. M. Dent & Sons.

CHAPTER 3

Programs for Infants and Toddlers

Donna S. Wittmer
University of Colorado, Denver

Sandra Petersen
Zero to Three

There is no trust more sacred than the one the world holds with children. There is no duty more important than ensuring that their rights are respected, that their welfare is protected, that their lives are free from fear and want, and that they grow up in peace.

—*Kofi Annan*

Infants and toddlers' well-being warrants careful attention by all who care about children and families. The infant and toddler years set a foundation for how children learn. The very architecture of the brain is formed during the first 3 years of life. Infants' (0–18 months) and toddlers' (18 months–36 months) early experiences influence later outcomes in all aspects of their development. The importance of the early years creates concern about the types and quality of programs provided as well as the effects of poverty, stress, and inadequate care on young children's development. Given the importance of the early years, infants and toddlers deserve quality care and education programs that emphasize positive relationships, family collaboration, and cultural sensitivity.

We discuss a number of issues in this chapter. Today there are more infants and toddlers attending early care and education programs. The increase in knowledge concerning the remarkable development of infants and toddlers helps parents and professionals understand how capable *and* vulnerable young children are as well as the importance of quality early experience. Even though we know more about the importance of the early years, stress, maltreatment, neglect, and abuse continue to have devastating effects on too many children. There is a proliferation of programs for young children and their families, and yet parents and professionals find that quality and availability are lacking, in part due to inadequate funding. Well-educated teachers and administrators for programs are essential. There is a need for professional development concerning cultural sensitivity, second language acquisition, and emotional and social development. Initiatives for improving quality are growing, professional development initiatives require higher standards for infant/toddler teachers and programs, and yet the workforce remains underpaid. A systems approach requires that professionals, the federal government, and individual agencies provide resources and set standards for program quality, adequate workforce compensation, and professional development.

In each of the following major sections, we identify what researchers, professionals, and families know; the challenges; and organizations, agencies, and initiatives that improve the quality of the programs attended by infants and toddlers. We first discuss the remarkable development of young children, second, the quality and availability of programs, and third, the workforce. To conclude, we highlight the implications of the research for practice as well as look into the future to see what might lie ahead for programs for infants and toddlers.

REMARKABLE DEVELOPMENT

Knowledge of child development increases the likelihood that professionals will provide the kinds of experiences infants and toddlers need to thrive. The new millennium opened with a landmark book by Shonkoff and Phillips (2000). *Neurons to Neighborhoods* summarized the science of early childhood development, with the authors stating, "An explosion of research in the neurobiological, behavioral, and social sciences has led to major advances in understanding the conditions that influence whether children get off to a promising or a worrisome start in life" (p. 1). The book's authors summarized the accumulating evidence for how infants and toddlers are both capable and vulnerable; products of both their genetic makeup and their environmental experiences; influenced greatly by their culture; and able to learn an astonishing amount in the context of nurturing relationships.

In infant research labs across the nation, in homes, and in programs, researchers and professionals are investigating the remarkable ways in which infants and toddlers learn how to communicate, how they think, and how they become social partners with adults and peers. For example, at Harvard University Dr. Elizabeth Spelke is studying how very young infants demonstrate mathematical understanding (www.wjh.harvard.edu/~lds/spelke.html), and at the University of Washington, Dr. Patricia Kuhl is studying how infants acquire language (http://ilabs.washington.edu/kuhl/research.html). Babies are no longer thought of as vegetables—"carrots that can cry" (Gopnik, Meltzoff, & Kuhl, 1999, p. 143), but as thinking and feeling human beings who do cry, but who, from birth, also actively attempt to understand their world.

Brain Development

What does the science tell us about brain development in the early years? Books such as *Rethinking the Brain—New Insights into Early Development* (Shore, 2003) and *Scientist in the Crib* (Gopnik et al., 1999), and Web sites such as www.zerotothree.org and www.PITC.com, summarize the remarkable development of the brain during the first three years and the experiences that enhance or diminish brain development.

We know that infants' and toddlers' brains develop at lightning speed during the prenatal period, and continue to grow at a rapid pace during the child's first 3 years of life. "A newborn's brain is about 25 percent of its approximate adult weight. But by age 3, it has grown dramatically by producing billions of cells and hundreds of trillions of connections, or synapses, between these cells" (Zero to Three, 2007). Prenatally and throughout the first years of life, the brain is rapidly forming these connections, or synapses, to store information and memories about experiences. As an event occurs and reoccurs, the synapses storing information about the event reactivate. With each activation, the synapses become stronger. A series of synaptic connections become very strong when over time the child experiences a favorite adult's quiet voice, songs, and gentle touches. Unfortunately, feelings of fear and hopelessness are also built into the structure of the brain if a baby cannot elicit comforting responses or lives in a violent or chaotic setting (Shore, 2003). According to Lally, Lurie-Hurvitz, and Cohen (2006), "Early experiences can and do influence the physical architecture of the brain, literally shaping the neural connections in an infant's developing mind" (p. 6).

Infants are born with an amazing capacity to learn with the help of supportive adults and peers. They are constantly developing—changing over time—and their behavior becomes more organized and more complex (Emde, 1998). They are growing in emotional, social, language, cognitive or thinking, and motor domains. Research on infants and toddlers' development in these domains is growing, too.

Emotional Development

"Emotions help define one's individuality." (Emde, 1998, p. 1236)

Infants are ready from birth to connect emotionally, interact, and start relationships with their primary caregivers. Both biologically and emotionally, children require adults who respond to their needs with protection and affection. Through responsive adults children learn whether they can trust others and whether they are worthy of love. They learn whether they can express their emotions in healthy ways or whether they need to exaggerate emotions or withdraw from others in order to be protected and emotionally connected. Children fall apart emotionally without responsive caregivers.

Achieving self-regulation of these emotions is an important task for infants and toddlers. When humans self-regulate they manage the emotions and physical responses necessary to be able to focus, learn, and interact successfully with others. Adults play a critical part in helping infants and toddlers gain self-regulation over the first 3 years (NICHD, 2004). By comforting a crying baby, soothing a hurt child, or talking gently to a fearful child, caring adults help children become calm again.

For emotional well-being, infants and toddlers need sensitive, responsive adult partners. They need warm, caring adults who are able to form enduring relationships (Honig, 2002). They need these relationships with family members, and if they are in early education programs, they need a strong positive relationship with their teachers. Caring relationships with adults are related to a child's sense of security (Howes, Galinsky, & Kontos, 1998; Howes & Hamilton, 1992; Howes, Hamilton, & Philipsen, 1998; NICHD, 2001d). While older children and even adults continue to need consistent, sensitive relationships in their lives, infants and toddlers "may be particularly vulnerable to very detrimental experiences that derive from aberrant caregiving and serious economic hardship" (Shonkoff & Phillips, 2000, p. 223). Rather than worrying about "spoiling" a child, teachers must be concerned about providing responsive care to help infants and toddlers feel they can have an impact on their environment, trust others, and learn that they are good at relationships.

Social Development

In addition to their ability to relate to caring adults, infants and toddlers are also interested in peers very early in their lives. They find children who are just their size fascinating. Through experience they learn that peers are not objects, but people who have ideas that are sometimes similar and often different from their own. Positive social behaviors and feelings (prosocial) emerge early and older infants and toddlers will comfort, protect, defend, help, and feel empathy toward their peers (Denham & Weissberg, 2004; Murphy, 1992; Quann & Wien, 2006; Wittmer, in press). Conflicts are often a valuable part of peer interactions as children learn to negotiate sharing toys and space with their peers in programs (Hay, 2006; Singer & Hannikainen, 2002). By 18 months of age, toddlers can take another person's perspective. Gopnik et al. (1999) found that 18-month-olds, who definitely preferred goldfish crackers to broccoli, would give an adult the broccoli if the adult indicated that she liked broccoli better than crackers. Between 2 and 3 years of age, toddlers learn to cooperate with each other to accomplish a goal (Brownell, Ramani, & Zerwas, 2006), for example, carrying a bucket or rolling a pumpkin across the room. Infants and toddlers become friends earlier than many have thought, as early as their first birthdays (Howes, 2000). Toddlers show "glee"—delight, joy, and hilarity with each other (Lokken, 2000a, 2000b). Infants and toddlers are active peer learners, constantly experimenting with what works and what does not work with peers.

Again, adults play a key role in supporting infants' and toddlers' rapidly increasing social skills. Children learn how to treat others from how adults treat them. One study found that toddlers (15-month-olds) who felt strongly and positively (securely) attached to mothers who were sensitive to their needs were more likely to play well with peers at 36 months of age (McElwain, Cox, Burchinal, & Macfie, 2003). The quality of the program the child attends also makes a difference. Child care quality predicts 36-month-old children's social skills, as reported by their caregivers (NICHD, 2002c).

Cognitive Development

The hypothesis is that babies and very young children use powerful techniques for learning about the world—actually the same techniques that adults use to find out about the world around them. That is, children have the capacity to make theories, formulate hypotheses, make predictions, test predictions, and even do experiments to test those predictions.

Babies are ready to learn about themselves, people, and objects from the moment they are born. They are curious and competent learners who are like little scientists, testing and creating rules (Talaris Research Institute, 2006). For example, infants at 7 months will turn a rattle repeatedly to see what it looks like from all sides and will then shake it in a variety of ways to see what sounds it makes. The next time they pick up a rattle they might shake it and then drop it to see what happens. They use all of their senses to learn. They learn both by actively experimenting and by imitating adults and peers.

Adults play an important role by providing emotional support and motivating materials for infants and toddlers to explore. Active infants and toddlers need time to freely explore their environments with loving adults nearby. Gopnik et al. (1999, p. 201) state that parents (and teachers) should be skeptical of playing Mozart tapes or using flash cards. Rather, by providing an environment where infants and toddlers can play with materials and people at their leisure, adults will see how even very young infants try out many different strategies to learn how to accomplish tasks. They are learning with each encounter with people, toys, and materials.

Higher-quality child care and education programs, with interesting environments and responsive teachers, are related to infants' higher cognitive scores (Tran & Weinraub, 2006). Warm, mutually enjoyable adult-child interactions and nonpunitive discipline rather than intrusive, harsh, coercive discipline also have a positive impact on young children's cognitive competence (Howes & Smith, 1995).

Communication and Language Development

The growth in language development and the ability to communicate in the first three years is remarkable, as well. Infants are "citizens of the world" (Kuhl, Stevens, Hayashi, Deguchi, Kiritani, & Iverson, 2006)—born with the capacity to distinguish between all of the sounds in all of the languages in the world, including sounds that they have never heard. By 7 to 12 months of age, however, they are focusing on and practicing the sounds in the language that they hear and lose the ability to distinguish all sounds in other languages (Kuhl et al., 2006). Infants are capable of learning several languages without hampering their development (Petitto, Katerelos, Levy, Gauna, Tetreault, & Ferraro, 2001).

By 12 months of age, they understand that when an adult points at an object they are supposed to look at it (Woodward & Guadjardo, 2002). They learn the names of objects at 13 and 18 months of age after hearing the name of the object nine times within 5 minutes, and they still remember the names after 24 hours (Woodward, Markman, & Fitzsimmons, 1994). Their rapid learning of words between 12 and 18 months is referred to as a language explosion (Woodward et al., 1994). Infants best learn language when an adult talks directly to them rather than to another adult (Thiessen, Hill, & Saffran, 2005), but by 18 months of age they also learn language by overhearing adults talk (Floor & Akhtar, 2006).

Adults play the key role in supporting language development by responding with great interest to children's sounds, babbles, words, and sentences. Offering a menu of rich language experiences is important. The more that adults talk *with* children in responsive ways and use different words, the higher the language development of the children (Hart & Risley, 1992, 1995).

Motor Development

Motor development progresses quickly as infants and toddlers try to solve the problems of moving, reaching, holding, pulling objects to them, and figuring out how they will fit in spaces, such as behind the couch or in a small chair. Motor and cognitive abilities go "hand in hand" as the young child figures out how to see a favorite face or crawl toward an interesting object (Thelan, 2001). When teachers provide an interesting environment to explore and appealing materials to use, motor development thrives.

Building on infants and toddlers' remarkable development, Zero to Three (1992) identified seven learning goals for infants and toddlers:

1. *Confidence and Courage:* A sense of control and mastery of one's body, behavior, and world; children's sense that they are more likely than not to succeed at what they undertake, and that adults will be helpful.

2. *Competence:* A sense of being effective; a sense of "I have the ability and skill to make things happen."

3. *Curiosity:* The sense that finding out about things is positive and leads to pleasure.

4. *Intentionality:* The wish and capacity to have an impact, and to act upon that with persistence. This is related to a sense of competence and of being effective.

5. *Self-Control (Self-Regulation):* The ability to modulate and control one's own actions in age-appropriate ways; a sense of inner control.

6. *Relatedness:* The ability and desire to engage with others based on the sense of being understood by and understanding others. Children should feel secure and trust important adults to take care of them. Children learn that relationships with others are satisfying and fun.

7. *Capacity to Communicate:* The wish and ability to exchange ideas, feelings, and concepts with others. This is related to a sense of trust in others and pleasure in engaging with others, including adults.

This also includes children's expression of feelings in ways that do not hurt others.

8. *Cooperativeness and Caring:* The ability to begin to balance one's own needs with those of others in a group develops as infants grow. As infants and toddlers develop, they become generally affectionate, friendly, loving, and kind with others. They want to be with peers and develop in their ability to play with peers in cooperative ways. They generally cooperate with adults during routines and play.

Developmental Challenges

Because of all of this exciting information on their developmental capacities, professionals, parents, researchers, and public policy makers are paying more attention to the importance of the infant and toddler years and more attention to the programs that they attend. They are also paying attention to the challenges that infants and toddlers face as they develop.

We know more now about the effects of stress on children's development. Too much stress (toxic stress) can change the architecture of the brain. In extreme cases, the brain becomes smaller; even in less severe toxic stress, children become more reactive to situations that typically do not cause stress in others (National Scientific Council on the Developing Child, 2005; Teicher, Andersen, Polcari, Anderson, & Navalta, 2002). Cortisol—the fight-or-flight hormone that indicates a person is stressed—rises in 71 percent of toddlers in child care while 64 percent of toddlers at home showed decreases in cortisol levels (Watamura, Donzella, Alwin, & Gunnar, 2003). Toddlers who were fearful or shy and did not play well with peers had the highest cortisol levels. However, as the quality of care increases, the likelihood that temperament (being fearful and shy) will affect the child's stress hormones decreases (Gunnar & Cheatham, 2003, p. 195).

Several characteristics of child care and education programs decrease cortisol levels. Gunnar & Cheatham (2003) found that sensitive and responsive caregiving helps infants and toddlers regulate or control their emotions, which in turn affects their levels of stress hormones. Legendre (2003) in a study of 113 children (18–40 months old) discovered that large group sizes (over 15), age differences of less than 6 months, and less play area increases cortisol levels in children. Sims, Guifoyle, and Parry (2006) found that with higher-quality care toddlers became less stressed during the day, but with satisfactory or low-quality care toddlers' cortisol levels increased. This means that toddlers in anything less than high-quality care felt more stressed as the day progressed.

The effects of maltreatment, abuse, and neglect can be devastating for infants and toddlers. For example, shaken baby syndrome (SBS) occurs when an adult shakes a child so hard that the child's brain is damaged, resulting in death, visual, motor, or cognitive impairment. The National Center on Shaken Baby Syndrome (2005) reports that between 1,200 and 1,600 children suffer from SBS each year.

Poverty can also have negative effects on the development of infants and toddlers. In families experiencing poverty, infants are less healthy (Sequin, Xu, Potvin, Aunzunegui, & Frohlich, 2003). The National Center for Children in Poverty (NCCP) (2007) reports that risk factors associated with poverty include inadequate nutrition, environmental toxins, trauma/abuse, and lower-quality child care. Programs that emphasize quality child care and education and provide family support to prevent child abuse can ameliorate the negative effects of poverty.

We often hear that we must treat infants and toddlers well because they grow up to be tomorrow's adults. While we do know that the infant and toddler years provide a foundation for learning and character in future years, we also know that how infants and toddlers experience their world today is important. "Children aren't just valuable because they will turn into grown-ups but because they are thinking, feeling, individual people themselves" (Gopnik et al., 1999). For this reason they have the right to be treated well today.

A number of organizations recognize the importance of the early years and work tirelessly for the well-being of infants, toddlers, families, and professionals. Notable among these are the United Nations (2002), which in 1989 introduced the United Nations Convention on the Rights of the Child to recognize the rights of infants and toddlers; Zero to Three, dedicated to the well-being of infants, toddlers, their families, and the professionals who work with them; and the Program for Infant Toddler Caregivers (PITC), which provides excellent materials about development for training those who provide infant and toddler care in group settings.

QUALITY AND AVAILABILITY OF PROGRAMS

Programs that serve infants, toddlers, and families struggle with a variety of issues. Funding, quality, and basic societal values about the family's rights and responsibilities concerning children under 3 years of age all affect the quality and availability of programs for this age group.

What We Know About Quality and Availability

There are four basic types of programs serving infants and toddlers: child care programs, family education and support programs, programs for children at risk, and early intervention programs for infants and toddlers with identified disabilities.

Child Care Programs.   Child care programs provide care and education for infants and toddlers while family members are employed outside the home. The primary purpose of child care is to allow parents to maintain employment, but child development and education are important components of these programs. Sometimes, child care is one element of a more comprehensive program to support families, such as school-based programs for teen parents or Early Head Start for families living in poverty.

Demand and Supply.   According to the National Survey of American Families in 1997, there were around 11.6 million American children under the age of 3. About

58 percent of those children, or 6.7 million children, lived with an employed parent and were in some form of out-of-home care arrangement every week (Macomber, Adams, & Tout, 2001). In a longitudinal study of 10,000 babies born in 2001, about half were already in child care by 9 months of age. Twenty-six percent were in relative care (most often with grandmothers), 15 percent in nonrelative care in their own or someone else's home, and 9 percent were in center-based care (Flanagan & West, 2004).

It is difficult to determine whether the supply of infant/toddler child care meets the demand because few states track the use or availability of child care slots by age group (NCCIC, 2007). The National Association of Child Care Resource and Referral Agencies monitors the cost of infant/toddler care but does not track capacity. In 2006, the average cost for a year of infant care ranged from just over $4,000 in family care in several states to just under $15,000 in center-based care in Massachusetts and the District of Columbia (NACCRRA, 2007). Anecdotally, resource and referral agencies often report that most of their requests are from families looking for infant/toddler care, even though research shows us that more than half of infants and toddlers are in family, friend, and neighbor care (Flanagan & West, 2004).

Variables of Quality.   The question of quality in available programs is a disturbing one for the infant/toddler field. The Cost, Quality, and Outcomes Study (Helburn, 1995), an in-depth study of child care programs in four states, found that only 8 percent of infant/toddler programs had mediocre or better quality. At the same time, and in a longitudinal follow-up, they found that the quality of the program is highly correlated to child outcomes (Peisner-Feinberg, 1999).

Researchers have been struggling to define exactly what elements contribute to quality in infant/toddler programs. One of the most enduring measures of quality is the Infant/Toddler Environmental Rating Scale (Harms, Cryer, & Clifford, 2005). This scale emphasizes observable elements such as group sizes, health practices, and suitability of materials. Others try to find ways to document and measure the effects of important but more subjective variables such as "the richness of 'turn-taking-talk' and the amount of warmth and cuddling between caregivers and babies" (Honig, 2002). Zero to Three: The National Center for Infants, Toddlers, and Families identified eight elements of quality care:

1. Health and safety
2. Small groups for infants and toddlers, with teachers responsible for no more than three young or mobile infants and no more than four children 18 months to 3 years old
3. Primary caregiving
4. Continuity of care
5. Responsive caregiving and planning
6. Cultural and linguistic continuity
7. Meeting the needs of the individual within the group context
8. A physical environment with developmentally appropriate materials and activities (Lally, Griffin, Fenichel, Segal, Szanton, & Weissbourd, 2003)

More information on these elements is provided throughout this chapter. Because each of these elements is, indeed, important to quality, infant/toddler care professionals must consider them all. However, some are easily observable and others are subtle and difficult to quantify. Therefore, it has become common practice to separate them into structural variables and process variables.

Structural Variables. Structural variables include ratios and group size, policies of primary caregiving and continuity of care, and teacher characteristics such as the amount of age-specific training and adequacy of compensation. Fewer children per teacher in infant/toddler classrooms is associated with more secure attachment to teachers, more complex play with peers and objects, more proficient adaptive language, and fewer behavior problems such as aggression and anxiety (Howes & Smith, 1995). Infants and toddlers find it difficult to concentrate with too much activity and noise around them, and teachers need time to be responsive to individual children. Ratios and group sizes are often determined by a combination of economics and state licensing regulations. NICHD researchers found adult-to-child ratios ranging from 1:1 to 1:13 across the states. (Phillips & Adams, 2001).

Even the best caregivers cannot provide quality care if too many children are in one space under the care of one adult. In an NICHD study (2002a), the strongest determining factor as to whether children were receiving warm, responsive, and stimulating attention was the adult-to-child ratio. The lower the ratio, the more sensitive and engaged the caregiver, regardless of whether the setting was relative care, home family care, or center-based care.

Primary caregiving is the policy of having one teacher assigned the main responsibility for routine care, observation, ongoing assessment, and communication with the family for each child. *Continuity of care* is the practice of keeping a group of children together with the same teacher over time, preferably the full 3 years of infant/toddler care. For relationships to be meaningful, they need to endure over time (Hinde, 1996). It takes time for a teacher to learn how each baby communicates, what he or she likes and dislikes, and to become a trusted partner to the baby. It also takes time for infants to feel secure with a special teacher—to trust, to feel safe, and to feel comfortable enough to explore and learn. The effect of relationship duration on secure attachment was studied in 61 teacher-child dyads with these findings:

❑ 91 percent of children who had been with their teacher for more than 1 year had secure attachments, compared to

❑ 67 percent who had been with their teacher for 9–12 months and

❑ 50 percent who had been with their teacher for 5–8 months (Raikes, 1993)

From the baby's perspective, it is challenging to have to learn and relearn the expectations of constantly changing teachers. With a national turnover rate in child care classrooms of over 40 percent, it can be very difficult to provide a stable interpersonal environment for babies in group care.

Teacher characteristics such as patience, a calm and gentle personality, and comfort with the intimacy of feeding, cleaning, and quieting a baby are all important but difficult to quantify. However, there is a correlation between a teacher's training and her or his behavior. Teachers with a higher level of education and specific training in the care and education of the age group tend to have cleaner and safer classrooms, be warmer and more developmentally appropriate with the children, and less authoritarian (Ulione, 1997; Whitebrook, Howes, & Phillips, 1998). In a study of the effects of child care, consistent findings related to teacher characteristics and positive caregiving. "Across ages and types of care, positive caregiving was more likely when child-adult ratios and group sizes were smaller, caregivers were more educated, held more child-centered beliefs about childrearing, and had more experience in child care, and environments were safer and more stimulating" (NICHD, 2000, p. 116).

Process Variables. Process variables are the elements that compose the moment-to-moment interactions that have so much impact on each child. These include the responsiveness of the teacher to the child, cultural and linguistic continuity, meeting the needs of the individual within the group, and a physical environment with developmentally appropriate materials and activities. Responsiveness describes an adult's ability to accurately read a child's expressions of needs and feelings and to respond sensitively and effectively. Responsiveness is more than being nice. Lally (1995) believes that every moment of interaction, and interactions over time, contribute to an infant or toddler's emerging sense of self.

Meeting the needs of individuals within the group requires teachers to observe and understand each child's culture, temperament, preferences in being fed and comforted, and abilities. Most importantly, teachers find moments throughout the day to demonstrate to each child that she or he is interesting, lovable, and greatly valued. Finally, the safety and appropriateness of the environment has an impact on the child's ability to engage in worthwhile learning about daily routines of life, how materials work, relationships with others, and acquisition of language and literacy skills.

Is child care harmful or beneficial to infants and toddlers? Questions concerning whether child care is harmful to infants and toddlers—especially with regard to the security of attachment to parents and to higher levels of aggression—have dominated the literature and research on child care (Belsky, 2001). Now, however, rather than asking if child care is harmful or beneficial to infants and toddlers, the question has become: Under what child, family, and program conditions is child care harmful or beneficial to very young children who are just forming their identity and attachment to significant others?

Child factors play a part. As discussed earlier in this chapter, children who are shy experience more stress in child care. Family risk factors, including poverty, play a part as they are the strongest predictors of children's later development (NICHD, 2000c, 2001d). As discussed earlier, the quality of the program is also a factor. In child care, the higher the program quality the higher the children's social, language, and cognitive skills at 36 months of age (Lamb, 1998; NICHD, 2001d, 2002b, 2002c). Higher-quality child care is also linked to math and reading achievement in third grade (NICHD, 2005). The number of hours of child care also makes a difference with more hours of child care in the early years related to poorer work habits and poorer social skills through third grade (NICHD, 2005). The amount of care, however, did not result in higher levels of aggressive behavior by third grade (NICHD, 2005).

Family Education and Support Programs.   Family education and support programs, often offered to all parents regardless of income or need, provide resources, support, and parent education, which may include group meetings, home visits, parent education opportunities, or all of these (as in the Parents as Teachers model; www.parentsasteachers.org). The purpose of these programs may also include supporting healthy parent-child interactions. Another example of a successful family education program is the Early Childhood Family Education program in Minnesota (www.ecfe.info/), which offers a variety of classes and resources for parents of children from birth through kindergarten. The program, a collaboration of the Minnesota Department of Education and local school districts, offers parent-child activity time, parent discussion time, and children's activity time. Home visitors also bring information on child development and parenting to the home. Family education and support programs play an important role in helping families understand typical child development so that they can better understand their children and enjoy parenting.

Programs That Support At-Risk Children.   Programs for infants and toddlers considered at risk for developmental delays or child abuse include parent education and support programs, infant mental health programs, teen parenting programs, and Early Head Start. These programs usually rely on a combination of child development activities, provide information to parents, and, in one way or another, develop relationships with parents that provide respectful, caring, and healthy models for the families' relationships with their children.

   Certain aspects of programming have been found to contribute to particular outcomes (Layzer & Goodson, 2001). Programs that provide some services directly to children are more likely to have a positive effect on children's cognitive development. Programs that provide opportunities for parents to meet with peers as well as work with professional staff have greater effects on children's cognitive and social-emotional development. According to Schorr (1997), successful programs

❑ Are comprehensive, flexible, responsive, and persevering

❑ See children within the context of their families

❑ Deal with families as parts of neighborhoods and communities

❑ Have a long-term preventative orientation, a clear mission, and continue to evolve over time

❑ Are well managed by competent and committed individuals with clearly identifiable skills

❑ Operate in settings that encourage practitioners to build strong relationships based on mutual trust and respect

❑ Train and support staff to provide high-quality, responsive services

Early Head Start.   Early Head Start (EHS), a federally funded program that provides a variety of supports and services to children and families considered at risk due to poverty, low education levels of family members, or other factors, appears to be a very effective program for families and children. The primary purpose of Early Head Start is to support parents in promoting their children's development.

Services include child development and parenting education and health, nutrition, and mental health services. Some Early Head Start programs offer full day child care; others offer home-based services. While EHS is currently serving nearly 100,000 (OHS, 2007) pregnant women, infants, toddlers, and their families, it has been estimated that the program is serving less than 5 percent of the children who are eligible (Fight Crime, 2007).

Rigorous research and evaluation of the EHS program reported by the Administration for Children and Families (2006) adds to evidence that early experiences can have positive long-term effects. A study that examined the effects of EHS in combination with prekindergarten education found that there were positive impacts remaining 2 years after the program ended, especially for children who first attended EHS and then prekindergarten care and education during years 3–5.

Two years after their involvement with the program was over, Early Head Start children continued to show the positive impact of the program. As they were entering kindergarten, children who had participated in EHS were more likely than a control group of children to demonstrate growth in intellectual, social, and emotional development. At the end of the preschool years, the EHS children liked to try new things, showed imagination in work and play, accepted friends' ideas in sharing and playing, and wanted to hear from adults that they were doing okay. Parents reported they were less likely to hit or fight with others, or be hyperactive or withdrawn.

In another study that followed families to the year their child was beginning kindergarten, researchers found that EHS continued to have impact on parenting. By the end of the preschool years, EHS parents were more likely to read to their children every day and play developmentally appropriate learning games. EHS parents were more likely to be involved in their child's formal preschool settings including events such as parent open houses.

Prevention of Child Abuse Program.   One of the most renowned prevention programs for infants at risk for abuse and neglect is the home visiting program developed by Olds and colleagues. The program uses nurses in home visits to first-time mothers living in poverty. The intervention begins in pregnancy and runs through the child's second birthday. Comprehensive services include health, quality of caregiving, maternal life course development, and social support. The model demonstrated an 80 percent reduction in child maltreatment, a 56 percent reduction in health care visits for children's accidental injuries, a 43 percent reduction in subsequent pregnancies, and a reduction in antisocial behaviors in the children at the age of 15 years (Goodman, 2006; Olds et al., 1997).

Infant Mental Health.   The purpose of Infant Mental Health services is to "enhance the development of very young children and to alleviate their suffering" (Zeanah & Zeanah, 2001). Infant mental health is defined as:

> The capacity of infants and toddlers to experience, regulate, and express emotions; form close and secure interpersonal relationships; and explore the environment and learn. Infant mental health is synonymous with healthy social and emotional

development. Infant mental health also refers to the mental wellness of the actual caregiving relationship between caregiver and child. (Onunaku, 2005)

The goal of infant mental health programs is to strengthen the caregiver-child bond by helping the caregiver learn to respond accurately and sensitively to the baby's cues. "The ability of the therapist to genuinely ally herself with a parent while still standing up for the baby may provide an entirely new kind of relational experience for the parent" (Wittmer & Petersen, 2005, p. 102).

Therapists work to develop a close, supportive relationship with the parent and other family members, listening with empathy and concern as the family members share their experiences. At the same time, the therapist continuously observes the baby, helping draw the family members' attention to the baby's experiences as well. Mental health specialists may also provide consultation to an infant or toddler teaching staff in a program.

Program for Infants and Toddlers with Disabilities. In addition to the kinds of programs we have just discussed, there are also programs available that provide support for infants and toddlers with disabilities. The Program for Infants and Toddlers (Part C of the Individuals with Disabilities Education Act; www.ideapartnership.org) provides services for infants and toddlers identified with developmental delays or medical or genetic conditions, such as Down syndrome. Part C programs consist of free assessments, an individualized family service plan that identifies the family's goals for their child, and supports for children and their families. Supports may include physical, occupational, or speech therapy; special education; or psychological services that support the family's priorities and the child's ability to learn. These supports are required by law to be delivered in "natural environments" such as homes, playgroups, parks, community swimming pools, child care programs, or other places where infants and toddlers without disabilities might be found.

Over 12 million children from birth through age 2 are receiving Part C services (NECTAC, 2007). The federal government allocates over $440 million to the states to provide these programs, and many states use additional state funds (NECTAC, 2007). It is difficult to assess efficacy of early intervention because disabling conditions may evidence themselves differently based on each child's personality, home life, and interpersonal and environmental experiences. Each state determines its own eligibility criteria so children who may qualify for services in one state may not be eligible in another.

Challenges to Quality and Availability

The greatest challenges to the quality and availability of programs for infants and toddlers are funding and workforce issues. Workforce issues are discussed more thoroughly in Part 3 of this book, but they are central to issues of quality. Most infant/toddler programs describe themselves as having insufficient funding to serve all the children who need services or to provide the quality they desire. Child care is largely paid for by the consumer—often young parents at the beginning of their wage-earning abilities. Offering quality infant/toddler child care requires many man (or woman) hours. Families need programs to be open from 6:00 A.M. to 6:00 P.M. Quality requires small groups of six to eight, with ratios of one teacher for every three or four children. Families cannot afford to pay the real costs of child care for infants and toddlers.

A report by the Children's Defense Fund (Schulman, 2000) describes how quality child care is out of reach financially for many American families, and even poor quality is out of reach for many:

> A survey of child care costs in the 50 states reveals that child care is one of the biggest expenses that families face in raising their children. Child care can easily cost an average of $4,000 to $6,000 per year. In certain areas of the country, families may be spending more than $10,000 a year on child care. Families with infants in care must grapple with particularly high costs. Among the cities surveyed, the average price of center care for infants is generally about $1,100 a year more than the average price of center care for 4-year-olds. These are only the costs for one child's care—yet, many families face child care expenses for more than one child. (p. 3)

In the United States, a challenge for child care has been that "[i]nfant/toddler care as a whole is not seen as a serious topic. In American society, at least, infant/toddler care is not considered a profession. It is seen as care that anyone can do, that until recently was done for no pay as part of daily family life, and that needs no training" (Lally, 1995, p. 59).

Initiatives Supporting Quality and Availability

Public policy and public demand have increased the number of programs for infants and toddlers and their families. In 1986, Congress added a section to the Individuals with Disabilities Education Act encouraging states to offer early intervention services to infants and toddlers with disabilities and their families. In 1994, in the reauthorization of the Head Start Act, Congress established Early Head Start, extending comprehensive child development services to pregnant women, infants, toddlers, and their families living in poverty.

In 1996, Congress passed the Personal Responsibility and Work Opportunity Reconciliation Act (PRWORA), which limited welfare benefits and required many women who would have been home with children to return to work. It also authorized the Child Care Development Fund (CCDF) to be provided in block grants to states to help subsidize the cost of child care. Between 1997 and 2001, the use of center-based care for infants and toddlers nearly tripled (Phillips & Adams, 2001). In response to the increased need and concerns about quality, Congress declared a set-aside for infant and toddler programs from the Child Care and Development Funds in 1999. Together these programs demonstrated a new interest on the part of the federal government in supporting programs that promote the healthy development of infants and toddlers and their families.

Most states are using a systemic approach to improving the quality of infant/toddler care and education programs. They are developing systems that can be utilized across all types of infant/toddler settings, providing outreach to both formal and informal caregivers, and creating incentives to entice people to participate in professional development experiences. Some of the most common quality initiatives are:

❑ *Early Learning Guidelines for Infants and Toddlers:* articulation of what infants and toddlers should know and be able to do
❑ *Core Knowledge:* description of infant/toddler teachers' skills and knowledge
❑ *Program Standards or Guidelines:* characteristics of quality in infant/toddler programs
❑ *Quality Rating Systems:* descriptions of levels of quality in programs used to inform consumers and guide technical assistance
❑ *Infant/Toddler Credential:* form of recognition for specialized training and experience
❑ *Infant/Toddler Specialist Networks:* systemic approach to providing training and technical assistance to infant/toddler providers in groups or in their own programs

THE INFANT/TODDLER WORKFORCE

Evidence is accumulating that positive child outcomes are linked to well-trained and responsive caregivers. Infant mental health and early intervention providers need specialized training and advanced degrees. However, coursework and degrees specializing in work with infants and toddlers are not readily available. Salaries and benefits, or even secure funding for specialized programs such as infant mental health, simply do not exist in ways that draw people to the field.

What We Know About the Infant/Toddler Workforce

Because of the unique nature of relationships as a context for all infant/toddler development, there are personal qualities that are of particular importance to this workforce. Warm and responsive interactions establish secure attachments and offer interesting and engaging learning experiences. Negative experiences, such as cries that are not answered, harsh treatment, and deprivation can have devastating impacts on vulnerable infants.

Child Care.   Caregivers' beliefs about child rearing, training, and years of experience affect how they provide experiences for young children. Caregivers with nonauthoritarian beliefs provided more positive experiences (NICHD, 1996). Toddler teachers were more positive and effective when they had higher levels of training, specialized training for the age group, and more recent educational experiences (Clarke-Stewart, Vandell, Burchinal, O'Brien, & McCartney, 2002). Training that carries college credit seems to increase quality when it is accompanied by technical assistance, especially for family child care providers (Adams & Buell, 2002).

Years of experience in child care and years on staff in the same program were also strong indicators of quality (NICHD, 1996). Personal commitment to a career in early childhood and to quality also contributed to positive outcomes for infants and toddlers served (Marshall, Creps, Burstein, Roberts, Glantz, & Robeson, 2004).

Wages and benefits vary greatly within the infant/toddler child care field. Teachers and directors may earn from $9,000 to $32,000 per year (PayScale, 2007). They may have no benefits, partial benefits, or strong benefit programs determined in part by the kind of program in which they work.

Programs for At-Risk Children—Infant Mental Health.   Providers in the relatively new field of infant mental health may be clinical social workers, psychologists, or psychiatrists. Infant mental health providers require some specialized skills in addition to basic clinical skills and understanding of mental health. These practitioners see infants and family members together, trying to understand what each contributes positively or negatively to the relationship. Mental health specialists use their own relationship with the family as an instrument of change, helping the family to see an infant's experiences and communications accurately. The mental health specialist may provide observations about the baby or anticipatory guidance about upcoming developmental changes (Weatherston, 2002, pp. 4–5).

There are a growing number of specialized courses or training programs for infant mental health but such training is still not readily available. Program directors usually have to provide considerable training in methods of clinical intervention to new staff. Families may use these services following mental health consultation through child care or if they are court-ordered in response to cases of abuse and neglect. This is emotionally trying but also gratifying work. Programs struggle both to hire qualified workers and to maintain funding. Infant mental health specialists earn an average of $35,000 per year (PayScale, 2007).

Programs for Infants and Toddlers with Disabilities.   Early intervention providers tend to have at least a bachelor's degree, or more often an advanced degree, in specialized fields such as special education; physical, occupational, or speech therapy; and psychology or social work.

In addition to being proficient in the basic skills and strategies of their professions, early interventionists need to know state and federal laws and regulations regarding early intervention, family-centered practice, and the unique developmental needs of infants and toddlers. They also need to know varying cultural beliefs and practices regarding disability, working in teams, providing services in natural settings, and maintaining ethical conduct (DEC, 1993). Early interventionists are usually employed through a state program and earn between $26,000 and $42,000 per year with benefits (PayScale, 2007).

Challenges to the Infant/Toddler Workforce

While providers in the infant and family field should have high levels of education, skill, and specific personal qualities, they work in uncertain circumstances and receive low to moderate wages. The list of skills and knowledge required for effective practitioners seems to grow every year as we learn more about infant development and the impact of early experiences.

This work requires the ability to form intimate and meaningful relationships with infants and their families. The vulnerability of infants and their willingness to form attachments requires a workforce of individuals who have a particular comfort level with emotional closeness.

It is difficult to recruit and maintain a workforce with this unique set of knowledge and personal qualities for the low wages available. Turnover in child care is determined to be over 40 percent each year (Kagan & Cohen, 1997). Despite the correlations between training and quality, the licensing requirements of the states are very low for infant/toddler child care providers.

Initiatives Supporting the Infant/Toddler Workforce

There are countless initiatives that support the infant/toddler workforce. This is somewhat ironic. The efforts offered as support in some ways add a burden to the workforce, requiring more training and more responsibility. Many initiatives do not deal with the basic issues of compensation and benefits that would attract more highly educated and skilled people. Nonetheless, there may be no other field in which a larger percentage of people are inspired to work out of a true love of children. For all of the frustration program directors may express over turnover and difficulty funding programs, one hears great admiration for the commitment and caring that those who care for infants and toddlers bring to their work.

Well-trained and -compensated teachers are the foundation of high-quality infant/toddler care and development programs. This means that states must offer an organized approach to professional development built on a core body of knowledge and competencies that addresses infants and toddlers. The core knowledge should then be integrated into the curricula offered through community colleges, resource and referral agencies, and other entities offering continuing education opportunities. These curricula should also be aligned with early learning guidelines for infants and toddlers, state licensing requirements, quality rating systems, and credentials or specialized certificates. To be effective, classroom learning experiences should be supported with on-site mentoring (Fiene, 2005).

However, core knowledge, early learning guidelines, increased licensing requirements, and higher degrees all increase the responsibility of the front-line worker. These offerings need to be supplemented with programs for grants, loans, and scholarships to assist providers in their professional development. They must also, ultimately, be linked with better compensation.

IMPLICATIONS FOR PRACTICE

There is a science to promoting the well-being of infants, toddlers, and families. The implications of this knowledge are that there is a need for ongoing professional development to increase the quality and availability of programs and a systems approach to increase the wages of the workforce.

The following quote summarizes the excitement those who care about infants, toddlers, and their families feel as they study babies:

> But in the end, the real reason for studying babies and young children is just that they are themselves intrinsically so valuable and so interesting. When we look attentively, carefully, and thoughtfully at the things around us, they invariably turn out to be more interesting, more orderly, more complex, more strange, and more wonderful than we would ever have imagined. (Gopnik et al., 1999, p. 207)

Need for Ongoing Professional Development

Professional development is a key to improving the quality and availability of programs, and ultimately to improving the wages of those who work with children and families. Professionals need to know about culture and diversity, how to support the development of young children, and how to develop relationship-based programs.

Knowledge of Culture and Diversity.   The United States is becoming more diverse. Therefore, those who work with young children need extensive training in cultural sensitivity, how young children acquire a second language, and other topics related to working with children and families from diverse cultural and racial backgrounds (Copple, 2003). Cultural sensitivity requires professional knowledge of how to dialogue with families about potential sources of conflict (Gonzalez-Mena, 2001). Professionals' attention to children's cultures is important because each child is in the process of developing his or her cultural identity. Gonzalez-Mena (2001) emphasizes that the identity of some children can be compromised in programs where they are not the dominant culture.

Knowledge of How to Support Children with Emotional and Social Challenges.   The National Scientific Council on the Developing Child (2004a) recommends that all teachers have training in identifying and dealing with emotional and behavioral challenges.

Early detection of emotional and behavioral problems is possible and important. Children who exhibit depression, who do not respond normally to touch or pain, who are fearful and overly sensitive, or who have difficulty relating to adults need early and ongoing intervention to reestablish their relationship and attention capabilities. For example, Fein (1995) found that infants who are depressed, distressed, and nonexpressive receive less attention from caregivers in child care than infants who are expressive and social, and that caregiver responsiveness and attention to withdrawn infants can positively affect their outcomes. With training, teachers are more likely to understand that infants who constantly soothe themselves and do not look to adults for comfort need intense intervention in order to learn to interact successfully with others.

Early intervention is important for toddlers who seem angry or withdrawn. Without support, they may continue to have difficulty with peers in the preschool years (Hay, 2006; Rubin, 2002). Infant mental health specialists can consult with child care programs to provide support for teachers, children, and families; while all infant/toddler professionals receive more education on how to meet children's emotional needs (Cohen & Kaufmann, 2000).

Knowledge of Relationship-Based Programs.   The importance of relationships for young children has strong implications for programs. In a relationship-based child care program and/or program for at-risk children or those with disabilities, infants and toddlers feel cherished, loved, and safe. Children have smiles, a spark in their eyes, and are learning. In a relationship-based program, teachers provide a responsive curriculum that is individualized for each child. Children are free to choose activities from a variety of interesting materials and books when they are not eating or sleeping. Warm, approachable teachers respond to children's cues for interaction, support, holding, and communication. In such a program, infants' and toddlers' motivation to learn thrives. In relationship-based programs, families are respected and supported (Honig, 2001, 2002, 2003).

New knowledge about infant development may tempt some early childhood educators to provide a downward extension of elementary and preschool programs with an emphasis on academic achievement. They may use inappropriate models to develop programs that are more like preschool (Lally, 1995). "Most out-of-home care experiences developed for infants and toddlers were created by people who were experienced in running programs serving older, preschool-age children. . . . Infant group experiences were routinely set up to mimic preschool, with yearly movement from grade to grade and attention placed on learning through experience or caregiver teaching" (Lally, 1995, p. 58). Infants and toddlers need primary care, continuity of care, and an emphasis on emotional and social development as a foundation for learning.

Need for a Comprehensive Systems Approach

To improve quality and workforce wages there is a strong need for "strategic approaches used to knit together the supports that families with young children need, especially families whose babies' development may be compromised by poverty and other risk factors" (Knitzer & Kreader, 2004, p. 318). A systems approach would develop programs that meet a variety of families' needs. For example, infants and toddlers who attend Early Head Start are receiving an educational experience. Their families also have access to child care, mental health programs, family support, and supports for their children who may have disabilities. A one-stop-shopping program provides comprehensive services that reduce family stress and enhance the well-being of infants and toddlers.

LOOKING AHEAD

If we could peer into the looking glass and see the future, what might it hold for programs for infants, toddlers, and their families? Would we see a world that is a good place for babies, families, and those who work with them? We have learned much about child development and what young children and families need:

> Here is what they [scientists] have learned. The early years are important. Early relationships matter. Even in infancy, children are active participants in their own development, together with adults who care for them. Experience can elucidate, or diminish, inborn potential. The early years are a period of considerable opportunity for growth, and vulnerability to harm. (Caring for Infants and Toddlers, 2001).

We look forward to a time when this knowledge about the importance of the early years will lead to a significant increase in the number of high-quality programs. We hope for a future in which child care programs are viewed as an educational experience and a worthy wage is paid to caregivers. We are optimistic that the emphasis on the importance of relationship-based practice and infant mental health will continue to grow.

More strong advocates for infants, toddlers, families, and the profession would help to ensure a bright future (Rappaport & Yarbrough, 2006). Greater recognition of the need and stronger advocacy will result in increased attention to and funding for infant, toddler, and family support programs. According to Sharon Lynn Kagan (2002), "The American public needs to see early care and education as a social imperative. There needs to be a sense that we are not doing right by our children or doing right for our future if we don't support such programs" (p. 31). The quality of programs for infants, toddlers, and families makes a difference in the quality of their lives!

REFERENCES

Adams, J. H. & Buell, M. (2002). *Project CREATE: Caregiver recruitment, education, and training enhancement.* Newark: University of Delaware, Center for Disabilities Studies. Retrieved May 14, 2007 from http://childcareresearch.org/location/ccrca5913

Administration for Children and Families, U.S. Department of Health and Human Services. (2006, April). *Early Head Start benefits children and families: Research to practice brief.* Retrieved September 14, 2007, from www.acf.hhs.gov/programs/opre/ehs/ehs_resrch/index.html

Belsky, J. (2001). Emanuel Miller lecture, developmental risks (still) associated with early child care. *Journal of Child Psychology and Psychiatry, 42*(7).

Brownell, C. A., Ramani, G. B., & Zerwas, S. (2006). Becoming a social partner with peers: Cooperation and social understanding in one- and two-year-olds. *Child Development, 77*(4), 803–821.

Caring for infants and toddlers. (2001). Retrieved May, 2007, from www.futureofchildren.org/information2827/information_show.htm?doc_id=79335

Clarke-Stewart, K. A., Vandell, D. L., Burchinal, M., O'Brien, M., & McCartney, K. (2002). Do regulable features of child-care homes affect children's development? *Early Childhood Research Quarterly, 17*(1), 52–86.

Cohen, E., & Kaufmann, R. (2000). Early childhood mental health consultation. Washington, DC: CMHS, U.S. Department of Health and Human Services.

Copple, C. (2003). *A world of difference. Readings on teaching young children in a diverse society.* Washington, DC: NAEYC.

DEC. (1993). Position statement: Personnel standards for early education and early intervention. Retrieved September 14, 2007, from www.decsped .org/pdf/positionpapers/PositionStatement_Pers Stan.pdf

Denham, S. A., & Weissberg, R. P. (2004). Social-emotional learning in early childhood: What we know and where to go from here. A blueprint for the promotion of prosocial behavior in early childhood. In E. Cheseborough, P. King, T. P. Gullotta, and M. Bloom (Eds.), *A blueprint for the promotion of prosocial behavior in early childhood* (pp. 13–50). New York: Kluwer Academic/Plenum Publishers.

Emde, R. N. (1998). Early emotional development: New modes of thinking for research and intervention. *Pediatrics, 102,* 1236–1243.

Fein, G. G. (1995). Infants in group care: Patterns of despair and detachment. *Early Child Research Quarterly, 10,* 261–275.

Fiene, R. (2005). *How on-site mentoring improves the quality of infant and toddler child care providers: A summary of the program and evaluation.* Paper presented at Society for Research in Child Development Biennial Meeting, Atlanta, Georgia. Retrieved September 14, 2007, from http:// childcareresearch.org/location/ccrca6026

Fight Crime. http://www.fightcrime.org/policy_ earlyed.php Fight Crime: Invest in Kids: Legislative Update March 19, 2007.

Flanagan, K., & West, J. (2004). Children born in 2001: First results from the base year of the Early Childhood Longitudinal Study, Birth Cohort (ECLS–B) (NCES 2005–036). Washington, DC: National Center for Education Statistics.

Floor, P., & Akhtar, N. (2006). Can 18-month-old infants learn words by listening in on conversations? *Infancy, 9*(13), 327–339.

Goodman, A. (2006). *The story of David Olds and the Nurse Home Visiting Program.* Retrieved April, 2007, from www.rwjf.org/files/publications/other/ DavidOldsSpecialReport0606.pdf

Gonzalez-Mena, J. (2001). Cross-cultural infant care and issues of equity and social justice. *Contemporary Issues in Early Childhood, 2*(3), 368–371.

Gopnick, A., Meltzoff, A. N., & Kuhl, P. (1999). *The scientist in the crib. What early learning tells us about the mind.* New York: HarperPerennial.

Gunnar, M., & Cheatham, C. L. (2003). Brain and behavior interface: Stress and the developing brain. *Infant Mental Health Journal, 24*(3), 195–211.

Harms, T., Clifford, R. M., & Cryer, D. (2005). *Early Childhood Environmental Rating Scale, Revised Edition, Updated (ECERS-R).* New York: Teachers College Press.

Hart, C., & Risley, T. R. (1992). American parenting of language-learning children: Persisting differences in family-child interactions observed in natural home environments. *Developmental Psychology, 28,* 1096–1105.

Hart, C., & Risley, T. R. (1995). *Before Head Start: Differences in the family experiences of 1- and 2-year-old children.* Baltimore: Brookes.

Hay, D. F. (2006). Yours and mine: Toddlers' talk about possessions with familiar peers. *The British Psychological Society, 24,* 39–52.

Helburn, S. W. (1995). *Cost, quality and child outcomes in child care centers.* (Technical Report, Public Report, and Executive Summary ED38697). Retrieved September 14, 2007, from www.eric.ed.gov/ ERICDocs/data/ericdocs2sql/content_storage_01/ 0000019b/80/14/22/e6.pdf

Hinde, R. (1996). On describing relationships. *Journal of Child Psychology and Psychiatry, 17,* 1–19.

Honig, A. S. (2001). Moving ahead and building relationships. *Scholastic Early Childhood Today, 22.*

Honig, A. S. (2002). *Secure relationships. Nurturing infant/toddler attachment in early care settings.* Washington, DC: NAEYC.

Honig, A. S. (2003). Helping babies feel secure. *Scholastic Early Childhood Today, 18*(1), 27–29.

Howes, C. (2000). Social development, family, and attachment relationships. Infants and toddlers in out-of-home care. In D. Cryer and T. Harms (Eds.), *Infants and toddlers in out-of-home care* (pp. 87–116). Baltimore: Brookes.

Howes, C., Galinsky, E., & Kontos, S. (1998). Child care caregiver sensitivity and attachment. *Review of Social Development, 7*(1), 25–37.

Howes, C., & Hamilton, C. E. (1992). Children's relationships with caregivers: Mothers and childcare teachers. *Child Development, 63,* 859–866.

Howes, C., Hamilton, C.E., & Philipsen, L. (1998). Stability and continuity of child-caregiver and child-peer relationships. *Child Development, 69*(2), 418–426.

Howes, C., & Smith, E. W. (1995). Relations among child care quality, teacher behavior, children's play activities, emotional security, and cognitive activity in child care. *Early Childhood Research Quarterly, 10,* 381–404.

Kagan, S. L. (2002). *Equal access to early learning.* Washington, DC: The National Black Child Development Institute.

Kagan, S. L., & Cohen, N. (1997). *Not by chance: Creating an early care and education system for America's children.* New Haven: Yale University Bush Center.

Knitzer, J., & Kreader, J. L. (2004). Strategic community and state action to promote the well-being of infants and toddlers. Lessons from the real world. *Infants and Young Children, 17*(4), 318–326.

Kreader, J. L., & Lawrence, S. (2006). *Toward a national strategy to improve family, friend, and neighbor child care.* Retrieved September 14, 2007, from http://nccp.org/publications/pub_676.html

Kuhl, P. K., Stevens, E., Hayashi, A., Deguchi, T., Kiritani, S., & Iverson, P. (2006). Fast-track report: Infants show a facilitation effect for native language phonetic perception between 6 and 12 months. *Developmental Science, 9*(2), F13–F21.

Lally, J. R. (1995). The impact of child care policies and practices on infant/toddler identity formation. *Young Children, 51*(1), 58–67.

Lally, J. R., Griffin, A., Fenichel, E., Segal, M., Szanton, E., & Weissbourd, B. (2003). *Caring for infants and toddlers in groups: Developmentally appropropriate practice.* Washington, DC: Zero to Three.

Lally, J. R., Lurie-Hurvitz, E., & Cohen, J. (2006). Good health, strong families, and positive early learning experiences. Promoting better public policies for America's infants and toddlers. *Zero to Three, 26*(6), 6–9.

Layzer, J., & Goodson, B. (2001). *National evaluation of family support programs.* Cambridge, MA: ABT Associates.

Legendre, A. (2003). Environmental features influence bioemotional reactions in day care centers. *Environment and Behavior, 35*(4), 523–549.

Lokken, G. (2000a). Tracing the social style of toddler peers. *Scandinavian Journal of Educational Research, 44*(2), 163–176.

Lokken, G. (2000b). The playful quality of the toddling style. *International Journal of Qualitative Education, 13*(5), 531–542.

Macomber, J. E., Adams, G., & Tout, K. (2001). *Who's caring for our youngest children? Child care patterns of infants and toddlers.* Washington, DC: Urban Institute. Retrieved May 20, 2007, from www.urban.org/publications/310029.html#exam

Marshall, N. L., Creps, C. L., Burstein, N. R., Roberts, J., Glantz, F. B., & Robeson, W. W. (2004). *The cost and quality of full-day year-round early care and education in Massachusetts: Infant and toddler classrooms.* Wellesley, MA: Wellesley Centers for Women. Retrieved August 15, 2007, from www.childcareresearch.org/location/ccrca5695

McElwain, N. L., Cox, M. J., Burchinal, M. R., & Macfie, J. (2003). Differentiating among insecure mother-infant attachment classifications: A focus on child-friend interaction and exploration during solitary play at 36 months. *Attachment and Human Development, 5*(2), 136–164.

Murphy, L. B. (1992). Sympathetic behavior in very young children. *Zero to Three, XII*(4), 1–5.

NACCRRA. (2007). *2006 price of child care.* Retrieved May 1, 2007, from www.naccrra.org/randd/data?2006PriceofChildCare.pdf

National Center for Shaken Baby Syndrome. (2005 January 1). Retrieved from www.dontshake.com

National Scientific Council on the Developing Child. (2004a). *Children's emotional development is built into the architecture of their brain: Working Paper No. 2.* Retrieved October 4, 2005, from www.developingchild.net/reports.shtml

National Scientific Council on the Developing Child. (2004b). *Young children develop in an environment of relationships.* (Working Paper No. 1). Retrieved April 23, 2006, from www.developingchild.net/reports.shtml

National Scientific Council on the Developing Child. (2005). *Excessive stress disrupts the architecture of the developing brain.* Retrieved May 2007, from www.developingchild.net/pubs/wp/Stress_Disrupts_Architecture_Developing_Brain.pdf

NCCIC. (2007). *Demand, supply, and quality: Trends in infant/toddler child care in the United States.* Retrieved May 2, 2007, from http://nccic.org/pubs/qcare-it/demand.html

NECTAC. (2007). *Annual appropriations and number of children served under Part C of IDEA Federal Fiscal Years 1987–2007.* Retrieved September 14, 2007, from www.nectac.org/PARTC/PARTCDATA.ASP

NICHD Early Child Care Research Network. (1996). Characteristics of infant child care: Factors contributing to positive caregiving. *Early Childhood Research Quarterly, 11*(3), 269–306.

NICHD Early Child Care Network. (2000). Characteristics and quality of child care for toddlers and preschoolers. *Applied Developmental Science, 4*(3), 116–135.

NICHD Early Child Care Research Network. (2001a). Before Head Start: Income and ethnicity, family characteristics, child care experiences and child development. *Early Education and Development, 12.*

NICHD Early Childhood Research Network. (2001b). Child care and children's peer interaction at 24 and 36 months. *Child Development, 72*(5), 1478–1501.

NICHD Early Child Care Research Network. (2001c). Child care and family predictors of preschool attachment and stability from infancy. *Developmental Psychology, 37.*

NICHD Early Child Care Research Network. (2001d). Nonmaternal care and family factors in early development: An overview of the NICHD Study of Early Child Care. *Journal of Applied Developmental Psychology, 22.*

NICHD Early Child Care Research Network. (2001e). Parenting and family influences when children are in child care: Results from the NICHD Study of Early Child Care. In J. Borkowski, S. Ramey, & Bristol-Power, M. (Eds.), *Parenting and the child's world: Influences on intellectual, academic, and social-emotional development.* Mahwah, NJ: Erlbaum.

NICHD Early Child Care Research Network. (2002a). *Child care from the child's perspective: Exposure and experiences.* Presentation at the Congressional Briefing, Washington, DC.

NICHD Early Child Care Research Network. (2002b). Child-care structure, process, outcome: Direct and indirect effects of child-care quality on young children's development. *Psychological Science, 13,* 199–206.

NICHD Early Child Care Research Network. (2002c). The interaction of child care and family risk in relation to child development at 24 and 36 months. *Applied Developmental Science, 6*(3), 144–157.

NICHD Early Child Care Research Network. (2004). Affect dysregulation in the mother-child relationship in the toddler years: Antecedents and consequences. *Development and Psychopathology, 16,* 43–68.

NICHD Early Child Care Research Network. (2005). Early child care and children's development in

the primary grades: Follow-up results from the NICHD Study of Early Child Care. *American Educational Research Journal, 42*(3).

Olds, D. L., Eckenrode, J., Henderson, C. R. Jr., Kitzman, H., Powers, J., Cole, R., Sidora, K., Morris, P., Pettitt, L. M., & Luckey, D. (1997). Long-term effects of home visitation on maternal life course and child abuse and neglect. Fifteen-year follow-up of a randomized trial. *Journal of the American Medical Association, 278*(8), 637–643

OHS. (2007). *Head Start fact sheet.* Retrieved May 2, 2007, from www.acf.hhs.gov/programs/hsb/research/2007factsheet.pdf

Onunaku, N. (2005). *Improving maternal and infant mental health: Focus on maternal depression.* Los Angeles: National Center for Infant and Early Childhood Health Policy at UCLA.

PayScale. (2007). *Compare your salary.* Retrieved September 2007, from www.PayScale.com

Peisner-Feinberg, E. S., Burchinal, M. R., Clifford, R. M., Culkin, M. L., Howes, C., Kagan, S. L., Yazejian, N., Byler, P., Rustici, J., & Zelazo, J. (2000). *The children of the cost, quality, and outcomes study go to school: Technical report.* Chapel Hill: University of North Carolina, Frank Porter Graham Child Development Center.

Petitto, L. A., Katerelos, M., Levy, B. G., Gauna, K., Tetreault, K., & Ferraro, V. (2001). Bilingual signed and spoken language acquisition from birth: Implications for the mechanisms underlying early bilingual language acquisition. *Journal of Child Language, 28*(2), 453–496.

Phillips, D., & Adams, G. (2001). Child care and our youngest children. *The Future of Children, 11*(1), 34–51.

Quann, V., & Wien, C. A. (July, 2006). *The visible empathy of infants and toddlers.* Retrieved September 8, 2006, from www.journal.naeyc.org/btj/100607/Quann709BTJ.asp

Raikes, H. (1993). Relationship duration in infant care: Time with a high-ability teacher and infant-teacher attachment. *Early Childhood Research Quarterly, 8*(3), 309–325.

Rappaport, D., & Yarbrough, K. (2006). Ensuring a bright future for babies: How to advocate effectively for infants and toddlers. *Zero to Three, 26*(6), 20–25.

Rubin, K. (2002). *The friendship factor.* New York: Penguin Books.

Schorr, L. B. (1997). *Common purpose: Strengthening families and neighborhoods to rebuild America.* New York: Anchor Books.

Schulman, K. (2000). *The high cost of child care puts quality care out of reach for many families.* Washington, DC: Children's Defense Fund.

Séguin, L., Xu, Q., Potvin, L., Zunzunegui, M., & Frohlich, K. L. (2003). Effects of low income on infant health. *Canadian Medical Association Journal, 168*(12): 1533–1538.

Shonkoff, J. P., & Phillips, D. (Eds.). (2000). *From neurons to neighborhoods: The science of early childhood development.* Washington, DC: National Academy Press.

Shore, R. (2003). *Rethinking the brain: New insights into early development* (rev. ed.). New York: Families and Work Institute.

Sims, M., Guilfoyle, A., & Parry, T. S. (2006). Children's cortisol levels and quality of child care provision. *Child Care, Health and Development 32*(4), 453–466.

Singer, E., & Hannikainen, M. (2002). The teacher's role in territorial conflicts of 2- to 3-year-old children. *Journal of Research in Early Childhood Education, 17*(1), 5–18.

Talaris Research Institute. (2006). *Testing 1, 2, 3.* Retrieved May 2007, from www.talaris.org/spotlight_testing123.htm

Teicher, M. H., Andersen, S. L., Polcari, A., Anderson, C. M., & Navalta, C. P. (2002). Developmental neurobiology of childhood stress and trauma. *Psychiatric Clinics of North America, 25*(2), 397–426.

Thelan, E. (2001). Dynamic mechanisms of change in early perceptual-motor development. In J. L. McClelland & R. S. Siegler (Eds.), *Mechanisms of cognitive development: Behavioral and neural perspectives* (pp. 161–185). Hillsdale, NJ: Erlbaum.

Thiessen, E. D., Hill, E. A., & Saffran, J. R. (2005). Infant-directed speech facilitates word segmentation. *Infancy, 7*(1), 53–71.

Tran, H., & Weinraub, M. (2006). Child care effects in context: Quality, stability, and multiplicity in nonmaternal child care arrangements during the first 15 months of life. *Developmental Psychology, 42*(3).

Ulione, M. S. (1997). Health promotion and injury prevention in a child development center. *Journal of Pediatric Nursing, 12*(3), 148–154.

United Nations. (2002). Convention on the Rights of the Child. Retrieved May 15, 2007, from www.unicef.org/crc/crc.htm

Watamura, S., Donzella, B., Alwin, J., & Gunnar, M. (2003). Morning-to-afternoon increases in cortisol concentrations for infants and toddlers at child care: Age differences and behavioral correlates. *Child Development, 74*(4), 1006–1021.

Weatherston, D. J. (2002). Introduction to the infant mental health program. In J. J. Shirilla & D. J. Weatherston (Eds.), *Case studies in infant mental health: Risk, resiliency, and relationships* (pp. 1–13). Washington, DC: Zero to Three.

Whitebrook, M. C., Howes, C., & Phillips, D. (1998). *Worthy work, unlivable wages.* Washington, DC: National Child Care Staffing Study, 1988–1997.

Wittmer, D. S. (in press). *A focus on peers in the early years.* Washington, DC: Zero to Three.

Wittmer, D. S., & Petersen, S. H. (2006). *Infant and toddler development and responsive program planning: A relationship-based approach.* Upper Saddle River, NJ: Merrill/Prentice Hall.

Woodward, A., & Guajardo, J. (2002). Infants' understanding of the point gesture as an object-directed action. *Cognitive Development, 17*(1), 1061–1084.

Woodward, A. L., Markman, E. M., & Fitzsimmons, C. M. (1994). Rapid word learning in 13- and 18-month-olds. *Developmental Psychology, 30,* 553–566.

Zeanah, C. H., & Zeanah, P. D. (2001). Towards a definition of infant mental health. *Zero to Three, 22,* 13–20.

Zero to Three. (1992). *Heart Start: The emotional foundations of school readiness.* Washington, DC: National Center for Clinical Infant Programs.

Zero to Three. (2007, April). Brain development. Retrieved from www.zerotothree.com

CHAPTER 4

QUALITY IN EARLY CHILDHOOD PROGRAMS

Gerrit Westervelt
Build Initiative

Annette Sibley,
Quality Assist, Inc.

Diana Schaack
Erikson Institute

The issue of quality in early childhood programs, including both home- and center-based child care settings, has become increasingly important in recent years, garnering attention from policy makers, practitioners, researchers, and parents. Quality has emerged as a central issue in early care and education circles, in part because more and more children are in out-of-home care. In fact, child care is second only to families in terms of where children spend their time. Use of child care has grown over the past 30 years as more women enter the workforce. Data collected in 2002 from the Survey of Income and Program Participation (U.S. Census Bureau, 2005) found that 18.5 million children (64 percent) were in some form of child care in a typical week, with almost one quarter of those children in formal care arrangements including licensed family child care homes and early care and education centers.

More children are also in care because of shifts in family policies, most notably the 1996 welfare reform law, the Personal Responsibilities and Work Opportunities Act (PRWOA). Welfare reform dramatically increased pressure on low-income mothers to work rather than stay at home with their children. In order to continue to receive state subsidies, women were required either to enter the labor market or to enroll in some form of job training or educational program. This requirement, along with the growing economic necessity for both parents to work, has increased the demand for child care and focused more attention on the quality of programs.

Program quality is also gaining attention because of the growing recognition on the part of the public and policy makers that quality of care affects children's well-being and developmental progress. The school reform movement, with its emphasis on standardized testing and increased accountability, has also fueled the drive for increased quality in early care and education. The Goals 2000: Educate America Act codified a set of national education goals, including Goal 1: "By the year 2000, all children will start school ready to learn" (Boyer, 1991). The No Child Left Behind Act (P.L. 107-110, 2002), with its focus on reducing educational disparities across racial and ethnic boundaries, ratcheted up the pressure still further. The public and policy makers began to see early education as a critical tool to help close the so-called achievement gap and increase the percentage of children who arrive at school prepared for the demands of a standards-based education system. This trend has increased pressure on all types of child care providers to demonstrate that their services can improve children's school readiness. The needs of working parents, the push for school readiness, and the widespread recognition of the developmental benefits of high-quality programs, have combined to put the issue of quality—what it is, how to measure it, and how to achieve it—squarely on the public agenda.

WHAT IS HIGH-QUALITY CHILD CARE?

While it may appear on the surface an easy task to define high-quality early care and education, different characteristics and levels of quality can be measured, and various stakeholders value different aspects of the quality of care. For example, policy makers and monitoring agencies, such as child care licensing departments, are interested in those aspects of quality that can be regulated, such as adult-to-child ratios, group sizes, and teacher training and education. Parents tend to define quality child care as places that keep their children safe (Helburn & Bergman, 2002), where their children are liked by their teachers, where teachers are warm and responsive to their children (Cryer & Burchinal, 1997), and as places that prepare their children for school (Ispa, Thornburg, & Fine, 2006). Providers of child care services, including teachers, administrators, and family home providers, may be interested in aspects of quality including the provision of developmentally appropriate curricula and approaches to teaching (Bredekamp & Copple, 1997). As professionals, they may also be interested in aspects of the work environment such as wages and turnover. And as demands for accountability have trickled down to early childhood education, more emphasis is being placed on child outcomes as an indicator of child care quality (Lambert, Abbott-Shim, & Sibley, 2006).

Layzer and Goodson (2006) suggest that "at the core of the definition are the experiences that promote children's physical, social, emotional, and intellectual development" (p. 558). Most child care research has focused on two distinct but interrelated aspects of child care quality. The first, *process quality*, involves the actual experiences of children in child care. It includes the emotional tone of the classroom, interactions between teachers and children, and interactions between peers. Process quality also includes how well teachers organize the environment to promote learning, how well and how often they respond to children's questions and scaffold their problem-solving skills and language development, and how well they manage and monitor the safety of the children in their care.

The second type of quality, *structural quality,* has to do with aspects of the child care environment that may support or constrain process quality. It can refer to teacher characteristics such as their training and education levels or their beliefs about caring for and teaching children. It can also include classroom characteristics such as adult-to-child ratios, the size of the group, the composition of children in the group, the safety of the physical classroom, and the learning materials available. Similarly, structural quality can also refer to aspects of the larger child care setting such as administrative leadership, overall program management, the wages that teachers earn, or the turnover rate in the child care center. Each of these structural variables can influence teachers' behaviors in the classroom, which can ultimately affect the experiences of children in care.

RESEARCH INTO CHILD CARE QUALITY: HISTORICAL PERSPECTIVES

Research into child care has generally followed two parallel tracks. The first track investigated whether high-quality child care could serve as an intervention to increase the chances of academic success for children from less advantaged home environments. From this perspective, early care and education is seen as a social program derived from a social responsibility to promote disadvantaged children's school and life success. In contrast, nonintervention child care has typically been viewed as a service to families to allow them to participate in the workforce (Brauner, Gordic, & Zigler, 2004). As such, early research into community-based child care originally stemmed from concerns among some developmentalists that prolonged separation of children from their mothers might interfere with the mothers' abilities to learn to read their children's emotional cues and become attuned to their children (Brazelton, 1986), which could thus damage the mother-child attachment relationship (Belsky & Rovine, 1988), long considered an essential component of children's healthy emotional development. However, as the social and political climate in the United States has shifted, increasing understanding that child care is a necessity for many families, current child care research primarily focuses on how child care quality affects children's developmental outcomes, including school readiness skills, as well as identifying the critical aspects of child care settings that promote developmentally appropriate caregiving and education.

Research on the benefits of high-quality child care stemmed from a growing concern in the mid-1960s that many children living in impoverished conditions were not succeeding academically in school. Two landmark studies—the High/Scope Perry Preschool Project and the Carolina Abecedarian Project—provided high-quality child care as an intervention. These programs offered play-based Piagetian approaches to instruction, delivered by teachers who had academic degrees with specialized training in early childhood education, in classrooms with low teacher-child ratios. Additionally, they provided home visits to parents and offered child development information to support parents in extending what was being learned in the early childhood program to the home setting. Consistent results across studies found that children in these programs had significantly higher IQ scores after the program and into the early elementary years, and consistently performed better on academic tests of achievement throughout high school as compared to children who did not receive these high-quality early child care experiences (Campbell & Ramey, 1995; Schweinhart, Barnes, Weikert, Barnett, & Epstein, 1993).

While these programs may not be typical of the majority of early care and education experiences in the United States, what they do show is that high-quality programs can have compensatory effects on school readiness skills for children living in poverty. They also provide guidance into the possible ingredients of high-quality care; namely an intentional, child-centered curriculum, well-qualified teaching staff, low adult-to-child ratios, and high levels of parent support and involvement.

Providing early care and education programs as a way to improve children's chances for academic success is also seen in such federally funded programs as Head Start and Early Head Start (Zill & Resnick, 2006). In this context, early care and education is seen as a social good that can help increase children's academic performance. School readiness has consistently been used as an indicator of program quality and as a goal of these programs. Recognizing the importance of high-quality early childhood programs in promoting school readiness, 25 percent of the national Head Start budget is directed toward improving child care quality (Shonkoff & Phillips, 2000).

Research into community-based, nonintervention child care, as noted earlier, originated from a much different tradition: concern that extensive time spent in child care could damage the mother-child attachment relationship. Early research in this area had inconsistent findings: Some researchers found that there were disproportionate amounts of insecure mother-child attachment relationships in children who were enrolled in child care for more than 20 hours a week (Belsky & Ravine, 1988), while others did not find similar results (Lamb, Sternberg, & Prodromidis, 1992). Researchers soon noted dramatic differences in children's experiences in child care and began to fine-tune their investigations of whether variations in quality could be an important factor to consider when examining the effects of child care on the mother-child relationship.

Born, in part, from a need to answer this question and many others regarding the effects of child care on children's development, the National Institute of Child Health and Human Development (NICHD) launched a multistate longitudinal study to investigate how children's family lives and child care experiences mutually influence children's development. They found that child care, in and of itself, did not present a risk to the mother-child attachment relationship. However, when poor-quality child care combined with insensitive parenting, children were more likely to be insecurely attached to their mothers (NICHD ECCRN, 1997). This situation presents a "dual risk" to children's development. Recent research has also found that when child care quality is extremely poor, it can present risks to the mother-child attachment relationship even when children experience sensitive and nurturing parenting. Children experiencing high levels of stress in poor-quality child care may not find their relationships with their mothers "good enough" to overcome the challenges and stresses of poor quality care (Love et al., 2003).

As more and more emphasis has been placed on children's school readiness skills, and as the use of early childhood programs has become more prevalent for many children and families, child care research has shifted from examining the effects of child care on the mother-child attachment relationship to examining how variations in program quality can impact children's social, cognitive, and language skills. The Cost, Quality and Child Outcomes Study (1995) tracked children from North Carolina, Colorado, California, and Connecticut from preschool through second grade. During preschool, researchers found that children's social and cognitive outcomes varied based on the quality of their child care experience; children in higher-quality programs had better receptive language skills, better emergent literacy skills, were more socially competent with their peers, and had better attentional skills. These results were consistent at all levels of income, ethnicity, and maternal education levels and among both boys and girls. Importantly, this study raised additional questions about whether certain children from more advantaged families were buffered from the negative effects of low-quality child care; as well as whether the effects of high-quality care were more pronounced for others (Peisner-Feinberg & Burchinal, 1997). No buffering effects for more advantaged children were found, suggesting that children from all backgrounds can be affected by poor-quality child care. However, children considered to be at risk of academic failure who were in high-quality education and care programs saw increased emergent literacy skills during their preschool years.

Children in high-quality care continued to show greater gains in their language development through kindergarten (Peisner-Feinberg, et al., 1999) and in their math abilities through second grade as compared to those in lower-quality care (Peisner-Fienberg et al., 2001). Developmentally appropriate teaching practices in preschool, as well as close preschool teacher-child relationships, were related to these increases in language and math scores, and close teacher-child relationships were related to fewer problem behaviors and more positive peer interactions in second grade. Children from less-advantaged backgrounds tended to see more benefits from high-quality preschool in their math abilities as well as reductions in problem behaviors in second grade. Similar results have been found in studies that have examined infant care as well (Burchinal, Roberts, Nabors, & Bryant, 1996; Field, 1991), suggesting that the quality of teacher-child interactions and the sensitivity of their care, as well as the provision of a stimulating learning environment, are related to better language skills and more positive peer interaction.

The NICHD Study of Early Child Care served to confirm some of the results of the Cost, Quality and Child Outcomes Study, particularly in the language and cognitive domain of children's development. Specifically, the NICHD team found that children who were in higher-quality child care, as characterized by adults who were sensitive and responsive, who frequently spoke with children, and who asked them questions and stimulated their problem-solving skills, had better vocabulary comprehension and expressive vocabulary at 15 months of age. Similarly, children in higher-quality care had larger vocabularies, used more complex sentences, and had better problem-solving and memory skills at 24 months of age and had better school readiness skills (such as letter identification, counting, and shape and color recognition skills) at 36 months of age, compared to children in lower-quality care (NICHD ECCRN, 2000). By 4.5 years of age and through transitions to kindergarten, better letter-word recognition and problem-solving skills, and better expressive vocabulary, comprehension, and memory were found in children who had consistently experienced high-quality child care (NICHD ECCRN, 2002; NICHD ECCRN, 2003). These results held true across all incomes, ethnicities, and home environments and among both boys and girls.

On the social-emotional front, the NICHD team found that children who were in higher-quality child care as toddlers were likely to have fewer behavior problems and were more likely to be socially competent with peers (NICHD ECCRN, 2001). By early preschool, children who had experienced more positive and responsive care from their teachers or family home providers were observed by researchers to be more positive and competent with peers; however, children who experienced more time in child care throughout their lives were reported by teachers to be more negative with peers, regardless of the quality of child care children experienced (NICHD ECCRN, 2001); these results carried forward throughout children's transitions to kindergarten (NICHD ECCRN, 2003).

These studies are just two prominent examples of the research into child care quality that has been conducted over the past several decades. However, as the amount of research has grown, most researchers, practitioners, and policy makers alike believe that high-quality child care is good for all children and can promote their school readiness skills and development. In a review of this research evidence, the National Research Council Institute of Medicine has concluded that "one of the most consistent and ubiquitous findings in this literature links the quality of child care children experience to virtually every measure of development that has been examined" (Shonkoff & Phillips, 2000, p. 310). One prominent researcher has noted, "in fact, the importance of child care quality is one of the most robust findings in developmental literature" (McCartney, 2004, p. 2). Most researchers also agree that families influence children's development more than child care, but that child care can exert unique influences on development above and beyond families (NICHD ECCRN, 2000, 2003), particularly in the cognitive and language domains and perhaps less so in the social-emotional domain (Howes & Sanders, 2006).

CORRELATES OF QUALITY

As research has pointed to the benefits of high-quality care for children, a parallel line of research has investigated factors in child care settings that can be used to predict the quality of classrooms and family child care homes.

Training and Education

It has long been assumed that specific training and education in early childhood education or child development contributes to better program quality. This assumption suggests that teachers with more education will be able to interpret children's actions from a developmental perspective, will be able to respond in age-appropriate ways, and will be able to facilitate learning activities that match the developmental levels of the children in their care. In fact, a great deal of research has found that teachers with bachelor's degrees in early childhood education are more sensitive and responsive to children and are less detached and restrictive in the care that they provide (Arnett, 1989; Howes, Smith, & Galinsky, 1995). Similarly, teachers with bachelor's degrees in early childhood education and a Child Development Associate credential (CDA) have been found to stimulate more language and literacy activities and to engage in more positive limit-setting and classroom management (Howes, et al., 1995).

Other studies have provided evidence that there may be alternatives to formal education that lead to effective teaching and sensitive caregiving. A recent study found that teachers who participated in community-based trainings and workshops, while not as effective as those with a bachelor's degree in early childhood education, still were more effective at teaching and facilitating emergent literacy skills than teachers who did not participate in any in-service trainings (Burchinal, Cryer, & Clifford, 2002). Others have found that teachers who have access to supportive reflective supervision by their directors or who have had access to mentoring were more responsive and sensitive to children and were more successful at facilitating developmentally appropriate literacy activities (Howes, James, & Ritchie, 2003). Similarly, the Cost, Quality and Child Outcomes Study (1995) found that the amount of time that directors spent with teachers supporting their curriculum planning was related to better classroom quality and more sensitive caregiving. These studies, while helping to identify key aspects of child care quality, also assist in identifying possible strategies to help improve program quality; namely through providing scholarships to teachers, offering comprehensive in-service trainings, and developing strong leadership skills in directors and mentors.

Ratios and Group Sizes

Ratios and group sizes are assumed to be important because as the number of children in care increases, a teacher's ability to individualize attention to children decreases—and managing large numbers of children can be stressful for even the most sensitive and knowledgeable teacher. Many studies have found ratios and group sizes to consistently predict more sensitive, responsive, and developmentally appropriate caregiving in care and education programs (CQCO, 1995; NICHD ECCRN, 2000). Ratios appear to be even more predictive of child care quality in infant classrooms (NICHD ECCRN, 1996), while group sizes appear to be more important in family child care homes (Kontos et al., 1995). Howes, Phillips, and Whitebook (1992) found that teachers were more likely to provide children with sensitive caregiving and provide developmentally appropriate activities when infant classrooms had a ratio of 1:3 and a group size of 6 or less, when toddler classrooms had a ratio of 1:4 and a group size of 12 or less, and when preschool classrooms had a ratio of 1:9 and a group size of 18 or less. Additionally, children in these classrooms were more likely to be securely attached to their teachers and have more positive relationships with their peers. As group sizes and ratios increased, even by just one child, the likelihood of these outcomes decreased significantly.

Work Environment

Many policy makers and researchers forget that child care is not simply a developmental setting for children, it is also a work environment for adults. A teacher's ability to respond sensitively to children and to provide appropriate learning experiences can be impacted by their working conditions. Having livable wages, a supportive work environment, health benefits, and paid time off, as well as paid time to plan for classroom activities, influences teachers' satisfaction with their jobs as well as commitment to their jobs (Phillips, Howes, & Whitebook, 1991).

Teachers with lower wages are more likely both to be less satisfied with their jobs and to leave their jobs (Phillips et al., 1991). Turnover can affect children's ability to form secure attachment relationships with teachers (Howes & Hamilton, 1993) and staff wages have been found to be consistently and strongly related to classroom quality; with higher teacher wages related to better classroom quality and more positive caregiving (CQCO, 1995; Goelman, Doherty, Lero, LaGrange, & Tougas, 2000; Mills & Ramono-White, 1999; Phillips et al., 1991).

Alarmingly, more than 27 percent of teachers and more than 39 percent of assistant teachers leave their jobs annually (Whitebook, Howes, & Phillips, 1998) because of dissatisfaction with working conditions. This can put stress on the entire child care center as new staff need to be trained and staff who have remained need to take on additional responsibilities.

DO WE HAVE QUALITY CHILD CARE IN THE UNITED STATES?

The Cost, Quality and Child Outcomes Study (1995) estimated that 58 percent of preschool classrooms and 84 percent of infant/toddler classrooms provide care that does not promote children's development and school readiness skills; with approximately 40 percent of infant/toddler classrooms and 10 percent of preschool classrooms considered of poor quality, that is, quality that falls below the minimum standards to protect children's health and safety. While the NICHD (2000) study painted a slightly brighter picture of child care quality, it still found that only 28 percent of infant classrooms, 22 percent of toddler classrooms, and 34 percent of preschool classrooms provided care that promotes healthy development and school readiness skills (NICHD ECCRN, 1996, 2000b). And disturbingly, two studies of family child care homes approximate the prevalence of poor-quality care to be between 35 and 41 percent (Kontos, Howes, Sinn, & Galinsky, 1995; NICHD ECCRN, 2000b).

IMPROVING CHILD CARE QUALITY

Financial realities have made child care a basic component of American family life across all economic sectors and substantial public investment has been required to increase child care's access, affordability, and quality. This investment has increased public expectations for accountability and a return on the investment. By the 1990s, the focus of the child care debate had substantially, although not fully, shifted from the detrimental impact on maternal attachment to identifying and measuring the critical features of child care quality and its cost. Today, as public investments to promote quality have increased, the focus is shifting again with a growing emphasis on measuring child outcomes and school readiness.

The U.S. General Accounting Office (GAO) reported that in fiscal year 2000, states spent $5.3 billion in federal Child Care and Development Funds for subsidized child care for low-income families and earmarked 4 percent of the funds for quality improvements (Shaul, 2002). By 2006, in addition to child care subsidies, quality improvement appropriations included $170 million for quality expansion, $98 million to improve the quality of care for infants and toddlers, and $19 million to improve school-age care and Child Care Resource and Referral Services. The GAO also reported that states have had wide latitude in deciding how to allocate funds for quality improvements and have funded initiatives to increase teacher compensation, provide teacher training, improve professional credentials, support compliance with state standards, offer training and technical assistance to achieve accreditation, provide incentives for exceeding state standards, and provide higher reimbursement rates for subsidized children served in accredited programs.

However, few states have systematically evaluated the effectiveness of these initiatives to increase the quality of early childhood programs. While current research provides promising directions for targeting funds and initiatives to improve quality, it offers little specific guidance on how to modify ongoing initiatives or the most cost-effective investments to improve quality. The National Research Council also reported that while state initiatives target aspects of child care settings that have the potential for enhancing developmental outcomes, there is insufficient information to conclude that the initiatives themselves have been effective (Shaul, 2002, p. 29).

Regulating and Promoting Quality

What policies, investments, or strategies drive quality? At the most basic level, the quality of child care is regulated by state child care licensing standards. State licensing standards establish a minimum "floor" of quality and are designed to protect the health and safety of children in care. When quality falls below the minimum standards, states have the authority and the responsibility to intervene on behalf of children. However, because each state establishes its own licensing standards and procedures for center-based and family-based child care, there is wide variation across states (Children's Foundation, 2000). Because regulatory standards set the baseline for quality, they also place a focus on compliance with the minimum acceptable level of quality. By definition, regulation has limited influence in "driving" or improving quality.

In contrast to mandatory licensing standards, voluntary national accreditation defines high-quality, professional standards for early care and education programs. The National Association for the Education of Young Children (NAEYC) introduced accreditation standards in 1985 and raised those standards in 2006. As a voluntary system, NAEYC accreditation set the bar high, with standards of quality that are nationally uniform and supported by early education and child development experts and scientific research. National accreditation is widely perceived to have been effective in stimulating improvements in quality. At the same time, the standards for quality are high and expensive to maintain, and the accreditation process itself is labor intensive and expensive. Consequently, as of 2006, only an estimated 8 percent of child care programs were nationally accredited. While licensing standards regulate from the floor with minimum standards, it was expected that the accreditation designation would inform child care consumers and market demand would drive quality upward. Market influence on quality has been slow and modest. The Institute for Families and Work found that in reality, working parents are likely to select child care based on practical considerations of geographic proximity and cost.

Quality Rating Systems, Rated Licenses, and Differential Reimbursement

To promote quality, a number of incentive approaches have emerged that attempt to bridge the gap between the mandatory, floor-level standards of licensing and the voluntary, ceiling-level standards of accreditation. These approaches have included quality rating systems, rated licenses, and tiered/differential reimbursement. Differential reimbursement has been the most commonly used strategy to improve quality. Under this system, states pay a higher reimbursement rate for publicly subsidized child care to those centers and family child care homes that exceed basic licensing requirements and demonstrate higher levels of quality based on predefined "tiers," or levels of quality. Rated licenses are statutory grading systems. The child care centers are "graded" based on quality standards that are delineated within the licensing regulations and therefore embedded in the state statutes. Quality rating systems assign centers a quality rating indicator based on established criteria and are intended to serve as a "report card" and guide for consumers.

Each approach attempts to drive quality: differential reimbursement relies on a funding strategy, rated licensing is a regulatory approach, and quality rating systems are primarily a market/consumer-based strategy. While these strategies can be implemented independently, states have begun to combine them into a systematic approach to improve quality under the umbrella of quality rating systems (QRS). The National Child Care Information Center (NCCIC) identified five common elements of quality rating systems: They (1) define quality standards; (2) invoke accountability; (3) offer program and practitioner outreach and support; (4) provide financial incentives linked to compliance with quality standards; and (5) educate parents. As of 2006, NCCIC reported that 13 states and the District of Columbia had implemented a statewide QRS, including Colorado, Iowa, Kentucky, Maryland, Montana, New Hampshire, New Mexico, North Carolina, Ohio, Oklahoma, Pennsylvania, Tennessee, and Vermont.

Gormley and Lucas (2000) examined the impact of differential reimbursement as an approach to improving child care quality. They reported that six states

(Florida, Mississippi, Nebraska, New Jersey, New Mexico, and Oklahoma) were able to demonstrate statistically significant, positive effects while four states (Kentucky, Ohio, Utah, and Wisconsin) found no statistically positive outcomes. They also concluded that (1) higher reimbursement rates produce greater results; (2) quality was linked to NAEYC accreditation and that when accrediting organizations and standards "fail to push the envelope beyond existing state licensing standards [it] is unlikely to yield any quality improvements; differential reimbursement most likely appeals to good centers that want to become excellent, but are unlikely to attract those centers that are in the most need of improvement and are struggling to comply with licensing standards; and that (3) differential reimbursement will, at best, affect a fairly small percentage of child care centers" (Foundation for Child Development, 2000, p. 16). In short, differential reimbursement will improve quality in "better" child care centers that are motivated to improve. However, alternative strategies are needed to improve the quality in lower-quality centers struggling to comply with state regulations and those of low-to-moderate quality that are showing no productive movement toward improving the quality of their services.

Professional Development

The discussion of quality and improving quality is not complete without considering the child care workforce. Child care teachers are the cornerstone of quality. The 1988 National Child Care Staffing Study (NCCSS) revealed that the quality of most child care centers was barely adequate and that those centers with "better" quality employed more educated and trained staff, provided teachers with higher wages, assigned fewer children to each teacher, and retained more teachers for longer periods of time. In 1997, nine years later, the NCCSS was updated following a significant increase in federal funding through the 1990 Child Care and Development Block Grant. Whitebook, Howes, and Phillips (1998) note that public block grant funds were "minimally targeted to improving quality child care or to retaining trained and qualified caregivers" (p. 5). Based on their data, Whitebook, et al. concluded that "public funds have had little, if any, effect in stabilizing the child care workforce" (p. 5). The 1997 NCCSS findings concluded that child care teachers continued to earn unlivable wages and turnover remained high. In addition, as welfare reform required parents to enter the workforce, the demand for child care services and caregivers increased. Ironically, former welfare recipients were encouraged to seek employment in child care, creating an influx of untrained, entry-level caregivers into the field. Approximately one-third of the centers in the 1997 sample employed welfare recipients with limited training and education. Centers paying the lowest teacher wages received the greatest increase in public subsidies for child care services. In other words, public funds, very likely, purchased child care services from lower-quality centers serving children with the greatest need of high-quality care and education. Whitebook, et al. recommended that public funds should target quality and compensation and that public funding for professional development and teacher credentialing should be linked to wage supplements and retention grants.

Still, the discussion of how staff turnover impacts quality warrants a more fine-tuned analysis. It is clear that turnover negatively impacts quality. Staff turnover is of particular concern when it results in skilled teachers, who love their work and would prefer to stay, being compelled to leave because of "unlivable" wages, lack of health benefits, and inadequate opportunities for professional development. Turnover can be positive when it involves teachers leaving who are burned-out from the demands of the job, ill-suited to the challenges of caring for large groups of children, or unwilling to learn new approaches and embrace changing standards of quality. It is essential to address the conditions that lead to workforce turnover and develop strategies to increase teacher retention. However, reducing turnover is, in itself, an inadequate benchmark of progress toward improving quality. A more effective measure of progress may be best represented by the increasing professional development of child care teachers, though even this approach is challenging.

Technical Assistance

Trohanis (2001) notes that "technical assistance projects are now recognized features in the landscape of government strategies to change and improve social service" (p. 57). Over the past 15–20 years, a wide variety of technical assistance initiatives have emerged and focused on improving child care quality. These initiatives have varied widely in terms of perception and approach, ranging from information dissemination to intensive consultation over time for the purpose of facilitating change.

The most comprehensive and informative resource on technical assistance systems was developed by the National Early Childhood Technical Assistance Center (NECTAC). NECTAC was established in 2001 to support implementation of the early childhood provisions of the Individuals with Disabilities Education Act (IDEA). Its mission is to "strengthen services systems to ensure that children with disabilities (birth through five) and their families receive and benefit from high-quality, culturally appropriate, and family-centered supports and services."

While NECTAC focuses on children and families with disabilities, their technical assistance recommendations and guidelines are relevant and applicable across settings. NECTAC defines *technical assistance* as

> a systematic process that uses various strategies involving people, procedures, and products over time to enhance the accomplishment of mutual goals of the state and those who request their help. Technical assistance is not a fragmented or reactionary strategy that addresses one need at a time. (Trohanis, 2001, pp. 39–40)

The NECTAC approach to technical assistance is distinctive because it focuses on systematic and systemic changes that endure over time.

There is substantial variation in the experience, expertise, and expectations across technical assistance initiatives. In addition, technical assistance initiatives for child care programs are generally dependent on short-term, one-shot funding, and therefore generally lack continuity in services. Statewide, coordinated systems for the delivery of technical assistance grounded in strategic vision and planning, professional standards for best practices, uniform evaluation and accountability, and continuity of services is virtually nonexistent. However, there is a growing interest in using technical assistance as a strategy to systematically improve child care quality. In fact, NAEYC reported that programs seeking national accreditation have a higher rate of success when supported by ongoing, on-site technical assistance.

In 2005, the National Association of Child Care Resource and Referral Agencies (NACCRRA) published a guide for technical assistance professionals detailing the basic processes and skills needed to provide on-site technical assistance. After considerable investment in technical assistance, a number of states have begun to develop competencies for technical assistance staff.

Technical assistance is a distinctive approach to improving the quality of child care. At its best, it is systematic and systemic in its approaches, diverse in strategies, and individualized to the needs of the recipients.

Public Policy and Quality

Early childhood programs operate within both a market and a regulatory context, with different sectors of the field affected by different policy, regulatory, and market levers. For example, depending on the mix of children who attend, a licensed child care center may be affected by state child care licensing regulations, state-funded preschool program rules, federal Head Start regulations, and private or faith-based accreditation requirements. Centers that accept public subsidies to serve poor children often have contractual relationships with cities, counties, or other governmental jurisdictions. Incentives and sanctions linked to quality measures such as rating systems may require centers to have contracts with one or more state agencies. Amid all of these potential constraints, centers must also operate within their local child care market, subject to constraints such as families' ability to pay, child mobility and other demographic shifts, and ongoing competition from other providers, both regulated and unregulated.

This complex environment means that the impact of public policy decisions on early childhood programs is not always straightforward. Goals and measures among different funding streams may be in conflict. Changing one variable (such as ratio requirements) within one public program or funding stream may not lead to the desired result, as there are many other policy variables that may also need to be changed—and unintended consequences are the rule rather than the exception. As Bardach (1977) said of the challenges of implementing public programs, "the maneuvers of the several parties both express conflict and create it—and with every maneuver aimed at reducing it there is an associated risk of actually making matters worse" (p. 53). Early childhood program quality thus presents unique challenges for both policy makers and technical assistance providers.

As the policy context for early childhood program quality has shifted toward increased accountability and increased public investment, the question of accountability for whom has emerged as a critical one for policy makers (see Elmore, Abelmann, & Fuhrman, 1996). The purposes of accountability, and therefore the policy choices that should be considered, are in the eye of the beholder. Parents may see accountability mechanisms such as quality rating systems and regulatory standards as tools to help them decide what care to purchase for their child. In this sense, accountability can be seen as a driver of market-based change. Early childhood markets are often "inefficient" in economic terms, lacking enough information about the product for consumers to make an informed choice. "Child care is a unique industry, as it has never responded to market pressures" (Colorado State Department of Human Services, p. 5). By enabling child care services to be differentiated from one another, and by encouraging increased public investment in early childhood, quality rating systems and other accountability tools help create a more transparent and efficient market for early childhood services.

Early childhood providers, on the other hand, have a built-in incentive to view accountability mechanisms as the means to a very practical end: more money and more technical assistance to improve classroom practice. This enlightened self-interest helps them respond to the accountability needs of policy makers, which often include the need to justify public investment decisions. Policy decision makers have in recent years adopted the "return on investment" (ROI) language common in the private sector as a framework to help shape funding allocation decisions. However, given the multiple perceived purposes of accountability—consumer education tool, market-based change mechanism, driver of incentives—measuring ROI becomes a complicated set of choices and trade-offs that must be made by policy makers and researchers alike.

LOOKING AHEAD

The next phase of the early childhood policy debate is likely to be characterized by a number of important questions related to program quality. As the early childhood quality movement continues to grow and attract more attention and resources from federal, state, and local policy makers, practitioners and researchers are likely to have to grapple with issues such as:

❑ What strategies and interventions work best to improve program quality, and how do these vary by program type, size, resource level, children served, and other variables?

❑ How should quality rating systems, tiered reimbursement and other incentives, national accreditation, and licensing rules relate to one another, and how can public policy help practitioners take maximum advantage of these tools?

❑ Whose job is it to improve program quality, and who should foot the bill? Government funding, especially federal, has historically been directed first at disadvantaged families. Who should be responsible for measuring, improving, and funding high-quality early childhood services for all children?

❑ How do these roles and responsibilities play out between state and local governments—or between municipal governments and school districts? And who decides?

❑ In an underfunded field, what role should financing strategies such as tax credits, rebates, and other indirect subsidies play in increasing the purchasing power of parents—and the resources available to providers?

❏ More and more states are adopting a "whole child" policy framework and seeking to establish "comprehensive early childhood systems" that cross different sectors such as health, mental health, nutrition, family support, and special needs services. How should quality improvement efforts be connected to these broader and more ambitious policy and regulatory changes?

The diversity, flexibility, and parent-child orientation that is widely seen as a strength of the early care and education system is, from a policy standpoint, one of its greatest challenges. Achieving high quality for all children and families is a tall order when the rules, regulations, standards, curricula, teacher qualifications, and funding streams for early childhood programs are all so different. However, just like the K–12 system before it, the early childhood field is moving toward increased standardization, accountability, and performance measurement—changes that are sure to bring both intended and unintended consequences. The movement toward high-quality care for all children who need it is likely to continue for many years, as policy makers, parents, and the general public recognize the critical importance of the early years.

REFERENCES

Bardach, E. (1977). *The implementation game: What happens after a bill becomes law?* Cambridge, MA: MIT.

Belsky, J. (1988). Non-maternal care in the first year of life and the security of infant-parent attachment. *Child Development, 59,* 157–167.

Boyer, E. L. (1991). *Ready to learn: A mandate for the nation.* Princeton, NJ: Carnegie Foundation for the Advancement of Teaching.

Brauner, J., Gordic, B., & Zigler, E. (2004). Putting the child back into child care: Combining care and education for children ages 3–5. *Society of Research on Child Development Policy Report, 18*(3).

Brazelton, T. B. (1986). Issues for working parents. *American Journal of Orthopsychiatry, 56,* 14–25.

Bredekamp, S., & Copple, C. (1996). *Developmentally appropriate practice in early childhood programs* (Rev. ed.). Washington, DC: National Association for the Education of Young Children.

Burchinal, M., Cryer, D., & Clifford, R. (2002). Caregiver training and classroom quality in child care centers. *Applied Developmental Science, 6,* 2–11.

Burchinal, M., Peisner-Feinberg, E., Pianta, R., & Howes, C. (2002). Development of academic skills from preschool through second grade: Family and classroom predictors of developmental trajectories. *Journal of School Psychology, 40*(5), 415–436.

Burchinal, M., Roberts, J., Nabors, L., & Bryant, D. (1996). Quality of center child care and infant cognitive and language development. *Child Development, 67,* 606–620.

Campbell, F., & Ramey, C. (1995). Effects of early intervention on intellectual and academic achievement: A follow-up study of children from low-income families. *Child Development, 62*(2), 684–689.

Children's Foundation. (2000). *Child Care Center licensing study.* Washington, DC: Children's Foundation.

Colorado State Department of Human Services. (1995). *Report of the Colorado Business Commission on Child Care Financing.* Denver: Author.

Cost, Quality and Child Outcomes Study Team (CQCO). (1995). *Cost, quality and child outcomes in child care centers* (Technical Report). Denver: University of Colorado.

Cryer, D., & Burchinal, M. (1997). Parents as child care consumers. *Early Childhood Research Quarterly, 12,* 35–58.

Elmore, R. F., Abelmann, C. H., & Fuhrman, S. H. (1996). The new accountability in state education reform: From process to performance. In H. F. Ladd, *Holding schools accountable: Performance-based reform in education* (pp. 65–98). Washington, DC: Brookings Institution.

Field, T. (1991). Quality infant day care and grade school behavior and performance. *Child Development, 62,* 863–870.

Goelman, H., Doherty, G., Lero, D. S., LaGrange, A., & Tougas, J. (2000). *You bet I care! Caring and learning environments: Quality in child care centres across Canada.* Guelph, Ontario: Centre for Families, Work and Well-Being.

Gormley, W. T., & Lucas, J. K. (2000). *Money, accreditation, and child care center quality.* (Working Paper Series) New York: Foundation for Child Development.

Helburn, S., & Bergman, B. (2002). *America's child care problem.* New York: Palgrave.

Howes, C., Galinsky, E., & Kontos, S. (1998). Child care caregiver sensitivity and attachment. *Social Development, 7,* 25–36.

Howes, C., & Hamilton, C. E. (1993). The changing experience of child care: Changes in teachers and in teacher-child relationships and children's social competence with peers. *Early Childhood Research Quarterly, 8,* 15–32.

Howes, C., James, J., & Ritchie, S. (2003). Pathways to effective teaching. *Early Childhood Research Quarterly, 18,* 104–120.

Howes, C., Smith, E., & Galinsky, E. (1995). *The Florida child care quality improvement study.* New York: Work and Families Institute.

Howes, C., Phillips, D., & Whitebook, M. (1992). Thresholds of quality: Implications for the social development of children in center-based care. *Child Development, 63,* 449–460.

Howes, C., & Sanders, K. (2006). Child care for young children. In B. Spodak & O. Saracho (Eds.), *Handbook of research on the education of young children* (2nd ed.). Mahwah, NJ: Erlbaum.

Ispa, J., Thornburg, K., & Fine, M. (2006). *Keepin' on: The everyday struggles of young families in poverty.* Baltimore: Brookes.

Kontos, S., Howes, C., Sinn, M., & Galinsky, E. (1995). *Quality in family child care and relative care.* New York: Teachers College Press.

Lamb, M. E., Sternberg, K. J., & Prodromidis, M. (1992). Nonmaternal care and the security of infant-mother attachment: A reanalysis of the data. *Infant Behavior and Development, 15*(1), 71–83.

Lambert, R., Abbott-Shim, M., & Sibley, A. (2006). Evaluating the quality of early childhood education settings. In B. Spodek & O. Saracho (Eds.), *Handbook of research on the education of young children.* Mahwah, NJ: Erlbaum.

Layzer, J., & Goodson, B. (2006). The quality of early care and education settings: Definitional and measurement issues. *Evaluation Review, 30,* 556–576.

Love, J., Harrison, L., Sagi-Schwartz, A., van Ijzendoorn, M., Ross, C., Ungerer, J., Raikes, H., Brady-Smith, C., Boller, K., Brooks-Gunn, J., Constantine, J., Kisker, E., Paulsell, D., & Chazan-Cohen, R. (2003). Child care quality matters: How conclusions may vary with context. *Child Development, 74,* 1021–1033.

McCartney, M. (2004, February 5). Current research on child care effects. In *Encyclopedia on early childhood development.* Retrieved April 15, 2007, from www.child-encyclopedia.com

Mills, D., & Romano-White, D. (1999). Correlates of affectionate and angry behavior in child care educators of preschool-aged children. *Early Childhood Research Quarterly, 14*(2), 155–178.

NICHD ECCRN. (1996). Characteristics of infant child care: Factors contributing to positive caregiving. *Early Childhood Research Quarterly, 11,* 296–306.

NICHD ECCRN. (1997). The effects of infant child care on infant-mother attachment security. *Child Development, 68,* 860–879.

NICHD ECCRN. (2000). The relation of child care to cognitive and language development. *Child Development, 71,* 960–980.

NICHD ECCRN. (2001). Early child care and children's peer interaction at 24 and 36 months. *Child Development, 72,* 1478–1500.

NICHD ECCRN. (2002). Early child care and children's development prior to school entry. *American Educational Research Journal, 39,* 133–164.

NICHD ECCRD. (2003a). Does quality of child care affect child outcomes at age 4.5? *Developmental Psychology, 39,* 451–469.

NICHD ECCRN. (2003b). Does time spent in child care predict social-emotional adjustment during the transition to kindergarten? *Child Development, 74*(4), 976–1005.

Peisner-Feinberg, E. S., & Burchinal, M. R. (1997). Relations between child-care experiences and children's concurrent development: The cost, quality, and outcomes study. *Merrill-Palmer Quarterly, 43,* 451–477.

Peisner-Feinberg, E. S., Burchinal, M. R., Clifford, R. M., Culkin, M. L., Howes, C., Kagan, S. L., & Yazegian, N. (2001). The relation of preschool child-care quality to children's cognitive and social development trajectories through second grade. *Child Development, 72*(5), 1534–1553.

Peisner-Feinberg, E., Clifford, R., Culkin, M., Howes, C., & Kagan, S. L. (1999). *The children of the Cost, Quality and Outcomes Study go to school.* Chapel Hill, NC: Frank Porter Graham Child Development Center, NCEDL.

Phillips, D., Howes, C., & Whitebook, M. (1991). Child care as an adult work environment. *Journal of Social Issues, 47,* 49–70.

Schweinhart, L., Barnes, H., Weikert, D., Barnett, S., & Epstein, A. (1993). *Significant benefits: The High/Scope Perry Preschool Study through age 27* (Monograph of the High/Scope Educational Research Foundation, Number 10). Ypilsanti, MI: High/Scope Educational Research Foundation.

Shaul, M. (2002, September). *Child care: States have undertaken a variety of quality improvement initia-tives, but more evaluations of effectiveness are needed* (GAO-02-897). Washington, DC: U.S. General Accounting Office.

Shonkoff, J., & Phillips, D. (2000). *From neurons to neighborhoods: The science of early childhood development.* Washington, DC: National Academy Press.

Trohanis, P. (2001). *Design considerations for state TA systems.* Chapel Hill, NC: National Early Childhood Technical Assistance System.

U.S. Census Bureau. (2005). *Who's minding the kids? Child care arrangements: Winter 2002.* Washington, DC: Author.

Whitebook, M., Howes, C., & Phillips, D. (1998). *Worthy work, unlivable wages: The National Child Care Staffing Study, 1988–1997.* Washington, DC: Center for the Child Care Workforce.

Zill, N., & Resnick, G. (2006). Low income children in Head Start and beyond: Findings from FACES. In N. Watt, R. Bradely, J. Puma, & W. LeBoeuf (Eds.), *The crisis in youth mental health: Critical issues and effective programs.* Westport, CT: Praeger.

CHAPTER 5

CHILDREN'S READINESS FOR SUCCESS IN SCHOOL

Catherine Scott-Little

University of North Carolina, Greensboro

Ms. Johnson, a kindergarten teacher, takes a moment of the first day of school to look around and think about her upcoming year. Her group of 21 children arrived on time, accompanied by teary-eyed parents, and eventually all found their seats. She noticed that Sally had difficulty separating from her parents, Juan eagerly ran into the room, Linlin seemed to be quite tired, and Eric, who has never been in a classroom, was slow to catch on to each new activity. As the day progressed she noted that Leanta picked up a picture book and began "reading" to a friend but Craig didn't seem to know how to open the book. Ms. Johnson wonders, Are these children ready for school? Am I ready for this group of children? What does readiness for school mean?

Ms. Johnson is not alone. As thousands of children start kindergarten each year, teachers, parents, and policy makers all wonder "are they ready for school?" In this chapter we will take a look at what school readiness is, what we have learned about children's readiness for school, the implications various school readiness issues have for policies and practice, and recent trends related to school readiness issues.

HOW DID SCHOOL READINESS BECOME A "HOT" ISSUE?

Although parents and teachers have wondered about whether their children would be successful in school from the time that compulsory education began in the 1800s, school readiness became a "hot" topic of debate among researchers, educators, and policy makers when the nation's governors established their first education goal as "all children in America will start school ready to learn" in 1989. They established a panel of experts to define what it meant for children to enter school "ready to learn," and to provide recommendations on children's readiness for school and how to know if children are "ready" (NEGP, 1990). Known as the National Education Goals Panel (NEGP), this policy initiative called attention to the importance of school readiness. Since that time the field has recognized the distinction between "ready to learn" and "ready for school" (Kagan, 1990) and the focus has shifted to children's readiness to succeed in school. The NEGP put school readiness "on the map" and set the stage for intense debates related to readiness.

At the federal level, the increased attention to preparing children for success in school led to a number of developments, particularly within the Head Start program. The Head Start Child Outcomes Framework (Head Start Bureau, 2000) was introduced to describe the specific skills and knowledge Head Start seeks to promote among the children it serves. Three years later, the National Reporting System (NRS) was initiated to provide data on the performance of 4-year-old Head Start children on specific academic tasks (Administration for Children and Families, 2003). In fact, the bill to reauthorize Head Start was titled the "School Readiness Act" in 2003, further calling attention to the importance of preparing children for school.

The focus on school readiness is evident in other federal policy initiatives. In 2002, President George W. Bush introduced his administration's early childhood initiative, known as Good Start, Grow Smart, to ensure that all children "begin school with an equal chance at achievement so that no child is left behind" (Bush, 2002). Among other efforts to strengthen the early childhood education system, the Good Start, Grow Smart initiative included provisions for states to develop "voluntary early learning guidelines" to define what children should know and be able to do at kindergarten entry in the areas of literacy, language, and prereading skills. Indirectly, the No Child Left Behind legislation also focused attention on children's readiness for school. Policy makers and educators realized that in order for schools to meet the required provisions for Adequate Yearly Progress on test scores in third grade and up, children need to start school with the skills and knowledge necessary to be successful. School districts across the country recognized the importance of early education and targeted their federal Title I funds to provide prekindergarten services (GAO, 2003). States have followed suit by expanding their services for children prior to kindergarten entry (Barnett, Hustedt, Hawkinson, & Robin, 2007). In short, policy developments in the field of early childhood education have focused increasing attention on the importance of the skills and knowledge children gain before starting school, further highlighting the importance of school readiness issues.

WHAT IS SCHOOL READINESS?

On one level, the question of what school readiness is may seem rather simple. We have numerous early childhood programs and have invested significant resources in services for children before they start school. Surely we know what children need in order to be successful in school. On the other hand, the question is complex and brings to mind many different responses. The answer to the question has changed over time and depends to some extent on whom you ask.

From the legal standpoint, children's readiness for school is determined by their birth date. Every state has a statewide cutoff date for when children can enter kindergarten or requires that districts set such a date. Thirty-nine states require that children turn 5 between August 15 and October 16, meaning that children entering kindergarten are 5 or will be turning 5 shortly after school starts. In recent years there has been a trend for states to adopt cutoff dates earlier in the year so that the cohort of children is older when they start kindergarten (Education Commission for the States, 2005).

Beyond the legal definition of school readiness, theorists, researchers, educators, parents, and policy makers have differing views of school readiness. One common element across the varying views is that school readiness "refers to the state of child competencies at the time of school entry that are important for later success" (Snow, 2006, p. 9). What varies across the different perspectives is the type of skills, abilities, and knowledge seen as important and views on how children develop the components of school readiness. We turn now to a brief summary of how school readiness has been defined from varying viewpoints.

Theorists

Early on, the maturationist perspective was highly influential on how educators and parents thought about school readiness. From this perspective, children are ready for school when they have matured and developed the skills needed to be successful. Readiness is not about a child's chronological age because each child's development unfolds according to a unique timetable. Instead, readiness is more like a threshold of certain skills or characteristics—when a child has the requisite skills, she or he is "ready" to start school (Gredler, 1992). Readiness screenings, red-shirting practices, and transition classrooms (discussed later in this chapter) emanate from this view—children are not "ready" for school until they reach a certain level of maturity and so less mature children should be discouraged from (or protected from) attending kindergarten.

A social constructivist view of school readiness focuses on the development of shared meanings and ideas about what is important related to readiness for school. Within this theoretical perspective, definitions of school readiness can vary from community to community or even from classroom to classroom. Individuals construct their own views of what is important for children's readiness based on their own experiences and the cultural, historical, institutional, and political forces operative in their environment. Individuals within a community may have some common views on readiness but also may have differing views depending on their own circumstances (Graue, 1993; Meisels, 1995, 1999; Smith & Shepard, 1988). Readiness is, within this model, not a fixed concept but something that is co-constructed by people within a particular community.

More recently, the focus has shifted to an ecological model of school readiness that focuses on the child within a broader context. While the skills, abilities, dispositions, and knowledge children bring to school are important, the environmental context within which a child exists and the relationships between the child and the environments are equally important. Child, family, school, and community factors are all interconnected and interdependent and greatly impact a child's success in school. This means that experiences children have before they enter school, the skills and abilities they bring with them, the characteristics and expectations of the school environment itself, and family supports all play a role in how ready a child is for school (Downer, Driscoll, & Pianta, 2006; Mashburn & Pianta, 2006; Ramey & Ramey, 1999; Rimm-Kaufman & Pianta, 2000). The primary focus in this model is on what adults are doing to support children's success rather than on a child's characteristics at the time of school entry, or on "ready schools" and "ready communities" in addition to "ready children."

Educators and Parents

Just as theorists differ in their views on readiness, so too do individuals who play various roles in children's lives. Research has noted some interesting differences in how teachers, administrators, and parents think about readiness. In general, teachers tend to focus on nonacademic aspects of school readiness—children being physically healthy, able to communicate their needs, able to follow directions, curious, and able to get along with their peers (Dockett & Perry, 2003; Heaviside & Farris, 1993; Lin, Lawrence, & Gorrell, 2003). Teachers' views on school readiness do, however, differ. Prekindergarten teachers tend to focus more on the importance of academic skills than kindergarten teachers (Piotrkowski, Botsko, & Matthews, 2000), although there is some more recent evidence that prekindergarten teachers may value social-emotional skills more than kindergarten teachers (Grace & Brandt, 2006). Some teachers report that the increasing focus on accountability and standards has caused them to place more emphasis on academic skills (Wesley & Buysse, 2003). This trend to emphasize academic skills as an important component of school readiness may be particularly pronounced among teachers working with low-income children (Wright, Diener, & Kay, 2000) and among teachers of color (Piotrkowski et al., 2000).

Like teachers, administrators tend to emphasize nonacademic related skills as important components of school readiness. Grace and Brandt (2006) found that preschool and kindergarten administrators reported that children's curiosity and approach toward learning new tasks, their health, and their motor skills are important. Taken together, teachers and administrators appear to feel that children who are healthy, who can communicate their needs, and who are able to regulate their behaviors are more ready for success in school, than children who are lacking in these factors. They tend to place more emphasis on these abilities than on basic knowledge or academic skills.

Parents, on the other hand, seem to consistently view academic skills as important elements of children's readiness for success in school (Grace & Brandt, 2006). For example, when asked about the importance of children being able to count to 20, 58 percent of parents rated this as being important while fewer than 10 percent of teachers indicated this skill was important (West, Germino-Hausken, & Collins, 1995). The emphasis on academic skills seems to be particularly important for parents from low-income families (Piotrkowski, 2004; Piotrkowski et al., 2000). Taken together, the research on parents', teachers', and administrators' views of school readiness supports the social constructivist view of school readiness. Persons in different types of roles differ in what they think is important for children's readiness for success in school.

Policy Makers

Just as educators, researchers, parents, and advocates have sought to define school readiness, so too have policy makers, sometimes explicitly but most often implicitly through policies and regulations. The NEGP (1997; Kagan, Moore, & Bredekamp, 1995) developed an explicit definition of school readiness that includes children's physical well-being and motor development; social and emotional development; approaches toward learning, communication, and language development; and cognition and general knowledge. In an effort to more specifically define important skills and knowledge for preschool-age children, the Head Start Child Outcome Framework published by the Head Start Bureau (2000) outlined 8 domains of children's learning that were broken down into 27 domain elements and 100 specific indicators of children's skills, abilities, and knowledge. The Head Start reauthorization bill, known as the School Readiness Act of 2005 (S1107; H.R. 2123), specified expectations for Head Start children at kindergarten entry in the areas of language, prereading, premathematics, cognitive abilities related to academic achievement, and social and emotional development, as well as progress learning English for limited-English-proficient children.

On the state level, policy makers have also been active in defining what is important for children's readiness for success in school. Known as "early learning standards," every state in the nation has developed a document to define what children should know and be able to do prior to or at kindergarten entry, and a growing number of states have developed similar documents to describe expectations for infants and toddlers. These early learning standards are being used for a variety of purposes—to guide curriculum and instruction decisions, to guide decisions about how children will be assessed, and to provide training/information to teachers and parents (Scott-Little, Kagan, & Frelow, 2003; Scott-Little, Lesko, Martella, & Milburn, 2007). Scott-Little, Kagan, and Frelow (2005, 2006) conducted content analyses on 46 early learning standards documents to determine what areas of children's development and learning have been addressed. Results suggested that early learning standards have emphasized language and cognitive domains, and that specific areas within domains of learning and development such as physical fitness, relationships, and reading comprehension have been addressed relatively less often. Many states have, however, included standards to address nonacademic areas of children's development and learning, including approaches toward learning and social-emotional competencies. It seems that policy makers at the state and federal levels have often focused on academically related skills when defining readiness for school success, whereas the persons who work most closely with children when they enter school—kindergarten teachers—tend to emphasize the importance of nonacademic competencies.

WHAT DOES RESEARCH SAY ABOUT CHILDREN'S READINESS FOR SCHOOL SUCCESS?

Having looked at what parents, teachers, administrators, and policy makers say is important regarding children's readiness for school, we now turn to the research literature to see what skills, abilities, and knowledge have been found to be important. Efforts to isolate particular skills associated with later success in school are complicated by a number of factors, including the lack of a clear-cut definition of school readiness, the limited number of assessments with evidence that they predict children's later success in school, and our limited understanding of how all of the elements of children's readiness for success in school "fit" together or impact each other (Snow, 2006, 2007). We do, however, have some understanding of the facets of children's development and learning that seem to be important. The following section summarizes research related to children's health and physical development, social and emotional development, approaches toward learning, language and preliteracy development, and cognitive skills and general knowledge, with particular emphasis on the skills and characteristics that research findings indicate are associated with later success in school.

Health and Physical Development

The NEGP (1997) advocated that children's health, nutrition, and physical development are important aspects of their readiness to succeed in school. Given that health and physical development set the stage for all other areas of development, the idea that children need to be healthy to learn seems self-evident. Most of the research literature in this area has examined the effects of health-related problems on children's learning and their success in school. Children with poor nutrition and children who are prone to health-related conditions such as asthma or other chronic health conditions, attention-deficit hyperactivity disorder (ADHD), and sensory deficits such as vision or hearing loss are more likely to be identified as having limited success in school (Currie, 2005). Furthermore, there is evidence that children exposed to environmental hazards such as chronic high-noise environments, pollution, lead, and pesticides may not perform as well in school (Pascoe, Shaikh, Forbis, & Etzel, 2007). The relationship between children's health and physical development and their readiness for school success may be direct (poor health may interfere with their capacity to process information and learn) and/or indirect (by impacting the level of energy children have to participate in school activities or causing them to be absent from school).

Social and Emotional Development

The beginning of kindergarten presents children with a number of formidable changes and demands: They must adapt to a new physical environment, the emphasis is often more on learning formal academic skills, the rules and expectations

Box 5–1 *Elements of Children's Early Learning and Development That Are Important for Success in School*

Health and Physical Development

❑ Good overall health and nutrition

❑ Absence of chronic health conditions

❑ Minimal exposure to environmental hazards

Social and Emotional Development

Social Development

❑ Social competencies with teachers

❑ Social competencies with peers

Emotional Development

❑ Emotional knowledge

❑ Emotional expression

❑ Emotional and behavioral regulation

Approaches Toward Learning

❑ Engagement and curiosity

❑ Initiative

❑ Ability to pay attention and persistence

❑ Creativity or imagination

❑ Ability to reflect on or interpret information

Language and Early Literacy Development

Language

❑ Expressive and receptive communication skills

❑ Vocabulary

❑ Pragmatics and social language skills

❑ Understanding of sequences of events

Early Literacy

❑ Phonological awareness

❑ Concepts of print

❑ Alphabet knowledge

❑ Invented spelling

❑ Comprehension

❑ Motivation to read

Cognitive Development and General Knowledge

❑ General knowledge about the world

❑ Cognitive processes

for behavior may be different, and they often lose connections with teachers/caregivers and friends they had in their child care setting or, if they have not attended a group care setting, they no longer are with their parents during most of their waking hours (Ladd, Herald, & Kochel, 2006). Children's social and emotional competencies are important aspects of their readiness for school because competencies in these areas impact how successfully children can surmount these and other challenges in school.

Social Competencies. Research suggests that the degree to which children demonstrate effective social skills and build relationships is associated with their success in school. Children who are able to initiate social interactions, respond to others, refrain from antisocial behaviors, and form constructive, supportive relationships are more successful in the school setting. Children who are able to establish warm relationships characterized by open communication with teachers are more comfortable in school, are more likely to approach their teacher, and are more likely to use their teacher as a resource for help with academic school work or social situations (Birch & Ladd, 1996, 1998; Burchinal, Peisner-Feinberg, Pianta, & Howes, 2002; Hamre & Pianta, 2001; Ladd et al., 2006).

In addition to relationships with teachers, children who are able to relate effectively with peers are also more successful in school (Ladd, Price, & Hart, 1988, 1990; Ladd, Birch, & Buhs, 1999). Children who are able to make and retain friendships in kindergarten typically adjust more easily to school and make greater gains in achievement (Ladd, 1990). To be socially successful in school, children must know how to initiate positive relationships with teachers and peers; demonstrate prosocial behaviors such as sharing, taking turns, and cooperating; refrain from antisocial behaviors such as aggression; and cope with instances of bullying or other forms of negative behaviors from peers (Ladd et al., 2006).

Emotional Competencies.   Children's emotional competencies are also key to their ability to adjust to and be successful in kindergarten and later grades. In fact, learning to express and control emotions appropriately are central developmental tasks of early childhood. Three types of emotional competencies that seem to be particularly important are emotional knowledge, emotional expression, and emotional and behavior regulation. Knowledge about emotions—the ability to recognize, label, and communicate about emotions—is an important element of school readiness. Children who understand emotions (their own and others') have an advantage in peer interactions. They can respond more appropriately to others, giving comfort when a peer is hurt or sad, steering clear of a situation when a peer is angry, and so on (Denham, 2006; Denham et al., 2003; Denham, Blair, et al., 2002; Denham, Caverly, et al., 2002). The importance of emotional knowledge seems to carry over into children's academic performance. Children with greater emotional knowledge tend to score higher on measures of academic success in later grades (Izard, 2002; Izard, Fine, Schultz, Moslow, Ackerman, & Youngstrong, 2001). In addition to having knowledge about emotions, children who learn to express emotions appropriately have an advantage in school. Children who express relatively more positive affect are perceived as more friendly and assertive by teachers, respond more prosocially to peers' emotions, and are seen as more likable by their peers. Positive emotional expression also seems to be associated with increased learning and effort when individuals are given difficult problems to solve (Denham, McKinley, Couchoud, & Holt, 1990; Isen, 2000; Izard, 2002; Park, Lay, & Ramsay, 1993).

Finally, emotional and behavior regulation play a key role in children's success in school. Children must learn to control emotions that are counterproductive in school settings and to call forth emotions that are helpful in school. Controlling anger, resisting self-gratification, and other types of emotional regulation are important because they are central to children's abilities to carry out a number of tasks necessary for learning—learning to share, taking turns, getting in line, waiting for instructions, and concentrating on learning tasks. The regulation of emotions and behavior is related to more positive social interactions, teacher's ratings of social effectiveness, and the ability to develop friendships. What's more, there is some evidence that children's brains are more receptive to new information when their emotions are regulated appropriately (Blair, Denham, Kochanoff, & Whipple, 2004; Raver, 2004; Raver, Garner, & Smith-Donald, 2007; Raver & Knitzer, 2002). Clearly children's social and emotional competencies are recognized as important elements of school readiness.

Approaches Toward Learning

Approaches toward learning are distinct behaviors related to how children engage in learning activities. When describing the behaviors that are included in how a child approaches learning tasks, researchers often identify children's motivation to engage in learning or curiosity, initiative to engage in new or challenging tasks, ability to pay attention and to persist on the task, creativity or imagination, capacity for reflection or interpretation, and their general attitude toward learning tasks. This is an important dimension of school readiness because while children may have the skills necessary to learn, their general approach toward learning influences whether they will actually put their skills to use in the classroom.

Children who were more highly motivated to demonstrate competence in learning tasks were also rated as more antonomous in the classroom. Children's approaches toward learning seem to be related to their success in school in a variety of ways, by impacting their peer relationships as well as the way they approach learning tasks (Coolahan, Fantuzzo, Mendez, & McDermott, 2000; Fantuzzo, Bulotsky-Shearer, Fusco, & McWayne, 2005; Fantuzzo, Perry, & McDermott, 2004; Kagan et al., 1995).

Language and Early Literacy Skills

The ability to communicate and to read and write are essential skills in school and in other settings. Children's language expands exponentially during the first years of life and they learn important skills that will serve them well as they learn to read and write. The following section summarizes what we've learned from research about the importance of children's language and early literacy skills for success in school.

Language Skills. A variety of skills are important for children to learn to communicate—to express their thoughts, ideas, and feelings and to understand messages other people express. Children's understanding of vocabulary and linguistic concepts—their ability to understand and use words and key concepts—is particularly important in paving the way for them to learn to read. The number of words children know in preschool and kindergarten is positively associated with their ability to read (Catts, Fey, Zhang, & Tomblin, 1999, 2001; Lonigan, 2006; Snow, Burns, & Griffin, 1998). As children acquire vocabulary knowledge, they also must learn to communicate more successfully. The ability to follow the "unwritten rules" about how to communicate is known as pragmatics and social language. This area includes understanding the norms that govern communication so that you can initiate and keep a conversation going and the ability to use language for different purposes. Children who are skilled in this area are exposed to more language (because they communicate more successfully, people talk to them more), have more positive relationships with peers and with teachers, and learn to read and write more successfully (Catts et al., 1999, 2001; Hempill & Siperstein, 1990; Ninio & Snow, 1999; Pianta & Nimetz, 1991). Finally, children's understanding and use of narrative (the sequence of stories and real life events) is associated with later reading and overall academic achievement. Children who can understand and produce narratives have stronger oral language skills and demonstrate greater competencies on a variety of school-related tasks (Catts et al., 1999, 2001; Zevenbergen, Whitehurst, & Zevenbergen, 2003).

Early Literacy Skills.   Development of early literacy skills—skills needed to recognize or decode print and to understand what one is reading—are essential for learning to read and the ability to read is essential for almost all other areas of learning in school. Early literacy skills that help children learn to read include phonological awareness (the ability to recognize and manipulate sounds in words), concepts of print (understanding how print is organized and how it is used), alphabet knowledge (the ability to recognize and name letters of the alphabet), invented spelling (the ability to guess how a word is spelled based on the sounds within the word), and comprehension (the ability to understand text that one hears as someone else reads or text that one reads) (Lonigan, 2006; Lonigan, Burgess, & Anthony, 2000; National Early Literacy Panel, 2005; Whitehurst & Lonigan, 1998). The final early literacy skill that is important is a child's desire or motivation to read—children who enjoy reading and want to read are more likely to read and to have more opportunities to practice their reading skills. Research suggests that the foundation for reading competencies begins very early in children's lives and that children who become competent readers reap benefits in many areas throughout their school careers, while those who have difficulty learning to read fall further and further behind their peers (Chall, Jacobs, & Baldwin, 1990; Snow et al., 1998).

Cognitive Development and General Knowledge

In general, children's scores on measures of what they know when they enter kindergarten are positively associated with various measures of student achievement at later grades. For instance, kindergartners participating in the Early Childhood Longitudinal Study-Kindergarten (ECLS-K) who scored higher on measures of reading, mathematics, science, and social studies had higher scores on measures of reading, mathematics, and science in the first, third, and fifth grades (Denton & West, 2002; Princiotta, Flanagan, & Germino-Hausken, 2006; Rathburn & West, 2004). There is, however, limited research to suggest specific content children should know. What seems more important is that children have opportunities to learn about a wide variety of topics through meaningful, hands-on experiences in order to set the stage for success later in school.

Recent research has also pointed to the importance of cognitive processes in children's success in school, suggesting that how children process information and learn tasks are important, in addition to the specific content they learn. "Executive functioning" refers to how an individual maintains and uses information from the environment and includes the individual's ability to pay attention to important information when learning or doing a specific task, analyzing what is needed to address the specific task or solve a problem, and remembering and using information they take in (Blair et al., 2007). In the area of cognitive development, general knowledge and cognitive processes are both important elements of readiness for success in school.

Variation in Children's Readiness for School

Although the majority of children who enter kindergarten come with age-appropriate cognitive, language, social, and emotional skills, research suggests that there is a great deal of variation in the skills and abilities that children bring with them to kindergarten and that this variation continues through the early grades (Denton & West, 2002; Princiotta et al., 2006; Rathbun & West, 2004; West, Denton, & Germino-Hausken, 2000). When asked about children's transition to kindergarten, kindergarten teachers seem to agree that most children make a smooth transition to kindergarten but some have difficulty adjusting to the new setting. In a national survey of 3,595 kindergarten teachers conducted in the late 1990s, the teachers reported that 16 percent of the children in the classrooms had difficult transitions into kindergarten and up to 46 percent of the teachers reported that half their class or more had specific problems during the transition process (Rimm-Kaufman & Pianta, 2000). Clearly, children do not start school equally "ready." We have looked at elements of children's learning and development that seem to be important for their readiness for success in school. We now turn to examining factors that seem to be associated with differences in children's readiness.

Family Characteristics.   Children from families living in poverty, families with low maternal education, and single-parent families are more likely to have lower scores on various measures of reading, mathematics, and general knowledge than children from families without these characteristics. These differences seem to persist at least through fifth grade. Children from these family circumstances are also less likely to be rated as having prosocial skills than children from more advantaged families (Denton & West, 2002; Princiotta et al., 2006; Rathbun & West, 2004; West et al., 2000). Children's performance on various measures of knowledge, achievement, and school adjustment at kindergarten entry and later in school is also associated with their racial/ethnic background, with results tending to favor white and Asian children over Hispanic and African American children (Brooks-Gunn, Rouse, & McLanahan, 2007).

Home Language.   Children from families that speak a language other than English also tend to score lower on measures of reading and mathematics but there is great diversity among children from families that do not speak English in the home. For instance, English language learners from European- or Asian-language-speaking families often have achievement scores comparable to their English-speaking peers. Children from Spanish-speaking homes score lower than all other language groups on measures of reading and mathematics achievement. In the area of social-emotional skills, however, Spanish-speaking children who enter kindergarten are often rated by teachers as having fewer emotional and behavioral problems than their peers. It seems that children from Spanish-speaking families in particular face a number of challenges related to academic achievement but often demonstrate social and emotional strengths associated with positive adjustment to school (Espinosa, 2007).

Early Education Experiences.   Research over the previous three decades indicates that early childhood education programs can have significant and sustained positive benefits for children. The same research, however, indicates that the quality of preschool classrooms where children are enrolled varies tremendously and that poor-quality early education experiences are not beneficial for children and do not prepare them well for success in school (Barnett, 1995; Guralnick, 1997; Karoly et al., 1998). Furthermore, it is estimated that approximately 32 percent of children do not attend a formal early care and education program (Rosenthal, Rathbun, & West, 2005). Children's readiness for school, therefore, varies according to the type and quality of educational experiences prior to kindergarten entry.

Children's readiness for success in school varies by all of these factors—family, language, and early education experiences—and many of the factors are interrelated. Children from single-parent families may have lower incomes and may be enrolled in lower-quality early education programs. White children tend to live in more economically advantaged families than African American children. Children whose families speak Spanish are more likely to have limited incomes and parents with lower education levels (Brooks-Gunn et al., 2007; Espinosa, 2007). The number of combinations of factors that can impact a single child's readiness for school are almost endless. We can summarize this section on what research says about children's readiness for school by saying that children who enter school with higher levels of cognitive, social-emotional, physical, and approaches toward learning competencies are more likely to be successful later in school but there is striking variation in the degree to which children across our country demonstrate these competencies and the variation is likely impacted by a number of interrelated factors within the child's environment.

HOW HAS THE ISSUE OF SCHOOL READINESS IMPACTED EARLY CHILDHOOD PRACTICES AND POLICIES?

The increasing attention and emphasis that the issue of school readiness has received over the past two decades has affected early education practices and policies in several ways. While the increasing recognition that the skills and knowledge children develop prior to entering school are important is a positive development, the increasing emphasis on school readiness has also led to challenges related to early childhood curriculum, to assessment of young children, and to decisions about when individual children start school and progress to first grade. The following section presents an overview of issues related to curriculum, assessments, and decisions about individual children.

Early Childhood Curriculum

Traditionally, early childhood educators have valued play-based curricula that emerge from teachers' observations of children's interests and developmental capabilities—a teacher develops the curriculum based on the children using her or his knowledge of child development and early education pedagogy. With the advent of standards-based education and various policies designed to "level the playing field" for children, there has been a dramatic movement to encourage teachers to teach in a way that helps all children learn a common set of knowledge and/or competencies described in standards. Kagan and Kauerz (2007) describe this as a shift toward "specifying what children should know and be able to do" rather than "evoking" the curriculum from the children themselves (p. 21). With the advent of the federal No Child Left Behind legislation that requires states to develop standards to define what children should learn and specifies that schools be held accountable for how well their children perform on standardized tests of achievement, there has been great pressure to emphasize academic skills and predetermined learning outcomes. Early childhood programs—both preschool and kindergarten—have not been exempt from this movement to hold educators accountable, and teachers often struggle to find a balance between their early childhood "roots" and the new expectations/requirements/pressures they face.

The impact of the emphasis on accountability has been most dramatic in kindergarten classrooms. Kindergarten was originally designed to provide a period of transition as children entered school, with enriched learning environments that afforded children opportunities through a play-based curriculum to develop cognitive, social, physical, and emotional competencies that pave the way for them to learn academic skills in first grade (Seefeldt & Wasik, 2002). Kindergarten classrooms today, however, typically are more focused on teaching academic skills. Known as the "push down" of curricula, there has been a strong emphasis on teaching children literacy, mathematics, and other academic skills at earlier and earlier ages. While kindergartens once looked similar to preschool classrooms with learning centers and lots of hands-on learning experiences, today they often more resemble first-grade classrooms with worksheets, whole-group rather than individualized or small-group instruction, and lots of time dedicated to helping children learn specific academic skills (Pianta, La Paro, Payne, Cox, & Bradley, 2002). This trend has been occurring for almost two decades—in 1991, Bryant, Clifford, and Peisner reported that approximately 80 percent of the kindergarten classrooms they observed were judged to be developmentally inappropriate—and has had tremendous implications for teachers.

Kindergarten teachers report feeling pressured to teach in a way that is counter to their own personal and professional philosophies about how children learn and how they should teach. While many kindergarten teachers come from an early childhood background that affirms variation in development that is typical for children of this age, emphasizes the importance of individualizing educational experiences, and promotes the use of play and hands-on learning experiences, they are being asked (often explicitly and sometimes more subtly) to teach children with a predetermined "one-size-fits-all" curriculum that emphasizes academic skills to the detriment of other areas. The "push-down-curriculum" pressures come from administrators, teachers in later grades who want to be sure that children start first grade having mastered certain skills, and from parents. The end result is that teachers feel pressure to cover specific content, worry that they are not being responsive to the developmental levels and individual learning styles they observe in children, and feel that they are not being true to what they think is best for children. It is not uncommon for teachers to think about leaving the profession or to actually resign rather than continue teaching in what they deem to be untenable circumstances. Many worry that the same push-down curriculum has reached or will soon reach preschool classrooms, subjecting even more teachers to personal and professional dilemmas about whether to continue teaching. The quest to improve children's readiness for school has somehow equated readiness with academic preparedness and has dramatically impacted the profession and the lives of early childhood teachers across the country (Goldstein, 2007; Wesley & Buysse, 2003; Wien, 2004).

Early Childhood Assessments

With the increasing emphasis on preparing children for success in school has come corresponding pressure to gauge how children are doing—are programs doing a good job teaching and are children ready for school? These important questions have forefronted issues related to assessment of children's readiness for school. Early childhood assessments are being implemented to evaluate program effectiveness and to determine the readiness for school of individual children. The end result is that young children are being assessed in a variety of ways for a variety of purposes. Issues related to assessment of children this age for purposes of program accountability and individual placement decisions are discussed in the section that follows.

Program Accountability.   Assessments of children's readiness for school that are used to gauge whether programs have been effective are increasingly common at the federal and state levels (this topic is elaborated on in Chapter 16). At the federal level, the Head Start National Reporting System (NRS) and the U.S. Department of Education Office of Special Education Program's (OSEP) Early Childhood Outcomes (ECO) initiative are examples of federal efforts to use child assessment to gauge the effectiveness of early childhood programs. The OSEP ECO initiative requires states to report outcome data for children served through Part B and Part C of the Individuals with Disabilities Education Act (IDEA) as part of their Annual Performance Report. States must report the percent of infants and toddlers with IFSPs and preschool children with IEPs who demonstrate improvements in positive social-emotional skills, knowledge and skills (including early language/communication and early literacy skills for preschoolers), and appropriate behavior to meet their own needs (ECO Center, 2007). Programs receiving federal funding to provide early childhood services are being asked to provide data on child outcomes.

Pressure to hold programs accountable for child outcomes is not limited to the federal level. State and local programs are also collecting child outcome data to evaluate the effectiveness of school readiness programs. The number of program evaluations has increased dramatically since the late 1990s. One recent review noted 86 state and local evaluation reports published between 1997 and the first half of 2006. The evaluations used a variety of measures to assess children's readiness for school. Children's language and literacy development was the area most commonly assessed, followed by children's mathematical knowledge. Fewer than half of the reports included a measure of children's social-emotional development and even fewer assessed children's physical development as part of the program evaluation process (Brown, Scott-Little, Amwake, & Wynn, 2007). Clearly many children are being assessed in efforts to hold programs accountable for how well they prepare children for success in school and many of these accountability-related assessments focus on children's academic skills, particularly in the areas of language, early literacy, and early mathematics knowledge.

Assessment to Gauge Individual Children's Readiness for School.   Apart from program evaluations, assessments are being conducted to gauge individual children's readiness for school. In 1999, 34 states either had a statewide kindergarten assessment system in place, directed local districts to have such as system, or were working to develop a kindergarten assessment system. The data from these assessment systems were used in a variety of ways—to guide teachers in making instructional decisions, to inform program decisions, and/or to make decisions about individual children (Saluja, Scott-Little, & Clifford, 2000). Analysis of the ECLS-K data found that an estimated 61 percent of schools administered some type of assessment to children prior to or at the start of kindergarten. Of these, 27 percent reported using assessment data to make decisions about whether age-eligible children should start kindergarten. Often children who do not score at a certain level on the assessment are deemed not to be ready for school and advised to delay school entry (Prakash, West, & Denton, 2003).

Unfortunately, the assessment of children is not an exact science and there are a number of issues that are of concern when assessments are conducted with very young children. Some issues that have been raised include the difficulty in assessing young children who are by nature growing and changing relatively rapidly, our limited agreement on exactly what skills and characteristics are important for school readiness, the importance of conducting authentic assessments to gain a good understanding of children's skills and abilities, and the limited number of valid and reliable assessment instruments available to assess particular areas of children's development such as physical health and social-emotional competencies (see Chapter 15 for further information about issues associated with child assessment). The bottom line is that preschool and kindergarten children are being subjected to more and more assessments designed to determine if they are ready for success in school. While the field has made progress in the area of early childhood assessment, questions remain about the best way to assess children at this age and the usefulness of the data that is collected, particularly if the assessment results are being used to predict the extent to which the child will be successful or whether the child should be excluded from starting school.

Implications for Decisions About Individual Children

The debate about children's readiness for school has important implications for decisions that are made about individual children—when they start kindergarten and whether they are promoted to first grade. Nationally, 6 to 9 percent of age-eligible kindergartners do not enroll in kindergarten the first year they are eligible (Bryant et al., 1991; Datar, 2003; Malone, West, Flanagan, & Park, 2006; Zill, Loomis, & West, 1997). This practice of holding children out of kindergarten to give them an extra year to get ready for school is known as "red shirting." Often children with birthdates close to the eligibility cutoff date (those who would be the youngest within their cohort of kindergartners) and boys are overrepresented among children who are red-shirted (Datar, 2003; Graue & DiPerna, 2000). The practice emanates from the maturationist view of readiness for school—the extra year will allow time for red-shirted children to catch up developmentally and be better prepared to meet the demands of the kindergarten classroom.

A number of research studies have been conducted to see if red-shirting children is beneficial in the long run. Unfortunately, the results from the research studies are mixed—some studies suggest that children benefit from this practice and others do not (Datar, 2006; Kinard & Reinherz, 1986; Malone et al., 2006; Morrison, Griffith & Alberts, 1997; Stipek, 2002; Zill et al., 1997). Some studies show that red-shirted children outperform their peers who started kindergarten on time on academic measures and other studies indicate no differences, particularly if they follow children through the early elementary grades. Red-shirted and non-red-shirted children tend to have a similar rate of progress on academic and achievement measures over the kindergarten and first-grade years but the non-red-shirted children are, of course, ahead of the red-shirted children by one year. There is some evidence to suggest that being a year older than peers in your grade may be associated with behavioral problems in later grades (Byrd, Weitzman, & Auinger, 1997).

A related and equally significant issue is the number of children who are retained in kindergarten—either repeating the kindergarten year or being enrolled in a transition kindergarten or a "kindergarten plus" year. Nationally, about 5 percent of kindergartners complete two years of kindergarten, often because of academic concerns or concerns about their social development. Children who repeat kindergarten are less likely to have attended a preschool the year before kindergarten, more likely to be male, and more likely to live in a family in poverty and have parents with less than a high school education. In the ECLS-K study, children who repeated kindergarten demonstrated lower scores on reading and mathematics measures at the end of first grade, even when differences in the children's family background, gender, and age were controlled (Malone et al., 2006). Several other studies have suggested that retaining children in kindergarten may not be helpful for children or may even be harmful (Dennebaum & Kulberg, 1994; Gay, 2002; Reynolds, 1992).

Taken together, the research related to children's delayed entry or retention in kindergarten indicates that decisions about when children start school and whether they go on to first grade should be made with great caution. Careful consideration must be given to the characteristics of the child and the family—what experiences he or she has had prior to kindergarten (particularly the type of preschool experience he or she has had); how he or she has progressed along various developmental milestones from birth; how family and caregivers describe his or her physical, social, emotional, language, and cognitive competencies; results from any assessments that have been conducted; and how the parents feel about delaying or retaining their child. In making decisions such as this, the characteristics of the setting where the child would be attending school should also be considered—will the classroom be highly structured with a focus on academic skills or will there be a more developmental approach with a curriculum that is play-based and focuses on individualization of learning experiences? The decision to red-shirt or retain a child has important implications for the child and his/her family and should be made after careful consideration of many factors, never solely on the basis of one assessment or school readiness test.

WHERE IS OUR THINKING ABOUT THE CONCEPT OF READINESS HEADED?

The previous pages describe what we have learned about children's readiness for school from research and summarize issues that have shaped policies and practices related to children's school readiness. We now begin to look forward—to consider some of the more recent trends related to school readiness. Generally, we can think of the field's views of readiness becoming broader and more sophisticated over time, both in terms of how we think about children's readiness for school and the importance of factors outside of children themselves.

More Refined Views of Children's Readiness for School

The National Education Goals Panel (1997) described a relatively broad view of the components of children's learning and development that are important for success in school in five domains—physical well-being and motor development, social and emotional development, approaches toward learning, communication and language usage, and cognition and general knowledge. Recent research has begun to define the elements of each of the domains more precisely, to explore how the various skills and capacities are both independent and interrelated, and to examine how the various skills and capacities vary across and within different populations of children. For instance, researchers looking at the relationship between children's abilities to regulate their behavior and reading outcomes have demonstrated that children who have better control of their behavior score higher on measures of reading competencies (Doctoroff, Greer, & Arnold, 2006; Fantuzzo, Bulotsky, McDermott, Mosca, & Lutz, 2003; Miles & Stipek, 2006; Rabiner, Coie, & Conduct Problems Prevention Research Group, 2000). Researchers have also begun to explore the relationship between children's language development and their comprehension of mathematical concepts (Carey, 2001, 2004).

At this point, there seems to be evidence that various components of children's readiness for success in school are interrelated. Research is, however, only beginning to explore the nature and cause of the observed relationships. For instance, do behavior problems cause children to have difficulty in learning to read or do children with reading difficulties act out as a result of their frustration with their limited success in reading or other subjects? Perhaps the observed relationships between various components of children's readiness for school are mediated by underlying processes that affect multiple areas of children's learning and development. Does a child's general approach to learning or his/her executive functioning impact his/her ability to learn to read, to understand mathematical concepts, or to control behaviors? If so, such "underlying processes" could perhaps be significant aspects of school readiness, along with the discrete skills and knowledge traditionally identified as important components of school readiness (Snow, 2007).

Using this logic, school readiness is viewed as a dynamic, multidimensional construct rather than an all-or-nothing construct that children reach at a specific point in time. Children are constantly learning and their learning within specific areas affects their learning in other areas. Taken together, the collective skills, abilities, knowledge, and competencies that a child has across and within the five domains determines his or her likelihood for success in school (Snow, 2006, 2007).

Broader and More Refined Views of the Role of the Environment in School Readiness

The role of the environment in shaping children's readiness for school has long been acknowledged by early educators—the skills and abilities children develop depend on their experiences and their readiness for success in school depends on the expectations of the school that the child will attend. In fact, the National Education Goals Panel recognized the importance of environmental contributions to children's readiness for school, set family involvement in the education of young children as a primary objective, and described features of a "ready school" (NEGP, 1997, 1998). As with our thinking about children's readiness for school, our understanding of environmental components of school readiness has broadened and become more refined. Current and future conceptualizations of school readiness emphasize the importance of children's transition experiences, the relationships they form, the nature of their classroom learning experiences, and policy-level developments that can promote children's readiness for school on a number of different levels. We turn now to recent trends in our understanding of environmental components of school readiness and the implications of what we have learned for policy and for practice.

Promoting Smooth Transitions.   The transition to school is a major event in the lives of children and their families. They often have to adjust to new classroom environments, new people, and new expectations. Previous research has suggested that teachers are aware of the importance of children's transition to school but most commonly report they have used "low-intensity" transition strategies such as talking with parents about school after school had started or sending a letter or flyer home to provide information to parents. "High-intensity" strategies such as making a home visit or a personalized phone call to families before school starts—the strategies that provide more support for children—were much less common, particularly for low-income children (Pianta, Cox, Taylor, & Early, 1999). Our understanding of the importance of helping children make the transition to kindergarten is growing. In analyses of data from the ECLS-K study, Schulting, Malone, and Dodge (2005) found that children's academic achievement in kindergarten was positively related to efforts that teachers made to help ease children's transition to school, particularly for low-income children. Teachers' transition practices were also linked to the degree to which families were involved with school activities during the year. It seems that helping children make a smooth transition to school not only makes the children feel more at ease but encourages family involvement, and may pave the way for children to learn more effectively during the year.

These findings have implications for individual teachers as they seek to help children transition to kindergarten and for policy makers and others who set policies and procedures that impact teachers' practices. At the community and program level, additional efforts are needed to implement policies designed to create continuity and smooth transitions for children. Interagency agreements, joint training and professional development shared between kindergarten and preschool teachers, and collaborative planning for transitions are needed to establish a climate that promotes effective transitions (Pianta & Kraft-Sayer, 2003). We must also examine kindergarten policies to ensure that they support children's transitions to school. For instance, kindergarten entry policies, kindergarten assessment policies, and kindergarten classroom requirements such as class size can all impact the extent to which children have positive transition experiences (Gallagher, 1999). Beyond the actual policies that dictate practice, professional development is needed to help teachers understand the importance of relationships during the transition period, child development and expectations for children who are kindergarten age, and specific transition practices (Clifford, 1999). As theoretical models and empirical evidence evolve and continue to emphasize the importance of children's transitions to kindergarten, we should seek to promote more intense transition practices and expand the number of schools and programs implementing effective transition practices.

The Importance of Relationships.   While traditional views of school readiness have focused on it as a set of skills and knowledge children bring to school, more recently researchers have begun to focus on the importance of relationships a child forms with others as a key factor in success in school (Mashburn & Pianta, 2006; Pianta, 2004). According to this model, the relationships children form with parents, with teachers (both preschool and kindergarten), and with peers have direct and indirect effects on how well children adjust to and succeed in school. Children with parents who are warm and supportive and who provide appropriate stimulation at home tend to be more successful in school. Children with close, nonconflictual relationships with teachers tend to do better in school. When teachers form close relationships with individual children, children feel more secure, are able to adjust to the expectations of the classroom, and can relate better with their peers. These positive aspects of close relationships between teachers and children can facilitate children's ability to learn. Relationships with teachers seem to be particularly important for children from circumstances that might place them at risk for difficulties in school. Strong positive relationships with teachers may serve as a protective factor for children from low-income families. Finally, children with positive peer relationships seem to have less difficulty transitioning to the school setting (Ladd et al., 2006).

Given the importance that relationships seem to make for children's success in school, a logical next step in our effort to promote children's readiness for school is to look closely at policies and practices that can help children develop close, supportive, and secure relationships. Careful consideration should be given to the adults in children's lives and how they promote relationships with and between children. Interventions that help parents understand the importance of their relationships with their children and provide guidance to promote cognitively stimulating home environments are important. To help children form close relationships with teachers, we need to think about the implications policies such as adult:child ratios and group size have for teachers' abilities to form close relationships with children. Large preschool and kindergarten classes may make it difficult for teachers to form and sustain positive relationships with individual children.

Furthermore, we need to think carefully about the qualifications of the teachers who are teaching in the classroom. Policies related to the qualifications of teachers teaching in prekindergarten and kindergarten should be examined to ensure that they maximize the likelihood that they are knowledgeable about child development and well prepared to foster close, caring relationships with children. The National Association of Early Childhood Teacher Educators (NAECTE) has developed a position statement, *Early Childhood Certification for Teachers of Children 8 Years and Younger in Public School Settings,* to emphasize the need for all teachers in prekindergarten, kindergarten, and the early grades to have specialized professional development in early childhood education (NAECTE, July 2007). Often kindergarten teachers (and teachers in the primary grades) are certified to teach in kindergarten through grades 4, 5, or 6. Typically, teacher certification programs that address the upper elementary school years provide students with less course material related to early childhood education and child development. The NAECTE recommends that teacher certification requirements be examined and revised as needed to ensure that teachers in kindergarten, first, second, and third grades have strong early childhood backgrounds. We also need ongoing professional development for teachers to help them understand the importance of forming warm and responsive relationships with each child in their care, and to develop interventions that teach children how to relate positively to adults and peers. Research suggests that these types of steps will have significant and long-lasting impacts on children's readiness for school success.

The Classroom Environment.   The field has long recognized that high-quality classrooms have positive impacts on child outcomes. We are, however, gaining a new understanding of the specific features of classrooms that make a difference for children. The importance of play and hands-on learning experiences have been recognized as key elements of quality early childhood classrooms and an important strategy for promoting children's readiness for success in school (see Chapter 12 for more information on the importance of play). Recent work by Robert Pianta and colleagues has further refined our understanding of the types of learning opportunities that are important for children (Hamre & Pianta, 2007). Evidence suggests that it is important for teachers to establish a classroom that has a positive emotional climate, that is organized to effectively engage children in learning activities, and that promotes children's understanding and higher-order thinking skills in a variety of areas. Future work in the area of school readiness should focus on how to support teachers in their efforts to provide highly interactive and stimulating play-based classrooms for children before they enter kindergarten and also in kindergarten classrooms in order to promote children's success in school.

Focus on Broadening the School's Role in Readiness.   From the very first discussions of school readiness, the National Education Goals Panel advocated that schools' readiness for children was just as important as children's readiness for school (NEGP, 1998). The focus, however, tended to be on how schools supported children during the transition to kindergarten and throughout the kindergarten year. Recent thinking about the school's role in the readiness equation suggests that our view of "ready schools" must be extended and reframed. In fact, many argue that in the near future school will not begin at kindergarten, but will begin with prekindergarten and that we now have an opportunity to rethink how we educate our children from age 3 through 8. Rather than continuing to view prekindergarten as an end of one stage in education or an "add-on" to public school, we should begin to look at children's experiences from age 3 through 8 as an integrated education system, with aligned standards, curriculum, and assessments to provide continuity in children's experiences so that children's learning in the early grades builds on what they have learned in preschool and kindergarten (Bogard & Takanishi, 2005; Pianta, 2007).

In an innovative new project known as "FirstSchool," the Frank Porter Graham Child Development Institute has partnered with a local school system to bring this new thinking about a school's role in readiness to reality (Ritchie, Maxwell, & Clifford, 2007). Together, they are building a new school that will integrate preschool education into the elementary school and reconceptualize the early grades, with a focus on alignment, attention to the "whole child," affirmation of diversity and inclusion, and strong partnerships with families and the community across all of the age/grade levels in the school. FirstSchool offers a new model to help policy makers and our field think more broadly about school readiness and what it means to be a "ready school." As we move forward in efforts to promote children's success in school, we must continue to advocate for efforts to make schools more responsive to young children and at the same time think about how recent advances in early education can help us rethink our vision of ready schools and elementary education.

Expanding Our Views of School Readiness in the Policy Arena.   As researchers and educators have expanded their views on what is important related to school readiness, there have been several efforts to expand the conceptualization of school readiness in the policy arena as well. In 2005, the National Governors Association (NGA) completed a multiyear process of studying school readiness issues and provided guidance to governors across the nation on how to address children's readiness for school. Among the key principles outlined in the NGA report were an affirmation of the importance of the early years to later development, the importance of addressing all areas of children's learning and development, and the recognition that school readiness is really not about children, but about what adults in children's lives do to support their development and learning. The NGA Task Force broadened the view of readiness beyond what schools, families, and the community can do by providing recommendations for "ready states" that develop strategic plans and the infrastructure to support children, families, schools, communities, and early education and intervention services in their efforts to promote school readiness.

The National School Readiness Indicators Initiative is another example of an effort to broaden the view of school readiness at the policy level. Operating as a partnership that included teams from 17 states, the Initiative developed recommendations for indicators that can be used to collect meaningful data and gauge trends related to school readiness. The partners developed indicators in the areas of Ready Children, Ready Families, Ready Communities, Ready Services (health and early care and education), and Ready Schools. In each of the areas the states agreed on types of data that could be collected to measure progress toward improved outcomes for children and families. Over time, the data can be used at the state and local level to focus resources and policies on areas that need attention in order to better support children's success in school (Rhode Island KIDS Count, 2005). Again, these are important developments at the policy level because they broaden the view of school readiness beyond just the skills and knowledge children have when they start school. This broader view of readiness recognizes the role that families, communities, service providers, and schools play in shaping children's readiness for success in school.

CONCLUSIONS

Looking back to Ms. Johnson, the kindergarten teacher considering school readiness issues on the first day of school, it is clear that her children reflect the diversity of kindergartners in this country—some have had experiences that prepared them for success and others have not. The factors that determine whether she and the children will be successful in this first year of formal schooling are complex. She likely is feeling pressure to structure her curriculum to address academic skills, perhaps to the detriment of an individualized, hands-on curriculum that addresses the wide variation of skills, knowledge, and dispositions of children in her classroom. As we have seen in this chapter, children's success is dependent on their competencies in every area of development and learning. Their success is supported or hindered by experiences they have had at home and in other early childhood education settings, and is impacted by the policies and programs in place (or lacking) to support their families in providing nurturing and stimulating environments. While Ms. Johnson may feel there is not much she can do to change these factors, there is a lot she can do once they enter her classroom, starting with her efforts to build connections with their families and other early childhood programs in the community to ensure children have a smooth transition to kindergarten. She also can set up her classroom to provide lots of choices for children among play and hands-on learning activities, seek to form warm and nurturing relationships with each child in her classroom, constantly assess and plan for individual children's particular strengths and areas that need additional support, teach social skills, and encourage children to develop higher-order thinking skills. She can continue to reach out to families to involve them in meaningful ways throughout the year. For, as it turns out, school readiness is multifaceted—not just what children know and are able to do when they enter kindergarten—and the adults in children's lives are key to whether children are ready for success in school.

REFERENCES

Administration for Children and Families. (2003). Developing the national reporting system. Head Start child outcomes—setting the context for the national reporting system. Head Start Bulletin #76. HHS/ACF/ACYF/HSB. Retrieved May 17, 2007 from http://eclkc.ohs.acf.hhs.gov/hslc/ecdh/eecd/Assessment/National%20Reporting%20System/edudev_art_00085_080905.html

Barnett, W. S. (1995). Long-term effects of early childhood programs on cognitive and school outcomes. *The Future of Children, 5*(3), 25–50.

Barnett, W. S., Hustedt, J. T., Hawkinson, L. E., & Robin, K. B. (2007). *The state of preschool 2006: State preschool yearbook.* Rutgers, NJ: National Institute for Early Education Research.

Birch, S. A., & Ladd, G. W. (1996). Contributions of teachers and peers to children's early school adjustment. In K. Wentzel & J. Juvonen (Eds.), *Social motivation: Understanding children's school adjustment* (pp. 199–225). New York: Cambridge University Press.

Birch, S. A., & Ladd, G. W. (1998). Children's interpersonal behaviors and the teacher-child relationship. *Developmental Psychology, 34*, 934–946.

Blair, C., Denham, S. A., Kochanoff, A., & Whipple, B. (2004). Playing it cool: Temperament, emotion regulation, and social behavior in preschoolers. *Journal of School Psychology, 42*, 419–443.

Blair, C., Knipe, H., Cummings, E., Baker, D. P., Gamson, D., Eslinger, P., & Thorne, S. L. (2007).

A developmental neuroscience approach to the study of school readiness. In R. C. Pianta, M. J. Cox, & K. L. Snow (Eds.), *School readiness & the transition to kindergarten in the era of accountability* (pp. 149–174). Baltimore: Brookes.

Bogard, K., & Takanishi, R. (2005). PK–3: An aligned and coordinated approach to education for children 3 to 8 years old. *Social Policy Report, XIX*(III). Washington, DC: Society for Research in Child Development.

Brooks-Gunn, J., Rouse C. E., & McLanahan, S. (2007). Racial and ethnic gaps in school readiness. In R. C. Pianta, M. J. Cox, & K. L. Snow (Eds.), *School readiness & the transition to kindergarten in the era of accountability* (pp. 283–306). Baltimore: Brookes.

Brown, G., Scott-Little, C., Amwake, L., & Wynn, L. (2007). *A review of methods and instruments used in state and local school readiness evaluations* (REL 2007, No. 4). Washington, DC: U.S. Department of Education, Institute of Education Sciences.

Bryant, D. M., Clifford, R. M., & Peisner, E. S. (1991). Best practices for beginners: Developmental appropriateness in kindergarten. *American Educational Research Journal, 28,* 783–803.

Burchinal, M. R., Peisner-Feinberg, E., Pianta, R., & Howes, C. (2002). Development of academic skills from preschool through second grade: Family and classroom predictors of developmental trajectories. *Journal of School Psychology, 40,* 415–436,

Bush, G. W. (2002). *Good Start, Grow Smart: The Bush administration's early childhood initiative.* Retrieved May 17, 2007, from www.whitehouse.gov/infocus/earlychildhood/toc.html

Byrd, R., Weitzman, M., & Auinger, P. (1997). Increased behavior problems associated with delayed school entry and delayed school progress. *Pediatrics, 100,* 654–661.

Carey, S. (2001). Cognitive foundations of arithmetic: Evolution and ontogenesis. *Mind & Language, 16,* 37–55.

Carey, S. (2004, Winter). Bootstrapping and the origin of concepts. *Daedelus, 133,* 59–68.

Catts, H. W., Fey, M. E., Zhang, X., & Tomblin, J. B. (1999). Language basis of reading and reading difficulties: Evidence from a longitudinal investigation. *Scientific Studies of Reading, 3,* 331–361.

Catts, H. W., Fey, M. E., Zhang, X., & Tomblin, J. B. (2001). Estimating the risk of future reading difficulties in kindergarten children: A research-based model and its clinical implementation. *Language, Speech and Hearing Services in the Schools, 32,* 38–50.

Chall, J. S., Jacobs, V., & Baldwin, L. (1990). *The reading crisis: Why poor children fall behind.* Cambridge, MA: Harvard University Press.

Clifford, R. M. (1999). Personnel preparation and the transition to kindergarten. In R. C. Pianta & M. J. Cox (Eds.), *The transition to kindergarten* (pp. 317–324). Baltimore: Brookes.

Coolahan, K., Fantuzzo, J., Mendez, J., & McDermott, P. (2000). Preschool peer interactions and readiness to learn: Relationship between classroom peer play and learning behaviors and conduct. *Journal of Educational Psychology, 92,* 458–465.

Currie, J. (2005). Health disparities and gaps in school readiness. *The Future of Children, 15,* 117–138.

Datar, A. (2003). *The impact of changes in kindergarten entrance age policies on children's academic achievement and the child care needs of families.* Santa Monica, CA: RAND.

Datar, A. (2006). Does delaying kindergarten entrance give children a head start? *Economics of Education Review, 25,* 43–62.

Denham, S. A. (2006). Social-emotional competence as support for school readiness: What is it and how do we assess it? *Early Education and Development, 17,* 57–89.

Denham, S. A., Blair, K. A., DeMulder, E., Levitas, J., Sawyer, K., Auerbach-Major, S., & Queenan, P. (2003). Preschoolers' emotional competence: Pathway to mental health? *Child Development, 74,* 238–256.

Denham, S. A., Blair, K. A., Schmidt, M. S., & DeMulder, E. (2002). Compromised emotional competence: Seeds of violence sown early? *American Journal of Orthopsychiatry, 72,* 70–82.

Denham, S. A., Caverly, S., Schmidt, M., Blair, K., DeMulder, E., Caal, S., Harnada, H., & Mason, T. (2002). Preschool understanding of emotions: Contributions to classroom anger and aggression. *Journal of Child Psychology and Psychiatry, 43,* 901–916.

Denham, S. A., McKinley, M., Couchoud, E. A., & Holt, R. (1990). Emotional and behavioral predictors of peer status in young preschoolers. *Child Development, 61,* 1145–1152.

Dennebaum, J. M., & Kulberg, J. M. (1994). Kindergarten retention and transition classrooms: Their relationship to achievement. *Psychology in the Schools, 31,* 5–12.

Denton, K., & West, J. (2002). *Children's reading and mathematics achievement in kindergarten and first grade* (NCES 2002–125). U.S. Department of Education, National Center for Education Statistics. Washington, DC: U.S. Government Printing Office.

Dockett, S. & Perry, B. (2003). The transition to school: What's important? *Educational Leadership, 60*(7), 30–33.

Doctoroff, G. L., Greer, J. A., & Arnold, D. H. (2006). The relationship between social behavior and emergent literacy among preschool boys and girls. *Applied Developmental Psychology, 27,* 1–13.

Downer, J. T., Driscoll, K., & Pianta, R. C. (2006). The transition from kindergarten to first grade: A developmental, ecological approach. In D. Gullo (Ed.), *Kindergarten and beyond.* Washington, DC: National Association for the Education of Young Children.

Early Childhood Outcomes (ECO) Center. (2007). *Outcomes 101: ECO Q & A.* Retrieved on May 23, 2007, from www.fpg.unc.edu/~eco/faqs.cfm

Education Commission of the States. (2005). *Access to kindergarten: Age issues in state statutes.* Denver, CO: Author. Retrieved May 17, 2007 from www.ecs.org/clearinghouse/58/27/5827.doc

Espinosa, L. M. (2007). English-language learners as they enter school. In R. C. Pianta, M. J. Cox, & K. L. Snow (Eds.), *School readiness & the transition to kindergarten in the era of accountability* (pp. 175–196). Baltimore: Brookes.

Fantuzzo, J. W., Bulotsky, R., McDermott, P., Mosca, S., & Lutz, M. N. (2003). A multivariate analysis of emotional and behavioral adjustment and preschool educational outcomes. *School Psychology Review, 32,* 185–203.

Fantuzzo, J. W., Bulotsky-Shearer, R., Fusco, R. A., & McWayne, C. (2005). An investigation of preschool classroom behavioral adjustment problems and social-emotional school readiness competencies. *Early Childhood Research Quarterly, 20,* 259–275.

Fantuzzo, J., Perry, M. A., & McDermott, P. (2004). Preschool approaches to learning and their relationship to other relevant classroom competencies for low-income children. *School Psychology Quarterly, 19,* 212–230.

Gallagher, J. J. (1999). Policy and the transition process. In R. C. Pianta & M. J. Cox (Eds.), *The transition to kindergarten* (pp. 351–362). Baltimore: Brookes.

Gay, J. E. (2002). The gift of a year to grow: Blessing or curse? *Education, 123,* 63–72.

General Accounting Office (GAO). (2003). *Title I preschool education: More children served but gauging effect on school readiness difficult* (GAO-00–171). Washington, DC: Author.

Goldstein, L. S. (2007). Beyond the DAP versus standards dilemma: Examining the unforgiving complexity of kindergarten teaching in the United States. *Early Childhood Research Quarterly, 22,* 39–54.

Grace, D., & Brandt, M. (2006). Ready for success in kindergarten: A comparative analysis of teacher, parent, and administrator beliefs in Hawaii. *Journal of Early Childhood Research, 4*(3), 223–258.

Graue, M. E. (1993). *Ready for what? Constructing meanings of readiness for kindergarten.* Albany: State University of New York Press.

Graue, M. E., & DiPerna, J. (2000). Redshirting and early retention: Who gets the "gift of time" and what are its outcomes? *American Educational Research Journal, 37,* 509–534.

Gredler, G. R. (1992). *School readiness: Assessment and educational issues.* Brandon, VT: Clinical Psychology Publishing.

Guralnick, M. J. (Ed.). (1997). *The effectiveness of early intervention.* Baltimore: Brookes.

Hamre, B. K., & Pianta, R. C. (2001). Early teacher-child relationships and the trajectory of children's school outcomes through eighth grade. *Child Development, 72,* 625–638.

Hamre, B. K., & Pianta, R. C. (2007). Learning opportunities in preschool and early elementary classrooms. In R. C. Pianta, M. J. Cox, & K. L. Snow (Eds.), *School readiness & the transition to kindergarten in the era of accountability* (pp. 49–84). Baltimore: Brookes.

Head Start Bureau. (2000). *The Head Start Child Outcomes Framework.* Washington, DC: Author. Retrieved May 18, 2007, from www.hsnrc.org/CDI/pdfs/ UGCOF.pdf

Heaviside, S., & Farris, S. (1993). *Public school kindergarten teachers' views on children's readiness for school.* Washington, DC: National Center for Education Statistics.

Hempill, L., & Siperstien, G. N. (1990). Conversational competence and peer response to mildly retarded children. *Journal of Educational Psychology, 82*, 1–7.

Isen, A. M. (2000). Some perspectives on positive affect and self-regulation. *Psychological Inquiry, 11*, 184–187.

Izard, C. E. (2002). Emotion knowledge and emotion utilization facilitate school readiness. *SRCD Social Policy Report, XVI*, 8.

Izard, C. E., Fine, S., Schultz, D., Moslow, A., Ackerman, B., & Youngstrong, E. (2001). Emotions knowledge as predictor of social behavior and academic competencies in children at risk. *Psychological Scenic, 12*, 18–23.

Kagan, S. L. (1990). Readiness 2000: Rethinking rhetoric and responsibility. *Phi Delta Kappan, 72*, 272–279.

Kagan, S. L., & Kauerz, K. (2007). Reaching for the whole: Integration and alignment in early education policy. In R. C. Pianta, M. J. Cox, & K. L. Snow (Eds.), *School readiness & the transition to kindergarten in the era of accountability* (pp. 11–32). Baltimore: Brookes.

Kagan, S. L., Moore, E., & Bredekamp, S. (Eds.). (1995). *Reconsidering children's early development and learning: Toward common views and vocabulary.* Report from the Goal 1 Technical Planning Group of the National Education Goals Panel. Washington, DC: U.S. Government Printing Office.

Karoly, L. A., Greenwood, P. W., Everingham, S. S., Hoube, J., Kilburn, M. R., Rydell, C. P., Sanders, M., & Chiesa, J. (1998). *Investing in our children: What we know and don't know about the costs and benefits of early childhood interventions.* Washington, DC: Rand Corporation.

Kinard, E. M., & Reinherz, H. (1986). Birthdate effect on school performance and adjustment: A longitudinal study. *Journal of Educational Research, 79*, 366–372.

Ladd, G. W. (1990). Having friends, keeping friends, making friends and being liked by peers in the classroom: Predictors of children's early school adjustment? *Child Development, 61*, 1081–1100.

Ladd, G. W., Birch, S. H., & Buhs, E. (1999). Children's social and scholastic lives in kindergarten: Related spheres of influence? *Child Development, 70*, 1373–1400.

Ladd, G. W., Herald, S. L., & Kochel, K. P. (2006). School readiness: Are there social prerequisites? *Early Education and Development, 17*, 115–150.

Ladd, G. W., Price, J. M., & Hart, C. H. (1988). Predicting preschoolers' peer status from their playground behaviors. *Child Development, 59*, 986–992.

Ladd, G. W., Price, J. M., & Hart, C. H. (1990). Preschoolers' behavioral orientations and patterns of peer contact: Predictive of peer status? In S. R. Asher & J. D. Cole (Eds.), *Peer rejection in childhood* (pp. 90–115). New York: Cambridge University Press.

Lin, H. L., Lawrence, F. R., & Gorrell, J. (2003). Kindergarten teachers' views of children's readiness for school. *Early Childhood Research Quarterly, 18*, 225–237.

Lonigan, C. J. (2006). Development, assessment, and promotion of preliteracy skills. *Early Education and Development, 17*, 91–114.

Lonigan, C. J., Burgess, S. R., & Anthony, J. L. (2000). Development of emergent literacy and early reading skills in preschool children: Evidence from a latent variable longitudinal study. *Developmental Psychology, 36*, 596–613.

Malone, L. M., West, J., Flannagan, K. D., & Park, J. (2006). The early reading and mathematics achievement of children who repeated kindergarten or who began school a year late (NCES 2006–064). Washington, DC: National Center for Education Statistics. Retrieved May 26, 2007, from http://nces.ed.gov/pubs2006/2006064.pdf

Mashburn, A. & Pianta, R. (2006). Social relationships and school readiness. *Early Education and Development, 17*(1), 151–176.

Meisels, S. J. (1995). Out of the readiness maze. *Momentum, 26*, 18–22.

Meisels, S. J. (1999). Assessing readiness. In R. C. Pianta & M. J. Cox (Eds.), *The transition to kindergarten* (pp. 39–66). Baltimore: Brookes.

Miles, S. B., & Stipek, D. (2006). Contemporaneous and longitudinal associations between social behavior and literacy achievement in a sample of low-income elementary school children. *Child Development, 77*, 103–117.

Morrison, F. J., Griffith, E. M., & Alberts, D. M. (1997). Nature-nurture in the classroom: Entrance age, school readiness, and learning in children. *Developmental Psychology, 33*, 254–262.

National Association of Early Childhood Teacher Educators (NAECTE). (2008). Position statement on early childhood certification for teachers of children 8 years old and younger in public school settings.

National Early Literacy Panel. (2005). *Report on a synthesis of early predictors of reading.* Louisville, KY: Author.

National Education Goals Panel (NEGP). (1990). *National education goals report executive summary: Improving education through family-school-community partnerships.* Washington, DC: Author.

National Education Goals Panel (NEGP). (1997). *Getting a good start in school.* Washington, DC: Author.

National Education Goals Panel (NEGP). (1998). *Ready schools.* Washington, DC: Author.

National Governors Association. (2005). *Building the foundations for bright future: Final report of the Task Force on School Readiness.* Washington, DC: Author. Retrieved May 18, 2007, from www.nga.org/Files/pdf/0501TaskForceReadiness.pdf

Ninio, A., & Snow, C. E. (1999). The development of pragmatics: learning to use language appropriately. In W. C. Ritchie & T. K. Bhatia (Eds.), *Handbook of child language acquisition.* San Diego, CA: Academic Press.

Park, K. A., Lay, K., & Ramsey, L. (1993). Individual differences and developmental changes in preschoolers' friendships. *Developmental Psychology, 29,* 264–270.

Pascoe, J. M., Shaikh, U., Forbis, S. G., & Etzel, R. A. (2007). Health and nutrition as a foundation for success in school. In R. C. Pianta, M. J. Cox, & K. L. Snow (Eds.), *School readiness & the transition to kindergarten in the era of accountability* (pp. 99–120). Baltimore: Brookes.

Pianta, R. C. (2004). Relationships among children and adults and family literacy. In B. Wasik (Ed.), *Handbook on family literacy programs* (pp. 175–192). Mahwah, NJ: Erlbaum.

Pianta, R. C. (2007). Early education in transition. In R. C. Pianta, M. J. Cox, & K. L. Snow (Eds.), *School readiness & the transition to kindergarten in the era of accountability* (pp. 3–10). Baltimore: Brookes.

Pianta, R. C., Cox, M. J., Taylor, L., & Early, D. (1999). Kindergarten teachers' practices related to the transition to school: Results of a national survey. *Elementary School Journal, 100,* 71–86.

Pianta, R. C., & Kraft-Sayre, M. (2003). *Successful kindergarten transition: Your guide to connecting children, families, and schools.* Baltimore: Brookes.

Pianta, R. C., La Paro, K. M., Payne, C., Cox, M. J., & Bradley, R. (2002). The relation of kindergarten classroom environment to teacher, family and school characteristics and child outcomes. *The Elementary School Journal, 102,* 225–238.

Pianta, R. C., & Nimetz, S. L. (1991). Relationships between children and teachers: Associations with classroom and home behavior. *Journal of Applied Developmental Psychology, 12,* 379–393.

Piotrkowski, C. S. (2004). A community-based approach to school readiness in Head Start. In E. Zigler & S. J. Styfco (Eds.), *The Head Start debates* (pp. 129–142). Baltimore: Brookes.

Piotrkowski, C. S., Botsko, M., & Matthews, E. (2000). Parents' and teachers' beliefs about children's school readiness in a high-need community. *Early Childhood Research Quarterly, 15,* 537–558.

Prakash, N., West, J., & Denton, K. (2003). *Schools' use of assessments for kindergarten placement: 1998–99.* Washington, DC: National Center for Education Statistics. Retrieved May 23, 2007, from http://nces.ed.gov/pubs2003/2003004.pdf

Princiotta, D., Flanagan, K. D., & Germino-Hausken, E. (2006). First grade: Findings from the fifth-grade follow-up of the Early Childhood Longitudinal Study, Kindergarten Class of 1998–99 (ECLS-K). (NCES 2006–038). Washington, DC: U.S. Department of Education, National Center for Education Statistics.

Rabiner, D., Coie, J. D., & Conduct Problems Prevention Research Group. (2000). Early attention problems and children's reading achievement: A longitudinal investigation. *Journal of the American Academy of Child and Adolescent Psychiatry, 39,* 859–867.

Ramey, S. L., & Ramey, C. T. (1999). Beginning school for children at-risk. In R. C. Pianta & M. J. Cox (Eds.), *The transition to kindergarten* (pp. 217–253). Baltimore: Brookes.

Rathbun, A., & West, J. (2004). *From kindergarten through third grade: Children's beginning school experiences* (NCES 2004–007). U.S. Department of Education, National Center for Education Statistics. Washington, DC: U.S. Government Printing Office.

Raver, C. (2004). Placing emotional self-regulation in sociocultural and socioeconomic contexts. *Child Development, 75,* 246–353.

Raver, C. C., Garner, P. W., & Smith-Donald, R. (2007). The roles of emotion regulation and emotion knowledge for children's academic readiness: Are the links causal? In R. C. Pianta, M. J. Cox, & K. L. Snow (Eds.), *School readiness and the transition to kindergarten in the era of accountability* (pp. 121–148). Baltimore: Brookes.

Raver, C. C., & Knitzer, J. (2002). *Ready to enter: What research tells policymakers about strategies to promote social and emotional school readiness among three- and four-year-olds*. New York: National Center for Children in Poverty.

Reynolds, A. (1992). Grade retention and school adjustment: An explanatory analysis. *Educational Evaluation and Policy Analysis, 14*, 101–121.

Rhode Island KIDS Count. (2005). *Getting ready: Findings from the National School Readiness Indicators Initiative, a 17-state partnership*. Providence, RI: Author.

Rimm-Kaufman, S. E., & Pianta, R. C. (2000). An ecological perspective on the transition to kindergarten: A theoretical framework to guide empirical research. *Journal of Applied Developmental Psychology, 21*, 491–511.

Ritchie, S., Maxwell, K., & Clifford, R. M. (2007). FirstSchool: A new vision for education. In R. C. Pianta, M. J. Cox, & K. L. Snow (Eds.), *School readiness & the transition to kindergarten in the era of accountability* (pp. 85–96). Baltimore: Brookes.

Rosenthal, E., Rathbun, A., & West, J. (2005). *Regional differences in kindergartners' early education experiences* (NCES 2005–099). Washington, DC: National Center for Education Statistics.

Saluja, G., Scott-Little, C., & Clifford, R. M. (2000). Readiness for school: A survey of state policies and definitions. *Early Childhood Research & Practice, 2*(2). Retrieved May 23, 2007, from http://ecrp.uiuc.edu/v2n2/saluja.html

Schulting, A. B., Malone, P. S., & Dodge, K. A. (2005). The effect of school-based kindergarten transition policies and practices on child academic outcomes. *Developmental Psychology, 41*, 860–871.

Scott-Little, C., Kagan, S. L., & Frelow, V. S. (2003). *Standards for preschool children's learning and development: Who has standards, how were they developed, and how are they used?* Tallahassee, FL: SERVE.

Scott-Little, C., Kagan, S. L., & Frelow, V. S. (2005). *Inside the content: The depth and breadth of early learning standards*. Greensboro: University of North Carolina, SERVE Center for Continuous Improvement.

Scott-Little, C., Kagan, S. L., & Frelow, V. S. (2006). Conceptualization of readiness and the content of early learning standards: The intersection of policy and research? *Early Childhood Research Quarterly, 21*, 153–173.

Scott-Little, C., Lesko, J., Martella, J., & Milburn, P. (2007). Early learning standards: Results from a national survey to document trends in state-level policies and practices. *Early Childhood Research and Practice, 9*(1). Available at http://ecrp.uiuc.edu/v9n1/little.html

Seefeldt, C., & Wasik, B. (2002). *Kindergarten: Fours and fives go to school*. Upper Saddle River, NJ: Merrill/Prentice Hall.

Smith, M. L., & Shepard, L. A. (1988). Kindergarten readiness and retention: A qualitative study of teachers' beliefs and practices. *American Educational Research Journal, 25*, 307–333.

Snow, C. E., Burns, M. S., & Griffin, P. (1998). *Preventing reading difficulties in young children*. Washington, DC: National Academy Press.

Snow, K. L. (2006). Measuring school readiness: Conceptual and practical considerations. *Early Education and Development, 17*, 7–41.

Snow, K. L. (2007). Integrative views of the domains of child function: Unifying school readiness. In R. C. Pianta, M. J. Cox, & K. L. Snow (Eds.), *School readiness & the transition to kindergarten in the era of accountability* (pp. 197–216). Baltimore: Brookes.

Stipek, D. (2002). At what age should children enter kindergarten? A question for policy-makers and parents. *Social Policy Reports, 16*, 3–13.

Wesley, P. W., & Buysse, V. (2003). Making meaning of school readiness in schools and communities. *Early Childhood Research Quarterly, 18*, 351–375.

West, J., Denton, K., & Germino-Hausken, E. (2000). *America's kindergartners* (NCES 2000–070). Washington, DC: National Center for Education Statistics. Retrieved May 30, 2007, from http://nces.ed.gov/pubs2000/2000070.pdf

West, J., Germino-Hausken, E., & Collins, M. (1995). *Readiness for kindergarten: Parent and teacher beliefs. Statistics in Brief* (NCES 93257). Washington, DC: National Center for Education Statistics. Retrieved May 30, 2007, from http://nces.ed.gov/pubs93/web/93257.asp

Whitehurst, G. J., & Lonigan, C. J. (1998). Child development and emergent literacy. *Child Development, 68,* 848–872.

Wien, C. A. (2004). *Negotiating standards in the primary classroom: The teacher's dilemma.* New York: Teachers College Press.

Wright, C., Diener, M., & Kay, S. C. (2000). School readiness of low-income children at-risk for school failure. *Journal of Children & Poverty, 6,* 99–117.

Zevenbergen, A., Whitehurst, G. J., & Zevenbergen, J. A. (2003). Effects of a shared-reading intervention on the inclusion of evaluative devices in narratives of children from low-income families. *Journal of Applied Developmental Psychology, 24,* 1–15.

Zill, N., Loomis, L. S., & West, J. (1997). The elementary school performance and adjustment of children who enter kindergarten late or repeat kindergarten: Findings from national surveys (NCES 98–097). Washington, DC: National Center for Education Statistics. Retrieved May 26, 2007, from http://nces.ed.gov/pubs98/98097.pdf

PART 3

WHO WILL TEACH
YOUNG CHILDREN?

W e all want the best for our children. The best food, shelter, clothing, health care, and especially the best education. As teachers are central to the process of education, any attempt to provide the best in education must focus on them.

What makes the best teacher of young children, however, is a long-standing debate in the field of early childhood education. Can anyone be an effective teacher? Are teachers born and not made as has often been said? Is a background of work with infants/toddlers necessary to prepare a person to become a teacher of young children? Is formal training necessary? If so, what kind of training and what should it cover?

Historically, there have been differing views about who is an effective teacher of young children. In the *School of Infancy,* John Amos Comenius (1632–1704) advocated that mothers are the first and primary teachers of young children. Certainly few would argue with the fact that learning begins at birth, with the people closest to an infant being the child's first teachers.

Attachment has long been regarded as a critical developmental task. Based on this theory, it was once believed that only women should teach young children; the idea being that female teachers would more closely resemble the mother figure a young child attached to during infancy. It was also believed that women would protect and maintain the child's emotional security once in a school setting. Female teachers were regarded as better able to provide the nurture and warmth young children required. "As the cliche goes, just love little children," wrote Almy (1975, p. 109). The theory was that women would be more likely than men to find wiping noses, cleaning up messes, comforting, and protecting—essential components of teaching young children—satisfying and rewarding.

However, in designing the kindergarten in Germany, Froebel (1887) rejected women as teachers. He hypothesized that only men could be effective teachers of children because only men had the ability to think, study, and understand philosophy. Women, even mothers, according to Froebel, would be unable to bring the necessary ability to think analytically so necessary to the intellectually demanding tasks of teaching kindergarten children.

Though he did not specify gender, Piaget (1969) agreed with Froebel's contention that teachers of the youngest children must have the ability to think analytically. He, too, believed the study of philosophy and psychology, and much more, was necessary preparation for teaching young children. In *The Psychology of the Child* (1969), Piaget wrote: "The younger the child the more difficult it is to teach him, and the more pregnant that teaching is with future consequences" (p. 127). Piaget suggested that

> the future primary-school teacher should begin by acquiring his baccalaureate and then go on to spend three years receiving his specialized training. During the first of these three years, the candidates take practical courses that enable them to become acquainted with the problems, and then, in the third year, they again return to practical work. The second year, on the other hand, is spent at the university, where the candidates take courses in psychology, pedagogy, and special courses in education. (pp. 128–129)

Today, we are still interested in identifying the best ways to prepare competent and nurturing teachers of young children. But in addition to the questions of who should teach and how we can best prepare teachers, we face the even more daunting concern of how to recruit and retain teachers who have the professional qualifications and personal qualities that will best support the development of young children.

The four chapters in Part 3 address a number of interrelated issues regarding to the question, Who will teach young children? The first two chapters concentrate on aspects of the early childhood workforce with a focus on those who teach children under the age of 5. In Chapter 6, "The Early Childhood Workforce," Kate Tarrant, Erica Greenberg, Sharon Lynn Kagan, and Kristie Kauerz describe the current workforce and explore in depth the thorny issues of how we can find, educate, and keep qualified teachers to staff programs for young children. The authors begin with examination of the early childhood workforce and the societal context that impacts it. Then they discuss two of the most critical issues facing the field of early care and education today—*recruiting* highly qualified teachers and *retaining* high-quality teachers. High-quality teachers are those who, once they enter the field, promote children's development and commit to continuously improving their practice. The implications of recruitment and retention issues for policy and practice are illustrated with examples of how these dual concerns are being addressed creatively in some states and communities. The chapter concludes with a look to the future, calling for innovation, research, and systemic reform to support the early care and education teaching workforce.

Chapter 7, "The Professional Development of Teachers of Young Children," by Nancy Barbour and Martha Lash, offers a detailed discussion of issues surrounding the provision of training for early childhood educators. The chapter begins by defining professionalism and examining the role of professional development in the evolution of a profession. The authors describe early childhood professional development as having three components—education (training that takes place in the formal educational system, generally leading to the acquisition of a degree), training (activities that take place outside the formal education system, often called "in-service" education), and credentialing (an external recognition of training that is often required to qualify for a position). The chapter goes on to discuss adult learner characteristics and adult learning theory, the history of early childhood professional development, and several views regarding what early childhood educators should know and be able to do. Research on what constitutes effective professional development is reported. The chapter concludes with discussion of the implications for the future of early childhood professional development.

Chapter 8, "What Do Early Childhood Educators Need to Know and Do to Work in Urban Settings?" written by Frances Rust, focuses on public school teachers (PreK–3) who are preparing to work, or who already work, in urban educational settings with culturally diverse groups of children. Because of changing demographics in cities, today many teachers are called on to teach groups of children who have very different backgrounds than their own. Rust explores some of the specific kinds of awareness, knowledge, and skill that will help teachers to function effectively in these settings.

The chapter begins by looking at the term *urban education* and the ways in which urban schools are different from other educational settings. The importance of teachers stepping outside of their comfort zone and being willing to get to know themselves, as well as the city and community in which they teach, are emphasized. Rust calls on teachers to learn about their own cultures and those of the children and families in the communities in which they teach. She believes that this is done best when teachers tell their own stories, and then listen to the stories of the children and their families. Her assumption is that by telling your own story you can learn about your own assumptions about power, race, class, and privilege and come to understand the nature of white privilege—an essential foundation for urban teaching. The next step is to get to know the children—including both solid knowledge of developmental theory and awareness of the social contexts that shape children's development in urban settings. Rust warns against arriving at judgments about children's readiness and/or competence based on middle-class assumptions and urges teachers to move from a concept of deficiency to a recognition of cultural competence. Examples of innovative teacher education programs that feature concepts of social justice and educational equity are described. The chapter ends with a call for more teachers who want to work with children who most need culturally sensitive, caring, and committed adults in their lives.

Finally, in Chapter 9, "Professionalism and Ethics in Early Care and Education," Nancy Freeman and Stephanie Feeney take a close look at the terms *profession* and *professional*, which are used frequently in discussions about those who work with young children. Some early educators refer to any person who works for pay in a group setting for children as a professional, while others reserve the term for those with advanced training. Some criteria that can be used to determine if an occupation is a profession are explored and the authors conclude that early care and education is an occupation that is moving toward professional status. They point out that professionalism can be a mixed blessing and explore some of the costs and benefits associated with this status.

The role of a code of ethics in emerging professions is discussed, as is the development and current status of the NAEYC Code of Ethical Conduct. Freeman and Feeney point out that because of the vulnerability of young children it is tremendously important for early childhood educators to be well trained in professional ethics and adhere to ethical guidelines in their practice. The chapter ends with a discussion of ethical implications of some current developments in the field of early care and education.

Together, these chapters highlight the need for a well-trained workforce committed to the welfare and development of young children. They underscore challenges relating to the provision of training, selection of content, and recruitment and retention of a competent, committed workforce.

Heightened demand for early childhood education has raised expectations and means that the demand for highly qualified teachers of young children will only increase in the future. The issue of who will teach young children leads to the related question of who will pay the cost if educational requirements are raised. Our examination of who will teach young children takes us full circle back to the issue of who will assume responsibility for the care and education of young children in our nation.

APPLY WHAT YOU LEARNED

As you read the following chapters, think about, talk about, and do additional reading and research regarding these questions:

❑ What knowledge, skills, and dispositions do you think teachers of young children should have?

❑ Should teachers of young children be required to complete a degree program? What degree? Why?

❑ What content should teacher preparation programs cover?

❑ Should in-service education be required for teachers of young children? What kind?

❑ Should teachers in all early childhood settings—preschools, child care centers, and prekindergarten, kindergarten, and primary grade programs in public schools—require the same level of training?

❑ Reflect on how your teacher education program prepared you to work with diverse learners. Do you think it should have done anything differently?

❑ What kinds of early childhood teacher preparation programs are available in your community? What degrees and credentials are granted? What guidelines do they follow (NCATE, WASC, NAEYC, etc.)?

❑ What kinds of in-service training program for teachers of young children are available in your community? Who sponsors them? How are they funded?

REFERENCES

Almy, M. (1975). *The early childhood educator at work.* New York: McGraw-Hill.

Froebel, F. (1887). *The education of man.* New York: Appleton.

Piaget, J. (1969). *The psychology of the child.* New York: Basic Books.

CHAPTER 6

THE EARLY CHILDHOOD WORKFORCE

Kate Tarrant
Teachers College,
Columbia University

Sharon Lynn Kagan
Teachers College,
Columbia University

Erica Greenberg
Teachers College,
Columbia University

Kristie Kauerz
Office of the Lieutenant Governor
in the State of Colorado

The early care and education (ECE) workforce comprises millions of adults who support the development of children under age 5 and their families. The ECE workforce is part of a broader early childhood workforce—including K–3 teachers; health workers; pediatric doctors and dentists; mental health professionals; family support professionals; and physical, occupational, and speech therapists—who also support young children's healthy growth. While all of these individuals are critical to supporting young children and their families, this chapter focuses on the issues unique to ECE *teachers* who guide young children's learning; this group includes lead teachers, assistant teachers, teachers' aides in center-based programs, family child care providers, and family, friend, and neighbor caregivers (Kagan, Kauerz, & Tarrant, in press).[1]

ECE teachers work in a wide range of settings, including home- and center-based child care, Head Start, preschool, school-based prekindergarten programs, and community-based organizations. Although they work in diverse settings, all ECE teachers share the common goals of protecting, nurturing, and advocating for

Note: This chapter is based on the book, *The Early Care and Education Teaching Workforce at the Fulcrum: An Agenda for Reform,* written by Sharon Lynn Kagan, Kristie Kauerz, and Kate Tarrant and published by Teachers College Press New York, NY (2007). This work was supported by funding from Cornerstones for Kids, Inc.

1. Early childhood education often includes kindergarten, first-, and second-grade teachers. Because these teachers are part of the highly regulated K–12 public school system, however, they experience different challenges and opportunities than teachers of children before kindergarten entry and so they are beyond the scope of the current chapter.

children's optimal growth and development. Their responsibilities are both complex and significant—to support the unique needs of children, families, and communities during the crucial period when positive interactions with adults have the greatest impact on children's lifelong learning (Shonkoff & Phillips, 2000). For these reasons, parents, families, community leaders, and policy makers have a stake in the quality of ECE teachers.

In this chapter, we provide an overview of the ECE teaching workforce, describing its characteristics and the context that affects it. We then turn to a discussion of the major issues facing today's ECE teachers. In this section of the chapter, we focus on *recruiting* highly qualified teachers and *retaining* high-quality teachers. Highly qualified teachers enter the field prepared for the challenges and opportunities of teaching young children because they have participated in professional development experiences specific to early childhood education and child development. High-quality teachers are those teachers who, once they enter the field, promote children's development and commit to continuously improving their practice. To illustrate the implications of these issues for policy and practice, we include real-life examples of how these dual concerns are being addressed. We conclude the chapter with a look to the future, calling for innovation, research, and systemic reform to support the ECE teaching workforce.

A Profile of ECE Teachers

Looking broadly at the ECE teaching workforce, several general characteristics emerge. The majority of ECE teachers are white women in their late 30s and early 40s. Most have at least an associate's degree and earn salaries that are extremely low compared with K–12 teachers and those in other fields that require similar levels of education. Painting an accurate portrait of today's ECE teachers, however, is far more nuanced than these generalizations convey. This complexity can be attributed to the configuration of the ECE system, which includes a range of programs, each with its own set of regulations and expectations for teachers.

ECE teachers are dispersed across home- and center-based settings: roughly half are family, friends, and neighbors (FFN) who care for children in homes; one-quarter works in regulated family child care (FCC) homes; and another quarter works in center-based settings (Burton, Whitebook, Young, Bellm, Wayne, & Brandon, 2002). Of center-based programs, 29 percent are for-profit programs, 22 percent are affiliated with a religious organization, 25 percent are independent nonprofit programs or those run by a public agency, 16 percent are public school-based, and 8 percent are Head Start programs (Saluja, Early, & Clifford, 2002). When we examine the teaching workforce across these different types of programs, tremendous variation emerges. Specifically, there are striking inconsistencies in ECE teachers' professional development and compensation, two major correlates of high-quality teaching (Barnett, 2003b).

ECE teachers' professional development, defined as formal education, training, and credentials (Maxwell, Feild, & Clifford, 2006), varies considerably across the different program types. Looking first at formal education, which refers to credit-bearing coursework provided by accredited 2- and 4-year educational institutions, one study of ECE teachers and administrators across program types estimates that one-third hold bachelor's or advanced graduate degrees, associate's degrees are held by 40 percent, and about one-third hold a high school degree (Herzenberg, Price, & Bradley, 2005). However, discrepancies are prevalent across different types of programs: 73 percent of teachers in state-funded prekindergarten programs for 3- and 4-year-old children have bachelor's degrees or more (Gilliam & Marchesseault, 2005), 36 percent of Head Start teachers hold bachelor's degrees or more (Hamm, 2006), and only 11 percent of FCC providers hold bachelor's degrees or more (Herzenberg et al., 2005). Training, which comprises educational activities that take place outside of the formal education sector (Maxwell, Feild, et al., 2006), also varies by program type. For example, a study of three states found that Head Start teachers participate in the most training of the ECE workforce: 62 hours of training per year, compared with 45 hours for teachers in state-funded prekindergarten and 27 hours for teachers in child care programs (Epstein, 1999). A four-state study found that, on average, FCC providers participate in 19 hours of training and FFN caregivers participate in 16 hours of training annually (Raikes et al., 2003). Finally, credentials, which attest to teacher competencies (e.g., Child Development Associate [CDA]), reveal large inconsistencies, as well: 57 percent of teachers in state-funded prekindergarten programs are certified by their states, whereas 44 percent of center-based teachers and 7 percent of FCC teachers hold the same credentials (Gilliam & Marchesseault, 2005; Workgroup on Defining and Measuring Early Childhood Professional Development, 2005). Although ECE teachers are more educated than many believe, striking variation permeates the workforce.

The tremendous diversity in teachers' professional development is accompanied by disparate compensation (defined as wages and benefits). ECE teachers in state-funded prekindergarten programs earn, on average, $30,998 per year; 89 percent receive health insurance; and 80 percent have retirement benefits (Gilliam & Marchesseault, 2005). On average, Head Start teachers earn $24,608 annually (Hamm, 2006), and one study of Head Start teachers in four midwestern states found that in 2001, 65 percent received health insurance and 48 percent had retirement benefits (Raikes et al., 2003). The level of compensation is generally even lower for FCC and FFN providers. In those same four midwestern states, FCC providers earned just $12,740, and FFN caregivers earned $7,920 (Raikes et al., 2003). Many ECE teachers live at or close to the poverty line. Across the board, ECE teachers' compensation pales in comparison to compensation for kindergarten teachers, who typically receive health and retirement benefits and earn an average annual salary of $47,040 (Bureau of Labor Statistics, 2007).[2] Yet, the disparity in earnings across different types of programs splinters the field. As teachers move from one ECE setting to the next in order to boost their earnings, retention problems mount.

2. Compensation also varies within the K–12 school system, with teachers for older children earning more than teachers for younger children. On average, kindergarten teachers earn $47,080, elementary school teachers earn $48,700, middle school teachers earn $49,470, and secondary school teachers earn $51,150 (Bureau of Labor Statistics, 2007).

ECE Teachers Matter

ECE teachers have the significant responsibility of supporting young children during the most impressionable stage of development—the early years. Indeed, research has found teachers to be essential to quality early education (e.g., Bowman, Donovan, & Burns, 2001; Schweinhart, Barnes, & Weikert, 1993); in center-based programs, teachers are more significant than classroom structure in promoting child development (Love, Schochet, & Meckstroth, 1996).

Quality teaching is both challenging and complex, combining a vast array of knowledge, skills, and dispositions (National Council for Accreditation of Teacher Education, 2006). For teachers, knowledge refers to an understanding of content, pedagogy, and professional concepts that inform instruction. In ECE, this knowledge begins with comprehensive and current understanding of typical and atypical child development (Hutchinson, 1994; Isenberg, 2000; Jones, 1995; Kramer, 1994; Lobman, Ryan, & McLaughlin, 2005; National Association for the Education of Young Children, 2006; Rowe, Early, & Loubier, 1994). Indeed, a deep understanding of how young children make meaning of their environments is crucial for scaffolding their learning. To promote the whole child, good ECE teachers have knowledge of numerous aspects of young children's growth and change, including physical and motor development, social and emotional development, cognitive development, language development, and approaches toward learning (National Education Goals Panel, 1994). Because of the centrality of family in young children's lives, ECE teachers must also understand the roles of family, community, and culture in children's development (AACTE Focus Council on Early Childhood Education, 2004; Isenberg, 2000; Kramer, 1994).

Knowledge, however, is not enough. High-quality ECE teachers possess complex skills to translate knowledge into practice. In doing so, they consider different approaches to teaching (e.g., child-centered and teacher-directed) and use a variety of instructional strategies to connect with all of their students (e.g., cooperative learning, independent learning activities). As skilled inquirers, they observe and assess children's learning and reflect on their teaching to meet students' needs (Bredekamp & Copple, 1997; Fein, 1994; Hutchinson, 1994; Isenberg, 2000; Lobman et al., 2005; Yonemura, 1994). They must be able to apply curricula to their particular learning environment and each of the unique children within it. Lastly, ECE teachers work with numerous other professionals who also support young children's learning and development, including administrators, special educators, and therapists, and they must have the interpersonal skills necessary for effective collaboration.

Teachers' dispositions—their prevailing emotional and mental tendencies and inclinations toward their work—also influence the quality of their teaching. Teachers who respect children as competent and creative learners create a classroom community in which teachers and students thrive. Teachers who approach their work with a highly professional attitude also make a commitment to continuous career and personal growth (Feeney & Freemen, 1999). As professionals, ECE teachers often balance their roles as teachers in the classroom with their dedication to advocacy in the broader practice and policy world (Grieshaber, 2001). Ultimately, ECE teachers have complex and demanding responsibilities that greatly impact young children's learning and development.

CONTEXT FOR THE ECE TEACHING WORKFORCE: A PUSH FOR QUANTITY AND QUALITY

The ECE teaching workforce is currently in need of more teachers who have the knowledge, skills, and dispositions to teach young children well. The push to expand the size of the ECE teaching workforce results from the growing demand for ECE programs. Meanwhile, there is a conflicting push to restrict the supply of teachers to only those teachers who are highly qualified. The confluence of four conditions contributes to these competing forces: (1) major demographic changes in the U.S. population; (2) the evolution and convergence of early *care* and early *education*; (3) the undervaluation of ECE teachers; and (4) heightened expectations for young children's learning.

First, the expansion of the population of young children and the increase in mothers' labor force participation has generated tremendous demand for ECE services, thereby raising demand for ECE teachers. Indeed, the number of ECE teachers has almost tripled over the last 25 years (Herzenberg et al., 2005). Yet, while the general population of teachers has swelled, the lack of funds in the ECE system limits the ability to recruit those who are truly high quality. Where high-quality teachers are in practice, parents are often unable to afford paying for their programs. Therefore, the demand for teachers is increasing at the same time that many qualified ECE teachers are leaving the profession to work in more lucrative fields or to retire altogether. Because of the fragmented ECE system, teacher shortages are felt most acutely in particular segments of the field. For instance, higher compensation levels offered in state-funded prekindergarten programs lure qualified candidates from lower-paying child care programs. In response to the growing overall demand for ECE teachers, and for child care providers in particular, policy makers have lowered entry requirements (LeMoine, Morgan, & Azer, 2003), thereby opening the door to underqualified and undercompensated teachers (Bellm & Whitebook, 2006). The need for more teachers has therefore directly diminished the quality of the ECE teaching workforce.

Second, the history of the ECE field influences the current quality of the ECE teaching workforce. Today's field has evolved from two distinct types of programs with different ideas about the function and value of quality ECE teachers: (1) child care focused on serving low-income children while mothers work; and (2) early education programs designed to offer educational experiences to middle- and upper-class children before they enter primary school. The former were mostly social welfare programs in which teachers were assumed to provide primarily custodial responsibilities (e.g., feeding); in the latter, teachers were assumed to be responsible for socializing and educating children (Cahan, 1989). Since the 1960s, distinctions between *care* and *education* have blurred so that there are no longer two distinct program types; today, early care *and* education (ECE) programs embrace child care, a necessity for many parents, and education, a benefit for children and society. This convergence stems from wide recognition that the knowledge, skills, and dispositions required to teach young children effectively are consistent across all types of programs (Caldwell, 1989). Despite the conclusion that good ECE teachers possess comparable capacities, discrepancies in ECE teacher quality for different types of ECE programs endure.

Third, policy makers and others are uncertain about the value of quality of ECE teachers—often because they are familiar with the low and inconsistent entry requirements that characterize the field (Bellm & Whitebook, 2006). Low social status stems from the public perception that today's ECE teachers are still the "babysitters" of yesterday. Indeed, social undervaluation is highly characteristic of all forms of "care work" (e.g., nursing; Albelda, 2002; Nelson, 2001). As a result, potential ECE teachers—in particular, highly qualified teachers—who seek more valued positions may choose to work in K–12 schooling or other occupations altogether. Social undervaluation has a direct and powerful effect on both the quantity and the quality of teachers in early care and education. Unless policy makers and the public appreciate the challenging and complex work of teaching young children, reward it with greater compensation, and raise expectations for the quality of teachers, the field will remain undervalued.

Fourth, heightened expectations for young children's learning have also contributed to a demand for quality ECE teachers, particularly in settings that serve disadvantaged children. Achievement gaps between socially privileged students and disadvantaged students appear well before children begin kindergarten and increase over time. ECE is one promising mechanism for ameliorating achievement for low-income and minority children. Moreover, No Child Left Behind's higher standards for K–12 have raised the stakes for ECE to prevent future academic failure. With greater attention to early learning, the majority of states have developed prekindergarten initiatives focused on improving children's skills so they enter kindergarten "ready" to succeed. Given their focus on closing the achievement gap, it is not surprising that state-funded prekindergarten programs that typically serve 4-year-old children are far more selective than other program types in hiring ECE teachers; this one segment of the ECE workforce *has not* seen a decline in the qualifications of ECE teachers (Barnett, Hustedt, Robin, & Schulman, 2005). Overall, increased attention to the quality of ECE has shone a spotlight on the need for ECE teacher quality.

Typically, greater demand and lower supply would increase the value and compensation of ECE teachers, thereby attracting more qualified individuals to the field. However, by establishing low entry requirements in particular segments of the ECE system, governments have enabled the pool of ECE teachers to expand. Thus, the tension between quantity and quality persists, raising the need to recruit more highly qualified teachers and retain more high-quality teachers.

CURRENT ISSUES: THE RESEARCH AND IMPORTANCE OF RECRUITMENT AND RETENTION

The four conditions outlined above have important consequences for the maintenance of a quality ECE teaching workforce. Because of the need for more quality teachers, the daily necessities of recruitment and retention are paramount—for program administrators who have clients to serve; for families, who need quality care and education for their youngest children; for children, who thrive when their teachers feel valued and stay in the classroom; and for society, which increasingly expects children to begin kindergarten with an array of knowledge and skills

(Cost Quality and Child Outcomes Study Team, 1995; Phillips, Mekos, Scarr, McCartney, & Abbott-Shim, 2001; Weber, 2005; Whitebook, Howes, & Phillips, 1990; Whitebook & Sakai, 2003).

Recruiting Highly Qualified Teachers

Recruitment of highly qualified teachers is primarily hampered by the undervaluation of ECE teachers. Prospective applicants to the field are dissuaded by low wages and benefits, low social standing, and high turnover among existing teachers. The challenge of recruiting highly qualified teachers is exacerbated by minimal and highly variable entry requirements and professional development programs that do not adequately prepare teachers for the diversity of students' needs.

Value of ECE Teachers.   Social and economic undervaluation of ECE teachers hinders efforts to recruit highly qualified teachers. Social undervaluation, the perception that ECE teaching is low-skilled work, prevents those who may want to teach young children from joining the field. Economic undervaluation, in the form of low wages and benefits, is a more concrete barrier to recruitment. It results from a tug-of-war among three competing factors: the costs of offering high-quality programs, affordability for parents, and compensation for ECE teachers (Mitchell, Stoney, & Dichter, 2001). These three issues are often referred to as the *trilemma* of early childhood education. To date, teachers actually subsidize the cost of ECE with their foregone wages—the difference between a teachers' compensation and the amount they could earn in other occupations that require similar qualifications. The median hourly earnings of child care teachers was $8.06 in May 2004 (Bureau of Labor Statistics, 2005). By comparison, just 22 occupations out of 820 surveyed by the Bureau of Labor Statistics reported lower mean wages than child care workers, with service station attendants, bicycle repairers, and locker-room attendants earning more (Center for the Child Care Workforce, 2006). In state-funded prekindergarten programs, which pay the highest wages in the field, 7 out of 10 teachers reported a salary below the threshold for "low-income" (Gilliam & Marchesseault, 2005). Not only are teachers' wages low, but benefits are also uncommon: only 28 percent of the ECE workforce have employer-provided health insurance, compared with 57 percent of workers in all industries (Herzenberg et al., 2005). Statistics like these send a signal to prospective ECE teachers that their work will not be valued, and that they may have to make significant sacrifices, for themselves and often for their own children, in order to work in the ECE field.

In order to raise teachers' compensation to levels that will enhance recruitment efforts without decreasing funding for other aspects of program quality, ECE programs need greater revenue. Limits to parents' ability to pay complicate this need, and public uncertainty about whether the government should subsidize ECE has done little to quell it. Nonetheless, to recruit highly qualified teachers, the tug-of-war between program quality, affordability for parents, and compensation for ECE teachers must be solved.

Entry Requirements.   Moving beyond economic barriers and social undervaluation, low and inconsistent entry requirements hinder the recruitment of highly

---

Box 6–1 **Policies and Practices from the Field**
Incentive Programs That Support ECE Teachers

To attract more teachers to the profession, some efforts provide financial incentives for ECE programs to value and support their highly qualified teachers. These programs hold high expectations for teachers' professional development qualifications, support teachers' professional growth, and compensate them based on the quality of their teaching.

Quality Rating Systems

Many states have developed quality rating systems (QRSs) to induce ECE programs to improve their overall quality, including the quality of their teachers. QRSs are typically publicly supported efforts to gauge ECE program quality based on factors such as classroom quality assessments, staff qualifications, and administrative procedures. As of November 2006, 13 states and the District of Columbia had adopted QRSs, and 31 states were in the process of designing one (National Child Care Information Center, 2007).

Not all QRSs are the same. The most comprehensive efforts cover center-based child care, family child care, after-school care, prekindergarten programs, and Head Start (Mitchell, 2005); some states' efforts embrace only a few of these program types. One state makes participation in the QRS mandatory, while others offer it on a voluntary basis. Some states offer higher reimbursements through the child care subsidy system or other financial awards to participating ECE programs that provide higher-quality care and education. Some states establish a QRS in statute while others do so in agency regulations (Mitchell, 2005). While each QRS has unique characteristics, they generally share three primary goals: (1) improving the overall quality of ECE programs, (2) raising public and consumer awareness about program quality, and (3) providing increased funding to encourage and reward programs that provide higher-quality ECE. Because teacher quality is central to program quality, each of these three goals directly and indirectly advances the ECE teaching workforce.

---

qualified ECE teachers. Indeed, the ECE field itself is divided on the issue of appropriate requirements: Many experts advocate the necessity of a BA for all teachers; some suggest that each group of children should have at least one teacher with a BA; and others advocate the AA degree. A substantial body of research has found that a BA corresponds with high-quality teaching and positive child outcomes (e.g., Whitebook, 2003). Recent research, however, complicates this seeming consensus: The National Center for Early Development and Learning has found little to no correlation between teachers' years of education and children's achievement, and only a marginal association between years of formal education and teacher quality (Early et al., 2006). To date, then, research neither confirms nor denies that a BA is essential for teacher quality.

Yet, many ECE experts agree that formal education does correlate with higher-quality care for young children (Barnett, 2003a; Howes, 1997; Tout, Zaslow, & Berry, 2006; Whitebook, 2003) and higher levels of formal education improve the overall standing of ECE teachers. Current policy does not reflect this understanding; inconsistent entry requirements are common across the entire ECE workforce. In prekindergarten, 20 states require teachers to have a bachelor's degree, 16 states require teachers to have a Child Development Associate (CDA) degree, and three states require teachers to have an associate's degree in ECE education (Gilliam & Marchesseault, 2005). For teachers in child care centers, no state requires teachers to have a BA degree, and just 12 states have minimum postsecondary education or training requirements for teachers (LeMoine & Azer, 2006a). Of these 12 states, 2 states require either a CDA or Child Care Provider (CCP) credential; 4 states require a credential plus experience; 2 additional states require the completion of a 2-year vocational child care course; and the remaining 4 states require some mix of training and experience in childhood development (LeMoine & Azer, 2006a).

To put ECE teachers' entry requirements in context, it is helpful to consider states' entry requirements for K–12 teachers. All 50 states require the vast majority of K–12 teachers to obtain teaching credentials prior to becoming licensed. Within each state, the requirements for those teaching the same grades and/or subjects are fairly consistent, irrespective of school or district. To achieve the requirements, teachers must have a bachelor's degree and complete an approved formal teacher education program that typically includes a specified number of credits, subject area coursework, and supervised practice teaching (Bureau of Labor Statistics, 2006). Most states also require K–12 teachers to pass a certification exam that assesses their skills and knowledge (Bureau of Labor Statistics, 2006). Within these K–12 regulations, there is some variation across the states, yet this variation pales in comparison to the diversity of entry requirements that characterizes ECE.

The possibility of high and consistent requirements in ECE is real, but scaling up from successful single-program or single-state efforts to policies that span the ECE field presents a serious challenge. Unless entry requirements are consistent across program type and geography, raising a requirement for one type of program would improve the quality of teachers in that program type but concomitantly decrease teacher quality in programs with less stringent requirements. For example, as highly qualified teachers are attracted into higher-paying jobs in state-funded prekindergarten programs, other ECE programs will attract less qualified teachers; since pre-K programs currently house a minority of children in ECE, policies that raise requirements for pre-K teachers may negatively affect the large population of children in alternative settings. The stratification of teacher quality creates inequities within ECE. Therefore, entry requirements must be set with careful attention to teachers in all types of ECE programs.

Teacher Preparation.   Professional development programs must prepare teachers with the knowledge, skills, and dispositions to successfully teach all young children. The current capacity and content of ECE teacher preparation programs across the country, however, raise concerns about the quality and consistency of prospective teachers' qualifications.

In terms of capacity, there is a severe shortage of early childhood faculty members within degree-offering programs nationally, with an average student to full-time faculty ratio of 61 to 1—60 percent higher than the student to full-time faculty ratio in institutions of higher education as a whole (Early & Winton, 2001). Furthermore, professors at 4-year institutions are more likely than professors at 2-year institutions to have doctorates, but less likely to have direct ECE classroom

Box 6–2 Policies and Practices from the Field
Raise Entry Requirements

Raising entry requirements ensures that prospective ECE teachers have adequate qualifications and enhances the overall professionalism of the workforce (Helburn, 1995; Phillips et al., 2001). Successful efforts to raise requirements couple regulatory changes with financial incentives and strategies for improving access to professional development (Ackerman, 2005).

Head Start

Head Start, the nation's major comprehensive child development and family support program for very low-income families, has raised ECE teachers' qualifications by raising requirements and offering professional development. Entry requirements for the teachers in Head Start programs are more stringent than those for child care. In 1998, Congress reauthorized the Head Start Act and required that 50 percent of its teachers have an associate's degree by September 2003. Head Start programs responded and exceeded this mandate. In 2005, 7 out of 10 Head

Start teachers had an associate's degree or higher: 33 percent held an AA, 31 percent held a BA, and 5 percent held a master's degree. Furthermore, many Head Start teachers are pursuing higher levels of formal education. One-fifth of Head Start teachers with an AA were enrolled in a BA program and one-half of Head Start teachers with a Child Development Associate (CDA) were pursuing either an AA or BA in 2005 (Hamm, 2006). Congress is likely to raise requirements when it reauthorizes the Head Start Act. A recent Senate proposal, for instance, would require 50 percent of teachers to have a BA, all assistant teachers to have at least a CDA, and all teachers to participate in at least 15 hours of ongoing training every year (Gish, 2007). To supplement these high entry requirements, Head Start has invested significant resources in supporting its teachers (Head Start Bureau, 2002). With its more stringent regulations and investments in teachers' professional development, many Head Start teachers have higher qualifications than their counterparts in other types of ECE programs.

experience (Early & Winton, 2001). Therefore, ECE teachers graduating from some programs may have had professors who emphasize content knowledge and theory, whereas graduates from other programs may have had professors who focus more on practice in ECE settings. Ideally, graduates from all programs would be exposed to theoretical *and* practical elements of ECE.

The content of teacher preparation programs needs to be expanded to keep pace with the contemporary realities of young children. Because of the diversity of children in ECE programs, teachers must be prepared to work with students of diverse cultural backgrounds and national origins; they must be trained to teach English language learners, and they must be sensitive to the development of infants, toddlers, and preschoolers with disabilities. Yet, many teacher preparation programs fall short of providing teachers with the knowledge, skills, and dispositions to carry out broadly inclusive practice. According to a national sample, the majority of master's, bachelor's, associate's, and credential programs (including the CDA) do not require a full course in working with children and families from diverse ethnic and cultural backgrounds *or* working with children learning English. The majority of MA, BA, and credential programs do not require students of ECE to

Box 6–3 Policies and Practices from the Field
Improve Teachers' Preparation

Standards for professional development ensure that prospective ECE teachers are prepared to successfully teach all children. To that end, the National Association for Child Care Resource and Referral Agencies is making progress on establishing standards for training, and the National Association for the Education of Young Children (NAEYC) and the National Council for the Accreditation of Teacher Education (NCATE) have established standards for formal education degrees in early care and education.

NAEYC and NCATE

To ensure that institutions of higher education provide high-quality education that incorporates elements of both practice *and* content knowledge, NAEYC and NCATE developed five standards for ECE teacher preparation programs: (1) Promoting Child Development and Learning; (2) Building Family and Community Relationships; (3) Observing, Documenting, and Assessing to Support Young Children and Families; (4) Teaching and Learning; and (5) Becoming a Professional (National Association for the Education of Young Children, 2001). Two- and 4-year colleges and universities that implement these standards in their ECE programs help ensure that students receive comprehensive content area coursework and field experience. Currently, 150 NCATE-accredited institutions of higher education across the country offer NAEYC-approved advanced degrees (Hyson & Biggar, 2006).

take a full course in the education and care of infants and toddlers, and the majority of MA and credential programs do not require a full course in the education and care of young children with disabilities (Maxwell, Lim, & Early, 2006). Furthermore, of all the training topics covered by local child care resource and referral agencies' workshops for child care providers, just 2 percent involve teaching children from diverse cultures or who speak languages other than English, and 4 percent involve teaching children of different age groups (Smith, Sarkar, Perry-Manning, & Schmalzried, 2006). As Ray, Bowman, and Robbins (2006) write, "perhaps 75% of the professional curriculum in bachelor's degree teacher education programs is primarily concerned with the development and education of White middle class, able bodied, monolingual children" (p. 36); "the developmental and educational needs of *all* children simply *do not* appear to be at the center of teacher preparation coursework and practice" (p. 39, emphasis in original).

Retaining High-Quality Teachers

Retaining teachers, especially high-quality teachers, may be the most pressing challenge facing the ECE workforce. Regardless of their preparation or qualifications, teachers who enter the ECE classroom or open their homes to infants and toddlers and other young children face a number of disincentives to remaining in their careers, including limited opportunities for professional growth, inadequate compensation, and poor working conditions. Turnover rates among ECE teachers hover around 30 percent (Bellm, Whitebook, Broatch, & Young, 2002)—nearly twice the rate of K–12 teachers (Provasnik & Dorfman, 2005). In ECE settings, higher staff turnover rates are associated with lower-quality services (Cost Quality and Child Outcomes Study Team, 1995; Kontos, Howes, Galinsky, & Shinn, 1995; Whitebook, Howes, & Phillips, 1990). In order to secure developmentally appropriate experiences for children, more responsive teacher-child interactions, better structural indicators of quality (e.g., child:staff ratios) and improved child development (Howes & Hamilton, 1993), retention strategies must be advanced.

Professional Growth.   Retention of quality teachers depends on treating and compensating ECE teachers as valued professionals. However, many ECE settings do not encourage even the most diligent and highly qualified teachers to take on additional duties, develop their leadership skills, or move into positions of authority. For example, one study of teachers in 10 ECE centers in urban and rural communities showed little differentiation in teachers', assistant teachers', and aides' compensation and responsibilities, suggesting that teachers have modest opportunities for meaningful career advancement (Kontos & Stremmel, 1988). As a result, many teachers experience feelings of stagnation and burnout that are not conducive to long careers in the field (Evans, Bryant, Owens, & Koukos, 2004). Without opportunities for professional growth, a career in ECE may be inherently dissatisfying.

To address the limited professional growth endemic to ECE, individualized professional development through mentoring and coaching programs has emerged. Mentoring programs support student teachers or newly employed teachers by providing them with individualized training and feedback from qualified supervisors or colleagues. They honor the experience and hard work of veteran teachers while orienting prospective and new teachers to ECE in order to improve their teaching and sustain their longevity in their programs and in the field. Mentorship appears to be positively related to teacher quality and improvements in children's developmental outcomes (Howes, James, & Ritchie, 2003), as well as to classroom quality: in one study, subscales of the Infant/Toddler Environment Rating Scale (ITERS) marked statistically significant improvement in areas such as learning activities, sensitivity, appropriate discipline, and routines (e.g., mealtimes, naptime, diapering/toileting) in the classrooms of mentored protégés (Fiene, 2002). Some form of mentoring program exists in at least 21 states (National Child Care Information Center, 2006b); given the proven effects of mentorship and the widespread problem of limited professional growth opportunities, ECE teachers across the country would benefit from having access to mentors.

While mentors induct new teachers into the ECE field, curriculum coaches provide individualized support for new and experienced teachers by introducing them to new teaching methods and guiding their application of new methods in the classroom. Research suggests that coaches and consultants play many distinct roles in supporting ECE teachers. They may serve as strategists, translators, advocates, nurturers, teachers, learners, professional role models, and curriculum developers (Rust & Freidus, 2001, in Ryan, Hornbeck, & Frede, 2004). Coaching

Box 6–4 **Policies and Practices from the Field**
Formalize Professional Growth

Programs offering both career ladders and individualized professional development create incentives for teachers to pursue higher levels of education and supports for teachers to improve their practices. Together, they encourage teachers to commit to professional growth and their careers in ECE.

Military Child Care

The U.S. Department of Defense (DoD) Child Development Program takes a thorough approach to supporting its ECE workforce as a result of the Military Child Care Act (MCCA), a measure passed by Congress in 1989. Improving teachers' compensation and training was a cornerstone of this reform (Campbell, Applebaum, Martinson, & Martin, 2000; De Vita & Montilla, 2003). In addition to establishing entry

requirements for ECE teachers, the DoD encourages teachers to pursue training and formal education through a wage scale that ties wages to training, education, and performance (Campbell et al., 2000). Once employed by the DoD, ECE teachers have opportunities for career growth through ongoing professional development, including individualized coaching and mentorship (Ackerman, 2006). To encourage stability of its ECE teaching workforce, teachers who stay within the DoD's child care system receive increases in their compensation. Evaluations of the DoD's reform demonstrate its success in improving the quality and stability of its ECE workforce. These reform efforts are ongoing, as the DoD continues to invest in certification, accreditation, staff compensation, and training (Pomper, Blank, Campbell, & Schulman, 2005).

initiatives have proven effective: In one Head Start program, for example, coaching improved both teacher quality and child outcomes (Lambert, O'Donnell, Abbott-Shim, & Kusherman, 2006).

Despite the preliminary success of mentoring and coaching efforts, these professional growth initiatives make limited headway against the lack of systematic career growth. To address this issue, career ladders, also called "career lattices" or "career paths," provide a unified framework for career growth by articulating levels of mastery that reflect workers' experience, training, and educational accomplishments. Compared to other professional fields, career ladders are widely absent from ECE settings, and are generally underutilized where they exist. The lack of career ladders discourages professional development and fosters feelings of stagnation among teachers who are not recognized for improving their practice. Indeed, because career ladders are crucial to the formation of professional development systems (Kagan, Tarrant, & Berliner, 2005; National Child Care Information Center, 2006b), improving the ECE teaching workforce depends on career ladders that new teachers and existing teachers are able and motivated to climb (Fitzgerald, 2006). Analysis of existing career ladders show that a complete ladder has three features: (1) discrete educational qualifications for each rung, (2) a manageable "distance" between each rung that builds on the credits earned at each previous rung, and (3) funding sufficient to reward each advance up the ladder (Fitzgerald, 2006). Programs that offer career ladders reap valuable benefits through lower levels of turnover and higher levels of program quality (Moon & Burbank, 2004).

Compensation.   As mentioned earlier, economic undervaluation already poses a significant barrier to teacher *recruitment*. The disconnect between teachers' classroom performance and compensation, along with low pay ceilings, further challenges *retention* and quality among teachers who have already entered the ECE workforce. While K–12 education and other fields generally compensate employees for increased educational attainment and experience in the classroom, ECE teachers are not consistently rewarded for advanced degrees or program tenure. Among ECE teachers in center-based programs in North Carolina, for example, the difference between having no college experience and having a BA or higher degree was associated with a pay increase of 50 percent—from $7.10 to $10.90 per hour; for FCC providers in that state, the associated pay increase was 9 percent—from $5.42 to $5.90 per hour (Child Care Services Association, 2003). Increased compensation for teaching experience is similarly low. Among nearly 8,000 staff members across licensed center-based programs in Ohio (including administrators, teachers, and assistant teachers), the pay raise associated with each year in the classroom was just $0.17 (T.E.A.C.H. Early Childhood Ohio and the Ohio Child Care Resource and Referral Association, 2005). Across the country, limited opportunities for higher compensation drive even the most dedicated ECE teachers from their jobs.

In addition to diminishing teachers' job stability, low compensation has strong negative effects on program and teacher quality. Looking at wages first, teachers who are poorly paid tend to work in lower-quality programs that provide a poorer educational experience for children; conversely, teachers earning higher wages have been linked to higher program quality, even when structural features such as student:teacher ratios are taken into consideration (Barnett, 2003b; Cost Quality and Child Outcomes Study Team, 1995; Whitebook et al., 1990). In fact, one study found that teacher wages were the strongest predictor of classroom quality in child care centers, stronger than any other structural indicator at either the center or classroom level (Phillips et al., 2001). The link between teachers' wages and classroom quality may be mediated by job stability: Teachers who earn higher wages are more likely to stay in their jobs (Whitebook et al., 1998; Whitebook, Sakai, Gerber, & Howes, 2001), and the stability of the teaching workforce is related to both teacher quality and child outcomes.

Turning to employment benefits, better and more comprehensive benefits increase teachers' nonwage compensation and, logically, contribute to greater job stability and lower turnover (Whitebook et al., 2001). Research has found that benefits, particularly health insurance and pension plans, influence teachers' decisions to stay at or leave their centers. When center-based ECE teachers who left their jobs between 1994 and 2000 were asked for their suggestions about reducing turnover, 75 percent recommended improving benefits (Whitebook & Sakai, 2003). Therefore, benefits affect quality through their effects on overall compensation and stability. In all, compensation has a significant effect on teacher retention and teacher quality.

Working Conditions.   The quality of working conditions is another factor influencing ECE teacher retention. Based on considerable research on productive work environments for ECE teachers, Paula Jorde Bloom (1988) has identified 10 dimensions of organizational climate that contribute to teachers' job satisfaction: (1) collegiality,

Box 6–5 Policies and Practices from the Field
Compensate for Higher Education and Commitment to the Field

Another strategy for retaining quality teachers provides compensation rewards for teachers' participation in professional development, attainment of higher qualifications, and commitment to the field. This strategy recognizes that attaining higher levels of training and formal education may not be possible without providing teachers with additional supports.

T.E.A.C.H. Early Childhood® Project

The Teacher Education and Compensation Helps (T.E.A.C.H.) Early Childhood Project is the most widespread program to enhance the formal education and compensation of ECE teachers in center-based facilities and licensed FCC homes. The model requires support from the state, the employer, and the ECE teacher. T.E.A.C.H. Early Childhood was developed in North Carolina by the Child Care Services Association in 1990. There are four components of the program:

1. *Scholarship.* The scholarship usually covers partial costs for tuition and books or assessment fees. Often, while states or private foundations pay for the scholarship, the employer is required to provide the scholarship recipient with paid release time and a travel stipend.

2. *Education.* In return for receiving a scholarship, each participant must complete a specified amount of education, usually in the form of college coursework, during a prescribed contract period.

3. *Compensation.* At the end of their contract, after completing their educational requirement, participants are eligible to receive increased compensation in the form of a one-time bonus (ranging from $100 to $700) or an ongoing pay raise (4 percent or 5 percent), usually paid by the early childhood employer.

4. *Commitment.* Participants must honor their commitment to stay in their current setting or the field for 6 months to 1 year, depending on the scholarship program.

In 2005, T.E.A.C.H. Early Childhood operated in 22 states and had served more than 80,000 ECE teachers, directors, and FCC providers (Child Care Services Association, 2005; Russell & Rogers, 2005).

(2) professional growth, (3) supervisor support, (4) clarity (of policies and procedures), (5) reward system, (6) decision making, (7) goal consensus, (8) task orientation, (9) physical setting, and (10) innovativeness (Jorde-Bloom, 1988). Compared with the research base on other characteristics of the ECE teaching workforce, limited data exist on work environment. Those that do exist show a need for improvement. For example, a study conducted by Cornille, Mullis, Mullis, and Shriner (2006) revealed that poor working conditions are an obstacle to teachers' classroom success. When asked to select their top three choices for work environment improvements, 36 percent of teachers chose increased supplies and equipment as crucial to their success as teachers, 27 percent requested more staff, 17 percent desired substitutes, 12 percent wanted to improve playgrounds, 12 percent preferred to stock a resource lending library, and 10 percent thought physical facilities or equipment could be improved. A study conducted by the North Carolina Child Care Services Association identified seven types of workplace support that ECE programs can provide and

linked them to teachers' likelihood of remaining in their jobs.[3] Only 11 percent of teachers in centers offering all seven types of support said they would leave the field within 3 years, compared with twice as many ECE teachers throughout North Carolina who said the same thing (Child Care Services Association, 2003). Poor working conditions are especially detrimental to retention efforts because of their strong correlation with high turnover.

Supervisors play an important role in efforts to retain teachers by creating work environments that are conducive to ECE teachers' professional growth. By placing teachers in positions they are qualified for and can succeed in, supervisors set teachers on the path to quality teaching. Supervisors who give teachers time to collaborate with their colleagues, a voice in decision making, and space to reflect on their practice create an effective work environment, which reaps benefits for the overall work environment and the quality of teaching. Indeed, research shows that ECE teachers supervised in a "reflective manner" are more likely to engage in language play and responsive involvement with their students (Howes et al., 2003). Furthermore, an evaluation of Head Start's Early Childhood Leadership Training Program found that training for directors and lead teachers significantly improved both classroom quality scores and the overall organizational climate of the centers, with staff expressing more positive attitudes about the climate of, and stronger levels of commitment to, their programs after the training period (Jorde Bloom & Sheerer, 1992). As with other ECE teacher supports, however, the requirements for supervisors' professional development could be improved: just 16 states require administrative training for center-based child care directors—2 of which specify only entry requirements, 8 of which specify only ongoing requirements, and 4 of which mandate both (LeMoine & Azer, 2006b). As a result, many ECE directors have not had the professional development necessary to create the work environment benefits described above.

Taken together, these findings confirm that teachers who have positive experiences in the workplace—who work in appropriate physical settings, feel that their input counts, and experience effective supervision and leadership—are more likely to find their jobs rewarding and remain committed to their work (Child Care Services Association, 2003; Howes et al., 2003; Hayden in Muijs, Aubrey, Harris, & Briggs, 2004). Though we may know what kinds of working conditions contribute to the retention of high-quality teachers, the data above show that few programs currently offer sufficient resources and support. As with limited professional growth and inadequate compensation, poor working conditions impede retention efforts across the ECE field.

LOOKING TO THE FUTURE

Failure to recruit and retain high-quality teachers renders ECE programs ill-equipped to meet the challenge of providing young children with high-quality ECE.

---

3. The seven types of support were (1) orientation, (2) written job descriptions, (3) written personnel policies, (4) paid education and training expenses, (5) paid breaks, (6) compensatory time for training, and (7) paid preparation/planning time.

Box 6–6 Policies and Practices from the Field
Build Supportive Work Environments

Work environment strategies are designed to improve the overall working conditions experienced by teachers in their programs. Because of the multidimensional nature of the work environment, these strategies are indirect, yet they have a crucial impact on teachers themselves.

Program Administration Scale

The Program Administration Scale (PAS) provides a comprehensive assessment of the overall administration of programs, examining 10 areas of administration: (1) human resources development, (2) personnel cost and allocation, (3) center operations, (4) child assessment, (5) fiscal management, (6) program planning and evaluation, (7) family partnerships, (8) marketing and public relations, (9) technology, and (10) staff qualifica-

tions (McCormick Tribune Center for Early Childhood Leadership, 2005). Although the PAS is a relatively new assessment instrument, it has become popular with local municipalities, state agencies, and Head Start grantees that seek to improve ECE workplace environments (T. Talan, personal communication, April 2006). Currently, Chicago's Department of Children and Youth Services is assessing the quality of all 400 of its Head Start and child care programs, using the PAS to measure administrative practices and the Early Childhood Environment Rating Scale (ECERS) to measure classroom practices. Building on this approach, Arkansas, Illinois, and Ohio have developed comprehensive plans to incorporate the PAS into their statewide quality rating systems ("Ohio, Arkansas, Illinois adopt NLU early childhood leadership quality rating tools," 2007).

Without new teachers to enter the field and move on to more advanced positions, the field currently suffers from a shortage of personnel in key positions—and will continue to suffer far into the future. The scarcity of mentors, coaches, directors, trainers, and teacher educators further exacerbates the quantity-quality crisis (Whitebook, 1997). Fortunately, as the boxed examples in this chapter illustrate, numerous efforts are under way to ameliorate recruitment and retention problems. From the federal government to individual programs, policies and practices are meeting these challenges throughout the country; in this chapter, we have highlighted only a few of the many exemplary efforts. In addition to bringing promising efforts to scale, however, research, innovation, and systematic reform are required to transform the ECE teaching workforce.

Innovation in Recruitment and Retention

New strategies for recruiting potential ECE teachers must be piloted and evaluated rigorously. Numerous innovations within the K–12 system entice individuals to consider a career in education. For example, school districts facing teacher shortages attract prospective teachers with financial incentives, such as signing bonuses, loan forgiveness, and housing assistance (Ingersoll, 2007). Alternative recruitment programs like "troops-to-teachers" and New York City's Teaching Fellows program attract and prepare new teachers for the profession; these programs could be applied to the ECE workforce. Some strategies, such as Teach for America, a program designed to appeal to graduates from elite colleges and universities, are just beginning to turn their attention to the early years (Jacobson, 2007). Although alternative route certification programs are plagued by high teacher attrition, lessons may be learned from these strategies that increase the pool of qualified candidates.

As articulated earlier, recruitment must be coupled with retention, and innovative retention strategies are also needed. ECE can look to K–12's induction programs to secure teachers' commitment to ECE. For example, to retain talented teachers, the Toledo Federation of Teachers created a peer assistance and review model in which consulting teachers mentor and evaluate new and/or struggling teachers. Due to the success of this induction effort, some form of Toledo's approach has been implemented in 75–80 programs across the country (Moses, 2006).

More and Better Research on All ECE Teachers

Existing research has limitations that inhibit our understanding of the challenge of recruiting and retaining quality teachers. First, current data focus on particular segments of the workforce (e.g., prekindergarten, Head Start) or on specific states. Second, research is limited because of imprecise and inconsistent definitions related to the ECE workforce. When studies define "staff," "teachers," "teacher assistants," and other groups differently, data are not broadly useful. Third, evaluations of strategies that promote teacher quality are also scarce. Without understanding how policies and practices can translate into better teaching and learning, ineffective approaches can survive while promising strategies flounder. Through greater investment in ECE research and sophisticated investigative techniques, some of the central questions about the ECE teaching workforce are starting to be answered.

Systemic Approaches to Enhancing the ECE Workforce

Because ECE teachers are one part of a broader ECE system, systemic efforts must lay the foundation for reform. Investments linked to consistent standards can equalize and improve ECE teachers' experiences (Mitchell & Stoney, 2004). Strategies such as quality rating systems, which hold all types of ECE programs to common program standards, have been adopted or are being designed in the majority of states (National Child Care Information Center, 2006a). Efforts that minimize fragmentation also minimize inequity among teachers in different types of ECE programs as they advance the entire field.

Lastly, reform cannot happen without the public's appreciation of the very real contribution that the ECE workforce makes to society. Associations like the National Association for the Education of Young Children provide an important vehicle for voicing concerns about today's teaching conditions. Unions have also successfully organized ECE teachers to win increased support for their work. The *entire* ECE workforce—including licensing professionals, resource and referral specialists, policy leaders, and others beyond the immediate delivery of services to children—must be engaged in a transformation.

CONCLUSIONS

The tension between having enough teachers and having high-quality teachers in programs for young children cannot be resolved without serious attention to recruiting highly qualified teachers and retaining those high-quality teachers once they have joined the ECE teaching workforce. This chapter has outlined the conditions that must be in place to fulfill the promise of early care and education: professional respect and social valuation, high and consistent qualifications, and effective professional preparation. Professional growth—career ladders and individualized professional development—combined with adequate compensation and positive working conditions can also improve ECE teachers' practice and sustain their commitment to young children. By creating a cadre of experienced professionals, the field will be able to staff key leadership positions with individuals who understand and respect the challenges of teaching. Targeted and systematic recruitment and retention strategies from ECE and allied fields are the only way to create a teaching workforce equipped to take on the challenge of educating and caring for young children.

REFERENCES

AACTE Focus Council on Early Childhood Education. (2004). *The early childhood challenge: Preparing high-quality teachers for a changing society.* Washington, DC: American Association of Colleges for Teachers of Education.

Ackerman, D. J. (2005). Getting teachers from here to there: Examining issues related to an early care and education teacher policy [Electronic Version]. *Early Childhood Research and Practice, 7.* Retrieved January 22, 2007, from http://ecrp.uiuc.edu/v7n1/ackerman.html

Ackerman, D. J. (2006). *"The learning never stops": Lessons from military child development centers for teacher professional development.* Paper presented at the Annual Meeting of the American Educational Research Association, San Francisco, CA.

Albelda, R. (2002). Under the margins: Feminist economists look at gender and poverty. *Dollars & Sense* (243), 30–35.

Barnett, W. S. (2003a). *Better teachers, better preschools: Student achievement linked to teacher qualifications* (Preschool Policy Matters, Issue 2). New Brunswick, NJ: National Institute for Early Education Research.

Barnett, W. S. (2003b). *Low wages = low quality: Solving the real preschool teacher crisis* (Preschool Policy Matters, Issue 3). New Brunswick, NJ: National Institute for Early Education Research.

Barnett, W. S., Hustedt, J. T., Robin, K. B., & Schulman, K. L. (2005). *The state of preschool: 2005 state preschool yearbook.* New Brunswick, NJ: National Institute for Early Education Research.

Bellm, D., & Whitebook, M. (2006). *Roots of decline: How government policy has de-educated teachers of young children.* Berkeley, CA: Center for the Study of Child Care Employment.

Bellm, D., Whitebook, M., Broatch, L., & Young, M. (2002). *Inside the pre-k classroom: A study of staffing and stability in state-funded prekindergarten programs.* Washington, DC: Center for the Child Care Workforce.

Bowman, B. T., Donovan, M. S., & Burns, M. S. (Eds.). (2001). *Eager to learn: Educating our preschoolers.* Washington, DC: National Academy Press.

Bredekamp, S., & Copple, C. (1997). *Developmentally appropriate practice in early childhood programs.* Washington, DC: NAEYC.

Bureau of Labor Statistics. (2005). *Occupational outlook handbook, 2006–07 edition: Child care workers.* Retrieved February 13, 2006, from www.bls.gov/oco/ocos170.htm

Bureau of Labor Statistics. (2006). *Occupational outlook handbook, 2006–07 edition: Teachers—preschool, kindergarten, elementary, middle, and secondary.* Retrieved June 5, 2006, from www.bls.gov/oco/ocos069.htm

Bureau of Labor Statistics. (2007). *Occupational employment and wages, 2006.* Retrieved June 20, 2007, from www.bls.gov/news.release/pdf/ocwage.pdf

Burton, A., Whitebook, M., Young, M., Bellm, D., Wayne, C., & Brandon, R. N. (2002). *Estimating the size and components of the U.S. child care workforce and caregiving population: Key findings from the child care workforce estimate* (preliminary report). Washington, DC, and Seattle, WA: Center for the Child Care Workforce and Human Services Policy Center.

Cahan, E. (1989). *Past caring: A history of U.S. preschool care and education for the poor, 1820–1965.* New York: National Center for Children in Poverty, Columbia University.

Caldwell, B. M. (1989). A comprehensive model for integrating child care and early childhood education. *Teachers College Record, 90*(3), 404–414.

Campbell, N. D., Applebaum, J. C., Martinson, K., & Martin, E. (2000). *Be all that we can be: Lessons from the military for improving our nation's child care system.* Washington, DC: National Women's Law Center.

Center for the Child Care Workforce. (2006). *Low salaries for staff, high costs to children.* Washington, DC: Author.

Child Care Services Association. (2003). *Working in child care in North Carolina: The North Carolina child care workforce survey.* Chapel Hill: Author.

Child Care Services Association. (2005). *T.E.A.C.H. Early Childhood® project.* Retrieved January 20, 2006, from www.childcareservices.org/teach/project.html

Cornille, T. A., Mullis, R. L., Mullis, A. K., & Shriner, M. (2006). An examination of childcare teachers in for-profit and non-profit childcare centers. *Early Child Development and Care, 176*(6), 631–641.

Cost Quality and Child Outcomes Study Team. (1995). *Cost, quality, and child outcomes in child care centers.* Denver: University of Colorado, Economics Department.

De Vita, C. J., & Montilla, M. D. (2003). *Improving child care quality: A comparison of military and civilian approaches* (Policy Brief: Charting Civil Society). Washington, DC: Urban Institute.

Early, D. M., Bryant, D. M., Pianta, R. C., Clifford, R. M., Burchinal, M. R., Ritchie, S., et al. (2006). Are teachers' education, major, and credentials related to classroom quality and children's academic gains in pre-kindergarten? *Early Childhood Research Quarterly, 21*(2), 174–195.

Epstein, A. S. (1999). Pathways to quality in Head Start, public school, and private nonprofit early childhood programs. *Journal of Research in Early Childhood Education, 13*(2), 101–119.

Evans, G. D., Bryant, N. E., Owens, J. S., & Koukos, K. (2004). Ethnic differences in burnout, coping, and intervention acceptability among childcare professionals. *Child and Youth Care Forum, 33*(5), 349–371.

Feeney, S., & Freeman, N. K. (1999). *Ethics and the early childhood educator: Using the NAEYC Code.* Washington, DC: National Association for the Education of Young Children.

Fein, G. G. (1994). Preparing tomorrow's inventors. In S. G. Goffin & D. E. Day (Eds.), *New perspectives in early childhood teacher education: Bringing practitioners into the debate.* New York: Teachers College Press.

Fiene, R. (2002). Improving child care quality through an infant caregiver mentoring project. *Child & Youth Care Forum, 31*(2), 79–87.

Fitzgerald, J. (2006). *Moving up in the new economy: Career ladders for US workers.* Ithaca, NY: Cornell University Press.

Gilliam, W. S., & Marchesseault, C. M. (2005). *From capitols to classrooms, policies to practice: State-funded prekindergarten at the classroom level. Part 1: Who's teaching our youngest students? Teacher education and training, experience, compensation and benefits, and assistant teachers.* New Haven, CT: Yale University, Yale Child Study Center.

Gish, M. (2007). *Head Start reauthorization: A side-by-side comparison of H.R. 1429, S. 556, and current law* (CRS Report for Congress). Washington, DC: Congressional Research Service.

Grieshaber, S. (2001). Advocacy and early childhood educators: Identity and cultural conflicts. In

S. Grieshaber & G. S. Cannella (Eds.), *Embracing identities in early childhood education: Diversity and possibilities* (pp. 60–72). New York: Teachers College Press.

Hamm, K. (2006). *More than meets the eye: Head Start programs, participants, families, and staff in 2005* (Head Start Series, Brief No. 8). Washington, DC: Center for Law and Social Policy.

Head Start Bureau. (2002). *Professional development: The cornerstone for trust and empowerment* (Head Start Bulletin #72). Washington, DC: Author.

Helburn, S. W. (1995). *Cost, quality, and child outcomes in child care centers.* Denver: University of Colorado, Economics Department.

Herzenberg, S., Price, M., & Bradley, D. (2005). *Losing ground in early childhood education: Declining workforce qualifications in an expanding industry, 1979–2004.* Washington, DC: Economic Policy Institute.

Howes, C. (1997). Children's experiences in center-based child care as a function of teacher background and adult:child ratio. *Merrill-Palmer Quarterly, 43,* 404–425.

Howes, C., & Hamilton, C. E. (1993). The changing experience of child care: Changes in teachers and in teacher-child relationships and children's social competence with peers. *Early Childhood Research Quarterly, 8*(1), 15–32.

Howes, C., James, J., & Ritchie, S. (2003). Pathways to effective teaching. *Early Childhood Research Quarterly, 18*(1), 104–120.

Hutchinson, B. L. (1994). The value of developmentally appropriate practice for all children. In S. G. Goffin & D. E. Day (Eds.), *New perspectives in early childhood teacher education: Bringing practitioners into the debate.* New York: Teachers College Press.

Hyson, M., & Biggar, H. (2006). NAEYC's standards for early childhood professional preparation: Getting from here to there. In M. Zaslow & I. Martinez-Beck (Eds.), *Critical issues in early childhood professional development* (pp. 283–308). Baltimore: Brookes.

Ingersoll, R. M. (2007). *Misdiagnosing the teacher quality problem* (CPRE Policy Briefs RB-49). Philadelphia: Consortium for Policy Research in Education.

Isenberg, J. P. (2000). The state of the art in early childhood professional preparation. In D. Horm-Wingerd & M. Hyson (Eds.), *New teachers for a new century: The future of early childhood professional*

preparation (pp. 15–58). Jessup, MD: U.S. Department of Education.

Jacobson, L. (2007, February 14). Teach for America setting sights on pre-k. *Education Week.*

Jones, H. A. (1995). Issues in early childhood education: Implications and directions for higher education. *Peabody Journal of Education, 70*(3), 112–124.

Jorde-Bloom, P. (1988). Closing the gap: An analysis of teacher and administrator perceptions of organizational climate in the early childhood setting. *Teachers and Teacher Education, 4*(2), 111–120.

Jorde Bloom, P., & Sheerer, M. (1992). The effect of leadership training on child care program quality. *Early Childhood Research Quarterly, 7*(4), 579–594.

Kagan, S. L., Kauerz, K., & Tarrant, K. (2008). *The early care and education teaching workforce at the fulcrum: An agenda for reform.* New York: Teachers College Press.

Kagan, S. L., Tarrant, K., & Berliner, A. (2005). *Building a professional development system in South Carolina: Review and analysis of other states' experiences.* New York: Columbia University, National Center for Children and Families.

Kontos, S., Howes, C., Galinsky, E., & Shinn, M. (1995). *Quality in family child care and relative care.* New York: Families and Work Institute.

Kontos, S., & Stremmel, A. J. (1988). Caregivers' perceptions of working conditions in a child care environment. *Early Childhood Research Quarterly, 3*(1), 77–90.

Kramer, J. F. (1994). Defining competences as readiness to learn. In S. G. Goffin & D. E. Day (Eds.), *New perspectives in early childhood teacher education: Bringing practitioners into the debate.* New York: Teachers College Press.

Lambert, R. G., O'Donnell, M., Abbott-Shim, M., & Kusherman, J. (2006, April). *The effect of the Creative Curriculum training and technical assistance on Head Start classroom quality.* Paper presented at the annual meeting of the American Educational Research Association.

LeMoine, S., & Azer, S. L. (2006a). *Center child care licensing requirements (October 2006): Minimum early childhood education (ECE) preservice qualifications and annual ongoing training hours for teachers and master teachers.* Retrieved May 7, 2007, from http://nccic.acf.hhs.gov/pubs/cclicensingreq/cclr-teachers.html

LeMoine, S., & Azer, S. L. (2006b). *Child care licensing requirements (October 2006): Minimum early childhood education (ECE) preservice qualifications, administrative, and annual ongoing training hours for directors.* Retrieved May 14, 2007, from www.nccic.org/pubs/cclicensingreq/cclr-directors.html

LeMoine, S., Morgan, G., & Azer, S. L. (2003, Winter). A snapshot of trends in child care licensing regulations. *Child Care Bulletin.*

Lobman, C., Ryan, S., & McLaughlin, J. (2005). Reconstructing teacher education to prepare qualified preschool teachers: Lessons from New Jersey [Electronic Version]. *Early Childhood Research & Practice, 7.* Retrieved November 10, 2007 from http://ecrp.uiuc.edu/v7n2/lobman.html

Love, J. M., Schochet, P. Z., & Meckstroth, A. L. (1996). *Are they in any real danger? What research does—and doesn't—tell us about child care quality and children's well-being.* Princeton, NJ: Mathematica Policy Research.

Maxwell, K. L., Field, C. C., & Clifford, R. M. (2006). Defining and measuring professional development in early childhood research. In M. Zaslow & I. Martinez-Beck (Eds.), *Critical issues in early childhood professional development* (pp. 21–48). Baltimore: Brookes.

Maxwell, K. L., Lim, C.-I., & Early, D. M. (2006). *Early childhood teacher preparation programs in the United States: National report.* Chapel Hill: The University of North Carolina, Frank Porter Graham Child Development Institute.

McCormick Tribune Center for Early Childhood Leadership. (2005). *Program administration scale: Measuring early childhood leadership and management.* Retrieved February 27, 2006, from http://cecl.nl.edu/technical/pasoverview.htm

Mitchell, A. (2005). Stair steps to quality: A guide for states and communities developing quality rating systems for early care and education: Alliance for Early Childhood Finance, United Way of America, Success by 6.

Mitchell, A., & Stoney, L. (2004). Financing early childhood care and education systems: A standards-based approach: Alliance for Early Childhood Finance. Houston, TX: Rice University, James A. Baker III Institute for Public Policy, Texas Program for Society and Health.

Mitchell, A., Stoney, L., & Dichter, H. (2001). *Financing child care in the United States: An expanded catalog of current strategies, 2001 edition.* Kansas City, MO: Ewing Marion Kauffman Foundation.

Moon, J., & Burbank, J. (2004). *The early childhood education career and wage ladder: A model for improving quality in early learning and care programs.* Seattle, WA: Economic Opportunity Institute.

Moses, A. R. (2006, December 1). Grading thy neighbor. *Teacher Magazine, 18,* 8.

Muijs, D., Aubrey, C., Harris, A., & Briggs, M. (2004). How do they manage? A review of the research on leadership in early childhood. *Journal of Early Childhood Research, 2*(2), 157–169.

National Association for the Education of Young Children. (2001). *NAEYC standards for early childhood professional preparation: Initial licensure programs.* Retrieved May 4, 2007, from www.naeyc.org/faculty/pdf/2001.pdf

National Association for the Education of Young Children. (2006). *Where we stand on standards for programs to prepare early childhood professionals.* Washington, DC: Author.

National Child Care Information Center. (2006a). *Quality rating systems: Definition and statewide systems.* Retrieved August 26, 2006, from http://nccic.org/pubs/qrs-defsystems.html

National Child Care Information Center. (2006b). *State professional development systems and initiatives for the early childhood workforce.* Retrieved February 2, 2006, from http://nccic.org/pubs/goodstart/state-ece.html

National Child Care Information Center. (2007). Introduction to quality rating systems [Electronic Version]. *Child Care Bulletin.* Retrieved June 30, 2007, from http://nccic.acf.hhs.gov/ccb/issue32.pdf

National Council for Accreditation of Teacher Education. (2006). *Professional standards for the accreditation of schools, colleges, and departments of education.* Washington, DC: Author.

National Education Goals Panel. (1994). *The national education goals report: Building a nation of learners.* Washington, DC: Author.

Nelson, J. A. (2001). *Why are early education and care wages so low? A critical guide to common explanations.* New York: Foundation for Child Development.

Ohio, Arkansas, Illinois adopt NLU early childhood leadership quality rating tools [Electronic (2007) Version]. *NCE Alumni Link-Up.* Retrieved January 22, 2007, from http://www.nl.edu/Alumni/nce-alumni-link-up-jan.cfm

Phillips, D., Mekos, D., Scarr, S., McCartney, K., & Abbott-Shim, M. (2001). Within and beyond the classroom door: Assessing quality in child care centers. *Early Childhood Research Quarterly, 15*(4), 475–496.

Pomper, K., Blank, H., Campbell, N. D., & Schulman, K. (2005). *Be all that we can be: Lessons from the military for improving our nation's child care system: 2004 follow-up.* Washington, DC: National Women's Law Center.

Provasnik, S., & Dorfman, S. (2005). *Mobility in the teacher workforce: Findings from the condition of education, 2005.* Washington, DC: U.S. Department of Education, National Center for Education Statistics.

Raikes, H., Wilcox, B., Peterson, C., Hegland, S., Atwater, J., Summers, J., et al. (2003). *Child care quality and workforce characteristics in four midwestern states.* Omaha, NE: Gallup Organization and the Center on Children, Families, and the Law.

Ray, A., Bowman, B., & Robbins, J. (2006). *Preparing early childhood teachers to successfully educate all children: The contribution of four-year undergraduate teacher preparation programs.* New York: Foundation for Child Development.

Rowe, D. J., Early, B., & Loubier, D. (1994). Facilitating the distinctive role of infant and toddler teachers. In S. G. Goffin & D. E. Day (Eds.), *New perspectives in early childhood teacher education: Bringing practitioners into the debate.* New York: Teachers College Press.

Russell, S., & Rogers, J. (2005). T.E.A.C.H. Early Childhood®: Providing strategies and solutions for the early childhood workforce. *Exchange, 162,* 69–73.

Ryan, S., Hornbeck, A., & Frede, E. (2004). Mentoring for change: A time use study of teacher consultants in preschool reform [Electronic Version]. *Early Childhood Research and Practice, 6.* Retrieved January 19, 2007, from http://ecrp.uiuc.edu/v6n1/ryan.html

Saluja, G., Early, D. M., & Clifford, R. M. (2002). Demographic characteristics of early childhood teachers and structural elements of early care and education in the United States [Electronic Version]. *Early Childhood Research and Practice, 4.* Retrieved January 19, 2007, from http://ecrp.uiuc.edu/v7n2/lobman.html

Schweinhart, L. J., Barnes, H. V., & Weikert, D. P. (1993). *Significant benefits: The High/Scope Perry Preschool study through age 27.* Ypsilanti, MI: High/Scope Press.

Shonkoff, J. P., & Phillips, D. H. (Eds.). (2000). *From neurons to neighborhoods: The science of early childhood development.* Washington, DC: National Academy Press.

Smith, L. K., Sarkar, M., Perry-Manning, S., & Schmalzried, B. (2006). *NACCRRA's national survey of child care resource & referral training: Building a training system for the child care workforce.* Arlington, VA: National Association of Child Care Resource & Referral Agencies.

T.E.A.C.H. Early Childhood Ohio and the Ohio Child Care Resource and Referral Association. (2005). 2005 Early Childhood Workforce Study [PowerPoint].

Tout, K., Zaslow, M., & Berry, D. (2006). Quality and qualifications: Links between professional development and quality in early care and education settings. In M. Zaslow & I. Martinez-Beck (Eds.), *Critical issues in early childhood professional development* (pp. 77–110). Baltimore: Brookes.

Weber, R. B. (2005). *Measurement of child care arrangement stability: A review and case study using Oregon child care subsidy data.* Unpublished dissertation, Oregon State University.

Whitebook, M. (1997). Who's missing at the table? Leadership opportunities and barriers for teachers and providers. In S. L. Kagan & B. T. Bowman (Eds.), *Rethinking leadership in early care and education.* Washington, DC: National Association for the Education of Young Children.

Whitebook, M. (2003). *Early education quality: Higher teacher qualifications for better learning environments—A review of the literature.* Berkeley: University of California, Center for the Study of Child Care Employment.

Whitebook, M., Howes, C., & Phillips, D. (1990). *Who cares? Child care teachers and the quality of care in America. The national child care staffing study.* Washington, DC: Child Care Employee Project (now the Center for the Child Care Workforce).

Whitebook, M., Howes, C., & Phillips, D. (1998). *Worthy work, unlivable wages: The national child care staffing study, 1988–1997.* Washington, DC: Center for the Child Care Workforce.

Whitebook, M., & Sakai, L. (2003). Turnover begets turnover: An examination of job and occupational stability among child care center staff. *Early Childhood Research Quarterly, 18*(3), 273–293.

Whitebook, M., Sakai, L., Gerber, E., & Howes, C. (2001). *Then and now: Changes in child care staffing, 1994–2000.* Washington, DC, and Berkeley: Center for the Child Care Workforce and the Institute of Industrial Relations, University of California.

Workgroup on Defining and Measuring Early Childhood Professional Development. (2005). *Defining and measuring early childhood professional development: Update and request for input.* Paper presented at the National Association for the Education of Young Children Annual Conference.

Yonemura, M. V. (1994). Accomplishing my work as a teacher educator: Hopes, practices, supports, and constraints. In S. G. Goffin & D. E. Day (Eds.), *New perspectives in early childhood teacher education: Bringing practitioners into the debate.* New York: Teachers College Press.

CHAPTER 7

THE PROFESSIONAL DEVELOPMENT OF TEACHERS OF YOUNG CHILDREN

Nancy Barbour
Kent State University

Martha Lash
Kent State University

What is early childhood professional development? The professional development of teachers of young children occurs across distinct age ranges, in a variety of settings, for a multitude of purposes, aimed at a diverse workforce. This chapter takes a close look at how, what, from whom, and where those who serve young children and families learn about their work. In so doing, we will explore what we mean by early childhood professional development, what research has to say about this process, and what implications that research has for the future of professional development.

CURRENT ISSUES AND WHAT WE NEED TO KNOW ABOUT THEM

The title of this chapter is evidence of the implications, but certainly not agreed-upon beliefs, that early childhood education is a profession and that there are early childhood teachers who represent a profession. Assumptions about professional development have been discussed and debated for many years, but are worthy of acknowledging up front. The first assumption is that early childhood education is a profession. The second assumption that we must acknowledge is that those who work with young children are professionals in need of development. The third, more pressing, assumption is that professional development for teachers of young children *does* have an impact on the outcomes for young children (Karp, 2006).

Is Early Childhood Education a Profession?

Our first assumption raises the question of whether early childhood education is a profession. As we focus on this assumption, we offer a caveat about our choice of language and meaning. We have used the term *early childhood education* to refer to all services for young children (ages birth through 8) and their families. Implied here is that "early childhood education" refers to one unified endeavor. Spodek, Saracho, and Peters (1988) discussed the historical evolution of the field as a series of early childhood movements from kindergarten to nursery school to child care and, finally, to early intervention. These movements, they suggest, have had a sense of separateness. The growth of kindergartens, nursery schools, and day nurseries during the early part of the 20th century was essentially parallel, serving different functions for different populations. And those employed in these settings had quite different professional preparation (Spodek et al., 1988). Almost 20 years later, we are still at a loss as we attempt to define "early childhood education" as a single phenomenon (Zaslow & Martinez-Beck, 2006).

Issues of Professionalism

The second assumption refocuses our attention on whether there are essential elements of working with young children that can be developed through education and experience or whether these are intuitive skills that can be polished via experience. Spodek et al. (1988) raise the question of whether early childhood practitioners should be viewed as "professionals, semi-professionals or craftsmen" (p. 8). Still, two decades later, there is an underlying need to explore what we mean when we talk about being an early childhood professional.

In defining professionalism, we look to a consensus understanding of what a profession and thus *being a professional* entails. Common characteristics include prolonged training based on principles that involve judgment for their application; a specialized body of knowledge and expertise; training delivered in accredited institutions; rigorous requirement for entry into training; code of ethical conduct; standards of practice; social necessity; altruism; autonomy; and self-regulation. Given these requisite components, is early child education a profession?

We do believe that within the field of early childhood education, there is consensus that we are moving in the direction of being a profession. However, questions remain about how far along on the continuum we are between being an occupation and being a profession (Feeney, personal communication, 2007; Katz, 1988; Spodek et al., 1988). It is clear that we meet some of the criteria very well (e.g., altruism) but are still a long way from achieving others (e.g., autonomy). Regardless of where one believes that early childhood educators land on the professionalism continuum, attempts to move the field toward a profession occur in a variety of ways commonly described as *professional development*.

Defining Early Childhood Education
Professional Development

As we have noted, identifying a common definition of early childhood education professional development is a complex process because there is great variation in how the term is used, understood, measured, and reported in a wide variety of care and education settings and systems. Maxwell, Field, and Clifford (2006) acknowledge that in the numerous professional development research articles and studies they analyzed, there was no agreed-upon or clearly stated definition for professional development, but rather implicit definitions depending on who was reporting and how they chose to report it. Maxwell et al. (2006) identify three components of professional development: *education, training,* and *credentialing. Education* signifies the professional development activities that occur within a formal education system and primarily addresses the overall education level and content-specific education, such as academic major and coursework. *Training* signifies the professional development activities that take place outside the formal education system. These activities do not lead to a degree and are commonly called in-service experiences. *Credentialing* is different from the other categories because the organizations that grant credentials are not the ones who offer the required knowledge. Although issues of professional development cannot always be neatly pigeonholed, these three categories nevertheless provide lenses for us to use to examine the current status of early childhood professional development.

Education that occurs within the formal education system is the clearest expression of professional development that we have in our field and is marked by education level attained and content covered. It is not clear, however, whether it is the level attained or the content covered that matters to the quality of children's environments and development (Maxwell et al., 2006; McMullen, Alat, Buldu, & Lash, 2004). While it is assumed that those who teach in public schools (pre-K, kindergarten through third grade) will have earned at least a bachelor's degree, there is no nationally standardized requirement for early childhood educators outside the public school system.

The category of training is frequently referred to in early childhood settings and again, without a standard definition, may be subjectively understood. In some cases training includes college courses, as well as workshops, on-site in-service experiences, conferences, and informal information sessions. However, as a way of moving the field toward greater professionalism, Maxwell et al. (2006) suggest that training is best defined as professional development experiences that take place outside the formal education system. There are four general things we need to look at to understand the nature of a training experience: type, content, amount (length), and timing (when received). There is some conjecture as to why training is not clearly defined. It may be that there is a lack of connection to actual classroom practices and children's development and learning. It may also be that programs are quite lenient in what they categorize and accept as training so that teachers can simply meet the clock training hours required by licensing agencies.

Like the two preceding categories, credentialing lacks a clear definition in the field. Terms such as *credential, certificate,* and *license* are often used interchangeably, although they are not necessarily the same. However, the issue is more complicated than interchangeable terms:

> Certification, or licensing, in early childhood education is complicated by the bifurcated nature of the field. Certification for those working with children younger than age 5 is often handled by state departments of health and human services, whereas certification for those working with children in the early childhood age range of 5–8 years (or those working in public school preschool classrooms) is usually governed by state departments of education. Some have referred to the early childhood system as trifurcated because the federal government sets standards for Head Start teachers (Goffin & Day, 1994). The inconsistencies in certification and licensing requirements across states and agencies make it very difficult to understand the meaning of a particular certificate or license. (Maxwell et al., 2006, pp. 34–35)

Aside from formal education degrees in early childhood education (i.e., associate, bachelor, master, doctorate), the Child Development Associate credential (to be expanded on later) is the most frequently discussed credential in programs for children under 5. It is a national credential specifically designed for teachers of young children from birth to age 5 and has been in existence for over 35 years. There are several certificate and credential programs within each state, but there is little consistency regarding type, content, and amount of training required.

If we are to make connections between specific professional development (e.g., teacher knowledge and practice) and relate it to children's improved development and learning, we will need to begin by clarifying and agreeing on definitions for *education* (both level of attainment and content), *training* (the category most in need of clearing up), and *credentialing*. Additionally, consistency in terms may assist our bifurcated and/or trifurcated system of recognizing professional development and as a consequence better serve the children around whom we rally.

DESCRIPTION OF THE WORKFORCE

Like the topics discussed thus far, the early childhood workforce is a complex and not clearly defined entity. Though a more thorough discussion of the early childhood workforce was provided in the previous chapter, we would like to raise several points that seem germane to the discussion of the professional development of teachers of young children. To begin, there is the issue of common language. The nomenclature of "teachers of young children," even within the profession, refers to unequally educated, unequally experienced, and unequally qualified individuals who may be called providers, teachers, and caregivers. Mitchell (2007) notes that "those outside our profession see it as two or three distinct professions: child care, preschool, and kindergarten/primary" (p. 6). She cites the U.S. Department of Labor's (DOL) occupation classification system in which child care workers fall into the major category of "Personal Care and Service Occupations" and preschool and kindergarten teachers fall into the category of "Education, Training, and Library Occupations." Her investigation of how the DOL actually describes the occupational work of child care workers and preschool teachers showed that the *work* is the same, though the preparation and compensation are different! Thus, in determining who makes up the workforce, multiple sources and occupational categories must be considered.

Brandon and Martinez-Beck (2006) consider these variations and more in estimating the size and characteristics of the paid early care and education workforce. They assert that the workforce for teachers of children under the age of 5 is large, representing approximately one-third of the paid instructional corps in the United States. Additionally they describe this section of the workforce as culturally diverse with lower educational qualifications than recommended. Public and private school (K–12) teachers represent 45 percent of paid instructors, although Brandon and Martinez-Beck do not specify K–3 separately (the remaining approximately 22 percent of paid instructors are at the postsecondary level). Thus, it would probably be fair to say that paid instructors for children from birth through third grade make up about 50 percent of the teaching workforce. The diversity of qualifications, education, and experience of this workforce is further complicated by the diversity of funding, settings, and governance of programs. One thing that is clear is that females dominate the profession, historically and currently, and as such, the profession struggles with inequity in wages, compensation, benefits, prestige, and the image of "women's work."

Although there are struggles associated with a female-dominated profession, it is also possible to consider the strengths of having a predominantly female profession. Osgood (2006) contends that professionalism, under the current regime of standardization, state regulation, and the demand for academic performance in the early years, is embedded in a masculine, managerialist perspective. She offers a critical perspective of the dominant construction of professionalism and expresses a feminist discourse perspective. She states that the language of feminist discourse defines professionalism in a way that is consistent with feminism: innovative, autonomous, collaborative, reflexive, wise/experienced, and collective. Osgood further stresses that governmental policies (standards, accountability, credentials, etc.) construct a teacher professionalism that controls the occupation. She urges practitioners to retain the intuitive, affective, and caring component of their work (Claxton, 1999).

ADULT LEARNER CHARACTERISTICS AND LEARNING THEORIES

Now that we have some clearer ideas about early childhood education as a profession, professional development categories, and a general overview of the workforce, we can begin to consider how adults learn and how this impacts the professional development that is offered to early childhood teachers from diverse backgrounds and teaching experiences. Malcolm Knowles, one of the best-known scholars of adult learning, is credited with popularizing the notion of *andragogy*, the art and science of helping adults learn in comparison to pedagogy (the art and science of teaching children). Knowles believed that adults learned differently from children and that this difference presents the basis for a distinctive field of inquiry.

Knowles's (1990) description of the adult learner includes the adult as self-directed; having a wealth of life experiences; possessing a great readiness to learn; voluntarily entering an educational activity with a life-centered, task-centered, or problem-centered orientation to learning; and possessing internal motivation. These attributes are advantageous for thinking about the professional development of adult teachers.

Long (1990) offers a critique of adult-learning theories, including that of Knowles, by noting that adults are variable in their behaviors and motivations and that it is erroneous to generalize about adult learners. Long also acknowledges that while all adult learners do not possess all of the characteristics described by Knowles, there is some benefit to identifying characteristics that pertain to adult learners. Thus, individual variation among adult learners is completely typical, though planning for groups of adult learners would benefit from consideration of these frequently shared attributes.

In addition to the characteristics of the adult learner, a number of theories of adult learning (behaviorist, cognitivist, humanist, social, and constructivist) are analyzed by Marquardt and Waddill (2004) for how they are utilized in professional development, particularly action learning. One could extrapolate from this that andragogy, like pedagogy, aligns with no one theoretical perspective that covers all aspects of development. Yet, Trotter (2006) is able to highlight the benefits of various theories for teacher professional development. Age and stage theory, cognitive theory, and functional theory provide useful frameworks for understanding adult development that can be considered in designing and implementing professional development.

Age Theory

Age theory states that people continue to learn throughout their lives, but that at different chronological ages they experience different problems and issues to which they react differently depending on their age. For example, age theorists believe that as teachers age they become more reflective about their lives and incorporate that reflection into decision making. Age theory considers that teachers in their late teens or early twenties will focus on independence-dependence issues, will think about fitting into the adult world, and will search for mentors. This suggests that staff development for this age group should provide clear definitions of what is expected, allowing for independence whenever possible, and offer opportunities for social activities. At this early-adult stage, it is very important not to encourage poor teachers to stay in the field. A proponent of age theory would view teachers in their early thirties quite differently. For example, these teachers are described as being stable and wanting to feel a sense of accomplishment. At the same time, they are interested in becoming their own person and are comfortable with interdependence. Meanwhile, family is a priority and time is limited. Thus, professional development for these teachers would consider career-family duality, acknowledge that social activities revolve around family, and recognize that some teachers may be returning to work or working for the first time and need support and mentors (Arin-Krupp, 1981).

Stage Theory

Stage theory promotes the notion that individuals go through life in stages instead of merely aging chronologically. The focus of stage theory is on the process of growing wiser rather than growing older. Stage theorists do not see knowledge as fixed, but rather as an evolving process. Piaget is recognized as the father of stage theorists for his work on the development of cognitive stages (Trotter, 2006). Also, the work of Erikson (emotional development) and Kohlberg (moral development) are clearly recognized as stage theories. While we tend to focus on the early stages of these pivotal theorists, Trotter also acknowledges Daloz for reviewing adult stage theorists' research overall into the following stages: preconventional (survival) to conventional (focused on fitting in) to postconventional (focused on thinking and evaluating).

Career Stages.   On a practical level, there are also career stages that adult learners experience that interface with stage theory of development. Lindstrom and Speck (2004) compiled a Career Stages and Developmental Needs of Professional Development. They surmise that the first career stage is the formative years (1–2 years) when teachers are learning the day-to-day operations of classroom and school. The second stage is the building years (3–5 years), when teachers develop confidence in their work and the multifaceted role of teaching. The third stage reflects the striving years (5–8+ years) when teachers develop professionally and achieve high job satisfaction. Additionally, they note that there are other issues that affect career stages and, consequently, professional development, such as crisis periods, when teachers burn out and need renewal; times when complacency sets in and innovation is low; career wind-down, when the teacher enjoys high status as a teacher without exerting much effort; and lastly, career end at retirement.

Katz's Stages of Teacher Development.   Katz (1972) wrote specifically about the developmental stages of preschool teachers' development and their training needs. Stage 1 is survival, which constitutes the first year or two in the profession when teachers need a high level of on-site support and technical assistance. Stage 2 is the consolidation stage, which builds upon the knowledge of the survival period to begin to differentiate tasks and skills to be mastered next; this lasts for approximately 1–3 years. Stage 3 is when teachers need renewal in the field and begin to ask what is new and who else they may learn from; this stage may overlap earlier stages and begin as early as the third or fourth year of teaching. Appropriate training might include conferences, professional associations, journals, films, and program visits. Stage 4, the final developmental stage, is that of maturity, when teachers come to terms with themselves as teachers. This may happen as early as the third year but others need 5 years or more. Training that teachers in this stage might enjoy most are seminars, institutes, courses, degree programs, books, journals, and conferences.

Cognitive Development Theory

Cognitive development theory centers on intellectual development. Adults move from concreteness to abstractness and from responding to external stimulation to internal understanding. Thus, in cognitive development theories, Trotter (2006) notes that veteran teachers, as compared to novice and midcareer teachers, were more likely to focus on self-affirmation than to look to externally generated achievements. She further notes that veteran teachers had survived changes and reform (and we would add, in many early childhood settings, poor compensation and benefits) and were still teaching, perhaps because of intrinsic satisfaction, in spite of the challenges like low prestige and increasing demands for children to perform academically.

Functional Theory

Functional theory posits that life experience is more significant than what a person learns in a book or workshop. Teachers, in view of their diverse backgrounds, should have individualized and self-directed professional development plans in their lifelong learning journey. Functional theory supports Knowles's (1990) view that adults prefer to plan their own educational paths and generally choose educational topics that they can apply directly to their own classrooms. Thus, attention to adult learner characteristics and adult learning theories may be helpful when considering the professional development of the early childhood educator. It is interesting to consider how or if attention was given to the learning theories of adults and teachers as we review the history of early childhood professional development.

HISTORY OF EARLY CHILDHOOD PROFESSIONAL DEVELOPMENT

Like today, those studying early childhood education in the early part of the 20th century did not have a common definition for who were the professionals in early childhood settings. Day nurseries (child care) were places where parents placed children for respite or custodial care, while nursery schools (preschools) served the purpose of providing learning experiences for young children (Whipple, 1929). Perhaps this was the beginning of the persistent division between early education and care over the last 80 years or so.

Training for early childhood professionals occurred in normal schools, colleges, and universities. Entrance requirements included an interest in young children, good health, scholastic excellence, a baccalaureate degree, and, in some cases, knowledge of psychology. The areas of study included child psychology, child hygiene, physical growth, educational measurements, clinical study, parent education, and curricula for young children. The programs had strong practical components with expectations that experiences with children would be closely supervised. The requisite personal characteristics (what we might now call dispositions) for nursery school teachers were listed under four categories: "personal adjustment to life, emotional control, social adjustment, and mental adjustment" (Whipple, 1929, p. 428).

These requirements may seem surprisingly rigorous. However, programs were preparing professionals to participate in the emerging field of child study, later to be called child development. The focus on this topic by the National Society for the Study of Education (NSSE) in its 28th *Yearbook* was just one of many pieces of literature from this time that elevated the value of child study because of what Sears (1975) deemed "external pressures broadly based on desires to better the health, the rearing, the education, and the legal and occupational treatment of children" (p. 3). We can infer from these writings that the professional development described was not applicable to the group that Whipple (1929) described as day nursery workers, so we do not have a full picture of professional development for teachers of young children. Likewise, we can also see that we have a long history of thinking separately about how we prepare professionals for "child care versus early education" rather than a unified system of "education and care."

We would be remiss if we did not note that, even from the beginning, the discussion about the professional development of teachers of young children is a discussion about the professional development of women. Both then and now, it is primarily women who comprise the workforce. And the history of their professional development exists within the context of our knowledge of women in society in general. As Finkelstein (1988) sees it,

> the role of women has been consistent. They have attempted to protect children by elevating motherhood, housekeeping, child rearing, and child nurture to a specialized moral status, and by equating professionalism with a capacity to discover the rules of child development and to provide good advice about how to promote it. (p. 11)

According to Finkelstein, women's commitments to the child advocate role in early childhood education created a pathway for women into academia to study and apply child development knowledge to the education of young children. Women like Lucy Sprague Mitchell, Anna Freud, Nancy Bayley, and others brought together the scientific study of children with applied practices in serving young children in higher education settings (Benham, 1985). Yet, Finkelstein (1988) notes, they did not manage to elevate the political or economic status of the field.

Need for Child Care During World War II

Services for young children and the professional development of those working with them in the 1940s and 1950s were influenced by the historical context of the nation and the world. With the advent of World War II, women who had been at home raising children were needed in the workforce. The U.S. government passed the Lanham Act in 1942 to help fund child care centers to accommodate the children of women employed in the war effort. Large child care operations such as the

Kaiser Centers in Portland, Oregon, were established to provide child care, often on a 24-hour basis, to the women workers needed for the war effort. The professionals employed in these 24-hour centers had degrees in child development. Hymes (1995) describes the radical shift in beliefs about what preparation was required to provide quality services for the young children of women working in the shipyards. In the planning and implementation of the programs, the notion that anyone could care for young children was quickly dispelled and the search for the very best staff, program, and facilities for these wartime child care centers was put in motion. The centers met the needs of this very special time in history. However, federal support for the centers disappeared after the war when these "model" centers were dismantled (Hymes, 1995).

Development of Child Study Laboratories

Evidence regarding early childhood professional preparation in the higher education system from the 1940s through the 1960s was documented in the case studies of five child study laboratory settings over 60 years (Benham, 1985). In particular, the Bank Street College of Education and the Merrill-Palmer Institute were actively engaged in preparing teachers for work with young children. Though the war and postwar years were lean ones for these institutions, they did seem to make their mark on early childhood teacher preparation.

Bank Street was intent on preparing teachers who connected theory with practice. In particular, the professional preparation was underpinned by those theories related to the mental health and ego development of the young child. The Merrill-Palmer Institute training focused on developmental knowledge of young children within the context of family (Benham, 1985). Both of these institutions placed a high premium on supervised field experiences, most often in their respective laboratory classrooms, as part of the training.

Though these are just two examples of the approaches used in preparing early childhood professionals, they demonstrate the continuing pattern of early childhood professional preparation in institutions of higher learning. Missing from much of the literature is any discussion of the preparation of those working in non-school early childhood settings or discussion of what we now refer to as in-service professional development for those on the job.

Creation of Head Start

With the advent of compensatory preschool education programs like Head Start in the 1960s, the field of early childhood education changed radically, and, consequently, so did early childhood professional preparation. Head Start was quickly set in motion in 1965 as part of the War on Poverty and many of the teachers serving in these early programs had little if any preparation to teach young children (Almy, 1988). In fact, the intention was to hire "indigenous non-professionals" to staff the programs (Peters, 1988).

Creation of CDA Credential

The need for more intentional preparation of professionals to work in Head Start and other programs for young children was answered by the then Office of Child Development and in 1971, the Child Development Associate (CDA) credential was created (Barbour, Peters, & Baptiste, 1995). The credential was the result of collaborative work by experts who identified competencies that they believed were necessary to work effectively with preschool age children. The nonprofit CDA Consortium was established to administer and oversee the credentialing system. It was the first successful national-level attempt at codifying what early childhood professionals should know and be able to do. It was intended to be a system that was comprehensive and flexible, one that could include higher education experiences if so desired. After administration of the program was moved out of the federal government, it went through several phases until it finally came under the direction of the independent, nonprofit organization known as the Council for Professional Recognition. Details regarding the content of this credential will be discussed later in the chapter.

During the 1980s, early childhood teacher education programs flourished around the country. The actual age ranges covered in university and college programs varied depending on the state teacher licensure structure. Likewise, the professional requirements for those working in nonschool early childhood programs varied with the individual state child care regulations; sometimes as little as a Graduate Equivalency Diploma (GED) was required. The CDA credential was voluntary, though heartily endorsed by the Head Start program. As Head Start began to increase the professional development requirements for its staff in the mid-1990s, the CDA credential became the first level of recognized professional development, with expectations that staff would continue on the path of formal preparation to achieve an associate degree, and finally a baccalaureate.

NAEYC's Influence

At about this time, the National Association for the Education of Young Children (NAEYC) began to use expert panels to create several kinds of standards. Among these were guidelines for early childhood teacher preparation (Bredekamp, 1994). The need for these guidelines came from those looking to professionalize the field. The development of standards was also one of the necessary conditions for the developing relationship with the National Council for the Accreditation of Teacher Education (NCATE; Hyson & Biggar, 2006). As one of the Specialized Professional Associations (SPA), NAEYC had to engage in the development and regular review and revision of standards for early childhood teacher education. Though these standards were part of the NCATE obligation, NAEYC was no stranger to the role of setting standards for teachers of young children, beginning with standards for nursery schools in 1929 (Hyson & Biggar, 2006). In the most recent revision approved in 2001, NAEYC made the shift to performance-based standards and clearly delineated what early childhood professionals at the associate, baccalaureate, and graduate levels need to know and be able to do (Hyson, 2003).

Since the early 1990s, much work has occurred within state departments of education, child care regulation agencies, and other organizations concerned with early care and education to develop viable systems of professional development. Inspired by Bredekamp and Willer's (1992) concept of a career lattice, as opposed to the linear notion of career ladder, state organizations began to explore ways that would welcome early childhood professionals from many different points in their professional career to enter and advance through a professional development pathway.

Themes in Early Childhood Professional Development

In summary, the history of early childhood professional development from the early part of the 20th century to the present day has several consistent themes. The first is that of bifurcated professional development. Those working in what we regard as school settings (e.g., laboratory schools, public school preschools, kindergartens, primary classrooms) are most likely to have participated in professional development delivered by an institution of higher learning. Those working in non-school settings (e.g., family child care, child care) are more likely to have little or no formal professional preparation. Head Start has been one exception, requiring more formal preparation, beginning with the CDA, as a way to ensure some external standard for professional development.

The second theme is that of child development knowledge as a staple of early childhood professional development. The child study movement established this trend and later professional development in both academic and nonacademic settings have included this as a mainstay.

The third and final theme evident here is the predominance of women in the early childhood workforce. Consequently, from the beginning the field has suffered from lack of political clout and lack of professional recognition. Whipple's comment from 1929 remains true today: "Since the preparation for nursery-school teaching is thus being offered almost universally upon a graduate level, a long period of preparation results, and this raises the problem of adequate salary compensation for students who have taken this long period of preparation" (Whipple, 1929, pp. 426–427).

WHAT SHOULD EARLY CHILDHOOD PROFESSIONALS KNOW AND BE ABLE TO DO?

What should be the content of professional development? What do early childhood educators need to know? There are no simple answers to these questions. It depends, as do most of our questions, on the kind of educational setting, on the age of the children served, and the auspices under which the program is sponsored. Yet there are particular areas of knowledge, skills, and dispositions that are named consistently in the literature on early childhood professional development. There are also persistent points of tension about the essential content and experiences that teachers should have: These include psychological emphasis versus academic content emphasis; intuitive content versus research-based content; and care versus education. At the center of these debates about content is the desire to prepare professionals who can create the best possible programs for young children and to ensure that they have the educational foundation they need to become lifelong learners.

Understanding of Child Development

Early accounts of early childhood teacher preparation (Hymes, 1995; Whipple, 1929) discussed the need for professionals to have a strong background in child development. This appears to be one of the constants in discussions about essential content for teachers of young children. More recently, the National Research Council's *Eager to Learn* report included the specific recommendation that "Education programs for teachers should provide them with a stronger and more specific foundational knowledge of the development of children's social and affective behavior, thinking, and language" (Bowman, Donovan, & Burns, 2001, p. 13). A similar recommendation appeared recently in the Foundation for Child Development's *Ready to Teach: Providing Children with the Teachers They Deserve* (2006). A panel of educators discussed what knowledge teachers of young children should have. They agreed that "knowledge of child development as a framework" for academic content and that the "context of cultural and linguistic diversity" are necessary (p. 4).

In Bredekamp and Copple's (1997) revision of NAEYC's position statement on developmentally appropriate practice, they describe three areas of knowledge that teachers of young children must master:

1. knowledge of typical or normative developmental sequences
2. knowledge of how one comes to identify and address individual developmental differences
3. knowledge of the social and cultural factors that might influence children's development

Critics have warned against viewing child development knowledge as a monolithic answer to curriculum rather than a reference point for understanding children (Charlesworth, 1998; Lubeck, 1998). Additional points of contention regarding how child development should be taught focus on issues of universality and consensus versus plurality and diversity (Charlesworth, 1998; Lubeck, 1998). In other words, do we need to have common beliefs and practices related to early care and education? Or is it best to focus on many approaches to educating young children that are sensitive to the great diversity among children and families? These points of intellectual discourse have raised questions and stimulated new thinking about the cultural content of professional development.

Content Addressed in Early Childhood Teacher Education Programs

Maxwell, Lim, and Early's (2006) report on early childhood teacher preparation offers a comprehensive look at programs that prepare individuals to work with children 5 years of age and younger. Though this is only a portion of the early childhood population, it is a useful snapshot of the content that is being addressed in early childhood professional development programs. Both 2-year (associate degree) and 4-year (baccalaureate) institutions were included in this study. There was an enormous range across the 1,179 participating institutions with regard to what and how much coursework was required. Eighteen different content areas were identified:

1. Education and care of infants and toddlers
2. Education and care of preschool-aged children
3. Education and care of young children with disabilities
4. Working with families
5. Working with children and families from diverse backgrounds
6. Working with bilingual children learning English as a second language
7. Assessment and/or observation of young children
8. Emergent literacy and literacy strategies
9. Numeracy and math for young children
10. Social and emotional development of young children
11. Physical health and motor development of young children
12. Classroom or behavioral management of young children
13. Early childhood program administration
14. Collaborating with professionals in other disciplines
15. Professional knowledge (e.g., confidentiality, ethics, code of conduct, etc.)
16. Adult learning and development
17. Leadership and advocacy
18. Research methods (Maxwell et al., 2006, pp. 12–13)

These authors make us aware of the range of recommended content and difficulty of preparing individuals to work across a broad age range.

In a recent policy brief from the Foundation for Child Development, Michael Sadowski (2006) presents recommendations for 10 components of core knowledge that all teachers of children birth through age 8 should have. Based both on professional association standards and research, Sadowski suggests that "rather than a discrete set of competencies, the elements of effective teaching outlined here point to an aligned set of standards, curriculum, instruction, and assessment both within and across developmental levels over the PK–3 continuum" (Sadowski, 2006, p. 1). The 10 areas of core knowledge are

1. Knowledge of child development
2. Methods for teaching diverse children
3. Use of multiple forms of assessment
4. Organization of learning environments
5. Curriculum design that helps children make connections
6. Strategic use of resources and technologies
7. Parent and family outreach
8. Professional collaboration and development
9. Reflection for enhanced teaching
10. Vertical alignment

NAEYC Standards for Professional Preparation

Since the mid-1990s, NAEYC has been the professional association defining early childhood teacher education standards for institutions of higher education. In the most recent iteration of the NAEYC standards for professional preparation, Hyson (2003) presents "consensus documents that rely for their credibility on the Association's members and other constituents within and beyond the field of early childhood education" (p. v). These documents provide guidance for everyone engaged in professional development of early childhood educators. The same five core standards apply to agencies providing training, individuals working on credentials such as the Child Development Associate, and institutions offering degrees (associate, baccalaureate, and advanced/graduate degrees). The standards "represent the early childhood field's best thinking about what young children need from teachers and other professionals if they are to develop and learn to their full potential" (Hyson, 2003, p. 9).

Professional preparation programs are expected to address all five standards in a comprehensive manner. The five individual standards are

1. Promoting child development and learning
2. Building family and community relationships
3. Observing, documenting, and assessing to support young children and families
4. Teaching and learning
   a. Connecting with children and families
   b. Using developmentally effective approaches

      c. Understanding the importance of each content area in young children's learning

  5. Becoming a professional

Though the standards are the same for each degree level, the expectations take into consideration the depth and breadth of experiences needed for each role. Each standard is accompanied by an explanation of its importance in the development of professionals, and has a set of rubrics that specify required levels of performance. The standards were constructed to allow for great flexibility in how professional preparation programs interpret and implement their training (complete standards are available online at www.naeyc.org/faculty/college.asp).

Putting the Content Together for Best Practice

The recommended content of early childhood teacher preparation appears to be relatively congruent across the literature with some differing opinions about particular emphases. In their volume of commissioned papers, Horm-Wingerd, Hyson, and Karp (2000) explored the state of the art of early childhood professional preparation at the preservice level in order to identify high-quality programs and make recommendations for the future of professional preparation for teachers of young children. Isenberg (2000) examined a number of programs and concluded that there were four major barriers to preparing teachers of young children: political, structural, institutional, and interpersonal. Political barriers include attempts by legislative bodies to mandate educational reform rather than allowing these changes coming from the profession. Another political barrier is the perceived absence of clear content requirements for training early childhood educators.

Structural barriers included low status of the profession, lack of uniformity regarding how early childhood is defined in terms of age range and services, few nationally recognized preparation programs, and difficulty in connecting the content of early childhood teacher preparation programs with the realities of the early childhood classroom. There are many institutional barriers to early childhood teacher preparation. The low status of early education in many universities often costs programs resources for enough faculty, supervision, and support for the desirable practice of interdisciplinary collaboration.

Finally, interpersonal barriers are noted. These have to do with how difficult it is to pull together the components of an exemplary early years teacher preparation program: interdisciplinary coursework, collaboratively taught courses, dynamic field experience and supervision, and funding for applied research to study the impact of programs. In other words, faculty must work intensively, collaboratively, and in a scholarly fashion. This can be discouraging if early childhood education and the work of the teacher educator are not valued or appropriately rewarded.

Isenberg (2000) also identified a number of exemplary early childhood teacher preparation programs. She chose them based on national recognition and their success in meeting national standards for accreditation. They were categorized by general features such as theoretical underpinnings (e.g., constructivist), primary focus (e.g., diversity, family), configuration (e.g., interdisciplinary), and program design (e.g., organization of course sequences). The comparison of these characteristics offers a glimpse into the diversity of approaches to teacher preparation. For instance, the program at George Mason University in northern Virginia emphasizes diversity in their "Unified Transformative Early Education Model (UTEEM) . . . which prepares students to teach children from birth through age 8 in inclusive, multicultural settings" (Isenberg, 2000, p. 31). In another example, Bank Street College of Education in New York City is presented as a program that emphasizes in-depth, intensive field experience across the program.

HOW AND WHERE DOES PROFESSIONAL DEVELOPMENT OCCUR?

Maxwell et al.'s (2006) discussion of the terms *education, training,* and *credentialing* described previously helps us define the various auspices of professional preparation. Less helpful are the distinctions made between *preservice* (i.e., preparation which occurs prior to employment in the field, often leading to a degree) and *inservice* (i.e., preparation that occurs while one is employed in an early childhood setting which may lead toward a credential, a degree, or certificate). Though these terms may not offer us clearly demarcated distinctions, they help to distinguish the differences among professional development experiences.

The fuzziness of these terms was noted as Maxwell et al. (2006) examined 13 articles regarding training published between 1988 and 2003. A wide range of approaches were described including traditional course-based instruction, media-based courses (Internet and television delivery), workshops, observations of programs for children, conference sessions, individual tutorials, and on-site supervision. Certainly, there is no good way to organize or compare these experiences since we have no clear way to know their purpose, duration, or timing. We find it more helpful to use the previously introduced terms *education, training,* and *credentialing* to examine different means and venues for professional development.

Education, as we have defined it, usually involves a pathway to a degree (vocational, associate, bachelor's, master's, doctoral). It most often takes place in an institution of higher learning. Many educational programs are monitored by accrediting organizations (e.g., state departments of education, systems of higher education, NCATE). Consequently, the program of study that is required for a person to receive the education degree offers some level of accountability and consistency to the process of professional education.

Though we have suggested that education is usually preservice professional preparation, this is not always so. For instance, a practicing teacher may seek a master's degree. Another example is the T.E.A.C.H. Early Childhood Project (Russell, 2006) designed for people who are employed in early education and care settings (confounding the distinction between pre- and in-service training). This program, in existence since 1990, was developed as a means of providing scholarship support and incentives for the early childhood workforce. The Program's

2005–2006 annual report indicates both the number of hours of education supported by the scholarships and increased levels of compensation in the 22 states involved in the program.

In recent years, there has been quite a bit of debate regarding whether it is necessary for those who work in early childhood settings to have education degrees. Certainly, those who are employed in public kindergarten and primary settings are required to have 4-year degrees as part of state teacher licensure structures. *Eager to Learn* (Bowman et al., 2001) reports on New Jersey's *Abbott* decision (Barnett, Tarr, Lamy, & Frede, 2002), and recommendations from the National Prekindergarten Center (National Prekindergarten Center, 2006), including recommendations for those employed in preschool settings to have a baccalaureate. The findings cited in these reports, based on examination of existing research, suggest that better-educated preschool teachers with specialized early years training are more effective than those without such training. They also found that preschool programs employing teachers with university degrees have children who demonstrate better academic achievement. These reports also note that better compensation is needed to hire and retain more effective teachers.

Training, or professional preparation that usually occurs outside of formal education settings (Maxwell et al., 2006), is typically for teachers already working in early childhood classrooms, and does not lead to an education degree. This kind of professional development consists of opportunities offered through many different venues (e.g., resource and referral agencies, state agencies, electronic media, and on-site by employers) which may or may not lead to any formal recognition. In-service training can involve many kinds of experiences. These are often provided for those who are employed in teaching positions but have not had prior formal educational experiences. This kind of training may or may not be regulated in a way that ensures quality and consistency, or requires demonstration of mastery. The impact of training is difficult to determine because it is not clearly defined (Tout, Zaslow, & Berry, 2006). However, there are some recommendations about what makes for high-quality training. According to Bowman (1990), "Effective in-service education [training] must be intensive and continuous, with opportunities to apply knowledge and receive individual feedback and mentoring in order to support improved teaching practices and positive outcomes for children" (p. 276).

King and Luebchow (2006), in a policy paper for the New America Foundation on teacher quality for pre-K–grade 3, make several comments regarding in-service training for early childhood educators. They state that it is generally believed that ongoing training will improve quality, but that the amount and type of in-service training needed to achieve this end has not been determined and is still up for debate. While most states require some in-service training for K–3 teachers to maintain licensure, it may be poorly monitored and clock hours completed often take precedence over content, quality, and types of activity.

Mentoring was shown to be valued by adult learners (Arin-Krupp, 1981) and an effective method for in-service training (King & Luebchow, 2006). Both informal and formal mentoring systems help early childhood teachers acclimate to teaching, help them learn teaching practices and school procedures, and provide moral support. At the K–3 level, formal and regulated mentoring programs for beginning teachers are available in a number of states, as well as informal networks of mentoring relationships. This formalized system is absent at the preschool level.

TAKING TRAINING AND EDUCATION TO A NEW LEVEL

The National Child Care Information Center (NCCIC), a service of the Child Care Bureau (now a part of the Office of Family Assistance in the U.S. Department of Health and Human Services Administration for Children and Families), has been a major force in supporting evolving state systems for early childhood professional development. They have developed a simplified framework depicting the elements of a professional development system for early care and education (see http://nccic.acf.hhs.gov/pubs/goodstart/pdsystem.html). These elements include funding, core professional knowledge, qualifications and credentials, quality assurance, and access and outreach. The metaphor of a tree, with funding as its roots and access and outreach as the leaves, demonstrates the interrelationship of these elements.

Issues regarding the education, training, and credentialing necessary for working with young children and families have motivated groups across the country to try to codify how individuals can engage in, and be recognized for, the work they do. One example of how states began to explore the early childhood professional development process as a continuous system is represented in the story of Ohio's journey. Kantor, Fernie, Scott, and Verzaro-O'Brien (2001) view this journey as growing out of the "educational reform across state agencies, across private and public sectors of the early childhood community, and across the types of institutions where professional development and teacher education takes place" (p. 157). They describe efforts to conceptualize the early childhood professional development process as a system rather than a series of discrete, unconnected experiences leading nowhere.

Dukakis and Bellm (2006) offer another state's example. They document the impact of the Comprehensive Approaches to Raising Educational Standards (CARES) in two California counties. This program provides money to early childhood personnel who make the commitment to increase their educational levels. In this case, the systems change focused on higher education institutions, exploring what and how communities can provide appropriate and accessible preparation.

Other states such as Utah, Alabama, Oklahoma, Wisconsin, Pennsylvania, Illinois, and Virginia, to name a few, provide descriptions of their state's version of career lattices (see http://nccic.acf.hhs.gov/pubs/goodstart/state-ece.pdf for a complete listing of state core knowledge and competencies). In each of these cases, the pathways to "professionalism" include education and training that is intended to prepare individuals who will provide high-quality services to children and families and who will be recognized for their expertise. The message in these efforts is that the professional development of teachers of young children should be a planned, intentional process that is worthy of organization, funding, and implementation.

The last, hard to define category of professional development, credentialing, refers to some formal recognition of professional development experiences. Teacher licensure in the early childhood age range varies from state to state, with some defining this credential for ages birth through 8, birth to 5, 5–8, and other configurations. The credential in most cases is a license to teach young children in public school settings. These particular credentials are governed by state departments of education. There is no national definition or set of requirements for the early childhood teaching credential.

Some early childhood credentials have emerged as states have created professional development systems in recent years. However, the requirement for these credentials and the recognition of them is quite variable and difficult to quantify across states.

There is, however, a widely known national credential in early childhood education—the Child Development Associate (CDA) credential. As previously mentioned, it arose from a need to recognize those in the field who did not hold an education degree. It was intended to acknowledge "a person who is able to meet the specific needs of children and who, with parents and other adults, works to nurture children's physical, social, emotional, and intellectual growth in a child development framework" (Council for Professional Recognition, 1997, p. 2). CDA training is based on competency goals and functional areas for both an infant/toddler endorsement and a preschool endorsement. While in some contexts the CDA credential involves informal training that would fall under the heading of in-service training, there is a component of formal education. The candidate must complete 120 clock hours to fulfill the CDA requirement.

As we review the literature, we see that there is little consistency in how the terms *preservice, in-service, education,* and *training* are used, making it very difficult to have common understanding of the impact and outcome of different forms of professional development. We have attempted to draw some reasonable conclusions from this morass in order to understand the present situation. A final note is that we should take heed of Karp's (2005) suggestion that we think about how we can link these various systems of training together so that there is a smooth, accessible means for individuals in the field to enter into professional development that has a clear pathway to recognition and reward.

WHAT PROFESSIONAL DEVELOPMENT WORKS?

Throughout this chapter we have attempted to draw on research about professional development practices. However, we know much more about the relationship of professional development to the quality of early childhood settings than we do about the actual impact on child outcomes. This takes us back to the question mentioned at the beginning of this chapter, of whether early childhood professional development has an impact on child outcomes.

In their introduction to *Critical Issues in Early Childhood Professional Development,* Zaslow and Martinez-Beck (2006) examine the strong relationship between the early childhood professional and the child as the central framework for discussions of quality and school readiness. The Good Start, Grow Smart initiative was begun in 2002 "as the early education reform companion of NCLB [No Child Left Behind]" (p. 2). The focus on the professional development of the early childhood workforce was seen as a means for improving learning and reducing the achievement gap. They note the gaps in our research to date: ". . . the research tends to stop at an examination of the relation of professional development to the quality of the early childhood environment, rather than asking whether professional development is related to children's development" (p. 12).

Tout, Zaslow, and Berry (2006) do a thorough job of sorting through the existing research for links between professional development and quality early childhood programs. They explore research on training and education and reach the following conclusions: (1) a relationship between more education (especially early childhood development) and higher-quality ECE programs and teacher-child interactions; (2) limitations of the research due to lack of identification of "thresholds" of preparation; and (3) a lack of deliberate and intentional study of training and its relationship to quality. Though their review of the research literature focused on professional preparation of those working with children younger than school age, they provide a comprehensive look at the body of research to date and suggest a need to "go beyond the 'more is better' approach to provide specific information on the thresholds of early childhood professional development that are linked to quality" (p. 105). They applaud the newest approach to research on professional development that looks at the content of both education and training. Snow (2006), in the same volume, challenges others to complete the logical connection between professional preparation and child outcomes by engaging in the necessary empirical investigations to see if, in fact, early childhood professional development improves the quality of early childhood environments which then results in improved child outcomes. He notes that the same dearth of research evidence appears in the K–12 professional development literature as well.

In recent years, the *Journal of Teacher Education* has focused on the research base for teacher education in general. In one meta-analysis, the conclusions were that there was little in the way of definitive research that could offer insight into the process (Wilson, Floden, & Ferrini-Mundy, 2002). The authors offer only one strong inference which suggests that a teacher's knowledge of subject matter seems to be a critical factor in defining quality in public school settings.

King and Luebchow's (2006) review of a K–3 study and a prekindergarten study showed consistent findings across these two systems. They cite a 2000 longitudinal study by the U.S. Department of Education (DOE) which indicates that professional development was found to be most valuable when it was ongoing, on-site, and involved observation and evaluation of actual teacher-child interaction and classroom activities. Additionally, it was found that if evaluation was conducted by a teacher in the same subject, grade, or school, the experience was even more beneficial. In contrast, ineffective professional development occurred when it was a one-time workshop, without follow-up, and without feedback on actual classroom implementation. This study reflected practices of K–3 teachers, but resonated with findings of the High/Scope Educational Research Foundation's 1999 study that showed effective in-service training for prekindergarten requires sustained, on-site activities combined with mentoring and feedback.

In summary, what we know about what works is somewhat limited at present. We hope that in the future we will see multiple approaches to investigating early childhood professional development that provide more clarity in definitions and language, and more focus on the nature of teacher-child interactions and their impact on child outcomes. Pianta's (2006) approach in which he proposes "connecting professional development, resources, evaluation, and curriculum to child outcomes and teacher outcomes through observational assessment of classroom processes" (p. 241) will help make the necessary connections.

THE NEED FOR A SYSTEMS APPROACH

Naomi Karp (2005) ties much of the thinking about early childhood professional development together as she argues that we are failing to prepare early childhood professionals as part of the contiguous educational system and that we have neglected to take into account the research, rigor, and respect that should be the foundation of professional preparation (p. 171).

In regard to research, she suggests a need to rely more heavily on the research that we have about child development and the impact of educational settings and teachers in those settings. But she affirms the need to make the connections between what we have learned in research and the policies we create around professional preparation. Karp also notes the dearth of doctoral-level professionals adequately prepared to engage in the next generation of research that would inform our professional development practices. Additionally, she points to the tension between the demands for research and practice facing those preparing to work in early childhood teacher preparation in higher education.

Rigor, according to Karp, refers to the sticky issue of uneven qualifications for professionals across the range of settings in which young children are served. This, she asserts, creates inconsistencies across state higher education systems, and across the nation. Rigor also addresses the inadequate preparation that many teachers have to work with all children, regardless of ability, culture, or language.

Karp's final point addresses the need for all early childhood educators to receive the respect and compensation that they deserve. This need has been a quiet echo throughout the history of early childhood professional development.

WHAT ARE THE IMPLICATIONS?

Throughout this chapter we repeatedly struggled with the lack of common language for professional development and related topics within the early childhood field. Clarification and consistency in terminology will make conversations, comparisons, decisions, and results easier to understand and more beneficial for children and their teachers.

We believe that the research about how adult development occurs can be useful in planning and supporting professional development. Research indicates that teachers do go through professional stages of development and that attention to these stages will be beneficial when considering professional development.

Based on our review of adult learner characteristics and adult learning theories, we believe that teachers should be given freedom to form their own professional development plans. Allowing teachers this latitude in professional development will increase their success, improve classroom practices, benefit children's development, and increase the likelihood of teachers becoming lifelong learners.

A serious commitment to study the connections between professional development and practice, as well as between practice and children's growth, development, and learning, needs to be undertaken by early childhood researchers. Professional development should result in a better-educated workforce. Improvements should be recognized not only by increased stature of early childhood professionals but also by increased compensation, benefits, and career lattices appropriate to the work of those in the field.

Due to the needs and sometimes geographical location of current students, distance education (online courses and interactive videoconferencing) is generating interest in various parts of the country and world. Yet there remains considerable debate among faculty and higher education regarding effectiveness, quality, ability to ascertain dispositions and other teacher qualities, and connection to children in early care and schools via distance education. It may be the wave of the future and a viable way to offer professional development in the workplace and/or the home, but it needs to be approached with caution.

The content area of child development knowledge as a staple for early childhood professional development has a long-standing prominance in our field. This needs to continue to be critically accepted as we teach and care for diverse, multilingual, and multiethnic children in a variety of settings.

In all settings, attention needs to be paid to the content and quality of in-service hours in addition to meeting the required clock hours and/or educational degrees.

Optimal in-service trainings for pre-K–3 teachers would show collaboration on effective practices, standards, curriculum, and assessment across the age span. This collaboration would be an indication that we are addressing our infant/toddler, preschool, and primary-age children regardless of the programs and systems of affiliation. This should improve the overall early childhood experience including transition between ages and grades of various educational and care programs.

CONCLUSIONS

In this chapter, we have explored the issues of relevance in the professional development of teachers of young children, noting the muddy quagmire that our lack of precision in language and concepts has created. We have also looked back at the history of this phenomenon and noted 20-year-old conversations about similar issues. We have acknowledged the serious attention given to these issues by the authors writing in the 1988 volume edited by Spodek, Saracho, and Peters. And yet, we have circled back to these issues in the equally informative 2006 volume edited by Zaslow and Martinez-Beck, looking at some of the very same concerns. It is our hope that we have identified a set of questions that helps move us forward.

We hope that these questions push us in new and productive directions so that, 20 years from now, we will be having different dialogues about professional development for early childhood educators.

REFERENCES

Almy, M. (1988). The early childhood educator revisited. In B. Spodek, O. N. Saracho, & D. L. Peters (Eds.), *Professionalism and the early childhood practitioner* (pp. 48-55). New York: Teachers College Press.

Arin-Krupp, J. (1981). *Adult development: Implications for staff development.* Manchester, CT: Adult Development and Learning.

Barbour, N. E., Peters, D. L., & Baptiste, N. (1995). The child development associate credential program. In S. Reifel (Ed.), *Advances in early education and day care* (Vol. 7, pp. 61–93). Greenwich, CT: JAI Press.

Barnett, W. S. (2003). Better teachers, better preschools: Student achievement linked to teacher qualifications. *Preschool Policy Matters, 2.*

Barnett, W. S., Tarr, J., Esposito-Lamy, C., & Frede, E. (2002). *Fragile lives, shattered dreams: A report on implementation of preschool education in New Jersey's Abbott districts.* New Brunswick, NJ: CEER, Rutgers University.

Benham, N. B. (1985). *An historical analysis of child study settings for policy relevant research potential.* Unpublished doctoral dissertation. University Park: Pennsylvania State University.

Bowman, B. T. (1990). Issues in recruitment, selection, and retention of early childhood teachers. In B. Spodek & O. N. Saracho (Eds.), *Early childhood teacher preparation* (pp. 153–175). New York: Teachers College Press.

Bowman, B. T., Donovan, M. S., & Burns, M. S. (Eds.). (2001). *Eager to learn: Educating our preschoolers.* Washington, DC: National Academy Press.

Brandon, R. & Martinez-Beck, I. (2006). Estimating the size and characteristics of the United States early care and education workforce. In M. Zaslow & I. Martinez-Beck (Eds.), *Critical issues in early childhood professional development* (pp. 49–76). Baltimore: Brookes.

Bredekamp, S. (1994). The competence of entry-level early childhood teachers: Teachers as learners. In S. Goffin & D. Day (Eds.), *New perspectives in early childhood teacher education* (pp. 59–63). New York: Teachers College Press.

Bredekamp, S., & Copple, C. (Eds.). (1997). *Developmentally appropriate practice in early childhood programs* (rev. ed.). Washington, DC: NAEYC.

Bredekamp, S., & Willer, B. (1992). Of ladders and lattices, cores and cones: Conceptualizing an early childhood professional development system. *Young Children, 47*(3), 47–50.

Charlesworth, R. (1998). Developmentally appropriate practice is for everyone. *Childhood Education, 74*(5), 274–282.

Charlesworth, R. (1998). Response to Sally Lubeck's "Is DAP for everyone?" *Childhood Education, 74*(5), 293–298.

Claxton, G. (1999). The anatomy of intuition. In T. Atkinson & G. Claxton (Eds.), *The intuitive practitioner: On the value of not always knowing what one is doing.* Buckingham, UK: Open University Press.

Council for Professional Recognition. (1997). *The child development associate assessment system and competency standards.* Washington, DC: Council for Professional Recognition.

Dukakis, K., & Bellm, D. (2006). Clearing a career path: Lessons from two communities in promoting higher education access for the early care and education workforce; Alameda and Santa Clara counties, California (pp. 1–34). Retrieved July 26, 2007, from www.iir.berkeley.edu/cscce/pdf/clearing_careerpath06.pdf

Early, D. M., & Winton, P. J. (2001). Preparing the workforce: Early childhood teacher preparation at 2- and 4-year institutions of higher education. *Early Childhood Research Quarterly, 16*(3), 285–306.

Feiman-Nemser, S. (2001). From preparation to practice: Designing a continuum to strengthen and sustain teaching. *Teachers College Record, 103*(6), 1013–1055.

Finkelstein, B. (1988). The revolt against selfishness: Women and the dilemmas of professionalism in early childhood education. In B. Spodek, O. N. Saracho, & D. L. Peters (Eds.), *Professionalism and the early childhood practitioner* (pp. 10–28). New York: Teachers College Press.

Foundation for Child Development. (2006). *Ready to teach: Providing children with the teachers they deserve.* New York: Foundation for Child Development. Retrieved June 19, 2007, from www.fcd-us.org/pdfs/2006AnnualReport.pdf

Galbraith, M. W. (1990). (Ed.). *Adult learning methods.* Malabar, FL: Krieger.

Horm-Wingerd, D., Hyson, M., & Karp, N. (2000). Introduction. In National Institute on Early Childhood Research and Education & U.S. Department of Education & Office of Educational Research and Improvement (Eds.), *New teachers for a new century: The future of early childhood professional preparation* (pp. 1–13). Washington, DC: U.S. Department of Education.

Hymes, J. L. (1995). The Kaiser child service centers—50 years later: Some memories and lessons. *Journal of Education, 177*(3), 23–38.

Hyson, M. (Ed.). (2003). *Preparing early childhood professionals: NAEYC's standards for programs.* Washington, DC: NAEYC.

Hyson, M., & Biggar, H. (2006). NAEYC's standards for early childhood professional preparation: Getting from here to there. In M. Zaslow & I. Martinez-Beck (Eds.), *Critical issues in early childhood professional development* (pp. 283–308). Baltimore: Brookes.

Isenberg, J. (2000). The state of the art in early childhood professional preparation. In National Institute on Early Childhood Research and Education & U.S. Department of Education & Office of Educational Research and Improvement (Eds.), *New teachers for a new century: The future of early childhood professional preparation* (pp. 17–58). Washington, DC: U.S. Department of Education.

Kantor, R., Fernie, D. E., Scott, J. A., & Verazo-O'Brien, M. (2000). Career pathways in Ohio's early childhood professional community: Linking systems of preparation inside and outside of higher education. In National Institute on Early Childhood Research and Education & U.S. Department of Education & Office of Educational Research and Improvement (Eds.), *New teachers for a new century: The future of early childhood professional preparation* (pp. 155–190). Washington, DC: U.S. Department of Education.

Karp, N. (2006). Designing models for professional development at the local, state, and national levels. In M. Zaslow & I. Martinez-Beck (Eds.), *Critical issues in early childhood professional development* (pp. 225–230). Baltimore: Brookes.

Karp, N. (2005). Building a new early childhood professional development system based on the 3 Rs: Research, rigor, and respect. *Journal of Early Childhood Teacher Education, 26,* 171–178.

Katz, L. (1972). Developmental stages of preschool teachers. *The Elementary School Journal, 73*(1), 50–54.

Katz, L. (1988). Where is early childhood education as a profession? In B. Spodek, O. N. Saracho, & D. L. Peters (Eds.), *Professionalism and the early childhood practitioner* (pp. 75–83). New York: Teachers College Press.

King, J., & Luebchow, L. (2006). *Teacher quality in grades PK–3: Challenges and options.* New America Foundation: Early Education Initiative Issue Brief #4. Retrieved May 23, 2007, from www.newamerica.net/publications/policy/teacher_quality_in_grades_pk_3_challenges_and_options

Knowles, M. S. (1990). *The adult learner: A neglected species* (4th ed.). Houston, TX: Gulf Publishing.

Lindstrom, P., & Speck, M. (2004). *The principal as professional development leader.* Thousand Oaks, CA: Corwin Press.

Lobman, C., Ryan, S., & McLaughlin, J. (2006). *Toward a unified system of early childhood teacher education and professional development: Conversations with stakeholders.* Available online at www.fcd-us.org/usr_doc/TowardAUnifiedSystem.pdf

Long, H. (1990). Understanding adult learners. In Galbraith, M. W. (Ed.), *Adult learning methods* (pp. 23–37). Malabar, FL: Krieger.

Lubeck, S. (1998a). Is DAP for everyone? *Childhood Education, 74*(5), 283–292.

Lubeck, S. (1998b). Is DAP for everyone? A response. *Childhood Education, 74*(5), 299–301.

Marquardt, M., & Waddill, D. (2004). The power of learning in action learning: A conceptual analysis of how the five schools of adult learning theories are incorporated within the practice of action learning. *Action Learning: Research and Practice, 1*(2), 185–202.

Maxwell, K. L., Field, C. C., & Clifford, R. M. (2006). Defining and measuring professional development in early childhood research. In M. Zaslow & I. Martinez-Beck (Eds.), *Critical issues in early childhood professional development* (pp. 21–48). Baltimore: Brookes.

Maxwell, K. L., Lim, C-I., & Early, D. M. (2006). *Early childhood teacher preparation programs in the United*

States: National report. Chapel Hill: University of North Carolina, FPG Child Development Institute.

McMullen, M. B., Alat, K., Buldu, M., & Lash, M. (2004). A snapshot of NAEYC's preschool professionals through the lens of quality. *Young Children, 59*(2), 87–92.

Mitchell, A. (2007). Developing our profession. *Young Children, 62* (4), 6–7.

National Child Care Information Center (NCCIC). (2006). State core knowledge and/or competencies. Retrieved July 31, 2007, from http://nccic.acf.hhs.gov/pubs/goodstart/state-ece.html

National Prekindergarten Center. (2006). *Early childhood teacher preparation programs in the United States.* Chapel Hill, NC: Frank Porter Graham Child Development Institute. Available online at www.fpg.unc.edu/~npc/pdfs/national_report.pdf

Osgood, J. (2006). Professionalism and performativity: The feminist challenge facing early years practitioners. *Early Years, 26* (2), 187–199.

Pianta, R. (2006). Standardized observation and professional development: A focus on individualized implementation and practices. In M. Zaslow & I. Martinez-Beck (Eds.), *Critical issues in early childhood professional development* (pp. 231–254). Baltimore: Brookes.

Peters, D. L. (1988). The child development associate credential. In B. Spodek, O. N. Saracho, & D. L. Peters (Eds.), *Professionalism and the early childhood practitioner* (pp. 93–104). New York: Teachers College Press.

Powell, D. R., & Dunn, L. (1990). Non-baccalaureate teacher education in early childhood education. In B. Spodek & O. N. Saracho (Eds.), *Early childhood teacher preparation* (pp. 45–66). New York: Teachers College Press.

Russell, S. (2006). *Early childhood workforce investments: A national strategy, 2005–2006 Annual Program Report.* T.E.A.C.H. Early Childhood. North Carolina: Child Care Services Association. Retrieved June 10, 2007, from www.childcareservices.org/_downloads/TEACH_annual_report_06.pdf

Ryan, S., & Ackerman, D. J. (2004). *Creating a qualified preschool teaching workforce. Part I: Getting qualified: A report on the efforts of preschool teachers in New Jersey's Abbott districts to improve qualifications.* New Brunswick, NJ: NIEER. Available online at http://nieer.org/resources/research/GettingQualified.pdf

Sadowski, M. (October, 2006). Core knowledge for PK–3 teaching: Ten components of effective instruction. Foundation for Child Development Policy Brief: *Advancing Pre-K,* 5. New York: Foundation for Child Development. Retrieved July 16, 2007, from www.fed-us.org/resources/resources_show.htm?doc_id=42123

Sears, R. R., (1975). Your ancients revisited. In E. M. Hetherington (Ed.), *Review of child development research* (Vol. 5, pp. 1–73). Chicago: University of Chicago Press.

Snow, K. (2006). Completing the model: Connecting early child care worker professional development with child outcomes. In M. Zaslow & I. Martinez-Beck (Eds.), *Critical issues in early childhood professional development* (pp. 137–140). Baltimore: Brookes.

Spodek, B., & Saracho, O. N. (1990). Preparing early childhood teachers. In B. Spodek & O. N. Saracho (Eds.), *Early childhood teacher preparation* (pp. 23–44). New York: Teachers College Press.

Spodek, B., Saracho, O. N., & Peters, D. L. (1988). Professionalism, semiprofessionalism, and craftsmanship. In B. Spodek, O. N. Saracho, & D. L. Peters (Eds.), *Professionalism and the early childhood practitioner* (pp. 3–9). New York: Teachers College Press.

Tout, K., Zaslow, M., & Berry, D. (2006). Quality and qualifications: Links between professional development and quality in early care and education settings. In M. Zaslow & I. Martinez-Beck (Eds.), *Critical issues in early childhood professional development* (pp. 77–110). Baltimore: Brookes.

Trotter, Y. (2006). Adult learning theories: Impacting professional development programs. *The Delta Kappa Gamma Bulletin, 72*(2), 8–13.

Whipple, G. M. (Ed.). (1929). Preschool and parental education. *The twenty-eighth yearbook of the National Society for the Study of Education, Volume 28* (Parts I and II). Bloomington, IN: Public School Publishing Company.

Wilson, S. M., Floden, R. E., & Ferrini-Mundy, J. (2002). Teacher preparation research: An insider's view from the outside. *Journal of Teacher Education, 53*(3), 190–204.

Zaslow, M., & Martinez-Beck, I. (Eds.). (2006). *Critical issues in early childhood professional development.* Baltimore: Brookes.

Zinn, L. M. (1990). Identifying your philosophical orientation. In M. W. Galbraith (Ed.), *Adult learning methods.* Malabar, FL: Krieger.

WHAT DO EARLY CHILDHOOD EDUCATORS NEED TO KNOW AND DO TO WORK IN URBAN SETTINGS?

Frances O'Connell Rust
Erikson Institute

Before you criticize someone, walk a mile in her moccasins. Then when you do criticize that person, you'll be a mile away and have her moccasins.

—Grey Owl

Walking in someone else's shoes is hard work—especially hard when the shoes are too small—but this is exactly what we must learn to do as educators and particularly as early childhood educators. While none of us might envision ourselves ever criticizing a little child or withholding needed support and guidance or failing to recognize her emerging know-how, we are likely to do so inadvertently and unintentionally by not taking the time to know the children in our care, by not learning to walk in their shoes. This chapter is designed to help teachers prepare to teach children in urban settings—children who may be from cultures that are not theirs, who may be from ways of knowing that are shaped by languages they may not speak, who may be from families that are very different from the ones in which they grew up.

This chapter is written for early childhood educators who currently, or may in the future, teach in an urban setting. There are two key understandings that undergird this chapter. The first is that learning to teach in urban environments is synonymous with multicultural education. The diversity of our school systems is such that even if you have grown up in a big city, and even if you plan to teach in the schools that you went to, things will have changed, and you will be coming back to those settings with new understandings and wearing the mantle of power if you are coming back as a professional. There will be new families with new languages, new ways of understanding child rearing and education, new sets of needs. There will be new political, economic, and social constraints that will affect you and the children and families in your care. Thus, to prepare yourself well to teach in urban settings, you must become a teacher who embraces multicultural education, which Banks (1993) defines as a *"total school reform* effort designed to increase education equity for a range of cultural, ethnic, and economic groups" (p. 6).

The second major understanding fundamental to this chapter is that preparing oneself to be an excellent early childhood educator in urban settings is essentially preparing oneself to be an "effective teacher for all children and to participate in the realization of inclusive conceptions of schooling" (NCREL, 2007, p. 3). There is no one, easy way to become an urban educator. There are, however, ways of preparing yourself to undertake this vital work and these are what I have tried to address in this chapter.

TEACHING AND LEARNING IN URBAN SETTINGS

The research on learning to teach in urban schools generally begins with a definition of urban education. So, the first thing that the reader might want to do is to unpack the word *urban*. What images does that word conjure? Many schools? Under-resourced schools? Hundreds, thousands of children? Many (maybe most) learners who are not native English speakers? Children of poverty? A different environment from that in which you grew up? Any of these? What else? It is important to think through the ways in which one uses this word and the meanings one attaches to it.

Something that you might try is making a list of all the answers that you can think of to these questions. Keep adding to your list over a period of days or weeks. Then, put it away, and revisit it after you have been teaching a while longer. See if any of your ideas and impressions have changed. Note the changes and write a little about how and why your ideas have changed. Keep the list, consult it again, and, again, note changes. Hopefully, there will be some changes that show you how you are growing as a teacher.

What Is Urban Education?

Often, we associate urban schools with diverse languages and with poverty. However, schools everywhere, even in the most affluent suburbs, are experiencing influxes of students whose native languages are not English. Many rural and inner-ring schools serve children of poverty and many of these schools are under-resourced. In fact, as the National Center for Children in Poverty (2001, as cited in Horm, 2003) makes clear, "America's children are more likely to live in poverty than Americans in any other age group" (Horm, p. 232).

So what makes urban schools different? Are they different? Peterman (2005) holds that they are and that the differences between schools in rural, inner-ring, and suburban districts have to do with *intensity* and *complexity* and with "interactions of these characteristics atop faltering physical, economic, and political infrastructures that present distinct challenges for new teachers" (p. 53). Urban schools, she writes, are often "bureaucratic and contradictory," "under-resourced," "poverty-bound," "multicultural, multiracial, multienthnic, and multilinguistic" (pp. 53–55). It is the intensity and complexity of these "multi . . ." urban environments, as well as the impact of poverty and racism on children and their families, that those who would go into these settings can and must prepare themselves to learn about and from (Carter & Goodwin, 1994; Cochran-Smith, 1995; Fennimore, 2001; Gonzalez, Moll, & Amanti, 2005; Goodwin, 1997; Irvine, 1991; Ladson-Billings, 1994; Weiner, 1994, 2002).

Knowing Yourself to Know Others

The complexity of most cities is such that even if you have grown up there, the impact of time and change will inevitably mean that others, and particularly young children, will have experiences of the place that are likely to be quite different from your own. Teaching all children well requires what Howard (1999) describes as the "inner and outer work of social transformation" (p. 6). Thus, coming to know yourself as well as the city and the community in which you will be teaching is a critical factor in preparing yourself as a thoughtful early childhood educator. It is the essential first step in developing an understanding of any new setting and particularly one in which language, ways of interacting, even ways of talking about, interacting with, and knowing about the world—any one or all of these—are different from those in which you may feel comfortable (Buck & Sylvester, 2005; Carter & Goodwin, 1994; Delpit, 1995; Goodwin, 2002; Howard, 1999).

Exploring Culture.   Culture has many meanings. As Nieto (1999) writes, "it is complex and intricate . . . it cannot be reduced to holidays, foods, or dances, although these are, of course, elements of culture" (p. 48). She describes culture as

> the ever-changing values, traditions, social and political relationships, and world
> view created, shared, and transformed by a group of people bound together by
> a combination of factors that can include a common history, geographic location,
> language, social class, and religion. (p. 48)

Culture, Nieto writes, "is dynamic, active, changing, always on the move" (p. 50). "It does not exist outside of human beings" (p. 50) and "when people of different backgrounds come in contact with one another, . . . change is to be expected" (p. 50). Nieto also describes culture as "multifaceted," "embedded in context," "socially constructed," "learned," and "dialectical" (pp. 49–59).

Each of us has a culture that has shaped us; each of us functions within many cultures. Exploring our own culture and its impact on the ways in which we respond to others and to events in our lives is something that is not done once and forgotten. It is the hallmark of a lifelong learner, and it is part of an ongoing inquiry stance that should guide our work as teachers of young children. For it is in recognizing and working with what Gonzalez, Moll, and Amanti (2005) describe as "funds of knowledge"—our own and those of the children we teach and their families—that we as teachers can make the most powerful and long-lasting connections with our students.

So how do we do this? Maxine Greene has long held that "We teach who we are." Thus, self-knowledge is a critical first step to becoming an effective educator and taking that step begins with telling our own stories. These stories provide a window for each of us about our own assumptions and particularly our often tacitly held beliefs about privilege (McIntosh, 1989), power (Delpit, 1995; Fennimore, 2001; Fruchter, 2007), and race (Buck & Sylvester, 2005; Carter & Goodwin, 1994; Cochran-Smith, 1994; Delpit & Dowdy, 2002). As well, stories enable us as teachers to articulate and examine our concerns and fears about going into urban schools.

Uncovering Assumptions

Stories of self enable an internal dialogue about beliefs and assumptions. When shared in the relative safety of a community of learners, they can be powerful catalysts for inquiry and learning. Goodwin (1997) used her students' stories as a way to assess the impact of the multicultural curricula of the Preservice Program in Childhood Education at Teachers College, Columbia University. What she discovered was that her students' stories about incidents in their lives were more powerful influences on their actions than her course and other courses in her program. She found that, in general, her students were drawing on one of two major narratives: the narrative of white privilege and the narrative of power, race, and class.

White Privilege.   Because the majority of teachers at all levels are middle-class white women, McIntosh's (1989) article "White Privilege: Unpacking the Invisible Knapsack" is used frequently in teacher education programs to raise preservice students' awareness of the privileges they enjoy by virtue of their class, race, and gender. Among these are assumptions of safety, goodwill, and freedom from humiliation in most everyday situations. Cochran-Smith (1995), Goodwin (2002), Delpit (1995), and others have used teachers' narratives and student journals to illustrate the extent to which the notion of "white privilege" shapes action and undergirds understanding. Piercing the bubble of unawareness is an essential part of preparation for urban teaching. As Howard (1999) has written,

> Too often, we place White teachers in multicultural settings and expect them to behave in ways that are not consistent with their own life experiences, socialization patterns, world views, and levels of racial identity development. Too often, we expect White teachers to be what they have not learned to be, namely, multiculturally competent people. (4)

If you have not read McIntosh's (1989) article, it might be helpful for you to read it. You might also read Gloria Ladson-Billings' (1994) book *Dreamkeepers* and Vivian Gussen Paley's (1979) *White Teacher*. Both of these are stories about teaching in urban settings written by teachers who were working very hard to understand their own cultures as well as those of their students. The books are quite different, which makes them interesting to read together, and they may help you to think through McIntosh's concept of white privilege. It might also be useful to you to find a couple of classmates who will also read these pieces with you so that you can discuss them together.

Power, Race, and Class.   Power in our society is intimately connected to race and class, and, as McIntosh's (1989) essay suggests, assumptions of privilege. It shows in the ways in which schools are organized (Fruchter, 2007; Oakes & Lipton, 2002; Orfield & Lee, 2005), the acceptance of language (Delpit & Dowdy, 2002), the availability of resources (Anyon, 1997; Delpit, 1995; Fruchter, 2007), the expectations of teachers (and society in general) for their students (Bowman, 1994; Fennimore, 2001; Goodwin, 1997), and the stature of public education in urban environments (Fruchter, 2007). And, as difficult as the awareness of white privilege is, awareness of inequities in schooling, efforts to understand the ways in which race and class intersect with power, the embrace of social justice—taking steps like these toward a principled stance as an educator is even more difficult. Goodwin (1997), Oakes and Lipton (2002), Rust (2002), and others suggest that this is not a short-lived undertaking. In the remainder of this chapter, you will learn about ways in which some thoughtful scholars are working to help new teachers do this difficult work.

EXPLORING FUNDS OF KNOWLEDGE

If you have begun to make a list or to write a narrative that incorporates your responses to the questions posed earlier, you will have taken the first steps toward developing ways of learning about your students, their families, and the communities in which they reside. Like you, they all have stories and, like you, they are the heroes of their stories. They are the ones who know best about their own strengths and ways of knowing. Learning how to elicit and hear these stories is best accomplished in three ways: through actual hands-on experience and interaction, through reading, and through reflection.

Situating Teaching and Learning in the Community

Gonzalez, Moll, and Amanti (2005) write, "We feel instruction must be linked to students' lives, and the details of effective pedagogy should be linked to local histories and community contexts. . . . Our perspective is that learning does not take place just 'between the ears,' but is eminently a social process" (p. ix). They go on to document ways in which teachers can learn about their students' lives outside of school so as to make their lives in school more relevant and their learning there more powerful. One of the major ways in which they do this is to visit children in their homes and communities.

Such inquiry on the part of teachers and others into children's lives outside of school has precedent in the work of anthropologists and ethnographers but it is different, too, in that it has special relevance for teachers and can be conducted by teachers as a form of action research or by teachers in concert with anthropologists, which is the way in which Moll, Amanti, Neff, and Gonzalez (2005) have shaped their work together.

When Moll and his colleagues visit children's families at home, they work systematically to develop relationships with the families, to learn from them about their children's interests, and to hear the families' stories so as to more effectively make a match between children's out-of-school and in-school lives. "This approach," they write, "is particularly important in dealing with students whose households are usually viewed as being 'poor,' not only economically but in terms of the quality of experiences for the child" (p. 71). These researchers are deeply interested in "how families develop social networks that interconnect them with their social environments (most importantly with other households), and how these social relationships facilitate the development and exchange of resources—including knowledge, skills, and labor—that enhance the households' ability to survive or thrive" (p. 73).

While Gonzalez, Moll, and Amanti (2005) and their colleagues have worked largely in the southwestern United States with U.S.-Mexican families, other similar investigations reported on in their book have taken place in communities throughout the country including New York City, Philadelphia, and South Florida. Such relationships are particularly relevant for early childhood educators whose traditional alliances with families and communities are among the major hallmarks of early childhood practice.

When I first started teaching in New York City, I was required by my school to make "home visits" to each of my students. I still remember each of those children in my first class. I remember where they lived, what I learned from them and their families, and how powerful those visits were in helping me work effectively with those children and their families during our year together. I went on from there to start two schools. My colleagues and I always visited each of our students before school began, and each time, we learned so much. We made connections with children that enabled a closeness that a visit to the teacher when she is setting up the classroom doesn't bring. Their space in their home is special and my being there was, even to most 3-year-olds, unforgettable. But I also learned about the families of my students. I can remember my surprise that women whose husbands went off to work at 5 or 5:30 in the morning had formed telephone support systems such that they had several hours of conversation with friends early in the morning before their little children, my students, woke up!

This was clearly one of those support systems that Gonzalez, Moll, and Amanti (2005) write about and it is discoveries like mine and like those that Gonzalez and colleagues write about that will enable you, as a new teacher, to develop relationships with families, with colleagues, and with other professionals that are both reciprocal and interactive. "This redefined relationship," write Gonzalez, Moll, Tenery, et al. (2005), "is that of colleagues, mutually engaged in refining methodology, interpretation, and practice" (p. 93).

However, gaining familiarity with any community takes time. One cannot know in one's first week or first year what immersion in the community over time provides, but being seen as interested, learning the rhythm and cadence of a place, getting a sense of how families live together can go a long way—even during one's first year—toward developing the trusting relationship between home and school that enables children to thrive. This is critically important in large urban areas where the pace of life outside of the classroom, the numbers of people, the pressures of daily life—the sheer complexity of the surroundings—often means that young children and their families will feel stressed and even alienated. In these settings, teachers can and often do provide critical support to young children and their families. Teachers' ability to bridge institutional and family cultures has everything to do with their understanding of and sensitivity to the children in their care.

Knowing Children

Knowing children, understanding their needs, and determining how to best guide their social, emotional, and cognitive development—these are the responsibilities of all teachers but especially of early childhood educators. In large part, the specialness of the early childhood educators' role has to do with the fact of our focus on very young children and the importance of engagement with families. As the work of Piaget and Vygotsky has made clear, from birth on, young children are actively engaged in making sense of their world (Bransford, Brown, & Cocking, 2000). In this process, children draw on both their native predisposition for learning and on others in their immediate surroundings. Parents, siblings, family, and the environment itself—all are teachers. Their effectiveness is determined by their ability to synchronize instruction with the child's developing capabilities. This is what Vygotsky (1978) described as operating in the child's "zone of proximal development," that is, "a bandwidth of competence that learners can navigate with aid from a supportive context including the assistance of others" (Bransford, Brown, & Cocking, 2000, p. 80). For teachers, developing a sense of the areas of conceptual development a child is pursuing and providing the appropriate scaffolding is critical.

Barbara Bowman (1994) writes, "Rules of development are the same for all children, but social contexts shape children's development into different configurations" (p. 236). She pushes teachers toward meshing the knowledge that they will have developed of the child, family, and community with knowledge of how children learn. This is incredibly complex work. Too often, as Bowman points out, the result is "a mismatch between what children know and can do and what is expected of them by schools that are organized to accommodate and reinforce white, middle-class values, beliefs, and behaviors" (p. 234).

This mismatch occurs in large measure because teachers have not done the deep work of knowing themselves and knowing the families and communities of their students. Hence, assumptions are made about children's readiness, competence, and potential. "Schooling," writes Bowman (1994), "is both individual and cultural. . . . schools should strive for a better understanding of the balance between a child's potential growth and the socializing practices of the child's home environment" (p. 236).

Bowman (1994) advocates that "Our thinking about the education of poor and minority children needs to begin not from an assumption of deficiency but from a recognition of cultural competence" (p. 236), which means that these are

> children whose acquisition of skills and knowledge matches the social demands of
> the communities in which they live. . . . The universal accomplishments of early

> childhood include establishing mutually satisfying social relationships with family and friends, learning language, organizing perceptions, beginning to think in terms of categories, imagining, and creating. These accomplishments are learned in a similar fashion by all children and occur in predictable sequences across various cultural and racial groups. (p. 237)

Skillful teachers shape their interactions with children by drawing on the child's developmental competence.

IMPLICATIONS FOR EARLY CHILDHOOD EDUCATORS

Learning how to recognize and support development in context as Bowman (1994) describes it should be an essential part of teacher preparation. In this section, we will look at ways in which various teacher education programs have been shaped to support the work of beginning teachers in urban settings. As you read about these programs, think about how they are similar to and different from the program that you attended. Think, too, about ways in which you have taken advantage of opportunities to learn about the children and families with whom you are interacting as a student or teacher.

We are learning that to prepare new teachers well for urban schools, experiential learning really counts. One or two courses cannot equip teachers to "assume . . . responsibility for becoming familiar with students' developmental, individual, and cultural characteristics so that they can diagnose the causes of children's behavior . . . [and ask] parents and community members to be informants regarding their children's knowledge and skills" (Bowman, 1994, p. 239). What is needed is a holistic approach that embraces an entire program and provides teachers with ample opportunities to explore their own cultural and racial identities as well as those of their students.

Examples from Teacher Education Programs

There are numerous examples in the research literature of ways in which various teacher education programs have worked to bring the concepts of social justice and educational equity into urban teacher preparation programs. However, most of the research that has been done on the preparation of teachers for urban settings focuses on teacher education for elementary and secondary schools. Early childhood is rarely addressed in these studies; it is rarely focused on in the major journals that relate to teacher education; and early childhood journals yield scant research on the preparation of teachers and caregivers specifically for urban settings. So, what I have done in this section is try to highlight findings from the research on teacher preparation for urban elementary and secondary schools and then to extrapolate from that to implications for early childhood.

Community Investigations at the High School Level. Medina, Morrone, and Anderson (2005), whose work at the Indiana University School of Education in

Indianapolis focuses on the preparation of teachers for secondary classrooms in an urban environment, begin their program with preservice teachers by engaging them in explorations of their own cultures. As they write,

> before preservice teachers can be expected to understand and address issues of diversity in the classroom, teacher education programs must provide these future educators with authentic opportunities for critical examination of their own entrenched values, belief systems, and cultural heritage. (p. 207)

Medina and colleagues (2005) shape their work with preservice teachers around a block of courses that engages their students working in teams in introspective, dialogic, and collaborative activities. When they introduce theories of psychosocial development, they ask their students to "prepare a poster that describes their view of the adolescent experience in American society" (p. 208). This poster preparation is followed by a simulation in which students take roles in different tribes that help them confront issues of race and gender, by journal writing using specific prompts, and by a deep reading of Kozol's *Amazing Grace* (1995) that is accompanied by extensive research on community assets—the funds of knowledge on which Gonzalez, Moll, and Amanti (2005) focus.

The students canvas the neighborhood of their school: housing, common areas, transportation, service centers, stores, race and ethnicity, religion, politics, media, and community personality; conduct an examination of written documents and interviews with key persons living or working within the community (planning in advance and making appointments); and prepare a written report as a PowerPoint presentation. When their students finish with these projects, Medina, Morrone, and Anderson (2005) write, "The majority of our students reported that their experiences in the Diversity and Learning block changed the way they define social justice. [Those experiences] provided the opportunity for critical reflection on their own views of teaching and social justice" (p. 209). And, when they went back to their posters of adolescent learning, they found that there were many ways of expanding their understanding and knowledge by using the material from the field investigations. These took them far beyond their own memories of adolescence.

Buck and Sylvester (2005) employ a similar strategy with their students in the University of Pennsylvania's Master's Program in Elementary Education. Like Medina and colleagues (2005), they focus on initial courses in their program and on a neighborhood investigation—here, two integrated summer courses, "Social Studies Methods" and "School and Society," that students take simultaneously. Students in the courses engage in an "investigative assignment" in which they "complete a study of the neighborhood that surrounds the school where they will student teach and, on the basis of that study, develop social studies curricula centered on a community-based fund of knowledge" (p. 216).

Other programs that work in similar ways and have a similar commitment to preparing teachers as advocates for social justice and equality of educational opportunity in urban schools include Center X at UCLA (Oakes & Lipton, 2002), Alverno College (Zeichner, 2000), and Mills College (Kroll et al., 2005). While these models seem to focus out, they begin by focusing preservice students inward and challenge them to continually compare and reflect on what they are seeing and learning relative to their own lived experience, for it is in doing so that tacit assumptions about race, gender, and class begin to emerge.

Each of these programs situates and embeds this important discussion across the entire program; they do not hold it to one or two courses. The faculty act in concert with commitment to a shared vision of quality teacher preparation. The programs have established strong working relationships with schools that take student-teachers' experience of urban schools far beyond a typical exposure to culturally diverse students. These are genuine partnerships that have been developed over time, that are perceived as mutually beneficial, and that are monitored constantly to maintain transparency and trust.

Learning to Teach to Enhance Learning in Specific Areas.   In a recent article, Cusumano, Armstrong, Cohen, and Todd (2006) describe preparing 29 Head Start teachers and day care personnel (some with coaches) to use research-based instructional strategies for literacy development. They taught these teachers a specific set of activities that required them to focus on children's emerging skills in the areas of picture naming, alliteration, and rhyming and measured the progress of the 271 students with whom these teachers interacted. What they show is that reading to children is simply not enough—particularly children who are not getting the academically oriented language environment that is the privilege of many middle-class children. What is required are teachers who know how to capitalize on what children know and can anticipate emerging skills.

The message for new teachers here is that you will need to learn how to teach the skills that children need to be literate and you need to be able to recognize these skills as they are emerging. The same is true for mathematics, science, and even for social skills. Focusing early childhood teachers toward thoughtful, high-quality instruction in the variety of areas that constitute the curriculum of early childhood is an essential aspect of urban teacher preparation. In combination with knowledge of how to work effectively with parents and community, it is one that could have the powerful effect of significantly narrowing the achievement gap.

WHAT DO EARLY CHILDHOOD EDUCATORS IN URBAN SETTINGS NEED TO KNOW AND BE ABLE TO DO?

Peterman (2005) writes that teachers of children in urban schools must be "creative problem solvers," "resourceful," "resilient and resistant," and "advocates for children, their parents, and their communities" (pp. 56–57). Early childhood educators in urban environments must embody all of these qualities with conviction and depth as so often they are the major advocates for young children and their families.

Young children in urban environments need the adults in their lives, especially their teachers, to know them and work from their strengths. Bowman (1994) writes,

> Children do not learn equally well from all adults. They learn best from adults who make an investment in them and in their learning. They learn best from adults who

are consistent and reliable figures in their lives. They learn best from adults who are able to present themselves in ways that children interpret as dependable and caring. (p. 240)

If you want to be the teacher that Bowman is writing about, you will need to prepare yourself so that you can serve as that critical link between the child's first teachers (their parents) and all of those who will follow. This is a high calling and is particularly important in areas where young children do not have all that is required to be successful in today's schools. Use this time of preparation as an opportunity to walk in others' shoes. By doing so, you will enable many young children to successfully take the critical first steps in their academic journeys.

REFERENCES

Anyon, J. (1997). *Ghetto schooling: A political economy of urban educational reform.* New York: Teachers College Press.

Banks, J. A. (1993). Multicultural education: Characteristics and goals. In J. A. Banks & C. A. M. Banks (Eds.), *Multicultural education: Issues and perspectives* (2nd ed., pp. 3–28). Boston: Allyn & Bacon.

Bowman, B. T. (1994). The challenge of diversity. *Phi Delta Kappan, 76,* 234–238.

Bransford, J. D., Brown, A. L., & Cocking, R. R. (Eds.). (2000). *How people learn: Brain, mind, experience, and school.* Washington, DC: National Academy of Sciences.

Buck, P., & Sylvester, P. S. (2005). Preservice teachers enter urban communities: Coupling funds of knowledge research and critical pedagogy in teacher education. In N. Gonzalez, L. C. Moll, & C. Amanti (Eds.), *Funds of knowledge. Theorizing practices in households, communities, and classrooms* (pp. 213–232). Mahwah, NJ: Erlbaum.

Carter, R. T., & Goodwin, A. L. (1994). Racial identity and education. In L. Darling-Hammond (Ed.), *Review of research in education* (Vol. 20, pp. 291–336). Washington, DC: American Educational Research Association.

Cochran-Smith, M. (1995). Uncertain allies: Understanding the boundaries of race and teaching. *Harvard Educational Review, 65*(4), 541–570.

Cusumano, D. L., Armstrong, K., Cohen, R., & Todd, M. (2006). Indirect impact: How early childhood educator training and coaching impacted the acquisition of literacy skills in preschool students. *Journal of Early Childhood Teacher Education, 27*(4), 363–378.

Delpit, L. (1995). *Other people's children.* New York: New Press.

Delpit, L., & Dowdy, J. K. (Eds.). (2002). *The skin that we speak: Thoughts on language and culture in the classroom.* New York: New Press.

Fennimore, B. S. (2001). Historical white resistance to equity in public education: A challenge to white teacher educators. In S. H. King & L. A. Castenell (Eds.), *Racism and racial inequality: Implications for teacher education* (pp. 43–50). Washington, DC: American Association of Colleges of Teacher Education.

Fruchter, N. (2007). *Urban schools, public will: Making education work for all children.* New York: Teachers College Press.

Gonzalez, N., Moll, L. C., & Amanti, C. (Eds.). (2005). *Funds of knowledge: Theorizing practices in households, communities, and classrooms.* Mahwah, NJ: Erlbaum.

Gonzalez, N., Moll, L., Tenery, M. F, Rivera, A., Rendon, P., Gonzales, R., & Amanti, C. (2005). Funds of knowledge for teaching in Latino households. In N. Gonzalez, L. C. Moll, & C. Amanti (Eds.), *Funds of knowledge. Theorizing practices in households, communities, and classrooms* (pp. 89–111). Mahwah, NJ: Erlbaum.

Goodwin, A. L. (1997). Multicultural stories: Preservice teachers' conceptions of and responses to issues of diversity. *Urban Education, 32*(1), 117–145.

Horm, D. M. (2003). Preparing early childhood educators to work in diverse urban settings. *Teachers College Record, 105*(2), 226–244.

Howard, G. R. (1999). *We can't teach what we don't know: White teachers, multiracial schools.* New York: Teachers College Press.

Irvine, J. J. (1991). *Black students and school failure.* New York: Praeger.

Kozol, J. (1995). *Amazing grace. The lives of children and the conscience of a nation.* New York: Crown.

Kroll, L., Cossey, R., Donahue, D. M., Galguera, T., LaBoskey, V. K., Richert, A. E., Tucher, P. (2005). *Teaching as principled practice: Managing complexity for social justice.* Thousand Oaks, CA: Sage.

Ladson-Billings, G. (1994). *The dreamkeepers.* San Francisco: Jossey-Bass.

McIntosh, P. (1989). White privilege: Unpacking the invisible knapsack. *Peace and Freedom, 49,* 10–12.

Medina, M. A., Morrone, A. S., & Anderson, J. A. (2005). Promoting social justice in an urban secondary teacher education program. *The Clearing House, 78*(5), 207–212.

Moll, L., Amanti, C., Neff, D., & Gonzalez, N. (2005). Funds of knowledge for teaching: Using a qualitative approach to connect homes and classrooms. In N. Gonzalez, L. C. Moll, & C. Amanti (Eds.), *Funds of knowledge. Theorizing practices in households, communities, and classrooms* (pp. 71–87). Mahwah, NJ: Erlbaum.

NCREL. (2007). *Critical issue: Preparing teachers for diversity.* North Central Regional Educational Laboratory—Learning Points Associates. Retrieved August 16, 2007, from www.ncrel.org/sdrs/areas/issues/educatrs/presrvce/pe300.htm

Nieto, S. (1998). From claiming hegemony to sharing space: Creating community in multicultural courses. In R. Chavez & J. O'Donnell (Eds.), *Speaking the unpleasant: The politics of (non)engagement in the multicultural education terrain* (pp. 16–31). Albany: State University of New York Press.

Nieto, S. (1999). *The light in their eyes: Creating multicultural learning communities.* New York: Teachers College Press.

Oakes, J., & Lipton, M. (2002). *Teaching to change the world* (2nd ed.). Columbus, OH: McGraw-Hill.

Orfield, G., & Lee, C. (2005). *Why segregation matters: Poverty and education inequality.* Cambridge, MA: Harvard University, Civil Rights Project.

Paley, V. G. (1979, 1989, 2000). *White teacher.* Cambridge, MA: Harvard University Press.

Peterman, F. P. (2005). Design principles for urban teacher assessment systems. In F. P. Peterman (Ed.), *Designing performance assessment systems for urban teacher preparation.* Mahwah, NJ: Erlbaum.

Rust, F. O'C. (2002). Professional conversations: New teachers explore teaching through conversation, story, and narrative. In N. Lyons & V. K. LaBoskey (Eds.), *Narrative interpretation and response: Teacher educators' stories.* New York: Teachers College Press.

Vygotsky, L. (1978). *Mind in society: The development of higher psychological processes.* Cambridge, MA: Harvard University Press.

Weiner, L. (1994). *Preparing teachers for urban schools: Lessons from thirty years of school reform.* New York: Teachers College Press.

Weiner, L. (2002). Evidence and inquiry in teacher education: What's needed for urban schools. *Journal of Teacher Education, 53*(3), 254–261.

Zeichner, K. (2000). Preparation in the undergraduate years. Alverno College. In L. Darling-Hammond (Ed.), *Studies of excellence in teacher education* (pp. 1–66). New York: National Commission on Teaching and America's Future.

CHAPTER 9

Professionalism and Ethics in Early Care and Education

Nancy Freeman
University of South Carolina

Stephanie Feeney
University of Hawaii

This chapter addresses two broad and interrelated topics—professionalism and ethics in early care and education. The first section explores what it means to be a profession. In it we consider how caring for and educating young children measures up as a profession and identify some of the advantages and disadvantages of professional status. The second part addresses the moral dimensions of working with young children, and in particular the role of ethics in professional practice. It identifies what early childhood educators need to know and be able to do to behave ethically in their work and considers how the early childhood field can support teachers and other caregivers to adhere to moral standards in their work.

Both of these topics, the status of early childhood on the professionalism continuum and the implications of practitioners' reliance on standards of ethical practice, will affect children, families, early childhood educators, and the field of early care and education now and into the future. Informed leaders and advocates should consider the implications of these subjects as they plan for that future.

Note: Thanks to Kerrie L. Welsh for her careful review and feedback.

WHAT IS A PROFESSION? WHERE DOES EARLY CHILDHOOD EDUCATION LIE ON THE CONTINUUM OF PROFESSIONALISM?[1]

Early childhood education is generally considered to be an "emerging" profession. It is not like the "paradigm professions" such as law and medicine, whose practitioners must complete prolonged programs of postsecondary education; whose contribution to society is unquestioned; and whose practitioners are usually accorded significant pay, power, and prestige. Nor are early childhood educators unskilled workers, such as day laborers or short-order cooks, who enter the workplace with little prior training or specialized knowledge and whose contribution to the workplace is not unique. The degree to which an occupation is considered to be a "profession" reflects its position along the professionalism continuum that has doctors and lawyers at one end and unskilled workers at the other. Below we identify characteristics of a profession and consider how early childhood education measures up when these criteria that have been identified by scholars who study professions are applied. In addition, as we examine the nature of professionalism and the movement to professionalize the early childhood field, we consider costs and benefits that will accompany a movement toward professional status.

Criteria for Determining if an Occupation Is a Profession

To understand where early childhood lies on the professionalism continuum we will consider how it meets eight of the criteria that are frequently used to define a profession.

1. *Professionals possess specialized knowledge.* They acquire this knowledge and skill in its application by following a course of *prolonged training.* Professional practice is not a precise set of easily learned behaviors applied by rote. Professional practice is characterized, instead, as behavior that is based on a firm foundation in the principles of the field and its recommended practices. Professionals make decisions and engage in professional practice by relying on their knowledge and expertise.

For many years, child development was considered the primary knowledge base of early care and education. Current research on the development of the brain has bolstered the conviction that the early years are of tremendous importance and have a great impact on later development and learning. In addition to their continuing reliance on the knowledge base related to children's growth, development, and learning, early childhood educators are now doing a better job articulating their own unique core knowledge related to the design of learning environments

---

1. Versions of this discussion have been published in *Young Children* and *Child Care Information Exchange.* See N. K. Freeman, and S. Feeney (2006) and S. Feeney, and N. K. Freeman (2002).

for young children, the use of appropriate strategies for guiding children's behavior, the planning and implementation of developmentally appropriate instructional and assessment practices, and the creation and maintenance of supportive and collaborative relationships with families. At this time the field of early care and education is working toward a more fully defined claim on a specialized body of knowledge and professional expertise.

Professions such as medicine and law require practitioners to earn undergraduate and gradate degrees and to pass rigorous examinations before entering practice. For many reasons related to the history and status of early care and education, entry into the field is not so closely controlled. One explanation is the fact that there is no recognized professional organization to play this gatekeeping role, as do the American Medical Association (AMA) and American Bar Association (ABA). Another explanation is the fact that eligibility to enter the field is determined on a state-by-state basis by licensing and regulatory agencies. Another explanation is the long-standing belief that caring for children is "women's work" and can be done by anyone.

Child care licensing often requires minimal training for those employed in settings serving children from birth through the preschool years. Some states stipulate only that teachers should have earned a high school diploma. Others require some specialized training, but it can be as little as 120 clock hours (NARA/NCCIC, 2006). As has been described in other chapters in this book, there are currently a number of efforts under way to require lead teachers in centers supported by public monies to hold a bachelor's degree in early childhood education or a related field.

State departments of education establish credentialing requirements for teachers who work with young children in public schools. There is wide variation, however, in how states define the early childhood years and in the requirements they establish for early childhood certification (Fields & Mitchell, 2007). Early childhood teachers who work in public schools are typically required to hold at least a bachelor's degree in education or a related field and to have completed an in-depth student teaching experience. There is, however, little agreement among states regarding the required coursework and experience specifically related to children from birth to age 8.

2. *Professions have rigorous requirements for entry into professional training and training is delivered in accredited institutions.* A number of early care and education's unique characteristics have prevented the field from enforcing rigid requirements for entry. First, we must consider the source of funding for early childhood programs. While the majority of 5- through 8-year-olds are served in state-run public elementary schools, most preschool education is supported in whole or in part by the fees or tuition paid directly by families. Realities of the marketplace mean it is usually impossible to generate enough revenue through fees and tuition to offer teachers professional wages and benefits, like health insurance and employer-supported retirement plans. As a result of these low salaries and the lack of benefits, many early care and education programs are able to attract only minimally trained personnel.

In addition, the field has always supported an early childhood career ladder (sometime called a lattice to suggest that it is not completely linear) and differentiated staffing patterns that make a place for caregivers with varied levels of specialized knowledge and expertise. That means that even though lead teachers might be required to have earned a bachelor's degree, entry-level opportunities remain for teaching assistants with very limited prior specialized training. The early childhood career ladder/lattice supports on-the-job training that offers practitioners opportunities to increase their skills and move up to positions requiring increased knowledge and expertise.

In addition to supporting a comprehensive career ladder, the field of early care and education has always appreciated how important it is for children to have teachers and caregivers who come from their community and share their culture and ethnicity.

We have found that striking a balance between efforts to increase educational requirements for early childhood practitioners while maintaining our time-honored commitment to inclusiveness and diversity is one of the biggest challenges facing early childhood today. This is a dilemma because on one hand early childhood advocates decry child care regulations that allow untrained or minimally qualified workers to care for children, claiming these minimal regulations demonstrate that the public fails to understand the difference between a babysitter and a trained early childhood educator. But, on the other hand, we realize we must be careful not to raise the educational bar for entrance so high that we create barriers discouraging practitioners from underrepresented populations from entering the field.

Finally, while certified teachers are generally graduates of accredited teacher preparation programs that easily satisfy this criterion of professionalism, child care providers' training is often a catch-as-catch-can arrangement. Their professional development might be delivered on-site by their program director or may include sessions offered at local early childhood conferences, or child care providers may participate in other trainings designed to help them meet their state's annual training requirement. Much of this training lacks cohesiveness. It certainly could not be described as the kind of systematic approach to professional development that could earn accreditation.

These are some of the reasons the field has never established rigorous requirements for entry and has not been able to ensure the quality of professional education and training available to the early care and education workforce.

3. *Members of a profession have agreed-upon standards of practice that guide them as they carry out their duties and meet their professional obligations.* There are three kinds of standards of practice that apply to working with young children. The first addresses how teachers of young children interact with their students, the second addresses what young children are expected to know and be able to do, and the third establishes levels of excellence for programs serving young children and those that prepare the early care and education workforce.

NAEYC's influential position statement on *developmentally appropriate practice* (DAP) is an example of the first kind of standard (NAEYC, 1996). It describes constructivist teaching strategies that actively involve young children with the people and things in their environment. DAP can be viewed as a first step toward creating standards of practice for the early childhood field.

States' content standards, which describe what children are expected to know and be able to do during the early years of schooling, are an example of the second type of standards. Most states now have early learning standards for children prior to entrance to the formal school system, and kindergarten through third-grade standards as a part of required K–12 standards. These standards are typically based on content standards developed by professional organizations such as the National Council for Teachers of English (NCTE), the National Council for Teachers of Mathematics (NCTM), the National Council for the Social Studies (NCSS), and the National Science Teachers Association (NSTA). (See Chapter 12 for more information about early learning standards.)

Federal *Good Start, Grow Smart Learning Standards* (GSGS) also fit into this category. They align expectations for what 3- and 4-year-olds are accomplishing in the areas of early literacy and mathematics with what they will be expected to have mastered when they enter public school as 5-year-olds. Some states have also developed *infant and toddler early learning guidelines* that provide a continuum of standards reaching from birth, through the early years, into elementary school and beyond.

The third kind of standards applies to programs. NAEYC has developed performance standards both for programs serving children and for institutions preparing teachers and caregivers to work with them. In 1985, NAEYC launched its voluntary accreditation system for school- and center-based programs serving young children. As the public's understanding of the importance of quality programming has grown, the number of NAEYC-accredited centers has increased. That accreditation system was revised in 2005. These new standards require extensive documentation and raise the bar, over time, on educational requirements for program administrators and teaching personnel (NAEYC, 2005a).

NAEYC has also addressed postsecondary teacher preparation since the 1980s, identifying what students graduating from associate, bachelor's, and advanced (master's and doctoral) degree programs in early childhood education should know and be able to do. The National Council for the Accreditation of Teacher Education (NCATE) awards accreditation to 4-year institutions that document their ability to meet these NAEYC standards. In 2006, NAEYC launched a program accreditation system for institutions that award associate degrees in early childhood education. Now NAEYC's accreditation programs address the preparation of teachers throughout their postsecondary professional preparation.

It is clear from this proliferation of standards relating to early care and education that the field is moving toward greater professionalism in the area of standards of practice—though in a somewhat piecemeal fashion. Some see the expectation that children, teachers, and programs meet standards as a positive development and evidence of the field's growing professionalism. Others fear that the standards movement represents a businessman's approach to education. They warn that it is built on the assumption that standardized "inputs" will create standardized results to ensure that all children are "ready" for school success. They warn that the trend to standardize children's school experiences ignores the cultural differences that enrich our pluralistic society and are designed to make parents question the goals and dreams they have for their children. These critics believe an overemphasis on standards stifles teachers' creativity and narrows the curriculum. Additional concerns center on standards-based assessments. When a school's success is measured by students' performance on high-stakes tests, teachers have an incentive to address discrete academic goals, like phonemic awareness, rather than provide experiences that invite engagement, challenge children intellectually, and provide opportunities to build meaningful understandings (Frost, 2007; Fuller, 2007; Katz, 2007).

Questions about the role standards should play in shaping early childhood practice are prompting important debates that are likely to shape the course of the field's journey toward increased professionalism in years to come.

4. *A profession has a commitment to meeting a significant societal need.* Early childhood educators have long known that they meet a significant societal need. They enhance children's growth, development, and learning; contribute to families' well-being; provide services that benefit parents' employers; and contribute to the financial health of the larger society. The recent growth in state-funded pre-K initiatives points to a growing appreciation for the contribution quality early childhood education makes to children, families, and society (Doctors, 2007).

But the fact remains that the patchwork system of for-profit, nonprofit, and publicly supported services for infants, toddlers, and preschoolers demonstrates that policy makers are not yet unanimous in their appreciation for the contribution early childhood education makes to the common good, nor in their commitment to support the care and education of children before they reach school age (Kagan & Cohen, 1999). When there is public support for making quality programs accessible to all young children whose families want to avail themselves of these services, and when early childhood educators' compensation is commensurate with their education and training, the field will have fully met this criterion of professionalism.

5. *Professionals are altruistic and service-oriented rather than profit-oriented. Their primary goal is to meet the clients' needs.* The criteria that call on professionals to be altruistic and service-oriented, rather than profit-oriented, are perhaps the easiest for early childhood educators to satisfy. This is the area in which we shine! It is safe to say early childhood educators are seldom, if ever, motivated by the expectation that they will realize substantial financial gain. In fact, they are known for putting the interests and needs of the children in their care before their own, almost to a fault. The salaries of many teachers of young children fall well below those earned by similarly qualified workers in other professions (Center for the Child Care Workforce, 2004), and the contributions of loyal, undercompensated employees have been shown to subsidize the programs they serve (Cost, Quality, & Outcomes, 1995).

The struggle to ensure worthy wages that compensate early childhood educators fairly for the important work they do is a focus of many advocacy efforts.

6. *Professionals provide an indispensable service and are recognized as the only group in the society who can perform its function.* Professionals in a given field are generally recognized by society as indispensable because they are the only individuals who

can perform a particular service. Doctors and lawyers easily satisfy these criteria. They, by law, have a monopoly on the important services they provide. Early childhood educators are not the only ones who care for children, however; parents, relatives, and babysitters can all play this role.

The field of early care and education is justified in taking the position that trained early childhood educators are the only group in our society with special expertise in supporting children's development and learning in out-of-home group settings. Gaining the public's respect for the unique services we provide and the specialized knowledge upon which our work is based is among our most pressing needs. As our field considers its place on the continuum of professionalism, these remain very serious issues.

7.   *A profession is characterized by autonomy—it has internal control over the quality of the services it offers and it regulates itself.* Members of professions control entry into their ranks and the quality of the services offered by their peers. Early childhood education is not yet doing this. Most early childhood programs serving children 4 years of age and younger are licensed by social workers employed in a state agency such as a department of human services. Teachers of children from 5 to 8 years old typically work in public schools where policies are created by states' boards of education which rarely include anyone with specialized knowledge in early childhood education. In fact, they are often led by individuals with no specialized expertise in education.

The early care and education field can move toward greater autonomy by encouraging these overseeing agencies to include experts in early childhood education when creating applicable regulations and policies. Additionally, early care and education leaders can claim increased autonomy for the field by participating in the political process through advocacy and activism, and in the future the field may achieve full responsibility for determining the policies impacting the programs that serve young children. A positive sign is that some professional initiatives, like 2- and 4-year teacher education guidelines and standards for accreditation of quality programs, have been developed by NAEYC, an association for early childhood educators, with extensive input from members of the field.

8.   *A profession has a code of ethics that spells out its obligations to society.* Since a profession may be the only group allowed to perform a particular societal function, it is important that the public have confidence that the members of the profession will behave morally and serve the public good.

A profession declares its commitment to moral conduct through its code of ethics—an agreed-upon document that spells out practitioners' obligations to society. A code of ethics, based on the field's collective and systematic reflections about its values and responsibilities, is an essential roadmap for practitioners when they encounter moral issues in the workplace. A code is critically important because it assures the public that a profession will meet its obligations to both the clients it serves directly and to the larger society.

We will elaborate further on the moral dimension of early childhood education and the role of professional ethics in the section that follows.

Is Increased Professionalism in the Best Interest of Practitioners, Children, and Families?

As you can see from this discussion, the field of early care and education can be considered to be moving toward professionalism because those who work with young children and families easily satisfy some criteria of being "professionals," but it fares less well on others. This is true, in some instances, because the nature of our work does not fit parts of the definition of "professional" and sometimes because, while aspiring to gain professional recognition, the field has not yet achieved that goal.

This consideration of the professional status of early childhood educators leads to the related issue of the impact this movement might have on the field. There is currently some debate regarding whether the movement toward increased professionalism in early childhood education is good thing.

On the positive side, greater professionalism would help to affirm the important and traditionally undervalued work that we do. We could capitalize on the ways we easily satisfy some criteria of professionalism such as our reliance on a code of ethics to guide decision making in the workplace and the existence of standards that set high expectations for performance. Additionally, if the field were to successfully raise the bar as to professional training required for entry, we could be assured that all workers would bring specialized skills and knowledge to their work. More training could also lead to higher status for early childhood educators, greater respect for early childhood educators and the work we do, and better compensation. It could also give us more control over the intellectual content and conduct of our field, which would ultimately improve our programs and services for young children.

Some fear, however, that becoming more like the paradigm professions such as law and medicine would make us focus on the technical requirements for entry into the field at the expense of the caring aspects of our work that make us unique. Silin (1988) expressed his concern some time ago that the movement toward professionalism could lead to the exclusion of some teachers who are already in the workforce and the voices of some groups of people concerned with the welfare of young children.

These efforts could also eliminate the field's unique career ladder that includes opportunities for beginners to acquire specialized knowledge and expertise on the job. Without a robust career ladder, we run the risk of creating a monocultural teaching force rather than one that reflects the communities we serve and welcomes diverse teachers, including those from populations who have been typically underrepresented because of their limited access to higher education. The early childhood career ladder/lattice has always been one of the field's most effective strategies for increasing access of traditionally underrepresented populations.

Ayers (2004) gives voice to these concerns. He advises that the move toward professionalism must be accompanied by a strong orientation toward social justice if it is to avoid discrimination against some groups of educators. He writes:

> If a concept of professionalism is built firmly on a base of respect for individuals and for community, of critique and compassionate regard, of connection and interaction,

perhaps teaching may become the model of a new kind of professionalism for others to aspire to and emulate. (p. 86)

We believe the field of early care and education is at a unique crossroads. As we advocate for the higher levels of professional preparation that we know increase the chances that children will benefit from their early educational experiences, we must build in strategies that keep doors of opportunity open to diverse populations who have traditionally played an important role in our efforts to serve young children.

MORAL AND ETHICAL DIMENSIONS OF CARING FOR AND EDUCATING YOUNG CHILDREN

The second topic addressed in this chapter relates to the moral and ethical dimensions of working with young children and their families. Whatever developments occur relating to the professional status of the field, early childhood educators agree that behaving ethically in our dealings with children is a commitment that every person in our field should make. This commitment is particularly important because our first and foremost responsibility is to care for children who are too young and too vulnerable to protect themselves. For that reason understanding and living by our ethical responsibilities is absolutely essential.

We begin our discussion of professional ethics by looking at resources designed to help teachers and caregivers who work with young children identify the core values, ideals, and principles of the field. Next, we identify what early childhood educators need to be able to do to behave ethically in their work with young children and their families. And finally, we consider the role ethics plays in the field of early care and education and explore recent developments that present new challenges to early childhood educators committed to the precepts of the field's ethical standards.

What Is Ethics? What Is a Code of Ethics?

It is helpful to begin conversations about morality and ethics with definitions of terms that are used in specific ways when discussing professional ethics. The field of early care and education has been working on professional ethics since the mid-1980s and has adopted the following definitions for frequently used terms:

❏ *Morality* is an individual's view of what is right and good. It concerns people's duties and obligations to one another. It is characterized by words such as *right, ought, just,* and *fair* and is based on personal values.

❏ *Values* are fundamental beliefs that individuals hold to be intrinsically desirable or worthwhile, that are prized for themselves and guide behavior (for example: truth, beauty, honesty, justice, respect). Values come from an individual's family, culture, community, faith, and society.

❑ *Ethics* is the study of right and wrong, duties and obligations. It involves critical reflection on morality, the ability to make choices between values and to examine the moral dimensions of relationships.

❑ *Professional ethics* involves reflection on professional responsibility that is carried out collectively and systematically by the membership of a profession. Professional ethical judgments are not statements of taste or preference, nor are they the same as laws. They tell us what we ought to do and what we ought not do as professionals.

While personal values and morality are a necessary foundation, they cannot be relied on to guide professional behavior. They need to be supplemented with professional values and standards of ethical behavior. Like individuals, professions have distinctive values and professional ethics.

❑ *Core values* are deeply held commitments that are embraced by members of a profession because they make a contribution to society. They are at the heart of the moral commitments of a profession.

❑ A *code of ethics* is a document that maps the dimensions of a profession's social responsibility and acknowledges the obligations its members share in meeting their responsibilities. (Feeney & Freeman, 1999/2005)

Codes of Ethical Conduct

A professional code of ethics can make a significant contribution to the quality of an occupation's practice and to its growing professionalism. Codes of ethics are important because they create a vehicle for the profession to speak with a collective voice. They extend individuals' personal and idiosyncratic sense of right and wrong by identifying how they agree, as professionals, with their colleagues.

Early childhood organizations throughout many parts of the English-speaking world have taken steps to guide practitioners' ethical decision making by adopting codes of professional ethics. A code provides a moral compass that helps educators make decisions that are fair to individual students as well as to groups of students, honor their responsibilities to families, guide collegial relationships, and are in the best interest of the community and the larger society.

Early childhood educators in the United States have the NAEYC Code of Ethical Conduct as a resource to guide their ethical decision making. Though it is not enforced like the codes of other professions such as law and medicine, the NAEYC code has become part of the field's core knowledge. NAEYC-accredited programs for young children must document their reliance on the code (NAEYC, 2005b) and students graduating from NAEYC-accredited associate degree and NCATE-accredited initial and advanced degree postsecondary programs are required to demonstrate their knowledge of the code and their ability to apply it to their work (National Council for the Accreditation of Education, 2006). In describing what master teachers must know and be able to do, the National Board for Professional Teaching

Standards (NBPTS) also emphasizes the importance of ethical practice (National Board for Professional Teaching Standards, 2002).

The NAEYC Code of Ethical Conduct

NAEYC has been a pioneer in efforts to map the ethical dimensions of early care and education. Founded in 1926, NAEYC has counted about 100,000 members on its rolls for more than a decade (NAEYC, n.d.). It is the largest and most influential professional organization devoted to the care and education of young children in out-of-home settings. NAEYC took the first step toward the establishment of the code of ethics in 1976 when its governing board passed a resolution calling for its development. Work on ethics did not begin to move forward, however, until after the 1978 publication, and 1991 expansion, of *Ethical Behavior in Early Childhood Education*, authored by Lilian Katz and Evangeline Ward. They identified two characteristics of the work of early childhood educators that are as important to consider today as they were more than 30 years ago.

The first and most important issue pointing to early childhood educators' need for ethical guidance is related to the power teachers and caregivers have over the vulnerable children with whom they work. Every aspect of children's days is in their hands: when and what they eat, when and where they sleep, when they can be noisy and when they must be quiet, when they go outside and when they come indoors. Katz and Ward (1978, 1991) advised that a code of ethics would remind early childhood educators to protect children from harm and to respect them in the ordinary and not-so-ordinary decisions they make every day.

A second issue identified by Katz and Ward is the multiplicity of clients served by early childhood educators who have responsibilities to children, families, their employing agencies, and the community. They recognized that early childhood educators need guidance about how to prioritize the needs of these different groups when their interests conflict. What is a teacher to do, for example, when a mother asks her to keep her child from napping even though the 4-year-old needs a nap to have a good afternoon? How should a committed early childhood educator respond when a family needs the services of her program even though they are temporarily unable to pay tuition? Katz and Ward realized that when teachers' resolutions to these kinds of dilemmas were based on a code of ethics, their decisions would reflect the field's history, values, and collective expertise.

The NAEYC board did not reach consensus about how to move work on the development of ethical guidelines forward until 1984. At that time they established an ethics commission and asked Stephanie Feeney to lead efforts to map the ethical dimensions of early childhood education. Working with Kenneth Kipnis, a professor of philosophy, Feeney guided a collaborative process which elicited input from NAEYC members to identify the core values, ideals, and principles guiding practitioners' work (Feeney & Freeman, 1999/2005). The first version of the *NAEYC Code of Ethical Conduct* was adopted as a position statement by the NAEYC governing board in 1989 (Feeney & Kipnis). The organization has continued to elicit broad-based participation and feedback during the code's three revisions (1992, 1997, and 2005) and during the development of supplements to the code that address the unique ethical responsibilities of adult educators (2004) and program administrators (2006).

The application and influence of the code has been expanded with the endorsement of the Association for Childhood Education International (ACEI) and adoption by the National Association for Family Child Care. In addition, early childhood professional organizations in Australia and Canada have relied on the NAEYC code and the process of its development to inform their work on ethics (Canadian Child Care Federation, 2003; Early Childhood Australia, 2006).

Even though the code remains unenforceable, NAEYC's leaders have taken the stance that, given the vulnerability of young children and the great disparity in power between children and their adult caregivers, even a voluntary code of ethics provides valuable safeguards for children participating in early care and education programs.

Making a Code of Ethics an Essential Part of Practitioners' Professional Repertoire

As noted by Katz and Goffin in 1990, "now that a code of ethics has been adopted, the issue of how it is to be 'learned' . . . will have to be addressed" (p. 201). The first, and most important, reason that every early childhood educator should learn the code and build it into their repertoire of professional actions is that the code is intended first and foremost to protect children. The first principle in the code (P-1.1) reads, "Above all, we shall not harm children. We shall not participate in practices that are emotionally damaging, physically harmful, disrespectful, degrading, dangerous, exploitative, or intimidating to children. *This principle has precedence over all others in this Code.*" This is a powerful statement that the first priority of every early childhood educator should be the well-being of children, and that every action and decision should first be considered in the light of potential negative consequences.

Engaging with professional ethics is beneficial for early childhood educators at every stage in their careers. A person entering the field may first encounter professional ethics in a preservice training program. It helps the beginner to focus on shared values and commitments. It makes it clear that they are not just learning a job—they are joining a community. Learning about professional ethics gives new practitioners a compass to guide them on a path toward ethical conduct in their work. It also helps them identify the ethical issues they are likely to encounter. Even at the earliest stages of professional life novices can begin to use the code to think through issues involving what is right, just, and fair.

Engagement with professional ethics is important for seasoned professionals as well. It reminds them of the shared values of the field, provides a framework for examining their practice more deeply, and raises the level of discussion by enabling intellectually productive dialogue about the real issues that they face daily in their work with children and families. Ethics can be the basis of some of professionals' most profound and engaging discussions as experienced teachers struggle with difficult dilemmas.

The code of ethics and the supplements addressing the particular responsibilities of adult educators, mentors, and program administrators also contribute
to the effectiveness of leaders in the field. These resources give them tools to speak
with an authority created by their reliance on position statements developed by the
field's largest and most comprehensive professional organization. When informed
by these ethical guidelines their leadership is not based solely on personal opinions, but reflects the wisdom of the field's commitment to children, families, the
workplace, and society.

NAEYC has made a concerted effort to disseminate information about professional ethics. The code is available online in English and Spanish and in brochures;
information about professional ethics can be found in articles in the journal *Young
Children,* and in two books written to help educators learn about the code, how to
use it, and how to teach it (Feeney & Freeman, 1999/2005; Feeney, Freeman, &
Moravcik, 2000). The code is also reprinted in a number of widely used introduc-
tory early education textbooks.

ISSUES TO CONSIDER

Two developments in the past decade have spotlighted early childhood care and
education as never before. They create opportunities and challenges that should be
considered from the perspective of professional ethics as practitioners decide how
they should, ought, and must respond. First, recent years have seen an unprecedented increase in support for publicly funded programs of early care and education. These increases have been fueled by complementary strands of research. Today
imaging technology provides even nonscientists previously unimagined glimpses
into the topology, formation, and function of the human brain. We now know that
children's earliest experiences create neural pathways that will determine, in large
measure, how their brains will function for their entire lives (Shonkoff & Phillips,
2000; Shore, 1997). There is also growing awareness of the substantial long-term
economic benefits the public can realize by investing in quality early childhood
programs (Heckman & Masterov, 2004; Rolnick & Grunewald, 2003; Schweinhart,
2004). These advances in our knowledge of how the brain develops as well as
documentation of the economic benefits of early care and education have resulted in
a 40 percent increase in the number of 4-year-olds served in public programs
between 2001 and 2006 (Barnett, Hustedt, Hawkinson, & Robin, 2007).

The second challenge facing today's early childhood educators is related to
the high levels of accountability that comes with public support (Pianta, 2006). The
first version of the NAEYC code of ethics adopted in the late 1980s identified the
field's responsibilities to children, families, colleagues, the community, and society.
However, the definition of *community* now, more than ever before, includes the legislators and public officials who have invested in early care and education. Regardless of the level of support they provide, policy makers expect children who
participate in publicly funded early childhood programs to show the same kinds of
gains reported in highly touted and very expensive benchmark studies such as the

Perry Preschool Project (Schweinhart, 2004). To document the efficacy of their efforts, well-meaning but uninformed policy makers sometimes mandate the use of inappropriate curricula, teaching methods, or assessments to measure child outcomes. These expectations bring with them unprecedented challenges for early childhood educators. It is more important than ever that they come to the classroom equipped with knowledge of child development, realistic expectations about what young children should know and be able to do, and appropriate instructional and assessment strategies. They must have the courage to be unyielding in the face of pressures to violate best practices that reflect what they know about young children and how they learn.

The 2005 revision of the NAEYC code of ethics addressed, in particular, the demands created by increased accountability by including nine new items related to assessment. Representative items remind early childhood educators:

- ❏ To use assessment strategies appropriate for the children to be assessed (I-1.6)
- ❏ To use assessments only for the purposes for which they were designed (I-1.6)
- ❏ To use appropriate assessment systems, which include multiple sources of information (P-1.5)
- ❏ To strive to ensure that decisions such as those related to enrollment, retention, or assignment to special education services, will be based on multiple sources of information and will never be based on a single assessment, such as a test score or a single observation (P-1.6)

In addition to new items on assessment, and in recognition of the pressures just discussed and the need for us to become more effective advocates for young children, the 2005 revision includes several new items on *collective* responsibilities to community and society. These include:

- ❏ To work through education, research, and advocacy toward an environmentally safe world in which all children receive health care, food and shelter; are nurtured and live free from violence in their home and their communities (I-4.3)
- ❏ To work through education, research, and advocacy toward a society in which all young children have access to high-quality early care and education programs (I-4.4)
- ❏ When policies are enacted for purposes that do not benefit children, we have a collective responsibility to work to change these practices (P-4.11)

Our response to the public's current interest and investment in programs for young children and the escalating levels of accountability that come with public funding may turn out to be a defining moment for the field of early care and education that will set its course in the years to come. Will we take a stand and make explicit our commitment to our code of ethics, or capitulate to demands that are not in the best interests of children? These are topics that deserve careful attention from today's leaders and the leaders of tomorrow as they shape the field for those to follow.

REFERENCES

Ayers, W. (2004). *Teaching toward freedom: Moral commitment and ethical education in the classroom.* Boston: Beacon Press.

Barnett, W. S., Hustedt, J. T., Hawkinson, L. E., & Robin, K. B. (2007). *The state of preschool in 2006.* New Brunswick, NJ: National Institute for Early Education Research. Retrieved October 12, 2007, from http://nieer.org/yearbook/pdf/yearbook.pdf

Canadian Child Care Federation. (2003). *Principles of the Code of Ethics.* Retrieved October 17, 2007, from www.cccf-fcsge.ca/practice/ethical%20dilemmas/codeofethics_en.htm

Center for the Child Care Workforce. (2004). *Current data on the salaries and benefits of the U.S. early childhood education workforce.* Retrieved October 17, 2007, from www.ccw.org/pubs/2004Compendium.pdf

Cost, Quality, and Child Outcomes Study Team. (1995). *Cost, quality, and child outcomes in child care centers public report.* Denver: Economics Department, University of Colorado.

Council for Exceptional Children. (1983). *CEC code of ethics for educators of persons with exceptionalities.* Retrieved May 18, 2007, from www.cec.sped.org/Content/NavigationMenu/ProfessionalDevelopment/ProfessionalStandards/EthicsPracticeStandards/default.htm

Doctors, J. V. (2007). *Leadership matters: Governors' pre-K proposals fiscal year 2008.* Washington, DC: Pre-K Now. Retrieved October 17, 2007, from www.preknow.org/documents/LeadershipReport_Apr2007.pdf

Early Childhood Australia. (2006). *Code of Ethics.* Retrieved October 17, 2007, from www.earlychildhoodaustralia.org.au/code_of_ethics/early_childhood_australias_code_of_ethics.html

Freeman, N. K., & Feeney, S. (2006). The new face of early childhood education: Who are we? Where are we going? *Young Children, 61*(5), 10–16.

Feeney, S., & Freeman, N. K. (1999/2005). *Ethics and the early childhood educator: Using the NAEYC Code of Ethics.* Washington, DC: NAEYC.

Feeney, S., & Freeman, N. K. (2002. Early childhood education as an emerging profession: Ongoing conversations. *Child Care Information Exchange, 143,* 38–41.

Feeney, S., Freeman, N. K., & Moravcik, E. (2000). *Resources for teaching the NAEYC Code of Ethical Conduct: Activity sourcebook.* Washington, DC: NAEYC.

Feeney, S., & Kipnis, K. (1989). *Code of Ethical Conduct and Statement of Commitment.* Washington, DC: NAEYC.

Fields, M., & Mitchell, A. (2007). *The ECE/Elementary licensure survey. National Association of Early Childhood Teacher Educators mid-year meeting.* Pittsburg, PA.

Frost, J. L. (2007). The changing culture of childhood: A perfect storm. *Childhood Education, 83*(4), 225–230.

Fuller, B. (2007). *Standardized childhood.* Stanford, CA: Stanford University Press.

Goffin, S. G., & Washington, V. (2007). *Ready or not: Leadership choices in early care and education.* New York: Teachers College Press.

Heckman, J. J., & Masterov, D. V. (2004). *The productivity argument for investing in young children.* Chicago: Invest in Kids Working Group, Committee for Economic Development. Retrieved October 15, 2007, from http://jenni.uchicago.edu/Invest/FILES/dugger_2004-12-02_dvm.pdf

Kagan, S. L., & Cohen, N. (1999). *Not by chance: Creating an early care and education system for America's children.* New Haven, CT: Yale Bush Center.

Katz, L. G. (2007). Viewpoint: Standards of experience. *Young Children, 62*(3), 94–95.

Katz, L. G., & Goffin, S. G. (1990). Issues in the preparation of teachers of young children. In B. Spodek & O. N. Saracho (Series Eds.) and B. Spodek & O. N. Saracho (Vol. Eds.), *Yearbook in early childhood education: Volume 1. Early childhood teacher preparation* (pp. 176–191). New York: Teachers College Press.

Katz, L. G., & Ward, E. (Eds.). (1978). *Ethical behavior in early childhood education.* Washington, DC: National Association for the Education of Young Children.

Katz, L. G., & Ward, E. (Eds.). (1991). *Ethical behavior in early childhood education* (Expanded ed.). Washington, DC: National Association for the Education of Young Children.

National Association for the Education of Young Children. (1996). *Developmentally appropriate practice in early childhood programs serving children from birth through age 8*. Retrieved October 17, 2007, from www.naeyc.org/about/positions/daptoc.asp

National Association for the Education of Young Children. (2004). *Code of Ethical Conduct and Statement of Commitment: Supplement for early childhood adult educators*. Washington, DC: Author. Retrieved October 17, 2007, from www.naeyc.org/about/positions/ethics04.asp

National Association for the Education of Young Children. (2005a). *NAEYC early childhood program standards and accreditation criteria: The mark of quality in early childhood education*. Washington, DC: Author.

National Association for the Education of Young Children. (2005b). *Code of Ethical Conduct and Statement of Commitment*. Washington, DC: Author. Retrieved October 17, 2007, from www.naeyc.org/about/positions/PSETH05.asp

National Association for the Education of Young Children. (2006). *Code of Ethical Conduct and Statement of Commitment: Supplement for early childhood program administrators*. Washington, DC: Author. Retrieved October 17, 2007, from www.naeyc.org/about/positions/PSETH05_supp.asp

National Association for the Education of Young Children. (n.d.). *History of NAEYC*. Retrieved October 17, 2007, from www.naeyc.org/about/history.asp

National Association for Regulatory Administration (NARA) & Technical Assistance Center (NCCIC). (2006). *The 2005 child care licensing study*. Conyers, GA: Author. Retrieved October 5, 2007, from nara.affiniscape.com/associations/4734/files/2005%20Licensing%20Study%20Final%20Report_Web.pdf

National Board for Professional Teaching Standards. (2002). *What teachers should know and be able to do: Policy statement and supporting statement*. Detroit, MI: Author. Retrieved October 17, 2007, from www.nbpts.org/the_standards/the_five_core_propositio

National Council for the Accreditation of Education (NCATE). (2006). *Professional standards accreditation of schools, colleges, and departments of education*. Retrieved October 17, 2007, from www.ncate.org/documents/standards/unit_stnds_2006.pdf

Pianta, R. C. (2006). Standardized observation and professional development: A focus on individualized implementation and practices. In M. Zaslow & I. Martinez-Beck (Eds.), *Critical issues in early childhood professional development* (pp. 231–254). Baltimore: Brookes.

Rolnick, A., & Grunewald, R. (2003). *Early childhood development: Economic development with a high public return*. FedGazette of the Federal Reserve Bank of Minneapolis. Retrieved June 21, 2006, from http://minneapolisfed.org/pubs/fedgaz/03-03/earlychild.cfm

Schweinhart, L. (2004). *The High/Scope Perry Preschool Study through Age 40: Summary, conclusions, and frequently asked questions*. Ypsilanti, MI: High/Scope Press.

Shonkoff, J. P., & Phillips, D. A. (Eds.). (2000). *From neurons to neighborhoods: The science of early childhood development*. Washington, DC: National Academy Press.

Shore, R. (1997). *Rethinking the brain: New insights into early development*. New York: Families and Work Institute.

Silin, J. (1988). On becoming knowledgeable professionals. In B. Spodek, O. Saracho, & D. Peters (Eds.), *Professionalism and the early childhood practitioner* (pp. 117–134). New York: Teachers College Press.

Whitebook, M. (2002). *Working for worthy wages: The child care compensation movement, 1970–2001*. Berkeley, CA: Center for the Study of Child Care Employment. Retrieved October 16, 2007, from www.iir.berkeley.edu/cscce/pdf/worthywages.pdf

PART 4

WHAT IS THE EARLY CHILDHOOD CURRICULUM?

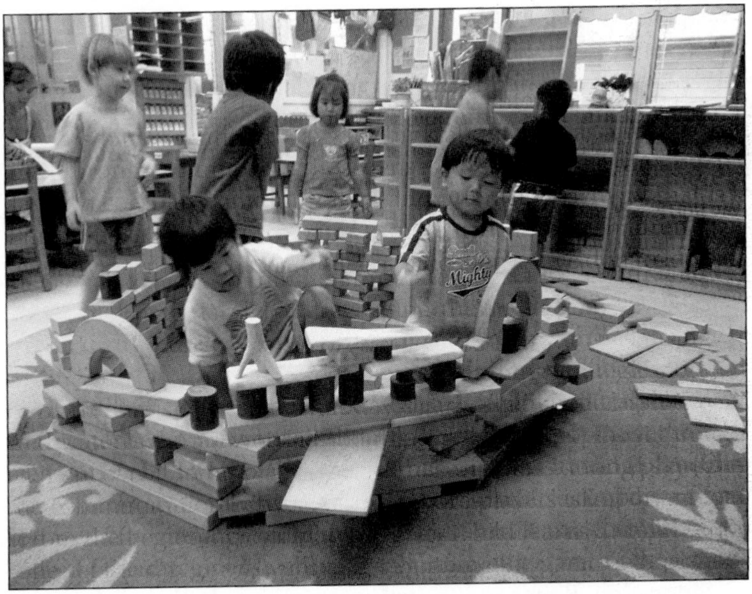

Controversy about curriculum has accompanied programs for young children since the first preschools and kindergartens were founded in our country. The chapters in Part 4 explore aspects of the long-standing debate about appropriate learning experiences for young children. Much of the controversy grows out of two conflicting views about practice in early childhood programs. One view, based on behaviorist theory and most prevalent in special education and elementary education, leads to a curriculum based on prescribed goals and objectives, and detailed instructions on how children are to achieve them. The contrasting view, held by the majority of educators who work with preschool children, is influenced by the theories of Piaget and Vygotsky that stress the necessity of social, physical, and mental activity in programs for young children. It is also influenced by the belief of progressive educators that curriculum should emerge from the child, and the community in which the child lives (Garrison, 1995; Prawatt, 1995). The three chapters in this section discuss some of the implications of these two views and explore some continuing issues related to defining best practices for early childhood education.

Chapter 10, "Curriculum in Early Childhood Education: Teaching the Whole Child," by Eva Moravcik and Stephanie Feeney, gives a broad overview of early childhood curricula. It includes a history of ideas about curricula in early education, an examination of the implications for practice of constructivist and behaviorist theories, and an overview of diverse viewpoints regarding the purpose of early childhood curriculum.

The chapter also examines some curriculum approaches that are widely implemented in early childhood programs today, with an emphasis on integrated approaches (including the developmental interaction [Bank Street] approach, emergent curriculum, the Reggio Emilia approach, and the project approach). The authors discuss similarities and differences between these and conclude,

> In truth the differences often are not very big. What the approach is called is not as important as how it is implemented. Any of these approaches can be implemented well by a skilled teacher who is sensitive to children's interests and ways of learning. And any of them may become stale and formulaic in the hands of a teacher who is not a good observer and who does not understand curriculum as a reciprocal process between teachers and children. (p. 233)

The chapter concludes with some thoughts about what educators need to know and do to provide worthwhile curricula for young children while also responding to current demands for adherence to early learning standards and preparation for the academic demands of elementary school.

In Chapter 11, "Play Theory and Practice in Contemporary Classrooms," Stuart Reifel and John A. Sutterby take an in-depth look at play, a topic which lies at the foundation of much of the practice and literature in the field of early childhood education. Reifel and Sutterby see play as both a developmental characteristic of early childhood and a tool for learning. They maintain that it should be a central component of any curriculum for young children. In this chapter they trace ideas about the important qualities of play for young children back to Plato, Socrates,

Froebel, and other pioneers of early childhood education. They point out that "the beliefs and theories that underlie contemporary early education are strongly tied to play."

Reifel and Sutterby present a history of ideas about the nature of play and its role in children's development. The value of play for children's learning is explored with an emphasis on its role in cognitive and social-emotional development. The authors also review the educational purposes of play materials.

A number of continuing issues relating to the role of play in early childhood education are presented. These include:

- ❏ Why there are so many views of play
- ❏ The value of play as a learning tool for young children
- ❏ The role of play in the early childhood curriculum
- ❏ How classroom play relates to the larger world
- ❏ Changing conceptions of play
- ❏ How ideas about play have influenced our current conceptions about developmentally appropriate practices (DAP)
- ❏ The impact of the movement for accountability on play in early education classrooms

The chapter concludes with reflections about and contemporary directions for play in early childhood programs and a call for educators to take children's play seriously—to observe it carefully, and to look at its multiple meanings for learning and education.

Chapter 12, "Early Learning Standards and Developmentally Appropriate Practice: Contradictory or Compatible?" by Sue Bredekamp, addresses the impact of the standards movement on early childhood education—an issue that is of major interest and concern to many early childhood educators at this time. The chapter begins with a discussion of continuing efforts to set standards for practice in early care and education and provides some historical context for the current discussions of this topic. Bredekamp considers potential negative consequences and positive benefits of early learning standards, and looks at the relationship between these standards and accountability.

The second part of the chapter reflects on developmentally appropriate practice and its relationship to content standards. Bredekamp argues that "developmentally appropriate practices not only reflect what is known about child development and learning, they *contribute* to children's development and learning" (p. 268). She maintains that developmentally appropriate practices, which derive from deep knowledge of individual children and the sociocultural context within which they develop and learn, are necessary to achieve standards of quality in early childhood programs.

Bredekamp maintains that standards that are challenging and achievable are clearly connected to best practices. The essential concept is "meeting children where they are," a concept that reflects the core early childhood value of responsiveness to individuals and the need to build curricula on children's interests. But she cautions that meeting children where they are is not intended to leave them there, but to help them get to where we want them to go.

Issues related to standards that need attention from early childhood educators include:

❑ The relationship between standards, curriculum, and assessment
❑ Research-based practice
❑ Alignment and transition between grades and between prekindergarten and the K–12 system
❑ Integration of curricula in the interests of more meaningful, connected learning
❑ Robust content in curricula for young children

These three chapters address issues that are at the heart of our endeavors in early childhood programs. They challenge educators to understand the value of children's play in all areas of development and to work to preserve our traditional commitment to it as a cornerstone of our practice. They also underscore the challenges of finding ways to preserve play and provide interesting and worthwhile learning experiences for children while also addressing standards that will help them meet later academic demands. More and more, this requires knowledgeable teachers who can manage a skillful balancing act between standards and curriculum and not lose track of the value of children's play in the process.

APPLY WHAT YOU LEARNED

As you read the following chapters, think about, talk about, and do additional reading and research regarding these questions:

❑ What do you think should be the curriculum content in early childhood programs?
❑ How can teachers balance children's play in a planned learning environment and planned curriculum? How will this vary for different age groups?
❑ To what extent is developmentally appropriate practice implemented in programs in your community? Is there a difference in programs for children of different ages? In different kinds of programs?
❑ What kinds of early childhood curricula are currently implemented in your program/your community? Do you think they are developmentally appropriate? How were they chosen?
❑ What kinds of early learning/content standards are in place in the programs in your community? What domains do they address? Do you think they are developmentally appropriate?

REFERENCES

Garrison, J. (1995). Deweyian pragmatism and the epistemology of contemporary social constructivism. *American Educational Research Journal, 32,* 687–716.

Prawatt, R. S. (1995). Misreading Dewey: Reform, projects, and the language game. *Educational Researcher, 24*(7), 12–23.

CHAPTER 10

CURRICULUM IN EARLY CHILDHOOD EDUCATION: TEACHING THE WHOLE CHILD

Eva Moravcik
Honolulu Community College

Stephanie Feeney[1]
University of Hawaii

"Would you tell me please which way to go from here?" asked Alice. *"That depends a good deal on where you want to get to,"* said the cat.

—*Lewis Carroll*

Curriculum, a word that evokes many images in the minds of teachers, families, administrators, and society as a whole, has long been controversial in the field of early childhood education. What is taught and how it is taught reflects beliefs about children and how they learn, views about the nature of childhood, and views about the role of education in a society.

In most early childhood programs[2] the curriculum is significantly different from that for older children. Central to understanding what makes early childhood curriculum so different and contentious is a question that has persisted since the earliest days of formal early childhood education. Should the childlike nature of children form the foundation of curriculum, or should adults determine curriculum content and impose it on children (Goffin, 1994)?

This question poses a number of related issues that are discussed in the pages that follow:

❑ Different conceptions of children's development and learning

1. The authors thank Marjorie Fields for reading this chapter and providing insights and assistance.
2. While the field of early childhood education defines early childhood as birth through age 8 (and hence early childhood programs as all school and child care for children from infancy through third grade), in practice the issues discussed here primarily concern preschool (programs for 3- and 4-year-olds) and kindergarten.

❏ Differing approaches to translating views of development and educational goals into curriculum

❏ Conflicting views about the purpose and goals of education

❏ Lack of consensus regarding what kind of curriculum is best for young children

As we thought about early childhood curriculum, it became clear to us that it is characterized by a major divide with the great majority of early childhood educators on one side and educators who teach older children, families, and policy makers concerned with academic achievement on the other. The situation is complicated by the fact that early childhood educators, while they share many basic assumptions about development and learning, often have very different ideas about curriculum.

We begin by providing some definitions of curriculum and a brief historical perspective. We then examine the issues listed above and attempt to explain why curriculum in early childhood education is often controversial and why it is now, and has been throughout its history, so consistently different in purpose, content, and structure from education for older children.

WHAT IS CURRICULUM FOR YOUNG CHILDREN?

When early childhood educators use the term *curriculum* they typically mean one of the following:

❏ Specific activities or lessons planned to accomplish desired outcomes for learning and development (these may be teacher created or commercially produced)

❏ A particular approach or model that guides an entire program and includes philosophy, principles for the design of the learning environment, teacher role, and curriculum (e.g., Montessori, Waldorf, developmental interaction approach, Creative Curriculum, Reggio Emilia approach, project approach, High/Scope)

❏ Everything in the early childhood program that children perceive and experience, whether planned or unplanned—sometimes described as "curriculum is what happens" (Jones & Nimmo, 1994).

In contrast to most elementary school teachers and the public, most early childhood educators embrace the idea of "teaching the whole child"—the view that all aspects of children's development (physical, social, emotional, cognitive) should be addressed in the learning experiences provided in good early childhood programs (Williams, 1987). This concern for children's overall development is an important distinguishing characteristic of early childhood education that sets it apart from most education for older children, in which curriculum is more narrowly defined as subject matter to be mastered with particular emphasis on teaching basic knowledge and skills. And while there are differences regarding preferred content and organization of the early childhood curriculum, there is a high degree of consensus about this central premise.

Another area of consensus among early childhood educators that contrasts with the views of educators of older children involves the teaching strategies and learning materials used to present the curriculum. Early childhood educators believe that the most appropriate way to teach young children is a holistic way that involves hands-on exploration, guided learning, and play in a carefully planned learning environment. For this reason most early childhood programs devote time, space, and equipment to play or play-like activities[3] (see Chapter 11 in this section for an in-depth exploration of the role of play in programs for young children.)

WHAT ARE THE ROOTS OF EARLY CHILDHOOD CURRICULUM?

Curriculum is a product of its time. As a society changes and as knowledge of children and learning evolves, so does curriculum. Educational values and practices are subject to influence by social and political forces. To understand the issues surrounding early childhood curriculum today it is useful to consider how views of curriculum have developed over time.

Many educators believe that there is an "educational pendulum" that swings between an emphasis on the nature and interests of the learner and an emphasis on the subject matter to be taught (Feeney, 2006). Each swing reflects a view of desirable practice that is frequently a reaction to perceptions of the shortcomings of the current educational approach.

Many of the philosophers and educators who were the founders of early childhood education were inspired by respect for children, a belief in the value of play, and a vision of education as helping children to become self-directed and creative. This can be heard in their words:

> The proper education of the young does not consist in stuffing their heads with a mass of words, sentences, and ideas dragged together out of various authors, but in opening up their understanding to the outer world, so that a living stream may flow from their own minds, just as leaves, flowers, and fruit spring from the bud on a tree. (John Amos Comenius, *Didacta Magna* [The Great Didactic])

> Play is the highest expression of human development in childhood for it alone is the free expression of what is in a child's soul. (Friedrich Froebel, *The Education of Man*)

The Kindergarten

Belief in individually relevant, play-based curriculum has by no means been universal or constant. The issue of whether the curriculum should be centered around

---

3. Note that in programs that follow the Montessori method, child-selected educational materials that appear similar to play materials are considered children's work, not play.

the child or centered around content first came to a head in the United States with the advent of the kindergarten. When the kindergarten was established in America it followed a program designed in Germany by Friedrich Froebel. It prescribed play with "gifts"—cubes and balls, beads, and pebbles—and "occupations"—paper weaving, folding or perforating, bead stringing, and block building. Even though described as play, the curriculum was didactic by the standards of many early childhood programs today.

Progressive Education.   It wasn't long before Froebel's followers were challenged. At a conference of the National Education Association in 1890, Anna Bryant criticized Froebelian rigid adherence to the prescribed gifts and occupations, and Patty Smith Hill (1902) argued that purposeful activities might hold more interest for young children. For example, Hill suggested giving the children "little problems designed to promote practical solutions; give paper dolls and ask them to make a bed to fit them using the blocks in the fourth gift" (p. 51). The uproar, hurt feelings, and open hostility that resulted from these seemingly benign suggestions were a precursor of the ongoing conflict over curriculum in the field of early childhood education.

Hill is associated with the American progressive education movement that had as its goal the improvement of society through fundamental changes in schools. John Dewey, progressive education's most influential spokesperson, included a kindergarten at the University of Chicago laboratory school. And though Dewey's kindergarten included some of the Froebelian materials, they were used in very different ways than as designed by Froebel. Dewey's approach emphasized greater freedom and spontaneity in play, and involvement in the social life of the classroom instead of Froebel's structured activities.

More controversy surrounded the curriculum when the kindergarten was institutionalized in the public schools. In St. Louis, Susan Blow and W. T. Harris opened the first public school kindergarten. Then, as now, the debate over curriculum revolved around the issue of school readiness. If children played little games with paper, folded paper into pretty shapes, and built with wooden cubes, how would they be ready for the rigorous work of first grade? In response, Alice Temple and S. C. Parker wrote *Unified Kindergarten and First Grade Teaching* (Parker & Temple, 1925), advocating a continuity of educational experiences from kindergarten through the primary grades. This refrain is still heard today.

The ideas of progressive education combined with research in child development triggered educational experimentation. In New York in 1916, Harriet Johnson, Caroline Pratt, and Lucy Sprague Mitchell organized the Bureau of Educational Experiments (which later evolved into the Bank Street College of Education) as an agency for research on child development. Mitchell, a friend of Dewey's and strong advocate of progressive education, directed Bank Street School and was influential in its evolution into a teacher training institution. She was deeply committed to the importance of children learning about their world through direct experience. Her book *Young Geographers* introduced the study of geography to young children through direct experiences in the community. This community study still characterizes the curriculum of the Bank Street children's school. Another member of this group, Caroline Pratt, was responsible for the design of the wooden unit blocks, which are standard equipment in early childhood programs today.

The Nursery School

The parallel growth of the nursery school was not without controversy either. Some of the nursery schools of the 1920s and 1930s based their curricula on the principles of John B. Watson, a behaviorist. These schools focused on teaching children the proper habits of hand washing, dressing, and eating. At the other end of the continuum were nursery school educators who used psychoanalytic theory as the foundation of their curricula. These schools encouraged children's self-expression through free play, finger painting, stories, music, and dance. There was great contrast between these two types of programs. The nursery school at Yale Psycho-Clinic or at Iowa State College stood in sharp contrast to those of the psychoanalytic tradition of the Nursery School for the Bureau of Educational Experiments in New York City (Weber, 1969). However, most nursery schools until the 1960s had a play-based curriculum closer to the psychoanalytic tradition.

Two European Programs

Two influential educational program models were developed in Europe at about the same time as progressive education and the kindergarten took hold in the United States—Waldorf education and the Montessori method. Neither of these had an exclusive focus on early childhood education though they did include it. Both Waldorf and Montessori schools can be found in the United States today. In common with Froebelian and progressive approaches, these programs focused on matching the curriculum to the developmental stages of children, and emphasized respectful relationships, hands-on learning, and child-initiated activity. Another European approach developed in the 1940s in Reggio Emilia, Italy, will be described later in this chapter.

Waldorf education was conceived in Germany by Rudolf Steiner, a philosopher, scientist, and educator who was interested in the intersection of science and spirituality. Steiner was deeply interested in the individual's search for self and the development of human potential. Steiner believed that childhood is a phase of life important in its own right. His philosophy emphasized balanced development, imagination, and creative gifts. Waldorf schools stress the development of the child's body, mind, and spirit (Feeney, Christensen, & Moravcik, 2006; Williams & Johnson, 2005).

Dr. Maria Montessori, a physician, was interested in the first years of life and believed that children went through sensitive periods during which they had interest and capacity for the development of particular knowledge and/or skills. She believed that children had an inherent desire to explore and understand the world in which they live. The Montessori approach is distinguished by carefully designed and sequenced learning materials, a series of learning experiences that actively involve the child, and a teacher role that involves observing and guiding rather than direct instruction. Activities are organized primarily for individual work, rather than group interaction. Purposeful activity is characteristic in a Montessori classroom. Children's work is taken seriously and is not considered play. Montessori was an innovative educator whose ideas had an impact on today's early childhood programs, in particular, the sturdy and responsive didactic materials, the use of sensory materials, and the design of a child-sized learning environment (Feeney, Christensen, & Moravcik, 2006; Montessori, 1965, 1967).

Programs for Children at Risk for School Failure

Debate over the nature of the curriculum arose again in the United States during the 1960s. The federally funded Head Start program grew out of the realization that many poor children did not have successful school experiences. Head Start was designed to provide these children with a good start in school. When first conceived and implemented, the Head Start curriculum was based on the same principles and views of child development as the psychoanalytic nursery school. Although immediate benefits of the Head Start program for children and their families were found, these gains appeared to dissipate by the time children completed the primary grades. To remedy this "fade-out" effect, Project Follow Through was established in the U.S. Office of Education. This program provided for the continuation of curriculum models from Head Start through grade 3 based on the premise that if Head Start children experienced continuity in learning, then academic gains made while in Head Start would be maintained. In an attempt to discover which approach to curriculum was most effective a number of educational models were selected and implemented (some were newly developed and some were adaptations of existing programs). These planned variations included models such as Bank Street and Education Development Center (EDC), descendents of progressive education; and basic skills models based on behaviorist theory such as DISTAR and the Kansas Behavioral Analysis model (Goffin, 2001; Maccoby & Zellner, 1970).

Results of the research were never definitive because families moved so often that the sample of children was not consistent over time, and because programs had such different educational goals that it was not possible to find appropriate assessments for all of them. There were no reliable assessment tools for program outcomes like curiosity, problem solving, autonomy, and social and emotional development. Children in the direct instruction programs showed immediate gains because it is much easier to test for specific skills. Later research suggested that as these children got older, those who had experienced the models based on behaviorist theory were less successful than those in the more child-oriented programs. In the end, no definitive answers emerged from the effort to compare such widely different educational approaches. Every group thought it was right and that the research showed that their program was best. The divide between the distinct approaches to curriculum studied in the planned variation programs still exists today.

Developmentally Appropriate Practice

In the 1960s and 1970s, elementary schools continued to stress skills-based learning and preschools continued to emphasize child-centered learning through play. Sue Bredekamp, in Chapter 12, describes an important landmark in early childhood education that occurred in the mid-1980s. Early childhood educators, through the auspices of the National Association for the Education of Young Children, published a position statement on developmentally appropriate practice (Bredekamp & Copple, 1997). Early childhood teachers, particularly in preschool but also some in kindergarten and primary grades, responded to the publication of *Developmentally Appropriate Practice* with a movement to focus curriculum on the needs and interests of children. Predictably, there was a backlash against this movement, which was regarded as lacking academic rigor. Today, the pendulum has swung again and public education has been molded by the demands of the No Child Left Behind legislation for skills-based learning and frequent administration of standardized testing to assess educational achievement.

TWO THEORIES OF DEVELOPMENT AND THEIR IMPLICATIONS FOR CURRICULUM

The two contrasting schools of thought about early childhood curriculum emerge from two very different theories of development and accompanying educational purposes and goals. It seems reasonable to assume that knowledge of how young children develop and learn should guide the design of early childhood programs. While it is not within the scope of this chapter to provide an in-depth account of theories of development, it is important to understand that disparate views of development and learning lead to very different assumptions about what should be taught to young children and how it should be taught.

Theory and educational purpose tend to go hand in hand; in fact, it is hard to know which one drives the other. And while there may be broad agreement that curriculum should help children to become productive citizens, there are stark differences apparent in the debate between those who embrace curriculum that grows from behaviorist theory, which focuses on the specific knowledge and skills to be learned, and curriculum that evolves from constructivist theory, focusing on the nature and developmental needs of the child.

It would make this discussion simpler if we could make a clear distinction between curriculum in early childhood programs and that for older children. But it is not possible to do so because the teaching strategies that have long been employed in settings for older children have increasingly been pushed down into early childhood programs including primary grades, kindergartens, prekindergarten programs in public schools, Head Start, and some preschools.

Behaviorist Theory and Its Implications for Curriculum

Behaviorist theory has had a profound impact on practice in early childhood programs and is even more influential in elementary education. The behaviorist school of psychology was founded by John B. Watson and elaborated by B. F. Skinner (Nye, 2000). Behaviorists contend that mechanisms of learning are the same for people of all ages and that behavior is controlled by the environment and can be modified by the application of scientific principles of conditioning; in educational settings this involves the use of external rewards.

Curriculum based on behaviorist theory is often referred to as academic, direct instruction, and traditional. Lilian Katz (1999) proposes the term *instructivist* to suggest that it is dependent on adults' instruction in academic knowledge and skills. The view of educators who hold this stance is that there is important content that children must learn as efficiently as possible. In this view curriculum should originate from adults (teachers, administrators, school boards) and should focus on "basic" subject matter. Behavioral conformity and the ability to follow rules are considered important for school success.

Early childhood curriculum that uses this approach tends to focus on the academic subjects of reading and math, a fairly limited constellation of concepts (letters of the alphabet, rote counting, naming colors and shapes), simple fine motor skills (holding a pencil, cutting with scissors, drawing lines and circles), and school behaviors (not speaking out of turn, walking in line, obeying instructions, raising hands). These skills, concepts, and behaviors are limited in number and not easily learned through children's play, which is regarded as having little to do with "real" school learning. Children are taught through direct instruction to achieve mastery. Educators who base instruction on this theory believe that every child learns in the same way, so structured teaching methods are appropriate for all children. Systematic reinforcement is used to shape behavior. Since this curriculum is not intrinsically motivating to young children, the use of rewards (like M&Ms, stickers, and frequent praise) is prescribed to keep children on task and to modify disruptive behavior (Bereiter & Engelmann, 1966; Moscovitz, 1968).

Curriculum based on direct instruction (used to a great extent in elementary and special education programs) include SRA's direct instruction programs, Success for All, precision teaching, and many commercial reading and math programs. These programs generally consist of scripted lessons for children who are grouped by ability level for efficient instruction.

Educators who subscribe to this approach use test results to demonstrate the success of the instructional programs they use. Since most existing tests assess the content taught in these programs there is ample data to support this position.

Constructivist Theory and Its Implications for Curriculum

Most early childhood educators today hold a constructivist view of the cognitive development of young children based on the premise that children construct understanding over time through reflecting on their interactions with people and the environment. Two well-known theorists have contributed valuable lenses for looking at development.

The first perspective comes from the work of Jean Piaget (1896–1980), a Swiss epistemologist (one who investigates the nature and origin of knowledge). Piaget was interested in mental activity. His focus was primarily on the nature and development of logical thought and on its construction as an individual activity. He believed that knowledge is not given to a passive observer; rather, it must be constructed through children's thinking about experiences that they have in the physical world (Ginsburg & Opper, 1988). Though Piaget focused to a great extent on individual tasks, constructivist scholars point out that peer exchange of viewpoints is also an important component of Piaget's view of learning, as are adult questions and adult-offered experiences that cause children to examine their current thinking (Piaget, 1963; DeVries, Zan, Hildebrandt, Edmiaston, & Sales, 2002).

The second view (called sociocultural theory) is based on the work of Lev Semenovich Vygotsky (1896–1934), a Russian psychologist, who focused on the social origins of language and thought. Vygotsky, like Piaget, believed that children are active in their own ongoing process of development. Vygotsky's premise that knowledge is created through interaction with other people teaches us that it is of utmost importance in understanding the processes of development to focus on the relationship between the adult and child (Berk & Winsler, 1995).

Most early childhood programs today are informed by constructivist theory, though some focus more on one or the other of these theorists. Many educators find that each contributes valuable insights and draw on both theories. Early childhood educators generally agree that knowledge of children's development, particularly in the area of language and cognition, is essential in designing educational programs.

Curriculum that grows from constructivist theory is called child-centered, developmentally appropriate, or informal. The child-centered point of view has been favored by early childhood educators throughout the history of the field and is supported by the theoretical contributions of Piaget and Vygotsky. The purpose of the early childhood curriculum is seen as fostering the development of the whole child and enhancing natural curiosity. Early childhood educators who embrace this approach believe that young children are active, self-motivated learners. They have learned from Piaget and Vygotsky that children construct understanding through their interactions with the world and learn from play in a planned environment with skilled guidance from a knowledgeable adult. These views are well represented in documents such as *Developmentally Appropriate Practice in Early Childhood Programs* (Bredekamp & Copple, 1997) and most contemporary early childhood teacher education textbooks.

Early childhood educators value the childlike nature of young children and the importance of early childhood as a stage in the life cycle, and believe that the natural play of young children is a valid means of learning. Play provides an opportunity for children's minds to process and make sense of sensory input and construct cognitive structures. Early childhood educators claim that learning which is tailored to the developmental stage and interests of children will nurture creativity and lead to true intellectual development as opposed to rote learning. Research on these programs had tended to be qualitative because the focus is on the process and quality of the learning and not scores on standardized tests.

Content in developmentally appropriate programs is, to a great extent, based on children's purposes, natural inclinations, and ways of learning. Planned activities emerge from observations of children and are responsive to their interests. Children have large blocks of activity time to play and explore in a safe and rich learning environment with many materials (including blocks, sand, water, paint, dramatic play props, puzzles, balls, and books). Teachers in these programs often construct their own curriculum based on knowledge of development, early childhood pedagogy, and sensitive observations of the children in their group. Since children are intrinsically motivated to learn in this way, external reinforcements are not considered to be necessary.

Today, because not all teachers are well grounded in child development and the construction of curriculum, some commercial materials have been developed to reflect a child-centered educational approach. One of the most widely used of these is Teaching Strategies' Creative Curriculum which places a great deal of emphasis on the provision of an appropriate environment. Others include the High/Scope Preschool Curriculum, Scholastic's Early Childhood Program, and Opening the World of Learning: A Comprehensive Early Literacy Program.

Issues Relating to Behaviorist and Constructivist Approaches to Curriculum

Proponents of behaviorist curriculum do not believe that constructivist approaches provide children with the necessary background for later schooling, particularly in the areas of literacy and numeracy. They believe that teachers who use curriculum based on children's interests, needs, and stages of development are abdicating responsibility for children's learning. There is a particular concern that while child-centered, play-based curriculum may be sufficient for children from affluent, educated homes, it is insufficient for children who are educationally "at risk" and need an academic "boost" from preschool and curriculum to ameliorate learning deficits. At best, proponents of skills-based curriculum see it as entertainment masquerading as education, an enjoyable waste of children's time; at worst, they believe that it cheats children of learning opportunities and puts educationally at-risk children further behind their better prepared peers.

Educators favoring constructivist educational approaches maintain that direct instruction ignores what we know about how children learn. They say that it teaches content that is out of context and therefore often meaningless to children (for example, practicing reading words that have no meaning). When tasks and information are joyless and meaningless they destroy children's motivation to learn.

Some commercial preschool and kindergarten curricula attempt to bridge the gap between the narrowly focused content and methods of direct instruction and the more child-focused developmentally appropriate curricula. These infuse typical play activities with an academic overlay or take academic content and attempt to make it "fun." These programs struggle to make skills-based learning palatable with movement activities (make your body into the letter *A*), songs and puppets that teach letters, numbers, shapes, and colors. Such an approach may initially seem to bridge the gap between play-based and academic curricula. On further investigation, it is clear that it provides neither the self-direction and joy of a child-centered approach nor the carefully sequenced, systematic approach of direct instruction.

Understanding these two approaches to early childhood curriculum helps to explain the great differences in theory and philosophy that can be observed in early childhood programs today, and why what is taught in early childhood education courses in colleges (regular education courses are most often based on constructivist theory) is often not what is practiced in schools. The current No Child Left Behind (NCLB) legislation has generated so much pressure on public schools to use direct instruction in an effort to raise test scores that the last vestiges of early childhood practice seem to be disappearing in public education. Most of us in early childhood education are hopeful that the educational pendulum will once again swing in the direction of a focus on development and needs of young children.

WHAT ARE THE PURPOSES OF EARLY CHILDHOOD CURRICULUM?

What should the early childhood curriculum be? What is its purpose? Or, to restate the question asked by the Cheshire Cat in *Alice in Wonderland*, "Where are we trying to get to?" What do we want the society of the future to be like? What kinds of people are needed to create that society? What knowledge and skills will children need to be productive citizens in society as it exists and as it will exist tomorrow?

In addition to looking at the theories of development that inform educational practice, we need to turn to philosophy and examine different views regarding the purpose and goals of education. These are based to a great extent on values (assumptions about what knowledge is of most worth). While there are many purposes for education, we have found that the four described below give a good overview of contemporary educational practice.

1. *Preserving cultural values and insights from great works and disciplines of knowledge.* Educators who embrace this educational purpose—the best known is E. D. Hirsch Jr.—are sometimes referred to as "traditionalists." They believe that the classics are the best expressions of human insight, understanding, and wisdom and that they stimulate human beings to probe deeply into great ideas (truth, beauty, goodness, liberty, equality, and justice). Their view is that the focus on individual differences neglects what all human beings have in common—the great ideas. They propose that the core of a preschool–grade 8 curriculum should consist of a body of lasting knowledge that includes, for example, the basic principles of constitutional government, important events of world history, essential elements of mathematics and of oral and written expression, widely acknowledged masterpieces of art and music, and stories and poems passed down from generation to generation (Hirsch, 2006). Preschool through high school curriculum, called the

core curriculum, has been developed as a resource for instruction that addresses this purpose.

2. *Efficient acquisition of knowledge and skills that are deemed important and that lead to success in future schooling and in society.* This view is associated with behaviorist theory, which views education as a science. Proponents of it are interested in specific learning outcomes and identifying behaviors that will help students to succeed in next year's classroom and in their future employment. They are concerned with behaviors that can be observed and assessed (usually with standardized tests). This point of view is often held by those concerned with the education of children from poor and minority communities (Delpit, 1995). Educators who value efficient acquisition of skills regard constructivist practices as designed to be consistent with the culture of the white middle-class majority and inadequate for the educational needs of poor and minority children. Constructivists counter this view with their concern that children who are already at risk for school failure may be limited by rote learning and by limited educational aspirations.

3. *Preparation for participation in a democratic society.* This view is held by progressive educators who embrace the philosophy of John Dewey. Progressives consider the purpose of early childhood curriculum to help children become intellectually active, socially engaged, lifelong learners. They believe that the natural way of learning springs from genuine interests and concerns. Progressive curriculum is not centered in authority outside of the learner, but derives from each learner's experience. The acquisition of skills is important, but they are taught in the context of children's exploration of meaningful content. Those who embrace this view today believe that education must be about developing problem-solving skills, creativity, learning to live in a democratic society, and becoming lifelong learners. The values of progressive education are most often linked with constructivist developmental theories.

Progressive educators view curriculum as a vehicle for improving society. Barbara Biber, who was a leading theorist at Bank Street College, describes the power of curriculum in this way:

> not only the excellence of intellect but in shaping the feelings, the attitudes, the values, the sense of self and the dreaming of what is to be, the images of good and evil in the world about and the visions of what the life . . . might be. (Biber, 1969, p. 8)

4. *Creating a more just and equitable society.* This view grows out of the values of progressive education but focuses more on remedying injustices in our society. Educators for whom this is a primary purpose are concerned with greater grassroots participation in the educational process including the exploration of injustices students feel deeply. The curriculum focus is social issues. An example of an approach to curriculum used widely in early childhood programs is the Anti-Bias Curriculum developed by Louise Derman Sparks and others.

All of these conceptions of the purposes of education are based on deeply held values and beliefs about what knowledge is of most worth. Views continue to shift and vie for recognition and influence in current curriculum debates. These positions reemerge in different forms and under different labels in every generation and in different places. Understanding the profound differences in values and beliefs about educational purpose provides educators with greater insight into current educational debates. We believe that answers lie in continuously asking what knowledge and experiences are most worthwhile at this time for all children in our society and for a particular group of children.

HOW SHOULD EARLY CHILDHOOD CURRICULUM CONTENT BE SELECTED AND ORGANIZED?

Despite their differences most early childhood educators agree to a great extent about the purposes and goals of early childhood programs and about the kinds of teaching strategies that are beneficial to children. They are committed to "teaching the whole child" and recognize the necessity of social, physical, and mental activity with both teachers and children taking an active role in the teaching/learning process. And most agree that play in a thoughtfully planned learning environment supervised by a warm, responsive teacher is optimal for infants and toddlers. They also agree that a more intellectually challenging educational approach is needed for older preschoolers.

Unanimity concerning goals and strategies and the commitment to teaching the whole child leads to another area of broad agreement. That is, the use of an *integrated* design for preschool and kindergarten curriculum in which both play opportunities and teacher-facilitated learning activities in different curriculum areas are planned to reflect a topic. Fundamental to the use of integrated curriculum is the belief that children will be motivated to learn something that is interesting to them and that basic skills and concepts can be acquired through experiences relating to the topic.

How a topic for curriculum integration should be selected and how integration should be achieved is more contentious. A number of approaches are widely used, and though there is much they have in common, each has its own emphasis and style. The differences between the various integrated curriculum approaches may appear arcane or insignificant to a layperson, but the distinctions are important to early educators; and there are real and heated debates regarding which particular approach, style of teaching, or relative emphasis is best.

The Unit or Thematic Approach

Perhaps the most familiar approach to integrated early childhood curriculum is the *unit* or *thematic* approach, sometimes referred to as "traditional" early childhood curriculum (Helm & Katz, 2001; Jones & Nimmo, 1994). In this approach a topic (sometimes called a "theme," e.g., transportation) is selected by the teacher as an organizing motif for a series of activities over at least a week. Theme-related play materials (e.g., puzzles, books, dramatic play, and block props) are added to the environment. Teacher-directed activities such as art projects, discussions, and songs are designed to reflect the theme. In theory each activity contributes to children's understanding of the topic while building other skills.

There are a number of criticisms of this approach. One is that topics are often chosen without regard for the particular interests and abilities of a group of children. It is typical for a theme to be scheduled for a predetermined, usually short, period of time so children have little chance to engage in inquiry. Short-lived themes rarely give teachers time to elaborate and extend children's learning. Often topics are superficially explored and there is little in-depth learning. Unit plans are often recycled each year, regardless of differences in groups of children. It is not uncommon for themes to be specified by a program administrator, or simply dictated by school tradition. Topics are sometimes trivial (e.g., teddy bears, parades, circus) and often focus on activities relating to holidays.

Another critique is that a theme may not offer (or teachers may fail to present) opportunities for children to have direct experience with the topic. For example, a week of a "bug" theme may involve playing with plastic bugs, singing songs about bugs, and reading fiction that features anthropomorphized bugs without ever providing any contact with real insects, or seeing insects in a natural environment. Related to this, activities sometimes do not provide appropriate learning opportunities. For example, children may be asked to complete workbook or coloring pages on the topic, an activity unrelated to any real learning.

A related problem is that teachers tend to misunderstand what "integration" means; they plug in activities that do not extend children's understanding of what is being studied. For instance, activities such as counting gummy bears during a study of bears do not help children learn about bears.

The Developmental Interaction, or Bank Street, Approach

The developmental interaction approach (DIA) is the direct descendent of progressive education as described by John Dewey and his protégé Lucy Sprague Mitchell, the founder of the Bureau of Educational Experiments (which evolved into Bank Street School and College). Like the unit/thematic approach, the DIA involves an integrated study of a topic selected for a class by a teacher. There are some significant differences. A DIA study is based on the teacher's knowledge of particular children and their community, as well as the learning potential of the topic. The topic is most commonly based on social studies concepts (for example, a study of stores). Like a unit or theme, the teacher plans many activities; however, in a DIA study a great deal of emphasis is placed on providing learning through real-world experiences. The topic is investigated in depth, over several weeks. Real experiences including a number of trips into the community are an essential component of this approach. Additionally, children are given multiple opportunities to reconstruct their experiences by building with blocks, writing or dictating stories, painting and drawing, and engaging in dramatic play. Questions that are raised during the study serve as the springboard for further study or new explorations (Biber, 1984, Mitchell & David, 1992).

The primary criticism of DIA is that it demands a great deal from teachers. It requires teachers to understand basic social science concepts and make sensitive and useful observations. It requires them to research, think, plan, and create materials. And it relies on resources from the school, community, families, and administrators. In a field in which most preschool teachers are minimally trained and woefully underpaid, this demand can be daunting.

Emergent Curriculum

Emergent curriculum (Jones & Nimmo, 1994) describes a child-centered approach to curriculum that involves integrated studies. In this approach, studies are conducted with a child or group of children based on their understanding and interests. While there is an element of teacher choice and guidance, emergent curriculum is more child directed. Teachers brainstorm ideas for activities, which are then modified in response to children's interests. Plans are changed as children's interests change. An emergent curriculum study may be quite small (jelly beans) taking a day or two, or may be more substantive (food) and last a few weeks or as long as the children remain interested. In an emergent curriculum, a teacher does not specifically attempt to address the range of subject areas. Advocates of this approach believe that all learning experiences should be based on children's interests and that the curriculum must emerge from daily occurrences.

Concerns regarding emergent curriculum are that children's interests may lead to superficial connections between activities, that they may not provide sufficient material for meaningful study, and that teachers may fail to understand what children are truly interested in. Another concern is that the subject of children's interest may exceed the teacher's knowledge, resources, or creativity.

The Reggio Emilia Approach

Another approach to integrated curriculum is based on the curriculum of preschools in the Italian city of Reggio Emilia. In the Reggio Emilia approach, integrated studies (projects) grow out of teachers' observations of and dialogues with children, each other, the community, and families. Teachers consider themselves children's partners in learning. Once a study topic is selected children are systematically encouraged to represent the topic through many "natural languages," or modes of expression, often referred to as "the Hundred Languages of Children" (Edwards, Gandini, & Forman, 1993). Teachers regard themselves as researchers, who conduct systematic study and prepare *documentation* of the children's work: photographs of children working, transcriptions of the children's questions and comments, and photographs and copies of children's work. These are mounted and displayed so that children and parents can examine them. The studies engaged in by children and teachers are conducted over fairly long periods of time and may be quite elaborate (the "playground for birds" project is a well-known example).

At this time, the Reggio Emilia approach is highly regarded for the quality of its intellectual content, responsiveness to children, the extraordinary aesthetic value of children's art production, and for the effectiveness of curriculum documentation. Some voice concerns about the uncritical way in which many Americans view the Reggio Emilia approach (Jipson & Johnson, 2000). Others suggest that while the approach is admirable it cannot easily be imported to American programs. We, the authors of this chapter, believe that as an Italian example of progressive education, it can be used to help American early childhood educators to reaffirm and rediscover their progressive roots.

The Project Approach (an American Interpretation of Reggio Emilia)

The project approach (Helm & Katz, 2001; Katz & Chard, 2000) translates the Reggio Emilia approach to an American setting. It focuses on in-depth investigation of a topic undertaken by a small group of children within a class, sometimes by a whole class, and occasionally by an individual child. The key feature of a project is that it is a research effort focused on finding answers to questions about a topic posed either by the children, the teacher, or the teacher and the children. The goal of a project is to learn more about the topic rather than to seek right answers to questions posed by the teacher. A teacher, with a group of children, selects a learning project that is highly motivating to the particular group (for example to "make" a car). Completing the project requires research to answer specific questions posed by the children or teacher and also requires the development of a host of skills and learning in many developmental areas. The project continues until the children reach a point of completion. The goal is not to "cover" predetermined content, but to help children develop skills for investigating a topic of interest.

Like its Reggio Emilia inspiration, the project approach is perceived favorably at this time. And like both the Reggio Emilia and developmental interactionist approaches, it requires a great deal of thought, ability, and time on the part of the teacher.

Similarities and Differences Among Integrated Approaches

What are the differences between these approaches to integrated curriculum? They differ in the extent to which the topic and initial questions for investigation are drawn from the children. They differ in the degree of teacher direction of children's investigation. And they differ in the extent to which the learning environment and daily program are devoted to study of a topic. In truth, the differences often are not very big. What the approach is called is not as important as how it is implemented. Any of these approaches can be implemented well by a skilled teacher who is sensitive to children's interests and ways of learning. And any of them may become stale and formulaic in the hands of a teacher who is not a good observer and who does not understand curriculum as a reciprocal process between teachers and children.

Integrated curriculum approaches are more notable for what they have in common. All evolved from the same progressive education roots. All have at their core investigation of topics that are of interest to children. All use play and hands-on learning as the core teaching strategies. All involve the modification of the classroom so that it is an interesting learning environment that builds children's desire to explore. And all integrate some, if not all, curriculum subject areas. Most important, all require a skillful and engaged teacher. Because there is such variation in how these approaches are understood and implemented, none of them is intrinsically "the best" and no program can be appropriately evaluated outside of the context of a particular setting or classroom.

The necessity of having a skilled teacher may be the primary challenge of integrated curriculum. A curriculum of investigation of the natural and social world is far more complex and requires greater knowledge and skill on the part of the teacher than either a scripted curriculum designed to teach basic skills or a curriculum consisting exclusively of play. To do it well involves observation skills, understanding of children and pedagogy, and the ability to design and implement meaningful and appropriate learning experiences. Although every functioning adult knows more about the world than a young child, a curriculum of investigation requires a teacher with broad knowledge and the ability to do research, as well as a lively mind and curiosity about the natural and social world that parallels those of the children she or he teaches. Sadly, as has been mentioned in the previous sections of this book, these characteristics are not always present among teachers who often have limited training, receive low wages, and labor under inadequate working conditions.

WHAT IS THE FUTURE OF EARLY CHILDHOOD CURRICULUM?

During the 20th century, society as a whole did not view early childhood education as particularly important. Early childhood programs received little attention and little funding. Because of this, teachers of young children were usually free to create or select curriculum they believed in. Today early childhood education is held in higher esteem and all educators are held to account for learning outcomes. As children enter kindergarten today they encounter expectations for reading and mathematics that until a few years ago would not have been introduced until first grade or later. The era of little attention and little interference has passed. The critical nature of the early years and the impact of early childhood education have been recognized and policy makers look to early childhood education as an important tool for improving educational and social outcomes for children. It is inevitable that in the future early childhood curriculum is going to be scrutinized, and often dictated, by others.

The challenge for early childhood education is how to provide the interesting and meaningful integrated curriculum that, as a field, we believe is best, while simultaneously helping children to acquire the foundational skills that will enable them to function successfully in later schooling. It is possible to identify some of what we must do to meet this challenge. We must recruit and train teachers who:

❏ *Know child development and how children learn.* In particular they must know the sequence of development in literacy and mathematical understanding.

Teachers who understand how children develop and learn can plan appropriate curriculum and articulate the reasons for curriculum that engages, excites, and educates children. They can resist pressure to use inappropriate strategies and content.

❑ *Know individuals.* If they are superb observers of children they will know each individual child's strengths, interests, and needs. Teachers who know their children and provide a curriculum that is individually appropriate will be able to help each child learn.

❑ *Understand curriculum and take it seriously.* There is no longer room for thoughtless or silly curriculum or activities that merely keep children busy and entertained. Teachers who understand curriculum and view it seriously will plan a curriculum that has meaning and purpose. They will use constructivist methods in the service of helping children learn.

❑ *Are experts on teaching emergent literacy and math.* They must know in the depths of their being that reading is more than reciting the alphabet and math is more than counting or doing worksheets. And they must be able to recognize when children are learning math and reading skills and capitalize on teachable moments.

❑ *Know, understand, and use standards.* Standards are here to stay. And they are not our enemies. Teachers who understand standards *and* child development *and* curriculum can use standards to help plan appropriate curriculum, *and* explain what they are doing and why.

Doing this will not be easy. It will not be cheap. It may not even be possible. But if early childhood curriculum in the future is going to be designed by early childhood educators, it is essential.

CONCLUSIONS

The debate over the curriculum in early childhood education—joyful play or grim labor, childhood enhancing or school preparation, individually worthwhile or dictated by authority, isolated facts or integrated knowledge—reflects the inconsistencies in society's views of children and childhood, and education and its purpose. The debate is not neutral, nor are the sides of the debate evenly weighted. Despite their many differences, early childhood educators value children, childhood, and integrated learning.

However, like many academic debates, the debate over the curriculum in early childhood is a false one. Young children learn actively *and* playfully. They prepare for later schooling in part by being children. And despite what authority dictates, each child learns as an individual—including ways to communicate like reading, and ways to order and organize like numbers. Today, with pressure to include academics in early childhood curriculum, a constructivist perspective provides a curriculum that is both intellectually substantive *and* child centered for early childhood educators to embrace.

REFERENCES

Bereiter, C., & Engelmann, S. (1966). *Teaching disadvantaged children in the preschool.* Upper Saddle River, NJ: Merrill/Prentice Hall.

Berk, L. E., & Winsler, A. (1995). *Scaffolding children's learning: Vygotsky and early childhood education.* Washington DC: NAEYC.

Biber, B. (1969). *Challenges ahead for early childhood education.* Washington, DC: NAEYC.

Biber, B. (1984). A developmental-interaction approach: Bank Street College of Education. In M. C. Day & R. K. Parker (Eds.), *The preschool in action: Exploring early childhood programs* (2nd ed., pp. 421–460). Boston: Allyn & Bacon.

Bredekamp, S., & Copple, C. (1997). *Developmentally appropriate practice in early childhood programs* (Rev. ed.). Washington, DC: NAEYC.

Comenius, J. A. (1967). *Didactica magna* (M. W. Keatinge, Ed. & Trans.). New York: Russell & Russell.

Cuffaro, H. K. (1995). *Experimenting with the world.* New York: Teachers College Press.

Delpit, L. D. (1995). *Other people's children: Cultural conflict in the classroom.* New York: New Press.

DeVries, R., Zan, B., Hildebrandt, D., Edmiaston, E., & Sales, C. (2002). *Developing constructivist early childhood curriculum.* New York: Teachers College Press.

Edwards, C., Gandini, L., & Forman, G. (1993). *The hundred languages of children.* Norwood, NJ: Ablex.

Feeney, S. (2006). Some thoughts about early childhood curriculum: Which way should we go from here? Beyond the Journal: *Young Children.* Retrieved from www.journal.naeyc.org/btj/200609/FeeneyBTJ

Feeney, S., Christensen, D., & Moravcik, E. (2005). *Who am I in the lives of children?* (7th ed.). Upper Saddle River, NJ: Merrill/Prentice Hall.

Froebel, F. (1885). *The education of man* (J. Jarvis, Trans.). New York: A. Lovell.

Ginsberg, H., & Opper, S. (1988). *Piaget's theory of intellectual development* (3rd ed.). Upper Saddle River, NJ: Merrill/Prentice Hall.

Goffin, S. G. (1994). *Curriculum models and early childhood education: Appraising the relationship.* Upper Saddle River, NJ: Prentice Hall.

Goffin, S. G., & Wilson, C. (2001). *Curriculum models and early childhood education: Appraising the relationship* (2nd ed.). Upper Saddle River, NJ: Prentice Hall.

Helm, J. H., & Katz, L. G. (2001). *Young investigators: The project approach in the early years.* New York: Teachers College Press.

Hill, P. S. (1902). The value of constructive work in the kindergarten. In *Proceedings of the Ninth Convention of the International Kindergarten Union* (pp. 107–135). New York: International Kindergarten Union.

Hirsch, E. D. (2006). *The knowledge deficit.* Boston: Houghton Mifflin.

Jipson J., & Johnson, R. T. (Eds.). (2000). *Resistance and representation: Rethinking childhood education.* New York: Peter Lang.

Jones, E., & Nimmo, J. (1994). *Emergent curriculum.* Washington, DC: NAEYC.

Katz, L. (1999, December). Curriculum disputes in early childhood education. *ERIC Digest.* Champaign, IL: ERIC Clearinghouse on Elementary and Early Childhood Education.

Katz, L., & Chard, S. (2000). *Engaging children's minds: The project approach* (2nd ed.). Stamford, CT: Ablex.

Maccoby, E. E., & Zellner, M. (1970). *Experiments in primary education: Aspects of project follow-through.* New York: Harcourt Brace Jovanovich.

Mitchell, A., & David, J. (Eds.). (1992). *Explorations with young children: A curriculum guide from the Bank Street College of Education.* Beltsville, MD: Gryphon House.

Montessori, M. (1965). *Dr. Montessori's own handbook.* New York: Schocken.

Montessori, M. (1967). *The absorbent mind.* New York: Holt, Rinehart & Winston.

Moskovitz, S. T. (1968). Some assumptions underlying the Bereiter approach. *Young Children, 24*(3), 24–31.

Nye, R. D. (2000). *Three psychologies: Perspectives from Freud, Skinner, and Rogers* (6th ed.). Pacific Grove, CA: Brooks/Cole.

Parker, S. C., & Temple, A. (1925). *Unified kindergarten and first grade teaching.* New York: Ginn & Co.

Piaget, J. (1963). *The psychology of intelligence.* New York: Harcourt Brace. (Original work published 1947)

Seefeldt, C., & Galper, A. (1998). What is early childhood curriculum? In *Continuing issues in early childhood education* (2nd ed., pp. 172–175). Upper Saddle River, NJ: Merrill/Prentice Hall.

Temple, A., & Parker, S. C. (1924, January). Unified kindergarten and first-grade teaching. *The Elementary School Journal, 24*(5), 333–347.

Weber, E. (1969). *The kindergarten.* New York: Teachers College Press.

Williams, C. L., & Johnson, J. E. (2005). The Waldorf approach to early childhood education. In J. L. Roopnarine & J. E. Johnson (Eds.), *Approaches to early childhood education* (4th ed., pp. 336–362). Upper Saddle River, NJ: Merrill/Prentice Hall.

Williams, L. (1987). Determining the curriculum. In C. Seefeldt (Ed.), *The early childhood curriculum: A review of current research.* New York: Teachers College Press.

CHAPTER 11

PLAY THEORY AND PRACTICE IN CONTEMPORARY CLASSROOMS

Stuart Reifel
University of Texas, Austin

John A. Sutterby
University of Texas, Brownsville

> Play *is the highest phase of child-development—of human development at this period: for* it is self-active representation of the inner—representation of the inner from inner necessity and impulse.
>
> *(Froebel, 1887/1902, pp. 54–55)*

Early childhood educators have a long history of valuing play as an important part of what we do. Both as a developmental characteristic of early childhood and a tool for learning, play appears in our practices and literature. Friedrich Froebel was not the first to note the important qualities of play for children; we can trace the appropriateness of play for young children's education to ancient philosophers like Plato and Socrates (Spariosu, 1989). More importantly, the beliefs and theories that underlie contemporary early education are strongly tied to play.

In this chapter, we explore continuing issues related to play and its connections to early childhood education. Among those continuing issues are debates about the value of play as a learning tool for young children, the role of play in classrooms (whether we can see play as children's work, what is being learned when children play, what types of play we should have in early childhood classrooms), and how classroom play relates to the larger world (family life and values, our culture and media, educational goals and practices) that children are growing into.

What is play, and how have people thought about it as a tool for early education? Why do we have so many views of play? What does it mean to have a play curriculum, or to have play in our curriculum? The fact is that there are many different definitions of play and numerous theories about what it means to play (Frost, Wortham, & Reifel, 2008). Notions of play change over time, just as what children do during play will transform as they grow older. Likewise, our thinking about early childhood curriculum has evolved over the years (Weber, 1969). In this chapter, we present continuing issues about play as it contributes to children's development and education. Throughout the chapter, we present the ways that ideas about play have become part of our developmentally appropriate practices (DAP) and the research that supports it (Bredekamp & Copple, 1997; Mallory & New, 1994).

PLAY'S HISTORY

"Let's play garage." "Well . . . O.K." Van bends down to arrange some blocks against the wall. Wallace runs to another corner and brings back some cars, buses, and trucks. "Here," says Wallace, "put them in here," pointing to a space between two blocks. "Wait, I'll make a stable for you." "I can fit them in here," insists Wallace, placing them in the empty space. Van doesn't like Wallace's aggressiveness and says, "Look here, I'm boss." Wallace does not budge. (Hartley, Frank, & Goldenson, 1952, p. 141)

While children's play was mentioned in ancient writings about learning, we have very few concrete examples of what philosophers like Plato and Socrates meant when they wrote of play (Spariosu, 1989). Over the centuries, philosophers return to the idea of play, suggesting that play contributes to children's good spirits and motivation (John Locke), human imagination and the arts (Immanuel Kant), and creativity (Friedrich von Schiller). How they would understand Van and Wallace's play is not known, although we can see imagination, desire, creativity, and much more in what these two boys were doing as they played. By the 19th century, thoughtful educators like Froebel were combining these ideas about play with beliefs in the natural development of the child (from Jean-Jacques Rousseau), the goodness of universal education (not just for nobility or the wealthy), and the particular needs of young children for hands-on "object lessons." Froebel was the first to create what he conceived of as a play-based curriculum for a school where children could naturally learn, like plants growing in the garden—his "children's garden" or kindergarten. Froebel began a debate that continues to this day about how children best learn: direct teaching versus "natural" learning by means of play.

Froebel and Play Curriculum

In Froebel's kindergarten curriculum, children were to play naturally with objects and each other so that they would gain understandings of the physical world, mathematics, and art; all three were conceived to be part of who we are in the larger spiritual world. Froebel based his ideas about play on what he saw as natural learning that takes place between mother and child. For this reason, women were viewed as the best teachers of young children. Froebel was the first to argue that women would bring important qualities to teaching. He wrote *Mother's Songs*,

Games, and Stories (1844/1897) to show his view of playful teaching, and he developed gifts and occupations that were to be the play objects that children would encounter in the classroom. The gifts and occupations (balls, wooden blocks and cubes, paper folding, bead stringing, and sewing cards) were devised so that children could begin to encounter the physical world, mathematics, and art (Brosterman, 1997). We still see circle time, a Froebelian innovation for teaching children their relationships to the larger social world, in many classrooms, as well as building blocks, sewing cards, and beads to string. But is the classroom play we see today, the kinds of things Van and Wallace do as they play with blocks, the same as we would have seen in Froebel's kindergarten?

Kindergarten was popular in Germany, and German immigrants brought it to the United States in 1856. At that time, private kindergartens brought us ideas about playful learning for young children. By the end of the 19th century, some cities and states had made kindergarten part of public schooling. With growth came differences of opinion and beliefs about the role of play in the curriculum, differences that continue to this day. Some kindergarten educators, like Susan Blow, argued for a traditional reading of Froebel, where the teacher might guide play directly. Others, like G. Stanley Hall and Patty Smith Hill, found the traditional reading to be too rigid; they preferred free play with Froebel's objects, or with newer objects that might speak to the contemporary interests of children. Was educational play the way children interacted with objects, under the close supervision of teachers? (Are Van and Wallace learning from building a garage?) Or was play what children chose to do, based on their interests? (Are Van and Wallace's play choices motivating them to explore interests about cars and transportation?) We still see both views of play in classrooms.

Differences about the meaning of play for early education contributed to heated debates in the field. Some members of the International Kindergarten Union (IKU; now the Association for Childhood Education International, ACEI) used this dispute as part of their reason for breaking away to form the National Association for the Education of Young Children (NAEYC), the eventual proponent of DAP. Froebel's ideas about play provoked strong feelings. IKU traditionalists wanted to maintain a prescribed use for gifts and objects, with the teacher guiding children toward patterns they could "discover" through play materials. Developmentalists who formed NAEYC wanted more free play and choice, so children could explore their many developmental needs; teachers were to use play as a way of studying children's needs and growth, using new research methods. Froebel's ideas had competition from the emerging field of child study. We continue to debate whether play leads to particular outcomes or if it supports a broad developmental foundation for later learning.

Science and Developmental Play

By the end of the 19th century, public education was expanding and there was a growing need for teachers. G. Stanley Hall, a founder of child study, included play as a key element in his recapitulation theory of child development. Hall argued that play in early childhood functions to help children get their inherited primitive culture out of their systems; children repeat the evolutionary history of humans as they play, and only during play can they get rid of humans' less civilized phases. Hall even identified stages of play that he associated with evolutionary stages: hide and seek with a savage stage, team games with a tribal stage. In essence, from Hall's view children needed to play to get the wildness out of their systems, before they could benefit from education. While none of the particulars of his theory remain with us (they never could be affirmed by research), he did leave us with the important idea that children and their play go through developmental stages. Van and Wallace would be viewed as getting their playful ideas out of their systems, before they can begin real school learning. This idea about play has guided research, teacher and parent education, and classroom practice for more than a century (Frost, Wortham, & Reifel, 2008).

Hall had many students who became teacher educators and researchers. The practice of doing research to create a scientific basis for teaching was becoming common. Child development laboratory schools were built at a number of universities where they served as places to train early childhood teachers. Play was at the center of research and practice. John Dewey established a laboratory school at the University of Chicago, where he wrote of play as the young child's learning experience. Disagreeing with Hall, Dewey saw play as a way that a child builds her ideas by doing: "The child does not get hold of any impression or any idea until he has *done* it" (Dewey, 1896/1972, p. 195). For Dewey, children do not play to get something out of their systems; they play to get something into their systems. Their actions are the bases for their thinking, and their play actions with other classmates serve many educational purposes: group problem solving, communication, negotiation, and ultimately formation of community. We see much of that occurring in Van and Wallace's block play. For Dewey, play is the enactment of ideas within a society, and the freedom of play is the foundation for social relationships in a democratic society (Cuffaro, 1995). In play, children learn social skills, how to clarify their own thinking, and also what their interests and strengths are. This multi-meaningful, doing-based view of learning is a foundation of progressive education.

Dewey did not conduct much research on play, but he inspired many others to study student interest, problem solving, and classroom community (Frost et al., 2008). And in laboratories across the country, researchers were describing social skills, learning, motor development, and thinking as they related to play (Jersild, 1933). Much of this research documented stages and ages in development of play, so that teachers and parents could have norms for understanding children's growth (Gesell, 1934).

Not all child study work was occurring in the United States. In Europe, Maria Montessori was elaborating her child-centered curriculum for disadvantaged children, where children would select hands-on activities in a carefully planned environment with child-sized furniture and equipment. Montessori's education program made its first big impact in the United States at the 1915 Panama-Pacific International Exposition's Palace of Education and Social Economy, held in San Francisco. The glass-walled demonstration classroom drew eager observers over its 4-month exhibition (Sobe, 2004).

Since that exhibition Montessori programs and schools have been created across the United States. Montessori curriculum does not specifically call the activities that children engage in "play activities," rather they are work activities designed to develop skills within the child (Cossentino, 2006; Saracho & Spodek, 1995). The use of specific materials and activities, and the carefully planned environment where they appear, were designed to develop order and attention in the child through the use of touch and stimulation of the senses. Children repeated activities over and over again in order to train the mind (Sobe, 2004). Montessori saw this activity as work, but many see it as a form of play. The work-play distinction in all its forms (e.g., play is the opposite of work, play is children's work, play is what you choose to do while work is what you must do) has been a continuing part of our thinking about play due to Dewey, Montessori, and others.

Science was giving play new meanings. Some theorists, like Hall, saw play as necessary but noneducative. Dewey saw play as the ideal form of education. Others, such as Karl Groos (1901), saw play as practice or preparation for future life. Sigmund Freud (1938) saw play as a necessary coping mechanism for children to use as they balance their own needs with social pressures as they grow. While not providing extensive connections with early childhood curriculum, these ideas about play have influenced more recent practices: Groos informed Jerome Bruner's work on development and education, and Freud called attention to children's emotions and play therapy for dealing with mental problems. Freud also taught Erik Erikson (1963), who invited many early childhood educators to visit the world of children's developing understandings of themselves as they proceed through the Eight Stages of Man. For Erikson, play is central to the earliest stages of psychological growth.

Different, often conflicting, ideas about play and education competed for years. For some, play is a stage prior to education, while for others it is the primary means of early education. Theorists and researchers continued to add to our ideas about play: social development (like Van and Wallace's cooperation using the blocks), emotional expression (Van's and Wallace's feelings about the other), motor skills (how they stack blocks), interest (their desire to understand garages and cars), creativity (how they put together their thinking about transportation), and others. And many educators still believe in the value of these aspects of play (e.g., Hohmann & Weikart, 1995; Isenberg & Jolongo, 2006; Van Hoorn, Scales, Nourot, & Alward, 2007). As we get closer to our own times, it is clear that a most persuasive understanding of play and early education comes from the connections that have been made between play and thinking. Cognition, or how we use our minds, becomes an important set of lenses that scholars and practitioners have used to understand what it means for children to play.

COGNITIVE LENSES ON PLAY

[U]sing interlocking bricks and rods she [J] built a big house, a stable and a woodshed, surrounded by a garden, with paths and avenues. Her dolls continually walked about and held conversations but she also took care that the material constructions should be exact and true to life. (Piaget, 1962, p. 137)

All the years that scholars spent arguing and theorizing about what play means, many teachers were discovering new ways to bring play into their classrooms. Caroline Pratt (1948) promoted dramatic play and created unit blocks so that children would have tools for constructing the ideas that interested them. Lucy Sprague Mitchell (1956) connected field trips and classroom play to geography. Vivian Paley (1981, 1984, 2004) explored connections between children's dramatic play and literacy. Play's meaning and role in early education became a major issue again when the federal government funded Head Start. Thousands of classrooms opened to tens of thousands of young children, and the question became what curriculum was good for them. What learning experiences would help young, disadvantaged children become better students when they entered school? What role might doll play and construction have in the curriculum? Are young children just students, or are they "whole" children with social, emotional, physical, language, and cognitive needs? (The idea of cultural needs did not emerge until later.) The "whole child" advocates tended to see play as an important unifying way of thinking about Head Start intervention, and they turned to a powerful theorist to support their case.

Piaget on Play

> Play also, especially from the point of view of "meanings" can be considered as leading from activity to representation (Piaget, 1962, p. 2)

Scholars had written about children's thinking, but Jean Piaget made a career of it. He observed his own children (including his daughter, J, playing with bricks and dolls, quoted earlier) and many others as they provided him evidence for his stage theory of cognitive development. Many find the four universal stages of thinking that he described (sensorimotor, preoperations, concrete operations, and formal operations) to be biased (they are based on a limited set of observations of white/European children), but his work still guides much research on learning and thinking. And play has an important place in how Piaget understands the origins of thinking. Play for Piaget is how children assimilate experience, on their way to constructing accommodated (learned) knowledge. Play is not how children learn; it is the way they practice their thinking, as his daughter J was practicing her thinking about her house, woodshed, garden, and other features of her world, rather than actually learning about it. While children do not learn about their world from their play, in Piaget's view, they do learn to explore meanings and how to represent their meanings. Pretend play in early childhood is how children begin to create symbols that reflect their thought. Symbolic play (sociodramatics and pretend construction) is critical for construction of thought in Piaget's preoperational stage, and it builds on the functional (repetitive, motoric) play of his sensorimotor stage and leads to the games with rules that guide moral thinking in his concrete operations stage.

Piaget's thinking about play made it a legitimate, theoretical part of thinking. He provided a reason for including pretend play as a necessary part of the curriculum for disadvantaged children and inspired research on the effects of play interventions (e.g., Schweinhart & Weikart, 1996; Smilansky, 1968). His stages of play (functional, symbolic, games with rules) also provided a familiar way for understanding children's play and development in terms of age-linked stages. His influence on appropriate practice has been profound, but he is not the only developmental theorist who ties play to cognition, or who inspires early educators to think of play as an educational tool.

Vygotsky on Play

> [T]hus, play creates a zone of proximal development of the child. In play a child always behaves beyond his average age, above his daily behavior; in play it is as though he were a head taller than himself. (Vygotsky, 1978, p. 102)

For Piaget, pretend play is the way children learn to represent what they are thinking about. For Lev Vygotsky, play for young children is learning itself. Vygotsky would have seen J's pretend about her real world, with her bricks and dolls, as a zone of proximal development (ZPD) where she could think about the world in a more advanced way than she would ordinarily do during daily experience. During daily experience, J would function in her world. During pretend, she would be forced to think about it, to learn about it, to construct it as an idea that is separated from any real experience around her house. Play, and play alone, has the power to separate our daily actions from what those actions mean, to begin to make actions objects of abstract learning. J can build houses and woodsheds in play that she cannot build in real life, and her dolls can converse in ways that she may not be able to; in play she can act a head taller than herself.

The power of play to become a tool of the mind is socially constructed in Vygotsky's theory. Children are predisposed to play, but their social contexts (culture, family, peers) provide play objects (toys are *pivots*, to use Vygotsky's term) and the social meanings that can be associated with those objects. Children's thinking will be connected to the objects they play with and the meanings of their actions by the language they use. J was given dolls that she learned could converse in play, and bricks that could be made into play buildings. Who those dolls might be in pretend and what the toy buildings might be (social meanings) are named and learned in the ZPD that play and other social relationships create. J's social context supported thinking at higher levels about the world around her, and it provided cultural tools (dolls, bricks) with which she could learn about that world. In different cultures, there will be different play tools (ABC blocks, handcrafted dolls, multiplayer online role-playing games) that connect to larger cultural ideas (school skills, living with nature, imaginary social worlds). Vygotsky makes pretend play in childhood the necessary developmental time when our thinking and learning begin to expand to the broader cultural world of meanings.

From this view, play is not just a stage children go through. Play opens children's minds to their society's world of ideas, where children will be supported in their ZPDs ("scaffolded") to be more capable and to think on higher levels. Vygotsky would have us think about play in terms of its talk, its actions, and the meanings that both action and thought reflect. This opens the door for seeing play as tool for supporting literacy (Dyson, 1997; Paley, 2004), self-control (Bodrova & Leong, 1998), and other desirable academic performance. He also helps us begin to see how play functions in slightly different ways depending on cultures and their meanings. Pretend play can be a context for learning cultural customs (Lin & Reifel, 1999), and it may reflect a culture's desire for academic achievement, such as when a preponderance of toys support academic skills and achievement (Tudge, Lee, & Putman, 1998). Play within Vygotsky's view is not just a developmental stage; it is a complex set of relationships and meanings that move children toward higher levels of intellectual functioning.

Piaget, Vygotsky, and others such as Jerome Bruner (1990) have provided a rich rationale for thinking about play as connected to thinking and learning. Combined with other ideas, such as Dewey's philosophy, these cognitive theories of play are an important part of a number of early childhood curricula, including the developmental interaction approach created at Bank Street College (Biber, 1984), High/Scope (Hohmann & Weikart, 1995), Reggio Emilia (Edwards, Gandini, & Forman, 1998), and many other programs. While different views of cognition do provide a number of lenses we can use for looking at children's play, there are equally powerful ways of thinking about play that can contribute to teaching and research.

SOCIAL AND COMMUNICATIONS LENSES FOR PLAY

Child 1. You come here. The babies are sleeping now.
Child 2. No, they'll cry when I leave 'cause they'll hear the car.
Child 1. Nooo. The car's broken. I have the car.
Child 2. All right, but one baby will have to take care of these little babies.
(Garvey, 1990, p. 137)

We often think of play in terms of pleasurable interactions, as a social activity. Many scholars have identified ways to think about play as a social event. We will look at play through a number of those lenses, to see how we can understand classroom play as a complex communicative and interactive activity that is laden with cultural meanings. Something as simple-appearing as two children playing house can have many meanings, depending on which lenses we don to look at it.

Signaling to Create Play

The current emphasis on literacy in today's early childhood classrooms is a concern to many educators who are worried about social skill development through play. One critical element of children's play is the role of social skills during play (Charlesworth, 2008). The communication between two or more players is important for the setting of play. From the beginnings of infant play, the child learns to smile and respond to the activities of the caregiver, eventually beginning the game of peekaboo (Bruner & Sherwood, 1976). Smiling, laughing, and the development of language are important for signaling someone else that play is going on (Garvey, 1990).

Gregory Bateson describes how players will use cues or signals to tell another player that "this is play" (1955, p. 120). Mammals like cats, dogs, and monkeys all participate in mock combat play. Although the moves they make during play (chasing, jumping on, hitting, and nipping) are all activities associated with fighting, the animals participating in the action know that play is going on and there is no real danger, because the players signal their play by wagging tails, keeping ears alert, or grinning. Bateson describes the "play frame" as a space where what is said is untrue, but that the players act on as if it were true. For example, a child says, "I am the mom, I'm going to cook dinner." All the other children present know that what is said is untrue (she is not a mother, and she will be preparing no food), but they all follow along in order to participate in the play (acting as if she were the mom cooking dinner). The simultaneous truth and untruth of play creates the foundation for paradox and paradoxical thinking, where we function with two incompatible notions at the same time. In the house play presented above, the children know that dolls aren't living, but they act as if dolls can sleep and hear; they function simultaneously with real and unreal by creating a play frame (playing house), acting "as if" their dolls were living babies and "as if" they had a car to drive.

Catherine Garvey (1990) extends Bateson's discussions of frames and signals by describing what children do with language during play. Children play with the sounds of their voices, rhyming, and nonsense. Children also use language to change themselves into someone else, and to plan what type of activity they will engage in, and what rules need to be followed for the activity. This language can be explicit when one child tells another, "I'm going to be the Blue Power Ranger," or it can be implicit when one child tells the other, "Dinner is ready now, let's eat." Garvey tells us that children can verbally signal one another about play in many ways, signaling intent to create a frame ("Let's play!") or a range of transformations about the intended play frame (who or what we will pretend to be, what our pretend actions will be, how we might transform objects or settings for pretense). Children's talk with one another can be about play (negotiating what they intend to do), or within pretend (speaking as if they were within role). In the example presented above, both children are speaking as play characters. In classrooms, we can overhear children spending an entire play period negotiating what they will play, and never actually enacting the pretend itself. In either case, the key role of different types of play language highlight how children's play is the context in which language can flourish in the service of play. The types of language children use in play may be a necessary foundation for later literacy (Paley, 2004).

Play as a Social Setting

Negotiating who gets to play and what roles to take is an important part of social communication. William Corsaro (1979, 1985) investigated the ways children negotiate with each other during play. This negotiation involved what roles each child got to take, where children would be able to play, and who would get to play. Children protect their play space by rejecting other children's attempts to enter a play group. Children who are socially adept are able to gain access to the group through the use of learned strategies. Other children may be allowed to play only if they take roles that have less value, like the baby or a pet. Over time, children's play negotiations contribute to their social statuses in the classroom, to how they are valued as playmates, what friendships they form, and who becomes the leaders or followers in the group. Scales (1996) looked at how children can change their strategies, with adult guidance, in order to be more successful at entering groups.

Over the past two decades, we have learned a great deal about the complexities of social relationships as they relate to play. For much of the past century, we were guided in our understanding of social play by age/stage conceptions such as the classic work of Mildred Parten (1932). Parten provided a set of stages through which children advance in the early childhood years, beginning with uninvolved and onlooker activity, through solitary, parallel, associative, and cooperative play. We can still see what she describes when we observe a 2-year-old playing by herself (solitary) in the midst of a group, or when we see two 3-year-olds playing side by side with puzzles, while not communicating with each other. Theorists such as Bateson, Garvey, and Corsaro give us guidance about how children use communicative abilities to develop their social relationships through play.

Culture and Social Play Communications

[Children played doctor in a Taiwanese kindergarten, including giving a bottle of medicine for treatment.] When she asked the doctor to return her bottle, the doctor regulated her behavior by saying, "Use both your hands to receive it." Here, the social custom of using both hands to give and receive an object from the other—a polite custom in Taiwanese society—regulated the partner's play behavior. (Lin & Reifel, 1999, p. 172)

The social relationships we form through our childhood and adult play create society (Huizinga, 1938). In play, we create our social groups, and play gives us the means for solidifying those groups. Shared communications are clearly a necessary part of how we bond with playmates, and how we acquire many aspects of our group identities. As the Taiwanese example of kindergarten doctor play shows, these children are not just learning to get along, to share with one another, and to cooperate; they are also relating to each other in a way that supports the customs of their society. Play like this is supported in classrooms when the teacher includes play objects (those pivots for meaning that Vygotsky describes) that prompt children to think about how to act and think within their cultures (Moon & Reifel, in press).

We have known for a half century that when children play together they form their own peer cultures (Opie & Opie, 1959, 1969). The games children play in their neighborhoods, the jokes and pranks they share, are created in a children's culture, usually separate from the values and desires of adults in the culture. Ring Around the Rosie has been transmitted since the time of the Black Plague in England over 500 years ago. If you say to a group of English speakers, "Ben and Jennifer sitting in a tree," and ask what the following line would be, you would get a chorus of "K-I-S-S-I-N-G." If you asked them where they learned that, they would usually mention friends or siblings. This oral language culture is rarely transmitted from adult to child, rather it is transmitted from child to child through many generations, in what we now call peer culture.

Peer culture is consistently a concern for adults and educators in that it often challenges authority. Adults want to shelter children from adult concerns such as sexuality, which is brought out in the kissing rhyme described above. At the same time children are playing out these same adult concerns in order to better understand them. Attempts to regulate children's play often end up forcing children into illicit play which they do out of the observation of adults (Frost et al., 2008; Sutterby, 2005). Adults often have little understanding of children's peer culture, as many worry today about children having cell phones, chatting online, or posting pictures on MySpace. The general fear that children's peer culture is out of hand or extreme has been a concern for years.

When we think of culture we often think of foods, styles of dress, or traditional festivals like Thanksgiving. What we often miss is the deep and subtle cultural meanings that are not transmitted publicly but become an important part of how we understand the world. This is especially true of play in classrooms and outside of school. As teachers, we often set up classroom play scenarios based on restaurant or grocery store themes that are familiar to children. A dramatic play of a hot dog street vender for a preschool in Chicago would be like a pretend taco stand in the southwest. The conflict often comes when the school culture does not match well with the home culture. Children who are used not to seeing geographical limits to play (play can occur anywhere in the house as long as an adult is present), often are confused when they see classrooms where there are separate centers for play like dramatic play or blocks (Sutterby & Frost, 2006; Woods, 2004). Overcoming these confusions for children involves the teacher coming to an understanding of what children (and their families) understand is appropriate play and how that relates to what the teacher expects for classroom play. It also involves closely looking at play for little, meaningful actions, such as a child passing on a custom during play, that makes play a powerful tool for understanding.

MATERIALS FOR PLAY

Educational Play Materials

Increased knowledge about the brain and brain development has impacted how materials are selected for classrooms. Brain development in childhood is considered to be critical to future ability to think. As the area of early childhood grows in importance, manufacturers of materials for play have begun to label toys as beneficial for the brain (Sutterby & Frost, 2006). Researchers looking into claims by some educational DVD manufacturers have found that DVDs not only are not helping children get "smarter," they may actually be harmful (Zimmerman, Christakis, & Meltzoff, 2007). Parents and educators looking to create learning environments for children have to evaluate the claims of these materials and decide if they really are beneficial.

Play materials have been incorporated for educational purposes for hundreds of years. For example, alphabet blocks were suggested as a learning tool by

John Locke in a publication from 1693 (Hewitt, 1979). As discussed earlier, Froebel created a complex set of play-based gifts and occupations. Maria Montessori designed materials to help the child gain understanding and self-organization through hands-on experiences. The closed-ended materials designed by Montessori are used to give children experiences with practical life activities, development of the senses, and literacy activities. Although Montessori programs generally use only Montessori materials, some teachers elect to integrate Montessori-type materials as a play center in their classroom or as a method to teach a specific concept area like mathematics (Guha, 2006).

Since the time of early designers of important play materials and environments, there have been a number of materials introduced for play in early childhood classrooms. Caroline Pratt (1948) is credited with developing unit blocks, the ubiquitous wooden blocks found in many classrooms. In addition to blocks, classrooms generally contain dramatic play materials (such as playhouses), small manipulative materials (beads for stringing, plastic connecting blocks), puzzles, and literacy materials, all associated with quality early childhood classrooms (Harms, Clifford, & Cryer, 2005). Contemporary classrooms also include technology in the form of computers and games.

Categories of Play Materials

Classroom materials can be included for many different reasons, and how to select play materials is a continuing issue. Play materials can be categorized as open ended, meaning the materials, like play dough or blocks, can be used in many different creative ways. Play materials can be closed ended like puzzles, which generally are used in only one way, for motor skills or problem solving. Play materials can be used for the different types of play, like costumes for dramatic play and Lego blocks for construction play.

Play materials can be more realistic, when they look more like the object that they are meant to represent. For example, a toy car will look more like a car than a wooden block will, but they can both be used as pretend cars. Realism has been found to promote more dramatic play in toddlers than have nonrealistic props. As children get older they are more able to play with materials that do not look like the object they are supposed to represent (Van Hoorn, Scales, Nourot, & Alward, 2007).

Play materials can also be included in order to support different domains of development. There can be cognitive reasons for including materials that encourage problem solving, like puzzles or blocks; these materials can also develop everyday math skills like comparison (Ginsberg, 2006). Play materials can be included for socioemotional reasons. Materials that encourage dramatic play, for example, can help children learn to negotiate interpersonally, which is an important social skill. Materials can also be included to develop physical skills, like scissors or Peg-Boards for fine motor development (Sutterby & Frost, 2006; Van Hoorn et al., 2007).

Researchers and educators have looked into how to select play materials for the classroom. Although there is no consensus on the best type of play materials, there is some consensus that children benefit from a balance of play materials (Harms, Clifford, & Cryer, 2005). A balance of materials that support cognitive, social, emotional, and physical development is of benefit to the most children (Doctoroff, 2001; Frost, Wortham, & Reifel, 2008).

Controversial Classroom Materials

[An example of Leo and Jeremy playing out an episode from the television series *Survivor*.]

Seven year old Jeremy and 6 year old Leo are playing in the outdoor lawn area of their elementary school playground. "I'll make you eat these worms!" snarls Jeremy, attempting to stuff a handful of leaves and wood shavings into Leo's mouth. When Leo protests, Jeremy counters, "But that's how your team can win! You want us to win, don't you?" (Van Hoorn et al., 2007, pp. 130–131).

When selecting materials for the classroom, teachers often have to make decisions about the materials included in the classroom that may be intentionally or unintentionally controversial. Children are exposed to different media out of the classroom that influence the type of play they engage in in the classroom. The most controversial play and play materials typically are toys that promote violence, racial or gender stereotyping, noneducational television shows, and technology. Many educators take the position that war play does not have a place in early childhood classrooms, while others see it as a part of children's emotional development and growing awareness of the world. One developmental view of play is that when children engage in war play or violent play they are meeting some emotional need that is being explored through their play. Sociopolitical theorists view war play as an expression of authoritarian power that teaches children that violence solves problems (Carlsson-Paige & Levin, 1987; Van Hoorn et al., 2007).

In addition to war play, teachers are often concerned about repetitive play that children engage in based on television programs. Children's television and children's toys based on television programs were gradually deregulated throughout the 1980s. Prior to this time, toy companies could not make television shows based on toy characters. Once deregulated, many children's programs essentially became program-length commercials for toys (Cross, 1997). Carlsson-Paige and Levin (1988) call this imitative play and suggest that it is a lower level of play than traditional play. The media's influence on children's play has been viewed negatively by many in that it encourages children to be more consumeristic, and encourages activities for younger children that are more appropriate for older children, such as encouraging dating or sexualized popular singing (Brown, Thornton, & Sutterby, 2004). Although media like television and movies influence children's play and play materials, it can also help children create a shared-play situation, as when they can use superheroes to help create a shared understanding of a script for play (Orellana, 1994; Paley, 1990; Scales, 1996).

Classroom teachers often struggle with how to control controversial play in the classroom. Banning this type of play often leads to it being conducted illicitly, in secret by groups of children who avoid adult interference. Although teachers have worked to ban or eliminate violent play, children often subvert class-room rules by ignoring them and continuing to play what they want to play (Sutterby, 2005).

CONTEMPORARY DIRECTIONS FOR EARLY CHILDHOOD PLAY

"Pretend we are walking in Egypt and there's no water but we see a big river."
   "Gulp, gulp, gulp, come on, drink it!"
   "No, I'm drowning. Help, help! Wait, there's a huge bullfrog jumping. Higher than the World Trade Center! He can't stay alive. There's no bugs to eat there any more. Hey, what's going on!"
   "It's exploding! . . . Get away from the fire. . . ."
   "Hey, you wanna bomb us?" (Paley, 2004, pp. 4–5)

Getting children to play (nicely or not) is one thing. Thoughtfully arranging the classroom, including appropriate materials, is important to that end. Understand-ing that play is another thing. Using all the theoretical lenses we have presented might help identify some of the cognitive, communicative, social, and cultural aspects of what happens during play. Building on play, for educational purposes, is a further challenge. How can we learn to observe children as they play, hear what they are saying, and decide how to respond? How do we make sense, when children play about rivers, frogs, the World Trade Center, and bombing? One thing we are learning from contemporary studies of play is just how complicated it can be.

The Multiple Meanings of Play

When children play, they think, they interact, they communicate, and they learn about schooling and their cultures. Traditional theories, as presented above, tell us how to understand those aspects of play as part of children's developmental stages. But pretend play, like all of the examples we have used throughout this chapter, reveals many different faces. Whether it is Van and Wallace playing with cars, J building her own house, the children playing with their baby and car, the Taiwanese children playing doctor, the American children playing *Survivor*, or the children blending frog jumping with the World Trade Center disaster, there is more going on than just children acting their ages. We can see the thinking they are doing, and the social jockeying that occurs as they play. They communicate and their feelings frequently emerge. Their play relates to our larger societies. Child-hood play is overflowing with meanings.
      Some contemporary scholars are trying to explore those meanings, drawing on older theories to interpret classroom play in new ways. When we look at dramatic play in classrooms, how do we (as adults) bring our thinking to that play? Paley's work, cited throughout this chapter, is one example. Others, like

VanderVen (2004); Reifel (2007); Reifel, Hoke, Pape, & Wisneski (2004); Reifel & Yeatman, (1991, 1993) argue that play is a text that we read, with layers of meanings. How can we look at children playing about the World Trade Center, without thinking of play as a Batesonian frame that children are trying to make sense of? How can we think about it without seeing what each of the players is bringing to that frame (is it just a tall building for some; a heroic setting for others; a bombing site for a few), and how their social relationships are contributing to their thinking about it? How do their relationships build the play story, from Egypt, to frogs, to tower? Given all the thinking, communicating, and feelings that can be involved in play, how can we bring together the play ideas of Vygotsky, Erikson, Bateson, and others to help us figure out what play means to children and to adults who work with them? Finding out more about how teachers can observe and make sense of play is a continuing issue—just as important for teaching as how the children are actually playing.

Postmodern Play Analyses

In contrast to the age-and-stage researchers discussed in the previous sections, a new direction for classroom play analysis strives to understand children and their educational play experiences from the perspective of social justice and equity. The questions for these play scholars are how classroom play becomes a context in which children confront larger social issues such as sexism, racism, and economic equity. Play is not just what children do; play becomes a tool for establishing and reinforcing society's inequities and biases.

From this point of view, researchers are seeing how children use race as a basis for deciding on desirable playmates, and what roles are appropriate for different races (Campbell, MacNaughton, Page, & Rolfe, 2004). Can a black boy be a prince? Can a brown girl be a doctor? Children make decisions about such things during play, and without adult supervision and guidance, they often come to ill-informed decisions. How does doll play, especially with dolls that resemble no human shape, influence girls' body image and identity (Hughes & MacNaughton, 2000)? The play objects we give girls and boys contribute to thoughtless, harmful stereotypes we seldom reflect on. The social interactions among children during free play can create powerful notions for girls and boys about what it means to be male, female, and heterosexual (Blaise, 2005). The often-ignored play lives of children in our classrooms are a potent melting pot for many issues that challenge our society.

While some play research has made efforts to tie children's play to the larger cultural customs that give it meanings (e.g., Chang & Reifel, 2003; Lin & Reifel, 1999), postmodern play scholarship has a social agenda that shows how many of our classroom practices, including something as "natural" as play, have connections to larger societal problems such as sexism and gender stereotypes, how people of different racial and ethnic backgrounds are treated with bias, and how poverty and wealth begin to be expressed through the toys and free play that we include in our classrooms. How do computers and computer games, for those who can afford them, establish inequities for learning? How does housekeeping play establish sex role expectations and biases for girls and boys? How do games and pretend marginalize the racial identities of minorities in multicultural schools? When we play about the World Trade Center, do children begin to think that all Arabs are bombers? These are the sorts of questions raised by this research, and they are a continuing issue for research and early childhood teachers.

Play in Contemporary Education

Play is challenged in today's educational settings. The accountability movement drew from the idea that our nation was at risk if we did not improve education for all children. In 1989, a state governors meeting began the idea of holding schools accountable for the education of all children, which culminated with the passage of the No Child Left Behind legislation in 2001 (Walberg, 2007). Currently, many teachers work in an environment where academic pressure is pushed down onto younger and younger children. Although many recognize the benefits of children's play, there is pressure to show results which may not pay off until many years from the date of the activity. Teachers can concretely show the results on a letter recognition task, but cannot show results for a child successfully negotiating a 25-minute play dialogue.

One of the most pronounced arenas for play that is the most threatened in contemporary schools is recess. The amount of time allowed for recess has declined dramatically since the advent of the accountability movement 17 years ago. Schools under pressure to improve test scores cut "noninstructional" time first, in order to improve test scores. Although recess has been demonstrated to improve on-task behavior and has many academic-related benefits, it is still under threat as a drain on time on task for teaching academic concepts (Pellegrini, 2005).

As a consequence children are developing more physical activity deficiencies, like obesity. This is directly related to the amount of physical activity that children engage in at school and are able to do at home. Frequently, children leave school with little time for physical activity and then spend many hours at home in front of television screens or computer monitors (Sutterby & Frost, 2002). What can we, as educators, do to bring a healthy balance to children's lives, including active play that can serve as a basis for a lifetime of vital participation in life?

Play is also threatened in the classroom. Direct instruction to teach literacy skills has become official government policy. Play activities that may improve children's skills in other developmental areas are being put aside to devote more time to direct instruction of skills. As a consequence, early childhood classrooms are beginning to look more like classrooms for upper-primary children, with children being encouraged to spend more time on paper-and-pencil tasks (Ohanian, 2002; Sutterby & Frost, 2006). The issue of what is the best curriculum for young children, play versus academics, continues as an issue, as it was when Froebel created the kindergarten.

CONCLUSIONS: THINKING ABOUT THE PLAY YOU SEE

It should be apparent to the reader that children's play as an educational tool has a rich, complicated history, with many different conceptions of play that theorists and educators have offered to guide our thinking and practice. Some old ideas have been discarded (play as recapitulation), while others have been updated (play builds on home experience). Developmental stages for cognitive, social, and language play still provide us with broad strokes we can use to understand children's growth. But now we see how all play is more than just a developmental marker. Play has multiple meanings for players and observers, including meanings for learning and education.

We hope that this chapter will help you take seriously ideas about what role play can have in early childhood education. We hope you can see some of the historical roots of play and education, and how those roots have sprouted more contemporary streams of thought about what it means to play and learn. These understandings should help you recognize how complex children's play is, and how it is further complicated by the contemporary world of education. At the same time, we hope that you have more tools for thinking about issues associated with play, in all its dimensions. Play brings together everything important and valuable about who we are—our ideas, our feelings for one another, our goals and ambitions. It takes much more than one idea to make sense of something so simply grand.

As you think about play, you can also plan your classroom settings where play will take place. How do you balance play with academics? What environments can you create for children to communicate and think together? Where can children express themselves and explore language? Where can they learn to get along with one another and to negotiate their identities? Where can they be physically active and safe? Where can they solve problems and spin the webs of narrative? And how can we understand what each player is contributing to her world and how he is benefiting? Even in an era of accountability, there is much interest in and support for play in early childhood classrooms (e.g., Frost et al., 2008; Jones & Cooper, 2006; Jones & Reynolds, 1992; Paley, 2004; Van Hoorn et al., 2007). We hope this chapter will lead you to resources that will help you explore all the continuing, evolving issues related to play, for the good of the children you teach.

REFERENCES

Bateson, G. (1955). A theory of play and fantasy. *Psychiatric Research Reports, 2,* 39–51.

Biber, B. (1984). *Early education and psychological development.* New Haven, CT: Yale University Press.

Blaise, M. (2005). *Playing it straight: Uncovering gender discourses in the early childhood classroom.* New York: Routledge.

Bodrova, E., & Leong, D. (1998). Development of dramatic play in young children and its effects on self-regulation: A Vygotskian approach. *Journal of Early Childhood Teacher Education, 20,* 115–124.

Bredekamp, S., & Copple, C. (1997). *Developmentally appropriate practice in early childhood programs* (Rev. ed.). Washington, DC: NAEYC.

Brosterman, N. (1997). *Inventing kindergarten.* New York: Abrams/Times Mirror.

Brown, P., Thornton, C., & Sutterby, J. (2004). Kids getting older younger: The adultification of children's play. In R. Clements & L. Fiorentino (Eds.), *The child's right to play: A global approach.* Westport, CT: Greenwood Press.

Bruner, J. (1990). *Acts of meaning.* Cambridge, MA: Harvard University Press.

Bruner, J., & Sherwood, V. (1976). Peekaboo and the learning of rule structures. In J. S. Bruner, A. Jolly, & K. Sylva (Eds.), *Play: Its role in development and evolution* (pp. 277–285). New York: Basic Books.

Campbell, S., MacNaughton, G., Page, J., & Rolfe, S. (2004). Beyond quality, advancing social justice and equity: Interdisciplinary explorations of working for equity and social justice in early childhood education. In S. Reifel & M. Brown (Eds.), *Social contexts of early education, and reconceptualizing play (II): Advances in early education and day care* (Vol. 13, pp. 55–91). New York: Elsevier/JAI.

Carlsson-Paige, N., & Levin, D. (1987). *The war play dilemma: Balancing needs and values in the early childhood classroom.* New York: Teachers College Press.

Carlsson-Paige, N., & Levin, D. (1988). Young children and war play. *Educational Leadership, 45*(4), 80–84.

Chang, L.-C., & Reifel, S. (2003). Play, racial attitudes, and self-concept in Taiwan. In D. Lytle (Ed.), *Play and culture studies: Vol. 5. Play and educational theory and practice* (pp. 257–275). Westport, CT: Praeger.

Charlesworth, R. (2008). *Understanding Child Development* (7th ed.). Clifton Park, NY: Thomson Delmar Learning.

Corsaro, W. (1979). "We're friends, right?" Children's use of access rituals in nursery school. *Language in Society, 8*(3), 315–336.

Corsaro, W. (1985). *Friendship and peer culture in the early years.* Norwood, NJ: Ablex.

Cossentino, J. (2006). Big work: Goodness, vocation and engagement in the Montessori method. *Curriculum Inquiry, 36*(1), 63–91.

Cross, G. (1997). *Kids' stuff: Toys and the changing world of American childhood.* Cambridge, MA: Harvard University Press.

Cuffaro, H. (1995). *Experimenting with the world: John Dewey and the early childhood classroom.* New York: Teachers College Press.

Dewey, J. (1896/1972). Imagination and expression. In *John Dewey: The Early Works, 1882–1898* (Vol. 5, pp. 192–201). Carbondale: Southern Illinois University Press.

Doctoroff, S. (2001). Adapting the physical environment to meet the needs of *all* young children for play. *Early Childhood Education Journal, 29*(2) 105–109.

Dyson, A. H. (1997). *Writing superheroes: Contemporary childhood, popular culture, and classroom literacy.* New York: Teachers College Press.

Edwards, C. P., Gandini, L., & Forman, G. (1998). *The hundred languages of children: The Reggio Emilia approach to early childhood education* (Rev. ed.). Stamford, CT: Ablex.

Erikson E. (1963). *Childhood and society* (2nd ed.). New York: W. W. Norton & Co.

Freud, S. (1938). *The basic writings of Sigmund Freud* (A. A. Brill, Ed. & Trans.). New York: Modern Library.

Froebel, F. (1887/1902). *The education of man.* New York: D. Appleton.

Froebel, F. (1844/1897). *Mother's songs, games, and stories* (F. & E. Lord, Trans.). London: Rice.

Frost, J., Wortham, S., & Reifel, S. (2008). *Play and child development* (3rd ed.). Upper Saddle River, NJ: Pearson/Merrill/Prentice Hall.

Garvey, C. (1990). *Play.* Cambridge, MA: Harvard University Press.

Gesell, A. (1934). *An atlas of infant behavior.* New Haven, CT: Yale University Press.

Ginsberg, S. (2006). Mathematical play and playful mathematics: A guide for early education. In D. Singer, R. Golinkoff, & K. Hirsh-Patek (Eds.), *Play = learning: How play motivates and enhances children's cognitive and social-emotional growth* (pp. 145–165). New York: Oxford University Press.

Groos, K. (1901). *The play of man.* New York: Appleton.

Guha, S. (2006). Using mathematics strategies in early childhood education as a basis for culturally responsive teaching in India. *International Journal of Early Years Education, 14*(1), 15–34.

Harms, T., Clifford, R., & Cryer, D. (2005). *Early childhood environment rating scale* (Rev. ed.). New York: Teachers College Press.

Hartley, R. E., Frank, L. K., & Goldenson, R. M. (1952). *Understanding children's play.* New York: Columbia University Press.

Hewitt, K. (1979). *Educational toys in America: 1800 to the present.* Burlington, VT: Queen City Printers.

Hohmann, C., & Weikart, D. P. (1995). *Educating young children: Active learning practices for preschool and child care programs.* Ypsilanti, MI: High/Scope Press.

Hughes, P., & MacNaughton, G. (2000). Identity-formation and popular culture: Learning lessons from Barbie. *Journal of Curriculum Theorizing, 16,* 57–67.

Huizinga, J. (1938). *Homo ludens: A study of the play-element in culture.* Boston: Beacon Press.

Isenberg, J. P., & Jolongo, M. R. (2006). *Creative thinking and arts-based learning: Preschool through fourth grade* (4th ed.). Upper Saddle River, NJ: Merrill/ Prentice Hall.

Jersild, A. (1933). *Child psychology.* New York: Prentice Hall.

Jones, E., & Cooper, R. M. (2006). *Playing to get smart.* New York: Teachers College Press.

Jones, E., & Reynolds, G. (1992). *The play's the thing: Teachers' roles in children's play.* New York: Teachers College Press.

Lin, S.-H., & Reifel, S. (1999). Context and meanings in Taiwanese kindergarten play. In S. Reifel (Ed.), *Play and culture studies: Vol. 2. Play contexts revisited* (pp. 151–176). Stamford, CT: Ablex.

Mallory, B., & New, R. (Eds.). (1994). *Diversity and developmentally appropriate practices: Challenges for early childhood education.* New York: Teachers College Press.

Mitchell, L. S. (1956). *Believe and make-believe.* New York: Dutton.

Moon, K., & Reifel, S. (2008). Play and literacy learning in a diverse language pre-kindergarten classroom. *Contemporary Issues in Early Childhood 9*(1), 49–65.

Ohanian, S. (2002). *What happened to recess and why are our children struggling in kindergarten?* New York: McGraw-Hill.

Opie I., & Opie, P. (1959). *The lore and language of school children.* Oxford: Clarendon Press.

Opie, I., & Opie, P. (1969). *Children's games in street and playground.* Oxford: Clarendon Press.

Orellana, M. (1994). Appropriating the voice of super-heroes: Three preschoolers' bilingual language uses in play. *Early Childhood Research Quarterly, 9,* 171–193.

Paley, V. (1981). *Wally's stories.* Cambridge, MA: Harvard University Press.

Paley, V. (1984). *Boys and girls: Superheroes in the doll corner.* Chicago: University of Chicago Press.

Paley, V. (1990). *The boy who would be a helicopter: The uses of storytelling in the classroom.* Cambridge, MA: Harvard University Press.

Paley, V. (2004). *A child's work: The importance of fantasy play.* Chicago: University of Chicago Press.

Parten, M. (1932). Social participation among pre-school children. *Journal of Abnormal and Social Psychology, 27,* 243–269.

Pellegrini, A. D. (2005). *Recess: Its role in education and development.* Mahwah, NJ: Erlbaum.

Piaget, J. (1962). *Play, dreams and imitation in childhood.* New York: Norton.

Pratt, C. (1948). *I learn from children.* New York: Harper and Row.

Reifel, S. (2007). Hermeneutic text analysis of play: Exploring meaningful early childhood classroom events. In J. A. Hatch (Ed.), *Early childhood qualitative research* (pp. 25–42). New York: Routledge.

Reifel, S., Hoke, P., Pape, D., & Wisneski, D. (2004). From context to texts: DAP, hermeneutics, and reading classroom play. In S. Reifel & M. Brown (Eds.), *Social contexts of early education, and reconceptualizing play (II): Advances in early education and day care* (Vol. 13, pp. 209–220). Oxford, England: Elsevier.

Reifel, S., & Yeatman, J. (1991). Action, talk, and thought in block play. In B. Scales, M. Almy, A. Nicologpoulou, & S. Ervin-Tripp (Eds.), *Play and the social context of development in early care and education* (pp. 156–172). New York: Teachers College Press.

Reifel, S., & Yeatman, J. (1993). From category to context: Reconsidering classroom play. *Early Childhood Research Quarterly, 8,* 347–367.

Saracho, O., & Spodek, B. (1995). Children's play and early childhood education: Insights from history and theory. *Journal of Education, 177*(3), 129–148.

Scales, B. (1996). Researching the hidden curriculum. In S. Reifel & J. Chafel (Eds.), *Advances in early education and day care: Theory and practice in early childhood education,* (pp. 237–262). Greenwich, CT: JAI Press.

Schweinhart, L., & Weikart, D. (1996). Lasting differences: The High/Scope preschool curriculum comparison study through age 23. *Monographs of the High/Scope Educational Research Foundation* (No. 12). Ypsilanti, MI: High/Scope Press.

Smilansky, S. (1968). *The effects of sociodramatic play on disadvantaged preschool children.* New York: Wiley.

Sobe, N. (2004). Challenging the gaze: The subject of attention and a 1915 Montessori demonstration classroom. *Educational Theory, 54*(3), 281–297.

Spariosu, M. (1989). *Dionysus reborn: Play and the aesthetic dimension in modern philosophical and scientific discourse.* Ithaca, NY: Cornell University Press.

Sutterby, J. (2005). "I wish we could do whatever we want!": Children subverting scaffolding in the preschool classroom. *Journal of Early Childhood Teacher Education, 25,* 349–357.

Sutterby, J., & Frost, J. (2002). Making playgrounds fit for children and children fit on playgrounds. *Young Children, 57*(3), 33–41.

Sutterby, J., & Frost, J. (2006). Creating play environments for early childhood: Indoors and out. In B. Spodek & O. Saracho (Eds.), *Handbook of research on the education of young children* (pp. 301–325). Mahwah, NJ: Earlbaum.

Tudge, J., Lee, S., & Putman, S. (1998). Young children's play in socio-cultural context: South Korea and the United States. In M. C. Duncan, G. Chick, & A. Aycock (Eds.), & S. Reifel, (Series Ed.), *Play and culture studies (Vol. 1): Diversions and divergences in fields of play* (pp. 77–90). Greenwich, CT: Ablex.

VanderVen, K. (2004). Beyond fun and games towards a meaningful theory of play: Can a hermeneutic perspective contribute? In S. Reifel & M. Brown (Eds.), *Social contexts of early education, and reconceptualizing play (II): Advances in early education and day care* (Vol. 13, pp. 167–208). Oxford, England: Elsevier.

Van Hoorn, J., Scales, B., Nourot, P. M., & Alward, K. R. (2007). *Play at the center of the curriculum* (4th ed.). Upper Saddle River, NJ: Merrill/Prentice Hall.

Vygotsky, L. S. (1978). *Mind in society: The development of higher psychological processes.* Cambridge, MA: Harvard University Press.

Walberg, H. (2003). Accountability unplugged. *Education Next, 3*(2), 76–79.

Weber, E. (1969). *The kindergarten: Its encounter with educational thought in America.* New York: Teachers College Press.

Woods, I. C. (2004). Lessons from home: A look at culture and development. In S. Reifel & M. Brown (Eds.), *Social contexts of early education, and reconceptualizing play (II): Advances in early education and day care* (Vol. 13, pp. 137–161). New York: Elsevier/JAI Press.

Zimmerman, F., Christakis, D., & Meltzoff, A. (2007). Television and DVD/video viewing in children younger than 2 years. *Archives of Pediatric Adolescent Medicine, 161*(5), 473–479.

CHAPTER 12

EARLY LEARNING STANDARDS AND DEVELOPMENTALLY APPROPRIATE PRACTICE: CONTRADICTORY OR COMPATIBLE?

Sue Bredekamp
Council for Professional Recognition

The early childhood profession has a long history of engagement with standard setting of all kinds: standards for programs, for professional preparation, for practice, and most recently, standards for children's learning. At the same time, the field of early childhood education has a profound ambivalence toward the concept of standard setting in general, as well as concern over specific standard-setting efforts, particularly those involving preestablished child outcomes. The familiar refrain is, standards or standardization? The implication of this question is that neither is a particularly attractive possibility (Carter, 2006; Catlett, Feeney, Gronlund, & Haggard, 2007; Wardle, 2007).

In June 2006, the National Association for the Education of Young Children (NAEYC) took "standards" as the theme for its annual professional development institute. The content of sessions covered a wide range of types of standard-setting efforts in the field. At the same time, the theme itself generated controversy. At a general session, for example, one participant reported that several "key leaders" in the field were boycotting the conference. Apparently, some individuals were affronted by NAEYC's presumed embrace of the concept of standards which they perceive as antithetical to the association's commitment to developmentally appropriate practice and responsiveness to individual and cultural variation among children and families (Carter, 2006).

The purpose of this chapter is to examine the complex issue of standards for children's learning and development. First, we examine the movement toward establishing early learning standards for children. Next, we describe the potential negative consequences as well as positive benefits of content standards, and the relationship between learning standards and accountability. Following this discussion of potential consequences, we describe the work that has been done setting standards for the standards. Finally, we address another ongoing standard-setting activity in the field—promotion of developmentally appropriate practice and its relationship with content standards. The chapter concludes with considerations for moving the debate forward, and future standard-setting work in the field.

EARLY LEARNING STANDARDS IN CONTEXT

One of the most influential trends in all of education in the last few decades has been the standards movement. The national trend began when then-President Clinton and the nation's governors established the National Education Goals in 1989. The first goal, clearly targeted at early childhood, was to have all children start school ready to learn by the year 2000 (NEGP, 1990). This goal was highly controversial in the field, with many early childhood educators objecting to the emphasis on children's readiness as opposed to the schools being ready for children (NAEYC, 1990/1995). Concerns were based on several issues: (1) the wide range of individual variation in the development of young children; (2) inequity of opportunities among diverse groups of children prior to school entry; and (3) the impact of linguistic and cultural diversity on children's development and learning.

Numerous debates at the time focused on whether and how readiness could or should be defined. A technical report of the goals panel offered a broad definition of readiness that included the following five dimensions: cognition and general knowledge; language and communication development; physical well-being and motor development; social and emotional development; and approaches toward learning (Kagan, Moore, & Bredekamp, 1995).

In retrospect, this broad definition has continued to be influential in subsequent efforts to define early learning standards for young children. For example, each of the five areas is included, along with others, in the Head Start Child Outcomes framework which was developed in response to the 1998 Head Start reauthorization (ACYF/Head Start Bureau, 2000). Prior to 1998, Head Start described its overall goal for children as the development of social competence, which was broadly understood to mean development of the whole child—physical, social, emotional, and cognitive. However, there were no specific learning goals articulated at the national level. In the 1998 reauthorization, Congress stepped in by mandating several specific goals in the areas of language, literacy, and numeracy. Most controversial and specific of these mandated child outcomes was that children needed to know at least 10 letters of the alphabet. Leaders at the Head Start Bureau responded to this mandate by articulating a more holistic child outcomes framework that encompassed the legislated requirements while also setting goals across all domains of children's development and learning (U.S. Department of Health and Human Services, 2003).

A parallel trend in standard setting was the development of standards by professional organizations and the promulgation of standards for learning in each state. The last decade of the 20th century saw each of the discipline-based content organizations develop standards for what students should know and be able to do at various grade levels. The National Council of Teachers of Mathematics (NCTM) led the way by first publishing principles and standards for school mathematics in 1989, and then revising them in 2000 (NCTM, 2000). Virtually every other discipline including science, history, the arts, physical education, and language arts/reading followed. The Web site of the Mid-Continent Regional Education Laboratory (www.mcrel.org) provides a complete chronology of content standards development.

Every state has established learning standards for K–12 schools and 46 states have developed early learning standards for the preschool level (Scott-Little, Kagan, & Frelow, 2006). The vocabulary of the standards movement encompasses several related terms. *Standards* is the broadest term referring to expectations for student learning. *Content standards* define the "knowledge, concepts, and skills to be taught at each age or grade level" (Bowman, 2006, 42). *Early learning standards* are content standards for young children, usually 3- to 5-year-olds (Scott-Little et al., 2006).

Performance standards, also called benchmarks, which sometimes accompany content standards, describe expected levels of student performance related to the content standard as illustrated by the following example. A content standard for preschool early literacy might state: *Children develop print awareness.* Accompanying performance standards might include: Children hold a book upright; identify the book's cover; turn the pages properly; understand that reading begins at the top of the page and follows as print moves left to right. Other performance standards related to print awareness might state: Children know that letters can be put together to form words, and know that in print, words have spaces between them. Performance standards are also sometimes called *mastery goals* because they are expectations for skills that children need to master by a given point in time.

The standards movement has affected all aspects of education. Standards are not curriculum; however, curriculum developers now design experiences and teaching strategies to help children achieve standards (Seefeldt, 2005; Wien, 2004). Similarly, assessment of children's learning is linked to accomplishment of the standards (Gronlund, 2006). Ideally, a program's goals for children's learning include, but are not necessarily limited to, the relevant early learning standards. Then as teachers plan and implement curriculum, they engage in ongoing assessment of children's learning in relation to the goals or standards. Finally, teachers adapt the curriculum and teaching strategies to ensure that children continue to make progress toward the standards. In such a scenario, standards guide but do not determine or standardize the curriculum and assessment tools.

Reality does not always conform to the ideal, however. The accountability movement in this country coincided with the explosion in standard setting at the state level. At the same time, state learning standards became closely associated with standardized testing for accountability, such as that required by the No Child Left Behind law. As a result, the stakes surrounding standard setting have been raised significantly. Schools, teachers, and even children are now held accountable for achievement of learning standards as defined by scores on standardized tests. These trends naturally have consequences, both negative and positive, which are described in the sections that follow.

Potential Negative Effects of Early Learning Standards

Early childhood educators have resisted setting specific goals for children's learning and development for several reasons. The most obvious reason is the fundamental variability in individual children's development. Because young children's development is episodic, uneven, and highly influenced by their prior experiences, early childhood educators tend to believe that no one set of age-related goals can be applied to all children (Bredekamp, 2004; NAEYC, 1990/1995). In addition, because development is so influenced by social and cultural contexts, concern exists that standards will not be sensitive to cultural and linguistic variation in young children. These concerns are legitimate because children from low-income families, children of color, and those who speak a home language other than English are more likely to be identified as unready for school or retained in kindergarten (West, Denton, & Germino-Hausken, 2000).

Another concern is that specifying learning outcomes will narrow the curriculum and negatively affect pedagogy. The concern is that teachers will attempt to directly teach narrowly defined skills and neglect important cognitive and social-emotional processes such as problem solving and self-regulation (Carter, 2006; Catlett et al., 2007; Wardle, 2007). Again, this concern has a basis in reality (Wien, 2004). If standards drive curriculum, it is essential that standards be comprehensive and developmentally appropriate. However, state early learning standards are not equally broad and holistic. An evaluation of state early learning standards found uneven attention to all areas of children's development and learning (Scott-Little et al., 2006). While every state addresses the areas of language and cognition, there is less consistent attention to social-emotional development, physical health and development, and approaches toward learning, such as curiosity and persistence.

At one extreme, standards can limit curriculum; at the other, they can overwhelm it. Some states list hundreds of discrete objectives for learning. Such lengthy lists can make the task of implementing and achieving standards nearly impossible. In addition, laundry lists of standards can lead to teaching discrete skills rather than focusing on larger conceptual understandings (Seefeldt, 2005; Wien, 2004).

A final negative consequence of standards is that they may not be at the right level to be challenging, even though they are achievable for most of the children within the age range. This criterion requires that standards be *developmentally appropriate.* However, some state standards underestimate children's competence whereas others overestimate it. For example, some states expect 4-year-olds to segment or blend phonemes, a task that is much too difficult for preschoolers and more appropriate for late kindergarten or first grade (Neuman, Roskos, Vukelich, & Clements, 2003).

Although all of these negative consequences are legitimate and warrant attention, each is based on the same assumption: that the standards which are set for children's learning and development will be the wrong standards. If, however, this assumption could be turned on its head, then many of the disadvantages of standards could be turned into advantages, as described in the next section.

Potential Benefits of Early Learning Standards

How can standards be most useful? Well-written learning standards clearly define what is to be taught and what kind of performance is expected. In other words, standards can provide useful guidance to curriculum developers and teachers about what and when to teach particular content.

Teachers of young children need guidance about appropriate expectations for children's learning in the various content areas. When standards are achievable and challenging (that is, developmentally appropriate), they provide a framework for planning and implementing curriculum and individualizing teaching. Such frameworks are especially important in curriculum areas where teachers' own knowledge of the content may be lacking, such as mathematics and science (French, 2004; Gelman & Brenneman, 2004; Greenes, Ginsburg, & Balfanz, 2004). When teachers are familiar with expected developmental continua and learning trajectories, they can more accurately assess children's learning and adapt their teaching to help children continue to make progress. Similarly, such information can help teachers identify children whose learning progress is outside the typical range, whether above expectations or indicative of a disability or special need.

The assumption that standards are inherently not developmentally appropriate is unfair and false. When standards are based on research and are developed with the input of knowledgeable and experienced teachers as well as families and community members, standards can provide excellent guidance for curriculum, teaching, and assessment (Neuman et al., 2003; Catlett et al., 2007).

One of the most powerful arguments in favor of standards is that they promote educational equity. Barbara Bowman (2006), a key leader in the field and founder of the prestigious Erikson Institute, advocates setting content and performance standards as a strategy for ensuring that professionals have high expectations for *all* children. Bowman (2006) points out a key fallacy in the arguments against standard setting:

> It is *not* true that programs that say they have no standards actually have no standards. What it means is that standards are implicit, embedded in the particular biases of a teacher, parent, or whatever other adults are making decisions. When a program has no standards, it really means that everyone gets to use their own standards without subjecting them to scrutiny. (p. 43)

Bowman raises a thorny ethical question about standard setting. Specified standards make it possible for administrators, teachers, families, funders, evaluators, and other interested parties to review, debate, and potentially revise a program's goals and expectations for children. If standards are in writing, they can be discussed, debated, and modified based on input from teachers and parents. Families can evaluate whether standards reflect their cultural values for their children. When expectations for children's learning are clear, teachers can evaluate whether they are not only achievable but also challenging for the children. For instance, if the standard calls for children to learn 10 letters in Head Start, teachers who know the children can determine that this expectation is too low for most of the children, but may be appropriate for some of the children with special needs. Other children who speak Spanish at home may learn the letters in their home language.

On the other hand, the absence of clearly articulated standards does affect curriculum and children's progress. Prior to the establishment of the Head Start Child Outcomes framework, for example, teachers did not recognize the importance of children learning the alphabet—which is one of the strongest predictors of later success in learning to read and write (National Early Literacy Panel, in press; Snow, Burns, & Griffin, 1998; Whitehurst & Lonigan, 1998). Early results from the Head Start Family and Child Experiences Survey (FACES) revealed that on average, children began Head Start knowing one letter and finished a year in Head Start knowing two letters (ACYF, 2001). Data such as these precipitated congressional action on mandated child outcomes in the Head Start reauthorization. In retrospect, it would have been much better if informed early childhood educators and child development experts had tackled the challenge of establishing early learning standards in the first place.

In summary, the potential benefits of learning standards include (Seefeldt, 2004; Gronlund, 2006):

❏ Enhanced clarity about what children can and should be learning

❏ Greater consistency in practice across diverse types of schools and programs serving young children

❏ Improved learning and developmental outcomes for all children

❏ Educational equity for those children who have not traditionally been served well by our nation's schools

❏ Enhanced continuity and alignment of curriculum from preschool through primary grades

❏ Increased professionalism among early childhood educators who become more intentional about their work, and capable of articulating its benefits for children

❏ Accountability among policy makers, administrators, and teachers for ensuring that all children achieve their potential

To ensure that content standards achieve these benefits and improve outcomes for children, the standards themselves must be the right standards. In other words, standards must meet standards, a description of which follows.

ENSURING POSITIVE OUTCOMES: SETTING STANDARDS FOR THE STANDARDS

In collaboration with early childhood specialists in state departments of education, NAEYC developed a position statement entitled, *Early Learning Standards: Creating the Conditions for Success* (NAEYC & NAECS/SDE, 2002). The position statement is supported by the Council of Chief State School Officers, National Association of Elementary School Principals, and the American Academy of Pediatrics. The statement effectively describes not only the essential features of standards themselves, but also the systems that are needed to ensure standards are successful in achieving goals for children. The essential features of an effective system of early learning standards follow (NAEYC & NAECS/SDE, 2002).

1. Effective early learning standards emphasize significant, developmentally appropriate content and outcomes that
   ❑ Emphasize all domains of development and learning
   ❑ Are meaningful and important to children's current well-being and later learning
   ❑ Are based on research
   ❑ Create appropriate expectations—achievable and challenging for most children
   ❑ Accommodate variations—community, cultural, linguistic, and individual

2. Effective early learning standards are developed and reviewed through informed, inclusive processes that
   ❑ Draw on valid sources of evidence
   ❑ Involve multiple stakeholders including families, community members, early childhood educators and special educators, and other professional groups
   ❑ Result from a thorough process of discussion and exchange of diverse views
   ❑ Are regularly reviewed and revised based on new research

3. Early learning standards gain their effectiveness through implementation and assessment practices that support all children's development in ethical, appropriate ways.
   ❑ Standards are connected to effective curriculum, classroom practices, teaching strategies, and assessment tools.
   ❑ Assessment information is used to benefit, not harm, children.

4. Effective early learning standards require a foundation of support for early childhood programs, professionals, and families.
   ❑ Needed resources are available for programs to provide high-quality environments for children.
   ❑ Families are involved in all aspects of standards implementation.
   ❑ Professional development is provided for teachers to effectively implement standards-based curriculum, assessment, and teaching.

This position statement sets a high standard for developing and implementing learning standards. The fundamental message is that standards can only achieve their full potential for children if certain conditions are met. One of the most important of these conditions is that teachers must be adequately prepared to implement standards effectively. If not, the negative consequences of standard setting are more likely to occur, regardless of the precautions taken in developing the standards in the first place (Wien, 2004).

To explore the consequences of standard setting, Carol Wien (2004) conducted several case studies of teachers as they implemented a major standard-based reform in Ontario, Canada. Although not an experimental study, these cases reveal what can actually happen in a standards-driven environment. A lengthy list of standards led to a standardized school curriculum. As a result, teachers' behaviors varied in four ways (Wien, 2004).

1. Some good teachers managed to figure out how to address standards and adapt the standardized curriculum to be responsive to children's needs and interests as best they could.

2. Some teachers succumbed to the demands and implemented an unvarying curriculum.

3. Some teachers attempted to juggle what they perceived to be conflicting demands: standards on the one hand and their commitment to developmentally appropriate practices on the other.

4. Some teachers left the field of education.

Even such a brief summary of possible outcomes for implementing standards in the real world demonstrates the necessity of addressing the topic of how to work with standards and adapt standardized curriculum in preservice preparation of teachers. Wien (2004) calls this process "negotiating standards." At the same time, most current teachers will need professional development opportunities to teach them to work effectively with standards (Gronlund, 2006; Seefeldt, 2005; Wien, 2004).

Another necessary condition for the success of standards is the involvement of diverse groups in setting and reviewing standards. One such example is the state of New Mexico, where early childhood leaders led by Dan Haggard at the state education department took several years to develop its early learning standards. They made a concerted effort to reach out to all groups in the state, including Native Americans. Haggard (Catlett et al., 2007) relates how involving tribal elders affected the process of identifying the most important standards, which originally included language, literacy, and numeracy. Discussions with tribal elders revealed their concerns that their children need to learn to "switch gears"—the ability to adapt their behavior and language in diverse contexts, such as when an elder enters a room (Catlett, 2007). This concept of switching gears is more broadly identified in the child development literature as self-regulation, a process that underlies all cognitive and social development, and is a strong predictor of academic success (Blair & Razza, 2007; McClelland, Acock, & Morrison, 2006; Shonkoff & Phillips, 2000). Thus, in New Mexico, input from tribal leaders resulted in adding this key concept of switching gears to the other important goals.

The standards movement no longer appears to be a current trend, but rather a reality that will continue to influence early childhood programs for the foreseeable future (Goffin & Washington, 2007; Seefelt, 2005). Given the potential negative consequences as well as real benefits of standards for promoting educational excellence and equity, it is essential that early childhood educators take the lead in setting standards for early learning. The alternative is for early childhood professionals to sit on the sidelines, wring their hands, and abdicate responsibility to others who are less informed (Goffin & Washington, 2007).

One of the most common reasons cited for rejecting learning standards is concern that they will lead to practices that are developmentally inappropriate. In the following section, we address the relationship of learning standards and developmentally appropriate practice.

DEVELOPMENTALLY APPROPRIATE PRACTICE AND LEARNING STANDARDS

Developmentally appropriate practice is a phrase that refers to another effort at standard setting by early childhood educators—the profession's attempts, led by NAEYC, to describe recommended teaching practices that reflect what is known about child development and learning (Bredekamp, 1987; Bredekamp & Copple, 1997). By definition, developmentally appropriate practices are ways of teaching that vary for and adapt to the age, interests, experiences, and abilities of individual children (Bredekamp, in press). Developmentally appropriate practices result from teachers' making decisions that draw on their knowledge of child development and learning, as well as their knowledge of individual children and the sociocultural context. A complete history of NAEYC's work on developmentally appropriate practice and related standard-setting work is beyond the scope of this chapter. (For a detailed history, see Bredekamp, 2001.)

The concept of developmentally appropriate practice has its origin in the child study movement during the early 20th century. Developmentally appropriate practice incorporates such cherished early childhood values as respect for the whole child; responsiveness to individual children; play as a key context for children's development; the importance of relationships to healthy development; respect for cultural diversity; and involvement of families (NAEYC, 2005).

NAEYC's position statement on developmentally appropriate practice (sometimes abbreviated as DAP) was first developed in the mid-1980s in the context of trends toward pushing down first-grade curriculum into kindergarten and preschool, and to help guide programs seeking NAEYC accreditation (Bredekamp, 1987). The position statement was revised in the mid-1990s to reflect new knowledge and in response to a changing social and political context, which included misunderstandings of the initial statement (Bredekamp & Copple, 1997). The 1997 revised position statement attempted to do a better job of addressing several key issues. These included awareness of the relationships between teaching, curriculum, and assessment; the intentional role of the teacher as decision maker; the role of culture in development; the importance of individually appropriate practices, especially for children with disabilities; and the need for reciprocal relationships with families. The 1997 position statement further challenged the field to go from either/or to both/and thinking to address some of the recurring false dichotomies that characterize the field: for example, moving from the belief that children benefit only from child-initiated learning experiences *or* only from teacher directed experiences, to the idea that children can benefit from *both* teacher-directed *and* child-initiated learning experiences.

NAEYC's position statements are regularly reviewed and revised in response to new knowledge and research, and to changing contexts and issues of controversy (Bredekamp, 2001). The 1997 DAP position is being revised as this chapter is written. In the interim, NAEYC has published a book to help entry-level personnel understand the basic concepts of developmentally appropriate practice (Copple & Bredekamp, 2006). The points that follow in this discussion are based on the conversations that have occurred regarding revisions to the position statement, as well as key provisions of the 1997 statement that are further clarified in the *Basics of Developmentally Appropriate Practice* (Copple & Bredekamp, 2006).

The Relationship of Developmentally Appropriate Practice and Learning Standards

One of the continuing confusions about developmentally appropriate practice is its focus. From the beginning the document has described *how* to teach, not *what* to teach. NAEYC's relative silence on curriculum content through the years led some to believe that goals for children's learning were unimportant. This misunderstanding grew in part from the field's ambivalence about specifying such goals, described earlier in this chapter. Attempts have been made to address this issue, with NAEYC developing curriculum and assessment guidelines in collaboration with the National Association of Early Childhood Specialists in State Departments of Education which were subsequently revised (NAEYC & NAECS/SDE, 2003). These statements provide general guidance for developing or selecting curriculum. They include criteria for curriculum such as evidence-based; individually and culturally appropriate; and validated by the disciplines (such as mathematics or science). But they do not say what children should know and be able to do at specific ages, the way state standards and Head Start outcomes do.

As already described, the early childhood profession took a stand on the specific issue of early learning standards—identifying standards for setting standards (NAEYC & NAECS/SDE, 2002). Among the criteria for such standards is that they be developmentally appropriate, that is, achievable and challenging for most children for whom they are intended. So we see that there is a bit of a circular relationship between setting standards for children and standards for teachers' practice. Standards need to be developmentally appropriate in the first place, and then teachers use developmentally appropriate ways of helping children achieve them.

One way of determining whether the learning standards themselves are developmentally appropriate is to ascertain whether they are research-based. In other words, standards should be built on a solid foundation of research in child development and early childhood education, as well as the particular discipline such as literacy, language, or mathematics (Neuman et al., 2003). For example, a preschool standard such as "comprehends and responds to stories read aloud" is research-based (Neuman et al., 2003). Studies have found that preschool children are capable of achieving this goal, and that the achievement predicts their later success in learning to read (Snow, Burns, & Griffin, 1998). On the other hand, a standard for prekindergarten such as "reads one-syllable and high-frequency words" is not research-based, because there is no evidence that this is a reasonable, achievable objective for 4-year-olds (Neuman et al., 2003).

Despite the lack of agreed-upon national learning standards, the 1997 DAP position statement contained an important inference about standards that has been somewhat overlooked. The position states: "Developmentally appropriate programs are based on what is known about how children develop and learn; such programs promote the development and enhance the learning of each individual child served" (Bredekamp & Copple, 1997, p. 8). In other words, developmentally appropriate practices not only reflect what is known about child development and learning, they *contribute* to children's development and learning. Therefore, if children are not making learning and developmental progress in a program, then the teaching practices are not developmentally appropriate. These clarifications beg the question of progress toward what? The most obvious answer is progress toward agreed-upon goals, or content and performance standards.

In the *Basics of Developmentally Appropriate Practice* text, we further clarified the relationship between practices and standards (Copple & Bredekamp, 2006). In that text, the complex concept of developmentally appropriate practice is reduced to three key ideas for teachers:

1. Meet children where they are
2. Help them achieve challenging and achievable goals
3. Use a variety of teaching strategies to ensure all children make continued learning and developmental progress

Here again, we have the idea of standards for children's learning and development—challenging and achievable, that is, developmentally appropriate, goals—clearly connected to ways of teaching. The concept of "meeting children where they are" reflects the core early childhood value of responsiveness to individuals and the need to build curriculum on children's interests. But implicit in that concept is a purpose for meeting children where they are. We meet children where they are, not to leave them there, but so that we can help them go where we want them to go. Effective teachers assess children's capabilities in order to plan and implement learning experiences and teaching strategies to help children achieve important goals, that is, learning standards.

So we see that in the past, an important relationship has existed between developmentally appropriate practices and learning standards. The current educational context places greater emphasis than ever on the role of standards and accountability that must be taken into consideration as the profession once again revisits its position on developmentally appropriate practice.

DEVELOPMENTALLY APPROPRIATE PRACTICE: THE NEXT ITERATION

A key part of the process of revising its position statements is for NAEYC to gather comments from the field regarding new trends to consider or issues in need of greater emphasis. In so doing, the association identifies the contextual factors that are most influential on early childhood practices, as well as the issues of controversy that a position statement is designed to address. Many of the themes of the mid-1990s continue to be issues, such as the both/and approach rather than the polarizing either/or stance; the need for consideration of the whole child, reflecting new research on the relationship of social-emotional development and school readiness; and teachers' decision making and intentionality in using the full range of effective teaching strategies. In addition, respondents have identified several issues in need of greater attention, reflecting the current accountability context in which schools and early childhood programs operate. These issues include:

❑ Standards, curriculum, and assessment

❑ Evidence-based (research-based) practice

❑ The fact that developmentally appropriate expectations and experiences are challenging as well as achievable and contribute to children's learning and development

❑ Focus on kindergarten through grade 3, and the alignment and transition between prekindergarten and the K–12 system

❑ Integration of curriculum in the interest of more meaningful, connected learning

❑ Robust content in curriculum for young children

Even such a cursory list of key issues as this indicates that early childhood professionals see the need for NAEYC to go beyond articulating *how* to teach to say more about *what* to teach. In particular, a need exists to help teachers and other educators understand the connections between the science of child development and the education of children (Bransford, Brown, & Cocking, 2000; Shonkoff & Phillips, 2000).

Given that NAEYC defines early childhood as birth through age 8, these issues are especially salient in light of the impact of No Child Left Behind (NCLB) on standards, curriculum, and assessment in the primary grades. One of the major purposes of NCLB is to ameliorate the intransigent achievement gap that exists in this country between white, middle-class children and children from low-income families and children of color—a gap that already exists before formal school entry (West et al., 2000). Research-based, developmentally appropriate, clearly written, and comprehensive standards of learning are one part of the solution. The other part is ensuring that teachers utilize an intellectually engaging curriculum and wide range of effective teaching strategies to help individual children achieve the standards. In conclusion, developmentally appropriate practice encompasses both the goals for children's learning and the means for helping children accomplish those goals.

REFERENCES

Administration for Children, Youth, and Families (ACYF). (2001). *Head Start FACES: Longitudinal findings on program performance*. Washington, DC: U.S. Department of Health and Human Services.

Administration on Children, Youth and Families/Head Start Bureau. (2000). *The Head Start path to positive child outcomes*. Washington, DC: U.S. Department of Health and Human Services, Head Start Information and Publications Center.

Blair, C., & Razza, R. C. (2007). Relating effortful control, executive function, and false belief understanding to emerging math and literacy ability in kindergarten. *Child Development, 78*(2), 647–663.

Bowman, B. T. (2006). Standards: At the heart of educational equity. *Young Children, 61*(5), 42–48.

Bransford, J. D., Brown, A. L., & Cocking, R. R. (Eds.). (2000). *How people learn: Brain, mind, experience, and school* (Expanded ed.). Washington, DC: National Academy Press.

Bredekamp, S. (Ed.) 1987. *Developmentally appropriate practice in early childhood programs serving children from birth through age 8* (Expanded ed.). Washington, DC: NAEYC.

Bredekamp, S. (2001). Improving professional practice: A letter to Patty Smith Hill. In M. Smith (Ed.), *NAEYC at 75: Reflections on the past, challenges for the future*. Washington, DC: NAEYC.

Bredekamp, S. (2004). Standards for preschool and kindergarten mathematics education. In D. H. Clements, J. Sarama, & A. M. DiBiase (Eds.), *Engaging young children in mathematics: Standards for pre-school and kindergarten mathematics education*. Mahwah, NJ: Erlbaum.

Bredekamp, S. (in press). *Effective practices in early childhood education*. Boston: Pearson/Allyn & Bacon.

Bredekamp, S., & Copple, C. (Eds.). (1997). *Developmentally appropriate practice in early childhood programs* (Rev. ed.). Washington, DC: NAEYC.

Carter, M. (2006). Standards or standardization: Where are we going? *Child Care Information Exchange, 169*, 32–36.

Catlett, C., Feeney, S., Gronlund, G., & Haggard, D. (2007, June). *Standards vs. standardization: Using early learning standards and authentic assessment to intentionally support a curriculum that is appropriate for all children*. Presentation at the annual NAEYC Professional Development Institute, Pittsburgh, PA.

Copple, C., & Bredekamp, S. (2006). *Basics of developmentally appropriate practice: An introduction for teachers of children 3 to 6*. Washington, DC: NAEYC.

French, L. (2004). Science as the center of a coherent, integrated early childhood curriculum. *Early Childhood Research Quarterly, 19*(1), 138–149.

Gelman, R., & Brenneman, K. (2004). Science learning pathways for young children. *Early Childhood Research Quarterly, 19*(1), 150–158.

Goffin, S. G., & Washington, V. (2007). *Ready or not: Early care and education faces new realities*. New York: Teachers College Press.

Greenes, C., Ginsburg, H. P., & Balfanz, R. (2004). Big math for little kids. *Early Childhood Research Quarterly, 9*(1), 159–166.

Gronlund, G. (2006). *Make early learning standards come alive: Connecting your practice and curriculum to state guidelines*. St. Paul, MN: Redleaf Press; Washington, DC: NAEYC.

Kagan, S. L., Moore, E., & Bredekamp, S. (Eds.). (1995). *Reconsidering children's early development and learning: Toward common views and vocabulary*. Washington, DC: U.S. Government Printing Office.

McClelland, M. M., Acock, A. C., & Morrison, F. J. (2006). The impact of kindergarten learning-related skills on academic trajectories at the end of elementary school. *Early Childhood Research Quarterly, 21*(4), 471–490.

Mid-Continent Regional Education Laboratory. Standards project. Retrieved June 8, 2007, from www.mcrel.org

NAEYC. (1990/revised 1995). *School readiness: Position statement*. Retrieved June 8, 2007, from www.naeyc.org

NAEYC & NAECS/SDE. (2002). *Early learning standards: Creating the conditions for success. A position statement*. Retrieved June 8, 2007, from http://ericps.crc.uiuc.edu/naecs/position/creatingconditions.pdf

NAEYC & NAECS/SDE. (2003). *Early childhood curriculum, assessment, and program evaluation: Building an effective, accountable system in programs for children birth through age 8; A joint position statement*. Retrieved February 8, 2008, from www.naeyc.org

NAEYC. 2005. *NAEYC Code of Ethical Conduct*. Washington, DC: Author.

Neuman, S., Vukelich, C., Roskos, K., & Clements, D. (2003). *The state of state prekindergarten standards in*

2003. Ann Arbor, MI: Center for the Improvement of Early Reading Achievement. Retrieved June 8, 2007, from www.ciera.org/library/archieve/2003-10/index.htm

Scott-Little, C., Kagan, S. L., & Frelow, V. S. (2006). Conceptualization of readiness and the content of early learning standards: The intersection of policy and research? *Early Childhood Research Quarterly, 21*(2), 153–173.

Seefeldt, C. (2005). *How to work with standards in the early childhood classroom.* New York: Teachers College Press.

Shonkoff, J. P., & Phillips, D. A. (Eds.). (2000). *From neurons to neighborhoods: The science of early childhood development.* Washington, DC: National Academy Press.

Snow, C. E., Burns, M. S., & Griffin, P. (1998). *Preventing reading difficulties in young children.* Washington, DC: National Academy Press.

U.S. Department of Health and Human Services, Administration for Children and Families, Head Start Bureau. (2003). *The Head Start leaders guide to positive child outcomes.* Washington, DC: Author.

Wardle, F. (2007, March/April). Math in early childhood. *Child Care Information Exchange,* 55–58.

West, J., Denton, K., & Germino-Hausken, E. (2000). *America's kindergartners: Findings from the early childhood longitudinal study, kindergarten class of 1998–99, fall 1998.* Washington, DC: U.S. Department of Education, National Center for Education Statistics.

Wien, C. A. (2004). *Negotiating standards in the primary classroom: The teacher's dilemma.* New York: Teachers College Press.

Whitehurst, G. J., & Lonigan, C. J. (1998). Child development and emergent literacy. *Child Development, 68,* 848–872.

PART 5

How Can We Meet the Needs of All Young Children?

"**M**aking room for everyone" in early childhood classrooms is perhaps the greatest challenge facing the early childhood community now and in the days and years to come. Not only are there federal and state laws that mandate inclusion (Individuals with Disabilities Education Act of 2004; No Child Left Behind Act of 2001), but as the authors of Chapters 13 and 14 strongly argue, diversity in early education rests on our very ideals as a people. It is the right, moral, and democratic thing to do. This right is viewed by authors Bruce Mallory, Beth Rous, Rebecca New, and Margaret Beneke as an ethical imperative that must be realized to achieve equitable and effective practice.

In Chapter 13, "Educating Young Children with Developmental Differences: Principles of Inclusive Practice," Mallory and Rous introduce the reader to a set of assumptions that guide the curriculum principles developed in later sections.

❏ Children with disabilities have the right to participate in high-quality early childhood programs that are developmentally and culturally appropriate.

❏ Inclusive early education programs benefit children's overall development and contribute to the acquisition of culturally valued knowledge and skills necessary for negotiating formal educational settings.

❏ There is an inextricable relationship between the conceptualization of curriculum and the success of inclusive practices.

❏ If we are to treat young children with disabilities as equals in early childhood classrooms, it may often be necessary to treat them differently. The goal is to create inclusive environments that acknowledge individual differences within a welcoming and supportive community of learners.

Mallory and Rous summarize the field of early childhood special education. Although there has been controversy along the way about a continuum of inclusion and what constitutes developmentally appropriate practice for young children with disabilities, by the mid-1990s the field of early childhood special education had become both an instigator and advocate for inclusive practices. In addition, there was a strong interest in ensuring that guidelines for high-quality early education include attention to the needs of children with both developmental and cultural differences.

Mallory and Rous argue that one of the primary factors contributing to the differential treatment and placement of young children with special needs has been the lack of a unifying theoretical framework that could guide inclusive early childhood practices. Principles of social constructivism lead to curriculum principles that address the needs of both adults and children in an inclusive early childhood program. They include the following:

❏ Effective early education programs are based on a coherent and integrated conceptualization of children's learning and development.

❏ The overarching goal of early education programs should be to increase young children's participation in the social contexts in which they live and learn on a daily basis. This goal requires strategies designed to enhance the frequency, intensity, and duration of interactions between children with disabilities and those without.

❏ Assessment of children's learning and development must be referenced to the skills and knowledge needed to participate successfully in a broad range of increasingly complex social contexts. The authors advocate the use of authentic assessment approaches involving the collaboration of various professionals.

❏ Inclusive curriculum and instruction are grounded in a dynamic balance between child-directed and teacher-directed activities.

❏ Small groups of two to four learners provide an optimal structure for fostering cognitive development and social participation in inclusive classrooms. Particularly interesting is the idea that small groups may act in an advocate role helping to identify the capabilities of classmates with disabilities and offering suggestions for ways to accommodate their classmates' needs.

❏ Domain-specific therapies support participation and inclusion when they are embedded within the context of the child's typical learning environment.

Mallory and Rous acknowledge that inclusion remains a difficult reality to achieve. The challenges are attitudinal and financial, and require a commitment to developing methodologies that work for all young children.

In Chapter 14, "Negotiating Diversity in Early Childhood Education: Rethinking Notions of Expertise," Rebecca New and Maggie Beneke argue for a new and more inclusive theory of human development that is strongly based in the sociocultural contexts of the lives of children and their families. If early childhood educators are to begin to solve the problems related to the vast differences in children's school achievement, they will have to acknowledge the expanding nature of diversity in contemporary society and then consider the implications for responding to the educational needs of all children.

The growing number and diversity of immigrants and their children contributes to both cultural and social class forms of difference. Associated with these dimensions of diversity are differences in values, beliefs, and goals for children's early education. Differences within immigrant groups and across generations appear to be critical in children's school success. In addition, there is an increasing understanding that factors like family structure and sexual orientation/gender identity play important roles in children's learning and the way they process social situations.

New and Beneke consider the past and present responses of the early childhood community to diversity. While they find many positive changes in the anti-bias curriculum that help children to learn how to recognize and challenge prejudice and stereotyping, they propose a number of specific initiatives that have the potential to make significant contributions to our field's understanding of the diverse population of children arriving in classrooms across the United States each day. These involve changes in research methodology and orientation including more studies on children and families not typically represented in the research, such as Muslims, and homes characterized by alternative lifestyles.

New and Beneke argue that just as sociocultural theory informs inquiry, the principles of sociocultural theory can be used as a basis for teaching and professional development. They cite instances of teachers undertaking ethnographic classroom studies, as well as embracing principles of documentation to learn about the children they are teaching. This leads to more effective communication with parents, teachers, and each other.

The ideas in these chapters can still be quite controversial. For Mallory and Rous, "making room" means full inclusion for young children (ages 3 to 8) with developmental disabilities, which they define as "conditions associated with cognitive, communicative, motoric, and socioemotional impairments that affect a child's ability to function at an age-appropriate level in family, school, and community settings" (p. 278). They use the term broadly to include those conditions caused by genetic, congenital, and environmental factors. Clearly, there are those who disagree with this position.

For New and Beneke, diversity refers to the myriad of "socially constructed" means by which groups of individuals in our society are distinguished, including race, ethnicity, language, gender, religion, sexual orientation, ability, and social class. To honor the diversity of all members of the early childhood community—children, families, teachers, stakeholders, and any others who may enter our doors—it is not enough to apply some quick fixes. A book about Martin Luther King, a new vocabulary word in Spanish, a song from the civil rights era might well be included in "just and caring" classrooms, but New and Beneke have a broader vision. They argue that early childhood teachers have both the responsibility and the potential to co-construct—with the help of children and their families—a curriculum that rejects prejudice and uncritical thinking, and creates the need for engagement, conversation, and collaboration.

APPLY WHAT YOU LEARNED

As you read the following chapters, think about, talk about, and do additional reading and research regarding these questions:

❏ Are you aware of any early care and education programs in your community that employ a full-inclusion model? If so, what techniques are used to "make room for everyone"? If not, use your research tools to find such a program.

❏ How do New and Beneke define the term *diversity*? Is this different than how you have understood the term in the past?

❏ How do schools in your community deal with issues of diversity? Do they employ quick fixes or do they appear to have an ongoing commitment to a curriculum that rejects prejudice?

❏ Do you believe that teachers of young children should have coursework in diversity issues?

❏ Can you alone, or in a small group, devise approaches that would foster full inclusion?

❏ Can you identify ways to eliminate the barriers (attitudinal, financial) to inclusion?

REFERENCES

Mallory, B. L., & New, R. S. (Eds.). (1994). *Diversity and developmentally appropriate practices: Challenges for early childhood education.* New York: Teachers College Press.

Paley, V. (1992). *You can't say you can't play.* Cambridge, MA: Harvard University Press.

EDUCATING YOUNG CHILDREN WITH DEVELOPMENTAL DIFFERENCES: PRINCIPLES OF INCLUSIVE PRACTICE

Bruce L. Mallory
University of New Hampshire

Beth Rous
University of Kentucky

The purpose of this chapter is to delineate principles of effective practice in early childhood programs that serve children with developmental disabilities.[1] The principles that are elaborated here are intended to assist practitioners who are seeking to understand and implement the practical, ethical, and legal dimensions of inclusive early childhood education. These principles are grounded in a particular theoretical framework that supports both the social aspects of inclusion and the specific learning goals that teachers typically hold for young children.

The chapter begins with a set of assumptions that serve to guide the curriculum principles developed in later sections. Then, following a brief overview of the field of early childhood special education from its initial conceptualization to its current manifestations, the basic tenets of social constructivist theory are explicated to create a context for the consideration of inclusive early childhood practices. In the subsequent section, six principles of curriculum and instruction are delineated that address the relationship between children's diverse characteristics and strategies for intervention, the goals and processes of social participation, the link between assessment and instruction, the use of both child-directed and teacher-directed learning, the role of group size as a key variable, and the integration of therapies within early childhood classrooms.

1. The term *developmental disabilities* is used in this chapter to refer to conditions associated with cognitive, communicative, motoric, and socioemotional impairments that affect a child's ability to function at an age-appropriate level in family, school, and community settings. The term is used broadly, and includes those conditions caused by genetic, congenital, and environmental factors. The term *early childhood* is used here to refer to the period between 3 and 8 years of age, when most children are in some form of group care for some part of the day.

It should be noted that this material is not meant to be comprehensive or exhaustive. There is a wealth of information about inclusive early childhood education that cannot possibly be captured in a single chapter. Rather, the goal here is to put forward a set of core principles that can serve as guideposts for curriculum decisions. The details can only be filled in during the particular moments that occur in classrooms every day, when diverse adults and children come together to make meaning of the complex and dynamic world that they are constantly reinventing. It is this process of cultural construction and reconstruction that is the core of teaching and learning, and it is a process that every learner—adults as well as children, able-bodied as well as those with disabilities—must participate in fully, without contingencies, if we are to achieve a truly inclusive educational experience.

GUIDING ASSUMPTIONS

Several assumptions inform the claims made in this chapter. First, children with disabilities have the right to participate in high-quality early childhood programs that are developmentally and culturally appropriate. This right has been codified in federal laws such as the Individuals with Disabilities Education Act of 2004 (IDEA, P.L. 108–446), the Americans with Disabilities Act of 1990 (ADA, P.L. 101–336), and the No Child Left Behind Act of 2001 (NCLB, P.L.107–110). In addition to the legal mandates that have been enacted, this right is viewed as an ethical imperative that must be realized in order to achieve equitable and effective practice (New & Mallory, 1994; Sandall, Hemmeter, Smith, & McLean, 2005).

The second assumption is that inclusive early education programs benefit children's overall development and contribute to the acquisition of culturally valued knowledge and skills necessary for negotiating formal educational settings. These benefits extend to children who are developing typically as well as those who have disabilities. The empirical support for this assumption is substantial (Guralnick, 1990; Jenkins, Speltz, & Odom, 1985; Odom et al., 2004), particularly when teachers or caregivers use explicit strategies to foster interactions among children with a broad range of abilities and dispositions.

The third assumption is that there is an inextricable relationship between the conceptualization of curriculum and the success of inclusive practices. Put simply, the successful inclusion of children with disabilities depends on the design and application of an inclusive curriculum (Buysse, Wesley, Bryant, & Gardner, 1999; Karagiannis, Stainback, & Stainback, 1996; Stainback & Stainback, 1992). An inclusive curriculum provides a context for positive social interactions and collaborative problem solving, which are seen as the heart of effective early childhood education. An inclusive curriculum is responsive to all developmental domains and integrates content or subject matter through contextualized instruction and such strategies as long-term projects that elicit sustained and complex problem solving (Katz & Chard, 1989; New, 1992).

A corollary assumption to the previous one is that the degree of curriculum modification to meet the needs of children with disabilities will be relatively minimal in high-quality early childhood programs. The evidence supporting this "minimal modification" assumption is that (1) materials for young children are usually applicable to a wide range of developmental abilities; (2) the discrepancy in ability between children with disabilities and their nondisabled peers is narrower when children are in the preprimary and primary years (compared to older children), and the majority of children diagnosed with disabilities have mild to moderate degrees of impairment; and (3) children with and without disabilities usually follow similar developmental trajectories (Hanline & Galant, 1993; Odom et al., 2004). This assumption has important implications when practitioners or family members express fears that the inclusion of children with special needs will require substantial changes in a program's curriculum or instructional strategies. Modifications become more a function of basic attitude, creative problem solving, and careful observation of children than of high levels of financial commitment, radical environmental rearrangements, or the use of discrete curriculum approaches for different groups of children in the same setting (Division for Early Childhood, 2007).

The final assumption that informs this chapter is paradoxical but nonetheless fundamental, thus it deserves greater elaboration. If we are to treat young children with disabilities as equals in early childhood classrooms, it may often be necessary to treat them differently. Inclusion does *not* mean providing identical educational experiences to all children present in a particular environment. In this sense, an inclusive curriculum is a form of affirmative action. Rather than being blind to young children's developmental differences, we are obligated to consciously seek out those differences and respect their meaning as a basis for the design of effective curricula. In fact, given the recognition of the importance of early intervening services, also defined as recognition and response, there has been increased emphasis on helping both parents and teachers respond early to learning difficulties in all young children (Coleman, Buysse, & Neitzel, 2006).

Another way to frame this paradox is to identify the limits inherent in an "individualized" approach. Because all young children with disabilities have either an individualized family service plan (IFSP) or an individualized education plan (IEP), our tendency has been to provide highly particularized or idiosyncratic services. Historically, this tendency has been manifested in "pull-out" programs (in which therapeutic services take place outside of the child's regular classroom) or in self-contained classrooms that serve only children with diagnosed developmental disabilities. Similarly, "compensatory" early education programs established in many states have been aimed at young children assumed to be at risk for developmental and educational difficulties because of their socioeconomic and ethnic status (and the correlation between these two factors). Head Start and many related state programs have created income-segregated settings that also have high proportions of minority children. The goal of these programs has been to give such children an educational "boost" that would allow them to "catch up" with their middle-class age peers. The good intentions that underlie these forms of intensive and targeted intervention must be balanced against the effects of social and academic segregation (New & Mallory, 1996).

Most recently, there have been increased efforts at the national and state levels to design more universal, comprehensive, and high-quality early care and education services (Goldstein, Lombardi, & Schumacher, 2006). More than ever before, states have begun to develop early care and education systems that cross traditional "program" or "agency" boundaries. This has been coupled with increased attention to articulating clear expectations for what young children should know and be able to do regardless of the setting in which children spend time. To this end, through the Good Start, Grow Smart initiative (2002), all states have developed early learning guidelines or standards, most of which take into consideration children of differing abilities (Harbin, Rous, & McLean, 2005; Scott-Little, Kagan, & Frelow, 2006). Our challenge is to design curricula that are responsive to the highly differentiated and sometimes unpredictable characteristics of children with disabilities *within* settings that foster interdependence and shared experiences among all the children present.

To unduly emphasize individual differences when those differences are manifestations of a deficit or impairment will likely result in stigmatization and isolation (e.g., Bogdan & Biklen, 1977; Goffman, 1963). However, to ignore such differences and apply uniform teaching methods and performance standards to all children is equally misguided. Thus, our goal is to create inclusive environments that acknowledge individual differences within a welcoming and supportive community of learners. The principles suggested in this chapter build on successful curriculum models that have demonstrated ways to address this paradox. These models stem from the newly evolved discipline of early childhood special education.

THE FIELD OF EARLY CHILDHOOD SPECIAL EDUCATION

Since the late 1960s, a new discipline concerned with the development and education of young children with disabilities has emerged in response to the increased awareness of the needs, capacities, and rights of such children. The field has evolved from its predecessor disciplines—special education and early childhood education—and has retained some of the advantages of each while conceptualizing new ways of responding to the characteristics of young children with special developmental needs. However, this merging of the two fields has not been a simple matter. In fact, at the surface it would seem that the two fields have quite divergent goals and means to accomplish those goals (Bredekamp, 1993; Mallory, 1992). Before defining the newer discipline, it is useful to examine some of the aspects of early and special educational practices that have actually *perpetuated* segregated services for young children.

Traditionally, the fields of early childhood and special education have emphasized a focus on individual differences through the application of separate teaching strategies for separate populations of learners. Children who were developing "normally" were most often found in "developmentally" oriented settings, where they interacted with objects and people in a relatively spontaneous manner and more value was placed on the child's exploration of the environment than on prescribing particular experiences and skill mastery. Children were assumed to move along a linear continuum of stage-based developmental milestones, and the curriculum and instructional context supported that movement with "facilitating" and "responsive" teaching. Children who were not maturing at the anticipated rate (who may have had a history of prematurity or be described as developmentally delayed) were either retained or placed in "readiness" or "transition" settings in order to benefit from the "gift of time." Once they demonstrated the ability to master the same material as their peers, these children were allowed to enter into the mainstream, albeit usually with younger aged "peers."

Children with more significant disabilities were often placed at the time of school entry in isolated, clinically oriented settings where specialists worked on their individual and idiosyncratic needs. Each specialist had responsibility for some discrete aspect of the child's body or mind, and learning goals were concentrated on the functional skills believed to be necessary for independent living. Contrary to the earlier examples, direct teaching or systematic instruction was often the primary means of improving a child's competence (e.g., Snell, 1987).

The social, physical, and temporal environments of early childhood classrooms can also have an excluding effect. Too often, children who do not fit the particular instructional approach in a given setting are subtly or overtly judged as troubled and/or troubling (Hobbs, 1982). A narrow range of materials and activities limits the diversity of cognitive capacities and creativities that may be recognized and fostered. Static, prescribed curricula designed by commercial enterprises have led to decontextualized, meaningless tasks that some children can tolerate but that, for others, create confusion, withdrawal, or resistance. Such curricula often emphasize the creation of teacher-modeled products rather than child-determined, developmentally appropriate and responsive processes and products. Finally, task completion within arbitrary time blocks has often been given greater value than sustained, complex projects that capture the interests of both adults and children. All of these characteristics—which are still found in too many early childhood classrooms—have resulted in the exclusion of children who cannot, for *whatever* reason, meet the expectations found in such environments. Ironically, the emphasis on individual differences, therefore, has on occasion led to the exclusion of children with special needs when their differences conflict with the nomothetic structure and expectations of the early childhood setting.

Early manifestations of the new discipline of early childhood special education reflected these legacies and emphasized specialized services to children with diagnosed disabilities or who were judged to be at risk for later educational problems. These models were often developed within the context of either early preventive programs for minority and/or low-income children such as the Milwaukee Project (Garber, 1988) or the Carolina Abecedarian Project (Campbell & Ramey, 1995), or in model demonstration programs targeted exclusively at children with particular disabilities. Many of these latter programs were a part of the First Chance Network funded by the Handicapped Children's Early Education Assistance Act of 1968 (P.L. 90–583). (A concise review of model intervention programs developed from the mid-1970s to mid-1980s is provided by Farran, 1990.)

By the late 1980s, most of these model projects had evolved from their status as small-scale demonstrations into state or locally funded preschool services housed within public schools and community-based early childhood programs. This shift occurred because of the mandates contained in federal and state laws (e.g., P.L. 99–457, the Education for All Handicapped Children Act Amendments of 1986) and because of growing empirical support for the value of integrated preschool services (e.g., Guralnick, 1990). Simultaneously, federally funded Head Start classrooms had been serving young children with diagnosed disabilities since the early 1970s, providing another model of early integration, albeit within the context of an income-segregated program. The lessons learned from the First Chance Network, Head Start, and integrated community early childhood programs have brought the field of early childhood special education to its present state of development.

By the mid-1990s, the field of early childhood special education had become both an instigator and advocate for inclusive practices. Contemporary interpretations of the field emphasize strategies that embed appropriate instructional practices tailored to individual characteristics *within* settings of interdependent learners. The field was historically and politically situated within the larger push toward inclusion that characterized not only public education but also national dialogues on matters of race (e.g., West, 1993) and cultural pluralism (e.g., Cornbleth & Waugh, 1995). For this reason, there was a strong interest in ensuring that prescriptions or guidelines for high-quality early education include attention to the needs of children with both developmental and cultural differences (New & Mallory, 1996; see also Chapter 14).

Beginning in the late 1990s, there was increased emphasis in the field of early childhood special education on inclusion, not only for preschool children but also for those receiving early intervention services as well. The reauthorization of Title I, through the No Child Left Behind (NCLB) Act of 2001, and the resulting Good Start, Grow Smart Early Childhood Initiative (2002) emphasized the needs and rights of all children, including those with disabilities, to have access to inclusive settings and curricula. This was coupled with increasing evidence that the inclusion of young children was beneficial to both those with and without disabilities (Odom et al., 2004). Concurrently, the U.S. Department of Education increased pressure on states to both address and document their efforts to ensure that children were served in inclusive settings through the development and implementation of State Performance Plans (SPP). SPP requirements include mandatory indicators related to inclusion, for which each state must set targets and identify strategies they will use to meet these targets. This process includes Annual Performance Reports (APR) that outline state progress toward meeting the targets and public reporting of progress.

As a result of the efforts within early childhood special education toward inclusive services, one of the most important contemporary trends, with respect to the focus of this chapter, is an interest in delineating what constitutes "developmentally appropriate practice" (DAP) for young children with disabilities. This interest was manifested in general critiques of the NAEYC guidelines for DAP published in 1987 (Bredekamp, 1987) from sociopolitical, theoretical, and pedagogical perspectives (e.g., Jipson, 1991; Mallory & New, 1994a; Walsh, 1991). Such critiques challenged the original DAP guidelines as being overly reliant on child development models based on Western cultural assumptions and theoretical paradigms and therefore as overly narrow in their conceptualization of children's growth and capacities. Mallory (1992, 1994) noted the particular inadequacies of the 1987 guidelines with respect to young children with disabilities.

A number of writers suggested ways to expand our understanding of developmentally appropriate practices in order to accommodate the needs of children with disabilities. These suggestions were concerned with the design of learning environments (Graham & Bryant, 1993a), the use of developmentally appropriate assessment strategies (Linder, 1990; Meisels, 1994), classroom instructional methods that blend systematic and more child-initiated models (Atwater, Carta, Schwartz, & McConnell, 1994; Novick, 1993), the use of transdisciplinary staffing models (Lyon & Lyon, 1980), and parent-child interactions as a context for teaching and learning (Mahoney, Robinson, & Powell, 1992; McCollum & Bair, 1994). What emerged from these efforts was a practical framework that acknowledged the particular and often unique needs of children with disabilities *and* the importance of creating classrooms based on shared understandings and common goals. Building on this and other work in the field, the Division for Early Childhood (DEC) of the Council for Exceptional Children (CEC) developed and published a set of recommended practices (Sandall et al., 2005) that takes into consideration DAP and the growing evidence base in early childhood special education. This convergence of understandings has resulted in the articulation of a theoretical framework that supports the pedagogical and social value of inclusive early childhood settings.

SOCIAL CONSTRUCTIVISM AS A THEORETICAL BASIS FOR INCLUSIVE PRACTICES

One of the primary factors that has contributed historically to the differential treatment and placement of young children with special needs noted earlier has been the lack of a unifying theoretical framework that could guide inclusive early childhood practice. In the 1990s, theories of social constructivism provided such a framework. Building on the cognitive-developmental/interactionist forms of constructivism developed by Piaget (1954), Bruner (1960), and Kohlberg and Mayer (1972), among others, more recent theoreticians have drawn on the sociocultural perspective of Lev Vygotsky (e.g., Forman, Minick, & Stone, 1993; Harris & Graham, 1994; Tharp & Gallimore, 1988; Wertsch, 1991). These interpretations have focused on the intersubjective, relational aspects of development, asserting that learning requires contexts rich with social interactions, reciprocal dialogues among children and adults, and the negotiation of problems that are related to the everyday experiences of those who are present.

Rogoff and her colleagues have illustrated the principles of social constructivism through their analyses of the ways in which children appropriate and participate in the rites, routines, and rituals of classrooms and community settings (Rogoff, 1990, 1992; Rogoff, Mistry, Goncu, & Mosier, 1993). It has been argued that these processes are applicable to the particular challenges associated with educating young children with disabilities (Bernheimer, Gallimore, & Weisner, 1990; Mallory & New, 1994b). What is most critical about these applications of social constructivism is their emphasis on the nature of learning as a cultural activity. From this perspective, learning involves the appropriation and mastery of "cultural tools" that enable learners to participate successfully in the daily routines of the community. Examples of such tools include literacy and social negotiation skills as well as material instruments such as books, markers, and computers. As Rogoff says, the tools "themselves must be adapted to the specific practical activities at hand, and thus both passed on to and transformed by new members of the culture" (1990, p. 16). In this light, to possess and know how to use such tools is to share in the currency of the culture, and thus be seen as a valued and competent contributor to it. This concept has important implications for teaching young children with disabilities and is explicated more fully in the next section of the chapter.

Another critical aspect of social constructivism for our present discussion is the necessity of diverse capabilities within a community of learners. The process of guided participation (Rogoff, 1990), which builds on what Wood, Bruner, and Ross (1976) earlier referred to as "scaffolding," entails a transactional relationship between teacher and learner whereby the teacher provides just enough direct support (information, modeling, prompting, etc.) to enable the learner to accomplish a task as independently and successfully as possible. The intensity and form of support vary in direct response to the cues and capabilities offered by the learner. In many cases, the teacher/expert is an adult and the learner is a child. However, this process also applies to age-peer relationships in heterogeneous classrooms. In this case, children of varying levels of competence work with each other to master specific tasks and/or content. The social and cognitive problems inherent in such peer tutoring extend *both* children's zones of proximal development. As such, the inclusion of children with a range of developmental abilities in a shared community enhances the learning of all those who are present.

This brief grounding of practices that can support inclusive early childhood classrooms is intended to assist practitioners who seek some congruence between the instructional decisions they make on a daily basis and the broader theoretical frameworks that influence those decisions. By being more self-reflective about the theories that are instantiated in classroom practice, teachers and therapists may approach the broad range of children found in inclusive classrooms with a common, and therefore communal, set of lenses for understanding and responding to developmental differences.

PRINCIPLES FOR AN INCLUSIVE CURRICULUM

Having established the historical and theoretical bases for inclusion in early childhood programs, it is now possible to delineate curriculum principles that build on and extend our past and present practices. These principles address the needs of both adults and children to participate in interesting, challenging, and culturally relevant activities that foster engagement, a sense of agentry, and mastery of increasingly complex skills and concepts. Thus, the six principles that follow focus on the interrelatedness of development and intervention strategies, the crucial importance of social participation as a determinant of instructional goals and strategies, the inextricable link between assessment and instruction, the dynamic balance between child-directed and teacher-directed learning, the use of group size and membership as a key instructional variable, and the necessity of embedding specialized therapies within the classroom setting.

The principles put forward here represent more specific, classroom-focused tenets than those suggested previously (Mallory & New, 1994b). In the earlier work, we articulated theoretically derived "principles for inclusive practice" based on social constructivism. These superordinate statements referred to the role of classrooms as communities of learners, the central role of social relations in learning, the content-context link in curriculum and instruction, and the role of authentic assessment. The propositions that follow reflect the present authors' thinking and are more grounded in everyday classroom practices.

The principles also take into consideration the growing body of evidence to support inclusive practices as articulated through the DEC Recommended Practices (Sandall et al., 2005). These practices are designed to support the right of all young children and their families to actively and meaningfully participate in the community. To that end, the recommended practices address all facets of the early care and education system as it relates to the needs of young children with special needs and disabilities: assessment, implementation of intervention and instructional strategies and curricula that cross disciplinary boundaries, and the respectful and meaningful involvement of families as primary decision makers in both planning and implementing services (see Figure 13–1, Inclusion Practices Recommended through the Division of Early Childhood).

It is important to stress that these six principles are not assumed to be comprehensive. Their greatest value may be that they can serve to provoke practitioners to construct their own principles of inclusive early education as they work with particular groups of young children in specific local settings.

Principle 1: Effective early education programs are based on a coherent and integrated conceptualization of children's learning and development. One of the attractions of social constructivism with respect to inclusive early education is its ability to incorporate the divergent developmental, maturational, and functional perspectives described earlier. Rather than relying on separate environments for children who are assumed to have diverse developmental trajectories, it is possible to design inclusive curricula that acknowledge the interrelated nature of psychosocial development, biological maturation, and behavioral functioning. In fact, it is essential that these three aspects of learning be explicitly and simultaneously addressed in order to establish a comprehensive and developmentally appropriate program. Young children's sociocognitive development (which includes such capacities as problem solving, communication, and self-understanding), their physical attributes (such as stamina, active-rest cycles, metabolism, strength, and coordination), and the adaptive skills they bring to various social contexts (such as self-care, social reciprocity, peer collaboration, and following directions) all should be considered and fostered in the process of curriculum design.

In doing so, the *common* elements of developmental, maturational, and functional models can be utilized. These elements include an emphasis on independent or assisted mastery of tasks, adaptation to environmental demands, the value of a contingently responsive social context, the aim of achieving social competence, and a concern for intervention that addresses individual differences (Mallory, 1992). These elements thus are viewed as discrete but interdependent components of a

FIGURE 13–1
Inclusion Practices Recommended by the Division for Early Childhood

I9. Team members focus on the individual child's functioning in the contexts in which he or she lives, not the service.

I15. Team members use the most normalized and least intrusive intervention strategies available that result in desired function.

I17. Team members plan to provide services and conduct interventions in natural learning environments.

C8. A variety of appropriate settings and naturally occurring activities are used to facilitate children's learning and development.

C9. Services are provided in natural learning environments as appropriate. These include places in which typical children participate such as the home or community settings.

C10. Interventionists facilitate children's engagement with their environment to encourage child-initiated learning that is not dependent on the adult's presence.

C11. Environments are provided that foster positive relationships, including peer-peer, parent/caregiver-child, and parent-caregiver relationships.

C18. Practices are used systematically, frequently, and consistently within and across environments and across people.

C19. Planning occurs prior to implementation, and that planning considers the situation (home, classroom, etc.) to which the interventions will be applied.

PS7. Public policies provide for sufficient, alternative, flexible fiscal and administrative requirements that facilitate: (a) the effective use of natural and inclusive settings, (b) interagency coordination at the "systems" level, and (c) interdisciplinary collaboration at the "direct-service" level (Medicaid waivers, child care subsidies, blended funding, itinerant services, etc.).

PS21. Program policies support the provision of services in inclusive or natural learning environments. Strategies are used to overcome challenges to inclusion.

PP13. Students/staff learn to apply instructional strategies in natural environments.

PP31. Field experiences occur in a variety of community-based settings in which children with and without disabilities and their families receive EI/ECSE services, including natural environments and inclusive programs.

PP63. Teachers and staff from early education programs and community child care centers are provided with knowledge and skills relative to the inclusion of young children with disabilities.

comprehensive curriculum for young children. In classrooms with high levels of heterogeneity, the *means* for addressing each element may vary across children. For example, some children may always require assistance with eating a meal or getting on a coat to go outdoors. However, this does not preclude the identification of common *goals* for all children, which brings us to the next principle.

Principle 2: The overarching goal of early education programs should be to increase young children's participation in the social contexts in which they live and learn on a daily basis.   The goal of participation in early childhood classrooms is too often misinterpreted to mean a superficial level of turn-taking and sharing of materials, or worse, an expectation that all children do the same thing at the same time (listening to a story, sitting in circle time, writing in journals). While each of these expectations may be appropriate for children for some portion of each day, when they become the end rather than the means, children as well as adults lose sight of their meaningfulness and value. The aim of participation requires a consciousness of the subtle exchanges and norms that are realized within peer and adult-child transactions. Artificial and coerced forms of participation (e.g., children are expected to share personal items from home on Fridays but are not allowed to on other days) do not create the sense of belonging that is crucial to the development of an inclusive classroom culture.

In fact, if classrooms are understood as cultural contexts, then the principle of participation can be more fully realized. In this light, the teacher's concern would shift from ensuring that everyone gets a chance to share something from home or that everyone draws a picture after a field trip to ensuring that the activities available to the children are connected to the children's and adults' personal and cultural experiences. Thus, an explicit recognition of what constitutes the rites, routines, and rituals in classrooms is a necessary prerequisite to enhancing the participation of children who may require direct assistance due to a particular disability (Kim, 2005; Mallory & New, 1994b). To the extent that the expectations associated with some routines (e.g., independently setting the table at snack time or sitting cross-legged on a rug square in circle time) exclude some children and call attention to their deficits, the classroom culture is not inclusive.

At the interpersonal level, dyadic and small-group transactions also must be more than turn-taking and sharing. Several strategies have been proposed for enhancing the frequency, intensity, and duration of interactions between children with disabilities and those without (Odom, Schwartz, & ECRII, 2002). Early work in the area of inclusion by Hanline and Galant (1993) stressed the necessity of structuring interactions between diverse children; close physical proximity is not a sufficient condition for meaningful participation. They further argued that inclusive arrangements that last for only portions of the day or "reverse mainstreaming" models in which there are greater numbers of children with disabilities than typical peers are not effective strategies for supporting social participation. General strategies to foster participation emphasize the need to structure the social environment through the use of cooperative tasks (mural painting, coauthoring a story), "family style" mealtimes, relying more on sociodramatic play materials (blocks, dress-up clothes) than materials that reinforce individual engagement (puzzles), arranging floor and table spaces to facilitate peer proximity, and giving children explicit feedback when they are engaged in reciprocal and sustained collaborative efforts (Cavallaro, Haney, & Cabello, 1993; Hanline & Galant, 1993).

Similarly, McEvoy, Odom, and McConnell (1992) suggest four specific approaches to fostering participation. These include:

1. *Teacher-mediated interventions* such as adult prompting and reinforcement of prosocial behaviors, assisting children with disabilities to initiate effective interactions and assisting children without disabilities to read and respond to these initiations, and adult determination of the composition of playgroups

2. *Peer-mediated interventions* that result when adults help children without disabilities to initiate interactions with children with disabilities, and teach the former specific scripts and reinforcement techniques to begin and sustain collaborative activities

3. *Affection training procedures* in which adults model and support children's expressions of affection toward each other, through verbal and physical means

4. *"Say-do" correspondence training* in which children are supported when they make a plan and then carry it out, as might occur when a nondisabled peer says that he or she will play with a child with a disability

The principle of participation thus requires attention to both the tacit cultural norms and practices in classrooms and the "subcultural" transactions that occur among diverse children and adults. To the extent that teacher-determined rituals exclude some children or that children's responses to one another are exclusionary, the goal of participation cannot be achieved. In Vivian Paley's (1992) terms, it may be necessary to establish a norm that "you can't say you can't play."

Principle 3: Assessment of children's learning and development must be referenced to the skills and knowledge needed to participate successfully in a broad range of increasingly complex social contexts.   A helpful framework for assessment that can support both individual progress and the goal of social participation for children with disabilities is that of ecobehavioral analysis (Carta & Greenwood, 1985; Odom, Peterson, McConnell, & Ostrosky, 1990; Schroeder, 1990). This framework, sometimes referred to as authentic or ecological, has been used to develop a number of new types of assessment tools, most often referred to as criterion- or curriculum-based. These types of assessments are designed to help ensure the use of both developmentally appropriate and culturally and linguistically responsive assessment methods (DEC, 2007) within environments and with materials that provide the best possible contextual match for both the child and family (Meisels & Fenichel, 1996; Neisworth & Bagnato, 2004).

The use of authentic assessment approaches relies on interviews, observations, and inventories. Parents, teachers, and other adults who know a child well are asked to describe the child's capacities in a variety of ecological domains (e.g., home, classroom, playground, shopping mall). Observations of those domains are conducted by those familiar with the child, over time, to identify the social and functional demands present and understand the behavioral norms for typical young children that are embedded within the respective domains. An inventory of functional skills is then produced that is domain-specific and age-appropriate. Finally, an analysis of the discrepancy between the child's present capacities and the demands of the relevant environments is conducted, leading to an intervention plan aimed at narrowing those discrepancies (Barnett, Carey, & Hall, 1993; Falvey, 1989). In this approach, child assessment is linked to functional criteria that are culturally, developmentally, and age appropriate.

To foster successful, interdependent participation in classrooms and elsewhere, the criteria for assessment must stem from proximal norms rather than distal, universal ones. This is especially true for children with disabilities, as their difficulties and strengths will be highly idiosyncratic and to some extent situation-specific, even when they share the same diagnostic labels. This assertion opens the door for new forms of assessment that are situationally relevant as well as geared toward individual children's development. Assessment that is focused on a child's capacities under conditions of assisted participation does not ask what a child can do independently at a given moment—the focus of traditional assessment. Rather, the assessment question becomes, "What is this child able to do within a supportive, responsive social context when presented with meaningful, interesting, and challenging problems?" (Mallory & New, 1994b, p. 333). Observation and analysis then are concerned with the degree and type of scaffolding or guided participation necessary for the child to master a task or skill (Brown & Ferrara, 1985). And, within an ecobehavioral framework, the concern shifts to the larger context, and analysis leads to questions about ways to modify the physical and social environment so there is a better match between the emerging competencies of the child and the demands and supports available in the child's world.

The structural process of assessment also needs to be considered to create congruence between assessment and an inclusive curriculum. When children with disabilities are assessed in order to develop an appropriate and valid educational plan, the various professionals who do the assessment must collaborate closely with each other if a complete, accurate picture is to emerge. This collaboration may take the form of arena assessments (Foley, 1990) in which the multidisciplinary team members observe a single facilitator interact with a child and present tasks that represent her development across all domains. Within an authentic assessment approach, children are provided with multiple opportunities to demonstrate a behavior or skill. These opportunities are provided across multiple settings and with objects and materials that are familiar to the child, thus helping establish a more valid estimate of their developmental status (Fewell, 2000). This process provides concise information that can be directly translated to IFSP/IEP development and curriculum and instructional planning.

These new assessment processes allow for greater reliance on clinical judgments of performance than on the measurement of specific behaviors thought to represent underlying developmental capacity. As well, the focus is on integrating diverse professional perspectives around observations that elicit optimal performance in a supportive social setting. In this way, not only can the team members get a clearer sense of a child's potentials, they also can transfer the tasks and supports provided in the assessment process to classroom intervention strategies.

Principle 4: Inclusive curriculum and instruction are grounded in a dynamic balance between child-directed and teacher-directed activities.   One of the most challenging aspects of defining the field of early childhood special education has been to articulate an effective relationship between what has traditionally been dichotomized as teacher-directed versus child-directed learning. By definition, many children with disabilities require, at least in the early stages of mastering new skills, greater assistance and direct instruction from adults than do their nondisabled peers. For children with more significant disabilities, continued adult intervention may be required for the maintenance and generalization of that learning. But an over-reliance on adult assistance can interfere with the goal of social participation described earlier. Spontaneous peer interactions are constrained when an adult is always present, and some children may acquire a sense of dependence and helplessness if they are not given opportunities to make choices, take risks, or assess the effectiveness of their own efforts.

This challenge has prompted a number of early childhood special educators to design teaching strategies that combine traditional views of DAP, which are predominantly child-directed, with the more teacher-directed approaches found in programs that serve children with disabilities (Cavallaro et al., 1993; DEC, 2007; Fox & Hanline, 1993; McLean & Odom, 1993). The central theme of most of this work has been the use of naturalistic teaching and authentic assessment within a context of teacher-determined manipulation of environmental and instructional variables, including the selection of reinforcement schedules and levels (DEC, 2007; Novick, 1993).

Routines, activity-based instruction (Sandall et al., 2005), and authentic assessment (Losardo & Notari-Syverson, 2001; Neisworth & Bagnato, 2004) are widely regarded among early childhood special educators as useful tools for reconciling the perceived tension between child-directed and teacher-directed methodologies. These approaches embed intervention on children's individual goals and objectives in routine, planned, or child-initiated activities, and use logically occurring antecedents and consequences to develop functional and generative skills (Bricker & Cripe, 1992, p. 40). It is helpful to elaborate on these approaches with respect to the purposes of the present chapter.

Traditionally, three types of activities were distinguished within a routines-based approach—routine, planned, and child-initiated (Bricker and Cripe, 1992). These activities are designed to occur on a predictable, regular basis and provide occasions for learning new skills while practicing those that are already established. Current recommendations related to ensuring that children with disabilities have access to curriculum within the early childhood setting include the infusion of aspects of universal design (Blackhurst et al., 1999; CAST, 2004).

This approach can help ensure that routines are seen as reflective of and congruent with the child's cultural and personal life. Thus, these routines are tools not only for managing the child's success in the classroom but also for fostering social participation both inside and outside of the classroom. In other words, classroom routines have a deeper meaning than as mere tools of individual or group manage-ment. Such routines should be consistent with children's cultural experiences. The rites, routines, and rituals of classrooms, to recall Rogoff's (1992) terminology, should mirror the rites, routines, and rituals that children encounter in their homes and communities. This not only can make the classroom a more authentic place, it can also serve to reinforce skills across settings and times, creating a kind of natural "distributed trials" approach that can lead to greater maintenance and generaliza-tion of the skills learned both at home and in school.

Planned activities, on the other hand, require adult initiation and organiza-tion. They are "designed events" (Bricker & Cripe, 1992). Planned activities may occur at the group level and can constitute either didactic instruction (e.g., teach-ing the words to a song or demonstrating the transformation of a liquid into a gas) or interactive sessions (e.g., discussing a book an adult has read to the class or deciding how to rearrange the classroom furniture). Planned activities also occur at the individual and small-group level, especially when an adult has decided to tar-get specific skills believed to be needed by one or more children (e.g., writing instruction or making a snack for the rest of the class). Planned activities offer opportunities to incorporate IEP objectives into the natural groupings and events that constitute the life of the classroom. For this reason, planned activities, while stemming from adult priorities and judgments, must also reflect the needs and characteristics of the individual children found in a particular setting.

Child-initiated activities are those introduced by children and then sup-ported or extended by other peers and adults. Sociodramatic play, block construc-tions, reading a book, telling stories, and pursuing the answers to questions asked by children are examples. Clearly these activities require adult responsiveness with respect to the physical and temporal arrangements of the classroom, and adults must be ready to supply the resources necessary for children to pursue their own goals (dress-up clothes, building materials, multilevel books, etc.). Children with more severe cognitive, motor, and sensory disabilities are less likely to initiate activities, or to communicate clearly their intentions with respect to such activities. In such cases, the onus is on adults to carefully observe and interpret the cues of nonverbal or nonambulatory children and then follow the children's lead. This is especially important in supporting attempts to enter into sociodramatic play or other child-initiated small-group events. Thus, adults must watch where children with severe disabilities are looking and infer where they are trying to move, and adults must listen closely to the vocalizations of such children as well as pay atten-tion to facial expressions, gestures, and muscle tone as cues to intent, desire, and satisfaction. Given the limitations inherent for children with more significant dis-abilities, and the tendency for adults to assume global incompetence when a child has a specific disability, the challenge of supporting child-initiated activities in this group of children represents one of the most important and complex aspects of an inclusive curriculum.

A common assumption of early childhood educators has been that children with more significant disabilities will benefit most from more structured, direct, and extrinsically reinforced activities. While this may be the case for older children who are trying to master academic skills, there is no evidence that this is true for younger children (Odom et al., 2004). For example, early studies of milieu (naturalistic) versus responsive (direct) language instruction for preschool children with varying degrees of disabilities indicate that younger and/or less competent children benefit more from child-initiated, milieu teaching strategies than from adult-directed approaches (Yoder, Kaiser, & Alpert, 1991; Yoder et al., 1995). More recent studies have also cast doubt on the assumption that children with severe disabilities must rely on artificial, adult-determined reinforcers rather than peer-mediated, natural reinforcements such as becoming part of a play group or being placed in charge of the daily attendance report (Odom et al., 2004).

To fully support the inclusion of young children with disabilities within the curriculum, three key principles of universal design are recommended (DEC, 2007): multiple means of representation, engagement, and expression. Children with disabilities (as well as those without disabilities) need a *generative* repertoire that will allow them to construct new responses or modify existing responses when they encounter new or changing conditions. This concept would seem to join Piaget's (1954) emphasis on accommodation with more topographical, behavioral dimensions of adjusting to new information or the demands of new settings. Classroom curriculum should therefore be constructed in ways that fully support young children with disabilities. Within the curriculum, learning opportunities are presented in a variety of formats and complexity levels that are *representative* of young children with a range of abilities and disabilities; address a range of interests and preferences through active *engagement,* which is supported as needed by adults in the environment; and include options for different means of *expression* in terms of responding to instructional cues and demonstrating skills and competencies. Curricula experiences that are constructed in this way, and through routines and activities included within the curriculum, can provide an appropriate balance between child-directed and teacher-directed events and where naturally occurring and authentic problems are encountered, and they can foster new or modified responses that serve to generate and maintain functional skills which are in turn transferable to other contexts.

In sum, the balance or tension (the two are interrelated—teaching is sort of a high-wire act) between child-directed and teacher-directed activities in inclusive classrooms is a critical, perhaps central, concern. Special education pedagogies have traditionally erred on the side of intrusiveness, wherein adults hover over learners and correct even the smallest errors in order to establish accurate and consistent responses, for fear both of losing time and allowing maladaptive responses to become fixed. But the laissez-faire approach in early childhood classrooms often does not provide a sufficient level of assistance and feedback to children with disabilities. Therefore, it is important to strive for greater degrees of child-directed activities, by using the least obtrusive and intrusive strategies possible for any given child (Falvey, 1989). Direct assistance and concrete reinforcements should be faded systematically as a child establishes generative, functional, and adaptable repertoires. Ultimately, power to make decisions and set standards is shared, within realistic developmental parameters, between the children and adults in inclusive classrooms.

Principle 5: Small groups of two to four learners provide an optimal structure for fostering cognitive development and social participation in inclusive classrooms. Too little attention has been given to group size and composition as key variables affecting the process of including children with disabilities in early childhood classrooms. The ways in which groups function also affect the establishment of an inclusive atmosphere that optimizes social participation. Group size generally may be categorized as either whole (the entire classroom) or small (typically ranging from two to five children); composition is either homogeneous or heterogeneous (with respect to the competencies needed to accomplish the tasks at hand); and function can be classified according to the dimensions of activity just discussed—routine, planned, or child-initiated. Each of these variables is subject to manipulation by teachers and therapists depending on the goals of the activities or projects in which the children are engaged, the characteristics of the children present, and the commitment among the children and adults to mutual assistance and collaboration.

Given the heterogeneity that exists in inclusive classrooms, it is logical to assume that whole-group activity is not likely to be an effective means for ensuring that the particular needs of individual learners will be met. Whole-group instruction is more likely to be didactic, to require prolonged periods of passive attention, to involve distracting and irrelevant contextual stimuli, and to be less responsive to children's cues as their interests vary over time and topic. While inclusive classrooms often have smaller adult-child ratios, the extra adults have typically played management roles during whole-group instruction. They intervene when children start getting restless, they provide physical support to help children face the teacher, or they remove children from the group when behavior becomes disruptive. In other words, much of the energy spent during whole-group instruction in heterogeneous classrooms is on reducing inappropriate behaviors rather than enhancing the quality and depth of the learning that could be taking place.

Small groups, on the other hand, are more likely to foster prosocial behaviors (Villa & Thousand, 1996), especially when they are made up of children with diverse capacities, interests, and temperaments. Disruptive behaviors decrease, students display more goal orientation, and there is a greater emphasis on cooperation and collaboration rather than competition and individual accomplishment (Stainback & Stainback, 1996).

These attributes of small groups are consistent with the claims of social constructivism outlined earlier in this chapter. Given the role of guided participation with more capable others, children who are less able benefit from the assistance available from one or more partners who can either model effective strategies or provide more direct instruction through verbal and/or physical prompting. As well, small groups create possibilities for the role of the more capable other to shift among the individual group members, depending on the nature of the task and the respective competencies within the group. In this way, children with disabilities can fulfill a particular role or contribute a special skill, and therefore become the more capable other. This will be especially true during times of child-initiated play, when roles are more fluid and open to negotiation, and when standards for performance can be adjusted spontaneously by the participants in light of what each member can accomplish.

Peer dyads are a particular subset of small groups that deserve special attention as a tool for effective inclusion. Two children who choose to work with each other or are assigned to do so by an adult may relate either as collaborators, in which each partner has equal status, or as tutor-learner pairs, in which one child is acknowledged to have some needed expertise (Forman & Cazden, 1985). Either of these relationships has the potential to lead to academic gains, positive social interactions, and increased self-esteem for both partners (Villa & Thousand, 1996). In addition, the child whose role is to guide his or her partner is likely to exercise higher-order thinking skills as he or she restates the problem or task, decides how to demonstrate or model it, makes suggestions, brings in related information that might be useful, and evaluates the results of his or her partner's efforts (Villa & Thousand, 1996). Again, it is important for adults to structure opportunities for children with disabilities so they can assume the role of expert whenever possible, to experience both the cognitive and social advantages inherent in this role.

Small groups are useful for another function in inclusive classrooms—that of acting as advocates and problem solvers relative to the process of inclusion itself. Villa and Thousand (1996, p. 181) refer to the role of students as "peer advocates" who can help to identify the capabilities of classmates with disabilities and who can offer suggestions for ways to accommodate their classmates' needs. Preschool and primary grade children are capable of filling this role, as they are the ones with the most direct experience of the physical, social, and cognitive demands of the environment. Sensitive teachers can create an atmosphere of collaboration and care in order for this process to be nonstigmatizing and nonpatronizing. Suggestions regarding the placement of furniture and materials, the assignment of classroom responsibilities, when to offer assistance, and how to adjust planned activities to make them accessible to all children are examples of ways in which young children can be advocates for their peers with disabilities.

Essentially, inclusive classrooms work best when both whole-group and individual instruction are used conservatively. When children work in pairs or small groups, opportunities for sociocognitive learning and social participation are maximized for all the children involved. Inclusive classrooms present occasions for natural experiments with regard to group size and composition, and these occasions should be systematically incorporated into the classroom curriculum as a means for both adults and children to learn more about themselves and the content they are investigating.

Principle 6: Domain-specific therapies support participation and inclusion when they are embedded within the context of the child's typical learning environment.   The preceding five principles have stressed the interrelatedness of development and intervention strategies, the importance of social participation, the connection between assessment and instruction, the balance between child and teacher-directed activities, and the value of small groups. These principles have direct implications for the roles and responsibilities of adults who work in early childhood classrooms. While some suggestions have been offered regarding the strategies that teachers might employ to foster an inclusive curriculum, we must also consider the particular roles of the related services personnel who are charged with supporting both children with disabilities and their teachers. Speech and language, physical, and occupational therapists are the most common such personnel; others who might be present include behavior specialists, nurses, and paraprofessional aides. As the number of adults assigned to focus on the particular needs of an individual child increases (in relation to the severity of the child's disabilities), so, too, does the complexity of integrating those adults and their aims into the life of the classroom. As daunting as this challenge may be, it is crucial that therapeutic assistance be seen as part of the fabric of the curriculum, not an add-on around which curriculum and instruction are scheduled.

Thus, domain-specific therapies must be woven into the activities of the classroom, with the dual and compatible aims of increasing social participation while developing functional communicative, motoric, and social skills in the individual child. This implies that therapeutic goals and processes must be realized within the context of the child's natural environments—school, home, and community. In this light, traditional forms of "pull-out" therapy that take place in isolation and are aimed exclusively at individual children and their deficits are viewed as developmentally and pedagogically inappropriate.

The challenge to therapists, then, is to bring their skills and insights into the classroom and community, where real problems of movement, communication, and social interaction are continuously present. Likewise, the challenge to teachers is to welcome these colleagues and incorporate their focus and expertise into what has traditionally been the teachers' sole domain. That is, inclusion is not just a concept that applies to children. Diverse adults, too, must feel that they are fully participating and valued members of the classroom community.

Therefore, ecobehavioral analysis includes input from therapists; and the identification of IEP goals and intervention strategies becomes driven by a commitment to assisting the child with a disability to participate in the rites, routines, and rituals of the regular classroom. Therapists and aides work with small heterogeneous groups of children. Some of this work is determined by the aims and priorities of the adults—who are responsible for the achievement of both idiosyncratic IEP and broad curriculum goals—and some is determined by the children, whose interests and capacities can become the basis for therapeutic activities. When therapeutic goals and processes are embedded within an emergent and integrated curriculum (Jones & Nimmo, 1995; New, 1992), instructional practices are more likely to be naturalistic and therefore effective.

The framework of routines or activity-based instruction elaborated earlier is a logical approach to the use of embedded therapies. This approach is, in fact, an extension of early traditions described as milieu intervention or incidental teaching (e.g., Kaiser, Hendrickson, & Alpert, 1991; Warren & Kaiser, 1986). However, there are distinct differences in these approaches, including a focus on groups of children rather than individuals, a more comprehensive approach that addresses all developmental domains rather than only those thought to be deficient, and the use of activities that children choose and enjoy rather than decontextualized materials and equipment. All of these features lead logically to the use of in-class therapies delivered by specialists from multiple disciplines.

The particular form that integrated therapies take may range on a continuum from interdisciplinary to transdisciplinary. In the former, specialists work directly with a child or children with disabilities in small groups with their peers on targeted skills. Often driven by third-party funding considerations and the perpetuation of clinically oriented models of intervention, interdisciplinary therapy emphasizes the separate, hands-on role of the specialist. Within this model, therapists may use their own approach; however, decisions about services are made collaboratively with other members of the child's team (e.g., family, classroom teacher).

A transdisciplinary model refers to "shared responsibilities and information to the extent that one team member can assume the role of another" (Sandall et al., 2005; p. 306). This approach encourages the use of a single plan for young children that is generated by all members of the team: families, developmental interventionists, and therapists. Advantages to this approach include increased consistency of interactions between the child and adult, better integration of therapies into classroom activities, and a greater likelihood of generalization and transference across settings (Vergara, Adams, Masin, & Beckman, 1993). Difficulties may be encountered, however, if therapists have not been trained to work collaboratively, if classroom curricula do not support integrated therapies, or if there are too few opportunities for planning and coordination among teachers and specialists. In practical terms, the style of interaction and collaboration will be determined by the individuals who make up the classroom team. Teams that have been together longer and that work within schools characterized by a climate of collaboration and professional development will be more likely to be transdisciplinary than teams whose members have less experience or who have worked in more compartmentalized settings. In any case, the ways in which adults work with each other and are a part of the learning that is occurring in early childhood classrooms will have a significant impact on the climate and consequences of those classrooms.

CONCLUSIONS

The six principles outlined here can serve as a framework for the design of inclusive early childhood curricula and instructional practices. They reflect current understandings of "recommended practice" in the field of early childhood special education, and build on the empirical research and practical experience. The central themes of these principles, and of the guiding assumptions with which this chapter opened, include (1) the right of all children to full and meaningful participation in high quality early childhood settings, (2) the value that accrues from interactions among diverse children and adults, (3) the close correlation between effective practices for children with and without disabilities, and (4) the need to provide individually responsive instruction within a participatory and caring community.

Before closing, it is important to note that families can and should play a crucial role in the design and implementation of inclusive early childhood curricula. Family members have special contributions to make in the areas of assessment, the selection of projects and activities, and the optimal use of therapists. Their particular expertise as observers and advocates for their own children should be valued and incorporated as much as possible. This process is complicated by the traditional problems that arise when family members and teachers of young children attempt to communicate and collaborate (Powell, 1989). Parents of children with disabilities are especially vulnerable to the judgments and practices of early childhood educators and therapists. Thus, the commitment to collaboration and participation that characterizes high-quality early childhood programs must be extended to parents and other key family members. And this commitment must stem not simply from legal prescriptions for consent and approval but also from an ethical stance that acknowledges parents of children with disabilities as genuine partners in the educational process. The goal and meaning of social participation encompasses all of the children and adults involved in an early childhood program, not simply those who are physically present on a daily basis.

This chapter has identified a number of recurring themes that are important to consider when designing educational and social supports for young children with disabilities and their families. First, there is a clear, prescriptive legal context that affirms the right of young children and their families to early childhood special education services. At the state level, there has been significant policy and program development that complements federal requirements and regulations, often to the benefit of all young children, not just those with disabilities. Second, there is continuing accumulation of evidence that classroom integration has educational and social benefits for all the children present. Third, there is an increasing consensus among educators and therapists about the processes of early development and the social, cognitive, and physical characteristics of young children, including those affected by early childhood disability. Fourth, there are continuing efforts to design developmentally and culturally appropriate curricula that are responsive to a wide range of needs, dispositions, and capacities in young children. Best practices in curriulcum and teaching have been articulated by the Divison of Early Childhood of CEC, providing guidance to teachers and caregivers serving young children with special needs. Fifth, it is recognized that families are crucial influences in early development and valuable partners with teachers and caregivers working with young children, especially those with early developmental difficulties.

Inclusion should not be viewed as yet another educational fad, or a "radical constructivist blueprint unsubstantiated by research" (Fuchs & Fuchs, 1994, p. 304). Inclusion is both a preferred best practice *and* a legal and moral mandate (Bricker, 1995). Yet inclusion remains a difficult reality to achieve. After more than 30 years of research conducted on effective ways to include children with disabilities in regular classrooms, we still have not implemented everything that we know, resulting in continuing educational mediocrity for all students, not just those with disabilities (Odom et al., 2004; Turnbull & Turbiville, 1995). The challenges are attitudinal, financial, and methodological. We must be committed, professionally as well as morally, to the democratic principles that underlie inclusive practices. We must find ways to reallocate existing resources and generate new ones to ensure access to specialists, materials, and time necessary for inclusive and integrated curricula. And we must continue to develop methodologies that are grounded in sound theoretical and empirical understandings about the human condition. Then, perhaps, we will create learning communities where the myriad manifestations of the human condition can be both celebrated and enhanced.

REFERENCES

Atwater, J. B., Carta, J. J., Schwartz, I. S., & McConnell, S. R. (1994). Blending developmentally appropriate practice and early childhood special education: Redefining best practice to meet the needs of all children. In B. L. Mallory & R. S. New (Eds.), *Diversity and developmentally appropriate practices: Challenges for early childhood education* (pp. 185–201). New York: Teachers College Press.

Barnett, D. W., Carey, K. T., & Hall, J. D. (1993). Naturalistic intervention design for young children: Foundations, rationales, and strategies. *Topics in Early Childhood Special Education, 13*(4), 430–444.

Bernheimer, L. P., Gallimore, R., & Weisner, T. S. (1990). Ecocultural theory as a context for the individual family service plan. *Journal of Early Intervention, 14*(3), 219–233.

Blackhurst, E., Carnine, D., Cohen, L., Kame'enui, E., Langone, J., Palley, D., Pisha, B., Powers, K., & Stewart, R. (1999, Fall). *Research connections in special education: Universal design.* Retrieved October 6, 2004, from http://ericec.org/osep/recon5/rc5cov.html

Bogdan, R., & Biklen, D. (1977). Handicapism. *Social Policy, 7*(5), 14–19.

Bredekamp, S. (Ed.). (1987). *Developmentally appropriate practice in early childhood programs serving children from birth through age 8.* Washington, DC: NAEYC.

Bredekamp, S. (1993). The relationship between early childhood education and early childhood special education: Healthy marriage or family feud? *Topics in Early Childhood Special Education, 13*(3), 258–273.

Bricker, D. (1995). The challenge of inclusion. *Journal of Early Intervention, 19*(3), 179–194.

Bricker, D., & Cripe, J. (1992). *An activity-based approach to early intervention.* Baltimore: Brookes.

Brown, A. L., & Ferrara, R. A. (1985). Diagnosing zones of proximal development. In J. V. Wertsch (Ed.), *Culture, communication, and cognition: Vygotskian perspectives* (pp. 273–305). Cambridge: Cambridge University Press.

Bruner, J. (1960). *The process of education.* New York: Knopf.

Buysse, V., Wesley, P. W., Bryant, D., & Gardner, D. (1999). Quality of early childhood programs in inclusive and noninclusive settings. *Exceptional Children, 65*(3), 301–314.

Campbell, F. A., & Ramey, C. T. (1995). Cognitive and school outcomes for high-risk African-American students at middle adolescence: Positive effects of early intervention. *American Educational Research Journal, 32*(4), 743–772.

Carta, J. J., & Greenwood, C. R. (1985). Eco-behavioral assessment: A methodology for expanding the evaluation of early intervention programs. *Topics in Early Childhood Special Education, 5*(2), 88–104.

Center for Applied Special Technology (CAST). (2004, March 12). *Universal design for learning.* Retrieved October 6, 2004, from www.cast.org/udl/

Cavallaro, C. C., Haney, M., & Cabello, B. (1993). Developmentally appropriate strategies for promoting full participation in early childhood settings. *Topics in Early Childhood Special Education, 13*(3), 293–307.

Coleman, M. R., Buysse, V., & Neitzel, J. (2006). Establishing the evidence base for an emerging early childhood practice: Recognition and response. In V. Buysse, & P. Wesley. (Eds.), *Evidence-based practice in the early childhood field* (pp. 227–246). Washington, DC: Zero to Three.

Cornbleth, C., & Waugh, D. (1995). *The great speckled bird: Multicultural politics and education policymaking.* New York: St. Martin's Press.

Division for Early Childhood (DEC). (2007). *Promoting positive outcomes for children with disabilities: Recommendations for curriculum, assessment and program evaluation.* Missoula, MT: DEC.

Falvey, M. (1989). *Community-based curriculum: Instructional strategies for students with severe handicaps* (2nd ed.). Baltimore: Brookes.

Farran, D. C. (1990). Effects of intervention with disadvantaged and disabled children: A decade review. In S. J. Meisels & J. P. Shonkoff (Eds.), *Handbook of early childhood intervention* (pp. 501–539). New York: Cambridge University Press.

Fewell, R. (2000). Assessment of young children with special needs: Foundations for tomorrow. *Topics in Early Childhood Special Education, 20*(1), 38–42.

Foley, G. M. (1990). Portrait of the arena evaluation: Assessment in the transdisciplinary approach. In

E. D. Gibbs & D. M. Teti (Eds.), *Interdisciplinary assessment of infants: A guide for early intervention professionals* (pp. 271–286). Baltimore: Brookes.

Forman, E. A., & Cazden, C. B. (1985). Exploring Vygotskian perspectives in education: The cognitive value of peer interaction. In J. V. Wertsch (Ed.), *Culture, communication, and cognition: Vygotskian perspectives* (pp. 323–347). New York: Cambridge University Press.

Forman, E. A., Minick, M., & Stone, C. A. (Eds.). (1993). *Contexts for learning: Sociocultural dynamics in children's development.* New York: Oxford University Press.

Fox, L., & Hanline, M. F. (1993). A preliminary evaluation of learning within developmentally appropriate early childhood settings. *Topics in Early Childhood Special Education, 13*(3), 308–327.

Fuchs, D., & Fuchs, L. S. (1994). Inclusive schools movement and the radicalization of special education reform. *Exceptional Children, 60,* 294–309.

Garber, H. L. (1988). *The Milwaukee Project: Preventing mental retardation in children at risk.* Washington, DC: American Association on Mental Retardation.

Goffman, E. (1963). *Stigma: Notes on the management of spoiled identity.* New York: Simon & Schuster.

Goldstein, A., Lombardi, J. & Schumacher, R. (2006). Birth to 5 and beyond: A growing movement in early education. *Zero to Three Journal.*

Good Start, Grow Smart (2002). A White House initiative.222.ed.gov. Retrieved July 27, 2007 from http://www.whitehouse.gov/infocus/earlychildhood/toc.html

Graham, M. A., & Bryant, D. M. (1993a). Developmentally appropriate environments for children with special needs. *Infants and Young Children, 5*(3), 31–42.

Graham, M. A., & Bryant, D. M. (1993b). Characteristics of quality, effective service delivery systems for children with special needs. In D. M. Bryant & M. A. Graham (Eds.), *Implementing early intervention: From research to effective practice* (pp. 233–252). New York: Guilford Press.

Guralnick, M. J. (1990). Major accomplishments and future directions in early childhood mainstreaming. *Topics in Early Childhood Special Education, 10*(2), 1–17.

Guralnick, M. J. (2005). *The developmental systems approach to early intervention.* Baltimore: Brookes.

Hanline, M. F., & Galant, K. (1993). Strategies for creating inclusive early childhood settings. In

D. M. Bryant & M. A. Graham (Eds.), *Implementing early intervention: From research to effective practice* (pp. 216–232). New York: Guilford Press.

Harbin, G., Rous, B., & McLean, M. (2005). Issues in designing state accountability systems. *Journal of Early Intervention, 27*(3), 137–164.

Harris, K. R., & Graham, S. (Eds.). (1994). Implications of constructivism for students with disabilities and students at risk: Issues and directions. A special issue of the *Journal of Special Education, 28*(3).

Hobbs, N. (1982). *The troubled and troubling child: Reeducation in mental health, education, and human services programs for children and youth.* San Francisco: Jossey-Bass.

Individuals with Disabilities Education Improvement Act of 2004, PL 108–446, 20 U.S.C. §§ 1400 *et seq.*

Jenkins, J. R., Speltz, M. L., & Odom, S. L. (1985). Integrating normal and handicapped preschoolers: Effects on child development and social interaction. *Exceptional Children, 52,* 7–18.

Jipson, J. (1991). Developmentally appropriate practice: Culture, curriculum, connections. *Early Education and Development, 2*(2), 120–136.

Jones, E., & Nimmo, J. (1995). *The emergent curriculum.* Washington, DC: NAEYC.

Kaiser, A., Hendrickson, J., & Alpert, C. (1991). Milieu language teaching: A second look. In R. Gable (Ed.), *Advances in mental retardation and developmental disabilities* (Vol. IV, pp. 63–92). London: Jessica Kingsley.

Karagiannis, A., Stainback, W., & Stainback, S. (1996). Rationale for inclusive schooling. In S. Stainback & W. Stainback (Eds.), *Inclusion: A guide for educators* (pp. 3–16). Baltimore: Brookes.

Katz, L., & Chard, S. (1989). *Engaging children's minds: The project approach.* Norwood, NJ: Ablex.

Kim, S. G. (2005). Kevin: "I gotta get to the market": The development of peer relationships in inclusive early childhood settings. *Early Childhood Education Journal, 33*(3), 163–169.

Kohlberg, L., & Mayer, R. (1972). Development as the aim of education. *Harvard Educational Review, 42,* 449–496.

Lincoln, Y. S., & Guba, E. G. (1985). *Naturalistic inquiry.* Beverly Hills, CA: Sage.

Linder, T. (1990). *Transdisciplinary play-based assessment.* Baltimore: Brookes.

Losardo, A., & Notari-Syverson, A. (2001). *Alternative approaches to assessing young children.* Baltimore: Brookes.

Lyon, S., & Lyon, G. (1980). Team functioning and staff development: A role release approach to providing integrated educational services to severely handicapped students. *Journal of the Association for the Severely Handicapped, 5*(3), 250–263.

Mahoney, G., Robinson, C., & Powell, A. (1992). Focusing on parent-child interactions: The bridge to developmentally appropriate practice. *Topics in Early Childhood Special Education, 12,* 105–120.

Mallory, B. L. (1992). Is it always appropriate to be developmental? Convergent models for early intervention practice. *Topics in Early Childhood Special Education, 11*(4), 1–12.

Mallory, B. L. (1994). Inclusive policy, practice, and theory for young children with developmental differences. In B. L. Mallory & R. S. New (Eds.), *Diversity and developmentally appropriate practices: Challenges for early childhood education* (pp. 44–61). New York: Teachers College Press.

Mallory, B. L., & New, R. S. (Eds.). (1994a). *Diversity and developmentally appropriate practices: Challenges for early childhood education.* New York: Teachers College Press.

Mallory, B. L., & New, R. S. (1994b). Social constructivist theory and principles of inclusion: Challenges for early childhood special education. *Journal of Special Education, 28*(3), 322–337.

McCollum, J. A., & Bair, H. (1994). Research in parent-child interaction: Guidance to developmentally appropriate practice for young children with disabilities. In B. L. Mallory & R. S. New (Eds.), *Diversity and developmentally appropriate practices: Challenges for early childhood education* (pp. 84–106). New York: Teachers College Press.

McEvoy, M. A., Odom, S. L., & McConnell, S. R. (1992). Peer social competence intervention for young children with disabilities. In S. L. Odom, S. R. McConnell, & M. A. McEvoy (Eds.), *Social competence of young children with disabilities* (pp. 37–64). Baltimore: Brookes.

McLean, M. E., & Odom, S. L. (1993). Practices for young children with and without disabilities: A comparison of DEC and NAEYC identified practices. *Topics in Early Childhood Special Education, 13,* 274–292.

Meisels, S. J. (1994). Designing meaningful measurements for early childhood. In B. L. Mallory, & R. S. New (Eds.), *Diversity and developmentally appropriate practices: Challenges for early childhood education* (pp. 202–222). New York: Teachers College Press.

Meisels, S. J., & Fenichel, E. (Eds.). (1996). *New visions for the developmental assessment of infants and young children.* Washington, DC: Zero To Three.

Neisworth, J. T., & Bagnato, S. J. (2004). The mismeasure of young children: The authentic assessment alternative. *Infants & Young Children, 17*(3), 198–212.

New, R. S. (1992). The integrated early childhood curriculum: New interpretations based on research and practice. In C. Seefeldt (Ed.), *The early childhood curriculum: A review of current research* (pp. 286–322). New York: Teachers College Press.

New, R. S., & Mallory, B. L. (1994). Introduction: The ethic of inclusion. In B. L. Mallory & R. S. New (Eds.), *Diversity and developmentally appropriate practices: Challenges for early childhood education* (pp. 1–13). New York: Teachers College Press.

New, R. S., & Mallory, B. L. (1996). The paradox of diversity in early education. In E. J. Erwin (Ed.), *Putting children first: Visions for a brighter future for young children and their families* (pp. 143–168). Baltimore: Brookes.

No Child Left Behind Act of 2001, P.L. 107–110, 115 Stat. 1425 (2002). Retrieved July 27, 2007, from www.ed.gov/policy/elsec/leg/esea02/107–110.pdf

Novick, R. (1993). Activity-based intervention and developmentally appropriate practice: Points of convergence. *Topics in Early Childhood Special Education, 13*(4), 403–417.

Odom, S. L., Peterson, C., McConnell, S., & Ostrosky, M. (1990). Ecobehavioral analysis of early education/specialized classroom settings and peer social interaction. *Education and Treatment of Children, 13,* 316–330.

Odom, S. L., Schwartz, I. S., & ECRII Investigators. (2002). So what do we know from all this? Synthesis points of research on preschool inclusion. In S. L. Odom (Ed.), *Widening the circle: Including children with disabilities in preschool programs* (pp. 154–174). New York: Teachers College Press.

Odom, S. L., Vitztum, J., Wolery, R., Lieber, J., Sandall, S., Hanson, M., Beckman, P., Schwartz, I., & Horn, E. (2004). Preschool inclusion in the United States: A review of research from an ecological systems perspective. *Journal of Research in Special Educational Needs, 4*(1), 17–49.

Paley, V. (1992). *You can't say you can't play.* Cambridge, MA: Harvard University Press.

Peck, C., Odom, S., & Bricker, D. (Eds.). (1993). *Integrating young children with disabilities into community programs: Ecological perspectives on research and implementation.* Baltimore: Brookes.

Piaget, J. (1954). *The construction of reality in the child.* New York: Basic Books.

Powell, D. R. (1989). *Families and early childhood programs.* Washington, DC: NAEYC.

Rogoff, B. (1990). *Apprenticeship in thinking: Cognitive development in social context.* New York: Oxford University Press.

Rogoff, B. (1992). *Observing sociocultural activity on three planes: Participatory appropriation, guided participation, apprenticeship.* Invited lecture presented at the Conference for Socio-Cultural Research, Madrid.

Rogoff, B., Mistry, J., Goncu, A., & Mosier, C. (1993). Guided participation in cultural activity by toddlers and caregivers. *Monographs of the Society for Research in Child Development, 58*(8, Serial No. 236).

Sandall, S., Hemmeter, M., Smith, B., & McLean, M. (Eds.). (2005). *DEC recommended practices: A comprehensive guide for practical application in early intervention/early childhood special education.* Longmont, CO: Sopris West.

Schroeder, S. R. (Ed.). (1990). *Ecobehavioral analysis and developmental disabilities: The twenty-first century.* New York: Springer-Verlag.

Scott-Little, C., Kagan, S. L., & Frelow, V. S. (2006). Conceptualization of readiness and the content of early learning standards: The intersection of policy and research? *Early Childhood Research Quarterly, 21,* 153–173.

Snell, M. (Ed.). (1987). *Systematic instruction of persons with severe handicaps* (3rd ed.). Upper Saddle River, NJ: Merrill/Prentice Hall.

Stainback, W., & Stainback, S. (1992). Using curriculum to build inclusive classrooms. In S. Stainback & W. Stainback (Eds.), *Curriculum considerations in inclusive classrooms: Facilitating learning for all students* (pp. 65–84). Baltimore: Brookes.

Stainback, W., & Stainback, S. (1996). Structuring the classroom to prevent disruptive behaviors. In S. Stainback & W. Stainback (Eds.), *Inclusion: A guide for educators* (pp. 343–348). Baltimore: Brookes.

Tharp, R. G., & Gallimore, R. (1988). *Rousing minds to life: Teaching, learning, and schooling in social context.* Cambridge: Cambridge University Press.

Turnbull, A. P., & Turbiville, V. P. (1995). Why must inclusion be such a challenge? *Journal of Early Intervention, 19*(3), 200–202.

Vergara, E. R., Adams, S., Masin, H., & Beckman, D. (1993). Contemporary therapies for infants and toddlers: Preferred approaches. In D. M. Bryant & M. A. Graham (Eds.), *Implementing early intervention: From research to effective practice* (pp. 253–287). New York: Guilford Press.

Villa, R. A., & Thousand, J. S. (1996). Student collaboration: An essential for curriculum delivery in the 21st century. In S. Stainback & W. Stainback (Eds.), *Inclusion: A guide for educators* (pp. 171–191). Baltimore: Brookes.

Walsh, D. J. (1991). Extending the discourse on developmental appropriateness: A developmental perspective. *Early Education and Development, 2*(2), 109–119.

Warren, S., & Kaiser, A. (1986). Incidental language teaching: A critical review. *Journal of Speech and Hearing Disorders, 51,* 291–299.

Wertsch, J. V. (1991). *Voices of the mind: A sociocultural approach to mediated action.* Cambridge, MA: Harvard University Press.

West, C. (1993). *Race matters.* Boston: Beacon Press.

Wood, D., Bruner, J. S., & Ross, G. (1976). The role of tutoring in problem-solving. *Journal of Child Psychology and Psychiatry, 17,* 89–100.

Yoder, P. J., Kaiser, A. P., & Alpert, C. (1991). An exploratory study of the interaction between language teaching methods and child characteristics. *Journal of Speech and Hearing Research, 34,* 155–167.

Yoder, P. J., Kaiser, A. P., Goldstein, H., Alpert, C., Mousetis, L., Kaczmarek, L., & Fischer, R. (1995). An exploratory comparison of milieu teaching and responsive interaction in classroom applications. *Journal of Early Intervention, 19*(3), 218–242.

CHAPTER 14

NEGOTIATING DIVERSITY IN EARLY CHILDHOOD EDUCATION: RETHINKING NOTIONS OF EXPERTISE

Rebecca S. New
University of North Carolina, Chapel Hill

Margaret Beneke
Early Childhood Educator

Setting: Block Area, Kindergarten, Summer 2007

"No, Nico, we aren't playing that way—it's an office! Maggie, tell him we made a medical office!" Jimmy shouted as Nico began rearranging the structure Jimmy and his friend had just created. I got down to Nico's level. "Nico," I said, looking in his eyes, "Jimmy wants you to stop now." Nico averted his eyes and continued to move around in the blocks, disrupting the "office." Soon, several children were claiming that Nico had ruined what they were doing. Without acknowledging my presence, Nico continued to launch his 5-year-old body in and out of the "fort" carrying various blocks and upturning the structure. "Build!" he cried. Moments later, he ran to me, and buried his head in my stomach—seeking silence? Or solace?

This was not the first mis-communication for Nico. Even though we had only known each other a week, I recognized his frustration with language. A 5-year-old with cognitive delays, his English-speaking Japanese parents had already enrolled him in an international school for kindergarten for the fall, where he would be expected to learn French. During the summer months, he was taking Japanese language lessons and speaking English at home and in our program. Not surprising, his language processing skills were constantly getting in the way of his ability to successfully interact with other children and teachers. Nico's linguistic challenges were not the only instance of diversity in the classroom. Of fifteen children, five came from biracial households, two were internationally adopted, five had sensory processing disorders to some degree, and three came from families with same-sex marriages.

Note: This chapter is dedicated to the memory of Leslie M. Williams, whose life-long commitment to social justice through multicultural education serves as a model for the field.

This classroom scenario is far from atypical. A 21st-century classroom in the United States without multiple linguistic, developmental, ethnic, and religious differences is increasingly rare. The last two decades have been marked by initiatives designed to guide the field in developing more culturally sensitive teaching practices and inclusive curricula within the context of welcoming educational environments for children. At the same time, growing numbers of policy makers recognize the critical importance of the period of early childhood for all children and universal preschool efforts are now under way in an increasing number of states. And yet the anxiety of educators and the public at large regarding the vast differences in children's school readiness and subsequent achievements highlights what we still do not know— how best to respond to the educational needs of *all* young children. In this chapter we consider the concept of diversity as both a challenge and a resource for early childhood education.

In the first half of the chapter, we briefly acknowledge the expanding nature of diversity in contemporary society; and then review responses from the field to diversity, particularly as it appears in the form of cultural differences. In the second half of the chapter, we propose a more purposeful orientation to diversity as informed by sociocultural theory, collaborative research, and inquiry-oriented practice. The chapter concludes with an image of early childhood settings as contexts in which adults learn to value and negotiate differences; and an image of early childhood educators as activists for more equitable responses to the diverse needs and capabilities of all young children.

A WORLD OF DIFFERENCES

When the concept of diversity is included in educational discourse, it is most often in reference to the challenges of teaching children who are poor, ethnic minorities, and/or English language learners. And yet, the presence and nature of the diversity of learners within educational settings has varied across historic periods. Early in this nation's history, educational privileges were limited to white males from established families and it was rare to find young girls in public schools. Long after girls were deemed eligible for formal schooling, it remained forbidden for children of color to attend schools created for white children. And it was not until a quarter-century ago that schools were legally obliged to include children with disabilities, albeit often in segregated classrooms where they received a "special" (and narrowly interpreted) education.

Today, girls outnumber boys in most educational settings and many gender-related concerns in early educational settings have been addressed in constructive ways, based not only on laws mandating equitable access to educational opportunities but also on increased understandings of the developmental course of gender differentiation (Liben, Lynn, & Bigler, 2002). Over the past several decades, tremendous gains have been made in the early education of young children with special needs (Hauser-Cram, Warfield, Erickson, Shonkoff, & Krauss, 2001), thanks to an expansion of federal laws as well as emerging understandings of the learning potentials of children with special needs when they participate in inclusive educational settings (see Chapter 13). In spite of these accomplishments, the challenges of diversity have expanded rather than diminished over the past several decades. This expansion is due in part to the changing nature of diversity in American society.

OLD AND NEW WAYS TO BE DIFFERENT

There are many reasons for the increasing diversity in U.S. early childhood settings. Recent demographic trends illustrate the changing nature of our national population, including longer life spans, immigration and accompanying cultural diversity, and expanding economic polarization. These changes have a direct impact on the population of young children entering schools today and present new challenges for the field of early childhood education. Increased globalization, medical progress, and expanded civil liberties also contribute to the diversity found in contemporary classrooms. And yet, the children in these settings are also distinguished by what they share—a desire to learn in a way that respects their personal lives even as it prepares them to participate in an increasingly global society. As is the case with most important social issues, designing effective ways to respond to these educational challenges is easier said than done.

Being Poor in the Richest Nation in the World

In spite of the American dream of equal opportunity for all, the reality is that some children have more and better opportunities than others. Throughout U.S. history, the greatest source of diversity in children's education has been associated with poverty and its correlate racial identity. Children of color now represent the majority in many publicly funded early childhood settings, most of which are mandated to serve children and families who are impoverished.

Head Start is one such program that has surely made a powerful difference in the overall quality of children's lives since its inception, and yet its contributions to children's school achievements remain equivocal. Evidence from the early childhood longitudinal study confirms previous findings that Head Start children perform better in kindergarten than do peers with similar socioeconomic circumstances but not as well as children from households with higher social class indicators (Pigott & Susman, 2005). That some Head Start programs now serve children from three-generation Head Start families further belies program aims to move families out of poverty. These facts, coupled with the reality that less than a third of eligible children have been served in the history of Head Start, make it difficult to proclaim Head Start as a successful means of fighting this most pernicious form of diversity.

As debates on Head Start continue (Zigler & Styfco, 2004), research persists in demonstrating the influence of poverty in children's lives, including their early learning (Larner & Collins, 1996). Compounding factors of poverty such as residential mobility, single-parent families, and the presence or absence of school-like activities at home (e.g., reading, computer time) have a major impact on children's school readiness (Lareau, 2003) and their subsequent learning and school achievement

(Lee & Burkam, 2002). In turn, recent research replicates and expands on decades-old findings of the positive consequences of middle-class parenting practices (described by Lareau, 2003, as "concerted cultivation") on children's school-like skills and dispositions. Variables associated with such "unequal childhoods" (Lareau, 2003) continue to be strong predictors of children's failure or success in school.

Children from low-income families also have unequal experiences in out-of-home early childhood settings, especially when teachers in these settings have different interpretations of childhood and the purposes of an early education (Lubeck, 1985). Perhaps the greatest form of inequity associated with social class is the unequal participation of children from low-income families in high-quality early childhood settings. One recent study found that preschool-age children from wealthy families are 23 percent more likely than children from low-income families to be enrolled in center-based child care (Bainbridge, Meyers, Tanaka, & Waldfogel, 2005). These and other findings reveal wide discrepancies in the general availability of early care and education facilities in wealthy versus less affluent neighborhoods, and the types of child care that are utilized in diverse communities (Kagan, forthcoming). At first glance, these disparities in children's early care and education mirror the vast inequalities in American schools (Kozol, 2005). And yet, this variation in child care quality, availability, and family preference adds a new wrinkle to the relationship between social class, cultural values, and child development—expecially although not solely among immigrant populations.

New Patterns of Immigration and Acculturation

As powerful as racial and social class predictors are in terms of children's educational opportunities, they are not the only influences. Another source of diversity underscores the changing dynamics of racial and economic dimensions when seen through a cultural lens. The United States is now experiencing the largest wave of immigration in its history and children of immigrants are currently the fastest-growing segment of the nation's population. Though some think of the United States historically as a "nation of immigrants," this newest trend is more than an echo of past challenges. In contrast to immigration patterns in the late 1800s, when most immigrants were of European origin, today a significant minority (approximately one-third) of U.S. immigrants are from Mexico. The remainder come from Latin America and Carribbean nations as well as Asia, Oceania, Africa, Canada, and Europe (Waldfogel & Lahaie, 2007).

The growing number and diversity of immigrants and their children contributes to both cultural and social class forms of difference, including new and sometimes perplexing cultural practices as well as new forms of cultural conflicts. Associated with these dimensions of diversity are differences in values, beliefs, and goals for children's early education. Some of these differences are also found among different generations from the same cultural group and sometimes within the same family. Depending on their length of time in the United States (i.e., first, second, or third generation), there are significant differences in parental interpretations of such things as the value of education, familial responsibilities (Wang,

Bernas, & Eberhard, 2005), and the parental role in children's education (Fuligni & Fuligni, 2007). As might be expected, parents' relationships with children's teachers and their school engagement experiences also vary as a function of time in the United States (Carreon, Drake, & Barton, 2005). These differences are often accompanied by other difficulties, for example, in accessing health and early education services for families of children whose first language is not English (Lee & Burkam, 2003).

Complicating educational responses to these new populations and in contrast to previous patterns of rapid assimilation, some immigrant groups reject the concept of the melting pot version of American society. These cultural groups, while hoping to be successful within their newly adopted culture, also establish their own communities-within-communities (Suarez-Orozco & Suarez-Orozco, 1995). One of the ways in which this resistance to mainstream American interpretations of child family life is manifest is through the under-utilization of publicly funded early childhood programs. Research among culturally distinct groups of subcultures in America reveals strong ethnic and household influences on parents' preferences, selection, and use of child care (Fuller, Holloway, & Liang, 1996; Hirshberg, Huang, & Fuller, 2005).

American society has also changed in terms of its response to these newcomers to the labor force. While immigrants come from a wide range of economic circumstances, poverty rates among immigrant households have dramatically increased in the past 25 years (Takanishi, 2004). This finding brings the challenge full circle: Children from culturally diverse families are also often from impoverished families. Collectively, research confirms what classroom teachers already know: We have yet to fully understand how best to promote the learning of all children regardless of racial, ethnic, or social class differences. Unfortunately, research hasn't helped teachers understand what they might do to break this cycle of poverty and educational failure.

Personal Proclamation of Difference

Contemporary discussions of diversity—including cultural diversity—now include another feature of children's lives subsumed under the category of gender identity. As possibilities for individuals expand to include the expression of homosexuality and sexual orientation, the number of children growing up in same-sex families is steadily increasing (Rowell, 2007). Regardless of the politicized nature of the current debate, same-sex marriages and reproductive technology (including egg donation, donor insemination, and in vitro fertilization) have had a significant impact on the social makeup of families. Although research suggests that children are not adversely affected by new family constellations (Meezan & Rauch, 2005), most assume that these factors (i.e., family structure and sexual orientation/gender identity) play important roles in children's learning. While this dimension of diversity is often less visible and even sometimes hidden (Fox, 2007), one thing is clear. Children from families with same-sex couples come to school with new understandings of and schemas for gender identity and "family" sometimes far-removed from the teacher's experience or even imagination.

Each of these types of diversity—the visible as well as the invisible—is a potentially powerful source of influence on children's learning opportunities. As a field, we have barely begun to consider how we might harness these new and diverse contributions to children's early learning.

ECE RESPONSES TO DIVERSITY

The early childhood field's responses to diversity have been as diverse as the construct itself. Children of low-income families, children with special needs, and children of middle- and upper-income families have been the targets of distinct theoretical interpretations of child development and, accordingly, different early childhood programs (New & Mallory, 1996). These differences mirror the larger field of education, with a long history of program differentiation for children labeled as "common," "delinquent," or "special" (Richardson, 1994). The diversity within the field of early childhood is not limited to differences in program design. Other differences—in program quality, affordability, and accessibility—mitigate against equal opportunities for the early education of young children. The economic auspices of programs also vary, such that for-profit centers (less likely to be affordable to low-income families) currently outnumber other types of centers, although the number of early childhood programs in public schools is increasing rapidly (Saluja, Early, & Clifford, 2002).

Many of the differences in the field are associated with images of the intended beneficiaries of various programs. The field was born in response to the perceived needs of children from poor and immigrant families (Beatty, 1995), and has continued to play a major role in attempting to redress some of the economic inequities in American society. Following the civil rights movement and associated school desegregation laws, the War on Poverty culminated in such initiatives as Head Start, designed to educate both children and families in mainstream values and developmentally appropriate ways of promoting social, emotional, and cognitive development (Ellsworth & Ames, 1998). Forty years after the initiation of Head Start, contemporary analyses continue to highlight the startling relationships between race, class, and cognitive status in the United States. These findings have sparked renewed debate about the role, costs, and presumed benefits of early childhood services for young children of impoverished families (Zigler & Styfco, 2004).

Some have suggested that the segregated nature of targeted programs such as Head Start—distinct in design as well as the population served—as well as more general tracking practices within school settings (Oakes, 1985) may "exacerbate the very problems they were designed to ameliorate" (New & Mallory, 1996, p. 150). Others critique the very discourse of "at-risk" children and families, suggesting that such labels often prove self-fulfilling (Swadener & Lubeck, 1995). And yet, when schools are required to serve diverse racial and economic groups, their integration has not always been successful. Research has found, at least in studies involving older children, that efforts to enhance racial mixing in schools have often been self-defeating (Caldas & Bankston, 2005). These scholars contend that a major premise of desegregation—to redesign American society—clashes with the goals of parents who are concerned only with benefiting their own children. The darker side of parents' hopes for their children to be competitive and successful may translate, for example, into opposition to progressive school reform initiatives (Perlstein, 1996) and middle-class parents who abandon schools that are desegregated.

Classroom responses to prejudices and a general rejection of cultural difference came in the 1970s and 1980s in the form of a multicultural education that emphasizes in a more purposeful way the fact that classrooms and societies are made up of all sorts of people with their own particular histories, traditions, values, and ways of knowing (Williams & DeGaetano, 1985). Analyses of various interpretations of multicultural education reveal a range of ideas and experiences deemed appropriate for schools to share with children (Sleeter & Grant, 1987). In response to calls to expand the meaning of diversity, more recent multicultural education efforts have included sexual orientation and religious identity. For the most part, early childhood interpretations of multicultural principles have continued to emphasize the commonalities and differences among various groups of people without addressing the social inequities that accompany those differences.

As it has become clear that multicultural education *inside* the classroom is not sufficient to producing an equitable multicultural education *outside* the school, some teachers have moved beyond the description of difference to a more explicit consideration of societal characteristics that have sustained prejudicial and discriminatory practices. Informed by principles of critical pedagogy (Sleeter & McLaren, 1995; Ladson-Billings, 1995), such culturally responsive teaching (Gay, 2000) assumes the stance of social activism (Sleeter, 1996).

Many early childhood educators joined this radical multicultural education movement, going beyond the focus on accepting differences to embrace a more purposeful and anti-bias curriculum to help children learn how to recognize and challenge prejudice and stereotyping (Derman-Sparks, 1989). Efforts within preschool settings, such as those promoted through the Start Small Teaching Tolerance project (1997), are demonstrating that it is never too early to help children understand and reject prejudice and social inequality. As teachers take more purposeful steps to address issues of diversity, many acknowledge the extent to which their anti-bias work influenced their own lives as adults (Alvarado, et al., 1999). And yet, by the 1990s the concepts of multiculturalism and a multicultural education were at the center of a national debate regarding the positioning of pluralism and the perceived failure of public education in America. Within an increasingly politicized context, some educators challenged the use of teaching strategies for minority children developed on the basis of middle class children's lifestyles and preschool learning experiences (Garcia, 1994; Delpit, 1995).

Surely one of the largest contributors to conflicts about teaching children from diverse family traditions and circumstances is the lack of diversity in the early childhood workforce. Demographic information on early childhood programs, including public preschool as well as Head Start and private programs, shows that the vast majority of teachers of 3- and 4-year-olds in the United States are women, and 78 percent are white. Approximately 50 percent of these teachers have earned a college degree, although educational attainment varies among program types (Saluja, Early, & Clifford, 2002). Although the explanation is not sufficient, few can argue with the premise that "we can't teach what we don't know" (Howard, 2006). The lack of men, teachers of color, and bilingual educators surely heightens the challenges of an effective multicultural education.

Within the field of early childhood education, there is a second critical issue beyond that of what happens inside the classroom: what to do about the large numbers of children with limited access to prevailing interpretations of high-quality early educational experiences. There are a number of critical social policy issues linked to the challenges of diversity in early childhood, foremost among them the need to level the playing field (Takanishi, 2004) by increasing the availability and quality of early childhood services so that all children have access to what is currently only available for a few. The disparities in the availability of high-quality early childhood services for children has been described as a 'national crisis' (Ramey, 2005) and particularly in the case of immigrant children, some now argue for a federal role in ensuring increased availability and quality of early childhood experiences (Takanishi, 2004), including both preschool and after-school programs (Waldfogel & Lahaie, 2007). And yet this recommendation comes with a number of caveats. Not only are some populations vastly underserved, others are not likely to be enrolled even when services are available (Fuller, Eggers-Pierola, Holloway, Liang, and Rambaud, 1996).

As the chorus grows for universal pre-K programs for young children in the United States, there are growing concerns about the false promise of a 'standardized childhood' in our pluralistic society (Fuller, 2007). There are widely different views on how to serve children of immigrant families. One recent study (Buysse, Castro, West, & Skinner, 2005) surveyed state administrators of a variety of early childhood education programs (including licensed child care, Head Start, and preschool special education programs) and found general agreement regarding the importance of supporting a child's home language, but significant differences in interpretations of the challenges of or approaches to diversity, including strategies for encouraging parental involvement. Research that helps to answer questions about how to best serve children of diverse family backgrounds comes from studies on specific immigrant populations. In advocating for a specific early care and education agenda for Hispanic children, for example, researchers point to the particular child care and early education needs of Latinos, including workforce issues, specific educational challenges, and culturally specific challenges for English language learners (Collins & Ribeiro, 2004). These concerns give rise to the second pressing question for our field: *What if what we know and believe in is rejected by other stakeholders in children's lives?*

WHAT NEXT? RECONCEPTUALIZING RESPONSES TO DIVERSITY

Given the extensive attention paid to diversity within early childhood settings over the last several decades, many educators are hard-pressed to imagine what else might be done. And yet many classroom teachers are feeling burdened by an increasing number of children whose characteristics don't match those children they are prepared to teach. Thankfully, there are a number of specific initiatives that have the potential to make significant contributions to our field's understanding of the diverse population of children arriving in classrooms across the United States. These initiatives draw on expanded understandings of human-development-in-context, otherwise known as sociocultural theory; the potentials of more purposefully guided research; and an expanded interpretation of early childhood settings as the locus for *adult* learning—about children, themselves, and the benefits of collaborative inquiry for a more equitable early education in a rapidly changing democratic society.

An Inclusive Theory of Culture and Child Development

If we wish to have more inclusive educational policies and practices—those that embrace the full variety of children and families residing in our communities—it is essential to have a theoretical interpretation of our common experiences as humans that can also help us to understand those ways in which we diverge from one another. While the field of psychology has done much to help us understand the individual mechanisms of behavior and development, even those understandings have been challenged by more recent work in the interdisciplinary field of cultural psychology. This work makes clear that what is highly valued and nurtured in one cultural setting may be considered improbable, if not inappropriate, from a cross-cultural perspective. Cumulatively, this work should give us pause in proclaiming expertise over what and how children should learn (New, 1999).

Over the past half-century, an impressive body of research has accumulated that demonstrates the dynamic relationship between sociocultural contexts and children's learning and development. It is now recognized by many in the field of child development that children's processes of learning and development include observation and participation in specific cultural settings (Rogoff, 2003). Scholars from a variety of social sciences—anthropology, child development, linguistics, sociology—have contributed empirical data supporting interpretations of human development as a cultural process, one in which individuals develop as they actively participate in social routines within specific cultural communities (Masten, 1999).

These cultural processes of development are structured and sustained in the form of family traditions and parenting practices. These practices, in turn, reflect parental values, beliefs, and priorities for children's early learning and development (LeVine, 1974) as defined by the 'moral goods' of particular cultural communities (LeVine et al., 1994). Thusly, adult ideologies are not isolated from the surrounding sociocultural context; rather, they are instantiated in the social and physical characteristics of the environment, including patterns of interaction and language use as well as other visible and tacit features of the child's "developmental niche" (Super & Harkness, 1986; Harkness & Super, 1996).

A century of ethnographic research on culture and child development (LeVine, 2007; LeVine & New, 2008) has consistently demonstrated the power of parental and communal beliefs about childhood as determinants in what and how children learn. In response to the slow-but-steady recognition of this body of work, scholarly images of previously homogeneous children growing up in the generic middle-class neighborhoods has been replaced with multiple images of children growing up in a wide array of settings that may nurture or inhibit their diverse biological predispositions (Shonkoff, 2000).

Culturally distinct interpretations of child development can be found in other nations' early childhood policies and practices, as described in ethnographic and comparative social policy research in European and Asian nations (c.f. Lubeck, 1995; Tobin, Wu, & Davidson, 1987). Studies on early care and education that examine adult belief systems support the premise of cultural diversity in adult conceptualizations of and responses to young children's needs and competencies (Kagitcibasi, 1996). A recent international review of early care and education programs confirms that program quality itself is interpreted differently in nations around the world (O.E.C.D., 2001). Discussions of curriculum, infant/toddler care, teacher education, and literacy, as well as many other features of the field's endeavors, represent distinct cultural values and national perspectives (New & Cochran, 2007).

The understandings garnered from this work have contributed to critiques of pan-cultural notions of optimal early care and education (Mallory & New, 1994; Dahlberg, Moss, & Pence, 2007). These critiques, in turn, have resulted in revisions to dominant interpretations of developmentally appropriate practices (Bredekamp, 1987; Bredekamp & Copple, 1997). And yet, the challenge persists of understanding and coordinating diverse perspectives about early childhood. Culturally grounded scholarship suggests new research questions as essential to effective responses to cultural diversity within our pluralistic society.

Social Science That Matters

In spite of the growing body of knowledge of children growing up in diverse cultural and national contexts, there remains a dearth of information about children growing up in diverse cultural communities within the United States. A bulk of the research (and accompanying discourse) on diversity continues to focus on racial and ethnic differences. Among immigrant populations, researchers have focused primarily on adolescents and their school achievement (Takanishi, 2004), with an overrepresentation of groups who represent extremes—i.e., those who end up in the penal system or those who constitute so-called model minority groups (Suarez-Orozco, 2007). Further limiting our understanding of child development within diverse cultural communities has been the tendency to group of families from diverse nations around the world into such categories as Latinos or Asians (Suarez-Orozco, 2007, p. 313). Thus, while some scholars point to the "extraordinary" diversity of children from immigrant households, with an "astonishingly wide array of languages, religious, cultural beliefs, and practices" (Suarez-Orozco, 2007, p. 313), there are significant gaps in research on immigrants (Lansford, Deater-Deckard, & Bornstein, 2007).

As questions of diversity increase in numbers and complexity, child development and education scholars have begun to direct more attention to young children as situated within home and school settings. This work has led to the recognition of specific research needs on the part of the early education community, including more studies on children and families not typically represented in research (e.g.,

Muslims), studies focused on the impact of early care and educational services on families at different stages of the immigration process, and more culturally sensitive research on the nature and quality of teacher-child interactions when they come from similar versus diverse backgrounds. Others have also called for attention to a broader range of outcomes for children (e.g., cognitive and socioemotional development as well as preacademic skills), and longitudinal studies that address the changing relationships among first-, second-, and third-generation immigrants with each other and with educators (Suarez-Orozco, 2007; Takanishi & Bogard, 2007). Still others emphasize the complex nature of the immigrant experience as a function of the interface between country of origin and the timing and reasons for immigration (Gibson & Ogbu, 1991). These and other documented differences among diverse populations of children have powerful implications for young children growing up in multigenerational immigrant families.

Most promising in terms of bringing diverse perspectives to bear on the topic of diversity are calls for a broader and multidisciplinary representation of the behavioral and social sciences (Takanishi & Bogard, 2007). Such research will go a long way to helping educators better understand the home environments and parenting goals and practices of these changing school and community populations.

Of course these research needs and the principles implied in the above recommendations are not limited to those children and families who represent culturally and linguistically diverse populations. Other groups of children and their families also remain poorly represented in child development and early education texts. Thus there are increasing calls for research on children growing up in homes characterized by alternative lifestyles, including calls for more studies on the effects of gay marriage in its various forms of union (civil union vs. same-sex couples vs. partner-benefit programs) (Meezan & Rauch, 2005). Regardless of the label assigned to the population under study, researchers are cautioned to consider parenting as both a dynamic and situated construct, in that parenting practices change over time as a function not only of children's development but also of contextual and anticipatory features (e.g., pending enrollment in kindergarten) of the larger environment (Son, 2007).

Parents are not the only targets of these new research pleas. Children, including those from diverse cultural and immigrant populations, warrant further study in their own right. Recent studies make clear that children play a powerful role in the construction of their own peer cultures and their transitions from one educational setting to another (Corsaro & Molinari, 2006). Studies focused explicitly on gender—now a relatively neglected topic—have also challenged common expectations, for example, about girls' "difficulties" in science (Jeffe, 1995). Few researchers have examined how children in diverse family structures interpret their family difference within the context of the peer culture. Those who do such work with culturally diverse populations of children and families emphasize the need for culturally sensitive tools in such studies, given that children's behavior (as well as how it is interpreted by adults) will likely be influenced by cultural values and social convictions (Chen, Rubin, & Sun, 1992).

These changes in research orientation and methodology represent a major paradigm shift in how science has traditionally viewed children, their parents, and their circumstances (Beatty, Cahan, & Grant, 2006). At the very least, such work adds to our knowledge of the cultural complexities in children's lives (Hyun, 2007). Adding to this paradigm shift are new interpretations of who may be best situated to study children as they explore educational environments and negotiate their positions and relationships. Whether it is called action research, teacher research, or qualitative inquiry, there is much to be gained by having classroom teachers—in collaboration with parents, other teachers, as well as university scholars—join the quest to learn more about the conditions and nature of effective and engaging learning environments for diverse populations of young children.

Teaching as Collaborative Inquiry

Teaching and professional development are another form of cognitive development in the sociocultural context. Teachers, too, come from particular cultural communities with life lessons about childhood, schools, adult-child relationships, and developmentally appropriate practices. Inspired by their own discoveries, an increasing number of teachers have begun to use classrooms as settings in which they can learn about the children they teach. Current research efforts by teachers include ethnographic, interpretive, and/or post-modern traditions of inquiry, each of which brings new insights into children's learning and development. For example, teacher research on children's literacy development underscores the multiple ways in which children from different cultural groups may approach language and adult authority figures as well as the critical need (and very real potential) for teachers to learn new and more culturally meaningful ways of teaching "other people's children" (Ballenger, 1999). Ethnographic studies of children's lives have helped teachers to understand the power of the peer culture within the classroom (Fernie, Kantor, & Whaley, 1995).

Teacher research does not necessarily need to focus on children's classroom activities. Teachers can utilize an ethnographic orientation to study cultural practices that take place outside of school (New, 1994), for example, in the family or neighborhood. Teacher-educators can also utilize an inquiry orientation to promote preservice-teacher awareness of children's diverse ways of learning—a form of research that is highly teacher-centric and entails a conscious deliberation of teacher discourse and patterns of relating (Moran, 2007b). Teacher research can also be intently focused on a single child, such as a recent case study of a Chinese girl's active role in learning English as a second language in a preschool setting (Konishi, 2007).

Many early childhood teachers, inspired by examples of teacher research in Reggio Emilia, have embraced the principles of documentation as a support to their efforts to learn about the children they are teaching, and to communicate more effectively with parents, children, and each other (Moran, 2007a). Collaborative encounters, particularly those supported by some form of documentation, facilitate the co-construction of knowledge and relationships as parents and teachers learn together about young children. By integrating their diverse perspectives to co-construct new understandings about children in areas such as technology, everyone has something to gain even "when no one is expert" (Bers, New, & Boudreau, 2004).

Such teacher inquiry is a valuable means of exploring and understanding diversity in children's learning, especially when documentation is used to support discussions among adults (parents *and* teachers) about their respective roles and relationships in children's learning. When teachers embrace an attitude of inquiry, they are more likely to be open to the cultural complexity of children's lives (Hyun, 2007), and have more information and provocation to search for multiple forms of "good" practice. From the perspective of diversity, such "good" educational practice is not only inquiry-based. It requires new partnerships (Castle, 1995) leading to new potentials for action.

Mediated Learning: Parent-Teacher and Parent-Parent Relationships

Throughout its history, parent involvement has been a fundamental component to many early childhood programs and particularly those designed for diverse populations of children. Parents are legally entitled to play a role in the determination of educational plans for young children with special needs. Parent involvement is central to the Head Start mission as instantiated through, for example, the Parent Advisory Council. And yet the premises of parent involvement and parent education have generally positioned parents as recipients of professional knowledge about child development in general and their own child in particular (Bloch, 1991; Lubeck, 1996). While Head Start's original goal was to create opportunities for impoverished parents to assume more active roles in restructuring society through their "maximum feasible participation," this aim has been hindered by the deficit theory guiding Head Start. The notions that professionals "know better" than lay parents and that "teaching and learning occur from staff to mom and child, and never vice versa" have translated into practices that maintain professionals' status and control at the expense of parent empowerment (Ellsworth & Ames 1998, p. 337). Similar findings of an emphasis on parental compliance have been noted in studies of special education services for African American populations (Harry, Allen, & McLaughlin, 1995).

More recent interpretations of anti-bias/multicultural education share the rejection of this deficit theory of children and families. Increasingly, multicultural materials and scholarship include greater attention to the adult learners in children's lives, and offer some additional guidance to teachers who want to promote tolerance and acceptance among adults as well as children (Kendall, 1983/1996; Ramsey, 2006). This is not to say that it is easy for educators to "get inside the heads" of immigrant parents or others whose life courses are so different from theirs. And it will surely be all the more challenging for educators to understand the nature and consequence of some of these differences as they might inform their own teaching practices. Indeed, as teachers learn of parenting beliefs and practices that strongly challenge their own views of ethical teaching and developmentally appropriate practices, the teaching of young children will inevitably become a more "risky business" (New, Mardell, & Robinson, 2005). And yet a vast majority of parents want happy and healthy children who can successfully traverse the distance between home and school environments. Reggio Emilia serves as a powerful illustration of what can happen when teachers remember this universal parental goal and take full advantage of conversations centered on children as powerful catalysts for respectful and productive adult relations (New, 2007).

PUTTING IT ALL TOGETHER: EARLY CHILDHOOD EDUCATION AS CAUSE AND CONTEXT FOR COLLABORATIVE INQUIRY

More inclusive theory and culturally grounded collaborative research both inside and out of the classroom will go a long way to addressing our need to know more so that we can do better with diverse populations of young children. There are challenges associated with these features that might be expected, given the complexity of the construct of diversity and its encounters with the long-standing tradition of American education as a primary source of socialization to a melting-pot society. But there is ample reason for optimism as we move beyond a quest for consensus to a quest for new understandings.

Recent research highlights both the challenges and the potentials of more collaborative partnerships with parents. Some Head Start programs, for example, have shown significant transitions with regard to increased levels of parent participation (Lubeck, Jessup, DeVries, & Post, 2001), with the potential for more open discussions regarding discontinuities between home and school (Bradley & McKelvey, 2007). When teachers in these and other early childhood settings shift from a position of *respecting* parents to *partnering* with family members as a means of understanding their differences, they are in a much better position to understand and negotiate conflicts that arise, for example when the school culture is more individualistic than the value system of the home (Trumbull, Rothstein-Fisch, Greenfield, & Quiroz, 2001). Such studies have major implications for classroom practice as well as teacher education. If the goal is to encourage meaningful parental presence and engagement in school settings (Carreon, Drake, & Barton, 2005), teachers must learn how to engage in the pedagogically and politically challenging task involving the sharing and negotiation of diverse goals and interpretations of children's development and early learning. And teachers will have new challenges in identifying necessary boundaries between parental and educator roles in children's school lives (Pomerantz, Moorman, & Litwack, 2007). This challenge extends as well to parent-parent relations, given the emerging research that shows class differences in the relations between schools and parent networks (Horvat, Weininger, & Lareau, 2003).

The principle of teachers as learners and participants in collaborative inquiry extends beyond partnerships with parents. Teachers also have much to learn from each other, within and beyond the boundaries of particular programs. Recent proposals build upon the early foundations of Head Start as national laboratory (Henrich, 2004, p. 517), and suggest, for example, that Head Start could be national model for future state and federal efforts to provide universal pre-K programs. Rather than be in direct competition as is the case in a number of states, such partnerships have the potential for adult learning and systematic coordination across programs and systems. Within such a context of collaboration, it may be easier to explore other recommendations specific to Head Start (Bowman, 2004) such as ending the mandatory segregation of low-income children and increasing educational requirements for teachers. Such collaborations also have the very real potential to create the conditions for success with early learning standards (Scott-Little, Kagan, & Frelow, 2003). For example, a growing body of research is now available to inform and support teachers' efforts in enhancing the early literacy skills of African American children (Bowman, 2002).

Of course, these recommendations have implications for the professional development of *all* teachers of young children, not just those of Head Start teachers. Federal guidelines for NCLB require that states have a highly qualified teacher in every public school classroom. And yet the definition of "highly qualified" (a teacher who has passed a state exam, has at least a bachelor's degree, and is state certified) does not ensure that this teacher will have the knowledge, skills, or dispositions to respond effectively and equitably to the diversity of children in his or her classroom. These qualifications rarely prepare teachers to successfully involve children's parents in their early education (Weiss, Kreider, Lopez, & Chatman, 2005).

In response to these concerns, inquiry-oriented practice has become a cornerstone of many teacher education programs in the United States (Tegano & Moran, 2005). When student teachers share their documentation with each other, much as when teachers share documentation with parents, images and recordings of children's and adults' thinking provoke extended examination and critique from multiple perspectives. There are a number of complex ethical issues associated with such collaborative inquiry, particularly when it is change-oriented (Clark & Moss, 1996). And yet, an increasing number of teachers and teacher-educators now recognize the value of documentation as a feature of such collaborative research due to its communicative and mediating potentials (Moran & Tegano, 2005).

IN CONCLUSION: BEYOND DEWEY

In spite of the vast new understandings that have emerged from the convergence of theory, research, and practice, as well as the expanding nature of diversity in the early childhood classroom, as a field and a nation we continue to struggle with some of the same problems that we have struggled with for the past 100 years. In spite of concerted efforts to promote more inclusive multicultural classrooms, the flight of middle-class families from urban school settings has yet to be reversed. In spite of the growing use of anti-bias and "teaching tolerance" materials, many teachers remain flummoxed about how best to respond to the multitude of differences among children in their culturally, linguistically, racially, and economically diverse classrooms.

And it's not just that we aren't doing enough. It may well be that we are contributing to the problem. Like clockwork, scholars of early childhood social policy regularly write compelling arguments for comprehensive national early care and educational policies (Kagan, forthcoming; Kagan & Cohen, 1997; Kagan & Zigler, 1987). In spite of heightened attention to the period of early childhood at the national level through such legislation as NCLB, the gaps in children's school readiness and subsequent academic performance continue to expand between children whose families are rich and those who are poor.

Many of the proposed solutions to these chronic problems are also not new. The notion of teacher inquiry as an essential component of a progressive education was a common theme of Dewey's work (1933). Two decades ago, teacher research was again proposed as an agency for change (Goswami & Stillman, 1987). Even increased parent involvement has not always proved to be the magic bullet in enhancing the academic achievements of all children. Indeed, none of these suggestions—improved theoretical understandings, increased parent participation, or preparation for teaching-as-inquiry—will be sufficient to make the needed changes in an early childhood education for a nation characterized by diversity. What it will take is a *synthesis* of these elements such that parents join teachers in learning about principles of emerging literacy, teachers join parents in learning about the oral and other literacy practices in the home, and teachers document these discoveries as they inform their own learning and that of children and *share* these new understandings with the larger public. In this sense, early childhood settings function as laboratories for and with the larger community.

Examples abound of such initiatives in other nations, including a number of western European countries with projects that actively seek alternative perspectives on children's education, for example, grassroots projects in Greece to enhance accessibility of preschool for refugees; in France, where parents and professionals routinely engage in pedagogical debate; in Germany, where a pilot project includes voices of children and parents; and in Italy, where parents and teachers explore the benefits of mixed-age groupings of infants and toddlers. Such an orientation to diversity—as something to seek out and explore—goes far beyond an anti-bias curriculum for children. It elicits and fosters curiosities and imagination among the adults, and encourages the sorts of connections that are rare between parents and teachers and community members; and responds to the plea for safer "bridges between the home culture and the institutional culture" (Vandenbroeck, 2007, p. 31). Reggio Emilia's early childhood program provides ample evidence of the benefits of projects that include adult as well as child learners (New, 1998; 2007).

To be truly collaborative, encounters with parents and other family members must entail more than a willingness to listen to parents as they share their perspectives (Edwards, 1999). These conversations must also include new voices as well as encouragement to share and then actively consider new visions (Williams, 1989). There are, of course, multiple language challenges in such discourse. The late early childhood activist Leslie Williams proposed, long ago and often, that we must be willing to change how we communicate. Our field's heavy reliance on the language of developmental psychology has not served us well in inviting parents to share their own views of their child's development. The language of progressive education, such as a child-centered or play-based curriculum, also fails to adequately describe the processes and goals of our dominant early childhood pedagogy. This failure to communicate inhibits our conversations with parents and policy makers; it also impedes our field's potentially collaborative relationship with other educators, including, for example, those in elementary classrooms.

But perhaps it is time for teachers to share their problems as well as their power. Surely the question of standards in the early childhood classroom is not just "the teacher's dilemma" (Wien, 2004). If educators are sincere about their intent to "appreciate and respect cultural diversity" (Fullinwider, 1996, p. 14), it will require a paradigm shift of major proportions, one in which parents and teachers are each respected as having valuable and specialized knowledge about children. This orientation of respect can lead to more than the development of friendly relationships with children's families. In such a context, notions of standards, quality, and developmentally appropriate practices shift from things to be counted or measured to things that invite debate, and that require exploration, innovation, and negotiation (New, 2005).

A pedagogy of collaborative inquiry has the potential to become a form of global exchange and a forum for civic engagement that is essential not only to effective teaching but also effective and ethical democratic society. And yet, we cannot wait for new knowledge to accumulate nor, even, can we take it for granted that what is learned by adults (scholars, teachers, parents) will get translated into more equitable social policies.

Some collaborative researchers find cause for optimism in the potentials of (local) practice to inform (local) policy (Ceglowski, 1999). There are a number of social policy issues, however, that will require more sustained and compelling advocacy. After multiple calls for action, we haven't come close to making the kind of changes necessary to "change the trajectory" of children of the working poor (Washington & Andrews, 1998). Nor have we responded in an effective manner to the national crisis in child care (Ramey, 2005). These two examples provide compelling reasons why we must, as a profession, embrace the principle of advocacy in our role and work for children both inside and out of the early childhood setting. The notion of such "everyday advocacy" is no longer a luxury activity for teachers with extra time (Goffin & Washington, 2007). Ready or not, we have an old but increasingly compelling mandate. Perhaps we will be more successful if we advocate in more subtle ways that belie traditional notions of professional expertise.

Some teachers may resist the expectation to more frequently and actively speak up on behalf of children and against inequities, although a vast majority of teachers are eager to demonstrate the early capabilities of young children who are eager to learn (Bowman, Donovan, & Burns, 2000). But there is another challenging aspect of this work that will cut to the heart of our identities as early childhood educators: the need to sometimes say "I don't know"; to often say "I wonder"; and to always share our platform with others who know and feel differently. As professionals, we have a particular responsibility to take a stand and go public with it (Fennimore, 2007). But this stance is not one of proclaiming our expertise. Rather, as soon as we go "beyond certainty" (Cochran-Smith & Lytle, 2001) we are in a better position to authentically invite others to join us in the sort of democratic discourse and collaborative inquiry so indispensable to our work.

REFERENCES

Alvarado, C., et al. (1999). *In our own way: How anti-bias work shapes our lives.* St. Paul, MN: Redleaf Press.

Bainbridge, J., Meyers, M. K., Tanaka, S., & Waldfogel, J. (2005). Who gets an early education? Family income and the enrollment of three- to five-year-olds from 1960–2000. *Social Science Quarterly, 86*(3), 724–745.

Ballenger, C. (1999). *Teaching other people's children: Literacy and learning in a bilingual classroom.* New York: Teachers College Press.

Beatty, B. (1995). *Preschool education in America: The culture of young children from the colonial era to the present.* New Haven CT: Yale University Press.

Beatty, B., Cahan, E., & Grant, J. (Eds.). (2006). *When science encounters the child: Education, parenting, and child welfare in 20th-century America.* New York: Teachers College Press.

Bers, M., New, R., & Boudreau, L. (2004). Teaching and learning when no one is expert: Children and parents explore technology. *ECRP, 6*(2).

Bloch, M. (1991). Critical science and the history of child development's influence on early education research. *Early Education and Development, 2(2),* 945–1008.

Bowman, B. (2002). *Love to read: Essays in developing and enhancing early literacy skills of African American children.* Washington, DC: National Black Child Development Institute.

Bowman, B. (2004). The future of Head Start. In E. Zigler & S. Styfco (Eds.), *The Head Start debates,* (pp. 533–544). Baltimore: Brookes.

Bowman, B., Donovan, M. S., & Burns, M. S. (Eds.). (2000). *Eager to learn: Educating our preschoolers.* Washington, DC: National Academy Press.

Bradley, R. H., & McKelvey, L. (2007). Managing the differences within: Immigration and early education in the United States. In J. Lansford, K. Deater-Deckard, & M. Bornstein (Eds.), *Immigrant families in contemporary society* (pp. 157–176). New York: Guilford Press.

Bredekamp, S. (Ed.). (1987). *Guidelines for developmentally appropriate practice in early childhood*

programs serving children from birth through age 8. Washington, DC: National Association for the Education of Young Children.

Bredekamp, S., & Copple, C. (Eds.). (1997). *Guidelines for developmentally appropriate practice in early childhood programs* (Rev. ed.) Washington, DC: National Association for the Education of Young Children.

Buysse, V., Castro, D. C., West, T., & Skinner, M. (2005). Addressing the needs of Latino children: A national survey of state administrators of early childhood programs. *Early Childhood Research Quarterly, 20,* 146–163.

Caldas, S., & Bankston, C. (2005). *Forced to fail: The paradox of school desegregation.* Westport, CT: Praeger.

Carreon, G. P., Drake, C., & Barton, A. C. (2005). The importance of presence: Immigrant parents' school engagement experiences. *American Educational Research Journal, 42*(3), 465–498.

Castle, K. (1995). Forming partnerships for action research. *Journal of Early Childhood Teacher Education, 16*(1), 18–20.

Clark, C. T., & Moss, P. A. (1996). Researching *with*: Ethical implications of doing collaborative change-oriented research with teachers and students. *Teachers College Record, 97*(4), 518–548.

Ceglowski, D. (1999). *Inside a Head Start center: Developing policies from practice.* New York: Teachers College Press.

Chen, X., Rubin, K. H., and Sun, Y. (1992). Social reputation and peer relationships in Chinese and Canadian children: A cross-cultural study. *Child Development, 63*(6), 1336–1343.

Cochran-Smith, M., & Lytle, S. (2001). Beyond certainty: Taking an inquiry stance in practice. In A. Lieberman & L. Miller (Eds.), *Teachers caught in the action: Professional development that works* (pp. 45–60). New York: Teachers College Press.

Collins, R., & Ribeiro, R. (2004). Toward an early care and education agenda for Hispanic children. *Early Childhood Research and Practice, 6*(2).

Corsaro W. A., & Molinari L. (2005). *I compagni: Understanding children's transition from preschool to elementary school.* New York: Teachers College Press.

Dahlberg, G., Moss, P., & Pence, A. (2006). *Beyond quality in early childhood education and care: Postmodern perspectives.* (2nd Ed.). Philadelphia: Falmer Press.

Delpit, L. (1995). *Other people's children: Cultural conflict in the classroom.* New York: New Press.

Derman-Sparks, L. (1989). *Anti-bias curriculum: Tools for empowering young children.* Washington, DC: National Association for the Education of Young Children.

Dewey, J. (1933). *How we think: A restatement of the relation of reflective thinking to the educative process.* Lexington, MA: D. C. Heath.

Edwards, P. A. (1999). *A path to follow: Learning to listen to parents.* Portsmouth, NH: Heinemann.

Ellsworth, J. & Ames, L. J. (Eds.). (1998). *Critical perspectives on Project Head Start: Revisioning the hope and challenge.* Albany: State University of New York Press.

Fennimore, B. (2007) Know where you stand and stand there: Everyday advocacy for children of diversity. *Childhood Education, 83*(5), 294–298.

Fernie, D., Kantor, R., & Whaley, K. L. (1995). Learning from classroom ethnographies: Same places, different times. In J. A. Hatch (Ed.), *Qualitative research in early childhood settings.* Westport, CT: Praeger.

Flyvbjerg, B. (2001). *Making social science matter.* Cambridge, UK: Cambridge University Press.

Fox, R. (2007). One of the hidden diversities in schools: Families with parents who are lesbian or gay. *Childhood Education, 83*(5), 277–281.

Fuligni, A. J., & Fuligni, A. S. (2007). Immigrant families and the educational development of their children. In J. Lansford, K. Deater-Deckard, & M. Bornstein (Eds.), *Immigrant families in contemporary society* (pp. 231–249). New York: Guilford Press.

Fuller, B. (2007). *Standardized childhood: The political and cultural struggle over early education.* Stanford, CA: Stanford University Press.

Fuller, B., Eggers-Pierola, C., Holloway, S., Liang, X., and Rambaud, M. F. (1996). Rich culture, poor markets: Why do Latino parents forgo preschooling? *Teachers College Record, 97*(3), 400–418.

Fuller, B., Holloway, S., & Liang, X. (1996). Family selection of child care centers: The influence of household support, ethnicity, and parental practices. *Child Development, 67,* 3320–3337.

Fullinwider, R. K. (Ed.). (1996). *Public education in a multicultural society: Policy, theory, critique.* New York: Cambridge University Press.

Garcia, E. (1994). *Understanding and meeting the challenge of student cultural diversity.* Boston: Houghton Mifflin.

Gay, G. (2000). *Culturally responsive teaching: Theory, research and practice.* New York: Teachers College Press.

Gibson, M. A., & Ogbu, J. U. (1991). *Minority status and schooling: A comparative study of immigrant and involuntary minorities.* New York: Garland.

Goffin, S. G., & Washington, V. (2007). *Ready or not: Leadership choices in early care and education.* New York: Teachers College Press.

Goswami, D., & Stillman, P. (1987). *Reclaiming the classroom: Teacher research as an agency for change.* Upper Montclair, NJ: Boynton/Cook.

Harkness, S., & Super, C. (Eds.). (1996). *Parents' cultural belief systems: Their origins, expressions, and consequences.* New York: Guilford Press.

Harry, B., Allen, N., & McLaughlin, M. (1995). Communication versus compliance: African-American parents' involvement in special education. *Exceptional Children, 61*(4), 364–377.

Hauser-Cram, P., Warfield, M. E., Shonkoff, J. P., & Krauss, M. W. (2001). *Children with disabilities.* Monograph of the Society for Research in Child Development, Serial No. 266, *66*(3).

Henrich, C. C. (2004). Head Start as a national laboratory. In E. Zigler & S. Styfco (Eds.), *The Head Start debates* (pp. 517–531). Baltimore: Brookes.

Hirshberg, D., Huang, S. S., & Fuller, B. (2005). Which low-income parents select childcare? Family demand and neighborhood organizations. *Children and Youth Services Review, 27,* 1119–1148.

Horvat, E. M., Weininger, E. B., & Lareau, A. (2003). From social ties to social capital: Class differences in the relations between schools and parent networks. *American Educational Research Journal, 40*(2), 319–351.

Howard, G. R. (2006). *We can't teach what we don't know: White teachers, multicultural schools.* New York: Teachers College Press.

Hyun, E. (2007). Cultural complexity in early childhood: Images of contemporary young children from a critical perspective. *Childhood Education, 83*(5), 261–266.

Jeffe, D. B. (1995). About girls' "difficulties" in science: A social, not a personal, matter. *Teachers College Record, 97*(2), 206–226.

Kagan, S. L. (forthcoming). *American early childhood education: Preventing or perpetuating inequity?* New York: Campaign for Educational Equity. Teachers College, Columbia University.

Kagan, S. L., & Zigler, E. (Eds.). (1987). *Early schooling: The national debate.* New Haven: Yale University Press.

Kagan, S. L., & Cohen, N. E. (1997). *Not by chance: Creating an early care and education system for America's children.* Full Report Quality 2000 Initiative. New Haven: Bush Center in Child Development and Social Policy.

Kagitcibasi, C. (1996). *Family and human development across cultures: A view from the other side.* Mahwah, NJ: Erlbaum.

Kendall, E. E. (1983/1996). *Diversity in the classroom: New approaches to the education of young children.* New York: Teachers College Press.

Konishi, C. (2007). Learning English as a second language: A case study of a Chinese girl in an American preschool. *Childhood Education, 83*(5), 267–272.

Kozol, J. (2005). *Shame of the nation: The restoration of apartheid schooling in America.* New York: Crown.

Ladson-Billings, C. (1995). Toward a theory of culturally relevant pedagogy. *American Educational Research Journal, 32*(3), 465–491.

Lansford, J., Deater-Deckard, K., & Bornstein, M. (Eds.). (2007). *Immigrant families in contemporary society.* New York: Guilford Press.

Lareau, A. (2003). *Unequal childhoods: Class, race, and family life.* Berkeley, CA: University of California Press.

Larner, M., & Collins, A. (1996). Poverty in the lives of young children. In E. J. Erwin (Ed.), *Putting children first: Visions for a brighter future for young children and their families.* Baltimore: Brookes.

Lee, V. E., & Burkam, D. T. (2002). *Inequality at the starting gate: Social background differences in achievement as children begin school.* Washington, DC: Economic Policy Institute.

LeVine, R. A. (1974). Parental goals: A cross-cultural view. *Teachers College Record, 76*(2), 226–239.

LeVine, R. A. (2007). Ethnographic studies of childhood: A historical overview. *American Anthropologist, 109*(2), 247–260.

LeVine, R. A., Dixon, S., LeVine, S., Richman, A., Leiderman, H., Keefer, S., & Brazelton, T. B. (1994). *Child care and culture: Lessons from Africa.* Cambridge UK: Cambridge University Press.

LeVine, R. A., & New, R. S. (Eds.). (2008). *Anthropology and child development: A cross-cultural reader.* Boston: Wiley-Blackwell.

Liben, L., & Bigler, R. (2002). *The developmental course of gender differentiation.* Monograph of the Society for Research in Child Development, Serial No. 269, *67*(2).

Lubeck, S. (1985). *Sandbox society: Early education in black and white America: A comparative ethnography.* Philadelphia: Falmer Press.

Lubeck, S. (1995). Nation as context: Comparing child-care systems across nations. *Teachers College Record, 96*(3), 467–491.

Lubeck, S. (1996). Deconstructing "child development knowledge" and "teacher preparation." *Early Childhood Research Quarterly, 11*, 147–167.

Lubeck, S., Jessup, P., DeVries, M., & Post, J. U. (2001). The role of culture in program improvement. *Early Childhood Research Quarterly, 16*, 499–523.

Mallory, B. L., & New, R. S. (Eds.). (1994). *Diversity and developmentally appropriate practices: Challenges for early childhood education.* New York: Teachers College Press.

Mallory, B., & Rous, B. (in press *this volume*). Educating young children with developmental differences: Principles of inclusive practice. In S. Feeney & A. Galper (Eds.), *Continuing issues in early childhood education* (3rd ed.). Upper Saddle River, NJ: Merrill/Prentice Hall.

Masten, A. (Ed.). (1999). *Cultural processes in child development: The Minnesota symposia on child psychology, 29.*

Meezan, W., & Rauch, J. (2005). Gay marriage, same-sex parenting, and America's children. *The Future of Children, 15*(2), 97–115.

Moran, M. J. (2007a). *Progetazzione* and documentation as sociocultural activities: Changing communities of practice. In Theresa Wilson (Ed.), *Theory to Practice: Special Issue on Reggio Emilia, 46*(1), 81–90.

Moran, M. J. (2007b). Teacher research. In R. New & M. Cochran (Eds.), *Early childhood education: An international encyclopedia* (pp. 793–798). Westport, CT: Praeger.

Moran, M. J., & Tegano, D. W. (2005). Moving toward visual literacy: Photography as a language of teacher inquiry. *Early Childhood Research and Practice, 7*(1).

New, R. S. (1994). Culture, child development, and developmentally appropriate practices: Teachers as collaborative researchers. In B. L. Mallory & R. S. New (Eds.), *Diversity and developmentally appropriate practices: Challenges for early childhood education* (pp. 65–83). New York: Teachers College Press.

New, R. (1999). What should children learn? Making choices and taking chances. *Early Childhood Research and Practice, 1*(2), 1–25.

New, R. (2005). Legitimizing quality as quest and question. *Early Education and Development 16*(4), 421–436.

New, R. (2007). Reggio Emilia as cultural activity theory in practice. In Theresa Wilson (Ed.), *Theory to practice: Special issue on Reggio Emilia, 46*(1), 5–14.

New, R., & Cochran, M. (Eds.). (2007). *Early childhood education: An international encyclopedia.* Vols 1–4. Westport, CT: Praeger Greenwood.

New, R. S., & Mallory, B. L. (1996). The paradox of diversity in early care and education. In E. J. Erwin (Ed.), *Putting children first: Visions for a brighter future for young children and their families* (pp. 143–167). Baltimore: Brookes.

New, R., Mardell, B., & Robinson, D. (2005). Early childhood education as risky business: Going beyond what's "safe" to discovering what's possible. *Early childhood research to practice, 7*(2). Online journal. http://ecrp.uiuc.edu/v7n2/new.html

O.E.C.D. (2001). *Starting strong: Early care and education.* Paris: Organization for Economic and Cooperative Development.

Oakes, J. (1985). *Keeping track: How schools structure inequality.* New Haven: Yale University Press.

Perlstein, D. (1996). Community and democracy in American schools: Arthurdale and the fate of progressive education. *Teachers College Record, 97*(4), 625–650.

Phillips, D., Voran, M., Kisker, E., Howes, C., & Whitebook, M. (1994). Child care for children in poverty: Opportunity or inequity? *Child Development, 65*, 472–492.

Pigott, T., & Susman, M. (2005). Head Start children's transition to kindergarten: Evidence from the early childhood longitudinal study. *Journal of Early Childhood Research, 3*(1), 77–104.

Pomerantz, Eva., Moorman, E., & Litwack, S. (2007). The who, whom, and why of parents' involvement in children's academic lives: More is not always better. *Review of Educational Research, 77*(3), 373–410.

Ramey, S. L. (2005). Human developmental science serving children and families: Contributions of the NICHD study of early child care. In The NICHD Early Child Care Research Network (Eds.), *Child care and child development: Results from the NICHD study of early child care and youth development* (pp. 427–436). New York: Guilford Press.

Ramsey, P. G. (2005). *Teaching and learning in a diverse world: Multicultural education for young children* (3rd ed.). New York: Teachers College Press.

Richardson, J. G. (1994). Common, delinquent, and special: On the formalization of common schooling in the American states. *American Educational Research Journal, 31*(4), 695–723.

Rogoff, B. (2003). *The cultural nature of human development.* New York: Oxford University Press.

Rowell, E. (2007). Missing! Picture books reflecting gay and lesbian families. *Beyond the Journal: Young Children on the Web.* Washington, D.C.: National Association for the Education of Young Children.

Saluja, G., Early, D., & Clifford, R. (2002). Demographic characteristics of early childhood teachers and structural elements of early care and education in the United States. *Early Childhood Research & Practice, 4*(2). University of Illinois at Urbana-Champaign: ERIC Clearinghouse on Elementary and Early Childhood Education.

Scott-Little, C., Kagan, S., and Frelow, V. (2003). Creating the conditions for success with early learning standards: Results from a national study of state-level standards for children's learning prior to kindergarten. *Early Childhood Research & Practice, 5*(2). University of Illinois at Urbana-Champaign: ERIC Clearinghouse on Elementary and Early Childhood Education.

Seefeldt, C. (1993). Social studies: Learning for freedom. *Young Children, 48*(3), 4–9.

Shonkoff, J. (2000). *From neurons to neighborhoods.* National Academic Press.

Sleeter, C. E. (1996). *Multicultural education as social activism.* New York: SUNY Press.

Sleeter, C. E., & Grant, C. (1987). An analysis of multicultural education in the United States. *Harvard Education Review, 57*(4), 421–444.

Sleeter, C. E., & McLaren, P. (Eds.). (1995). *Multicultural education, critical pedagogy, and the politics of difference.* Albany: SUNY Press.

Son, S. (2007). Getting children ready for kindergarten: The nature and impact of changes in the home learning environment on growth of early literacy and language skills. *EECD Newsletter, 2*(4), 4.

Suarez-Orozco, C. (2007). Afterword: Reflections on research with immigrant families. In J. Lansford, K. Deater-Deckard, & M. H. Bornstein (Eds.), *Immigrant families in contemporary society* (pp. 311–326). New York: Guilford Press.

Suarez-Orozco, C., & Suarez-Orozco, M. (1995). *Children of immigration* (4th ed.). Cambridge, MA: Harvard University Press.

Super, C., & Harkness, S. (1986). The developmental niche: A conceptualization at the interface of child and culture. *International Journal of Behaviorial Development, 9*, 545–569.

Swadener, B. B., & Lubeck, S. (Eds.). (1995). *Children and families "at promise": Deconstructing the discourse of risk.* Albany: SUNY Press.

Takanishi, R. (2004). Leveling the playing field: Supporting immigrant children from birth to eight. *The Future Of Children, 14*(2), 60–79.

Takanishi, R., & Bogard, K. L. (2007). Effective educational programs for young children: What we need to know. In N. Eisenberg (Ed.), *Child Development Perspectives, 1*(1), 40–45.

Teaching Tolerance Project. (1997). *Starting small: Teaching tolerance in preschool and the early grades.* Montgomery, AL: Southern Poverty Law Center.

Tegano, D. W., & Moran, M. J. (2005, October). Conditions and contexts for teacher inquiry: Systematic approaches to preservice teacher collaborative experiences. *The New Educator, 1*(4), 287–309.

Tobin, J., Wu, D. Y., & Davidson, D. H. (1989). *Preschool in three cultures.* New Haven: Yale University Press.

Trumbull, E., Rothstein-Fisch, C., Greenfield, P. M., & Quiroz, B. (2001). *Bridging cultures between home and school: A guide for teachers.* Mahwah, NJ: Erlbaum.

Vandenbroeck, M. (2007). Beyond anti-bias education: Changing conceptions of diversity and equity in European early childhood education. *European Early Childhood Education Research Journal, 15*(1), 21–35.

Waldfogel, J., & Lahaie, C. (2007). The role of preschool and after-school policies in improving the school achievement of children of immigrants. In J. Lansford, K. Deater-Deckard, & M. Bornstein (Eds.), *Immigrant families in contemporary society,* (pp. 177–193). New York: Guilford Press.

Wang, X., Bernas, R., & Eberhard, P. (2005). Maternal teaching strategies in four cultural communities. *Journal of Early Childhood Research, 3*(3), 269–288.

Washington, V. & Andrews, J. D. (1998). *Children of 2010.* Washington, DC: Children of 2010.

Weiss, H. B., Kreider, H., Lopez, M. E., & Chatman, C. (2005). *Preparing educators to involve families.* Thousand Oaks, CA: Sage.

Wien, C. A. (2004). *Negotiating standards in the primary classroom: The teacher's dilemma.* New York: Teachers College Press.

Williams, L. R. (1989). New visions, new voices: Future directions in the care and education of young children. In F. Rust & L. Williams (Guest Eds.), *The care and education of young children: Expanding contexts, sharpening focus* (pp. 138–139). New York: Teachers College Press.

Williams, L., & DeGaetano, Y. (1985). *ALERTA: A multicultural, bilingual approach to teaching young children.* Menlo Park, CA: Addison-Wesley.

Zigler, E., & Styfco, S. (Eds.) (2004). *The Head Start debates.* Baltimore: Brookes.

PART 6

How Will Early Childhood Education Be Evaluated?

*I*n the past, it was assumed that children would grow and mature given a pleasing school environment and the support of the teacher. There are still many such schools for young children in our country, but the early childhood enterprise has changed radically as a result of both internal and external factors. With the changes have come continuing issues (and sometimes bitter quarrels) among stakeholders about how to assess the growth and development of a diverse population of young children and to evaluate early childhood programs.

In Chapters 15 and 16, Alice Galper (with Carol Seefeldt) and Cynthia Paris examine the issues involved in assessment of children and program evaluation. The authors highlight historical perspectives while emphasizing demographic change. Today's centers for young children are serving audiences far different from those described above. Paris highlights the fact that early childhood programs are serving a population that is becoming more culturally diverse, and one with increasing numbers of young children identified with disabilities and developmental delays and those growing up in poverty. Add to this the many children for whom English is not their primary language. Additionally, because of a new focus on early brain development and the large numbers of parents in the workforce, programs for infants and toddlers are being created and evaluated and even the youngest children are being assessed.

Chapter 15, "Assessing Young Children," was revised by Alice Galper, drawing on the chapter on assessment in the previous edition of this book that was written by Carol Seefeldt. In this updated version of the chapter, Galper emphasizes the fact that assessing young children is a complex process at best. Continuing issues abound and are centered on the disagreement among experts as to whether "formal assessment," which uses only standardized instruments such as intelligence or achievements tests, or "authentic" or "performance-based" assessments, which emphasize exhibitions, investigations, demonstrations, anecdotal records, journals, and portfolios, should be used in assessing young children. Many argue that formal assessments are being misused in making high-stakes decisions about children and early childhood programs. Such decisions include school readiness, placement of children in special programs, and denial of funding to state and federal programs on the basis of children's scores. There is also concern that when federal and state funding are at stake, teachers will teach to the test and funding will be denied to needy students on the basis of a score on a test. Formal assessments fail to take into account the culture and primary language of children, as well as the many dimensions of intelligence and achievement.

As of April 2007, Congress suspended the implementation and terminated the further development and use of the hastily constructed National Reporting System for Head Start, which had been the focus of heated debate between most early childhood professionals and policy makers intent on providing an assessment instrument for Head Start children. The National Academy of Sciences has taken a positive step by convening a panel of independent experts to review and provide guidance on appropriate outcomes and assessments for young children.

According to Galper (and Seefeldt), on the basis of the research it would seem that some combination of quality authentic measures subject to systematic evaluation for reliability and validity may provide an answer to the question of how to assess young children. Yet, because of the lack of teacher training, sufficient funding, and differing beliefs and expectations about assessment among the various stakeholders, it is unlikely that developmentally appropriate assessment approaches will find their way today into the little nursery school described at the beginning of this discussion.

In Chapter 16, "Evaluating Programs for Young Children," Cynthia Paris revisits an issue raised in other chapters, that a national evaluation of over 400 center-based child care programs revealed that many were of poor quality and 74 percent were deemed to be mediocre. Given this finding, it would seem that program evaluation is an essential tool for building high-quality programs for all children from birth through age 8. The issues treated in this chapter are grouped into the following categories:

❏ Issues of assumptions and values. When assumptions and values are not articulated and shared, the result is poorly designed evaluations that are of limited usefulness.

❏ Issues of power and voice. Some stakeholders hold more power in the evaluation process and the interpretation of results.

❏ Issues of technical quality of program evaluations. Evaluating programs is technically challenging and depends on tools that have not been perfected.

❏ Issues of costs, benefits, and risks. Program evaluation is extremely costly and can incur risks to vulnerable children.

The chapter examines a century of early childhood program evaluation based on varying views of child growth and development. It discusses the establishment of the role of the early childhood profession in developing recommendations for creating and maintaining quality programs for young children and monitoring and documenting the quality of those programs. As Paris points out, the advent of large-scale federal programs for young children and a new emphasis on accountability significantly altered the practice of program evaluation.

The author also discusses the push for licensing standards and the role of the National Association for the Education of Young Children (NAEYC) in creating standards for voluntary accreditation of programs. As a result of the No Child Left Behind Act, program evaluation in early childhood is now standards based, focusing on both program characteristics and child outcomes. In addition, professional organizations in math, science, social studies, and the arts have adopted large standards documents.

While evaluation design and tools have improved, Paris cautions that it is important to keep in mind the current imbalance between the high-stakes decisions that may be made on the basis of program evaluation and the limited but improving tools and processes available. It would appear to be in the interest of the early childhood profession and the children it serves to move quickly to correct the imbalance.

APPLY WHAT YOU LEARNED

As you read the following chapters, think about, talk about, and do additional reading and research regarding these questions:

❑ Given what you know about child development and the diversity in early care and education centers, which assessment techniques make sense to you?

❑ Is it possible to create a framework for evaluation of programs and assessment of children that would be consistent with child development, diverse cultures, and the need for accountability?

❑ What types of child assessments are being used in the early childhood programs in your community? How are they used?

❑ How are early care and education programs being evaluated in your community? How is the data used?

❑ Are families and teachers informed about evaluation strategies and assessment techniques?

❑ What types of child assessments have you examined or used? What is your reaction to them?

REFERENCES

Mindes, G. (2007). *Assessing young children* (3rd ed.). Upper Saddle River, NJ: Pearson/Merrill/ Prentice Hall.

NAEYC & National Association of Early Childhood Specialists in State Departments of Education. (2003). *Joint Position Statement. Early childhood curriculum, assessment, and program evaluation: Building an effective, accountable system in programs for children birth through age 8.* Washington, DC: Authors.

CHAPTER 15

ASSESSING YOUNG CHILDREN

Alice R. Galper

Educational Consultant

Carol Seefeldt

Grownups love figures. When you tell them that you have made a new friend, they never ask you any questions about essential matters. They never say to you, "What does his voice sound like? What games does he love best? Does he collect butterflies?" Instead they demand: "How old is he? How many brothers has he? How much does he weigh? How much money does his father make?" Only from these figures do they think they have learned anything about him.

Antoine de Saint-Exupéry

Historically, experts in child study (later child development and early childhood education) have searched for ways to measure and describe the developing child's physical, intellectual, social, and emotional growth and development. Further, there has been debate about which domains are most important for us to know about if the child is to be successful in school, in the social group, and in life. The Little Prince clearly believes that the social-emotional life of the child holds the key to understanding a "new friend." There are child development experts today who agree with that position. This leads them to believe in the efficacy of certain types of child assessments and even to the position that some aspects of the child are indeed not measurable by any tools that we possess at this time.

Early childhood educators tend to favor this position, although most find it reasonable to ask for evidence of how young children are developing and learning and whether early childhood programs are serving them well. To do this, they tend to favor authentic measures such as teachers' anecdotal records and samples of children's work over time as proof of children's progress or lack thereof.

In contrast, another group of researchers and educators embrace more predictable and exact measures such as standardized intelligence and achievement tests to measure child growth and development. Standardized tests are instruments that are administered, scored, and interpreted in a standard manner. They may be either norm referenced or criterion referenced. Because of the difficulty in testing young children, they are often administered on an individual basis for this age group. Since they have proved not to be as accurate and reliable for younger children as for elementary-age groups, it is often recommended that they not be used alone to make decisions about school placement or special programs at least until grade 3 (Guddemi & Case, 2004).

Americans have been highly interested in what was once considered the "scientific" measurement of young children. "Having a number associated with something makes it sound worthwhile, even if the number isn't all that valid," said Robert Sternberg, dean of Tufts University's School of Arts and Sciences and former president of the American Psychological Association, in attempting to explain our country's fascination with tests and test scores (Strauss, 2006).

WHAT IS ASSESSMENT?

Assessment as we know it today is complex and difficult to define, although some early childhood educators favor some forms of assessment over others. The Early Childhood Education Assessment Consortium On-line Glossary defines assessment as a "systematic procedure for obtaining information from observation, interviews, portfolios, projects, tests, and other sources that can be used to make judgments about characteristics of children or programs" (p. 43). It is possible to distinguish "formal assessment," which uses only standardized instruments, from "authentic" or "performance-based" assessment, which emphasize methods other than standardized intelligence and achievement tests such as exhibitions, investigations, demonstrations, written or oral responses, journals, and portfolios. The latter tend to be based on evidence of what a child can do and what skills have been mastered rather than assessing the child's performance by comparing it with a prespecified standard or the performance of a group of peers who have previously taken the same test. Further, this performance-based information is gathered in the child's everyday environment rather than an artificial testing situation.

Alternative assessment refers to accommodations made to enable children with disabilities to participate in the assessment process, while developmental screening assessments identify at an early point which children may have learning problems or disabilities that could keep them from realizing their potential. Screening involves the use of procedures or instruments designed to identify those who may need further assessment or to verify developmental or health risks. Developmental screening—particularly for children younger than age 6—is often a mandated service under federal guidelines. "Screening can indicate only that a child *might* have a problem that should be further investigated. . . . Screening must be followed by further diagnostic assessment in order to confirm or refute any suspicions that the screening raises about a child" (Meisels & Atkins-Burnett, 2005).

School readiness assessment typically refers to assessment of young children around school entry—right before kindergarten, at kindergarten entry, or very early in the kindergarten year (Maxwell & Clifford, 2004). Many early childhood educators are alarmed at the prospect of denying school entrance to young children who would otherwise qualify on the basis of age. The National Education Goals Panel (1997) suggests that it is a school's responsibility to educate all children who walk through its door, regardless of whether children are deemed ready. In fact, many early childhood educators take the position that it is the school that must be ready, not the child (Maxwell & Clifford, 2004). Most states use age, not skill level, to determine whether a child is eligible to attend public school. Yet practice does not always follow this philosophy. Research does suggest that delaying school entry does not generally benefit children (Stipek, 2002).

Because the assessments of infants and toddlers pose myriad challenges, they are often treated differently. Dichtelmiller and Ensler (2004) point to the Ounce Scale, designed to be used in Early Head Start programs, child care centers, Even Start programs, home visiting programs, and family child care homes, as a developmentally appropriate way to assess the youngest children. It not only more accurately measures a very young child's performance in the context of daily routines, it also includes the family in the assessment process through a Family Album in which parents are encouraged to write notes and stories, keep photographs, and save drawings that illustrate the young child's growth and development (Meisels, Dombro, Marsden, Weston, & Jewkes, 2003).

HISTORICAL PERSPECTIVES

Given that assessing young children, much less infants and toddlers, is a challenging task at best, one wonders why psychologists and early childhood educators have persisted so long in devising ways to do so, and why each step is met with controversy. Assessment as we know it today has roots in several events occurring around the 1900s.

The Child Study Movement

G. Stanley Hall (1907) was instrumental in the development of the child study movement that emerged after the turn of the century. Hall was influenced by Charles Darwin's theory of evolution which provided an impetus for the scientific study of the child's development. Darwin completed a case study of his son William, and although Darwin's conclusions that the infant's behavior was a living record of the evolution of our species were discredited, his belief that the case study could yield a valuable understanding of humans was not. Today, students of child development and education are trained in how to build a case study of a child and use it to draw conclusions about that child's growth and development.

As president of Clark University, Hall established a major center for child study. For the psychologists who adhered to his ideas about growth and development, intelligence was a concrete, invariant entity that could be measured with accuracy by an intelligence test. Hall (1907) was impressed with the idea of measuring intelligence through testing.

A student of Hall, Arnold Gesell (1925), was the first to attempt a description of the knowledge, skills, and behavior that developed in children at each chronological age level. Gesell focused his research on the extensive study of a small number of children. At his clinic, he trained researchers to collect data and produce reports that resulted in the development of the Gesell Development Schedules.

Gesell was criticized for basing his work too rigidly on the observation of a small number of research subjects who were all children of white, middle-class parents in a single New England city. He was also faulted for the failure to consider individual and cultural differences in growth patterns. Such criticisms of other measures continue today. Nonetheless, Gesell is recognized for advances in the methodology of observing and measuring child behavior. He inaugurated the use of photography and observation through one-way mirrors as research tools which are used today as authentic indicators of intelligence and achievement.

A further development in the study of young children was the establishment of laboratory schools or institutes for child development at academic centers around the country. Here children were observed in group settings and often the observations were used as a basis for curriculum development and teacher training. With the establishment of these schools, researchers could include the family to broaden the study of children. Family input is thought of as crucial today in providing another view of the child and in the development of portfolio assessment techniques.

Standardized Tests

Long a source of heated debate, standardized testing began when the French educational establishment instituted compulsory education in 1904 and needed a way to identify children with learning difficulties. Some of the problems with these tests were, and continue to be, not test content per se but how the results were used and what practices they were used to justify. Alfred Binet, with the help of Theodore Simon, created a test to determine which children were developing at normal rates within their age group.

Examples of the misuse of the Binet test abound. American psychologist Henry Goddard, who believed that intelligence was hereditary and invariant, began using the Binet test in U.S. public schools at the turn of the century. In 1913, he applied intelligence testing to immigrants arriving at Ellis Island to determine who should be admitted to the United States. According to Goddard's results, four-fifths of Jews, Hungarians, Italians, and Russians were "feeble-minded." Goddard declared that Alpine and Mediterranean "races" were "indeed intellectually inferior to the representatives of the Nordic race" (Kevles, 1984a, p. 79). Test results were in turn used to influence immigration law and the placement of children in schools.

While criticism of intelligence tests began as early as 1920 and focused on racial/cultural bias and the self-fulfilling prophecy that people who are expected to score low generally will do so, Stanford University professor Lewis Terman made major revisions in the original Binet test and presented it as a valid and reliable measure of IQ. The test, which is individually administered to children aged 2 through 8, asks children to identify parts of the body, build a tower with blocks, recognize objects in terms of their functions, string beads, and copy simple geometric designs. Examiners believe that it yields valuable information about young children. "Coming to know more about a child through administration of the Binet is not the issue, however. The issue stems from how the Binet scores are used" (Seefeldt, 1998, p. 327).

Another topic that has occupied theorists is whether intelligence tests measure an innate core of mental ability or are too narrow to capture the many dimensions of intelligence. Today, intelligence is more often viewed as being composed of many separate mental abilities that operate more or less independently. Thurston (1938) identified seven factors he believed made up intelligence. Guilford (1982) argued that intelligence consists of 150 separate mental abilities. The widely used Wechsler Preschool and Primary Scale of Intelligence (2002) is an example of an intelligence scale based on the concept of intelligence as consisting of a number of discrete abilities.

Although the controversy between a global view of intelligence and a discrete abilities view continues, Sternberg (1996) believes that the weight of evidence at this time is that intelligence is multidimensional and relates to mental mechanisms in the internal world of the individual. Further, intelligence is largely related to the ability to achieve the goals one wants to achieve. Gardner (1999) posits that children have seven (possibly eight) areas of intellectual competence that are relatively independent of each other. His multiple intelligences (MI) theory, however, does not provide support for the assessment of particular intelligences in children or adults. Both theorists continue to explore new constructs in search of new measures that might better predict real-world performance to supplement existing measures of intelligence.

CONCERN ABOUT ASSESSMENT

As reported above, concern about assessment in early childhood is not new. Decades of debate are summarized by Bredekamp and Rosegrant (1992) in *Reaching Potentials: Appropriate Curriculum and Assessment for Young Children.* What appears to be new, however, is the heightened attention on testing young children as a means of holding programs accountable for their learning (Epstein, Schweinhart, & Debruin-Parecki, 2004) and the corresponding fear on the part of early childhood educators that the instruments are inadequate and the scores misused.

The rapid proliferation of prekindergarten IQ and achievement tests and school readiness assessments adds the large and profitable testing industry to those who favor early and frequent testing of young children. According to Wortham (2008), the expanded use of tests has resulted in the establishment of giant corporations that are able to assemble the resources to develop, publish, score, and report the results of testing to a large clientele. Questions also continue to arise about how the scores on the Binet and other standardized tests are being used. More recently, for example, early childhood educators have wondered if the assessment of school readiness on a large scale is a legitimate use of standardized tests.

ARE THERE OTHER WAYS?

Historically, no other method of assessing children may have had as powerful an impact on the field of child study as that of observation. Jablon, Dombro, and Dichtelmiller (2007) define observation as "watching to learn" (p. 1). In the broadest sense, teachers learn about children by carefully watching them, listening to them, and studying their work. This process also helps them to understand what children are feeling and thinking, as well as what they are learning.

Gesell pioneered work in measuring the mental abilities of infants. He and his coworkers at Yale University listed 915 items that were used to appraise the mental, motor, and social development of infants between 3 to 30 months, highlighting the great complexity of the undertaking. Nancy Bayley (1969) and her colleagues at the Berkeley Growth Study developed the Berkeley Scales of Infant Development to measure the mental, motor, and behavioral aspects of infant intelligence. Checklists and scales based on observation are widely used today by both teachers and professional researchers.

Later, Piaget (1952) observed young children to determine what tasks they could do at certain ages, and how they learned and behaved when faced with a novel task or problem. Observations of his own three children led Piaget to develop the clinical method that combined observing children complete a task, questioning and probing their reasoning, and observing still more. Piaget interviewed children at length with an interest in the how and why of children's answers. The case study continues to have validity as an assessment tool today, as do structured interview techniques. They are especially popular with teachers and researchers who are more interested in the strategies that children use to solve problems than whether the answer is "right" or "wrong."

As standardized intelligence tests purport to assess a child's ability, standardized achievement tests should assess what a child has been taught or learned. A variety of achievement tests are available and are widely used in the field of early childhood education. Achievement tests are available in every variety, for every category, and for any purpose. Just a few of the more popular measures include the Metropolitan Readiness Tests, the Cooperative Preschool Inventory, and the Woodcock-Johnson Tests of Basic Skills. Even though abundant and unique, all standardized achievement tests share common characteristics. They all have standardized materials such as forms, instructions for administration, and scoring procedures. They usually have a manual that contains statistical data to support the test. Finally, they are commercial, designed to be marketed and sold for the purpose of making a profit.

Achievement tests are favored by school systems and researchers because of their established validity and reliability, and the relative ease in administering them. Comparison is possible with standardized achievement tests. The achievement of an individual or group can be compared with others. However, national norms also presume that all children in all schools in all parts of the country are presented with the same knowledge, information, and skills which are measured by one of these national achievement tests and that they will process new information in the same ways (Burns, 1979; Mitchell, 1992).

Many experts acknowledge that these tests have been translated into many different languages to represent the primary language groups used by children in this country, and see that as a big improvement. Yet others suggest that professionals need to deepen their understanding of the impact of culture on the assessment process (Santos, 2004). This type of assessment problem often stems from a lack of training, awareness, and sensitivity on the part of professionals who plan and conduct the procedures. The Early Childhood Research Institute on Culturally and Linguistically Appropriate Services (CLAS) offers valuable Internet-based resource materials designed to assist professionals, family members, and policy makers in ensuring that assessments are culturally and linguistically appropriate.

Standardized achievement tests have the potential to provide some important information about the quality of a curriculum and how well subject matter is being taught. As with intelligence tests, however, serious questions can arise about how the scores are being used, whether a desire for a high level of performance by their students will cause teachers to teach to the test, and if funding will be denied to needy students on the basis of a number.

A NEW AND MORE INTENSE FOCUS

It is unlikely that researchers and early childhood educators will ever reach consensus on the issue of assessing young children. Yet, recent articles on the topic are beginning to ask some fundamental questions such as, Why are young children assessed? There appears to be some agreement not only that assessment is an important educational tool, but also that it informs a variety of stakeholders including parents and teachers about best practices in early childhood education. In addition, researchers such as Epstein and colleagues (2004) believe that "like traditional tests, authentic measures must meet psychometric standards of reliability and validity" (p. 47).

Further, according to Meisels and Atkins-Burnett (2005), "experience has taught us that we must never remove ourselves from the process of assessment to rely on tests alone to make important decisions about children's lives. Testing is not a natural environment, particularly for young children. Whenever possible, we should use test data in conjunction with information from parents, teachers, other professionals, and firsthand observations of children" (p. 3).

Why Are Young Children Assessed?

The joint position statement of the National Association for the Education of Young Children (NAEYC) and the National Association of Early Childhood Specialists in State Departments of Education (NAEYC & NAECS/SDE, 2003) suggests that policy makers, the early childhood profession, and other stakeholders in young children's lives have a shared responsibility to make ethical, appropriate, valid, and reliable assessment a central part of all early childhood programs. To assess young children's strengths, progress, and needs, methods must be developmentally appropriate, culturally and linguistically responsive, tied to children's daily activities, supported by professional development, inclusive of families, and connected to specific, beneficial purposes: (1) making sound decisions about teaching and learning, (2) identifying significant concerns that may require focused intervention for individual children, and (3) helping programs improve their educational and developmental interventions.

Jones (2004) states that "appropriate assessment is an integral part of the teaching/learning process, and sound assessment practices can

❑ highlight children's knowledge, skills, and interests
❑ document their growth over time
❑ describe children's progress toward specified learning goals
❑ provide constructive feedback to instructional programs

Done well, the assessment process can be a powerful tool for teachers. By providing a record of children's growth over time, assessment can become an advocate for children and the centerpiece for meaningful conversations between families and educators." (p. 5) Instead, the topic of assessment has often become the centerpiece for bitter quarrels between major stakeholders in early childhood educational programs and policy makers.

Why Is the Assessment of Young Children a Major Issue?

As mentioned earlier, some of the explanation lies in questions about how assessment results were used in the past and are to be used today. With increased federal dollars for educational achievement at all levels, many early childhood educators are concerned that a number based on a standardized measure will serve as the basis for important decisions about which children and schools are funded, a child's promotion or retention, and rewarding teachers and administrators. Further, this number does little to inform teachers about strengths and weaknesses in the curriculum and in teaching strategies. Yet, administrators, legislators, and the tax-paying public (knowing little about child development and learning) want to know that their investment has been profitable. This need, in turn, gives new meaning, pressures, and import to the assessment of young children. Early childhood educators are on the line to gather this information in developmentally appropriate ways.

How Are Early Childhood Educators Dealing with the Issue?

Interest in the assessment of young children has clearly increased in recent years. While several major texts on assessment in early childhood are in their third or fourth editions (Mindes, 2007; Puckett & Black, 2008; Wortham, 2005), the focus has changed. Several books on continuing issues or major trends in early childhood education deal with new challenges and issues in assessment. Several organizations have issued position statements delineating their beliefs about assessment and the assessment process. In the position statement *Standardized Testing of Young Children 3 Through 8 Years of Age,* the National Association for the Education of Young Children (NAEYC, 1987) summarizes a number of challenges in assessing young children. First, the paper stresses the importance of using quality instruments in the assessment process. Further, since young children are difficult to test, these instruments must be administered individually to elicit accurate and useful information. The position statement also emphasizes careful interpretation and reporting of results. No decision about a child's placement or special needs should be based on the administration of a single test.

Where We Stand on Curriculum, Assessment, and Program Evaluation (NAEYC & NACES/SDE, 2003) makes the following recommendations for the assessment of young children:

❑ Ethical principles guide assessment practices.

❑ Assessment instruments are used for their intended purposes.

❑ Assessments are appropriate for ages and other characteristics of children being assessed.

❑ Assessment instruments are in compliance with professional criteria for quality.

❑ What is assessed is developmentally and educationally significant.

❑ Assessment evidence is used to understand and improve learning.

❑ Assessment evidence is gathered from realistic settings and situations that reflect children's actual performance.

❑ Assessments use multiple sources of evidence gathered over time.

❑ Screening is always linked to follow-up.

❑ Use of individually administered, norm-referenced tests is limited.

❑ Staff and families are knowledgeable about assessment.

Misunderstandings About Assessment and Accountability

Although young children in the United States are not strangers to testing, the No Child Left Behind Act of 2001 (NCLB) raised the stakes higher than ever. NCLB mandates assessment and accountability at all levels of public school, although in theory testing begins in third grade. Additionally, early in 2003, the Bush administration announced its intention to require every 4-year-old in the federal Head Start program to be tested on literacy, math, and language skills at the beginning and end of each program year. Early childhood educators became alarmed as they envisioned serious cuts in the Head Start program due to assessments based solely on standardized tests of achievement and used for the wrong purposes.

According to Meisels and Atkins-Burnett (2004), "Unfortunately this test, called the National Reporting System (NRS), includes items that are rife with class prejudice and are developmentally inappropriate. This is particularly troubling because the test is used by Head Start officials as a quality assurance system. In fact, the idea that a narrow test of young children's skills in literacy and math can represent a quality indicator of a holistic program like Head Start shows a stunning lack of appreciation for the comprehensive goals of the 38-year-old program" (p. 64).

As of April 2007, Congress suspended the implementation, and terminated further development and use, of the NRS test and authorized the National Academy of Sciences to convene a panel of independent experts on Developmental Outcomes and Assessments for Children Birth Through Age 5. Catherine Snow of Harvard University will chair the panel (NAEYC, 2007).

The Committee on Developmental Outcomes and Assessments for Young Children will respond to a congressional mandate for a National Research Council panel to review and provide guidance on appropriate outcomes and assessments for young children. The committee will focus on two key topics: (1) the identification of key outcomes associated with early stages of child development for children from birth to 5; and (2) the quality and purpose of different state-of-the-art techniques and instruments for developmental assessments (National Academies of Science, 2006).

The committee will review the research on developmental outcomes in different domains, including the physical, cognitive, social, psychobiological, and emotional. The committee will further examine the available range of techniques and instruments for assessing these outcomes. Particular attention will be paid to the empirical evidence available about the reliability, validity, fairness, and other considerations related to the quality and use of developmental assessments.

Issues related to the use of assessments in screening the developmental status of special populations of children (such as children with developmental disabilities, children from minority cultures, and children whose home language is not English) will be considered. The committee will also examine the criteria that should guide the selection of assessment techniques for different purposes, such as:

❑ Guiding curriculum and instructional decisions for individual children
❑ Program evaluation and program accountability
❑ The ability to link early childhood interventions such as Head Start with wider community goals for young children

Special consideration will be given to the training requirements for using assessments in different program settings and with different child populations. The committee will, to the extent possible, identify opportunities to link measurement improvement strategies within diverse settings (such as educational, developmental, and pediatric programs for young children) to avoid duplication and to maximize collaboration and efficiency.

The committee will provide recommendations to practitioners and policy makers about criteria for the selection of appropriate assessment tools for different purposes, as well as how to collect and use contextual information to interpret assessment results appropriately for young children. They will also develop a research agenda to improve the quality and suitability of developmental assessment

tools that can be used in a variety of early childhood program and service environments (National Academies of Science, 2006).

The charge to this committee and the agenda that it has formulated for itself
are daunting. Because of its composition, any results it reports will be of great benefit to the early childhood community in resolving issues around assessment. Yet,
to complete the outlined agenda will take time, and not everyone will agree with
the results. It is likely that the accountability/testing debate will continue, but with
much more attention on the part of all parties paid to the careful development of
instruments that are not only valid and reliable but also take into account gender,
socioeconomic status, race/ethnicity, language, and age.

In the meantime, it is productive for the discussion to continue in the larger
arena of early childhood stakeholders and to be framed by a few fundamental and
critical issues. For starters, all parties must come to agreement on the definitions of
terms. There can be no productive dialogue without a common understanding of
meaning.

How Can We Continue the Discussion and Frame the Debate?

In January 2004, NAEYC devoted its journal, *Young Children*, to the topic of assessment. The articles raised a number of issues that were new to the debate and also
emphasized the importance of framing the assessment discussion. According to
Jones (2004),

> In the current climate, responsible early childhood educators need to reach beyond
> their skills in observation and documentation to developing what Stiggins (1991) calls
> *assessment literacy*—a deep understanding of the uses and limitations of the full range
> of assessment options, the knowledge to select the most appropriate methods to
> describe the development of young children. (p. 4)

The author suggests a framework that includes the following questions:

❑ What is the purpose of the assessment?
❑ What content and type of knowledge are being assessed?
❑ What is the most appropriate assessment method?
❑ How will assessment results be evaluated?
❑ Are assessment results reported clearly and accurately?
❑ How will assessment results be used?

In 2004, NAEYC issued *Spotlight on Young Children and Assessment*, which
included the articles from the January 2004 issue of *Young Children*. This booklet
provides a broad perspective on the assessment discussion, which the Committee
on Developmental Outcomes and Assessment for Young Children will undoubtedly take into account.

Further, it is clear to early childhood educators that any discussion about the
assessment of young children must include some very basic issues concerning

culturally and linguistically appropriate assessment and screening. Santos (2004) suggests that lack of awareness and sensitivity can inadvertently lead to the selection and use of assessment materials and tools that fail to take into account variations in children's skills and knowledge based on cultural and linguistic differences.

Wortham (2003) questions how appropriate our tests and assessment strategies are when one considers the diversity of young children attending early childhood programs in our country. Meisels and Atkins-Burnett (2004) describe an item in the NRS in which the facial features of all four images are Caucasian, ignoring the fact that facial expressions differ in different cultural and ethnic groups. Many researchers and early childhood experts agree that the NRS was put together in great haste. This is clearly a lesson that any assessment system created for young children requires extensive study, care, and review.

The growing number of children from low-income families and the influx of people from other countries, especially Southeast Asia, Mexico, and Central and South America, raise important questions about the fairness of existing tests for children who are school-disadvantaged and linguistically and culturally diverse. Recently, in a county adjacent to Washington, DC, teachers refused to administer a test in English to nonnative speakers. They relented only when faced with a loss of federal funding to their schools. In large numbers, teachers have become concerned about the use of test data and the possible damage that it can do to them, the children they teach, and developmentally appropriate curriculum.

WHAT IS THE MOST APPROPRIATE ASSESSMENT METHOD?

While we have considered the drawbacks of standardized tests of intelligence and achievement, they are quick and easy to administer and yield scores that teachers and researchers can understand and work with. Yet, since assessment often drives curriculum, teachers frequently lament the fact that traditional multiple-choice or one-word answer tests tend to narrow curriculum to decontextualized academic skills (Bredekamp & Rosegrant, 1995). Concern about the role of assessment in improving early childhood education is part of a widespread conviction that much of standardized testing in elementary and secondary education has served education poorly by emphasizing low-level reading, writing, and math skills isolated from a context of meaning, critical thinking, and problem solving.

Bredekamp and Rosegrant (1995) believe that because young children should be exposed to an integrated curriculum, more authentic assessment strategies—teacher observation, portfolios, three-way conferencing (teachers, parents, and children)—provide excellent tools for assessment. "For teachers to observe children's problem-solving behavior and social interaction, children must engage in solving real problems or negotiating social situations with peers" (p. 171). Further, for teachers to collect, analyze, and evaluate children's work over time and use portfolios adequately, children must engage in the production of meaningful products (representations, journals, project work).

Authentic Measures

Authentic assessments "engage children in tasks that are personally meaningful, take place in real-life contexts, and are grounded in naturally occurring learning activities" (Epstein et al., 2004, p. 46). According to Epstein and her colleagues (2004), one of the best ways to undertake meaningful student assessment is through the use of a well-constructed portfolio system. "A portfolio is a purposeful collection of evidence of a child's learning, collected over time that demonstrates a child's efforts, progress, or achievement" (McAfee, Leong, & Bodrova, 2004, p. 52). Some believe that portfolios can contain anything that teachers or children want them to include. Others believe that decisions about what to include should be made prior to the creation of a portfolio.

Since portfolio systems must meet psychometric standards of reliability and validity, there must be guidelines for the selection of items, criteria for judging merit, and multiple sources of data collected over a period of time. Teachers are increasingly developing and using rubrics to describe levels of performance of children's work by defining varying levels of quality or mastery and providing indicators of each level. More formal entries in portfolios can include checklists, rating scales, and anecdotal records compiled by the teacher at regular intervals. Anecdotal records capture what a child says and does during the course of a learning experience. For older children, journal entries provide excellent documentation of their understanding of an experience or experiences.

Examples of less formal authentic measures include photographs, videotapes, audiotapes, writing samples, artwork of all kinds, and lists of books that a child has read. When using photographs or items of children's work, teachers add a note about what the artifact means in terms of growth and development in the subject matter area. Although there is some debate about who should choose items for the portfolio, many early childhood educators believe that portfolios should be shared with children and their families because they can and should be used to interpret strengths, weaknesses, and progress over time.

Despite considerable progress in the creation of valid and reliable authentic measurement systems, there are still concerns associated with their use, even though it is unlikely that they can harm young children in the same way that the use of standardized tests of intelligence and achievement have. They, too, may become standardized in a way that would fail to capture the essence of the child.

This chapter has raised issues of training and the time associated with collecting observational and performance-based evidence of growth, development, and achievement. There remains the issue of teacher bias, whether intentional or unintentional. In their zeal to do the best for their students, teachers may believe that they detect evidence of a learning disability. Or children with poor social skills or less developed control mechanisms may receive a poorer rating on achievement. Everything that is observed has to pass through the filter of the observer's mind, perspective, and unique way of viewing the world.

The use of multiple observers can limit bias. Teachers may worry less about the issue of time as they integrate authentic measures into the curriculum and practice their use. Teacher bias may not be eliminated entirely, but Jones and

Courtney (2002) suggest that there are three guiding principles in documenting early learning that may help:

1. Collect a variety of forms of evidence. This is necessary because children vary in how they best convey their ideas.
2. Collect the forms of evidence over a period of time. A teacher who collects evidence over a period of time can see the evolution of a concept or an idea.
3. Collect evidence on the understandings of groups of children as well as individuals. The early childhood classroom is interactive and children contribute to each other's understanding through acting on objects and discussion of solutions to problems posed by the environment.

Children may be asked to assess their own learning. Even 3-year-olds can be asked to think about what they did during the day. Four-year-olds, in addition to thinking about things they did, can also begin to think about how they have grown and what they have learned. By 5 years of age, children can pick out their best work to include in a portfolio, decide how completely they gained a skill, and rate themselves on how well they accomplished specific tasks. They can also be asked to tell about all the things they know now that they did not know at the beginning of the year, or when they were younger (Seefeldt, 1998).

On the basis of the research, it would seem that some combination of quality authentic measures, subject to systematic testing for reliability and validity, may provide the answer to the assessment question. They certainly have the potential to answer the important questions posed by the Little Prince. Observations, audio- and videotapes, and photographs will tell us what his new friend's voice sounds like, what games he loves best, and whether he collects butterflies. To many early childhood educators, this type of information is crucial if we are to understand a child.

CONCLUSIONS

At present, the differing beliefs and expectations about assessment among the various stakeholders in early childhood education make it difficult to envision wide acceptance of developmentally appropriate assessment approaches. Yet, by 1995, Bredekamp and Rosegrant (1995) cited progress in the development and use of more appropriate, authentic assessment strategies:

> For example, the Work Sampling System (Meisels, 1992, 1993) is a complete assessment system designed for preschool through third-grade classrooms or schools that use integrated curriculum to help children learn important knowledge and skills from the disciplines. This system includes developmental checklists, portfolio collection, and summary reports for parents that are framed around seven domains of development and learning: personal/social development, language and

literacy, mathematical thinking, scientific thinking, social and cultural awareness, art and music, and physical development. (p. 171)

Shillady (2004) lists seven appropriate assessment systems that are in use and points to a wide variety of assessments to choose from with a great deal of information available online. Mindes (2007) provides a portfolio template that should help considerably in providing validity and reliability to authentic measures of development and learning. Yet, reform and improvement of assessment systems requires time and effort. The Committee on Developmental Outcomes and Assessments for Young Children is just beginning its work.

Most teachers in early childhood classrooms lack systematic training in the new conceptions of assessment. Data collection, coding, entry, and analysis can take a lot of time and cost a lot of money. While Epstein and colleagues (2004) believe that the investment is reasonable and necessary to yield valid information, it may be difficult to convince administrators, school board members, funding agencies, and parents that the cost is justified.

In addition, some teachers may be concerned about systems that require observation, recording, and narrative reports of children's progress because they believe their workload is already too heavy even without additional assessment tasks. Unfortunately, many early childhood programs rely on paraprofessionals who have neither the knowledge nor skills in child development to implement an authentic assessment system. While early childhood educators demand developmentally appropriate assessments for children, they often complain about the time it takes to administer them and the resulting loss of instructional time in the classroom. However, when quality tests mirror quality instruction, assessment and teaching become almost seamless, complementing and informing one another (Neuman, Copple, & Bredekamp, 2000). Authentic assessments must be built into the daily schedule and become a natural and familiar part of the early childhood program.

One would think that parents would warm to authentic measures since they would participate in their creation and interpretation. They are also easy to interpret to parents who see concrete examples of their children's work. Yet, many parents have faith in standardized tests. They may fear teacher bias in anecdotal records, narrative reports, teacher observations, and checklists.

Then too, school board members, elected officials, and administrators must face issues of accountability. They may rely entirely on standardized testing programs to determine whether school programs justify the public expenditures that support them because they believe that the tests are scientific and objective and thus lead to accurate inferences about student achievement.

Clearly, any measure or combination of measures used to assess young children's progress should benefit the children and the program. Implementation of any assessment system should not be at the whim of federal government agencies. Nor should the results of child assessments be used to withhold funding to programs serving children living in poverty or nonnative speakers or to punish teachers inappropriately. Undoubtedly, the Committee on Developmental Outcomes and Assessments for Young Children will emerge with significant recommendations. Hopefully, they will include a call for an integrated, well-financed system of early education and supports for professional preparation and ongoing professional development for teachers. The time has come to replace bitter quarrels among stakeholders with communication and collaboration.

REFERENCES

American Educational Research Association, American Psychological Association, National Council on Measurement in Education. (1999). *Standards for educational and psychological testing.* Washington, DC: Authors.

Bredekamp, S., & Rosegrant, T. (1992). Reaching potentials: Introduction. In S. Bredekamp & T. Rosegrant (Eds.), *Reaching potentials: Appropriate curriculum and assessment for young children* (Vol. 1, pp. 2–8). Washington, DC: NAEYC.

Bredekamp, S., & Rosegrant, T. (1995). Reaching potentials through transforming curriculum, assessment, and teaching. In S. Bredekamp & T. Rosegrant (Eds.), *Reaching potentials: Transforming early childhood curriculum and assessment* (Vol. 2, pp. 15–22). Washington, DC: NAEYC.

Bayley, N. (1969). *Bayley scales of infant development.* Cleveland, OH: Psychological Corporation.

Burns, E. (1979). *The development, use, and abuse of educational tests.* Springfield, IL: Charles E. Thomas.

Dichtelmiller, M. L., & Ensler, L. (2004). Infant/toddler assessment: One program's experience. In D. Koralek (Ed.), *Spotlight on young children and assessment* (pp. 17–21). Washington, DC: NAEYC.

Early Childhood Education Assessment Consortium. (2007). *On-line Glossary* (p. 43). Retrieved June 5, 2007, from www.ccsso.org/projects/SCASS/Projects/Early_Childhood_Educaton_Assessment_Consortium

Epstein, A. S., Schweinhart, L. J., & DeBruin-Parecki, A. (2004). Assessing children's development: Strategies that complement testing. In D. Koralek (Ed.), *Spotlight on children and assessment* (pp. 45–53). Washington, DC: NAEYC.

Gardner, H. (1999). *Intelligence reframed: Multiple intelligences for the 21st century.* New York: Basic Books.

Gesell, A. (1925). *Guidance of mental growth in infant and child.* New York: Macmillan.

Guddemi, M., & Case, B. J. (2004). *Assessing young children. Harcourt Assessment Report.* San Antonio, TX: Harcourt Assessment, Inc.

Guilford, J. P. (1982). Cognitive psychology's ambiguities: Some suggested remedies. *Psychological Review, 89,* 48–59.

Hall, G. S. (1907). *The contents of children's minds.* Boston: Ginn.

Jablon, J. R., Dombro, A. L., & Dichtelmiller, M. L. (2007). *The power of observation for birth through eight* (2nd ed.). Washington, DC: Teaching Strategies, NAEYC.

Jones, J. (2004). Framing the assessment discussion. In D. Koralek (Ed.), *Spotlight on young children and assessment* (pp. 4–8). Washington, DC: NAEYC.

Jones, J., & Courtney, R. (2002). Documenting early science learning. *Young Children, 50*(5), 34–40.

Kevles, D. J. (1984a, October 5). Annals of eugenics. Part II. *New Yorker,* pp. 52 on.

Kevles, D. J. (1984b, October 24). Annals of eugenics. Part III. *New Yorker,* pp. 92 on.

Maxwell, K. L., & Clifford, R. M. (2004). School readiness assessment. In D. Koralek (Ed.), *Spotlight on young children and assessment.* Washington, DC: NAEYC.

McAfee, O., Leong, D., & Bodrova, E. (2004). *Basics of assessment: Primer for early childhood educators.* Washington, DC: NAEYC.

Meisels, S. J., & Atkins-Burnett, S. A. (2005). *Developmental screening in early childhood* (p. 13). Washington, DC: NAEYC.

Meisels, S. J., Dombro, A. L., Marsden, D. B., Weston, D. R., & Jewkes, A. M. (2003). *The ounce scale.* New York: Pearson Early Learning.

Mindes, G. (2007). *Assessing young children* (3rd ed.). Upper Saddle River, NJ: Pearson/Merrill/Prentice Hall.

Mitchell, R. (1992). *Testing for learning.* New York: Free Press.

National Academies of Science, Board on Children, Youth, and Families, Board on Testing and Assessment. (2006). *Committee on developmental outcomes and assessments for young children.* Washington, DC: Author. Retrieved June 11, 2007, from www7.nationalacademies.org/boycf/head_start.html

NAEYC. (1987). *Standardized testing of young children 3 through 8 years of age* (Position statement). Washington, DC: Author.

NAEYC, & National Association of Early Childhood Specialists in State Departments of Education. (1990). *Guidelines for appropriate curriculum content and assessment on programs serving children ages 3 through 8* (Joint Position Statement). Washington, DC: Authors.

NAEYC, & National Association of Early Childhood Specialists in State Departments of Education. (2003). *Early childhood curriculum, assessment, and program evaluation: Building an effective, accountable system in programs for children birth through age 8* (Joint Position Statement). Washington, DC: Authors.

NAEYC. (2007, February 15 and April 17). *Children's champions update.* Washington, DC: Author.

National Education Goals Panel. (1997). *Getting a good start in school.* Washington, DC: Government Printing Office.

Neuman, S. B., Copple, C., & Bredekamp, S. (2000) *Learning to read and write developmentally appropriate practice for children.* Washington, DC: NAEYC.

Piaget, J. (1952). *The origins of intelligence in children.* New York: International Universities Press.

Puckett, M. B., & Black, J. K. (2008). *Meaningful assessments of the young child* (3rd ed.). Upper Saddle River, NJ: Pearson/Merrill/Prentice Hall.

Santos, R. M. (2004). Ensuring culturally and linguistically appropriate assessment of young children. In D. Koralek (Ed.), *Spotlight on young children and assessment* (pp. 38–41). Washington, DC: NAEYC.

Saint-Exupéry, A. de (1971). *The little prince* (K. Woods, Trans.). New York: Harcourt Brace Jovanovich.

Seefeldt, C. (1998). *Assessing young children.* In C. Seefeldt & A. Galper (Eds.), *Continuing issues in early childhood education* (2nd ed, pp. 314–348.). Upper Saddle River, NJ: Merrill/Prentice Hall.

Shepard, L. A., Kagan, S. L., & Wurtz, E. (Eds). (1998). *Principles and recommendations for early childhood assessments.* Washington, DC: National Goals Panel.

Shillady, A. L. (2004). Choosing an appropriate assessment system. In D. Koralek (Ed.), *Spotlight on young children and assessment* (pp. 54–57). Washington, DC: NAEYC.

Sternberg, R. J. (1996). Myths, counter myths, and truths about intelligence. *Educational Researcher, 25*(2), 11–16.

Stipek, D. (2002). At what age should children enter kindergarten? A question for policy makers and parents. *Society for Research in Child Development Social Policy Report, 16*(2), 3–16.

Strauss, V. (2006, October 10). The rise of the testing culture. *The Washington Post,* p. A9.

Thurston, L. L. (1938). *Primary mental abilities* (Psychometric Monographs, No. 1). Chicago: University of Chicago Press.

Wortham, S. C. (2003). Assessing and reporting young children's progress: A review of the issues. In A. P. Isenberg and M. R. Jalongo (Eds.), *Major trends and issues in early childhood education* (2nd ed., pp. 97–113). New York: Teacher's College Press.

Wortham, S. C. (2008). *Assessment in early childhood education* (5th ed.). Upper Saddle River, NJ: Pearson.

EVALUATING PROGRAMS FOR YOUNG CHILDREN

Cynthia Paris
University of Delaware

A preschool staff asks: Are we doing the best job we can for our children and families?

A community wants to know: Which of our early care and education programs are doing a good job? Which are the best?

Legislators ask: If we invest taxpayers' money in expanding a statewide program for young children, will the results justify the cost?

An oversight agency asks: Is this early childhood program in compliance with our requirements?

Growing numbers of young children are being served in a variety of early care and education programs. As the questions above suggest, many individuals or groups are involved in, affected by, or have invested in programs for young children. These stakeholders include families, communities, legislatures, agencies, private foundations, and providers of care and education for children from birth through age 8. All have different reasons for wanting to know if programs serving young children are "good."

Interest in providing high-quality early care and education programs has intensified in recent years as more has been learned about early neurological development and the role of early experience in supporting cognitive, social, and emotional development (National Research Council, 2001; National Research Council and Institute of Medicine, 2000). Professional standards for high-quality programs have been established and revised (NAEYC, 2005a) and public and private investment in programs for young children has increased (Fuller, Holloway, & Bozzi, 1997).

But children's needs are great, and providing all children with the high-quality programs they deserve is challenging. We are seeing increasing numbers of children with identified disabilities and developmental delays (Odom & Diamond, 1998), large numbers of young children growing up in poverty (Douglas-Hall, Chau, & Koball, 2006), a population that is becoming more culturally diverse (U.S. Department of Education, 1996), and a persistent achievement gap between the most advantaged children and those with multiple risk factors. Existing programs are often not of sufficient quality to meet children's needs. A national evaluation of over 400 center-based child care programs, for example, produced alarming results (Helburn, 1995). Of those evaluated, only 14 percent were judged to be of sufficient quality to support children's development, 74 percent were deemed to be mediocre, and 12 percent of such poor quality that children's health and safety needs often were not being met. The situation for programs serving infants and toddlers was worse. Only 8 percent of the classrooms serving the youngest children were found to be of good quality and 40 percent were of low quality (Helburn & Howes, 1996).

Within the early childhood field, program evaluation is considered to be an essential tool for building an effective and accountable early care and education system that will ensure that all children from birth through age 8 experience high-quality programs (National Association for the Education of Young Children & National Association of Early Childhood Specialists/State Departments of Education, 2003). Program evaluation can provide incentives and supports for increasing quality and cultivating a culture of continuous improvement. It can increase understanding of what makes programs good, can identify areas that need improvement, and it can be used to determine if public and private investments in early care and education lead to the outcomes intended. Its potential for contributing to increasing the quality of programs for young children is great (Lambert, Abbott-Shim, & Sibley, 2006).

In practice, program evaluation is a form of research. It provides tools and procedures for systematically examining settings and services, making judgments about their merit, and informing decisions that range from day-to-day decisions in a single program to state and federal early childhood policy. Given what is at stake in terms of children's well-being and expanding public and private investment, it is not surprising that early childhood program evaluation is fraught with difficult and often contentious issues.

OVERVIEW OF ISSUES IN PROGRAM EVALUATION

Some of the issues surrounding program evaluation have been with the early childhood community for some time. Others have arisen or become more visible in light of new knowledge of the importance of the early years and increasing government and private sector involvement. The issues explored in this chapter can be grouped in the following categories:

❑ *Issues of assumptions and values*—The assumptions and values held by individual stakeholders shape their definitions of high-quality programs and their purposes for conducting program evaluations. When assumptions and values are not articulated or remain unexamined, poorly designed evaluations and findings of limited usefulness may result.

❏ *Issues of power and voice*—Program evaluation is a political enterprise. Some stakeholders will have more power than others to determine what constitutes high quality, how it will be measured, and how the results will be used.

❏ *Issues of technical quality of program evaluations*—Evaluating programs serving young children is a technically challenging task. While tools for evaluating programs are becoming more sophisticated, there remain limitations that can affect the trustworthiness and usefulness of those evaluations.

❏ *Issues of costs, benefits, and risks*—Program evaluation can yield significant benefits, but use of the best evaluation tools and processes is time-consuming, costly, and not without risks.

Each of these issues requires thoughtful examination, careful analysis, and informed action by all stakeholders. Early childhood professionals, however, have unique knowledge to share and responsibilities to uphold. A joint position statement by the National Association for the Education of Young Children (NAEYC) and the National Association of Early Childhood Specialists/State Departments of Education (NAECS/SDE) states that regular engagement in program evaluation is a professional responsibility (2003). But engagement is just the first step. NAEYC's Code of Ethical Conduct charges that by virtue of the vulnerable status of children and our specialized knowledge of children, development, learning, and assessment, we have a collective obligation to advocate for practices that benefit children and work to change those that do not (NAEYC, 2005b).

Before considering each of these issues, the following section provides a brief history of evaluation of programs for young children in the United States. It is followed by an introduction to concepts and definitions useful in understanding program evaluation.

A CENTURY OF EARLY CHILDHOOD PROGRAM EVALUATION

Evaluation of programs has long been part of the fabric of early childhood education, serving as a means of determining, maintaining, and increasing the quality of programs for young children. Conceptions of what constitutes high quality and how best to measure it have changed over the decades as knowledge of child development has advanced, measurement tools and procedures have improved, contexts of children's lives have changed, attention has focused on different populations, and more and different stakeholders have entered the early childhood arena. What follows are some events of the past century that have shaped the ways program evaluation is currently conducted and used and the issues surrounding that work.

Evaluating Program Characteristics

Early in the 20th century, maturationist views of child development were waning. Progressive perspectives on the role of experience on development and the emerging field of scientific study of children challenged prevailing views that children's development unfolded naturally. Attention turned to creating environments and experiences that would foster early development and learning. As the quality of those environments and experiences became salient, interest in evaluating those programs serving young children emerged.

In this context, the International Kindergarten Union conducted its influential evaluation of progressive kindergarten programs and traditional Froebelian kindergartens to determine which programs merited their endorsement. Evaluation was based on comparisons of the assumptions about child development and learning on which each program was based and how well those assumptions aligned with prevailing theories of early childhood. Although unable to come to consensus, their 1913 report marked the emerging role of the profession in evaluating the quality of programs for young children (Spodek & Saracho, 1997).

The early part of the century also saw the proliferation of nursery schools, the growth of the field of scientific study of children's development and learning, and the emergence of university-supported child development laboratory schools. Each contributed to the evolving articulation of characteristics of high-quality programs and tools for documenting and improving quality. The rapidly increasing number and diversity of nursery schools raised concerns among early childhood leaders that the uneven quality of these programs threatened to weaken early childhood education as a whole. In 1929, they published *Minimum Essentials for Nursery Education*. This small volume, the result of more than 2 years of study and deliberation by the group, set out current knowledge about nursery school environments that best supported young children's development and learning (NAEYC, 2001). By the time the document was published, the group had formally organized as the National Association for Nursery Education (NANE), the forerunner of NAEYC. Their document stands as an early example of standards for practice within the profession.

Influenced by both progressive approaches and the child study movement, university-supported child development laboratory schools were developing scientific measurement tools to document and evaluate early environments for young children. Programs like the one at the Bureau of Educational Experiments (later, Bank Street College of Education) developed the use of systematic observation, anecdotal records, and analyses of children's work to increase understanding of and make improvements to program quality. Their work and that of other child development laboratory schools contributed to growing understanding of the elements of high-quality programs for young children.

Two periods of rapid expansion of programs for young children followed and early childhood professional groups again expressed concern about quality as new programs proliferated. They responded by developing guidelines to guide the creation and evaluation of these programs. During the Depression, the federal Works Progress Administration (WPA) created emergency preschool programs to provide jobs for unemployed workers and secure and stable environments for children. For the most part, the programs were staffed by unemployed elementary and secondary school teachers. NANE produced recommendations for creating the physical environment and providing experiences that focused on development of the whole child. They recommended that these standards be used as well to guide professional training and support for the teachers. Subsequently, early childhood professionals were deployed as regional supervisors who, in addition to providing staff support, assessed programs and filed field reports on the quality of the emergency preschools (Beatty, 1995).

As the economy recovered prior to World War II and the number of WPA nursery schools declined, large numbers of women entered the wartime labor force creating unprecedented needs for child care. To attract and keep women in crucial sectors of the wartime economy, the federal government created numerous children's centers. Like the WPA nursery schools, these centers employed many teachers who were untrained and served children with multiple vulnerabilities, again raising concerns within the profession about program quality. Guidelines for child care programs were published jointly by three early childhood professional organizations: NANE, the Association for Childhood Education International (ACEI), and the National Council of Parent Education. These detailed guidelines addressed appropriate design of the physical space, selection of equipment, daily schedules, and pedagogy for children who would spend long days in these centers (Beatty, 1995).

The first half of the 20th century, then, saw the establishment of the role of the early childhood profession in developing recommendations for creating and maintaining quality programs for young children and monitoring and documenting the quality of those programs. The use of scientific measures, site visits, field reports, and the practice of linking evaluation to improving program quality laid a foundation for the evaluation of early care and education programs in the second half of the century.

Evaluating Program Accountability

At mid-century, against the backdrop of equal rights movements, legislation was passed creating programs for young children living in poverty and for children with special needs. Federal involvement in funding and oversight of these large, highly visible, and politically charged programs shifted the emphasis in program evaluation from assessing program characteristics against standards of practice to accountability defined in terms of compliance with federal requirements set out as conditions of funding and documentation of intended outcomes.

Head Start was created in 1965 as an important component of the federal War on Poverty. Its aim was to support local communities in offering comprehensive programs for young children living in the poorest areas of the country. Programs were designed to support all domains of children's development and to strengthen families and communities as a means of mitigating the effects of poverty on children's lives. As a condition of continuing federal funding, program evaluations were conducted to determine if Head Start programs produced intended outcomes. Early evaluations, however, depended largely on IQ tests which failed to evaluate the broad goals of the program. Further, these tests were ill-suited for use with young children, especially children from nonwhite, non-middle-class populations. Not surprisingly, the quality of the early evaluations was considered "uneven at best" (Gullo, 2005, p. 10).

Between 1970 and 1990, in response to calls for equal access for all children to publicly supported education, federal legislation created programs for young children with special needs. The Education for All Handicapped Children Act of 1975 (Public Law 94-142) guaranteed access to public education programs for all children with disabilities ages 3 and older. The 1986 Education for the Handicapped Act Amendments (Public Law 99-457) extended services to children with special needs between birth and 2 years of age. And the 1990 Americans with Disabilities Act (Public Law 101-576) required that all programs serving young children include those with identified special needs. Like Head Start, programs were required to demonstrate compliance with stipulations of the laws as well as achievement of measurable outcomes. The challenges of assessing children with disabilities and evaluating programs that served them were legion and existing tools and procedures were not sufficient to meet these demands (Wortham, 2008).

The advent of large-scale federal programs for young children and the focus on accountability significantly altered the practice of program evaluation in the early childhood field and the definitions of program quality on which it was based. Compliance with legislated requirements for receiving funding and the ability to produce measurable outcomes shaped definitions of program quality. Quantifiable indicators of child outcomes came into widespread use, highlighting the limitations of existing tools and processes for evaluating program quality.

Standards and Program Quality

Concerns about the quality of programs for young children persisted. Rapidly rising numbers of mothers of young children in the workforce through the 1970s and 1980s called attention to the alarming variation in the quality of child care programs. After an unsuccessful attempt by the federal government to regulate child care, the responsibility for evaluating and licensing child care devolved to the states (Spodek & Saracho, 1997). By 1985, all states and the District of Columbia had established licensing standards and systems for evaluating child care and preschool programs serving children from birth through kindergarten in nonpublic school settings. Licensing standards, for the most part, established minimum health and safety requirements.

Higher standards of quality for center-based programs were established within the profession. In the mid-1980s, NAEYC initiated a national voluntary program accreditation system based on standards of practice and procedures for evaluating programs against those standards (NAEYC, 2001). Standards for accreditation were set high and were intended to stimulate and guide programs toward continuous improvement. The National Association for Family Child Care issued *Quality Standards for Family Child Care* in 1994 and began accrediting child care programs based in private homes (National Association for Family Child Care, 2005). In 2005, NAEYC released a reinvented accreditation system outlined in *Early Childhood Program Standards and Accreditation Criteria: The Mark of Quality in Early Childhood Education* (NAEYC, 2005a). Its ten standards, focusing on children's experiences in programs, teaching staff, program administration, and relationships with families and community, constitute a comprehensive and detailed definition of program quality (NAEYC, 2005a).

A spate of national reports in the 1980s charged that the educational systems in the United States were of such poor quality that they were failing children and society. A series of sweeping federal education initiatives followed. The Goals 2000: Educate America Act of 1994 introduced incentives for states to adopt standards for student achievement and to evaluate programs based on those standards. The first goal stated that "by the year 2000, all children will start school ready to learn" and as an intermediate step toward school readiness for all, "all children will have access to high-quality and developmentally appropriate preschool programs to prepare them for school" (Kagan & Rigby, 2003). Readiness was defined in terms of children's cognitive achievement and program quality in terms of children's scores on tests of discrete cognitive tasks.

In 2001, the Elementary and Secondary Education Act, reauthorized as the No Child Left Behind Act (NCLB), guaranteed "every child in America, regardless of race, economic background, language or disability, the opportunity to get a world-class education" (U.S. Department of Education, 2002). As a condition of receiving federal funds, states were now required to develop content and achievement standards and assessment plans aligned with those standards. Also in 2002, the Good Start, Grow Smart initiative was introduced, requiring states to develop early learning guidelines for preschools with emphasis on language and literacy skills. By 2005, 49 states and the District of Columbia had established standards for prekindergarten aligned with their K–12 standards, 26 states had standards that included 3-year-olds, and 14 states had standards for infants and toddlers (Scott-Little, Martella, Lesko, & Milburn, 2007).

At the beginning of the 21st century, program evaluation in early childhood is standards-based, and focused both on program characteristics and child outcomes. Standards have been established by professional organizations and states have adopted their own standards in response to federal requirements. As the number and types of programs are increasing, the number of stakeholders and their various interests are increasing as well. The following section provides some concepts and categories to help sort through and better understand this diversity.

CONCEPTS AND CATEGORIES

Evaluation of programs in early childhood takes many forms and serves many purposes. First, program evaluation may be conducted at the local, state, or federal level (Lee & Walsh, 2004). *Local-level* program evaluations may be conducted at a single center or school, at multiple sites of associated child care facilities, or within a single school district. *State-level* program evaluations may be conducted at all or a sample of related sites throughout a state by a state agency or others contracted by that agency. *Federal-level* evaluations are conducted at all or a sample of related sites throughout the country by federal agencies or those contracted by a federal agency.

Program evaluations can vary by who initiates and conducts them. *Internal* evaluations are conducted by participants in an early childhood program. Internal program evaluations may involve teaching and support staff, administrators, and families as well as others with interests in the program. *External* evaluations of programs may be called for and conducted by program oversight boards, monitoring or regulating agencies, or independent researchers.

Evaluations of programs also vary in how they are used. *Formative* evaluations gather information in order to improve program quality. *Summative* evaluations yield summary judgments about program quality at one point in time. Often summative evaluations are initiated and conducted externally for use by policy makers to make high-stakes decisions about future funding or the continuation, expansion, or limitation of programs.

Program evaluations may focus on program inputs, the structural or process features of a program (Helburn, 1995; Howes, Phillips, & Whitebrook, 1992), and/or program outcomes. *Structural features* include teacher:child ratios, group size, training and education of personnel, and indoor and outdoor physical space and materials. *Process features* include child-staff interactions and relationships, peer interactions, and activities. Together they constitute the program *inputs*. Program *outcomes* may include impact on children, families, or other stakeholders. Impact on children, for example, may focus on social and emotional development, cognitive growth, or school readiness.

Finally, program evaluations vary by their purposes and the forms that follow from those purposes. Common forms of program evaluation in early childhood include self-study, accreditation, licensing, quality rating, accountability, and policy studies.

Self-Study for Program Improvement

Self-studies are internal evaluations initiated and conducted by staff, often along with other stakeholders, in order to improve the quality of their programs. Those closely involved with programs pose the questions that guide the self-study and collect and examine data to answer those questions. Many self-studies make use of rating scales such as the Infant/Toddler Environment Rating Scale (ITERS; Harms, Cryer, & Clifford, 1990), the Early Childhood Environment Rating Scale-Revised (ECERS-R; Harms, Clifford, & Cryer, 1998), and the Assessment of Practices in Early Elementary Classrooms (APEEC; Hemmeter & Ault, 2001) to gather data on current practices. Self-studies may also draw on existing documentation, as in the case of a preschool staff who sought to improve their work with children with special needs. Examination of children's records, school policy documents, and family surveys led to changes in administrative policy, staff support, relationships with families, and daily planning for children (Paris, Eyman, Morris, & Sutton, 2007). Self-studies can serve as formative evaluations that yield information that can be used immediately to improve quality and, at their best, become part of programs' continuous improvement efforts.

Program Evaluation for Accreditation

Evaluation for accreditation is a voluntary form of program evaluation that can result in public recognition for programs that meet accreditation requirements. Accreditation by NAEYC begins with a self-study by a program's staff to evaluate the quality of the program against NAEYC's standards and make necessary improvements. An external review follows in which a team evaluates the program based on documentation and observations conducted during a site visit. Programs that achieve accreditation must file periodic reports and applications for reaccreditation in order to assure sustained quality. Evaluation of programs for accreditation is summative insofar as a judgment is made about program quality at the times of accreditation and reaccreditation; however, the overall intent of the accreditation process is formative with the goal of supporting a culture of continuous improvement (NAEYC, 2005a).

Evaluation for Licensing Programs

Licensing requirements are most often established and administered by state departments with responsibility for regulation of care and education programs serving young children. Criteria for licensure focus primarily on basic health, nutrition, and safety requirements; indoor and outdoor facilities and materials; and group size and teacher-child ratios (National Resource Center for Health and Safety in Child Care and Early Education, n.d.). Evaluation of programs for licensing involves on-site inspections and examination of records by state agency representatives to determine compliance with licensing requirements. Efforts are made in many states to provide consultation, technical assistance, and training throughout the process to help programs increase quality and meet criteria for licensing.

Evaluation to Rank and Reward Quality

Whereas state licensing criteria most often represent minimal standards, many states are developing program evaluation systems that recognize levels of quality above those required for licensing. Quality rating systems (QRS) are used to assist families in the selection of early care and education programs. They may also be used by state governments to determine the level of reimbursement they will pay programs for services provided, or by potential funders to select programs in which to invest. These systems support increased quality by providing significant incentives as well as supports in the form of training and technical assistance. While in some states, schools and centers can elect to participate in the QRS, in others participation is mandatory. Such is the case in North Carolina, which has one of the oldest QRS programs in the country (Stoney, 2004).

Program Evaluation to Determine Accountability

Programs created and/or funded by legislative bodies, corporate foundations, community organizations, and other agencies are subject to evaluation to demonstrate accountability in terms of compliance with requirements for program operation, management, and demonstration of achievement of intended outcomes. Judgments made as a result of these evaluations are linked to high-stakes decisions to continue, expand, decrease, or withdraw funding. Programs created by the No Child Left Behind Act fall into this category.

Studies to Inform Policy

Program evaluations may be conducted to inform policy decisions about creating, maintaining, expanding, terminating, managing, and funding programs. Legislatures considering increasing the number of full-day kindergartens in their states, for example, have conducted evaluations comparing outcomes of their part-day and full-day programs to inform their decisions (Plucker et al., 2004). The national child care Cost, Quality and Child Outcomes follow-up study has yielded policy recommendations on expenditures for early childhood programs; preservice and in-service professional development, certification, compensation of teachers, and changes in licensing and accreditation (Peisner-Feinberg et al., 1999).

Cost-benefit analyses evaluate programs to determine if the costs are justified by the benefits they provide. These economic program evaluations are used to inform policy decisions regarding funding levels for existing programs or investment in new programs. Legislatures currently considering investments in publicly funded prekindergarten programs are looking at cost-benefit analyses such as those of the Perry Preschool, Abecedarian Project, Chicago Child Parent Center prekindergarten programs, and Head Start. Cost-benefit evaluations of these programs suggest that investment in high-quality preschool programs, over time, yield significant benefits to society in terms of reduced costs of remedial programs, special education, welfare, and crime, as well as increase in participants' incomes and taxes paid (Lynch, 2007).

Judgments and actions stemming from program evaluations are not without consequence. Much is at stake. Young children constitute a vulnerable population whose development is highly sensitive to the quality of care and education they experience. Programs judged to be of sufficient quality, when that is not in fact the case, may put children at risk. Programs judged to be of insufficient quality when in fact they are serving children and families well may face withdrawal of funding or have their licenses revoked. Given what is at stake, program evaluation must, itself, must meet high standards of quality.

PROFESSIONAL GUIDELINES FOR PROGRAM EVALUATION

In a joint position statement on curriculum, assessment, and program evaluation, NAEYC and NAECS/SDE (2003) outlined indicators of effective program evaluation. This document reflects concern for technical quality and ethical responsibility to children, families, communities, and the profession. The following features of program evaluation were determined to be essential:

❑ Evaluation of programs must be the shared responsibility of all stakeholders, conducted for the purpose of continuous improvement, and guided by sound standards for high-quality early childhood programs.

❑ The design of program evaluations must reflect the goals of the stakeholders.

❑ The design of program evaluations should employ multiple measures and document multiple perspectives.

❑ Where tests are used, they must be valid (measuring what it is intended to measure), and reliable (doing so accurately), and carefully chosen to be developmentally appropriate, culturally sensitive, and administered in children's dominant languages.

❑ When individual tests of children's progress are used, a matrix sampling scheme should be employed, administering only portions of a test to each child to minimize the amount of time each child is tested.

❑ Individual children's scores should be aggregated to represent a combined measure of the impact of the program on all the children.

❑ All data on children's outcomes should be collected over time rather than just at the completion of a program in order to inform judgments of progress toward intermediate as well as ultimate goals.

❑ Those who conduct the evaluations should be well trained in the processes and measures to be used and the quality of their data collection and analysis should be checked frequently.

Additionally, Walberg and Reynolds (1997) have called for the use of longitudinal evaluations when evaluating program impact, arguing that outcomes of greatest import may not be evident in the short term. Evaluations of the long-term benefits of model programs for children deemed at risk, such as the High/Scope Perry Preschool Project (Schweinhart, Barnes, & Weikart, 1993) and the Chicago Child Parent Centers (Reynolds, 1994, 2000) found substantial benefits to the children who are now adults and to society.

The federal General Accounting Office has recommended that evaluations of federally funded programs measure program impact by employing experimental and quasi-experimental evaluation designs (U.S. GAO, 2002). Program evaluations using experimental designs randomly assign children to groups so that outcomes of the group that participated in a program can be compared to those that did not. Quasi-experimental designs also compare groups. However, rather than randomly assign children and families to a group, naturally occurring groups are compared. While this second approach avoids the ethical dilemma of manipulating who has access to potential benefits of a program and who does not, random assignment permits evaluators to conclude with greater certainty that outcomes for children who attended a program can be attributed to the program alone and not to other factors. But both approaches are costly and require specialized skills to conduct.

ISSUES

Some of the most challenging issues surrounding program evaluation in early care and education have to do with the assumptions and values that underlie the design and use of evaluations. Others have to do with whose assumptions and values are dominant, raising concerns about power and voice. Limitations and choices of tools and procedures used to evaluate programs raise other issues. And finally, there are considerations of the costs and benefits to stakeholders and potential risks.

Assumptions and Values

All program evaluations are based on assumptions and values. While not all designers and consumers of program evaluations make them explicit, assumptions and values shape the questions stakeholders ask about programs, the tools and methods chosen to answer them, and how the findings are understood and used.

Assumptions are beliefs, often unacknowledged and unquestioned, about what *is*. Assumptions about children and how they develop and learn, for example, may vary greatly based on knowledge of child development, personal experience, and culturally based beliefs. For example, if stakeholders believe that children learn primarily when adults direct their activity, then evaluation will most likely focus on parts of the program in which the teacher is giving information rather than on child-directed activity.

Values are reflected in what we deem to be of great importance or worth. Goals, desired outcomes, and definitions of high quality are grounded in stakeholders' values. The NCLB goal of increasing school readiness suggests that high value is placed on school achievement. Defining school readiness in terms of acquisition of academic knowledge and skills suggests greater value is assigned to cognitive development than to social, emotional, and physical development when preparing children for success in school. Evaluating programs on the basis of children's academic readiness for school suggests the view that program quality rests primarily on a program's capacity to promote cognitive development.

Without clearly articulated and carefully considered assumptions and values, program evaluations may yield results of limited credibility and usefulness. This was the case in the early studies of Head Start. The Westinghouse study (Westinghouse Learning Corporation, 1969), like many other evaluations of Head Start, was criticized for its misalignment with the program's assumptions, values, and purposes. The original conception of Head Start was based on assumptions about the interdependence of all domains of children's development, the impact of family and community in children's development, the value of improving children's well-being now and later in life, and the long-term goal of eliminating poverty. The Westinghouse evaluation, which focused on children's cognitive outcomes, failed to accurately reflect the assumptions, values, and goals of the program.

In their study of 141 evaluations of early childhood programs, Lee and Walsh (2004) found that few program evaluation reports included clear statements of the values that shaped the purposes or methods of the evaluations or definitions of program quality. When assumptions and values are not articulated, they are not available for examination or critique. Once made public, assumptions and values may be reviewed, and perhaps contested, by stakeholders, then used intentionally to shape program evaluations aligned with those assumptions and values. Issues arise, however, when some stakeholders' voices are not heard and others' perspectives prevail.

Power and Voice

Both early childhood professional organizations and public policy makers wield considerable power in defining what counts as high-quality programs for young children and determining how programs should be evaluated. As the largest early childhood professional association, NAEYC's (2005a) recently revised *Early Childhood Program Standards and Accreditation Criteria: The Mark of Quality in Early Childhood Education* are considered by some to be the "gold standard" for program quality (Bowman, 2006). In addition to serving as the basis for determinations of accreditation, the association's standards have influenced many states' early learning standards, licensing regulations, and quality rating systems. Although NAEYC's standards are intended to represent both recent research and consensus of the organization's members, they are considered by some to reflect only mainstream American perspectives (Cryer, 1999), failing to include others' values and assumptions (Dickinson, 2002; Lee & Walsh, 2005).

State and federal policy makers exert considerable power in determining how the quality of programs they regulate and fund are evaluated and the standards against which program quality will be assessed. Fuller, Holloway, and Bozzi (1997) argue that early childhood program evaluation today primarily serves the purposes of policy makers who define program quality in terms of their own purposes. The Head Start National Reporting System, a test used to measure the quality of Head Start programs throughout the country, for example, reflects the federal government's focus on early literacy and numeracy in the NCLB and Good Start, Grow Smart early childhood initiatives (Meisels & Atkins-Burnett, 2004). As Fuller and his colleagues point out, such definitions of quality often fail to represent those of the programs, their families, and their teachers.

Teachers and families occupy unique positions as partners in programs, as potential sources of local knowledge of program values and purposes, and as providers of insider perspectives on program operation and outcomes. It is likely that these groups, representing diverse socioeconomic and cultural backgrounds, bring different perspectives on indicators of program quality. Definitions of good relationships between children and adults, appropriate guidance strategies, and best ways of supporting learning, for example, have all been found to vary across cultures (Bowman & Moore, 2007; Delpit, 1995). Yet the voices of teachers and families are rarely heard, and, if they are, their perspectives are often overridden by those with greater power (Fuller et al., 1997).

Whose perspectives should be heard? Whose should prevail? Bowman (2006) asks if all voices should be equal when defining high quality. She suggests that early childhood professionals have both the right and responsibility to take the lead. Lee and Walsh (2004) ask if there can or even should be universal definitions of quality. Does failure to open dialogue about values and purposes and what constitutes quality in early childhood programs limit the possibility of coming to richer, more potent conceptions that would reflect the views of all stakeholders?

Technical Quality of Program Evaluations

Methodological limitations have plagued program evaluation in the past and, in spite of considerable progress in the field of evaluation design and instrumentation, they continue to do so today. Gilliam and Zigler (2001), in a meta-analysis of evaluations of state-funded preschool programs from 1977 to 1998, found that many evaluations suffered such serious methodological weaknesses that it was difficult to have confidence in their findings. Methodological challenges in evaluations of early childhood programs include the absence of theoretical foundations and weaknesses in design, instrumentation, and implementation.

Theories provide the foundations of well-designed program evaluation. Theories may focus on child development and learning, organizational behavior, or social change. They call attention to contexts, processes, players, and other aspects of early childhood programs that should be attended to and offer explanations for what is found. The use of ecological theory has been seen as a significant methodological advance in early childhood program evaluation (Marshall, 2004; Ramey & Ramey, 1998). Ecological theory focuses attention on the multiple, interdependent, and changing contexts of children's development and learning. Program evaluations guided by ecological theory look beyond a discrete set of classroom features or child outcomes and attend, for example, to relationships between a program and the various populations it serves, relationships with and supports provided by the surrounding community, and the wider context of state and federal level requirements, regulations, and supports (Marshall, 2004).

Yet few documented evaluations of programs are guided by a sound theoretical base (Lee & Walsh, 2004). NAEYC and NAECS/SDE (2003) recommend the use of theory-driven logic models to guide program design, implementation, and program evaluations. When building a logic model, stakeholders engage together in articulating the theories that guide the program, clarifying short-term and long-term goals, identifying activities that lead to achievement of those goals, and measuring progress using formative evaluations along the way (United Way of America, 1996; W. K. Kellogg Foundation, 2004). Kagan and Rigby (2003) provide an example of how program evaluations guided by a logic model might look in their recommendations to policy makers planning large-scale school readiness programs. Grounded in articulated theories about children, development, and learning, their logic model identifies indicators of school readiness and links specific program and policy characteristics to the development of those indicators of readiness, thus setting out what might be measured to evaluate progress toward program goals and summative evaluation of the impact of the program.

The timing of data collection is significant as well. In the current political context there are pressures to demonstrate accountability sooner rather than later. But only mature programs that have had adequate time to consolidate their work and accrue measurable outcomes should be evaluated. Evaluations of programs that depend on measures of child outcomes must also consider how long children have been enrolled in a program before their performance is a true measure of program quality.

The use of tests to measure child outcomes poses particular challenges due to the fluid nature of early development and learning and the diversity of experiences, language, culture, and ability of young children. Given the challenges of measuring and aggregating data on infants' and toddlers' development, the National Educational Goals Panel (1998) recommends that evaluations of program quality depend on indirect measures of program characteristics known to support development. For preschoolers, both indirect and direct measures are feasible but currently neither are of sufficient quality to be used to make high-stakes decisions about programs. After age 5, they suggest, using direct measures of children's learning is possible, but not until age 8 should they be used for making high-stakes decisions. In addition, the use of multiple measures, representing multiple perspectives, can provide context for interpreting otherwise unreliable or questionable child outcomes measures (NAEYC & NAECS/SDE, 2003).

Finally, high-stakes decisions require high-quality instruments (NEGP, 1998). But the availability and quality of existing evaluation instruments is limited (Lambert et al., 2006). Some of the most widely used evaluation instruments do not reflect recent research in the fields of emergent literacy, the learning experiences of children for whom English is not their home language, children living in poverty, and children with special needs (Dickinson, 2002; Lambert et al., 2006). Yet, some instruments have achieved "incremental validity" or acceptance by long use rather than proven quality (National Research Council, 2001).

High-stakes program evaluations that do not meet high standards of design and instrumentation have not gone unchallenged. Meisels and Atkins-Burnett (2004) and others have challenged the use of the Head Start National Reporting System (NRS) to inform decisions about the reauthorization of Head Start. Numerous weaknesses have been found in this test of discrete early literacy and numeracy skills designed to be administered individually to all 4- and 5-year-olds enrolled in Head Start twice a year. As challenges to the NRS escalated, its use was suspended.

Benefits, Costs, and Risks

The potential benefits of program evaluation are significant. Evaluations of programs help policy makers create and support high-quality programs for children, funders to direct funds to programs that may have the greatest impact, families to choose the best placements for their children, and program staff to engage in continuous assessment and improvement of their programs. And the greatest potential benefit of program evaluation lies in what it might contribute to the understanding of why and how programs affect children and families. Comprehensive evaluations that take into account program structures and processes as well as child outcomes may allow causal links to be found between program features and specific outcomes. Such evaluations yield findings that teachers and others can put to immediate use to improve program quality (Lambert et al., 2006; National Research Council & Institutes of Medicine, 2000).

However, comprehensive evaluations are costly in terms of materials, personnel, and time expended. So, too, are longitudinal studies and large-scale studies. In its first year alone, the use of the Head Start National Reporting System cost more than $16 million (Meisels & Atkins-Burnett, 2004). On a smaller scale, costs to small schools or centers to engage in licensing or accreditation evaluations may include direct fees to the evaluators as well as expenditures required to bring programs into compliance with regulations or to meet standards. With limited funds, what other expenditures must be delayed or foregone? With limited staff, what activities might be suspended as all are required to participate in the evaluation? And does the investment of money, time, and staff yield sufficient benefits in terms of improving program quality? Few cost-benefit analyses of this sort have been done (National Research Council & Institutes of Medicine, 2000).

For all the potential benefits to children, there are risks as well. The NEGP (1998) and NAECS/SDE (2003) both stress that measures designed to gather samples of children's performances to be aggregated for the purpose of program evaluation may not be appropriate or sufficiently reliable for making high-stakes decisions about an individual child's placement, promotion, or eligibility for services. Yet sometimes this is done. There are risks as well in terms of opportunity costs to children. When definitions of quality are narrowly drawn and measurements of outcomes focus on narrow goals, time and resources are directed away from other experiences that, in fact, are of greater worth. Narrowing of program content in order to ensure that children perform well on what is tested is widespread (Scott-Little et al., 2007) and richer opportunities for development and learning are lost.

IMPLICATIONS FOR THE FIELD

The NAEYC Code of Ethical Conduct (2005b) provides the following guidance relevant to conducting program evaluation and participating in policy decisions about program evaluation. Early childhood educators should:

❑ Be knowledgeable about the appropriate use of assessment strategies and instruments and interpret results accurately to families (P-4.5)

❑ Use assessment instruments and strategies that are appropriate for the children to be assessed, that are used only for the purposes for which they were designed, and that have the potential to benefit children (I-1.6)

❑ Develop written policies for the protection of confidentiality and disclosure of children's records (P-2.12)

❑ Inform families about the nature and purpose of the program's child assessments and how data about their child will be used (P-2.1)

❑ Inform families of and, when appropriate, involve them in policy decisions (P-2.3)

❑ Work to ensure that appropriate assessment systems, which include multiple sources of information, are used for purposes that benefit children (P-1.5)

❑ Support policies and laws that promote the well-being of children and families, and work to change those that impair their well-being; to participate in developing policies and laws that are needed, and to cooperate with other individuals and groups in these efforts (I-4.7)

In other words, we must be knowledgeable about the processes of program evaluation, engage in program evaluation in ways that maximize its many benefits, remain alert to potential risks to children, and work with families and other stakeholders to ensure that program evaluation processes and uses serve children and families well.

Some have questioned the overall quality of program evaluation in early childhood as compared to the field of educational evaluation as a whole (Spodek & Saracho, 1997). And it is true that we have more experience evaluating programs for preschool children than for infants and toddlers and children in primary grades. But others see value and potential in what has been achieved. Early childhood program evaluation, with its long history, its definitions of quality, and range of tools for measuring program characteristics, may in fact provide models and guidance for program evaluation in kindergarten and primary grades (Lambert et al., 2006).

As program evaluation in early childhood education continues to evolve, it is important to keep in mind the current imbalance between the high-stakes decisions that may be made on the basis of program evaluations and the limited but improving tools and processes available. When program evaluations are based on standards, we should take seriously the caution that accompanied NANE's publication of *Minimum Essentials for Nursery Education* in 1929: "It is undesirable at this stage in the development of nursery school education that details and practices should become crystallized or even that objectives and standards should be fixed" (NAEYC, 2001, p. 47). And, we should bear in mind Hills's (1998) advice that judgments made on the basis of program evaluations today, given the tools available, the data before us, and our current understanding of quality, should be viewed humbly as hypotheses to be revisited and retested as we come to know more about providing high-quality programs for all children.

REFERENCES

Beatty, B. (1995). *Preschool education in America: The culture of young children from the colonial era to the present.* New Haven, CT: Yale University Press.

Bowman, B., & Moore, E. K. (2007). *School readiness and social-emotional development: Perspective on cultural diversity.* Washington, DC: NAEYC.

Bowman, B. T. (2006). Standards at the heart of educational equity. *Beyond the Journal, Young Children on the Web.* Retrieved July 11, 2007, from www.journal.naeyc.org/btj/200609/BowmanBTJ.asp

Cryer, D. (1999, May). Defining and assessing early childhood program quality. *Annals of the American Academy of Political and Social Science, 563,* 39–55.

Delpit, L. (1995). *Other people's children: Cultural conflict in the classroom.* New York: New Press.

Dickinson, D. K. (2002). Shifting images of developmentally appropriate practice as seen through different lenses. *Educational Researcher, 31*(1), 26–32.

Douglas-Hall, A., Chau, M., & Koball, H. (2006). *Basic facts about low-income children: Birth to age 18.* National Center for Children in Poverty. Retrieved June 23, 2007, from www.nccp.org/publications/pub_678.html

Fuller, B., Holloway, S. D., & Bozzi, L. (1997). Evaluating child care and preschools: Advancing the interests of government, teachers, or parents? In B. Spodek & O. N. Saracho (Eds.), *Issues in early childhood educational assessment and evaluation. Yearbook in early childhood education* (Vol. 7, pp. 7–27). New York: Teachers College Press.

Gilliam, W. S., & Zigler, E. F. (2001). A critical meta-analysis of all impact evaluations of state-funded preschool from 1997 to 1998: Implications for policy, service delivery, and program evaluation. *Early Childhood Research Quarterly, 15,* 441–479.

Gullo, D. (2005). *Understanding assessment and evaluation in early childhood education.* New York: Teachers College Press.

Harms, T., Clifford, R., & Cryer, D. (1998). *Early Childhood Environment Rating Scale, Revised Edition.* New York: Teachers College Press.

Harms, T., Cryer, D., & Clifford, R. (1990). *Infant/Toddler Environment Rating Scale.* New York: Teachers College Press.

Helburn, S. (Ed.). (1995). *Cost, quality and child outcomes in child care centers. Technical report.* Denver, CO: Department of Economics.

Helburn, S. W., & Howes, C. (1996). Child care cost and quality. *The Future of Children: Financing Child Care, 6*(2), 62–82.

Hemmeter, M. L., & Ault, M. J. (2001). *Assessment of Practices in Early Elementary Classrooms.* New York: Teachers College Press.

Hills, T. W. (1998). Finding what is of value in programs for young children and their families. In C. Seefeldt & A. Galper (Eds.), *Continuing issues in early childhood education* (2nd ed., pp. 293–313). Upper Saddle River, NJ: Merrill/Prentice Hall.

Howes, C., Phillips, D. A., & Whitebrook, M. (1992). Thresholds of quality: Implications for the social development of children in center-based care. *Child Development, 63*(2), 449–460.

Kagan, S. L., & Rigby, E. (2003). *Improving the readiness of children for school: Recommendations for state policy.* Washington, DC: Center for the Study of Social Policy.

Lambert, R., Abbott-Shim, M., & Sibley, A. (2006). Evaluating the quality of early childhood settings. In B. Spodek & O. Saracho (Eds.), *Handbook of research on the education of young children* (pp. 457–476). Mahwah, NJ: Erlbaum.

Lee, J.-H., & Walsh, D. J. (2004). Quality in early childhood programs: Reflections from program evaluation practices. *American Journal of Evaluation, 25*(3), 351–373.

Lee, J.-H., & Walsh, D. J. (2005). Quality from the perspective of stakeholders: Quality in early childhood programs? Underlying values. *Early Education and Development, 16*(4), 449–468.

Lynch, R. G. (2007). *Enriching children, enriching the nation: Public investment in high-quality pre-kindergarten.* Washington, DC: Economic Policy Institute.

Marshall, N. (2004). The quality of early care and education and children's development. *Current Directions in Psychological Science, 13*(4), 165–168.

Meisels, S. J., & Atkins-Burnett, S. (2004). The Head Start National Reporting System: A critique. *Beyond the Journal, Young Children on the Web.* Retrieved June 23, 2007, from www.journal.naeyc.org/btj/200401/meisels.pdf

National Association for Family Child Care. (2005). *Quality Standards for NAFCC Accreditation* (4th ed.). Retrieved July 20, 2007, from www.nafcc.org/documents/QualStd.pdf

National Association for Nursery Education. (1929). *Minimum essentials for nursery school education.* Chicago: Author.

National Association for the Education of Young Children (NAEYC). (2001). *NAEYC at 75: Reflections on the past, challenges for the future.* Washington, DC: NAEYC.

National Association for the Education of Young Children (NAEYC). (2005a). *NAEYC early childhood program standards and accreditation criteria: The mark of quality in early childhood education.* Washington, DC: NAEYC.

National Association for the Education of Young Children (NAEYC). (2005b). *Code of ethical conduct and statement of commitment: A position statement of the National Association for the Education of Young Children.* Retrieved June 23, 2007, from www.naeyc.org/about/positions/PSETH05.asp

National Association for the Education of Young Children/National Association of Early Childhood Specialists in State Departments of Education. (2003). *Early childhood curriculum, assessment, and program evaluation: Building an effective, accountable system in programs for children birth through age 8.* Retrieved June 23, 2007, from www.naeyc.org/about/positions/pdf/pscape.pdf

National Education Goals Panel, Shepard, L., Kagan, S. L., & Wurtz, E. (1998). *Principles and recommendations for early childhood assessments.* Washington, DC: National Education Goals Panel.

National Research Council. (2001). *Eager to learn: Educating our preschoolers.* Committee on Early Childhood Pedagogy. B. T. Bowman, M. S. Donovan, & M. S. Burns (Eds.). Commission on Behavioral and Social Sciences and Education. Washington, DC: National Academy Press.

National Research Council and Institute of Medicine. (2000). *From neurons to neighborhoods: The science of early childhood development.* Committee on Integrating the Science of Early Childhood Development. J. P. Shonkoff & D. A. Phillips (Eds.), Board on Children, Youth, and Families, Commission on Behavioral and Social Sciences and Education. Washington, DC: National Academy Press.

National Resource Center for Health and Safety in Child Care and Early Education. (n.d.) *Individual states' child care licensure regulations.* Retrieved on July 30, 2007, from http://nrc.uchsc.edu/STATES/states.htm

Odom, S. L., & Diamond, K. E. (1998). Inclusion of young children with special needs in early childhood education: The research base. *Early Childhood Research Quarterly, 13,* 3–26.

Paris, C., Eyman, A., Morris, L., & Sutton, T. (2007). Facing the storm, turning the tide: Using practitioner research to meet children's and families' needs in inclusive settings. *Journal of Research in Childhood Education, 21*(4), 406–419.

Peisner-Feinberg, E. S., Burchinal, M. R., Clifford, R. M., Culkin, M., Howes, C., Kagan, S. L., Yazejian, N., Byler, P., & Rustici, J. (1999). *The children of the Cost, Quality, & Outcomes Study go to school: Technical report.* Chapel Hill: Frank Porter Graham Child Development Center, University of North Carolina-Chapel Hill.

Plucker, J. A., Eaton, J. J., Rapp, K. E., Lim, W., Nowak, J., Hanson, J. E., Bartleson, A. (2004, January). *The effects of full-day and half-day kindergarten: Review and analysis of national and Indiana data.* Retrieved July 11, 2007, from www.doe.state.in.us/primetime/pdf/fulldayreport.pdf

Ramey, S. L., & Ramey, C. T. (1998). Evaluating educational programs: Strategies to understand and enhance educational effectiveness. In C. Seefeldt & A. Galper (Eds.), *Continuing issues in early childhood education* (2nd ed., pp. 274–292). Upper Saddle River, NJ: Merrill/Prentice Hall.

Reynolds, A. J. (1994). Effects of preschool plus follow-on intervention for children at risk. *Developmental Psychology, 30,* 787–804.

Reynolds, A. J. (2000). *Success in early intervention: The Chicago Child-Parent Centers.* Lincoln: University of Nebraska Press.

Schweinhart, L. N., Barnes, H. V., & Weikart, D. P. (1993). *Significant benefits: The High/Scope Perry Preschool study through age 27.* Ypsilanti, MI: High/Scope Press.

Scott-Little, C., Martella, J., Lesko, J., & Milburn, P. (2007). Early learning standards: Results from a national survey to document trends in state-level policies and practices. *Early Childhood Research and Practice, 9*(1). Retrieved July 23, 2007, from http://ecrp.uiuc.edu/v9n1/little.html

Spodek, B., & Saracho, O. N. (Eds.). (1997). Evaluation in early childhood education: A look to the future. In B. Spodek & O. N. Saracho (Eds.), *Issues in early childhood educational assessment and evaluation. Yearbook in Early Childhood Education* (Vol. 7, pp. 198–206). New York: Teachers College Press.

Stoney, L. (2004, September). *Financing Quality Rating Systems: Lessons learned.* Alliance for Early Childhood Finance for United Way of America Success by 6. Retrieved July 20, 2007, from www.earlychildhoodfinance.org/handouts/Louise_Stoney_QRS_Financing_Paper.pdf

United Way of America. (1996). *Measuring program outcomes: A practical approach.* Alexandria, VA: United Way of America Press.

U.S. Department of Education. (1996). *National education longitudinal study, 1988: Third follow-up (1994).* Washington, DC: National Center for Education Statistics.

U.S. Department of Education, Office of Elementary and Secondary Education. (2002). *No Child Left Behind: A Desktop Reference.* Washington, DC: Author.

U.S. General Accounting Office. (2002). *Early childhood programs: The use of impact evaluations to assess program effects* (GAO-01-542). Washington, DC: Author.

W. K. Kellogg Foundation. (2004). *W. K. Kellogg Foundation Logic Model Development Guide.* Battle Creek, MI: Author. Retrieved July 24, 2007, from www.wkkf.org/Pubs/Tools/Evaluation/Pub3669.pdf

Walberg, H. J., & Reynolds, A. J. (1997). Longitudinal evaluation of program effectiveness. In O. Saracho & B. Spodek (Eds.), *Issues in early childhood educational assessment and evaluation* (Vol. 7, pp. 28–47). New York: Teachers College Press.

Westinghouse Learning Corporation. (1969). *The impact of Head Start: An evaluation of the effects of Head Start on children's cognitive and affective development* (Vol. 1 & 2). Washington, DC: Office of Economic Opportunity.

Wortham, S. C. (2008). *Assessment in early childhood education* (5th ed.). Upper Saddle River, NJ: Merrill/Prentice Hall.

PART 7

WHAT IS THE ROLE OF FAMILIES IN EARLY CARE AND EDUCATION?

R ecently the National Association for the Education of Young Children published a book by Janis Keyser entitled *From Parents to Partners: Building a Family-Centered Early Childhood Program.* The title tells us a lot about where the profession stands regarding the role of families in early care and education. First, the term *family* is increasingly being substituted for *parents* in recognition of the many different individuals who today assume the primary responsibility for rearing the children who participate in early childhood settings. Next, the goal of early childhood programs is to include parents and other family members as true partners in children's care and education in school. The emphasis is now on building a "family-centered" program, not the "child-centered" program that early childhood educators and teachers were so accustomed to hearing about.

Much was written in the past about various layers of parent involvement in a child's education (from playing with the child at home to volunteering in the classroom), and educational programs of various kinds designed to enhance parenting skills. Later, early childhood educators became interested in a less direct (but perhaps more powerful) type of involvement in which family members assumed at least partial responsibility for the philosophy and direction of programs by serving in decision-making capacities through PTAs/PTOs, school committees, and other parents' organizations. Head Start and some other programs for poor children mandated and employed a model in which parents played important roles at all levels. Researchers studied the effect of parent involvement on parental efficacy or feelings of control over their child's education and behavior which, in turn, could be related to child academic outcomes. Another term that was often used was *empowerment.*

Despite general agreement among early childhood leaders that a truly collaborative approach to family engagement is desirable and even necessary in programs for young children, the challenges to implementing it are great and require adaptations in early education programs as well as approaches to family involvement. Some of the issues include the incorporation of parent beliefs, sensitivity to the language and culture of the family, the ability to build on family strengths, and involving the family in setting goals and evaluating outcomes.

In her chapter "Family-Centered Early Care and Education," Janet Gonzalez-Mena paints a complex picture of families and ECE including the benefits of bringing the two groups together and some of the issues that get in the way. One issue is that the term *parent involvement* is open to interpretation. It leaves room for teachers who would rather not have parents as true participants to devise involvement strategies such as bake sales and bulletin boards to keep parents busy. Other excuses may include no time, no training, and no space.

Additional issues revolve around diversity—language differences, communications barriers, cultural differences, and power differentials. But, according to Gonzalez-Mena, research on stress, social support, and parenting behavior has given advocates plenty of reasons to push for more family-focused programs that address parents' needs.

After outlining the benefits of family-centered approaches for children, teachers, families, and communities, she takes a deeper look at the issues involved in bringing professionals and families together, and concludes that the reality is that many of those who work with children and some of those who administer programs have very different ideas about the roles they want families to play in their programs. In addition, caregivers and parents both have protective feelings toward the children they care for which makes it difficult for the two to communicate. The author is candid about her own early experiences as a teacher when she tried valiantly to save the children from their parents. She outgrew that phase, but states that many ECE programs are still about "fixing parents."

Gonzalez-Mena devotes a good deal of attention to diversity issues that also apply to gay, lesbian, bisexual, and transgender parents. To step out of your comfort zone, to have a relationship with each family and learn from them—about their culture or other differences, and to prepare by reading about—differences those may spare young children the identity issues that stand in the way of growth and learning. Some families, too, may need help in overcoming cultural norms that prevent them from relating positively to the school or accepting the concept of partnership with it. NAEYC and other organizations are focusing on the tools to make a family-centered focus a reality in programs for young children. The author speculates about what will have happened in the field when the next edition of this book is ready for the press.

APPLY WHAT YOU LEARNED

As you read the following chapter, think about, talk about, and do additional reading and research regarding these questions:

❑ How can parents be effectively involved as partners in their children's education? What do you think constitutes being an equal partner?

❑ To what extent do families participate in early care and education centers in your community?

❑ What types of programs for family involvement are you aware of? To what extent do they incorporate parent beliefs, native language, and culture?

❑ What can teachers do to increase their sensitivity to diverse families?

❑ What can be done to enhance families' trust in school programs?

❑ What are the benefits to children and teachers of family involvement? Do you know of any research that supports the benefits? Have you experienced any of these benefits as a teacher or parent?

❑ What are some barriers to family involvement? Have you ever experienced any of these barriers?

❑ Can you envision ways to lessen or remove barriers?

REFERENCES

Epstein, J. L. (2001). *School, family, and community partnerships: Preparing educators and improving schools.* Boulder, Co.: Westview.

Keyser, J. (2007). *From parents to partners: Building a family-centered early childhood program.* Washington, DC: NAEYC.

CHAPTER 17

FAMILY-CENTERED EARLY CARE AND EDUCATION

Janet Gonzalez-Mena
Napa Valley College

"The parents at my son's school need a workshop," wrote a friend of mine recently. "They have no empathy for the teachers and there seems to be a lack of trust." As a new parent board member at her son's school she had gotten an earful from the teachers about the parents. My friend is an infant/toddler specialist and she defined the issue between the parents and teachers in terms of "protective urges." Her solution for the problem, as she perceived it, was simple. She said, "All fears arise from lack of information. Once we give parents information about what the teachers are doing in the classroom, and create empathy, we can have a harmonious, trusting group."

I opened her message on my e-mail just as I sat down to write the first draft of this chapter. It couldn't have been more timely. My initial reaction was to smile at her innocence and tell myself that it would be easy if it were just that simple. Obviously a lot more than just a one-way information flow was needed. My thoughts about this chapter came tumbling in as I worked on my answer to my friend's e-mail.

Certainly a major goal for families in any early care and education program, as my friend said, is to become "a harmonious, trusting group" in tune with the professionals involved with their children. Before that can happen teachers have to work on the many issues between families and professionals that get in the way of that goal. That particular outcome depends on the professionals seeing themselves as partners with the families of the children and working to create good relationships. Exchanging information is important, but it goes much further than teachers merely delivering information to parents in a workshop. This chapter is about the complex picture of families and early care and education (ECE) including the benefits of bringing the two groups together and also some of the issues that get in the way.

My friend's vision is a limited one, though the fact that she is on the board as a parent member shows that the school is involving parents even up at the top levels of the organization. Yet my friend perceives a problem with the attitudes of the other parents and proposes solving it by a one-way transfer of information from teachers to parents. She isn't looking at the whole picture. What she proposes is one aspect of what is called parent involvement. She also shares her vision—parents and program coming together with common goals and working together in harmony. That vision is one shared by others. A number of early childhood leaders perceive that the path to reach that vision leads in the direction of family-centered early care and education programs (Bloom, Eisenberg, & Eisenberg, 2003; Epstein, 2001; Fitzgerald, 2004; Keyser, 2006; Lee & Seiderman, n.d.; McGee-Banks, 2003). These are people and organizations that see the importance of including the families in all aspects of their children's care and education.

Douglas Powell was already writing about this movement in 1986. He said, "This shift toward family-oriented programs is typical of the direction many programs in the field of early childhood are taking" (Powell, 1986, p. 50). He uses Head Start as an example because it moved from a child-focused program to a variety of program models that see the family as the client. The vision was already established but the reality hadn't caught up when 12 years later Powell wrote,

> Imagine an early childhood program as a woven fabric made of three different colors of threads representing children, parents, and staff, respectively. A common pattern weaves the child and staff threads together, but most or all of the parent threads are woven into a separate section as a parent-involvement component. (Powell, 1998 p. 60)

Powell proposes a better design, one in which parent threads are woven throughout the pattern. In this design the child and parents are redefined as *family* and their threads are an integral part of the whole pattern, not just a special section. This design represents a lovely image of the family-centered concept. When I first read that metaphor, it stuck in my mind. It's not only a description of Bronfenbrenner's (1994) ecological model, in which the child is seen as embedded in an ever-increasing context of family and community, but it also describes what happens in family-centered programs.

Family-centered care is a giant step forward from what is the more common approach to parent involvement as described by Powell's pattern of parent threads woven into a separate section, or component. A quick overview of the issues shows what gets in the way of programs and individuals gaining and sharing a bigger vision of families being vital parts of their children's care and education.

ISSUES AND CHALLENGES TO FAMILY-CENTERED CARE

One issue is that the term *parent involvement* is open to interpretation and gives room for professionals who are uncomfortable having parents around to limit their involvement to bake sales or performing little tasks that save the teachers time.

Another issue that gets in the way is confining the idea of parents to biological parents alone instead of broadening it to other family members and parental substitutes who play important roles in a child's life.

Other issues come pouring out when early care and education professionals are asked why they can't focus more on parents. Unless they are already doing it, most of them can give a list of the reasons it can't be done. There's no time. There's no space in the environment to make a place for parents—and there are the younger siblings they usually bring along. There's no training for working with parents. A big reason for avoiding having parents around is that children are hard to manage when their parents are present. The list goes on and on.

Then there are the diversity issues. Those are numerous—language differences, communication barriers, cultural differences, power differentials. Just one example involves some families' ideas about role separation. Some cultures view the school and teachers as separate and apart from the lives of the families they serve. There's no point in families becoming involved in schools because the belief is that teachers know best about teaching and families know best about child rearing.

WHY BOTHER WITH INVOLVING FAMILIES?

Why should programs bother with family involvement at all, with all these issues getting in the way? Why not just focus on the children? The National Association for the Education of Young Children (NAEYC) has an answer for that question:

> Young children's learning and development are integrally connected to their families. Consequently, to support and promote children's optimal learning and development, programs need to recognize the primacy of children's families, establish relationships with families based on mutual trust and respect, support and involve families in their children's educational growth, and invite families to fully participate in the program. (NAEYC, 2005, p. 11)

What does the research say? Does parent involvement make a difference? The answer is, yes and no. A massive amount of research has been done and is in progress on the relationship of parent involvement to its effect on children. The Harvard Family Research Project, for example, has been and is still aggressively working on linking families to their children's educational programs.

When parent involvement takes the form of family support, there is evidence that it can lower stress levels in parents and make their lives easier. Parent Services Project (Lee & Seiderman, n.d.; Link, Beggs, & Seiderman, 1997), started by Ethel Seiderman in the 1980s in the San Francisco Bay area, has as its mission to strengthen families to provide for and take leadership in ensuring the well-being of children, families, and communities. Now in eight additional states, Parent Services Project (PSP) provides training, technical assistance, and consultation to help programs and schools engage families. When they work with programs they train them to take the approach of providing the kinds of services that families need and ask for. Instead of a set parent involvement curriculum, each program is encouraged to respond to the interests and needs of the families enrolled. The families are involved in making decisions and planning and organizing the activities. PSP services result in increased parent involvement, leadership, and participation, as well as strengthening community ties and effective community building (Pope & Seiderman, 2001; Seiderman, 2003).

One of the effects of providing support and relieving stress is to decrease the risk of child abuse. The Doris Duke Foundation and the Center for the Study of Social Policy (2004) take the approach of supporting protective factors in families through a project called Strengthening Families Through Early Care and Education. Protective factors include parental resilience, social connections, parenting and child development knowledge, and support in times of need (Olsen 2007). Like the Parent Services Project, this project sees ECE professionals as a logical group for working with parents to prevent child abuse. The project is based on a body of research that focuses on protective factors with the idea that early care and education professionals can support parents, provide resources, and teach coping strategies that will then reduce stress and lower the risk of child abuse.

Early care and education programs work better when professionals understand families and involve them in respectful ways and when there is two-way information sharing. This is true for general ECE programs and also for special education. Parents spend more time with their children than early interventionists and should take an active role in the interventions. When parents are involved they have many more opportunities to influence their children's learning and development. There is evidence that parent involvement is a critical factor in intervention (Mahoney & Wiggers, 2007; Turnbull, Turbiville, & Turnbull, 2000).

I can use my own history as an involved parent (I'm mother of five children) as an example of what doesn't work. I resisted teachers who weren't supportive and understanding of who I was and what I was already doing. I was not happy to be asked to do fund-raising for five different programs and schools. I have to admit that I spent energy on trying to limit my involvement. Also, whenever I was told my job was to take responsibility for my children doing their homework, I rebelled. That didn't fit my belief system. My approach to homework was to consider it the child's responsibility, not mine. But I'm a bit of a rebel and see *learning* as the goal of school, not *grades*. I believe more in intrinsic rewards than extrinsic ones, which fit as long as my children were in preschool, but put me at odds with some of their teachers from kindergarten on.

My children grew up in a middle-income family, and I was the third generation in my family to have a college education, so I had some confidence that my children would figure out how to get the education they needed to earn a living. That's a very different situation from many low-income families. Middle-class children are more likely to succeed even if their parents aren't involved. But one thing about my story does translate to all parents: It makes a difference when families feel understood and find support from their children's programs. Most important of all is for families to have the voice to say what they need. When they are listened to and their beliefs respected, then involvement works better. Instead of asking for their support of the school or program's goals and told to help their children with homework, the better route is to take a collaborative approach (Gonzalez-Mena & Stonehouse, in press). A collaborative approach means that change not only occurs within the families, but also within the program as it begins to reflect those enrolled rather than just predetermined policies and practices (Powell, 1998). The push for family-centered programs isn't just about child outcomes improving, however you state child outcomes—grades, test scores, enhanced development, confidence, self-esteem, and lower risk of abuse are some of the desired outcomes, depending on who is asked. Advocates for collaborative parent-staff relations include those who come from the perspective of parental rights, parent empowerment, and respect for diversity. Research on stress, social support, and parenting behavior has given advocates plenty of reasons to push for more family-focused programs that address parents' needs.

WHERE WE HAVE BEEN

Long ago when Lilian Katz and I were much younger, I believe it was 1967, she taught a class at San Francisco State College (as it was then called). That was the first early childhood class I ever took. I remember that she said, "Your client is not the child but the family." I've never forgotten that. It has taken a long, long time for that message to be widely heard.

A Quick History Lesson

We learned years and years ago that families are important to children and that importance doesn't diminish when children are separated from those families. John Bowlby (1969, 1973) convinced the medical profession that it was important to keep parents and children connected when children were hospitalized. We know about attachment and hospitalization. We're still learning about attachment and education.

Another research base for involving families in their children's education comes from psychology and Uri Bronfenbrenner, cofounder of Head Start, who wrote a book in 1979 called *The Ecology of Human Development*. He helped us in the ECE field see that children are always part of a context and that it is important to never think of "the child" in the abstract without considering the family, the community, and the society (Bronfenbrenner, 1979, 1994; Bronfenbrenner & Morris, 1998).

Ira J. Gordon set out to improve child outcomes through involving parents of infants back in the 1960s. In 1968, he focused on compensatory education (Gordon 1968, 1976). He studied parent education and involvement and eventually came up with six types of involvement (Olmsted, Rubin, True, & Revicki, 1980). Gordon looked at parent involvement as a hierarchy moving from less to more involvement, with parents

1. Being mere recipients of information
2. Learning new skills
3. Being the teacher of their own children
4. Taking the role of volunteer in the classroom
5. Being a paid semiprofessional
6. Being decision maker and policy advisor

All these levels remain valid descriptions of the roles professionals assign to parents today. Parent education classes are common; certainly part of the goal of delivering information is for parents to learn new skills in relating to their children. Discipline is always a hot topic and most parents are eager to expand their repertoire. "The parent is the child's first teacher" is a motto and now a widespread notion. It can be interpreted in many ways, from reading to little ones in the name of early literacy, to helping children with their homework, to sitting them down and giving them lessons or drilling them with flashcards. But it can also be interpreted in another way which includes supporting them by organizing their lives so they get their basic needs met for nutrition, exercise, and rest—that way they have the energy to learn. Parents can support older children by finding a quiet place for homework and figuring out what else they need to do their homework, and also by showing an interest in school and what children are learning. As parents move up the "involvement ladder," they move beyond thinking about their own children and becoming an advocate for them, to looking at advocating for all children including ways to improve the program, the school, or the system.

The Epstein model was based on Gordon's roles for parent involvement and expanded on by Joyce Epstein (2001), who wrote a handbook called *School, Family, and Community Partnerships*. The handbook lists the six types of partnerships that reflect Gordon's hierarchy using a little different language. Here is Epstein's list:

1. Parenting
2. Communicating school-to-home and home-to-school
3. Volunteering
4. Helping students learn at home
5. Decision making (including families as participants in school decisions, governance, and advocacy through PTAs/PTOs, school councils, committees, and other parent organizations)
6. Collaborating with the community

Head Start, born during the mid-1960s War on Poverty, is a comprehensive preschool and social services program with a mandate for parent involvement as well as built-in devices for parents to have some say in the education of their 4-year-olds. Several generations have now been through Head Start. Some of today's teachers are grown-up Head Start children, as are some of the directors.

Special education law PL 94-142 (the Education for All Handicapped Children Act of 1975) gave a boost to involving parents in their children's education by mandating parental participation with professionals in developing Individualized Educational Plans (IEPs) for children and Individualized Family Service Plans (IFSPs) for infants/toddlers that emphasize both strengths and needs. According to the law and reauthorizations of the Individuals with Disabilities Act (IDEA) in 1990 and 1997, parents must be involved in all aspects of their children's education. In 2004, PL 108-446 aligned special education with No Child Left Behind (NCLB) legislation, retaining the parent involvement and its inherent power. Parents have the power to call a hearing if they disagree with a diagnosis or placement.

THE BENEFITS OF FAMILY-CENTERED APPROACHES

When family-centered approaches provide services that support what the families need, as individuals and as a group, they begin to become a replacement for the old-fashioned extended family, which continues to disappear from large segments of the population. But family-centered approaches offer more than just services, they offer partnerships in which professionals and parents share power and become allies. Collaboration is a pattern as each side brings special skills that enhance the partnership. Such partnerships provide consistency, enhance communication, and result in mutual learning as both sides share resources and information with each other. Everyone benefits.

Benefits to Children

When people who are closest to children work together for their mutual benefit, their relationship and actions serve to enhance children's emotional security, which in turn makes it easier for them to learn. The collaboration and mutual information exchange between professionals and family members helps both groups better understand the children's strengths and needs. The relationship of teacher and parent provides greater continuity between home and out-of-home program, which can result in greater cultural continuity, or at least understanding and respect of differences. A sturdy identity formation process is more likely when children don't have to experience great discrepancies between what they learn at school and what they learn at home.

Another important benefit comes when adults model for children healthy, equitable relations in their interactions with each other. It's not just about being polite to each other, but having rich, authentic exchanges and even disagreements and showing children that you can resolve them. When adults on both sides are skilled and aware, children, and everyone around them, gain an increased understanding of equity in action. It isn't about just teaching an anti-bias curriculum to children and waiting for them to grow up and make the world a better place. It's about the adults in the children's lives dealing with their own biases and increasing their ability to communicate across differences. The children are always watching. They learn as much from adults interacting with each other as they do from lessons about being fair and empathetic.

The number 1 item in the NAEYC Accreditation Standards is relationships, because positive relationships are important to development, security, and getting along with others. What better way to encourage positive relationships than to model them every day as professionals and other adults interact and collaborate.

Benefits to Teachers

Teachers, caregivers, and family child care providers who understand children within their families can do a better job of teaching and working with those children. This deeper understanding of children relates to gains in self-confidence on the part of children and effectiveness in teaching on the part of teachers. When families and professionals exchange information and observe each other in action, teachers can learn new and effective teaching and behavioral management strategies from families. Cindy Ballenger (1992) changed her approach to guidance when she came to understand the strategies used by the Haitian families she worked with. Making connections with the families helps build trust.

By having close contact with families and the kinds of interactions that create partnerships, teachers can receive acknowledgment and appreciation of their skills that they might not receive otherwise. As professionals learn more about other cultures they can expand their views and gain knowledge and insights about child development, education, desired outcomes, and approaches related to these views. Families add richness to a program and provide resources to professionals. Through relationships with families, teachers can become more a part of the local community, if they aren't already.

Benefits to Families

When families are empowered and able to become a vital part of their children's education, they can find ways to make a better fit with their personal, family, and cultural goals and desired outcomes for their children. Barbara Rogoff, author of *The Cultural Nature of Human Development*, said, "The goals of human development— what is regarded as mature or desirable—vary considerably" (2003, p. 18). With pressures to conform to prescribed outcomes and results desired by policy makers and funding sources, it becomes even more important to pay attention to what parents want for their children. Paying attention creates stresses and challenges, but it's worth it because families then feel more secure and confident about their children's education and life outside the home and family. They also can feel empowered when teachers take on the challenge of figuring out together what to do when there is a mismatch between what a parent wants and what the program is doing.

Just as teachers can learn teaching and behavioral management strategies from parents, so too can parents learn them from teachers. Seeing one's child in an environment with other children gives a broader view than simply knowing that child within the context of home and family. Teachers' knowledge of child development can be a benefit to parents. Families can gain greater knowledge of resources from the professionals in their children's program. Sometimes it is the parents who have resources that teachers don't have. For example, a family with a child who has special needs may already be connected to a number of resources that the teachers need to know about and have contact with. Finally, just as parents can help teachers become part of the local community, teachers can help parents be part of the school community.

Mutual Benefits

Both families and professionals gain from collaborative relationships in a number of ways. Communication is enhanced as the groups relate to each other around shared power and decision making. Creating supportive relationships can be a huge benefit that leads to networks of mutual support. The community also gains from families and ECE programs working together. A better-educated population is the ultimate outcome and one to constantly strive for. A more pluralistic society is another benefit as everyone gains from the richness of diversity. When families and professionals work at getting together, greater understanding and acceptance of diversity at all levels of the population can result. When equity and social justice grow from understanding and acceptance, everyone gains a great deal.

If there are so many benefits to families and professionals coming together in ECE settings, why don't all programs have a family-centered focus?

A DEEPER LOOK AT THE ISSUES IN BRINGING PROFESSIONALS AND FAMILIES TOGETHER

The biggest issue in what is generally called parent involvement is defining the concept and recognizing to what extent families should be involved in programs. Related issues arise from differences between the vision and the reality. The vision of leaders in the field, as mentioned previously, is of a movement from child-centered programs to family-centered ones. The reality is that many of those who work with children and some of those who administer programs have very different ideas of the roles they want families to play in their programs.

Conflicting Ideas of the Role Families Should Have in Relation to Professionals

Parent involvement is the all-encompassing term that ECE professionals use when talking about working with parents. The term rolls easily off their tongues if they believe in it, less so if that involvement is mandated by funding sources. The question is, What is parent involvement anyway? The term doesn't mean much until it is defined because it varies widely from program to program. It can mean as little as asking parents to take paint smocks or bedding home to wash or to repair equipment and clean up the play yard. It can also mean parent education, from which parents are expected to gain information and skills from teachers. It can also mean as much as parents creating policy and hiring staff.

Why the Conflicting Ideas? It Can Boil Down to Attitudes

Many people go into the ECE field because they enjoy being with children. Not all of those who become teachers enjoy parents to the same degree. The trend is to create child-centered programs. It's easy to spot a child-centered program simply by observing and reading the parent handbook. A quick look shows most programs set up the environment for children and children are the entire focus of the teacher, even when parent involvement is a stated program component. The parent handbook usually verifies that the focus is on the children, not adults. Sometimes that fact is stated in writing using the term *child-centered program*. Further evidence comes by listening to teachers talk when no parents are around. In my experience, it is common to hear complaints about how difficult it is to work with children when their parents are present. When it comes to parent involvement, minor or major, mandated or chosen, teacher and administrator attitudes can be a big issue no matter what the official policy says.

One explanation for potential difficulties between parents and the professionals who work with their children is, as my friend who complained about the parents in her son's school at the beginning of this chapter put it, "protective urges." The idea comes from an infant/toddler training program, the Program for Infant/Toddler Care, headquartered in WestEd's Center for Child and Family Studies in California. According to their literature, "Caregivers and parents both have protective urges toward the children they care for that underlie much of the stress of the parent/caregiver relationship. Understanding that these feelings are normal and actual can help to ease the tension" (WestEd and the California Department of Education, 1997, p. 165). Of course, this information is directed at those who work with the youngest children. The feelings may be more intense with infants and toddlers, but they don't necessarily go away when children get older.

Another way to look at protective urges is by looking at the developmental stage of the teacher. I remember myself as a beginning teacher wanting to save children from their parents. I'll never forget the one child I would have tried to adopt if such a thing were possible. That's how strong my protective urges were, not just with the one child, but with many others whose families I thought weren't doing a good enough job. Luckily, I eventually moved from that stage to one of deciding to save the children through educating their parents instead of just looking down on them. I went wholeheartedly into parent education, to help those who knew so much less than I did gain my knowledge about how to parent. Of course, that was when I had my teacher hat on. I was much more humble when I remembered that I was also a parent and far from perfect, in spite of all my knowledge (Gonzalez-Mena, 1995). Maybe realizing that about myself got me to the third stage when I finally began to see the *families* as my clients, instead of their children, just as Lilian Katz said back in that first early education class. It is embarrassing to look back and think about how long it took me to begin to recognize that parents and other family members of children in ECE programs also had knowledge and strengths to support that knowledge—ones that I didn't necessarily have. That was when I opened my vision to family-centered care. I'm now an advocate, as are others in the field.

Diversity Issues

I can look at my own experiences and see how they reflect a period in the ECE field of wanting to fix parents. I outgrew that phase, but many ECE programs, especially compensatory ones, are still about fixing parents. They work from a deficit model instead of a strength-based one.

That is in contrast to Head Start's origins during the civil rights movement. Called the Mississippi Freedom Schools, the statewide programs were run by parents and civil rights workers. The original Head Start's parent-run schools, with some help from outsiders, set an amazing example for programs everywhere and is an important part of the history of early childhood education. It wasn't the same after the federal government stepped in (Greenberg, 1968).

Although Head Start has done good work since the mid-1960s and influenced the profession in many positive ways, especially with the comprehensive approach to early childhood education, it is still a deficit model. It suggests that something is wrong with these children and families that needs to be fixed. It's also a segregated model—by income level. But Head Start also mandates parent involvement at all levels, as mentioned earlier, and has always given both families and communities some say in their programs, so that's a big plus in its favor. Head Start offers a model for how we can implement standards and regulations and still have effective parent and community involvement, though in reality it doesn't always work out that way, in Head Start or other places either. It has the chance to work, though the regulations have some built-in conflicts because parents have some power and at the same time regulations mandate the way things have to be.

It may seem like a paradox or a double bind to have potential contradictions built into the regulations, but those contradictions invite dialogue. Here's an example. Head Start regulations mandate "family style meals," which is greatly open to interpretation about whose family and whose style. At the same time, the regulations say that the nutrition program must serve a variety of foods which consider cultural and ethnic preferences, and that parents must be involved in planning, implementing, and evaluating the agencies' nutritional services. In a program where there is true parent involvement, whoever is interpreting that regulation about family-style meals can have a dialogue with parents who disagree with the interpretation. That's true empowerment of parents.

Isaura Barrera and Rob Corso in their book *Skilled Dialogue* (2003) have some good ideas about how to work through those kinds of conflicts. Barrera (personal communication, 1997), instead of using the term *cultural conflicts,* calls them "cultural bumps," which puts a more positive spin on what happens when program and families disagree with each other. When I used the term *cultural bump* with my colleague Marion Cowee, she explained why she thought it was a good metaphor. The term made her think of a speed bump. "It's good when you can see it coming in the road ahead and you slow down and pay attention as you cross it, before you speed up again. If you don't see it coming, you can hit it hard and get hurt or wreck your car" (Cowee, personal communication, 2002). Another aspect of the speed bump metaphor is that it protects children. That's why early childhood professionals need to talk to parents and understand their perspectives when they hit a cultural bump.

Children's identity formation can be affected if teachers are taking children in a different direction from where their parents want them to go (Lally, 1995). It happens all the time. Just one small example is when teachers say, "Look at me when I'm talking to you," and the child comes from a culture in which he or she has been taught not to look an elder in the eye.

One particular story brings home the point about how much cultural differences can affect children—even to their questioning who they are and where they belong. When teachers and parents disagree, children can feel caught in between and that's not a good feeling!

Here's the story. I was at a conference and during a break I ended up talking to someone I didn't know. I read her name tag, Ana. I made a remark that her name was spelled with one *n*. I was thinking to myself that she probably had roots in a Spanish-speaking country. I was surprised when she suddenly started talking emotionally about her childhood. She told me that when she went to kindergarten, she already knew how to write her name. She proudly wrote it on the first day for the teacher. The teacher corrected her by saying, "This is the way Anna is spelled" and putting a second *n* in her name. Ana had tears in her eyes when she told me she went home and told her mother that her name was spelled wrong. Her mother was adamant that it was spelled correctly. Ana had been named for her Croatian grandmother and the correct spelling in Croatian was Ana. A tear ran down her cheek as she told me she had to make a choice between her teacher and her mother. She chose her teacher. Then she said, with a deep sigh, "It took me until I was 15 years old to get the guts to spell my name the proper way." By then she had fire in her eyes—"And I've been doing it ever since!" Such a simple mistake on the part of the teacher had such huge repercussions. One little *n* became a huge identity issue and left a child with a feeling of having betrayed both her mother and grandmother.

Although we don't think of such things as spelling of names or eye contact as issues of power, or of equity and social justice, in some ways they are. And those issues can start the day children go into out-of-home care or a school where the professionals don't know about cultural differences and don't find out about them. That's why family-centered care is so important.

Speaking of equity and social justice, there is a group of parents who deserve the same respect and acceptance as those who are culturally different from the professional or the program. No matter how educators feel about sexual orientations that are different from their own, it's important to recognize that all children have the right to have their family accepted. Gay, lesbian, bisexual, and transgender parents have children in our programs. Everything in this chapter applies to them as well as everyone else.

Sometimes working with parents causes early educators to step out of their comfort zones, especially those who are new at it. Tamar Jacobson (2003) gives advice about just that subject in her book *Confronting Our Discomfort: Clearing the Way for Anti-Bias in Early Childhood*.

Certainly the best way to find out is to have a relationship with each family and learn from them about their culture or other kinds of differences. It doesn't hurt though to prepare ahead of time by reading more about differences. A number of books have been published on this topic that give information to teachers (Akbar, 1985; Bhavnagri & Gonzalez-Mena, 1997; Casper, 2003; Chao, 1994; Clay, 2004; Delpit, 1995; Eggers-Pierola, 2005; Gelnaw, Brickley, Marsh, & Ryan, 2004; Gonzalez-Mena, 2005; Gonzalez-Mena & Shareef, 2005; Harwood, Miller, & Irizarry, 1995; hooks, 2003; Kagiticibasi, 1996; Lin & Fu, 1990; Tan, 2004).

Other Factors That Get in the Way

There are many more challenges related to turning a child-centered program into a family-centered one. Here are some additional issues from both the professional and family perspectives.

Issues from the Early Educator's Perspective.   First, there is the time factor. There just isn't enough time in a teacher's day to work with children and spend time with their families as well. Home visits would be nice to get to know families better and connect school to home, but how many programs have that kind of time built into teachers' schedules? And even if time to build relationships with parents exists, where are the money and resources to create environments that welcome adults? If there is no support for a family focus, trying to implement it is nearly impossible for teachers.

Training is another factor. Most of the coursework required to become a qualified teacher focuses on children and on curriculum. Some teacher training courses don't even have one class on working with families. Where do teachers learn how to build relationships with adults? Or develop communication skills? And, of course, status and salaries always enter in. "How can I do even more than I'm doing and get paid so little?" is a lament of teachers across the country.

If a teacher is younger than the parents and has no children, relating to parents as an equal may be difficult, especially if parents don't treat the teacher as an equal. One common put-down by parents goes something like this, "You don't understand because you're not a parent yourself." Similarly, classism can be a problem if a parent has a high-paying job and comes from a different socio-economic level from the teacher. Feelings related to these issues can get in the way of forming relationships.

Issues from the Family Perspective.   Again, time is a factor. How do families who work full time find extra time to get involved? How do they even manage to come to conferences held during the day if their job doesn't allow them to take time off for such things? For some families a translator is vital. If there is no translator, there's no communication.

Depending on the family members' own school experiences, the classroom or child care center can be an uncomfortable place to be. Or just being around educators can cause discomfort. Some parents feel they have nothing to contribute and are afraid they'll just be in the teacher's way if they come into the classroom. Some parents feel insecure about their own education and social status, or their children's abilities. A common issue occurs when parents try to manage children's misbehavior in the presence of the teacher.

Some parents put teachers on a pedestal and can't imagine playing any kind of teacher role themselves in the face of such expertise. This can be due to cultural differences in the relative status of teachers and parents. Some parents wouldn't dream of trying to collaborate with a teacher, when the teacher is the one with the knowledge about child development and education. Then there are the parents who see themselves superior to the teacher. All these factors can be barriers to communication, let alone developing a relationship and actually collaborating with each other.

Issues Related to Both Families and Early Educators.   School readiness pressures are huge these days, with everyone wanting to ensure that children arrive from prekindergarten programs and other ECE settings "ready to learn" as the saying goes. Of course, those who use that phrase are ignoring that babies are born ready to learn. Furthermore, children don't stop learning, no matter what happens.

School readiness has been a big issue in early childhood education for a long time. Certainly there is no magic bullet to get children ready for school, though some have banked on parent involvement being that bullet. There are too many outside factors besides what happens in ECE programs including socioeconomic level, race, culture, language, and family stability. As long as babies are born into unequal situations, the goal of equal education for all is an issue the entire society must deal with. It can't be left to care and education systems alone, though we keep trying.

WHERE ARE WE NOW?

The current trend and mandate is to make connections between professionals and families in the many types of programs falling into the category of early care and education. Though in the past educational programs for young children were sometimes thought to be different from child care programs, that can no longer be the case. All programs for young children have the potential to be educational. Therefore this chapter hasn't only been about school, kindergarten, and preschool but instead about all ECE programs including full-day programs for working parents and also family child care. That's the reason I used the term *teacher* sometimes, but not exclusively. I also used ECE professional, early educator, and a variety of other terms, including caregiver—to remind the reader that programs for infants and toddlers fall under the heading of ECE and need to be regarded as educational, even though they may not look anything like programs for older children.

Another trend is to move away from separate programs for children with additional (or special) needs and toward full-inclusion programs that integrate those children with their typically developing peers. Of course, that trend also includes integrating the families into the program as well (O'Shea, O'Shea, Algozzino, & Hammittee, 2001).

The reader may have noticed that instead of using the term *early childhood education* for the acronym ECE, I used *early care and education* which is more inclusive of the broad range of programs. There's an integration theme working here. Just as we shouldn't be separating families from programs that serve their children, so we shouldn't separate care from education. Nell Noddings, a Stanford professor of education, is a strong advocate for linking care and education. She makes scholarly arguments in her 2005 book *The Challenge to Care in Schools,* proposing that school should be about caring and caring should be educational. She is writing about older students—through college age. As I read her book, I kept thinking about how she was describing quality ECE programs. Some people do continue to separate child care programs from educational ones, but there's no reason that child care programs can't be highly educational. Training the staff is key (Lombardi, 2003).

The NAEYC, always a leader in the field, focuses two of their program standards, numbers 7 and 8, on adults other than early care and education professionals and includes diversity in both standards. The family standard reads: "The program establishes and maintains collaborative relationships with each child's family to foster children's development in all settings. These relationships are sensitive to family composition, language, and culture" (NAEYC, 2005, p. 11).

In 2005 and 2006, NAEYC identified 40 early childhood leaders as part of a Supporting Teachers, Strengthening Families Initiative. These leaders were people interested in working with families and designing action plans for use in strengthening the approaches to families in their local communities. Implementation followed (Olson, 2007).

At this writing, NAEYC is in the beginning stages of developing training in working with families as partners, which could help not only to spread the concept but also to give tools to programs and individuals for improving what they're already doing in the area of parent involvement or for implementing something new.

CONCLUSIONS

When I try to envision the future, I see the need for the ECE field to work harder to integrate families into their programs and in order to do that, we have to pay even more attention to diversity than we have in the past. NAEYC agrees. Their *Families and Community Relationships: A Guide to the NAEYC Early Childhood Program Standards and Related Accreditation Criteria* says, "Partnering with families is essential to high-quality early childhood programs. A successful partnership requires that programs . . . seek to understand families' personal and cultural backgrounds" (NAEYC, 2005, p. 23).

A broader and perhaps different kind of training is needed. In addition to specific courses on working with families, I see integrating working with families (and the accompanying subject of respecting and understanding diversity) into all classes. Further, I see teaching present and future early childhood professionals more about family systems theory. Understanding family systems is a key component in working effectively with families. No matter how different families are, there are certain characteristics that all families share, but they play out in different ways. Boundaries are one example. Families teach their children, often unconsciously, about boundaries, which may be narrow or extremely broad. These lessons include how individuals relate to each other and to groups. Boundaries and identity are tied together and answer the question, Where do I end and where do you start? Roles is another example. What roles children and other family members play may be quite different depending on the family. Family systems theory looks at these characteristics as a way to help professionals work with families in ways that are effective (Christian, 2006).

The focus of future efforts needs to be on creating relationships (Baker & Manfredi/Pettit, 2004), which is the first of NAEYC's Program Standards and also part of Standard 7 on Families. Communication is an important path to relationships. NAEYC says, "a successful partnership requires that programs . . . create and maintain effective communication with respect to all aspects of the child's develop-ment and learning both in school and at home" (NAEYC, 2005, p. 23). Some of these conversations may be difficult ones. It's important that both teachers and parents be open to two-way communication, use the opportunity to share the information that they have, and at the same time listen to the other (Lawrence-Lightfoot, 2003; Keyser, 2006).

Honoring diversity is the key to communication and the relationships. There are ways to find out where the differences lie (Zepeda et al., 2006), and skills that can be used to handle conflicts that arise when partners share their differences (Bredekamp, 2003; Kreidler & Whitall, 2003; Tobiassen & Gonzalez-Mena, 1998).

One idea that could be considered by funders and policy makers is that of expanding environmental requirements to make room for parents to be on site. Jim Greenman (2003), always thinking about the messages the environment gives, sug-gests that parents feel more welcome when there is an area set up for them.

How can we make all this happen? NAEYC suggests that one key is to "sup-port and nurture family members to be effective advocates for their children" (NAEYC, 2005, p. 23). Advocacy starts when parents begin to advocate for their own child. When a parent doesn't perceive this as an appropriate role, it behooves the ECE professional to help him or her understand that this is not only appropri-ate, but a right. Parents who are advocates for their own children may end up becoming advocates for the group their child is in. With support and encourage-ment, some may go on to become advocates for all children. One thing they can advocate for is that conditions support families as partners with professionals (Robinson & Stark, 2002; Sanders, 2003).

I have hope that the field will continue to move toward increasing numbers of programs that have a family-centered focus. I speculate about what might be in the next edition of this book. When it comes out, will that movement have hap-pened? And how would we know if it had? Future research is called for. I also won-der if the issues, challenges, and barriers to increasing family focus will be the same or whether some will have been surmounted and others will have emerged. I can't see into the future, so it's a matter of spreading the word, increasing the informa-tion and funding for training, then waiting to see what will happen.

REFERENCES

Akbar, N. (1985). *The community of self.* Tallahassee, FL: Mind Productions.

Ballenger, C. (1992, Summer). Because you like us: The language of control. *Harvard Educational Review* 62(2), 199–208.

Bhavnagri, N., & Gonzalez-Mena, J. (1997, Fall). The cultural context of caregiving. *Childhood Educa-tion* 74(1), 2–8.

Baker, A. C., & Manfredi/Pettit, L. (2004). *Relationships, the heart of quality care: Creating community among* adults in early care settings. Washington, DC: NAEYC.

Barrera, I., & Corso, R. (2003). *Skilled dialogue.* Balti-more: Brookes.

Bloom, P. J., Eisenberg, P., & Eisenberg, E. (2003, Spring/Summer). Reshaping early childhood pro-grams to be more family responsive. *America's Family Support Magazine*, 36–38.

Bowlby, J. (1969). *Attachment and loss.* Vol. 1. *Attach-ment.* New York: Basic Books.

Bowlby, J. (1973). *Attachment and loss.* Vol. 2. *Separation: Anxiety and anger.* London: Hogarth.

Bredekamp, S. (2003). Resolving contradictions between cultural practices. In C. Copple (Ed.), *A world of difference.* Washington, DC: NAEYC.

Bronfenbrenner, U. (1979). *The ecology of human development: Experiments by nature and design.* Cambridge, MA: Harvard University Press.

Bronfenbrenner, U. (1994). Ecological models of human development. In T. Husen & N. Postlethwaite (Eds.), *International encyclopedia of education, Vol. 3* (2nd ed., pp. 1643–1647). Amsterdam: Elsevier.

Bronfenbrenner, U., & Morris P. A. (1998). The ecology of developmental processes. In W. Damon (Series Ed.) & R. M. Lerner (Vol. Ed.), *Theoretical models of human development: Vol. 1. Handbook of Child psychology.* New York: Wiley.

Casper, V. (2003). Very young children in lesbian- and gay-headed families: Moving beyond acceptance. *Zero to Three, 23*(30), 18–26.

Chao, R. (1994). Beyond parental control and authoritarian parenting style: Understanding Chinese parenting through the culture notion of training. *Child Development, 65,* 1111–1119.

Christian, L. G. (2006). Understanding families: Applying family system theory to early childhood practice. *Young Children, 61*(1), 12–20.

Clay, J. (2004). Creating safe, just places to learn for children of lesbian and gay parents: The NAEYC Code of Ethics in action. *Young children, 59*(6), 34–38.

Center for the Study of Social Policy (CSSP). (2004). *Protecting children by strengthening families: A guidebook for early childhood programs.* Washington, DC: Author. Retrieved April 15, 2007, from www.cssp.org/doris_duke/index.html

Delpit, L. (1995). *Other people's children: Cultural conflict in the classroom.* New York: New Press.

Eggers-Pierola, C. (2005). *Connections and commitments: A Latino-based framework for early childhood educators.* Portsmouth, NH: Heinemann.

Epstein, J. L. (2001). *School, family and community partnerships: Preparing educators and improving schools.* Boulder, CO: Westview.

Fitzgerald, D. (2004). *Parent partnership in the early years.* London: Continuum.

Gelnaw, A., Brickley, M., Marsh, H., & Ryan, D. (2004). *Opening doors: Lesbian and gay parents and schools.* Washington, DC: Family Pride Coalition.

Gonzalez-Mena, J. (1995). *Dragon mom: Confessions of a child development expert.* Napa, CA: Rattle OK Publishing.

Gonzalez-Mena, J. (2005). *Diversity in early care and education: Honoring differences.* New York: McGraw-Hill

Gonzalez-Mena, J. & Shareef, I. (2005, November). Discussing diverse perspectives on guidance. *Young Children, 60*(6), 34–38.

Gonzalez-Mena, J., & Stonehouse, A. (in press). *Making links: A collaborative approach to planning and practice in early childhood programs.* New York: Teachers College Press.

Gordon, I. J. (1968). *Parent involvement in compensatory education.* Chicago: University of Illinois Press.

Gordon, I. J., & Breivogel, W. F. (1976). *Building effective home-school relationships.* Boston: Allyn & Bacon.

Greenberg, P. (1968). *The devil has slippery shoes.* New York: Macmillian.

Greenman, J. (2003). Places for childhood include parents too. In B. Neugebauer & R. Neugebauer (Eds.), *The art of leadership.* Redmond, WA: Exchange Press. Retrieved June 29, 2007, from www.gse.harvard.edu/~hfrp/

Harwood, R. L., Miller, J. G., & Irizarry, N. L. (1995). *Culture and attachment: Perceptions of the child in context.* New York: Guilford.

Hooks, B. (2003). *Rock my soul: Black people and self-esteem.* New York: Atria.

Jacobson, T. (2003). *Confronting our discomfort: Clearing the way for anti-bias in early childhood.* Portsmouth, NH: Heinemann.

Kagiticibasi, C. (1996). *Family and human development across cultures.* Mahwah, NJ: Erlbaum.

Keyser, J. (2006). *From parents to partners: Building a family-centered early childhood program.* St. Paul, MN: Redleaf and Washington, DC: NAEYC.

Kreidler, W. J., & Whitall, S. (2003). Resolving conflict. In C. Copple (Ed.), *A world of difference: Readings on teaching children in a diverse society* (pp. 52–56). Washington, DC: NAEYC.

Lally, J. R. (1995, November). The impact of child care policies and practices on infant/toddler identity formation. *Young Children,* 58–67

Lee, L. (2006). *Stronger together: Family support and early childhood education.* San Rafael, CA: Parent Services Project.

Lee, L., & Seiderman, E. (n.d.) *Families matter: The Parent Services Project.* Cambridge, MA: Harvard Family Research Project.

Lawrence-Lightfoot, S. (2003). *The essential conversation: What parents and teachers can learn from each other.* New York: Ballantine Books.

Lin, C. Y., & Fu, V. (1990). A comparison of child rearing practices among Chinese immigrant, Chinese, and Caucasian-American parents. *Child Development, 61,* 429–433.

Lombardi, J. (2003). *Time to care: Redesigning child care to promote education, support families, and build communities.* Philadelphia: Temple University Press.

Mahoney, G., & Wiggers, B. (2007). The role of parents in early intervention. *Children and Schools, 29*(1), 7–15.

McGee-Banks, C. A. (2003). Families and teachers working together for school improvement. In J. A. Banks & C. A. McGee-Banks (Eds.), *Multicultural education: Issues and perspectives* (4th ed., pp. 402–410). New York: Wiley.

National Association for the Education of Young Children (NAEYC). (2005). *Families and community relationships: A guide to the NAEYC early childhood program standards and related accreditation criteria.* Washington, DC: Author.

Noddings, N. (2005). *The challenge to care in schools.* New York: Teachers College Press.

Olmsted, P. P., Rubin, R. I., True, J. H., & Revicki, D. (1980). *Parent Education: The Contributions of Ira J. Gordon.* Olney, MD: Association for Childhood Education International.

Olson, M. (2007). Strengthening families: Community strategies that work. *Young Children 62*(2), 26–32.

O'Shea, D. J., O'Shea, L., Algozzino, R., & Hammittee, D. (2001). *Families and teachers of individuals with disabilities: Collaborative orientations and responsive practices.* Boston: Allyn & Bacon.

Pope, J., & Seiderman, E. (2001, Winter). The child-care connection. *Family Support, 19*(4), 24–35.

Powell, D. R. (1986). Research in review. Parent education and support programs. *Young Children, 41*(3), 47–53.

Powell, D. R. (1998). Research in review: Reweaving parents into the fabric of early childhood programs. *Young Children, 53*(5), 60–67.

Robinson, A., & Stark, D. R. (2002). *Advocates in action: Making a difference for young children.* Washington, DC: NAEYC.

Rogoff, B. (2003). *The cultural nature of human development.* New York: Oxford University Press.

Sanders, M. G. (2003). Community involvement in schools: From concept to practice. *Education and Urban Society, 35*(2), 161–180.

Seiderman, E. (2003). Putting all the players on the same page: Accessing resources for the child and family. In B. Neugebauer & R. Neugebauer (Eds.), *The art of leadership.* Redmond, WA: Exchange Press.

Tan, A. L. (2004). *Chinese American children and families: A guide for educators and service providers.* Olney, MD: Association for Childhood Education International.

Tobiassen, D. P., & Gonzalez-Mena, J. (1998). *A place to begin: Working with parents on issues of diversity.* Oakland: California Tomorrow.

Turnbull, A. P., Turbiville, P. V., & Turnbull, H. R. (2000). Evolution of family-professional partnerships: Collective empowerment as the model for early twenty-first century. In J. P. Shonkoll & S. J. Meisels (Eds.), *Handbook of early childhood intervention* (pp. 630–650). New York: Cambridge University Press.

WestEd and the California Department of Education. (1997). *The Program for Infant/Toddler Caregivers' trainer's manual, module IV: Culture, family and providers* (Rev. ed.). Sausalito & Sacramento, CA: WestEd and California Department of Education.

Zepeda, M., Gonzales-Mena, J., Rothstein-Fisch, C., & Trumbull, E. (2006). *Bridging cultures in early care and education: A training module.* Mahwah, NJ: Erlbaum.

PART 8

HOW CAN WE ADVOCATE FOR YOUNG CHILDREN?

*I*n this third edition of *Continuing Issues,* we have moved the chapter on advocacy to the end in the hope that readers will be inspired to apply their knowledge and skills to the role of child advocate. Linda Buck and Barbara Willer believe that child advocacy is an ethical imperative for members of the early care and education field. The editors of this book believe strongly that all of us who are concerned with young children should be in the forefront of advocacy for best practices in children's health, education, and welfare.

Who are child advocates and what do they do? Traditionally, early childhood educators were generally seen as well-meaning and highly dedicated to children. Unfortunately, at the same time they possessed little knowledge of how to advocate for children in the public and private arenas.

Organizations such as the Children's Defense Fund changed that image by gathering the statistics and performing the analytical studies that documented the position of children and families in our society. Their publications, as well as those from the National Association for the Education of Young Children and other advocacy organizations, presented the hard facts to those who determine public policy. At the same time, several major research studies demonstrated that monies spent early in children's lives result in benefits much later on, and are crucial to the development of productive and compassionate citizens. Many researchers and representatives of national organizations present compelling testimony at the state and local levels. The efforts of advocates are not always successful in implementing or changing public policy, but the "children's cause" is much stronger than it was in years past and evidence that the work has paid off can be seen in the federal, state, local, and private sectors.

In Chapter 18, Buck and Willer introduce the concept of advocacy in three arenas (public, private, and personal), present a framework for viewing the process of policy making, and recommend strategies that child and family advocates can use in each of the three arenas. According to the authors, advocates in the public policy arena have spent the last two decades envisioning coherent, comprehensive systems of education and care that will benefit all young children. "The National Association for the Education of Young Children, the world's largest association working to improve early childhood program quality, believes that such systems must include access for all young children to high quality early care and education programs staffed by qualified, nurturing professionals who are appropriately compensated" (p. 396). The authors posit that the major question today is how, rather than whether, the public will support early care and education programs.

Effective advocacy efforts must take into account that public policy decisions affecting young children and early childhood programs are made at local, state, and federal levels of government. At both the state and federal levels, judicial decisions may also have important impacts on children and their families. At the same time, it is important to understand that policy is made incrementally, and it may be wise for advocates to focus on policy initiatives that will build toward comprehensive change step by step. The authors propose a model through which advocates can view and understand which problems will make it onto the decision agenda.

The chapter presents many informed and helpful strategies for personal and public policy advocacy that are invaluable to all child advocates. Some of those that novices may not have considered include:

❑ Consider your personal spheres of influence.
❑ Listen before you speak.
❑ Prior to testifying before a public policy-making body, research the history of the group's previous positions and decisions.
❑ Counter preexisting frames (ways of interpreting a message) with new frames that expand understanding.
❑ Use different messages for different audiences.

Buck and Willer urge readers to put their child advocacy tools to work immediately and regularly. While individuals may not believe that their efforts can be effective, when an entire core of individuals join together, it can be a powerful force for change.

APPLY WHAT YOU LEARNED

As you read the following chapter, think about, talk about, and do additional reading and research regarding these questions:

❑ Do you agree with the authors of this chapter that early childhood professionals are ethically required to advocate for the well-being of young children?
❑ What are you and your colleagues doing now to be child advocates in the personal, public policy, and private sector arenas?
❑ Are you aware of all of the various arenas in which public policy decisions are made? Where do you think your input could be most valuable?
❑ Why is it sometimes difficult to be a child advocate?
❑ Can you, individually or in a small group, identify people or groups with whom you might build a coalition?
❑ What preparation might you make before you tackle an issue? How would you begin the process?
❑ What is some common jargon that we use in ECE that you could best omit in approaching persons with little or no early childhood background?
❑ How can we become effective advocates for young children in the many settings in which we must function today?

REFERENCES

Children's Defense Fund (2005). E-Advocacy. *In child care and Head Start organizer's toolkit.* Washington, DC: Author.

Dorfman, L., Woodruff, K., Herbert, S., & Ervice, J. (2004). *Making the case for early care and education: A message development guide for advocates.* Berkeley, CA: Berkeley Media Services Group.

National Association for the Education of Young Children. Access their articles on advocacy online at www.naeyc.org

ADVOCACY FOR
YOUNG CHILDREN

Linda Buck

Honolulu Community College

Barbara Willer

National Association for the Education of Young Children

Please think of the children first. If you ever have anything to do with their entertainment, their food, their toys, their custody, their day or night care, their health care, their education—listen to the children, learn about them, learn from them. Think of the children first.

—*Fred Rogers*

This quote from Mister Rogers sums up what advocacy for young children is all about—considering the needs of children and then acting to be sure that those needs are met. Childhood by its very nature is a time of tremendous vulnerability. Children rely on caring adults, especially family members, teachers, and caregivers, to nurture and protect them. But the responsibility for nurturing and protecting children does not end with the daily interactions between children and familiar adults. Often the decisions of others—sometimes far removed from the home, center, or classroom—greatly affect children's opportunities for development and learning. Such public and private policy decisions include decisions by a school board regarding school entry policies, by state government regarding preservice educational requirements of child care staff, by the federal government regarding policies and funding for preventive health care for children of low-income families, by a company regarding support for the early childhood programs used by their employees, or by a city regarding the use of a children's park.

Public opinion polls and other social science research provide strong evidence that the general public and most policy makers are now convinced of the importance of early brain development to the future of children's lives in school and in society. The public will to support and finance early childhood education and care as a social responsibility seems to have reached a tipping point—a majority of

Americans favor such an effort (Dorfman, Woodruff, Herbert, & Ervice, 2004; Klein, 2004). Now the challenge is making the broad vision of high-quality care and education for all children and families a reality.

In the previous edition of this book, this chapter detailed the impact on early care and education of broad social programs such as welfare reform which included the Child Care and Development Fund, and efforts in the private sector to influence policy makers through research and reports such as the Cost, Quality, and Child Outcomes Study (1995), the Committee for Economic Development reports regarding the importance of investing in children's earliest years (1987, 1990, 1993), and the National Education Goals Panel's first goal, adopted in 1989, that by the year 2000 all children would enter school ready to learn. Readers of the current edition should be well grounded in the critical issues in early care and education today that provide background knowledge for advocacy efforts. Chapter 1 provides an overview of the history and current status of efforts to create comprehensive, coordinated systems of early care and education in many states.

This chapter introduces the concept of advocacy in three arenas—public, private, and personal—briefly presents a framework for viewing the policy-making process, and recommends strategies that advocates can use in any of the three arenas.

Advocacy: Influencing Decisions

The fundamental purpose of early childhood advocacy is to make sure that decisions which affect children and families—in both the public policy arena and the private sector—support children's development and learning. Robinson and Stark (2005) identify three spheres in which early childhood professionals can affect opportunities for children and families: personal, public policy, and the private sector. According to Robinson and Stark, *personal advocacy* is about sharing one's personal views and philosophies with other individuals and groups; *public policy advocacy* is about influencing public policies and practices so that they are more responsive to issues affecting large numbers of children; and *private-sector advocacy* is about changing private-sector policies and practices to support children and families.

Many of the concepts and strategies explored in this chapter are relevant to all three types of advocacy. For example, teachers of young children advocate for them when they help families understand how quality early childhood programs support children's learning in developmentally effective ways, as opposed to the models of "school" and academic learning that many adults have in their minds. This example of personal advocacy provides families with a new "frame" for their ideas about how children learn. Framing is the same technique that those working in the public policy arena use to help legislators and public officials understand and support the policies that will result in good outcomes for large groups of children. Those working to influence workplace policies or business contributions to early care and education in the private sector can also use message framing and other advocacy strategies to influence decision makers in the private sector.

Advocacy: A Professional and Ethical Responsibility

Now more than ever early childhood professionals must see themselves as committed, effective advocates for children. It is no longer a choice. For many, especially those just beginning the advocate's journey, the issues confronting young children and families and early childhood programs seem overwhelming and far too large for any individual to truly make a difference. It is important for beginners to consider advocacy in a light similar to the one in which they considered their decision to become an early educator. What personal and professional values will guide you? What might be the impact of your cultural background—do you come from a culture in which speaking out is acceptable and encouraged, or from one in which it is discouraged in order to maintain harmony? Practical considerations might play a role in the ways and arenas in which you choose to advocate. For example, one young teacher described her concerns about job security before she had achieved tenure in a public school setting. She chose to focus on building relationships within that setting so that when she felt the need to speak out, her opinion would be valued. Like this young teacher, many individuals will find personal advocacy more comfortable at first. But early childhood professionals have an ethical responsibility to act in ways that benefit all children, not just those we know. To do so requires tackling forms of public policy and private-sector advocacy. Some of the same techniques important in personal advocacy can also be helpful in the policy and private-sector arenas, with the opportunity to gain new knowledge and skills in these areas as well. And the skills of a highly qualified early childhood professional—the abilities to observe, reflect, assess, and act—are also those of effective advocates.

Although it may appear that political orientation—liberal, conservative, progressive—should also be considered, ensuring children's well-being is not the exclusive purview of any particular political orientation. It is not necessary or useful to be partisan. Instead, credibility comes from advocating on the basis of research and evidence and experiences. Most Americans agree that, whether they like it or not, the majority of young children will spend some time in the care of adults who are not their parents. And all Americans agree that the early childhood years are critical to the development of productive and compassionate citizens. The goal of providing experiences and environments that achieve this outcome is a shared one even though there are likely to be differences in opinion as to how the goal should be achieved. The job of advocates is to determine mutually acceptable approaches to achieving goals in whatever arena they choose to work.

INFLUENCING PUBLIC POLICIES TO EFFECT SYSTEMIC CHANGE

More than ever, early childhood professionals are called on to pay attention to and speak out for policies and actions that affect the quality, affordability, and accessibility of early childhood programs both as services to children and families and as *systems* of care and education. Parents need information to make good choices for their children. The general public and community leaders need information in order to understand how investing in early education benefits society. Policy makers and implementers need information in order to provide funding and support for a system of early care and education that ensures young children have the opportunity to become productive citizens and nurturing parents to the next generation of children.

Advocates in the public policy arena have spent the last two decades envisioning coherent, comprehensive systems of education and care that will benefit all young children. The National Association for the Education of Young Children, the world's largest association working to improve early childhood program quality, believes that such systems must include access for all young children to high-quality early care and education programs staffed by qualified professionals who are appropriately compensated (NAEYC Vision Statement, www.naeyc.org/about/mission.asp). Advocates have also mounted public awareness campaigns to persuade the public of the importance of the early years. The evidence that their work has paid off can be seen in the current burgeoning in many states of quality rating systems for child care programs (National Childcare Information Center, 2007) and publicly supported prekindergarten programs (Barnett, Hustedt, Hawkinson, & Robin, 2007; Pre-K Now, 2007).

The question these advocates must address now is *how* rather than *whether* there will be public support for early care and education programs. The focus for advocacy is more community mobilization than persuasion (Klein, 2004). As Kagan and Kauerz point out in Chapter 1, the proliferation of programs and initiatives from federal, state, and local governments and the private sector has made the advocate's job more complex. In a growing number of states, the envisioned comprehensive systems are being constructed policy decision by policy decision.

The Policy-Making Process

Understanding policy and the policy-making process is one of the keys to effective advocacy in the public arena. This section presents a brief introduction that is intended to provide beginning advocates with a framework for viewing the policy process.

Public policy can be described as the collection of decisions by public officials that result in laws, regulations, and court decisions designed to implement a social goal—a goal that is intended to support or improve the welfare of society (Lippitt, 2001).

Public policy decisions affecting young children and early childhood programs are made in many different arenas. Locally, decisions by school boards, municipalities, and counties daily affect the lives of children and families. At the state level, decisions by state governments include those made by legislatures (laws) as well as administrative decisions made by governors and their administrations (regulations and executive orders). At the federal level, decisions are made by Congress as well as the president and the administration. At both the state and federal levels, judicial decisions through the courts may also influence the lives of children and their families.

Formal policy exists in the form of laws, rules and regulations, and court decisions. Some argue that policy is also the ways in which these formal delineations of policy are implemented. This is sometimes called "experienced policy" or formal policy translated into action and experienced by the intended beneficiaries. The way rules for child care subsidies are implemented and the impact they have on the ability of families to obtain and keep stable child care are examples.

Incrementalism, a widely accepted view of the policy-making process, assumes that policy is constructed by making small adjustments along the margins of what already exists. In the incremental model, policy changes occur very gradually, in small steps. Policies that are built incrementally reflect compromise among those interested in an issue and may also be less threatening strategies to advance a broader agenda. Anne Mitchell and Louise Stoney, two experienced policy advocates, have advised early childhood advocates working for comprehensive system change in the states to focus on policy initiatives that will build toward that change step by step. Efforts to improve the quality of child care, to offer prekindergarten for all children, to build professional development systems, and to help families pay for child care are examples of policy elements that lead toward overall system change. Mitchell and Stoney, writing in an issue brief for the Smart Start National Technical Assistance Center, describe the incrementalist strategy perfectly. "Our challenge as advocates of whole system reform is to maintain our focus on the whole system we desire to implement—knowing what the parts are, how they fit together, which comes first, etc.—and to understand clearly which parts are moveable when" (Mitchell & Stoney, 2006).

Of Streams and Windows.   John Kingdon, the author of a classic text on public policy, proposes a model for viewing the policy process that complements the incrementalist approach and reflects the reality of a diverse, democratic country with policy making and implementation spread among different branches of federal, state, and local governments (Kingdon, 2003). This model is particularly useful in helping advocates understand that how the policy agenda is determined and solutions identified are as important as the procedure by which a bill becomes a law. Kingdon uses the metaphor of three streams to describe the policy-making process: the *problem stream,* the *policy or solutions stream,* and the *political stream.* Action on an issue takes place when the three streams converge to open a "policy window."

The *problem stream* is the list of subjects or problems to which people in government and others closely associated with them are paying serious attention at any given time. The broad agenda is usually a long list that includes items such as Social Security reform, health care, and education reform, including school readiness. Within the broad agenda is a shorter list of issues that are up for an active decision, for example, Head Start reauthorization (at this writing) and support for prekindergarten education at both the state and federal levels. Problems on the policy decision agenda may be defined by values (we're not doing the best we can for our children), comparisons (there is an achievement gap between children from poor families and those from better-off families; the children in the United States are behind children from other countries in science and math), and existing frames or organizing principles that are socially shared and persistent over time (the welfare of children is primarily a family responsibility).

This shorter list of problems and their possible solutions make up the *policy or solutions stream*. Possible solutions often arise from groups of specialists in a policy area (what Kingdon terms policy communities). Advocates may play a key role in policy communities along with government officials, researchers, consultants, and academics. The *political stream* impacts the issues or problems that appear on the decision agenda and the process of making decisions. This stream includes perceived swings of national mood, public opinion, election results, organized political interests, changes of administration, and turnover in the legislatures or Congress.

According to Kingdon's analysis, the political stream largely determines which problems will make it onto the decision agenda. Coalitions in the political stream are formed through negotiation and bargaining. Issues seem to "tip" onto the decision agenda from the political stream when those in the stream perceive some movement, such as change in the national mood, often as revealed by opinion polls, and don't want to be left out of what they perceive as a building trend. Advocates in the political stream are likely to use mobilization of interest groups, pressure, and influence, especially through frequent and intense communication with decision makers.

The issue of universal health care in this country provides a striking example of activity in the political stream that may have some relevance for early childhood advocates in the public policy arena. In the mid-1990s an overwhelming majority of Americans said they were in favor of a comprehensive health care reform bill that was introduced in Congress by the Clinton administration. Then the now-famous "Harry and Louise" ads began appearing on television depicting a middle-aged couple at their kitchen table becoming disenchanted with the complexity and potential costs of the proposal. Within weeks, public support for the bill collapsed. The Health Insurance Association of America, sponsor of the ads, was not the only interest group lobbying to defeat the proposal, but the ads made the opposition visible and tapped into the seemingly deep-seated fears of many Americans who already had health coverage. At this writing, health care reform looks as if it will again be a major issue, this time in the 2008 presidential election campaign. Stakeholders on both sides of the issue learned much from the experiences of the mid-1990s, but once again the success or failure of various proposals will depend on the influence of stakeholders in the political stream and the ability of interest groups to mobilize support for their positions, for or against (Toner, 2007).

The opening of a *policy window* (when the three streams converge) may be due to crises (like 9/11), institutionalized events such as elections and budget cycles, or the gradual accumulation of knowledge such as the purposeful dissemination of information about the critical importance of early brain development to children's learning.

When a policy issue or problem, such as health care reform or education reform, tips and reaches the decision agenda, advocates must be prepared to recommend proposals and solutions. It is at this stage that the incrementalist approach may have its greatest strength as a policy strategy.

Policy communities work to influence the decisions of policy makers once an issue surfaces on the decision agenda. They lay out alternative solutions in conferences, commissions, reports, and briefings attempting to persuade and develop consensus about acceptable solutions. The policy community around an issue may be tightly knit and share a similar agenda, or it may be fragmented. Consensus building within a policy community consists of persuasion through dissemination of ideas and subjecting possible solutions to the tests of survival: technical feasibility (will it work?), compatible values among the members of the community, and a reasonable chance for acceptance by elected officials (Kingdon, 2003).

As can be seen by this discussion, the policy-making process is complex and may seem confusing, but it is intensely human and is often driven by relationships among the participants as much as it is the evidence regarding the efficacy of a policy solution or its cost (although cost is always a major consideration). Early childhood professionals who become advocates in this sphere already understand the importance of building relationships. The three stream model may provide a perspective that will help to temper expectations of the short-term outcomes of the process. Advocates must have or develop acceptance that the process will often be frustrating, while keeping their hearts and minds focused on the goal of the best possible outcomes for children. Fortunately there are many things that beginning advocates can do to participate while learning about the policy-making process.

Participating in the Public Policy Sphere

It is beyond the scope of this chapter to outline the specific processes of decision making in the public policy arena. Readers are referred to *Advocates in Action* by Robinson and Stark (2005) for more detailed information. The section that follows offers suggestions and guidance for effective participation in advocacy efforts. It is written in the second-person imperative to emphasize the importance of taking personal and professional responsibility as an advocate.

Many states have coalitions of groups working toward early childhood systems change that can provide entry to public policy advocacy for early childhood professionals. A good place to start is as a volunteer helping the public policy committee of an NAEYC affiliate or a local early childhood coordinating council. The opportunities for involvement will be numerous, and even if you are a beginning advocate you are likely to find something suited to your level of development and expertise. Participating as a volunteer in advocacy events; conducting research on a policy issue to help the organization determine or support its position; writing testimony for others to give or providing testimony in person, by fax, or even e-mail for legislative, municipal, or school board hearings; and helping to convene a forum or focus group to find out how specific groups feel about issues are examples of public policy advocacy.

Be sure that you understand the positions of the organization or coalition so that you can represent them accurately. If you disagree with a position, work from within to try to achieve change or respectfully agree to disagree and find another way to make a contribution. You may find that your perspective and depth of understanding change as you work through issues with others more experienced than yourself. Continue to apply the strategies of a highly qualified early childhood professional: observe, assess, and reflect before taking action.

As you observe the policy-making process, spend some time figuring out how the decisions are made and who the decision makers are. How can you, individually or through your sphere of influence, "connect" with the decision makers? What issues are meaningful to the decision makers and how can you relate to them with your area of concern? Who are the allies that you can draw on to bolster your support? Who are the potential adversaries? Are there areas of common agreement that might serve as a foundation for working out mutually acceptable strategies for action? These questions are the same kind that early childhood professionals rely on every day in making decisions about appropriate teaching strategies for individual children or about effective communication with the families with whom they work.

STRATEGIES FOR ADVOCACY

Early childhood professionals, regardless of role, setting, or auspices (public, private, for-profit, not-for-profit), should keep in mind three overarching advocacy strategies: (1) create greater understanding and commitment among all decision makers (whether in public or private arenas) regarding the rights and needs of young children, (2) influence specific decisions by the individuals and groups with which one has direct contact, and (3) influence broader public policy decisions to achieve positive outcomes for children and families. As important as public policy advocacy is, it often seems the most removed from the day-to-day lives of early childhood educators and is the form of advocacy with which they feel the least comfortable. Perhaps as a result, advocacy is often not well-addressed in professional preparation programs, and many successful advocates have had to learn the process "on the job" throughout their professional careers while lamenting the fact that few others are joining them in their efforts. Stressing the importance of influencing the decisions of individuals with whom one has direct contact as an essential part of the advocacy process underscores the fact that it can and must be part of the daily work of all professionals. As early childhood professionals develop advocacy knowledge and skills, their spheres of contact and influence will likely expand. With the accessibility of information about issues and advocacy efforts, largely through the World Wide Web, it is anticipated and critical that many more early childhood professionals will find themselves in the arena of public policy advocacy. But regardless of where advocacy efforts are focused (personal, public, or private sector) the specific strategies that follow will help to ensure successful outcomes. They apply to *all* early childhood professionals in all arenas of advocacy.

Consider Your Personal Spheres of Influence

A good way to begin is to make a list of all of the groups and organizations to which you currently belong: professional groups, civic organizations, and/or religious groups. Also consider the various individuals with whom you regularly have contact—neighbors, board members, principals or program administrators, teachers, parents and grandparents of students, your physician. Are there "unlikely allies" within your sphere of influence? For example, merchants that you regularly patronize, high school or college alumni groups, hobby or craft groups, book clubs, sports teams, arts organizations? What opportunities do you have to speak out on behalf of children to each of these groups or individuals?

Listen Before You Speak

Before approaching a group or individual with an issue, problem, or potential solution, stop and listen. Use this information, from individual conversations or perhaps written descriptive information about the group, to help you frame your message and target the information that you provide. This is an absolutely essential step, and one that beginning advocates may overlook. Yet this step is analogous to one of the basic principles of developmentally appropriate education—to first observe and assess children's abilities and interests in order to provide the most appropriate type of learning activity.

Personal Advocacy.   For example, when meeting with parents, first ask them to talk about their issues and concerns. Listening first and carefully taking into account what you've heard helps you to make your message more appropriate, especially if more than one cultural group is involved.

Also listen as you attend meetings of various groups and organizations for relevant information about the group's strengths and interests. Ask about previous successful projects or commitments, and find out about pet projects of the group's leader or personal characteristics that may affect individual interest (for example, a local journalist who is a new parent or a chief executive officer with several young grandchildren).

Public Policy Advocacy.   Before you testify before a public policy-making body such as a school board, municipal council, or legislative committee, research the history of the group's previous positions and decisions on the issue for which you will provide testimony. Try to learn about the group's and individual members' concerns by reading news accounts or testimony and reports from previous hearings, which are a matter of public record and now often available on the Internet.

Use Language and Message Frames That Will Have Meaning for Your Audience

After you have carefully listened to or otherwise researched the positions and opinions of those you want to persuade, use the information you gather to tailor a message that will effectively reach your audience. Regardless of the sphere of advocacy, communication is one of the most important tools you will use to effect change. Even beginning advocates will have greater success if they understand some of the key concepts that communications research on messages about early childhood has identified.

A great deal of research about message frames that are effective with different audiences to promote the cause of early care and education has become available in the past few years. Research on framing has found that people respond to new information from preexisting mental shortcuts (frames) that are socially or culturally shared and help individuals make sense of the world. People will make facts fit these frames, not vice versa. The Frameworks Institute, a leading research organization in this area, has found that even though most people agree that the first 5 years of life are critical, they have a limited understanding of child development and think of child rearing as solely the responsibility of the family, that the goal of child rearing is to raise independent children who can stand on their own two feet, and that the main priority is to protect children from harm. The advocates' job—whether as a teacher or caregiver talking with parents, or as a spokesperson for an organization involved in advocating for systems change—is to counteract these preexisting frames with new frames that more accurately portray child development as the result of interactions between the developing brain and the broader environment, and that expand understanding that the successful development of children is a social, not just a family responsibility (Frameworks Institute, 2005).

Use Simplifying Models.   Effective message frames contain a simplifying model, a concrete mental picture based on something familiar that is linked to the new information. "Brain architecture" has been found to be one of the most powerful simplifying models for helping people understand child development. The analogy of architecture helps people make sense of the complex scientific information about how the human brain develops. (For accessible information about brain research findings and their implications for policy and practice see *The Science of Early Childhood Development,* a publication of the National Scientific Council of the Developing Child at www.developingchild.net.) The brain architecture model explains that early experiences and interactions create either a solid or weak structure (architecture) in the brain that provides the scaffolding for subsequent development (Frameworks Institute, 2005; National Council on the Developing Child, 2007).

Avoid Jargon.   As you assess how to frame your message, consider what you want to say and review it for jargon. All groups have their "in-group" terms and definitions that their members understand but others often find confusing. Early childhood professionals are no exception. For example, terms such as *group size* and *staff-child ratio* are commonly used within the field but may not convey appropriate meaning to others. Similarly, *developmentally appropriate practice,* or DAP, is likely to need further explanation. Research has shown that the phrase *the whole child* is misunderstood and confusing to many people. A good rule of thumb is to think about family members or neighbors of yours with no previous knowledge of early childhood issues. If you used the term, would they know what you were talking about? If you were trying to put the term into words that they could understand, what would you say?

Use Values to Help Others Connect with the Message.   The Frameworks Institute and others have also found that people are primed to adopt the brain architecture and other models when they are introduced with statements about values that they consider important such as stewardship of resources (children as resources), future prosperity for society, and reciprocity (if we invest in children now, they will give back to society in the future). The importance of values in any interaction about the welfare of children cannot be emphasized enough. For example, in the area of personal advocacy, a group of new and experienced teachers recently were discussing the ways in which they ask parents to express their ideas about how their children learn. All of the teachers agreed that asking parents to talk about their hopes and dreams for their children was more effective than asking them to identify their goals and objectives for the children's learning. While many parents do not know a great deal about how children learn, they do know what they value for their own children in the future, which provided the teachers with an opening to talk about the things they were doing that were supporting the children's development in line with the parents' hopes and dreams. In the area of public policy advocacy, successful advocates remind policy makers of the value of educated citizens in a democratic society and connect this to the importance of investing in the education of young children to support our democratic ideals.

Use Different Messages for Different Audiences.   If we only communicate in professional terms or on the basis of our professional values, we run the risk of failing to communicate our message. Sometimes listening first and framing the message to fit the audience can make professionals uncomfortable. Consider the term *school readiness,* in the sphere of public advocacy. When the national education goals were adopted in 1989, many early childhood professionals were very uncomfortable with how the following goal was worded: By the year 2000, all children will enter school ready to learn (Willer & Bredekamp, 1990). Many early childhood professionals felt that this statement presumed that learning could only occur once children reached the school door. Participating in an ongoing dialogue that further shaped the message, early childhood professionals were among the first to point out that readiness is at least a two-way street. Not only are the skills and resources that children bring to school important, but the expectations of the school and classroom teachers will also determine children's success and achievement. Unless the school's and teacher's expectations for children in kindergarten and first grade are appropriate individually, developmentally, and culturally, not all children will fully achieve their potential. Public policy advocates succeeded in reframing the message to incorporate a broader context. For example, Maxwell and Clifford (2004) were quoted in the NAEYC's position statement on school readiness, "School readiness in the broadest sense is about children, families, early environments, schools and communities." By working within the framework of the readiness message, this additional information was successfully communicated in a way that might not have been possible if the message began by focusing strictly on the responsibilities of the school and teacher.

In a more recent development, research has shown that while the school readiness message is a powerful one for policy makers, it is little understood by parents and by the public in general, unless it is accompanied by language that tells in vivid and values-based terms what it is and why it is important. The Berkeley Media

Services Group gives an example of such language: "Children need to be prepared for school because school prepares children to participate in life: as engaged citizens in a democracy, and as contributing members of their neighborhoods, workplaces and society" (Dorfman et al., 2004). Others have found that the school readiness message is more effective when it is connected to information about child development and brain architecture.

This example underscores again the importance of tailoring the message to the audience, beginning with what they care about and value, and providing them with a frame to understand the point that you are trying to make. This principle applies whether you are working in the personal or public policy advocacy spheres; whether you are trying to convince parents that the way you are teaching early reading skills is developmentally appropriate, or trying to convince a legislator to fund additional scholarships for early educators.

Provide for Hands-On Learning

Drawing again from a key tenet of developmentally appropriate practice, don't just talk about what's good for children, look for ways that people can discover the knowledge for themselves. One example in the personal advocacy arena is a teacher's approach to convincing parents about the importance of exploration versus memorization and drill as teaching strategies. During a parent meeting, parents were divided into two groups and were told they were going to learn about fruits. One group was given a set of flash cards that named various fruits and also received worksheets that asked them to color and count various pictures of fruit. Some of the fruit were unusual varieties that were unfamiliar to the parents. Members of the second group each received an actual piece of fruit and were asked to come up with a group project using the fruit. Not surprisingly the first group didn't take long to complete their task, while the second group became tremendously engaged with the project and wanted to keep working long after the allotted time. Reporting back what they learned, members of the first group could only show their worksheets. All they had learned about the exotic fruits were the names. The second group had much more information about the color and size of the fruit, its internal appearance, and its taste. They had graphed the number of pieces that they had cut from each fruit, written their recipe for fruit salad, and discussed fractions as they divided up their treasure. After this experience, there was little question among either group of parents as to which teaching approach was more effective!

To provide hands-on learning in the public policy arena, advocates have successfully arranged field trips for policy makers and business leaders to see early childhood programs in action and to talk with the staff and families of the programs. This activity takes careful planning to execute effectively and often requires an advocacy initiative involving coalitions of organizations. *How to Plan a Site Visit,* a resource from the Zero to Three Policy Center, provides useful information on this kind of advocacy activity. Beginning advocates might become involved as volunteers or as spokespeople for their programs if they are featured on the field trip.

Suggest Potential Actions

In addition to creating better understanding about the needs of young children and their families and the benefits of early education experiences, think strategically about how you might influence actions and potential actions by the groups and individuals in your personal sphere of influence. Review the types of decisions that these groups or individuals already make that have an impact on children and families. What information or resources do you have that would help them improve their decisions with regard to their impact on children?

Examples in the Personal Advocacy Arena.   For example, the school principal is considering the adoption of a controversial new curriculum that provides little flexibility for teachers, but you and other teachers would prefer one with a strong research base that provides more opportunity for individualization. In this era of strong demands for accountability, how could you persuade the principal to consider your ideas? To what values could you appeal? What kind of evidence of the effectiveness of this approach could you offer that would have credibility with this school leader? Who else could you engage to help you?

Perhaps your religious organization leases space to a child care program that meets only minimal quality standards. To what fundamental values could you appeal to help the organization's leaders understand the impact of their decision? What information could you provide that would help them understand the importance of providing for more than children's basic safety? What alternatives could you suggest? Who could you enlist to help you?

Other examples where you may have the potential to influence decisions: Suppose a civic organization to which you belong is choosing a new service project and may be willing to consider one focused on young children. A local employer may be willing to support centers and schools seeking NAEYC accreditation. A religious organization may provide space for expansion of an after-school program. A softball league might agree to sponsor a neighborhood park cleanup day. These are just a few of the myriad possibilities for taking action within the personal sphere of influence.

Examples in the Public Policy Arena.   Working with coalitions in the public policy arena, you may find your expertise as an early educator with practical experience of the impact of policies on children crucial when the group is considering a policy position. Collect examples of the impact of "implemented policy" from your daily work to share with other advocates who may not have that perspective. For example, how would a proposal to fund a limited number of hours daily for a prekindergarten initiative affect children whose parents or guardians work full-time? How would such a proposal affect the ability of early childhood programs in the private sector to maintain their level of service to families?

Spread the Word—Again and Again and Again

It's been said that people need to hear new information seven times or more before they really remember it. Look for ways to continue to repeat your messages about children and early childhood program quality, accessibility, and affordability. In *Building Support for Your School,* Judy Harris Helm and Amanda Helm (2006) introduce the concepts of strategic communication and show how teachers and administrators can use the principles and techniques of documentation to create effective and powerful messages that can help parents and community members understand how children learn. The same strategies can be used in the public policy arena to create powerful displays and messages about the needs of young children for building consensus within the policy community on issues or for informing policy makers in briefings and conferences. Beginning advocates may want to explore this avenue to spreading the word through activities that are already part of your repertoire as a teacher.

One of the key principles of effective communication is to choose a messenger who has credibility with the intended audience. For example, in the area of personal advocacy, if you are a preschool teacher, the kindergarten teachers in the schools your children are likely to attend may be some of your most effective allies in spreading the message of the importance of good preschool programs to children's successful transitions to formal schooling. You will already be building relationships with those teachers to support transitions. Enlist their assistance in spreading the word to their own networks. In the area of private-sector advocacy, you may know a small-business owner who would be willing to meet with other business owners to discuss strategies for improving the quality of life for children within the community. You could volunteer to provide assistance with helping them understand how children learn and how that could be enhanced through their efforts. For example, a group of small businesses might be willing to support distribution of information packets to customers with young children or grandchildren or to sponsor a family day in the park. Business leaders who may be the parents or grandparents of children who are enrolled in your program are other allies in spreading the word. They are likely to carry additional weight with some audiences, such as other business leaders or even policy makers. Invite them to participate in family activities sponsored by your school or program and use the opportunity to educate them and enlist their support. Consider how you might be able to move any of these "unlikely allies" from support for individual early childhood programs to public policy advocacy for a system that will provide early learning opportunities for all children.

Develop a Broad-Based Network

If you begin with all of the groups and individuals within your own sphere of influence and then consider all the personal spheres of influence of each of the individuals within your sphere, you will quickly amass a very large group! Creating this type of broad-based network is an essential element for successful advocacy in any sphere. Marian Wright Edelman, founder and president of the Children's Defense Fund, has often referred to children's advocates as a "flea corps." Individually, one person's actions may seem insignificant, but joined together with many others they become a powerful force for change, as in the children's book *Swimmy* by Leo Lionni (1973).

In the popular book *The Tipping Point* (2000), Malcolm Gladwell presents a framework for considering the particular expertise of individuals within your expanded network. Some may be connectors, people who know lots of other people and enjoy making connections among them. Others may be mavens, experts who have deep and broad knowledge of things that are important to your issue that they enjoy sharing. Still others are salespeople, the persuaders who can convince individuals and groups to take action—to buy a product, to vote for a candidate, to participate in a social movement. Use the strengths of those within your broad network to advance the advocacy issues on which you are working. For example, in the area of private advocacy, if an early childhood program that meets a significant need in your community is about to close because it has lost the lease on the facility it uses, who in your broad network are the connectors that could help find new space at a reasonable price, what mavens could assist with design for a new facility, and what salespeople could convince potential donors to contribute to the cost of a new lease and renovations?

Build on Your Success

Nothing breeds success like success! Once you discover that your actions *do* make a difference, it empowers you to use your skills and knowledge to work for further change in new arenas. This fact is one of the reasons why it is so important to view advocacy as a continuum with many different potential actions and strategies at many different levels. We need to recognize the connections and similarities of actions and strategies at all levels so that we also recognize that if we can convince a parent of the importance of developmentally appropriate teaching strategies, we have the basic skills that can be built upon to convince a legislator of the need for a comprehensive system of early care and education. The actions that create positive change in our daily lives can also be the ones that help to create systemic change that can improve the lives and experiences of large groups of children and families.

CONCLUSIONS

Early childhood professionals do not have a choice: They are ethically required to advocate for the well-being of all children. The key point to remember is that the knowledge and skills of early childhood professionals as the teachers and caregivers of young children—building relationships, effective communication, and educating others using developmentally effective pedagogy—can be put to use in advocating for the needs and rights of children in all three spheres of influence: personal, private, and public policy. By recognizing these similarities and focusing on them in professional preparation programs as well as in our daily professional lives, the early childhood profession can build a strong and effective group of champions for children that includes not only professionals but all who are concerned with the well-being of children.

REFERENCES

Barnett, W. S., Hustedt, J. T., Hawkinson, L. E., & Robin, K. B. (2007). *The state of preschool 2006.* New Brunswick, NJ: National Institute for Early Education Research. Retrieved September 20, 2007, from http://nieer.org/yearbook/

Children's Defense Fund (2005). E-Advocacy. In *Child care and Head Start organizer's toolkit.* Washington, DC: Author. Retrieved July 15, 2007, from www.childrensdefense.org/site/DocServer/cc_hs_toolkit.pdf?docID=201

Committee for Economic Development (1987). *Children in need.* New York: Author.

Committee for Economic Development (1991). *The unfinished agenda: A new vision for child development and education.* New York: Author.

Committee for Economic Development (1993). *Why child care matters: Preparing young children for a more productive America.* New York: Author.

Doggett, L., & Epstein, D. (2006, November/December). Turning advocacy into action for children. *Exchange,* 66–67.

Dorfman, L., Woodruff, K., Herbert, S., & Ervice, J. (2004). *Making the case for early care and education: A message development guide for advocates.* Berkeley, CA: Berkeley Media Services Group. Retrieved July 15, 2007, from http://bmsg.org/pdfs/YellowBook.pdf

Frameworks Institute (2005, July). *Talking early child development and exploring the consequences of frame choices: A frameworks message memo.* Retrieved July 15, 2007, from www.frameworksinstitute.org/products/frameworksmemo1.pdf

Gilliam, F. D., & Nall Bales, S. (2004). Framing early childhood development: Strategic communications and public preferences. In N. Halfon, T. Rice, & M. Inkelas (Eds.), *Building state early childhood comprehensive systems series, No. 7.* National Center for Infant and Early Childhood Health Policy. Retrieved July 15, 2007, from www.healthychild.ucla.edu/PUBLICATIONS/NationalCenterPubs.asp

Gladwell, M. (2000). *The tipping point: How little things can make a big difference.* New York: Little, Brown.

"Harry and Louise," the Sequel? The Universal Health Care Debate Is Back. Knowledge@Wharton. Retrieved June 27, 2007, from http:// knowledge.wharton.upenn.edu

Helm, J., & Helm, A. (2006). *Building support for your school: How to use children's work to show learning.* New York: Teachers College Press.

Jacobson, L., & Simpson, A. (2007). Communicating about early childhood: Lessons from working with the news media. *Young Children, 62*(3), 89–92.

Kingdon, J. W. (2003). *Agendas, alternatives, and public policies* (2nd ed.). New York: Longman.

Kirwan, A. (2001). The art of the possible: Getting involved in policy change. *Zero to Three, 21,* 9–15.

Klein, E. C. (2004). *Mobilizing support for child care: Five key messages.* Berkley, CA: Berkley Media Services Group. Retrieved August 15, 2007, from http://bmsg.org/pdfs/YellowBookAppendix.pdf

Link, G., Beggs, M., & Seiterman, E. (1997). *Serving families.* Fairfax, CA: Parent Services Project, Inc.

Lionni, L. (1973). *Swimmy.* New York: Random House Children's Books.

Lippitt, J. (2001). Policy and policy making for infants, toddlers, and their families: A primer for practitioners. *Zero to Three, 21,* 4–8.

Maxwell, K., & Clifford, R. M. (2004). Research in Review: School readiness assessment. *Young Children, 59*(1), 42–46.

Mitchell, A., & Stoney, L. (2006, March). *Framing our message to communicate effectively.* Smart Start National Technical Assistance Center. Retrieved July 15, 2007, from www.earlychildhoodfinance.org/2006%20Early%20Childhood%20Finance%20Learning%20Community/2006FinanceMeeting/8-FramingMessageBrief.doc

National Association for the Education of Young Children (NAEYC). (n.d.). *Mission and goals.* Washington, DC: Author. Retrieved October 1, 2007, from www.naeyc.org/about/mission.asp

National Association for the Education of Young Children (NAEYC). (2004). *Advocacy toolkit.* Washington, DC: Author. Retrieved July 15, 2007, from www.naeyc.org/policy/toolbox/pdf/toolkit.pdf

National Association for the Education of Young Children (NAEYC). (1995). *Where we stand on school readiness.* Washington, DC: Author. Retrieved July 15, 2007, from www.naeyc.org/ece/critical/readiness.asp

National Childcare Information Center. (2007, July). *Quality rating systems: Definitions and statewide systems.* Retrieved August 1, 2007, from http://nccic.acf.hhs.gov/pubs/qrs-defsystems.html

National Council on the Developing Child. (2007, February). *The science of early childhood development.* Retrieved July 15, 2007, from www.developing child.net

National Education Goals Panel. (1994). *The national education goals report. Building a nation of learners.* Washington, DC: Author.

Pre-K Now. (2007, April). *Pre-K across the USA.* Washington, DC: Author. Retrieved July 15, 2007, from www.preknow.org/advocate/presentations.cfm

Robinson, A., & Stark, D. R. (2005). *Advocates in action: Making a difference for young children* (Rev. ed.). Washington, DC: NAEYC.

Rogers, F. (2003). *The world according to Mister Rogers: Important things to remember.* New York: Hyperion Books.

Toner, R. (2007, September 16). Unveiling Health Care 2.0, again. *The New York Times.* Retrieved October 20, 2007, from www.nytimes.com/2007/09/16/weekinreview/16toner.html

Voices for America's Children. (2005, September). *Translating school readiness: How to talk about investing in young children* (Issue Brief). Washington, DC: Author. Retrieved July 15, 2007, from www.voicesforamericaschildren.org/Template.cf?Section=BrowsebyOrganization&CONTENTID=6318&TEMPLATE=/ContentManagement/Content Display.cfm

Voices for America's Children. (2006, October 31). *Understanding research: Top ten tips for advocates and policymakers.* Washington, DC: Author. Retrieved July 15, 2005, from www.voices foramericaschildren.org

Voices for America's Children. (2006, December). *Child advocacy primer: Tips and tools for improving your child advocacy skills* (3rd ed.). Washington, DC: Author. Retrieved July 15, 2007, from www .voicesforamericaschildren.org/Content NavigationMenu/CAI/Advocacy_Tools/Child_ Advocacy_Primer1/Child_Advocacy_Primer.htm

Willer, B., & Bredekamp, S. (1990). Redefining readiness: An essential requisite for educational reform. *Young Children, 45*(5), 22–24.

Zero to Three Policy Center. (n.d.). *How to plan a site visit: Inviting policymakers to see your work with infants, toddlers & their families.* Washington, DC: Author. Retrieved July 15, 2007, from www .zerotothree.org/site/PageServer?pagename=ter_ pub_advocacytools&AddInterest=1159#primers

INDEX